SEARCH THE SCRIPTURES

SEARCH THE SCRIPTURES

A THREE YEAR BIBLE STUDY COURSE

GENERAL EDITORS

THE REV. G. T. MANLEY

THE REV. H. W. OLDHAM

THE INTER-VARSITY FELLOWSHIP

39 BEDFORD SQUARE, LONDON, W.C.1

First Edition in one volume	.	.	.	.	1949
Second Edition	.	.	.	.	.	1951
Third Edition (revised order of study)	.	.	1955
Fourth Edition	.	.	.	.	.	1960
Reprinted	.	.	.	.	.	1962

The course can also be obtained in three separate volumes bound in limp covers. Each provides one year's study.

Made and printed in England by
STAPLES PRINTERS LIMITED
at their Rochester, Kent, establishment

PREFACE

THIS course of Bible reading was first issued in 1934 in response to a widespread demand from Christian students and others for a systematic plan which could be used daily in the Quiet Time. Its aim is to guide the reader through the whole Bible in three years and it first appeared in six parts, each of which provided six months' study. The late Archdeacon H. E. Guillebaud compiled two of these booklets, Dr. B. F. C. Atkinson, the Rev. R. J. Cobb, Dr. F. D. Coggan, and the Rev. A. M. Stibbs, one each, and the Rev. G. T. Manley acted as General Editor.

This new and revised course is the work of the late Rev. H. W. Oldham, assisted by a small band of helpers. Experience showed that the value of the course to students of the Bible would be increased if more explanatory notes were introduced, especially in those sections dealing with the more difficult biblical books. This has now been done with the twofold aim of simplifying the course generally and of directing attention more closely to the actual text of Scripture.

The course has also been issued in three separate volumes (instead of six as previously) each of which provides one year's study. These are bound in limp covers. The plan of study, which is simplicity itself, is set out in the General Directions, which should be carefully read. In the third (1955) edition some changes were made in the order in which the books are studied during the first two years with the object of introducing more New Testament material during the early months. The original compilers and those who have assisted in preparing this revised edition are in close touch with the needs of students and know well the difficulty of sustained Bible study, and how many a hindrance Satan will put in the way. But they pray that the guidance here given, by the grace of God, may stimulate such a taste for His Word as to make the time daily spent upon it a delight as well as a source of strength.

G. T. MANLEY

CONTENTS

THIRD YEAR

GENERAL DIRECTIONS FOR STUDY

THE AIM OF THE COURSE

THIS is quite definite—to provide for university students and others a working scheme which will cover the text of the whole Bible in three years. There are many schemes which provide more extensive commentaries and notes, but the purpose here is to stimulate the personal study of those who will give to it at least twenty minutes daily.

A major question which arises at once is the relationship between intellectual study of the Bible and the Quiet Time.

'Your object in the Quiet Time is not so much to gather information as inspiration, and so you should discover what is the application of what you read to your then present circumstances and need. Turn the truth into terms of life, and use the Word to light and feed the fire of devotion.'*

As far as the present course is concerned, while the intellectual need certainly has not been disregarded, the compilers have endeavoured especially to provide for those who will desire to use the course *as part of their Quiet Time*, and to this end daily questions have been designed to bear as far as possible on the spiritual meaning and application of the passages. The great need is to gain a real knowledge of the text of the Bible itself, and this is where the whole emphasis is being placed day by day. Yet foremost for our practical lives must be the thought of the need of the Bible for *spiritual life and power*.

The following suggestions, originally put forward by Dr. Griffith Thomas, are offered for this devotional study:

* Dr. Graham Scroggie in *The Inter-Varsity Magazine*, Michaelmas Term, 1933.

ix

1. Open all such occasions with prayer for the Holy Spirit's light (Ps. cxix. 18). This is most important. The knowledge of what the Bible says, or even a correct understanding of its meaning, will not of itself bring spiritual life and power. 'What is needed,' says Andrew Murray, 'is very simple: the determined refusal to attempt to deal with the written Word without the quickening Spirit. First, in a quiet act of worship, look to God to give and renew the workings of the Spirit within you; then, in a quiet act of faith, yield yourself to the power that dwells in you, and wait on Him, that not the mind alone, but the life in you, may be opened to receive the Word.'

2. Ask to be guided to some definite thought for *yourself*.

3. Dwell prayerfully on this thought thus given—Is it a counsel, a precept, a warning, a promise, an experience, a command?

4. When its meaning is clear, use it as the basis of a prayer for grace to realize it in experience.

5. Yield the whole soul in full surrender to its truth and power.

6. Link it on to truths already known, and thereby strengthen the chain of experience.

7. Trust God to reproduce it in your life that day.

THE NATURE OF THE COURSE

Keeping the above aims in view, the three sections of the Course each provide a year's study, in which the ground covered is grouped in weeks so that the Course may be started at any time, irrespective of date. The time is divided more or less equally between the New Testament and Psalms and the rest of the Old Testament. The assumption is made that not less than twenty minutes will be spent on the portion and questions daily, but, of course, the amount of text covered varies from day to day. When reading the Old Testament the portions are, roughly speaking, twice the length of those in the New Testament books.

THE USE OF THE COURSE

(a) *Requirements.*

While the Course can be used with the Authorized Version only, the following additional equipment will help the student to obtain the best results:

(i) *Authorized Version* and *Revised Version.* The Course is, in general, based upon the Authorized Version of the Bible, and can be profitably used with this alone; but to obtain the best results it is necessary also to have a Revised Version for consultation, preferably one with references. Indication is given in the daily questions and notes where the rendering of the Revised Version is of importance in the study of the portion.

There are also a number of modern translations, such as those by Moffatt, Weymouth, Way (Paul's Epistles only), and the recently published American Revised Standard Version to which occasional reference is made in the Course. It is not necessary for the user of the Course to possess these, but if he already has any of them, or has access to them, they will often throw light upon the meaning of a difficult passage.

(ii) *Two note books,* one an exercise book for rough notes and references, the other a loose-leaf or other good note book for more permanent records.

(iii) *A good concordance.*

(iv) *The New Bible Commentary,* a one-volume commentary on the whole Bible published by the Inter-Varsity Fellowship and designed primarily to enable the student to understand the meaning of the text.

(v) *The New Bible Handbook,* published by the Inter-Varsity Fellowship, which takes into account the latest results of biblical and archaeological research. While no special time has been allowed in the Course for external reading of this kind, the Handbook will be found invaluable as a book of reference, and any additional time given to it will be amply rewarded. It contains a series of chapters dealing with general biblical subjects, and with the historical background of the Bible story; and provides also a much fuller introduction to the Bible books than is given in the present Course.

(vi) *The New Bible Dictionary*, a comprehensive reference work of more than 1,400 pages, designed to give easy access to background information on the Bible and its teaching. Up-to-date in its scholarship, accurate in its facts, profusely illustrated, this volume has been specially prepared to assist Bible study, and is published by the Inter-Varsity Fellowship.

(b) *The Material Supplied in the Course.*

(i) *Introduction* and *Analysis* at the beginning of each book, to give some grasp of the contents at the outset. These should be read before beginning the study of the book and may be referred to again with advantage from time to time.

(ii) *The daily portions*, accompanied by questions, notes and references. The notes have been kept down to a minimum, and the attention of the student should be given to the questions, rather than to the notes.

(c) *The Actual Procedure.*

This must be settled individually, but an indication of two ways in which the material has been used may be valuable as a suggestion.

(i) Read the portion through, and jot down in the book for rough notes the main subject or subjects with which it deals. When a clear grasp of the general contents of the passage has been obtained, then write out answers to the questions, leaving a brief time at the end for practical application.

(ii) Look at the questions first and deal with them during the first reading of the passage, jotting down rough notes on them. Perhaps there will be time for a second reading.

Whatever the actual procedure may be, it is essential to realize that answering questions is simply a means to an end. Hence, at some stage, time should be given to such prayerful meditation as will lead to a personal appropriation of the spiritual message, and if desired, the recording of spiritual impressions.

There will be days when a section proves too much for the allotted time. In such cases a choice between the questions should be made, and one of the questions be left over. It is inadvisable to carry the question over into the next day, so as to fall out of step with the progress of the Course. A better plan is to devote some extra time on Sundays, both for going back to questions that have not been dealt with, and also for writing up the rough notes made n the daily study into a permanent record.

(d) *Comparing Results.*

A final note may be added regarding sharing results with others. While our own individual work in seeking to get to know the Word of God for ourselves is the most important thing, and worth any number of analyses or points which we obtain second hand, nevertheless there are great advantages also in comparing notes with others working on the same basis at the same time. By this is not meant organized Group study, which is another method of studying the Bible, and for which specially prepared outlines are issued by the Inter-Varsity Fellowship. What we are speaking of now is informal exchange of thought with one or more friends on points arising out of our private Bible study. Mutual discussion of this kind is the most effective and profitable method of checking our own individual ideas; it also deepens mutual fellowship in the things of Christ, and it provides a fresh stimulus to continue in the study of the Word, that we may become 'those who, by reason of use, have their senses exercised to discern' (Heb. v. 14).

LIST OF ABBREVIATIONS

Books of the Old Testament: Gn., Ex., Lv., Nu., Dt., Jos., Jdg. Ru., 1, 2 Sa., 1, 2 Ki., 1, 2 Ch., Ezr., Ne., Est., Jb., Ps., (Pss.), Pr., Ec., Ct., Is., Je., La., Ezk., Dn., Ho., Joel, Am., Ob., Jon., Mi., Na., Hab., Zp., Hg., Zc., Mal.

Books of the New Testament: Mt., Mk., Lk., Jn., Acts, Rom., 1, 2 Cor., Gal., Eph., Phil., Col., 1, 2 Thes., 1, 2 Tim., Tit., Phm., Heb., Jas., 1, 2 Pet., 1, 2, 3 Jn., Jude, Rev.

A.V. Authorized Version (1611).

cf. Compare.

Gk. Greek.

Heb. Hebrew.

LXX. Septuagint Version, that is, translation of the Old Testament into Greek, about 250 B.C.

mg. Margin.

Moffatt. Moffatt's translation of the Bible.

R.S.V. Revised Standard Version of the New Testament (1946).

R.V. Revised Version (1885).

Way. Translation of St. Paul's letters and Hebrews by Arthur S. Way.

Weymouth. New Testament in Modern Speech by Weymouth.

INDEX OF BIBLICAL BOOKS

Note.—First Year contains pages 1–144; Second Year contains pages 145–332; Third Year contains pages 333–544.

FIRST YEAR

GENESIS

INTRODUCTION

(See New Bible Handbook, pp. 79-88, 115-133)

THE title Genesis comes from the Septuagint Greek translation of the Old Testament and means "Origin" or "Beginning." The book justifies its title in three ways.

(a) As *history* it tells the story of the creation, of the earliest civilization, of the flood, and of the origins of the chosen people of God.

(b) As *revelation* it teaches primary truths about God and Man: and with regard to the way of salvation it tells first of the coming of sin into the world through the fall; then of the utter failure of early man to save himself, culminating in the flood; and finally of God's choice of one family in which all families of the earth should be blessed. The fact of God's redemptive purpose, first foreshadowed in the garden of Eden (Gn. iii. 15), shines out from time to time with increasing clearness as the book proceeds.

Genesis is thus the story first of man's need of salvation, and then of the early stages in the unfolding of God's wonderful plan of redemption.

(c) As *practical teaching* it introduces us to personalities of profound and universal religious significance, such as Abel and Cain, Noah, Abraham, Jacob and Esau and Joseph, and by its unforgettable stories teaches lessons of abiding value, showing God at work in human life.

AUTHORSHIP

The Pentateuch or Five Books, of which Genesis is the first, was attributed to Moses by universal tradition of the Jews, which our Lord takes for granted and endorses with His own authority, e.g. Mk. xii. 26; Jn. v. 46, 47. This is not the place to attempt to discuss the questions raised by modern criticism, but the following remarks may be made here.

(1) To put the composition of the Pentateuch centuries after the time of Moses means much more than a judgment on its authorship; it inevitably involves surrendering its claim to be

See *New Bible Handbook*, pp. 40-56.

reliable history, and, moreover, it involves the unreliability of a great part of Bible history outside the Pentateuch, as the course of modern criticism shows.

(2) There is an important external check on the claim of the Pentateuch to be historical, namely, its representation of the customs of ancient Egypt. Archaeology has shown that these were just such as they are represented in Genesis to be in the period referred to, but that in many respects they had become quite different long before the exile. How could a late writer have attained such accuracy? Not assuredly by archaeological research, which was not dreamed of in ancient times.

Those who desire to study a brilliant exposure in considerable detail of the weakness of the critical hypothesis and of the arguments by which that hypothesis is maintained, cannot do better than read Finn's *Unity of the Pentateuch*. See also Chapter IV of *The New Bible Handbook*.

ANALYSIS

i–xi. Primaeval history.

xii–l. The ancestors of the chosen people. There is some overlapping, but each patriarch is the leading figure within the section to which his name is attached below:

xii–xxv. 18. Abraham.
xxv. 19–xxvi. Isaac.
xxvii–xxxvi. Jacob.
xxxvii–l. Joseph.

Week 1. GENESIS I–XI. 9

Day 1. Gn. i–ii. 3.

(1) Having read the chapter, try to picture the story as a succession of acts or scenes. As you survey these in turn, what truths stand out regarding God and His relation to nature and to man?

(2) 'And God said'—found eight times. Cf. Ps. xxxiii. 9; Heb. xi. 3. What further light upon the mode of creation do we get from Jn. i. 1-3; Col. i. 15-17?

Day 2. Gn. ii. 4–iii. 24.

(1) What does Gn. iii teach about (a) Satan's methods, (b) the first false steps which lead to sin in act, (c) the results of sin?

(2) What prophecy of the Lord Jesus do we find in this section ?

Day 3. Gn. iv and v.

(1) Trace in chapter iv the growth of sin and also the evidences of its power and of its effects.

(2) Abel died and Cain lived. But what had Abel that Cain had not? Cf. 1 Jn. iii. 12.

(3) Try to picture to yourself the life of Enoch as told in Gn. v. 21-24. What new light does Heb. xi. 5, 6 throw upon it?

Day 4. Gn. vi.

(1) What do we learn from today's portion of the fallen condition of human nature, of the need of a divine way of salvation, and also of God's attitude to sin? See Mt. xxiv. 37-39; 1 Pet. iii. 20; 2 Pet. ii. 5.

(2) 'Noah found grace in the eyes of the Lord.' What were his characteristics? Cf. Heb. xi. 7.

Notes.—(1) In Gn. vi. 3, the words 'an hundred and twenty years' probably refer not to the average length of human life, but to the respite for repentance which the race was to have from that time to the flood.

(2) The value of the N.T. references is specially great in this portion.

Day 5. Gn. vii–viii. 19.

(1) How long was Noah in the ark?

(2) Once Noah was in the ark, what was God's part in his salvation and what Noah's? See vii. 16, viii. 1, 15, 18. What may we learn from these things regarding our own salvation in Christ? See Eph. ii. 8; 1 Pet. i. 5.

Day 6. Gn. viii. 20—ix.

(1) What did Noah's altar and burnt offerings signify? To what would they correspond in our own life today?

(2) Reflect on Noah's position after the deluge. In what two ways, according to chapter ix, did God encourage him?

(3) How does this chapter teach also the need of *continued* faithfulness, day by day, and that a past experience of the grace of God is no guarantee against present failure?

Notes.—(1) Observe God's care for 'every living creature' (ix. 10, 12, 15. Cf. Lk. xii. 6).

(2) ix. 13. This does not imply that the rainbow was now seen for the first time, but that God now gave it as a token of His covenant of promise to Noah.

Day 7. Gn. x–xi. 9.

(1) What does chapter x teach about the origins of the nations and of their relation to one another and to God? Mt. xxviii. 19; Acts xvii. 26; Rom. iii. 29.

(2) How does xi. 1-9 show the peril of living without God in pride and selfish ambition? What does it reveal also of God's attitude towards all human organization that leaves Him out of account? With xi. 9 contrast Rev. xxi. 24-27.

Week 2. GENESIS XI. 10–XXI. 21

The Book of Genesis passes here from the story of the race as a whole to one line, one family, and finally one man as the chosen instrument of God's purpose of redemption.

Day 1. Gn. xi. 10–xiii. 4.

(1) What light is thrown upon Abram by the fact that such promises made any appeal to him? Consider also the inseparable intermingling of promise and command in God's call and the importance of Abram's obedience, not only for his own life, but in the world purpose of God. See Heb. xi. 8.

(2) Compare and contrast xi. 31 with xii. 5. See also Acts vii. 1-4. On which side of the Euphrates was Haran? Are we ready to cross every barrier and to go the full way with God?

(3) In what two respects did Abram's faith fall short under the tests of famine and of fear? Do you find a special significance in xiii. 3, 4, especially in the words 'where his tent had been at the beginning'? Cf. Rev. ii. 5.

Day 2. Gn. xiii. 5–xiv.

(1) Put yourself in Lot's place when Abram's offer was made to him. What was the motive that decided his choice and how did it end? On the other hand, did Abram suffer any real loss through his unselfishness? Cf. Mt. xvi. 25.

(2) What fresh light do the events of chapter xiv throw on Abram's character?

Day 3. Gn. xv.

(1) Do you find indications in the story that Abram was at this time discouraged? He had incurred the enmity of powerful kings and had refused the spoil of Sodom and Gomorrah. How do God's words in verse 1 exactly meet his need?

(2) See verses 5, 6. Could anything seem less likely to human judgment than the fulfilment of verse 5? Yet Abram believed in the Lord. What great spiritual truth of the gospel does Paul find set forth here? See Rom. iv; Gal. iii. 6-8.

(3) What double ground for faith did God give Abram in verse 7? What *more* did Abram crave and what more did God

give him? See verse 18. The whole chapter is full of God's loving-kindness towards His servant.

Note.—Verses 9, 10, 17 describe an ancient form of agreement or contract; see Je. xxxiv. 18, 19. The smoking furnace and burning lamp represent the Lord passing between the divided animals and thus ratifying the covenant.

Day 4. Gn. xvi and xvii.

(1) Another wrong step on Abram's part brings suffering on others. What attributes of God's being and character are revealed in His dealings with Hagar? See Pr. xv. 3; Col. iii. 22; 1 Pet. ii. 20.

(2) Under what name does God reveal Himself in xvii. 1 and what does He require of His servant? Do you find indications that Abraham at this time needed some such reminder? Consider the strain imposed upon his faith by the passing of the years (xvi. 16; xvii. 1). Notice Abram's change of name in verse 5.

(3) In what respects are God's promises in xvii more definite, more complete, and more gracious than on any earlier occasion? Notice Abraham's prompt obedience in xvii. 23.

Day 5. Gn. xviii.

(1) How do verses 1 and 2 show that 'the three men' collectively were a manifestation of Jehovah Himself? What other evidence do you find that it was indeed 'the Lord'? Cf. Ps. xxv. 14; Jn. xiv. 21-23, xv. 15.

(2) What are the chief characteristics of Abraham's intercession? Can you find at least seven which should mark also our praying? With verses 22, 23, compare Heb. x. 19-22. What did Abraham's intercession effect? See xix. 29.

Day 6. Gn. xix.

(1) What is revealed in this chapter about the evil latent in the heart of man and about the certainty of divine judgment? See Lk. xvii. 28, 29; 2 Pet. ii. 6; Jude 7.

(2) What did Lot gain for himself and his family by his association with Sodom? How does his life warn us?

Day 7. Gn. xx–xxi. 21.

(1) What may we learn from chapter xx of the weakness of human nature, even in a believer, and of God's protecting care? See Ps. xciv. 18; Mk. xiv. 38; 1 Cor. x. 12.

(2) What spiritual lessons does Paul draw from the choice by God of Isaac rather than Ishmael? See Rom. ix. 6-9; Gal. iv. 28–v. 1.

(3) How does chapter xxi illustrate God's faithfulness to His promise both in regard to Isaac (verse 1) and in regard to Ishmael (verses 13, 18)? See Heb. x. 23, xi. 12.

Week 3. GENESIS XXI. 22–XXVIII

Day 1. Gn. xxi. 22–xxii.

(1) Read the incident in xxi. 22-32 in the light of Rom. xii. 17 (R.V.); Col. iv. 5; Eph. v. 15; 1 Pet. ii. 12. What new aspect of God's name was revealed at this time to Abraham? Cf. xiv. 22, xvii. 1; Is. xl. 28.

(2) Reflect on the severity of the test that God gave to Abraham. Notice how often the parental bond is emphasized (verses 2, 3, 6, 7, 16, etc.). See also Heb. xi. 17, 18. Reflect also on Abraham's response, and on the promises renewed to him because of it. See Heb. vi. 11-15.

Day 2. Gn. xxiii.

(1) What is Sarah's character as shown in Genesis? Cf. Heb. xi. 11; 1 Pet. iii. 6.

(2) What features in Abraham's character does the story of this chapter bring out? With verse 4 compare Heb. xi. 13-16.

Day 3. Gn. xxiv. 1-60.

(1) Consider Abraham's servant (a) in his attitude towards his master and (b) in the way he carried through his mission. What may we learn from him regarding our service of Christ?

(2) What picture do you get of Rebekah?

Day 4. Gn. xxiv. 61–xxv.

(1) What light do we get from this portion on the kind of man that Isaac was? See especially xxiv. 63-67, xxv. 28.

(2) Contrast Jacob and Esau, as described in xxv. 27-34, in their habits, character and spiritual outlook. What lesson is drawn in Heb. xii. 14-17 from Esau's conduct in regard to his birthright?

(3) Review Abraham's life. What gives him an outstanding place in world history and makes him a conspicuous example to us all? See Is. xli. 8, li. 2; Gal. iii. 9; Jas. ii. 21-24.

Day 5. Gn. xxvi.

(1) Why did Isaac fail so grievously just after receiving gracious promises from God? What did he not do after this first appearance of God to him which he did do when God appeared to him the second time? See verses 24, 25 and cf. Ps. cxvi. 12-14.

(2) Can you think of any spiritual wells in our day, which were dug by our fathers and which the enemy has stopped up? What can we do to repair those old wells, such as family worship, for example, and also to dig others?

Day 6. Gn. xxvii. 1-45.

(1) Trace the part played by each of the actors in this story. What motive actuated each?

(2) Consider the story in the light of Nu. xxxii. 23.

Day 7. Gn. xxvii. 46-xxviii.

(1) How does the fundamental difference between the two brothers now manifest itself increasingly?

(2) What fourfold assurance did God give to Jacob? Has there been some 'Bethel' in our experience, some conscious transaction with the Lord Jesus Christ, when He declared to us His love and we promised to serve Him?

Week 4. GENESIS XXIX–XXXV

Day 1. Gn. xxix. 1-30.

(1) What evidences are there in this portion of Jacob's exceptional energy and of his zeal in pursuing the object of his desire?

(2) God is not mentioned. Yet in what ways may we discern Him at work in training and disciplining Jacob through the experiences of life?

Note.—xxix. 27 seems to mean that Jacob had to fulfil the week of wedding festivities for Leah; then he received Rachel and served seven more years for her after marrying her. See xxx. 25, xxxi. 41.

Day 2. Gn. xxix. 31-xxx.

(1) Which of Jacob's wives was the ancestress of the Lord? Cf. Pr. xvi. 9.

(2) How does today's portion show the evils of polygamy and supply an answer to the question heard in some mission fields, 'Why should we not have many wives like men of God in the Bible?'

Day 3. Gn. xxxi–xxxii. 2.

(1) It has been said that when inward desire, favouring circumstances and the divine word agree, we may venture forth with sure confidence. How were these three factors present in Jacob's return to Canaan?

(2) In spite of all his cunning and trickery, what qualities in Jacob are to be commended? See especially verses 6, 38-42. How was he superior to Laban in character?

Notes.—(1) xxxi. 42, 53. 'The fear of Isaac', that is, the God whom Isaac reverently worshipped.

(2) xxxii. 1, 2. Cf. xxviii. 12, xxxi. 11; Ps. xxxiv. 7.

Day 4. Gn. xxxii. 3-32.

(1) What is good and what is defective in Jacob's prayer in verses 9-12? Was he relying most upon God, or upon his own resourcefulness? If the former, why was he so greatly afraid? See verse 7; Mk. iv. 40; Is. xxvi. 3.

(2) God wrestled with Jacob at the entrance to the land. Why? Was it that He could not give the land to Jacob *while he was still Jacob,* but only to a Jacob humbled and renewed in heart? How did Jacob 'prevail' in the conflict—by his own strength, or by faith? See Ho. xii. 3-6.

Day 5. Gn. xxxiii.

(1) What is the importance of the title which Jacob gives to God in verse 20? How has he named Him before this time? See xxxi. 5, 42, 53, xxxii. 9.

(2) In the story of this chapter did Jacob behave worthily of his new name of Israel? In what three points especially did he come short? Compare verse 14 (last clause) with verse 17 (first clause); verse 19 with Heb. xi. 9; and verses 18, 19 with his vow at Bethel, xxviii. 22. See 2 Pet. i. 1-11.

Notes.—(1) In other cases of change of name in Scripture the new replaces the old, e.g. Abram to Abraham; Simon to Peter; Saul to Paul. But after Penuel the old name Jacob is found seventy times in Genesis and Israel only forty times.

(2) Jacob's stay at Succoth and Shechem must have extended over several years.

Day 6. Gn. xxxiv.

(1) In this sordid story, which appear the more honourable: Shechem and his father, or the sons of Jacob? How contrary to 1 Pet. ii. 12, iv. 15!

(2) What evidence is there that Jacob left everything to his sons, instead of taking action himself as head of the family? When he did finally rebuke them, about what was he chiefly concerned?

Day 7. Gn. xxxv.

(1) Reading verses 1-7 in the light of 2 Cor. vii. 10, 11, do you find evidence of true repentance in Jacob at this time? In what ways was it manifested?

(2) What new revelation was given to Jacob after his repentance? How does this whole story reveal the loving-kindness and faithfulness of God to His covenant promises, and at the same time His inexorable insistence upon true holiness of life in His people? See Ho. xiv. 4, 9; 2 Tim. ii. 19, 22.

(3) Observe the record of sorrows in this chapter, all of them touching Jacob intimately.

Week 5.   GENESIS XXXVI–XLIII

Day 1. Gn. xxxvi.

In chapter x, before the writer concentrates on the line of Abraham, the names of other nations are recorded. In a similar way in this chapter, before any concentration on the family of Jacob, a list of Edom's descendants is given.

(1) It was foretold from the beginning that each of Rebekah's twin sons would beget a nation (xxv. 23), and so it came to pass. Was it the case with the nations, as it was with their progenitors, that the one was chosen of God and the other rejected? See Heb. xii. 17; Mal. i. 2-4; Rom. ix. 10-13.

(2) Jacob and Esau were both sinners. What was the vital difference between them and between the nations that sprang from them? Contrast this chapter with xlix, especially verse 18.

Day 2. Gn. xxxvii.

(1) What three things specially aroused the envy and hatred of Joseph's brothers? To what other sins did their envy lead them? See Jas. iii. 16.

(2) Observe the depths of Jacob's sorrow for the loss of Joseph. Is such unrelieved gloom justifiable for those who believe in God?

Note.—A coat of colours; better 'a tunic with sleeves'. Cf. R.V. mg. It was a garment of distinction, perhaps implying freedom from manual toil. The ordinary tunic had no sleeves.

Day 3. Gn. xxxviii and xxxix.

(1) From what initial false step on Judah's part did all the events of sin and shame in chapter xxxviii originate? What may we learn therefrom? Cf. Gn. xxiv. 3, xxvi. 34, 35, xxvii. 46–xxviii. 4.

(2) It has been pointed out that in Joseph were combined the best qualities of his ancestors: the faith and faithfulness of Abraham, the meekness of Isaac, the ability and energy of Jacob, and the personal beauty of his mother. How is this illustrated in chapter xxxix?

(3) Over what temptations did Joseph gain the victory?

Notes.—(1) In xxxviii. 21, 'harlot' is literally 'holy woman', i.e. consecrated to a Canaanite god; contrast Jehovah's holiness, verse 10.

(2) See Ps. cv. 17, 18, which shows how Joseph's imprisonment began.

Day 4. Gn. xl–xli. 13.

(1) What qualities in Joseph are shown in today's portion? Find at least five.

(2) How did God make Joseph's prison experiences 'work together for good'?

Note.—xl. 2. 'Chief of the butlers' and 'Chief of the bakers' were titles for high officials of Pharaoh's court.

Day 5. Gn. xli. 14-57.

(1) What in Joseph so impressed Pharaoh and his court that he was made ruler of Egypt? What impresses you most in Joseph? When you lay your own character alongside his, wherein do you fail?

(2) If we have found in Christ the Bread of Life and men around us are perishing, what spiritual lesson may be drawn from verses 54-57?

Day 6. Gn. xlii.

(1) What was the motive of Joseph's apparent harshness towards his brethren? For his real feelings see verses 24, 25. Have we not here an illustration of methods which God also uses? See Heb. xii. 6, 11; Je. xxxi. 18, 19.

(2) What brought Joseph's brothers to the recognition and acknowledgment of their guilt? See verse 21.

(3) How mistaken the attitude of Jacob in verse 36! What may we learn from this in regard to our own attitude when 'all things seem against us'? See Ps. xliii. 5; Rom. xv. 13.

Day 7. Gn. xliii.

(1) Why did Jacob yield to Judah's appeal when he had refused the earlier appeal of Reuben in xlii. 37, 38?

(2) Why do you think Joseph gave Benjamin portions five times as large as those given to the others? Was it affection for Benjamin, or was it a further test of his brothers? See xxxvii. 4.

Week 6. GENESIS XLIV–L

Day 1. Gn. xliv.

(1) How do the actions of Joseph's brothers in this chapter show that they were indeed changed men? Contrast their former behaviour towards their father and towards a young brother in xxxvii.

(2) Observe how in all this second visit to Egypt Judah takes the lead; see xliii. 3, 8, xliv. 14, 16, 18. What qualities are revealed in his speech before Joseph in verses 16-34? And how does this teach us that we should not despair of any? See xxxvii. 26, 27, xxxviii. 1; Ps. cxix. 59, 60, 176.

Day 2. Gn. xlv.

(1) Consider the parallel between verses 1-15 and the story in Acts ii. 22-39. We have, for example (a) Joseph made known to his brethren (cf. Acts ii. 36); (b) Joseph's brethren troubled in his presence (cf. Acts ii. 37); (c) reconciliation following on repentance (cf. Acts ii. 38).

(2) What blessings did the restoration of family harmony and fellowship bring in its train?

Day 3. Gn. xlvi–xlvii. 12.

(1) See Week 4, Day 3 (1). Do you find the same three lines of especial guidance converging in Jacob's going down to Egypt? What larger plan had God in view than was in the thought of Jacob and his sons?

(2) What trait in Joseph is revealed by his whole management of Jacob's arrival in Egypt? See Pr. xiii. 16; Is. xi. 2, lii. 13.

(3) How does this portion illustrate, typically or otherwise, (a) Jn. xiv. 6; (b) 2 Cor. iv. 17, 18?

Day 4. Gn. xlvii. 13–xlviii.

(1) What did Joseph, by their own confession, do for the people of Egypt? How was it that in his exalted position and amid the pressure of secular duties he remained true to his father's God?

(2) Contrast the two retrospects given by Jacob of his life in xlvii. 9 and xlviii. 15, 16. What are the differences between them and which is the one most worthy of our imitation?

(3) Chapter xlviii should be read in the light of Heb. xi. 21. What quality is revealed in Jacob by the fact that, when dying, he 'worshipped' and 'blessed' (that is, conveyed to his grandsons the inheritance promised to Abraham and to his seed)? See 1 Jn. v. 4; 1 Cor. xv. 55-57.

Day 5. Gn. xlix.

(1) Three features characterize this chapter: (a) the unity of the family, cleaving by faith to the God of their fathers and to the promises made to Abraham and to his seed; (b) the sins and blemishes of individuals; (c) the glorious hope for the future. Consider these facts, and note how, because of the first, God in His grace can fulfil the third, in spite of the second. Cf. Ps. cxxx. 3, 4, 7, 8; Mt. xvi. 15-18; 1 Cor. vi. 9-11.

(2) What picture of a victorious fighter is given in verses 23-25a, and what is the secret of his victory? Have you learned this secret? See Eph. vi. 10; Phil. iv. 13.

Note.—Verse 10, 'till Shiloh come', should perhaps be rendered 'till He come whose it is'. Cf. Ezk. xxi. 27, which is possibly an intentional reference to this verse.

Day 6. Gn. l.

(1) Comparing l. 1-13 with xxviii. 10-15, reflect how faithful and gracious God had been in the fulfilment of His promises even in Jacob's own lifetime. See Ps. cxlvi. 5, 6.

(2) Why were Joseph's brothers so slow to believe that Joseph had really forgiven them? What evidence is there that Joseph was grieved by their unbelief, and what light does this cast upon the pain our own unbelief towards God must cause Him?

(3) How long a time elapsed between Jacob's coming to Egypt and Joseph's death, and what was taking place in those years? See verses 22, 23; Ex. i. 7. How does this make Joseph's faith, expressed in verses 24, 25, the more conspicuous? See Heb. xi. 22.

Day 7. Revision.

Consider Joseph as a type of Christ. How many parallels can you find?

LUKE

INTRODUCTION

(See New Bible Handbook, pp. 319-322, 333-338)

THIS Gospel is proved by its style and language to have been written by a *Greek doctor*, who was identical with the writer of the Acts of the Apostles, and, as the latter book shows, was a companion of Paul. Only Luke, 'the beloved physician', fits these conditions, and as he was not a man of note, there would have been no inducement to attribute the Gospel to him had he not actually been the author.

The most probable explanation of the abrupt ending to Acts is that Luke brought that book up to date, and that Paul was still in his first imprisonment at Rome when Acts was finished. This would give a date of about A.D. 62 for Acts, and a year or two earlier as the latest date for the Gospel.

This Gospel lays a special emphasis on the human nature of the Lord Jesus, though witnessing also with no doubtful voice to His Deity; see, e.g. x. 21, 22, xxiv. 26, 49. His sympathy with the suffering and bereaved, the despised and the outcast, is brought into clear view: and the universal nature of the gospel, intended for Samaritan and heathen as well as the Jew, is strongly emphasized. The free offer of salvation and the impossibility of acquiring merit come out again and again, e.g. xv. 11-32, xvii. 7-10, xviii. 14, xxiii. 39-43.

ANALYSIS

i, ii. The birth and childhood of our Lord and the Baptist.

iii–iv. 13. The preaching of John; the baptism and temptation of the Lord.

iv. 14–ix. 50. The ministry in Galilee.

ix. 51–xix. 28. Journeyings towards Jerusalem; ministry outside Galilee.

xix. 29–xxi. Last days of public teaching.

xxii–xxiv. The last supper, the arrest, trial, death, and resurrection of the Lord.

Week 7. LUKE I AND II

Day 1. Lk. i. 1-23. See R.V., especially in the preface (verses 1-4).

(1) What do we learn from the preface as to (a) the sources of Luke's information, (b) the care which he took to verify his facts,

(c) the importance which he attached to giving a truthful record?

(2) What was the mission assigned to John the Baptist? What was the nature of his greatness (verse 15)? See also verses 66, 67; Mt. xi. 10, 11, 13.

Day 2. Lk. i. 24-38.

(1) Verses 31-33 and 35. What seven things are said in these verses about the person and destiny of the promised Child?

(2) Contrast Mary's reception of the angel's message with the attitude shown by Zacharias. Cf. verse 45.

Day 3. Lk. i. 39-56.

(1) What three divine attributes does Mary extol in verses 49, 50?

(2) What principle of God's working is revealed in the *manner* of the Saviour's coming? See verses 51-53 and 1 Cor. i. 26-31.

(3) What features in Mary's character shine forth in this song?

Day 4. Lk. i. 57-80.

The song of Zacharias may be divided thus: verses 68-70, thanks to God for the coming of the Messiah; verses 71-75, the purpose of the Messiah's coming; verses 76, 77, the mission of John; verses 78, 79, further picture of Messiah's coming.

(1) The song refers primarily to the Jewish nation. On what principle has the Christian Church appropriated it for its own use? See Rom. xv. 8, 9; 1 Pet. ii. 9.

(2) What divine attributes are extolled in Zacharias' song?

(3) What, according to verses 74-75 and 77-79, is the *purpose* of salvation? Who, in the application of the song to ourselves, are our enemies? How much of the salvation here spoken of are we experiencing?

Note.—Verse 69. 'A horn of salvation', that is, one who has strength to effect salvation; the horn of an animal was a common symbol of strength and power.

Day 5. Lk. ii. 1-20. In verses 10 and 14 see R.V.

(1) Verses 1-7. How do these verses illustrate the control of God over all, bringing to pass His own purposes through the free actions of men? See i. 70; Mi. v. 2; Tit. i. 3.

(2) What may we learn from the angel's message and the rejoicing of the heavenly host concerning the *importance* of the birth of Jesus? How are the shepherds an example to us in the manner of their response to the divine word of revelation?

Day 6. Lk. ii. 21-39.

(1) In what ways did Mary and Joseph show their punctilious obedience to God's law? What evidence does the portion give also of the existence among the people of a hidden company of devout souls in whose breasts burned a living flame of pure religion? Cf. Mal. iii. 16, iv. 2.

(2) What did Simeon see in the child that lay in his arms (verses 30-32, 34 and 35)? Whence had the aged saint this insight?

Notes.—(1) Verses 21-24. After the circumcision of the child two rites had to be performed: first, his presentation to God, and redemption by a money payment (verse 23; Ex. xiii. 2, 13; Nu. iii. 44-47); and second, the sacrifice of purification for the mother (verse 24; Lv. xii).

(2) Verse 25, 'waiting for the consolation of Israel', i.e. for the coming of the Messiah. For other phrases of similar meaning, see verse 38 and xxiii. 51.

(3) Verses 34, 35, 'is set', i.e. 'is appointed'. Three things are said: (a) through this child many will fall (cf. Is. viii. 14) and many will rise up according as they reject or receive Him; (b) He will be a sign from God, unwelcome to many; and (c) through Him the secret thoughts of many will be brought to light.

Day 7. Lk. ii. 40-52. Verse 49, see R.V. mg.

(1) What consciousness of a unique relation to God shines out in Jesus' words, and what does He say must be the necessary consequence in His life? How far do His words apply to us, who are sons of God in Him? Cf. Jn. xx. 21.

(2) How does this portion show the Lord's perfection at each stage of His human growth?

Week 8.   LUKE III–V. 26

Day 1. Lk. iii. 1-20. With verses 3-6 cf. i. 16, 17, 76, 77.

Verses 1 and 2 show the holy land divided among alien rulers and the high priesthood shared by two men (see verse 2, R.V.). 'What a frame for the picture of the appearing of the Restorer!' (Godet).

(1) What is the Restorer's message? According to his teaching in verses 2-14 neither the forms of religion nor a godly ancestry are of any avail in providing an escape for the sinner from divine judgment. What alone suffices? As regards verses 16 and 17, verse 16 has been fulfilled. How far has verse 17 been fulfilled?

(2) What features in John's character stand out in this passage?

Notes.—(1) Verse 12. 'Publicans', i.e. 'tax-gatherers'.
(2) Verse 14. 'Soldiers'—these were Jewish soldiers, possibly armed police.

Day 2. Lk. iii. 21-38.

(1) What does the 'opened heaven' signify and what is implied in the words 'in bodily form as a dove'? What threefold testimony is given to Jesus by the voice from heaven? See Ezk. i. 1; Jn. iii. 3, 4; Mt. xii. 29, 30; Col. i. 13 (R.V.).

(2) With verse 23 (R.V.) cf. ii. 42. What had Jesus been doing in these intervening years? See Mk. vi. 3. Was He not ready for God's service at twenty-one years, or twenty-five, or twenty-seven? Why did He wait until He was about thirty years?

Note.—An obvious explanation of the difference between the genealogies in Matthew and Luke is that Luke's is really that of Mary, Joseph being son of Heli by marriage; a woman's name by itself would be impossible in a Jewish genealogy. There is no exception to this rule in Mt. i. 3, 5. Notice that Zerubbabel and Shealtiel come into both genealogies: in Matthew, Shealtiel is probably son by adoption of the childless Jehoiachin (see Je. xxii. 30).

Day 3. Lk. iv. 1-13.

(1) What proof do we find in this story that temptation is not sin, and that it may come most strongly after some special experience of God? Observe in verses 2 and 3 the special moment chosen by the devil for his attack. Cf. Mk. xiv. 38.

(2) Jesus was entering upon a life and ministry, the foundation principle of which was faith in, and loving obedience to, God His Father. What light does this throw upon the nature of the devil's attack, and upon his twice-repeated challenge 'If thou be the Son of God'? Cf. iii. 22.

(3) Looking at the three temptations separately, what was the special subtlety of each, and how did Jesus parry the thrust in each case? Cf. Eph. vi. 17.

Day 4. Lk. iv. 14-30. A sabbath day in Nazareth.

In verses 14-44 of this chapter is given a general statement of a preaching tour in the synagogues of Galilee, with a detailed account of two momentous sabbaths.

(1) Verses 16-21. Jesus speaks to the people of His own home town of Nazareth. With what startling claim does He begin, and how does He describe His mission?

(2) Verses 22-30. The people were moved but not convinced. Cf. verse 22. How did Jesus interpret to them their unspoken thoughts (verse 23), and what did He go on to imply (verses 25-27)? What made the people so angry?

Note.—Verses 18 and 19 are quoted from Is. lxi. 1, 2. Note where Jesus stopped: the 'day of vengeance' had not yet begun.

Day 5. Lk. iv. 31-44. A sabbath day in Capernaum.

(1) Try to picture the scenes in the synagogue, in Peter's house, and at sunset. What two facts about Jesus particularly impressed the people in the synagogue?

(2) The reception of Jesus at Capernaum was outwardly very different from that at Nazareth. But was the result very different in the end? See x. 13-15.

(3) Is the theory that demon possession is a form of madness and nothing more reconcilable with the facts here narrated and with our Lord's words and actions?

Note.—Verse 40. The Jewish sabbath ended at sunset. The people waited until the sabbath was over and then brought their sick for healing.

Day 6. Lk. v. 1-11. An eventful morning.

(1) Consider what happened from the point of view of the disciples and especially of Simon Peter: (a) Simon helping the Lord in His work; (b) Simon obedient to the Lord's word in the sphere in which he was expert and against his own judgment; (c) Simon astonished at the Lord's power, and made to feel that he was no fit companion for such a Master; (d) Simon summoned to a new task; (e) Simon and the others forsaking all and following Jesus. Reflect on the change this last step would bring about in their lives.

(2) Consider the incident in relation to Christ's work, and note how it marked a new development. The people were thronging round (verse 3). He needed helpers. How and where did He find them?

Day 7. Lk. v. 12-26. Two outstanding miracles.

(1) Sometimes men doubt Christ's *power* to save, and sometimes His *willingness*. Of which was the leper doubtful, and how did Christ reassure him? What may we learn from this incident in relation to our own need?

(2) Verses 17-26. In how many different respects do you find this miracle remarkable?

Week 9. LUKE v. 27–VIII. 21
Day 1. Lk. v. 27–vi. 10. Various grounds of opposition.

(1) The word 'why' occurs three times in this portion, introducing three grounds of offence which His critics found in Jesus' conduct. What are they, and how do Jesus' answers reveal the principles on which He acted?

(2) The new revelation which Jesus brought raises three questions: (a) Can it be combined with the old? (b) Who are the kind of men to whom the new can be entrusted? (c) What will be the reaction of those who are accustomed to the old on hearing the new? How are these questions answered in the three short parables of verses 36-39?

Note.—vi. 1. This was allowed on other days (Dt. xxiii. 25), but according to the scribes it was not lawful on the sabbath.

Day 2. Lk. vi. 11-38.

(1) Verses 11-19. The excitement of the people was increasing (verses 17-19) and the hostility of the scribes and Pharisees growing more intense (verse 11). What special action did Jesus take? See verses 12 and 13.

(2) Verses 20-38. A picture of the new society of the kingdom of God. Who are welcome to it and who are not? See verses 20-26 and cf. i. 53. What is its basic principle, and in what ways does it manifest itself? See verses 27, 31. How does it exceed the ordinary standards of men, and to what standard does it aspire? See verses 35-38. Are you a practising member of this society of the blessed?

Day 3. Lk. vi. 39-49.

(1) Verses 39-45. If we aspire to be guides to others, what two faults do the two parables in these verses teach us to avoid? Further, on what will our spiritual usefulness depend?

(2) Verses 46-49. When the house of our life is tested, what alone will enable it to stand? Cf. Jas. i. 22.

Day 4. Lk. vii. 1-17. Two outstanding miracles.

(1) How had this centurion come to believe on Jesus? And how did he conceive of Him in relation to the unseen world and its powers? Why was the Lord so astonished at his faith?

(2) Picture the two processions meeting at the city of Nain, and the scene that followed. What features in Jesus' character shine out in this story?

Day 5. Lk. vii. 18-35.

(1) What exactly was the doubt in John's mind? Do you find a clue to his perplexity in iii. 16, 17? Observe how our Lord took him back to the Scriptures (see verses 21-23 and cf. Is. viii. 14, 15, xxxv. 4, 5, lxi. 1).

(2) Note Jesus' testimony to John. If John in his mission was greater than all the prophets, consider how our Lord's words bring

out the surpassing privilege of the 'new covenant' believer. See
x. 23, 24; 2 Cor. iii. 7-11.

(3) What does this portion teach (a) about the longsuffering
mercy of God, and (b) about the personal responsibility of the
hearer?

Day 6. Lk. vii. 36-50.

(1) How did Jesus prove to this Pharisee that it was not
ignorance which made Him tolerate this woman's touch? What
do you think his attitude to Jesus really was? Did he believe in
Him?

(2) What evidence is there that something had already happened in this woman's life and that she was acting under deep
emotion?

(3) What does Jesus look for in those who receive forgiveness
of sins?

Note.—The conjunction 'for' in verse 47 means 'as is shown by the fact that'

Day 7. Lk. viii. 1-21.

(1) What light do verses 1-3 throw upon the way our Lord and
the twelve were at this time supported? What evidence is there
that Jesus at this time deliberately adopted a new method of
teaching? Contrast the method of teaching here with that of vi.
17-49, and compare Mt. xiii. 11. Note in verse 4 the size of
the crowd.

(2) What experience have you of the truth of this parable in
yourself and in others? What sorts of people do the four soils
represent?

(3) Taking the 'candle' or 'lamp' (R.V.) as denoting the revelation brought by Jesus, what is the application of verses 16-18 to
those who are His disciples?

Week 10. LUKE VIII. 22–X

Day 1. Lk. viii. 22-39.

(1) Verse 25. 'Where is your faith?' Jesus asked. In what was
the disciples' faith defective? Did they not seek Christ's aid?

(2) Verses 26-39. What was the man's condition before and
after he met Jesus? What may we learn from this about our
Lord's power to save?

(3) Why did Jesus grant the request of people who had no
desire for Him, and refuse the request of the man He had saved?

Day 2. Lk. viii. 40-56.

(1) What two kinds of touching the Lord are spoken of here? To what do they correspond in a spiritual sense?

(2) How do the incidents in this portion show the importance of faith and of continuing in faith?

Day 3. Lk. ix. 1-17.

(1) What new development in method is recorded in verses 1-6? Picture the twelve itinerating as here described. What lessons would they learn as a training for their future work and what would be the effect upon the places visited?

(2) What light is thrown in verses 10-17 upon our Lord's unselfishness (the R.V. is clearer here) and upon His concern for both physical and spiritual need? Which kind of need, however, was in His eyes the more important? See Jn. vi. 26, 27.

Day 4. Lk. ix. 18-36.

(1) What was the difference between the popular view of Jesus and that of the apostles? If Jesus were to ask you 'Whom do you say that I am?' what would be the answer of your heart?

(2) What new disclosure did Jesus now make concerning His future path? And what demands did He make upon those who would follow Him? Observe also what claims He makes for Himself.

(3) In the transfiguration scene notice (a) the revelation of Jesus' essential glory; (b) the witness given by Moses and Elijah (representing the law and the prophets) to His death; and (c) the divine approval upon His person and His teaching. In what ways would these facts strengthen the disciples' faith? See 2 Pet. i. 16-18.

Notes.—(1) 'Deny himself' means to refuse to recognize the claim of self.

(2) 'Take up his cross', that is, as those condemned to die were made to do on their way to execution.

Day 5. Lk. ix. 37-62. With verse 42 cf. Lk. vii. 15.

(1) In what five ways, as recorded in verses 37-56, did the twelve (or some of them) fail? Are you failing in any of these ways?

(2) How would you describe the three different types referred to in verses 57-62? Why was Jesus not satisfied with the response of these men to His summons to follow Him? Contrast Jesus' own attitude as described in verse 51.

Day 6. Lk. x. 1-24. The mission of the seventy—a further development in method. See Day 3 above.

(1) What do verses 1-16 show of the passion for evangelism in
our Lord's heart (see especially verses 1, 2)? Note also the importance of the message, the responsibility of the hearers, and the
principles of divine judgment.

(2) Contrast our Lord's joy in verse 21 with His sorrow in ix.
41. What grieves Him and what makes Him glad? What do
verses 17-24 teach concerning (a) the greatness of our privilege
in Christ; (b) the Father's method of working (verse 21, R.V.; cf.
1 Cor. i. 26-28); and (c) Jesus' unique relationship to the Father?

Note.—Verses 18, 19. The language here is highly symbolical. 'Heaven',
as in verse 15, signifies the height of power and prosperity. The language of
verse 19 signifies complete triumph over the powers of evil (cf. ix. 1, 2, xi. 21,
22; Ps. xci. 13; Rom. xvi. 20).

Day 7. Lk. x. 25-42.

(1) What two words show that this lawyer was not a genuine
enquirer? How does the whole incident reveal that men cannot
escape from the condemnation of the law by whittling down its
requirements, which this lawyer tried to do? This was the great
mistake of the scribes. Jesus, on the other hand, showed that the
law's meaning is far deeper and higher than men thought.

(2) This incident gives the answer of the *law* to the lawyer's
questions. What is the answer of the *gospel*? See Jn. iii. 16; 1 Jn.
v. 11, 12. Does the gospel exempt men from the obligation to
love, or what does it do? See Rom. iii. 31, viii. 4.

(3) With what differing matters were Martha and Mary concerned? Which did Jesus think the more important, and how
did He solve the issue? See verse 40, R.V. mg.

Week 11. LUKE XI–XIII. 21

Day 1. Lk. xi. 1-13.

(1) Verses 6-9. Do we not often find ourselves, as Christians,
in exactly this position? Someone comes across our path and we
feel we ought to help, but we are utterly unable. How does this
parable tell us what to do?

(2) How does our Lord's teaching emphasize that it is enor-
mously worth while to pray? Have you grasped the force of His
argument, and are you praying? For what supreme gift does
Jesus encourage us to ask in absolute assurance of receiving it?

Day 2. Lk. xi. 14-36.

In verses 15 and 16 are recorded two attacks upon Jesus: the one a charge of collusion with Satan, the other a challenge to give a sign 'from heaven'. Jesus deals with the first in verses 17-26, and with the second in verses 29-32.

(1) How does the Lord show the unreasonableness and falsity of the charge that He cast out devils by the devil's aid?

(2) What was the sign of Jonas the prophet? The Ninevites would regard him as one who had almost risen from the dead, and they repented at his preaching. How would the generation to whom Jesus preached stand in comparison in the judgment day, when they refused to repent even when He did actually rise from the dead? See Mt. xii. 40; 1 Cor. xv. 4.

(3) What was wrong with the generation to whom Jesus spoke? The light shone, but they did not see. Why?

Notes.—(1) Verse 19. 'Your sons', i.e. Jewish exorcists. Verses 20-22 show Jesus' complete mastery over Satan in comparison with the imperfect cures of the exorcists in verses 24-26.

(2) Verse 36. Jesus here describes the man who is wholly open to the light as himself transformed by it, so as to become 'full of light'. Cf. 2 Cor. iii. 18.

Day 3. Lk. xi. 37-54.

In verses 39-44 Jesus addresses the Pharisees, and in verses 45-52 the lawyers (or scribes).

(1) How would you translate His accusations against the Pharisees into terms of modern life?

(2) What three charges does He level against the lawyers, and what judgment does He say is on its way?

Notes.—(1) Verse 41. A loving spirit is the true purifier.

(2) Verse 44. Contact with a grave was defiling (Nu. xix. 16). Hence the Jews were accustomed to whitewash their graves that people might avoid them.

(3) Verse 49. 'The wisdom of God', probably meaning 'God in His wisdom'. Cf. Pr. i. 20-31.

Day 4. Lk. xii. 1-12.

(1) In the light of xi. 49, 53, 54 and xii. 1, consider what need there must have been to steady and strengthen the disciples.

(2) What is Jesus' teaching here concerning (a) the final triumph of His word; (b) the security of His people; (c) the final difference between faithful confessors and those who deny or blaspheme; (d) the divine help that will be given in the hour of need?

(3) What, then, should be the inner attitude of the disciple in the face of threatening danger?

Day 5. Lk. xii. 13-34.

(1) In what does a man's life consist? See verse 15 and cf. Jn. xvii. 3.

(2) Where did the rich man in the parable go wrong? Was he wrong to pull down his barns and build greater?

(3) What should be the central motive in the life of a Christian? And if this is functioning rightly, what about other things? Why need not the Christian 'be anxious'?

Notes.—(1) Verse 22. 'Take no thought'; follow R.V.: 'Be not anxious'.
(2) Verse 31. 'The kingdom of God'; see Rom. xiv. 17.

Day 6. Lk. xii. 35-59.

The thought of the kingdom leads naturally to the return of the King.

(1) What exactly is meant by being ready for the Lord's return? What aspects of readiness and unreadiness are shown in the three parables in verses 35-48?

(2) Consider (a) the suddenness of the return; (b) the greatness of the rewards to the faithful; and (c) the principle on which judgment is inflicted on the unfaithful.

(3) Before the return can take place, Jesus must endure the cross which, while it brings salvation, brings also division and judgment. What warning does the Lord give to His disciples about the former (verses 51-53), and what to the multitude about the latter (verses 54-59)?

Notes.—(1) Verse 49. Follow R.S.V. here: 'I came to cast fire upon the earth, and would that it were already kindled!'
(2) Verse 50. The suspense and agony of anticipation are meant; the thought of Calvary was already a Gethsemane to the Lord.
(3) Verses 58, 59. The meaning is 'Be reconciled to God before the day of judgment.'

Day 7. Lk. xiii. 1-21.

(1) What is the connection of thought between verses 1-5 and 6-9? Cf. verses 3 and 5 with verse 9.

(2) Work out in detail the comparison between the woman and the beast, showing in what respects her claim was higher than its admitted right.

Note.—Verses 6-9. Cf. Rom. ii. 4, 5.

Week 12. LUKE XIII. 22–XVII. 19

Day 1. Lk. xiii. 22-35.

With verse 22 cf. ix. 51; x. 1. Note the *solemn* character of Jesus' teaching in these chapters.

(1) The kingdom is here represented as a palace to which

admission may be obtained by entering through a narrow gate. What is meant by this narrow gate (cf. Jn. x. 9), and what is Jesus' answer to the question of verse 23? See verse 24 ('many') and verse 29.

(2) How does this portion remind us of the truth of 2 Cor. vi. 2b, and that opportunities neglected may never return?

(3) Verse 34 is a window giving an insight into the heart of Jesus. What do you see there?

Note.—Verse 33. The three days cannot here mean literal days; perhaps they indicate a definite short period. 'Out of Jerusalem'; outside Jerusalem.

Day 2. Lk. xiv. 1-24.

A vivid narrative of a meal in a Pharisee's house. First, the assembling of the guests (verses 1-6); second, taking seats at the table (verses 7-11); third, Jesus' counsel to His host about the guests he should invite (verses 12-14); and fourth, the remark of someone present, giving occasion to the parable of the supper (verses 15-24). With verse 5 cf. xiii. 15.

(1) What attitude and disposition of heart is commended in verses 7-11 (cf. Mt. xi. 29; Lk. xxii. 26, 27; Phil. ii. 7)? And what in verses 12-14?

(2) What is the connection between the parable (verses 16-24) and verse 15? Notice the 'but' in verse 16, R.V. Were the excuses which the guests made genuine? If not, what was their real reason for not coming? Cf. Jn. xv. 24.

(3) Who finally participated in the feast? Cf. xiii. 29; Acts xxviii. 25-28; Rom. xi. 11.

Day 3. Lk. xiv. 25-35.

(1) Why did Jesus thus emphasize the cost of discipleship at this time?

(2) What, according to verses 26, 27, does discipleship involve? Was this teaching only for the time or is it always true?

(3) How do the two parables in verses 28-32 enforce the wisdom of counting the cost before embarking upon a life of following Jesus? What picture of Jesus do we get from this whole passage?

Note.—xiv. 26. Hate, i.e. love less than Me, especially if there should be a conflict between their claims and Mine.

Day 4. Lk. xv.

(1) What was the occasion of these parables being spoken? And how do they provide a complete justification of our Lord's attitude to the fallen and the despised?

(2) What led the prodigal son to leave home and what led him to return? During all this time how had his father regarded him?

(3) What is the spiritual equivalent of the robe, the ring, etc., when the sinner returns to God? How do the closing verses show that the Pharisees also might have enjoyed all these things, but missed them through a legal spirit? Cf. Ps. lxxxi. 10, 11.

Day 5. Lk. xvi. 1-13.

(1) To whom was this parable spoken, in contrast to the parables of chapter xv? From the fact that the parable gives instruction about the right use of money, do you think there may have been converted 'publicans' present (cf. xv. 1)? There is an almost playful touch in this story, very different from the tone of the next parable spoken to the Pharisees.

(2) For what did the steward's master commend him? And in what way is this steward an example to disciples? See verses 8, 9.

(3) How do verses 10-12 show that Jesus was not in any way condoning dishonest practices in His references to the unjust steward?

Notes.—(1) The *details* of the parable have no special significance.

(2) Verse 9. To be read as in R.V. 'Friends'—perhaps a reference to such people as the 'Lazarus' of the next parable. 'The Mammon of Unrighteousness.' Weymouth renders 'the wealth which is ever tempting to dishonesty'.

(3) Verse 13. A further reason for generous giving, namely, that Mammon, if master, will steal the heart from God. The best way of ensuring that wealth is not master is to give it away with a liberal hand.

Day 6. Lk. xvi. 14-31. The end of a selfish life.

(1) Contrast the earthly scene (verses 19-21) and the scene beyond this life (verses 22, 23). What was the sin for which the rich man was punished? Can you see a connection of thought between this parable and that of the unjust steward?

(2) What does the parable teach about (a) the opportunity of repentance; (b) the reality of future punishment; (c) the authority of the Old Testament Scriptures?

(3) Verse 31. What is the principle lying behind these words? See Jn. v. 36, 38, 40.

Notes.—(1) Verses 16-18. From the days of the Baptist the privilege of the Jew was over; men of every race could press into the kingdom. Yet the moral law stood unshaken as ever, as, for instance, the sanctity of marriage.

(2) Verse 23. Hell: as R.V. shows, the Greek word is not Gehenna but Hades, i.e. the state before the Judgment.

Day 7. Lk. xvii. 1-19.

(1) What four subjects are spoken of in verses 1-10? And what kind of spirit do they pre-suppose in a true disciple, if he is to live according to this teaching?

(2) Study the story of the lepers as an illustration of the way of salvation from sin, asking yourself such questions as 'How did their healing begin? What brought it to pass?' etc.

Notes.—(1) Verse 3, see Lv. xix. 17, 18.
(2) Verse 12, see Lv. xiii. 45, 46.
(3) Verse 14, see Lv. xiv. 2.

Week 13.   Luke xvii. 20–xx. 18

Day 1. Lk. xvii. 20-37.

(1) Verses 20, 21. What do our Lord's words reveal as to the essential nature of the kingdom of God? Cf. Jn. iii. 3; but see also Lk. xiii. 19, and verse 24 below.

(2) What aspects of our Lord's return are emphasized in to-day's portion? How will His return find the world, and how should it find His own people?

Notes.—(1) Verse 21. 'Within you'. The words may also mean 'among you' or 'in your midst' (see R.V. mg.). The general sense is not affected.
(2) Verse 37. Where a society is dead, judgment follows. Cf. Jb. xxxix. 30.

Day 2. Lk. xviii. 1-14.

(1) Verses 1-8. What condition of the people of Christ is implied in the comparing of them to a widow?

(2) The parable is a powerful argument for persistent un-wavering continuance in prayer. To bring out its full force, contrast the widow with the elect and God with the unjust judge.

(3) Verses 9-14. How does this parable illustrate 1 Sa. xvi. 7 and lay bare a fundamental error of the Pharisees? What lesson does Jesus draw from it?

Day 3. Lk. xviii. 15-34.

(1) See verse 17. To what characteristics of children do you think our Lord was referring?

(2) What did this ruler 'lack'? And how did the challenge of Jesus bring it to light? Cf. ix. 23, 24; xiv. 26, 27, 33.

(3) What subject filled the Lord's mind in these days, and how did He seek to fortify the twelve in face of it? Looking at today's portion as a whole, what demands are made upon, and what promises are made to, disciples who are willing to go all the way with the Lord?

Day 4. Lk. xviii. 35–xix. 10.

(1) Compare and contrast the two men whose stories are told in this portion. With all these differences what had they in common? What may we learn from the different way in which Jesus dealt with each?

(2) What important part of repentance (in the case of the one who has wronged others) is here shown to us?

Day 5. Lk. xix. 11-28.

(1) What evidence do you find of a growing excitement and expectancy among the people? What was the main purpose of this parable?

(2) What does the parable teach about the present responsibility of every follower of Christ and about future judgment? Cf. 2 Cor. v. 9, 10.

(3) On what ground was the servant who made no use of the pound given to him condemned? Was the excuse he gave for his inactivity a valid one?

Notes.—(1) Verse 14. Observe the hostile conditions under which the servants laboured.

(2) The phrase 'taking up', etc., in verses 21, 22 was probably a current expression for a grasping person.

Day 6. Lk. xix. 29-48.

(1) What was Jesus' purpose in making this public entry into Jerusalem? See Zc. ix. 9. What picture of the nature of His kingship did He give by it?

(2) How does this portion show that love and judgment are not mutually exclusive, as many suppose, and that opportunities for salvation do not last for ever? Cf. xiii. 24-30.

Day 7. Lk. xx. 1-18.

(1) How would a right reply to our Lord's question (verse 4) answer the question of the deputation?

(2) Verses 9-18. To whom and to what does this parable refer? What claim does Jesus openly make for Himself?

(3) Compare verse 18 with Lk. xix. 10. What may we learn by combining these two sayings?

Week 14. LUKE XX. 19–XXII

Day 1. Lk. xx. 19-47.

(1) Observe in what an atmosphere of hostility, intrigue, and suspicion our Lord moved. Consider carefully the meaning of both halves of His answer about the tribute (verse 25). How far are you obeying both commands?

(2) The doctrine of the resurrection appeared to the Sadducee ridiculous, because of the practical complications it seemed to

them to entail. Nor did they find it set forth in the Pentateuch, which they regarded as alone authoritative. How did the reply of Jesus meet their objections on both grounds? For verse 37, see R.V.

(3) What is the answer to the question in verse 44? See Rom. i. 3, 4.

Day 2. Lk. xxi. 1-19.

(1) What do we learn from verses 1-4 as to how God regards the gifts of His worshippers? Cf. 2 Cor. viii. 2, 12.

(2) Verses 5-19. The divisions are as follows: verse 6, complete destruction of the temple foretold; verse 7, two questions by the disciples; verses 8-19, an outline of what will happen before the temple is destroyed.

What teaching does the Lord give (a) as to the treatment which His disciples would receive; (b) as to their attitude under these trials? What promises does He make to them? Cf. Jn. xv. 18-27. With verse 19, R.V. cf. Lk. ix. 24, 25.

Day 3. Lk. xxi. 20-38.

(1) Verses 20-24. This is the answer to the disciples' question in verse 7. How clear was Jesus' vision of what would happen! With verse 22 cf. xi. 49–51; and with verse 24 cf. Rom. xi. 25.

(2) Verses 25-28. Jesus takes a forward look to His return. Contrast the attitude of Christians at that time with that of the ordinary man. What makes the difference?

(3) Yet Christians also may fail. What solemn warning is given in verses 34-36?

Note.—Verse 32. Some take this verse to apply only to the earlier part of the prophecy, which speaks of the destruction of the temple. Cf. xi. 50, 51. Others take the Greek word '*genea*' to mean 'race' and translate 'this (Jewish) race'; and again others take it to refer to the generation in which the signs begin to appear.

Day 4. Lk. xxii. 1-23.

(1) It is important to keep the different parties and figures in these final scenes clearly in view. Who are mentioned in verses 1-6 and what is the attitude of each towards Jesus?

(2) Comparing what is said of Judas in this portion with the references to him in Jn. xii. 4-6, xiii. 2 (R.V.), 26, 27, can you trace a progressive power of Satan over him? See also Jn. vi. 70, 71.

(3) Jesus, conscious that His death is at hand, discloses that His death is 'for them' (verses 19, 20). What further light is thrown upon the meaning of His death by the fact that He connects it (a) with the passover (see Ex. xii), and (b) with the new covenant prophesied by Jeremiah (Je. xxxi. 31-34)?

Day 5. Lk. xxii. 24-38.

(1) In what various ways does Jesus' love and concern for His disciples reveal itself in this portion? See Jn. xiii. 1. How does He thereby illustrate what He says of Himself in verse 27b?

(2) What root evil, prevalent in the world, does Jesus deal with in verses 24-27? Have you let Him deal with it in your own life? And are you living in this matter after His example?

(3) Can you identify in this passage (a) a special danger to which a backslider under conviction of sin is exposed; (b) the greatest help against that danger; (c) an important duty of the restored backslider?

Notes.—(1) Verse 32. Our Lord's prayer referred not to the denial (He knew Peter *would* deny Him), but to what would follow it. A.V. 'converted' is too strong; read with R.V. 'turned again'.

(2) Verse 36. The command to buy a sword symbolizes the time of insecurity and danger that was at hand: it was not an encouragement to resistance (see Mt. xxvi. 52).

Day 6. Lk. xxii. 39-53.

(1) What great facts about our Lord Himself and about the nature of His sufferings on the cross are indicated by the agony in Gethsemane? Could the prospect of physical pain and death by themselves have appalled Him so? Think of your share in responsibility for that agony.

(2) What is meant by the 'power of darkness'? What other references to the activity of Satan are there in this chapter? Cf. also Col. ii. 15 and i. 13, and consider the bearing of this on the answer to question (1).

(3) What facts show our Lord's mastery of the situation and the truth of His claim in Jn. x. 17, 18?

Day 7. Lk. xxii. 54-71.

(1) Trace out the various stages in Peter's downfall from verses 33-60. What brought him to repentance?

(2) Consider what our Lord had to endure, as described in verses 63-71. Meditate also on His sayings. Especially ask yourself, 'What does it mean to *me* that the Son of *Man* is seated at the right hand of the power of God?'

Note.—Verse 70. 'Ye say that I am', that is, 'It is as you say, I am He.'

Week 15.   LUKE XXIII AND XXIV

Day 1. Lk. xxiii. 1-25.

(1) What evasions of duty did Pilate make? We blame him; but if we reflect on what happens still, when people are faced by the claims of Jesus, what analogies should we find? Have you ever been guilty of similar evasions or compromise?

(2) How does this portion illustrate ii. 35b? How did the religious leaders of the Jews, Pilate, Herod, and the crowd show their true inward character and attitude when they had to say 'Yes' or 'No' to Jesus?

Day 2. Lk. xxiii. 26-49.

(1) Verses 26-31. 'In the Via Dolorosa Jesus experienced two alleviations of His suffering: the strength of a man relieved His body from the burden of the cross and the pain of His soul was cooled by the sympathy of women. Is it not a parable—a parable of what men and women can do for Him still?' (Stalker).

(2) What different attitudes towards our Lord are represented among those who were gathered round His cross?

Note.—Verse 31. A proverbial expression, which probably means: 'If the Romans treat one whom they admit to be innocent thus, what will they do to this city, when it rises up in rebellion against them?'

Day 3. Lk. xxiii. 26-49 (again).

(1) Verses 39-43. What brought this robber to penitence and faith? Was it anything that he had seen or heard on the way to or at Calvary? Consider the greatness of his faith, exercised in such surroundings. Notice also how the answer given by Jesus to his prayer far exceeded what he asked. Cf. Eph. ii. 4-7.

(2) What other words of our Lord on the cross are recorded by Luke, and what do we learn from each?

Day 4. Lk. xxiii. 50–xxiv. 12. With xxiv. 5, R.V. mg. cf. Rev. i. 18, A.V.

(1) What do we learn from verses 50-56 as to the attitude of Joseph and the women to the Lord at a time when His work seemed to have failed?

(2) Try to put yourself in the place of the women and imagine their experience on Easter morning. Ought they to have been perplexed (verses 6-8)? Is the Lord 'He that liveth' in your personal experience?

Day 5. Lk. xxiv. 13-35. With verse 34 cf. 1 Cor. xv. 5.

(1) Why do you think the Lord appeared to Peter before any of the other apostles? Cf. Mt. xii. 20.

(2) What do we learn from the story of the two disciples and from verses 44, 45 about the unity and inspiration of the Scriptures of the Old Testament, and about their trustworthiness? Also, what is needed in us if we are to gain in full measure what the Scriptures have to give?

Day 6. Lk. xxiv. 36-53.

(1) What was the first reaction of the disciples to the resurrection, as narrated in this chapter? What proofs convinced them that Jesus was indeed risen?

(2) What are the fundamental facts of the gospel to which witness must be borne 'the wide world o'er'? Who are to bear that witness, and in what power?

Note.—Verse 43. To be able to receive food is not necessarily the same as to need it.

Day 7. Revision.

EXODUS I–XX

INTRODUCTION

(See New Bible Handbook, pp. 89, 108, 115-123, 133-137)

THE name 'Exodus', taken from the Septuagint translation, means 'going out'. If we apply the word 'redeem' to the great deliverance from Egypt (Ex. vi. 6, xv. 13), the book itself shows us in which direction to look for the spiritual meaning lying behind the historic fact. These twenty chapters are indeed full of types: not only Egypt itself and the deliverance from it, but also the Red Sea, Marah, Elim, the manna, the rock, and the life-giving water, to name only the chief examples, all speak to us of spiritual truth.

In these chapters we read:

(a) Of redemption from bondage by power, and from death by blood; two parts of one whole.

(b) Of the love of God: manifesting itself first in compassion for His suffering people, then in action for their deliverance, and in wonderful patience with their faithlessness and obstinacy.

(c) Of the holiness of God demanding consecration, separation and purity, and giving a law which must be observed.

(d) Of the amazing ingratitude of man, despite the countless benefits showered upon him, and of a ready promise (so soon broken) to do *all* that Jehovah commanded.

(e) But also of one man, Moses who, like Abraham and Joseph, lived in the consciousness of God's presence and showed steadfast fidelity and conspicuous faith.

ANALYSIS

i–vii. 7. Israel in bondage; the call and training of Moses.

vii. 8–xv. 21. Israel redeemed; the plagues, the passover, and the crossing of the Red Sea.

xv. 22–xviii. Israel in the wilderness; needs met, despite ingratitude and unbelief.

xix, xx. Israel at Sinai; the revelation of the majesty of Jehovah; the ten commandments.

Week 16. EXODUS I–XI
Day 1. Ex. i and ii.

(1) What was the situation and outlook for the people of Israel, judging by human standards? But what four things are said of God in ii. 23-25? And what evidence is there in these chapters that faith was present and operative in some hearts? Cf. Heb. xi. 23-25.

(2) By what varied means from birth onwards was Moses prepared for his life work? See Acts vii. 20-29.

Day 2. Ex. iii–iv. 17.

(1) After considering God's self-revelation in the incident of the burning bush, in the declaration of His Name, and in His promises, how would you sum up God's being and character?

(2) What made Moses so reluctant to accept God's call? Was his attitude to be commended? See 2 Cor. iii. 5; Rom. xii. 3. But why, then, was the anger of the Lord kindled against him?

Note.—iii. 22. A.V., 'Borrow' correctly rendered 'ask' in R.V., so also xi. 2, xii. 35.

Day 3. Ex. iv. 18–vi. 9.

(1) Contrast iv. 29-31 with v. 20-21. What had intervened to

effect such a change in the people's attitude? Consider how Moses must have felt it. In his distress what did he do?

(2) How did God answer Moses' cry? Make a list of God's sevenfold 'I will' in vi. 2-9. If, as He did, He fulfilled these promises to Israel, what encouragement should this give us in regard to His promises to us in Christ?

Notes.—(1) Ex. iv. 24. This seems to mean that Moses was struck down by a severe and dangerous illness, the result of his neglect to circumcise his son, and his life was saved by Zipporah's prompt action. He could not act as God's instrument while in disobedience to His covenant.

(2) Ex. vi. 3. 'Known', r.v. mg. 'made known', i.e. in the meaning of the Name: there was no Jehovah-revelation to them. Once only in Genesis did God use that name of Himself, and then without emphasis or explanation (Gn. xxviii. 13).

Day 4. Ex. vi. 10–vii.

(1) How does God answer Moses' despairing plea in vi. 30? See vii. 1-5, and compare Is. xlii. 13.

(2) On what power did Pharaoh rely in his opposition to God's command? See vii. 11-13 and 22-23. In what form does this same kind of opposition manifest itself now? See 2 Tim. iii. 1-9.

Note.—vi. 12. 'Of uncircumcised lips'—uncircumcision symbolizes unfitness for God's service and hence, more generally, unfitness. Cf. iv. 10.

Day 5. Ex. viii.

(1) What is mentioned in this chapter as the double purpose of the plagues? See also Is. xlv. 22-25.

(2) What new evidences are given of God's power, and how would these hearten the people of Israel?

Note.—Verse 26; a reference to the sacrifice in Israelitish worship of bulls, cows or oxen, which in Egypt were sacred to Isis and therefore sacrosanct.

Day 6. Ex. ix.

(1) How does Pharaoh's attitude show the difference between sorrow for the consequence of sin and true repentance?

(2) What illustration is given in this chapter of the difference between faith in the word of God and unbelief, and of the consequences in each case?

Note.—ix. 15, 16. It is specially important to consult the r.v. here.

Day 7. Ex. x and xi.

(1) What was the result in the life of Pharaoh of persistent rejection of warnings sent by God? See Pr. xxix. 1; Is. xxx. 12-14.

(2) What spiritual lesson may we learn from Moses' refusal to

accept a compromise, where God's command is concerned? See
1 Thes. v. 22, 23.

(3) What was the secret of Moses' great courage? See Heb.
xi. 27.

Week 17.   EXODUS XII–XX

Day 1. Ex. xii. 1-36.

(1) What determined the passing over by the destroying angel
of the houses of the Israelites? And how is this a type of our
redemption in Christ? See 1 Pet. i. 18, 19.

(2) How were the Israelites to use the lamb's blood, and how
its flesh? What is the gospel counterpart of this?

(3) What is the significance of the unleavened bread? See 1
Cor. v. 6-8; 2 Tim. ii. 19.

Day 2. Ex. xii. 37–xiii.

(1) What further aspect of redemption is set forth in xiii. 3, 14,
16? See Lk. xi. 21-22; Eph. i. 19, 20. Are you proving both
aspects in personal experience?

(2) What lessons about guidance are taught in xiii. 17-22?

Day 3. Ex. xiv–xv. 21.

(1) Chapter xiv is one of the most vivid stories in the Bible.
Try to picture what happened, stage by stage. What does the
story teach us about God, about faith, and about the completeness
of God's salvation? See Rom. vi. 12-14.

(2) What does the song of triumph in xv declare concerning
God's character, and concerning what He has done and what He
will do? To what does this correspond in the life of the Christian?

Day 4. Ex. xv. 22–xvi.

(1) What reason is given twice in this passage why God allowed
His redeemed people to suffer thirst, disappointment, and hunger?
Cf. Dt. viii. 2, 16; 1 Pet. i. 6, 7.

(2) In what respects is the manna a type of the Lord Jesus?
See Jn. vi. 32-35, 48-51.

Day 5. Ex. xvii and xviii.

(1) What may we learn from the sequence of the two incidents
recorded in xvii? Amalek was a powerful foe (see Nu. xxiv. 20).
How would the experience at Rephidim strengthen Israel's faith
to meet the Amalekite attack?

(2) What, according to xvii. 15, was the lesson Israel was meant
to learn from the fight with Amalek?

(3) What does chapter xviii teach concerning the necessity of applying common sense to the management of church affairs? And what kind of men should be chosen as rulers? Cf. Acts vi. 1-4.

Day 6. Ex. xix.

(1) Study God's message to the people in xix. 3-6. What does He bid them remember? What does He promise them, and on what conditions? Cf. Tit. ii. 14; 1 Pet. ii. 5-9.

(2) How does this chapter emphasize the holiness of God?

(3) What was the new feature in God's revelation at this time? See verses 9, 11, 19; Dt. v. 22-27.

Day 7. Ex. xx.

(1) What do we learn from the ten commandments as to what God does not want to find in His people?

(2) In the light of Mk. xii. 29, 30; Gal. v. 14, 22, what may we learn concerning the life God does want His people to live and how it may be accomplished?

THE ACTS

INTRODUCTION

(See New Bible Handbook, pp. 344-350)

THE key to the book is found in the opening verses (i. 1-11), where attention is drawn to (1) the continued activity of Jesus, risen and ascended; (2) the apostles as the leaders chosen by Him (verse 2); (3) the Holy Spirit as the source of power; (4) Jesus' programme for the future. These facts are dominant throughout the book. It tells how the gospel spread from Jerusalem—the capital of the Jewish world—to Rome—the metropolis of the Gentile world; and shows also how Christianity, step by step, emerged from within the framework of the Jewish nation to become a universal religion; and these developments are consistently traced to the continued activities of the ascended Christ, and to the working of the Holy Spirit.

ANALYSIS

The book of Acts falls into two main parts: chapters i–xii, which give the story of the rise of the Church in Jerusalem and its extension to Judæa, Samaria, and Antioch; and chapters xiii-

xxviii, which describe Paul's three missionary journeys, his arrest
in Jerusalem, imprisonment in Cæsarea, and journey to Rome.
A more accurate analysis, however, reveals that there are (apart
from the introductory paragraph, i.1-11) six divisions or periods,
each concluding with a brief summary of progress. We then get
the following outline:

	i. 1–11.	Introduction.
1.	i. 12–vi. 7.	Progress in Jerusalem.
2.	vi. 8–ix. 31.	Extension to Judæa and Samaria.
3.	ix. 32–xii. 24.	Reception of Gentiles into the Church.
4.	xii. 25–xvi. 5.	A door of faith opened to the Gentiles.
5.	xvi. 6–xix. 20.	Extension to Macedonia, Achaia, and Asia.
6.	xix. 21–xxviii. 31.	Paul's journey to Rome.

Week 18. ACTS I–VI. 7

Day 1. Acts i. 1-11.

(1) What further preparation for their mission did the apostles
receive during the forty days mentioned in verse 3? In regard to
what matters were they instructed and enlightened?

(2) What is said in these verses about God the Father, about
the Holy Spirit, and about Jesus? The whole story of this book
flows from these facts. Are they transforming your life?

(3) What is taught in verse 11 about the fact and the manner
of our Lord's return?

Day 2. Acts i. 12–ii. 13.

(1) In the period between the ascension and the coming of the
Spirit, what did the disciples do? Note that they made no impact
upon the world outside, nor attempted to do so. What difference
did the coming of the Holy Spirit make in this respect, and what
may this teach us?

(2) What three signs were given in connection with the coming
of the Spirit? See ii. 3, 4 and 6, 8, 11. They express in symbol
what our Lord had already stated in word (see i. 8), that the
coming of the Spirit would lead to power, inspired utterance, and
universal testimony.

Note.—Pentecost was the Greek name for the feast called in the Old Testament 'the feast of harvest' (Ex. xxiii. 16) or 'the feast of weeks' (Dt. xvi. 9, 10).
It marked the end of the grain harvest, and began on the fiftieth day from the
day after the passover sabbath (Lv. xxiii. 15, 16). The season of the year being
favourable for travelling, Jerusalem was crowded with Jews from all parts
(Acts ii. 9-11).

Day 3. Acts ii. 14-47.

(1) What three passages of the Old Testament does Peter quote and what conclusions does he draw from each?

(2) What twofold offer is made in verse 38, and on what conditions?

(3) Summarize the results of the day of Pentecost. How would you describe the Church of the first days?

Day 4. Acts iii.

(1) The story of verses 1-11 vividly illustrates the gospel way of salvation. Observe how it shows, for example, man's *need*, the method of salvation, and its result. Have you ever been the link between Christ and a soul in need, as Peter was that day? How was the miracle wrought? See verses 12-16.

(2) In addressing these people of his own nation, what sins does Peter charge against them? And what promises does he make to them, and on what conditions? How far are his words applicable to us who are not Jews?

Note.—Verse 13. The word 'Son' (A.V.), 'Servant' (R.V.) is the word used in the Septuagint version for 'servant' in Is. lii. 13 and other similar messianic passages (xlii. 1-4, xlix. 1-6, l. 5-10), and seems to indicate that Peter had these passages in mind. Cf. Acts iii. 26; iv. 27, 30 (R.V.).

Day 5. Acts iv. 1-22.

(1) What caused the beginning of persecution and what form did it take?

(2) Picture the scene described in verses 5-21. Contrast the position, influence, and training of the judges with that of the two apostles. Yet with whom did victory lie? It will be helpful to write out Peter's defence in your own words. See also Lk. xxi. 12-15; 2 Tim. i. 7.

Note.—Verses 1-3. Peter was still speaking to the people when he and John were arrested by 'the captain of the temple', that is, the priest in charge of the temple guards, and by other Sadducees, who were the high priestly party among the Jews. They resented this teaching in the temple independently of their authority, and still more the teaching itself, which was not only contrary to their beliefs (Acts xxiii. 8) but a condemnation of their treatment of Jesus.

Day 6. Acts iv. 23–v. 16.

(1) On what facts is the prayer of the apostles based? And what three petitions did they make?

(2) What were the essentials of the Christian fellowship described in verses 32-35?

(3) What exactly was the sin of Ananias and Sapphira, and what led to it? If such a spirit had spread within the Church, what would have been the result? But what, in fact, did result from the divine judgment upon the sin? See verses 11-16.

Notes.—(1) v. 4. This verse shows that the giving spoken of in iv. 34 was entirely voluntary.

(2) v. 9. 'Tempt'. The word means to put God to the test, to challenge Him, as it were (see Ex. xvii. 2, 7; Acts xv. 10).

Day 7. Acts v. 17–vi. 7.

(1) Verses 17-42 give the answer to the petition 'Behold their threatenings'. Consider in what varied ways God brought help and deliverance to His servants while not wholly exempting them from suffering. Cf. Phil. i. 29.

(2) What purpose did the miracle of verses 19 and 20 serve? Consider its effect upon (a) the apostles; (b) the general body of believers; (c) the people; and (d) the rulers.

(3) How did the apostles deal with the incipient trouble mentioned in vi. 1? What lessons may we learn from their handling of it?

Note.—(1) vi. 1. 'Grecians' denotes Jews who had lived abroad and spoke Greek. 'Hebrews' were Jews of Palestine who spoke the Jewish tongue.

Week 19. ACTS VI. 8–IX. 31

Day 1. Acts vi. 8–vii. 16.

(1) Contrast this persecution in its origin and method with those that have gone before. Why was Stephen singled out for attack?

(2) What was the charge against Stephen? Do you think Stephen may have said something of the kind and that the witnesses are called 'false', not because what they alleged was wholly untrue, but because they twisted Stephen's words? Was not the real question at issue whether or not Jesus is the Messiah?

(3) Stephen goes back in his defence to a time in Israel's history before law and temple existed. Where, in that far-off time, does he find a foreshadowing of the experiences of Jesus?

Note.—vi. 11. Describes a whispering campaign by hired agitators who roused the anger of the people and of their leaders against Stephen, and this led to his arrest and trial (verse 12).

Day 2. Acts vii. 17-43.

Stephen now passes on in his review of Israel's history to the time of Moses.

(1) What does Stephen say regarding Moses as to the time and manner of his birth, his reception at the hands of his brethren,

God's appointment of him, and the services which he rendered? Consider in all these things the close parallel between Moses and Christ.

(2) Ponder the tragedy of Israel's unbelief, as described in verses 39-43. How did it manifest itself first in thought, will, and desire (verse 39), and finally in action (verses 40-43)? What was its penalty?

Day 3. Acts vii. 44–viii. 4.

(1) What two things does Stephen say about the tabernacle and temple, recognizing on the one hand their divine origin, and on the other their inadequacy? Cf. Heb. viii. 4-6.

(2) Consider the likeness between Stephen and his Lord in his life and character and in his death. Whence sprang that likeness? Cf. 2 Cor. iii. 18.

(3) What were the results for the Church of Stephen's witness (a) in suffering, (b) in extension? In regard to (a), see viii. 1, 3, ix. 1, xxvi. 10, 11; Gal. i. 13; and in regard to (b), see viii. 4, 5, xi. 19. May we not say that all the developments, recorded in later chapters, flowed from Stephen? Augustine said: 'If Stephen had not prayed, the Church would not have had Paul.'

Day 4. Acts viii. 5–25.

(1) Measure the greatness of Philip's success in Samaria by the difficulties against which he had to contend. Cf. Jn. iv. 9. To what was his success due? See Jn. xiv. 12; Acts i. 8.

(2) Simon was intellectually convinced of the truth and power of the gospel, but his heart was unchanged. How did this come to light?

Note.—Verses 14-17. The reason, no doubt, why the Holy Spirit had not yet fallen upon the Samaritan believers was that, as this was the first extension of the Church *beyond the borders of the Jewish people*, it was fitting that the seal of the Spirit (Eph. i. 13) should be given through Peter and John, as representing the apostles. In a similar way Peter was chosen to go to Cornelius (x. 5), though Philip was probably in Cæsarea at the time.

Day 5. Acts viii. 26-40.

(1) Consider well this Ethiopian official! An Ethiopian, yet a worshipper of the God of Israel; a eunuch, yet humble and sincere; a man of wealth and position, yet full of spiritual hunger. Does he not rebuke us, who excel him in spiritual advantage, yet fall short of him in faith and devotion?

(2) Learn from Philip how to win a soul. What qualities are here portrayed?

(3) A moment before, these two men were separated by seemingly impassable barriers; a moment after, they are sitting together in absorbed conversation about Jesus Christ. If Christ be not alive and working with His people (Mk. xvi. 20), how could such things happen? But if Christ is alive, may they not happen with us also?

Day 6. Acts ix. 1-16.

(1) What do these verses reveal of Christ's power, majesty, and glory, and also of His compassion, love, and grace? Cf. 1 Tim. i. 12-14.

(2) In what way is Ananias an example to us? Consider what great issues may result from one act of trustful obedience.

Day 7. Acts ix. 17-31.

(1) How did Paul prove his sincerity from the very beginning of his Christian life? Cf. 1 Jn. iii. 14; Ps. xvi. 2, 3 (R.V.); Acts xxvi. 19, 20. What word is twice used of his preaching?

(2) What two marks of healthy spiritual life in a church or individual are found in verse 31? Comparing this verse with vi. 7, notice how the Church has extended.

Notes.—(1) The visit to Arabia of which Paul speaks in Gal. i. 17 should probably be fitted in between verses 21 and 22 of the story in Acts.

(2) Verse 29. 'Grecians', i.e. Greek-speaking Jews, probably the same persons as are mentioned in vi. 9.

Week 20.   ACTS IX. 32–XII. 24

Day 1. Acts ix. 32-42.

(1) What evidences do you find in these verses that a widespread revival was going on at this time, and that Christ, dwelling in His people, still moved among men as Saviour, Teacher, Healer, Friend?

(2) How do you picture Dorcas? What ideals of Christian character and service are exemplified in her?

Note.—How reminiscent Peter's words and actions are of his Master! With verse 34 cf. Mk. ii. 11; Jn. v. 8; and with verses 40, 41 cf. Mk. v. 35-43.

Day 2. Acts ix. 43–x. 22.

(1) Contrast the two towns, Joppa and Cæsarea, and the two men, Peter and Cornelius. It has been said that this chapter represents in miniature the whole story of the Acts. Do you agree?

(2) What practical action did their visions involve for Cor-

nelius and for Peter? Are we also willing, on receiving new light from God, to follow Christ along new paths?

Notes.—(1) ix. 43. This verse really belongs to the Cornelius story. Joppa was a very Jewish town, loyal to ancient tradition; Cæsarea a semi-pagan city, modelled on Rome.

(2) x. 1. Cornelius was a Gentile, a Roman soldier of 'the Italian cohort' (R.V. mg.), so called, probably, because composed of men born in Italy.

(3) x. 4. 'For a memorial'. The word is that used in Lv. ii. 2, etc., in connection with the remembrance offering. The angel's message assures Cornelius that though, in his uncircumcision, he had no share in the sacrifices of the temple, yet his prayers and alms were acceptable before God.

Day 3. Acts x. 23-48.

(1) What new truth had Peter learned from the vision? See verses 28 and 35. Are we retaining through prejudice distinctions which God has removed?

(2) When Peter addressed Jews, what truths did he use to awaken their conscience (see ii. 36, iii. 13-15)? What truth did he use now? Do you find any other indications in this address that it was spoken before a Gentile audience?

(3) Consider the character of Cornelius as revealed in this chapter. If he was such a devout man before, what did he gain by believing on Jesus? See xi. 14.

Note—Verses 34, 35. The meaning of Peter's words is not that men can be saved by their own good works, but that men like Cornelius and his friends are not excluded from God's favourable regard on the ground of their nationality. Their devout spirit is just as pleasing in God's sight as a similar spirit and behaviour would have been in a Jew.

Day 4. Acts xi. 1-18.

(1) On what does Peter lay emphasis in his story of what happened? Note, for example, what he was doing when he saw the vision, whence the sheet came and whither it went, why the men came seeking him, and why he went with them. Note, too, the phrase 'the angel standing in his house'. If an angel stood there, might not an apostle do so?

(2) Verse 16. 'Ye shall be baptized'. When the words were spoken by Jesus (see i. 5) the apostles had no idea that any who were not Jews could be included in the 'ye'. But what, in fact, had now happened? This is the climax of Peter's argument, and it leads on logically to the doctrine of Eph. iii. 6.

Note.—Verse 2. 'They that were of the circumcision'—an indication that there was in the church in Jerusalem a conservative party who insisted on the necessity of circumcision for all. Cf. xv. 1, 5.

Day 5. Acts xi. 19-30.

(1) What was the distinctive feature that from the beginning marked the preaching of the gospel at Antioch (see note below)? And what was the result?

(2) What three stages marked the establishing of the church there?

(3) What evidences are found in the story of the vitality and influence of the church in Antioch and of its Christian spirit? Cf. ii. 44, 45, iv. 34-37.

Notes.—(1) Verse 22. The city of Antioch, capital of the Roman province of Syria, was one of the three largest cities of the empire. It was famous for its commerce, art and literature, and infamous for its vice and frivolity.

(2) 'Grecians', better as in R.V., 'Greeks'. What is meant is not Greek-speaking Jews, but Greek-speaking *Gentiles*.

(3) Verse 26. 'Christians'—a name probably given first by the heathen populace, but accepted later as a name in which to glory (1 Pet. iv. 16).

Day 6. Acts xii. 1-17.

(1) What evidence is there in this portion of changes (a) in the government of Palestine; (b) in the mood of the people of Jerusalem towards believers; and (c) in the organization of the church in Jerusalem?

(2) Was ever deliverance so unlikely? Consider how many obstacles lay between Peter and liberty. What was the church's resource?

(3) Can you bear witness that intercessory prayer has not lost its efficacy? Cf. 2 Cor. i. 8-11; Eph. iii. 20, 21.

Notes.—(1) Verse 1. 'Herod the king', a grandson of Herod the Great, who was made king over all the territory ruled by his grandfather.

(2) Verse 6. The deliverance took place on the last possible night and, as verse 18 possibly suggests, in the last watch of the night.

Day 7. Acts xii. 18-24.

(1) How would you estimate the character of Herod from this chapter?

(2) How do these verses show that behind all that happens, God is watching and working? What may we learn from Herod's end?

(3) Review the progress made in this third period. What great new developments have taken place in the forward march of the gospel?

Week 21. Acts XII. 25–XIV

Day 1. Acts xii. 25–xiii. 12.

With the return of Barnabas and Saul to Antioch (xii. 25) begins the story of a great expansion of the gospel among *Gentiles*, from Antioch as a base.

(1) What was the part played by the Holy Spirit in the initiation of the new advance, and in the victory over the sorcerer Elymas?

(2) What was the special significance of the facts recorded in verses 11b and 12?

(3) What evidences are there that Paul now stepped into the place of leadership of the Gentile mission? Contrast, for example, verse 1 (where his name is last on the list) with the phrase in verse 13, 'Paul and his company'.

Notes.—(1) Verse 2. They may well have been praying about the future of the work when guidance came, possibly through a prophet inspired of the Spirit.

(2) Verse 6. Bar-jesus or Elymas was a representative of a numerous class of men who practised sorcery and magic and claimed to control the powers of the unseen world. Their influence was at the time widespread and powerful, as is shown by the fact that a Roman procurator had one of them in his entourage.

(3) Verse 9. 'Saul, who also is called Paul'. The change over, at this point in the narrative, from Paul's Jewish name to his Gentile and Roman name seems to indicate that in Luke's judgment this incident marks the beginning of Paul's special ministry as apostle of the Gentiles.

Day 2. Acts xiii. 13–29.

(1) How does Paul show that the coming of Jesus was the culminating point of Israel's history?

(2) How does he account for our Lord's rejection by the leaders of His own nation?

(3) Contrast in these verses God's grace and Israel's sin.

Notes.—(1) Verses 13 and 14. From Perga to Antioch in Pisidia involves an ascent of 3,600 feet from the sea coast to a high plateau, which at the time was a flourishing region of Græco-Roman civilization. Possibly this was more than John Mark had contemplated when the journey began, and hence his return to Jerusalem.

(2) Verse 16. 'Men of Israel, and ye that fear God'. The synagogue congregation consisted of two classes: Jews and God-fearing Gentiles. Paul, throughout his address, expressly includes both. See also verse 26.

Day 3. Acts xiii. 30-43.

(1) What proofs does Paul give that, notwithstanding His death upon a tree, Jesus is the promised Messiah?

(2) What offer does Paul make to his hearers? And what warning does he give?

(3) What was the immediate effect of Paul's words? See verses 42 and 43 (R.V.). What counsel did the apostles give to those who followed them?

Notes.—(1) Verse 34. A quotation from Is. lv. 3 (LXX), which may be translated 'I will give you the holiness of David that fails not' (Moffatt). That points to an enduring holiness, incompatible with corruption and decay (cf. verse 35.). This was not fulfilled in David himself (verse 36), but has been fulfilled in Jesus (verse 37).

(2) Verse 39. Paul here sets side by side two contrasted methods of justification: the one, by the works of the law, failing to achieve the end desired; the other, through faith in Jesus, introducing the soul into the immediate blessing of full justification. Cf. Phil. iii. 6-9.

Day 4. Acts xiii. 44-52.

(1) Picture the scene described in verses 44 and 45. What bold action did Paul and Barnabas now take, and on what grounds did they justify it? See verses 46, 47. Consider with what sorrow of heart they must have seen the unbelief of their fellow countrymen. Cf. Rom. ix. 1-5.

(2) What results followed the decision to turn to the Gentiles (a) in the wider proclamation of the gospel and ingathering of believers; (b) in the stirring up of persecution of the missionaries; and (c) in the experience of the converts?

Notes.—(1) Verse 49 covers a considerable period, probably some months.
(2) Verse 50. 'Devout and honourable women', that is, women of high social position who had become worshippers of the God of Israel.

Day 5. Acts xiv. 1-12.

(1) Observe carefully the course of events in Iconium. Each verse of verses 1-6 describes a fresh development. Do you notice three main stages in the work?

(2) Comparing the work in Iconium with that at Pisidian Antioch, what points of similarity and what of contrast do you find?

(3) Signs and wonders had been done in Iconium, and were continued at Lystra in a notable miracle. What was the effect upon the people? With regard to gifts of healing and working of miracles, see 1 Cor. xii. 4, 9, 10, 11, 29, 30, xiii. 2.

Notes.—(1) Iconium was a prosperous commercial city on one of the main trade routes from east to west. Hence the presence there of many Jews. Lystra was a smaller and more rustic town, with a simpler and less-educated population.
(2) Verse 1. 'So spake'—possibly for a number of sabbaths.

Day 6. Acts xiv. 13-28.

(1) What five elementary truths about God, suited to a heathen audience, are set forth by Paul in verses 15-17?

(2) In what ways did the apostles seek to strengthen the churches they had founded? What may we learn from this?

Notes.—(1) Verse 19. Cf. Acts ix. 16; 1 Thes. ii. 15, 16.

(2) Verse 21. 'Taught many', better 'made many disciples' (R.V.).

Day 7.

Consider afresh this model missionary enterprise, recorded in Acts xiii and xiv (a) in its origin, progress, and results, and (b) in the character, aims, methods, and teaching of the missionaries.

Week 22. ACTS XV–XVII. 21

Day 1. Acts xv. 1-12.

(1) The question at issue was: 'On what terms can Gentiles be saved?' What answer did Paul and Barnabas give (see xiv. 27, last clause)? And what answer did the teachers from Judæa give?

(2) Of what three facts did Peter remind the council (verses 7-9)? And what conclusion did he deduce from them (verses 10, 11)? Try to state the argument in your own words.

Notes.—(1) Verse 7. 'Much disputing'. The discussion may have extended over some days and been marked by considerable heat and fire (cf. verse 2 and verse 12, 'all the multitude kept silence'). Luke records only the closing speeches.

(2) Peter's speech contains in germ two truths which find fuller expression in the Epistles to the Hebrews, Romans, and Galatians. The first is that the Gentiles, in receiving Christ through faith, had received the full messianic blessing, hence law and circumcision were unnecessary (see Heb. viii. 6, 13). The second is that the law had not brought salvation to the Jews, who themselves were saved by faith. Why therefore impose the law upon Gentile believers? The two principles of law and grace—or works and faith—are incompatible (see Rom. iv. 13-16; Gal. v. 2-6).

Day 2. Acts xv. 13-33.

(1) How does James show that God was doing a *new* thing, yet one that was in full accord with His eternal purpose as declared in the prophets? What, then, was his judgment on the question at issue?

(2) What evidence do you find in the whole discussion, and in the decision arrived at, of the Holy Spirit's guiding and controlling? The whole chapter provides a striking illustration of Christian comity.

(3) The bigness of the issue at stake may be seen by asking what might have happened if the decision had been otherwise. As it was, what was the result? See verse 31 and xvi. 5.

Notes.—(1) 'James', the Lord's brother, who, as head of the church in Jerusalem (cf. xii. 17; xxi. 18), may have been presiding on this occasion.

(2) Verse 20. Gentile believers were enjoined to refrain from practices abhorrent to their Jewish brethren.

(3) Verse 21. James seems here to be answering an implied objection, which may have been raised in the discussion, that if the Gentiles were not required to keep the law, the law would fall into neglect. James shows that this would not be so.

Day 3. Acts xv. 34–xvi. 5.

(1) What was the contention between Paul and Barnabas? Which was right, or were both right? Cf. 2 Tim. iv. 11.

(2) What provision did God make for Paul in the loss of Barnabas and John Mark? See xv. 40 and xvi. 1-5.

(3) What great developments took place in this fourth period (xii. 25–xvi. 5)? See *Analysis*.

Note.—Verse 3. Paul firmly opposed the circumcising of Gentile believers, but Timothy in Jewish eyes was a Jew by birth; and it would cause needless offence if he did not wear the sign of his Jewish nationality. Circumcision in itself was indifferent. Cf. 1 Cor. ix. 20, vii. 18; Gal. v. 6, vi. 15.

Day 4. Acts xvi. 6-15.

A new period begins here, recording Paul's greatest missionary effort and achievement: the evangelization of three important Roman provinces— Macedonia, Achaia, and Asia.

(1) By what various means was Paul guided at this time? Trace on a map how remarkable the guidance was, both in what was forbidden and in the final result. What indication does Luke, the writer of the Acts, give that he joined Paul at this time?

(2) Does verse 13 seem an anti-climax after the hopes excited by the vision of verses 9 and 10? Contrast the beginning of Paul's ministry in Philippi with that at Antioch and Iconium, as described in chapters xiii and xiv. Cf. Zc. iv. 10a.

(3) How did Lydia show the reality of her faith? Are we equally courageous and wholehearted?

Note.—Verse 14. Lydia, a native of Thyatira, a city famous for its dyeing. She now lived in Philippi, and carried on a business in purple-dyed garments. She was probably a woman of position and means.

Day 5. Acts xvi. 16-34.

(1) What was the origin of this persecution, and in what way did it differ from all those hitherto recorded? Note the successive stages of it, as described in Luke's very vivid narrative.

(2) What enabled the missionaries to triumph over their sufferings (verse 25) and to remain calm and cool in the midst of terrors (verse 28)? Cf. Heb. xi. 33, 34; 2 Tim. i. 7.

(3) What do you think brought the jailer to ask the question of verse 30? How did the change wrought in him by believing on the Lord Jesus Christ express itself? Cf. viii. 39, xiii. 52; Ps. xvi. 3 (R.V.).

Notes.—(1) Verses 20, 21. Philippi, as a Roman 'colonia' (see verse 12 R.V.), was proud of its Roman connection and privileges. Hence the charges here brought against the missionaries would excite the people and the magistrates.

(2) Verse 22. Read as in R.V. A beating with *rods* was very severe. Cf. 2 Cor. xi. 25.

Day 6. Acts xvi. 35–xvii. 9.

(1) Why did Paul act as he did in xvi. 37? In answering this question consider how different the situation would have been if the missionaries had left in the way which the magistrates proposed.

(2) Verse 40. Who were these 'brethren'? How does their existence show that Paul's work in Philippi was far more fruitful than is here recorded in detail? Cf. Phil. iv. 15.

(3) What resulted from Paul's preaching in Thessalonica (a) in converts, (b) in further persecution? As regards the former, compare Paul's own account in 1 Thes. i–ii. 12; and as regards the latter, how did it arise and what was its method and issue?

Notes.—(1) Thessalonica was the metropolis and most populous city of Macedonia, a centre for both inland and maritime trade.

(2) Verses 6 and 7. Revolution and treason—a subtle and dangerous charge!

(3) Verse 9. 'Taken security'. Probably in the form of a deposit of money, to be forfeited if there was any disturbance.

Day 7. Acts xvii. 10-21.

(1) 'Immediately—by night'. Were the missionaries then in great peril? See verses 13, 14 below. The persecuting malice and hatred of the Jews in Thessalonica seems to have been specially bitter. Cf. 1 Thes. ii. 15, 16.

(2) How are those who attended the Jewish synagogue in Berea described, and why are they commended? Is this spirit and attitude any less rare today?

(3) What stirred Paul to action in Athens, even though he was alone? And what two methods did he use? Nothing is said of any

result from his synagogue ministry, but what came out of the other kind of witness in which he engaged?

Notes.—(1) Verse 14. Read as in R.V.

(2) Verse 17. 'The market'—the famous Agora, the chief place of concourse in Athens.

(3) Verse 19. 'Areopagus', meaning the Hill of Ares; the name of a hill where, according to legend, the god Ares (in Latin, Mars) was once tried by a council of twelve gods. It became the meeting place of an important council of citizens called 'The Council of the Areopagus', but there is evidence that this became shortened to 'the Areopagus' and that the council later met in a building in the Agora. If this is so, Paul did not speak on the hill as A.V. indicates (verse 22), but before the council in the building where they assembled.

Week 23. ACTS XVII. 22–XX.

Day 1. Acts xvii. 22-34.

(1) How do Paul's sympathy and tact appear in the opening words of his speech?

(2) What does Paul say about God (a) in relation to the universe, and (b) in relation to man? And how does he show the error of idol temples, sacrifices, and images in the light of these truths?

(3) What then does he say is the present duty of man, and why?

Notes.—(1) Verses 22, 23 should be read as in R.V. So also verse 30.

(2) Verse 34. 'Dionysius the Areopagite', that is, a member of the Council of the Areopagus, and consequently a man of high position and influence.

Day 2. Acts xviii. 1-17.

(1) Try to put yourself in imagination in Paul's place as he entered Corinth alone. Had ever any missionary a harder task? How did he find a home, a means of maintaining himself, and an opportunity for preaching? As to his inward feelings, see 1 Cor. ii. 3.

(2) What distinct stages can you trace in Paul's work in Corinth? What encouragements came to him, and what hindrances did he encounter?

Notes.—The city of Corinth was the capital of the province of Achaia, and one of the greatest cities in the empire. It was famous for commerce and learning, but also infamous for its wickedness. Cf. 1 Cor. vi. 9-11.

Day 3. Acts xviii. 18-28.

(1) Consider with the aid of a map what long journeys are recorded in verses 18-23. They must have occupied many months. What various ministries did Paul undertake during this time, and what purposes did they serve?

(2) What was Apollo's life story, as indicated here? What were his special gifts, and what three characteristics are noted regarding his preaching? Have you a desire to be mighty in the Scriptures?

(3) How did Aquila and Priscilla help Apollos, and with what result? What may we learn from their action as to our attitude to those who are earnest, but have not had the full gospel set before them?

Note.—(1) Verse 18. 'He had a vow'. It is not known why Paul made a vow. The practice was, however, common among the Jews.

(2) Verse 22. 'Gone up', that is, to Jerusalem. Cf. verse 21.

(3) Verse 25. 'Diligently', better as in R.V. 'carefully', that is, with care and accuracy.

Day 4. Acts xix. 1-20.

(1) What twofold difference between John's baptism and Christian baptism is brought out in verses 1-7? Have you entered into the full heritage offered in Christ?

(2) What methods did Paul use in Ephesus? And what special incident led to a great victory for Christ? What was the effect (a) on the people; (b) on believers; (c) on those who practised magic?

(3) Consider the great results achieved in Ephesus and in the whole period from xvi. 6 to xix. 20. By what power were they wrought? See xvi. 14, xviii. 9, xix. 11, 20.

Notes.—(1) Ephesus was the metropolis of the large and wealthy province of Asia, a centre of commerce and religion, and famous also for its magic. Cf. verses 18, 19 (R.V. mg.).

(2) Verse 2. Read as in R.V.

(3) Verse 9. 'The school of Tyrannus', probably the lecture hall of some pagan teacher.

(4) Verse 10. 'All they that dwelt in Asia'—the province was evangelized. The seven churches of Asia mentioned in Rev. i were probably among those founded at this time.

(5) Verses 13 and 14. Read as in R.V.

Day 5. Acts xix. 21-41.

(1) What were Paul's plans for the future? Whither was his eye turned? But what two things must first be done? Cf. Rom. xv. 19, 23, 24.

(2) How did persecution suddenly arise? What was its cause, and how was it quieted?

(3) What witness is borne by this story to the success of Paul's work and to the influence which he exerted, and also to the cost of missionary service? Cf. 2 Cor. i. 8-11.

Notes.—(1) Verse 24. 'Silver shrines of Diana' (R.V.). The Ephesians were very proud of their temple to the goddess Diana, and of the image of the goddess within it (verses 27, 35). Small shrines containing her statue provided a lucrative trade.

(2) Verse 31. 'The chief of Asia' or 'Asiarchs' (R.V. mg.), high officials of the province.

(3) Verse 33. It would seem that the Jews were afraid that the excited populace would turn against them, and sought to exculpate themselves.

Day 6. Acts xx. 1-16.

(1) What was Paul's original plan? See xix. 21. How was it modified, and why?

(2) Try to picture yourself in the church gathering depicted in verses 7-12, and follow what was done, step by step. Do you find the same spirit in these Gentile believers as that in the first Jewish believers, as described in ii. 42?

(3) What qualities are revealed in Paul throughout this whole section? Cf. 1 Thes. ii. 7, 8; 2 Cor. xi. 28; Rom. xv. 18, 19.

Notes.—(1) Verse 2. This tour in Macedonia lasted probably several months. Paul had not revisited the churches in that province since their founding.

(2) Verse 3. Paul was about to board a vessel sailing for Syria, when it was revealed to him that the Jews had a plot to kill him, probably on board the vessel.

(3) Verse 4. These were doubtless delegates from the Gentile churches, bearing the money raised for the poor in the church in Jerusalem. See Rom. xv. 24-27.

Day 7. Acts xx. 17-38.

(1) How does this address to the elders of the church in Ephesus confirm and add to your answer to question (3) of yesterday? As you measure your outward service and inward spirit against Paul's, in what respects especially do you feel you come short?

(2) What counsel does Paul give those to whom God has given positions of leadership how they may guard the flock against the dangers that threaten?

(3) Have you begun to find in experience the truth of our Lord's words quoted at the end of the address?

Week 24. ACTS XXI–XXV. 12

Day 1. Acts xxi. 1-16.

(1) Follow this voyage on a map. Picture especially the moving scene in verse 5. What a memory for the children through life!

(2) How are we to understand these warnings of the Spirit? To Paul's friends they seemed to say 'Do not go to Jerusalem', but Paul himself did not so interpret them. Is the explanation

perhaps this: that the Spirit gave clear warning of peril and suffering, and Paul's friends, in their human affection, interpreted this
in one way, while Paul regarded it in another and deeper way?
Cf. xx. 23, 24; Mt. xvi. 21-23.

Note.—Verses 15, 16. Read as in R.V. Cæsarea was sixty-four miles from
Jerusalem. The meaning seems to be that the party rested for a night on the
way at the house of Mnason, who was one of the early disciples.

Day 2. Acts xxi. 17-36.

(1) It was Paul's hope and desire that a closer unity of spirit
might be established between the church in Jerusalem and the
Gentile churches. What initial difficulty did James and the elders
feel must be removed, and how did they suggest it might be dealt
with?

(2) In verse 14 Paul refused to yield to the counsel of friends.
In this case he yielded willingly. What was the principle that
determined his action in both cases? See xx. 24; 1 Cor. ix. 20-23,
x. 32, 33.

(3) What happened? Try to picture the vividly described scene.

Note.—Verse 23. 'We have four men'. These men were Jewish Christians
who were about to complete a Nazirite vow by offering the prescribed sacrifices
(see Nu. vi. 13-21). It was considered a meritorious act to defray the expenses
of poor Nazirites.

Day 3. Acts xxi. 37–xxii. 21.

(1) As you consider the circumstances under which this speech
of Paul was made, what impresses you most in regard to it?

(2) What was Paul's main aim, and how do the different parts
of his speech contribute to it?

(3) What practical lessons may we learn from the fact that, in
spite of Paul's arguments in verses 19, 20, the Lord gave him the
command in verse 21?

Day 4. Acts xxii. 22–xxiii. 10.

(1) In Philippi Paul allowed himself to be scourged, and only
later mentioned the fact of his Roman citizenship. Why did he
act otherwise in this instance? In what respect were the circumstances different?

(2) How did Paul twice attempt to get a hearing before the
Jewish council when he was brought there by the Roman chief
captain, and how was he foiled on each occasion?

Notes.—(1) xxii. 26. It was one of the privileges of Roman citizens that they
were exempt from the punishment of scourging. If the chief captain had

scourged a citizen of Rome he would have put himself seriously in the wrong. Cf. verse 29.

(2) xxiii. 1. 'Lived', literally 'lived as a citizen'. Paul's meaning was 'Men and brethren, I have fulfilled my duty to the commonwealth of Israel in all good conscience, in the sight of God, until this day'

(3) xxiii. 5. This was not a formal meeting of the Jewish Council, at which the high priest was presiding, but a meeting summoned by the chief captain and no doubt presided over by himself. Paul therefore did not know that the voice that spoke was that of the high priest.

Day 5. Acts xxiii. 11-35.

(1) Consider how greatly Paul must have needed comfort and cheer (a) because of the physical strain he had undergone; (b) because of the pain of Israel's unbelief; (c) because of the seeming failure of his witness; and (d) because of the danger that he was to become aware of next day. How would the vision and the words spoken by the Lord meet all these needs?

(2) God sends deliverance in many different ways. How did He send deliverance in this case? Think how much it must have meant to Paul to have this touch of human kindness amid the sea of hatred that surrounded him, and consider how true is the saying 'Man is immortal till his work is done', as illustrated in Paul's life.

Day 6. Acts xxiv. 1-21.

(1) The Jewish prosecution employed on this occasion a trained advocate. What four charges were brought against Paul?

(2) Notice in Paul's defence what answer he gave to each charge: to the first and second in verses 11-13, to the third in verses 14-16, and to the fourth in verses 17, 18.

(3) What three things does Paul assert in verses 14-16 concerning the Christian faith (a) in its relation to the Scriptures; (b) in its hope concerning the future; and (c) in its effect upon the personal life and character of those who practise it?

Notes.—(1) Verse 8. In the A.V. the preposition 'whom' refers to Lysias, but in the R.V. to Paul.

(2) Verse 18. 'Purified'. Cf. 'profane', verse 6.

(3) Verses 19-21. Paul ends on a strain of irony. 'These' (pointing to his accusers) 'cannot witness to what I did in the temple, for they were not there. All they know is what I did at the council meeting. Are they accusing me of declaring my faith in the resurrection of the dead?'

Day 7. Acts xxiv. 22–xxv. 12.

(1) Why did Felix not acquit Paul? What may we learn from his behaviour of the peril of putting off doing right because it is inconvenient?

(2) Notice how 'righteousness, self-control, and judgment to come' are part of 'the faith in Christ'. Does your presentation of the gospel to others include these elements?

(3) Why did Paul refuse Festus' offer for a trial in Jerusalem, and instead, as a Roman citizen, claim his right of appeal to Cæsar? See verses 9 and 10; also verse 3.

Week 25. ACTS XXV. 13–XXVIII

Day 1. Acts xxv. 13-27.

(1) How would you describe Festus, as seen by his words and actions in this chapter? In what is he to be commended? And wherein did he fail, like Pilate and Felix before him? Cf. Mk. xv. 15; Acts xxiv. 27, xxv. 9.

(2) Taking the Lord's words in xxiii. 11 as the key to Paul's experiences at this time, while to human judgment he might seem a friendless and unwanted outcast, tossed to and fro between Jew and Roman, in reality before what various important persons and audiences did he fulfil his rôle as a witness to Jesus Christ? Cf. ix. 15, 16, xxii. 15.

Day 2. Acts xxvi. 1-23.

(1) In his defence Paul answers three questions: (a) What was he before his conversion (see especially verses 5 and 9)? (b) How did his conversion come about? (c) What did he do after his conversion, and why?

(2) The real question at issue was, Is Jesus the Christ? How does Paul's witness help to answer that question? Can his conversion and after-life be explained on any other ground?

(3) How does the Lord, in the commission He gave to Paul (verses 16-19), describe (a) the lost condition of mankind; (b) the content of salvation; (c) the method of salvation?

Notes.—(1) Verse 6. 'The hope of the promise', etc., i.e. the hope of the Messiah and His kingdom.

(2) Verse 18. 'By faith in Me'; words giving the essential condition by which the whole process described in this verse is to be achieved. The full force of the phrase is 'by the faith, which has Me for its object'.

Day 3. Acts xxvi. 24–xxvii. 8.

(1) The challenge and invitation of the gospel came to Felix (xxiv. 24, 25), Festus, and Agrippa, and was rejected by all. It had come also to Paul, and was accepted (xxvi. 19). What did he gain and what did they lose? Cf. verse 29.

(2) Follow the voyage on a map. What encouragements did Paul receive in the early part of the journey? Who were with him?

Notes.—(1) Verse 24. Paul had not concluded his speech when Festus interrupted him.

(2) Verse 28. The R.V. should be followed here. Agrippa sought to turn the edge of Paul's thrust by raillery.

(3) xxvii. 3. 'Unto his friends', i.e. the Christians at Sidon. Cf. xxiv. 23.

Day 4. Acts xxvii. 9-44.

(1) What were the outstanding events of the voyage, as Luke describes it? The passage should be read in R.V.

(2) When human skill and energy had done their utmost (see verse 20), what did faith do? What may we learn about faith as we see it exemplified here in Paul? On what does it rest? What does it give to him who has it? How does it work? Cf. Is. xl. 29-31.

(3) Life on shipboard, particularly in time of danger, reveals the true character of men. What spirit did the sailors show, and what the soldiers? How did Paul stand the test? And to what was it due that he, a prisoner, became the leader and deliverer of all on board?

Note.—Verse 9. 'The fast', i.e. the day of atonement, which came in the latter part of September and was considered by the Jews as marking roughly tne close of the safe season for sea travel.

Day 5. Acts xxviii. 1-16.

(1) What evidences of the Lord's activity do you find in these verses—watching over His servant, opening for him opportunities of service, and giving him inward encouragement?

(2) 'So we came to Rome' (verse 14, R.V.)—triumphant words. Cf. xix. 21, xxiii. 11; Rom. i. 13, xv. 22, 23; also Ps. cvii. 29-31. Has God set some goal before you, and as you pursue the way (it may be a devious one) by which He is leading you to it, are you seeking to help those around you, as Paul did?

Notes.—(1) Verse 2. 'The barbarous people': not 'barbarians' in the modern sense, but non-Greek-speaking.

(2) Verse 15. 'The market of Appius' (R.V.), a town forty-three miles from Rome. 'The three Taverns', a large village thirty-three miles from Rome.

(3) Verse 16. 'The soldier that guarded him' (R.V.), who was bound to him by a chain (see verse 20; Eph. vi. 20, R.V. mg.).

Day 6. Acts xxviii. 17-31.

(1) What was Paul's chief concern on reaching Rome?

(2) What was Paul's message to the Jews in Rome? And what reason does he give for the persistence of so many in unbelief?

(3) In what seven facts does Luke summarize Paul's ministry as a prisoner in Rome? See verses 30 and 31.

Day 7. Acts xix. 21–xxviii. Revision.

(1) Consider more closely the inner spirit of the apostle, as revealed in such passages as xx. 18-35, xxi. 13, 14, xxiii. 1, xxiv. 16, xxvi. 19-23, 29, xxvii. 22-25. What qualities in him are outstanding?

(2) There is a close parallel which extends even to points of detail between Paul's sufferings in this period and those of the Lord Himself. How many such can you trace? Cf. Col. i. 24.

EXODUS XXI-XL—LEVITICUS

INTRODUCTION

(See New Bible Handbook, pp. 115-123, 133-142)

THIS section is sometimes considered by those who first come to it as uninteresting and unprofitable. Readers are anxious to pass on to the narrative portions of the Book of Numbers.

It will be our chief object in this study to find the key that turns these chapters from a dull list of laws that seem to have little practical or devotional interest to living words radiant with the picture of the Saviour. The Lord Jesus Christ is the key to these chapters. While this is true of the whole Bible, we shall find in this section some of the clearest and most poignant pictures of the Saviour and of His suffering for us, definitions of holiness not less plain because expressed in vivid type rather than in direct language, and a concise summary of the great principles and doctrines of atonement. As soon as we understand the spiritual principles that lie behind these chapters they become transformed for us into one of the most precious and wonderful of all sections of the Old

Testament. They draw out our hearts to the Saviour, they fill us
with reverence for the holiness of God, and they become powerfully influential in inducing within us that separation from sin and
all its ways that is necessary in order that our lives may please
God.

We should note carefully the context of this section. Although
the twentieth chapter of the Book of Exodus divides the book into
two distinct parts, we must remember that the book is really one.
The narrative of the opening chapters leads up to the law-giving
of the later ones, and is bound to it with an intimate connection.
When our section opens, Israel is encamped at the foot of Sinai.
Behind them are the great experiences of God's judgments upon
Egypt, the passover, the passage of the Red Sea, and the wilderness
journey. 'Not a hoof' was 'left behind' (Ex. x. 26). This was a
great separation preparatory to a great santification. The whole
book rings with the note of holiness. God had delivered Israel
from bondage and separated them from Egypt, that He might call
them to Himself and make known His will to them. And these
things are an allegory.   God has called us from the bondage
of sin and the world, redeemed us with the precious blood of
Christ, baptized us with His Holy Spirit, and separated us unto
Himself. Israel met with God on Sinai. We have met with Him,
too, not among the thunders of the law, but in the face of Jesus
Christ. Holiness is His intention for us, as it was for them.

The Immediate Context

The voice of God had proclaimed the ten commandments from
Sinai (Ex. xx. 1-17). On account of the people's fear they fled
from the mountain (xx. 18, 19) and asked that Moses should tell
them God's commands. Moses therefore went up into the mountain (xx. 21, 22), and the words of chapter xxi—where our section
begins—are the words of God spoken to Moses alone on the mountain, with the command that he is to pass them on to the people.

ANALYSIS

Exodus.

xxi–xxiii. 13.	Civil and criminal laws.
xxiii. 14-33.	Various religious laws and promises.
xxiv.	Making of the covenant.
xxv–xxxi.	Directions for making the tabernacle and for its worship.
xxxii–xxxiv.	The people's sin and its forgiveness.
xxxv–xl.	Making of the tabernacle.

Leviticus.

i–vii.	The offerings.
viii–x.	Consecration of the priests.
xi–xv.	Laws of cleansing.
xvi.	Day of atonement.
xvii–xxii.	Various laws as to ceremonial and social purity.
xxiii–xxv.	Laws of sabbaths, jubilee, etc.
xxvi.	Blessings and curses and their condition.
xxvii.	Redemption.

Week 26. Exodus xxi–xxix

Day 1. Ex. xxi. 1-32.

The laws in this portion concern relations between human persons, particularly those between slaves and masters. While slavery is tolerated, its severity is mitigated in various ways.

(1) What kind of relationship between slave and master is contemplated in verses 2-6? See further Dt. xv. 12-18; also Je. xxxiv. 12-17, where is seen God's displeasure at the transgression of this law. With verses 5, 6 cf. 2 Cor. v. 14, 15.

(2) For what kinds of transgression was the death penalty to be surely inflicted? See also xxii. 18-20, xxxi. 15.

(3) If a person be wronged, what does *justice* demand? But if *love* reign, what will the wronged person do? See Mt. v. 38-48.

Note.—xxi. 6. 'Judges'. The Hebrew word is Elohim, as also in xxii. 9, 28. Cf. Dt. i. 16. 'Judges' in xxi. 22 is a different word.

Day 2. Ex. xxi. 33–xxiii. 19.

The laws in xxi. 33-xxii. 15 relate mainly to questions of property, and the remainder of the portion contains miscellaneous precepts.

(1) What instances of careless neglect, leading to injury or loss for other people, are given in xxi. 33–xxii. 15, and what does God demand of the offender in such cases?

(2) Gather out from xxii. 16–xxiii. 19 illustrations of the claims God makes for Himself at the end of xxii. 27 and in xxiii. 7. Against what sin does He say that His wrath will wax hot?

Note.—Some of these laws are similar to those found in the famous Code of Hammurabi,[1] but the provisions are much more merciful. Notice in xxii. 31 the reference to being 'holy men'. Cf. xix. 6.

[1] See *New Bible Handbook*, pp. 136, 137.

Day 3. Ex. xxiii. 20–xxiv.

(1) What does God promise to His people in xxiii. 20-23, and what does He require of them? Can you think of corresponding spiritual promises made to us in Christ and of requirements still more searching? For a somewhat parallel New Testament passage, see 2 Pet. i. 2-11.

(2) xxiv. Why was this day significant in Israel's history? See verse 8, and cf. Heb. ix. 18-20.

(3) Consider the symbolism by which the covenant was ratified in the light of Heb. ix. 19-22. To what measure of nearness to God did it lead? See Ex. xxiv. 9-18. How immeasurably greater our privileges in Christ (Heb. x. 19-22)! But are we entering into them as fully as did the elders of Israel into theirs that day?

Day 4. Ex. xxv.

(1) From where was God speaking and in what form had He hitherto been present with the children of Israel? See xiv. 19, xxiii. 23. What change does He now propose to make? See verse 8 and xxix. 45, 46. How have we in Christ something far better still?

(2) Deduce from the words 'sanctuary', 'meet', 'commune' the purpose for which the tabernacle was designed.

(3) Note the three articles of furniture described in this chapter, but observe specially the ark and what is said of it in verses 20, 22. What is the significance of the fact that only above the mercy seat could God and man meet and commune together? See 1 Jn. ii. 1, 2.

Note.—The 'mercy seat' or propitiatory covering was a slab of pure gold, with cherubim at either end, covering the tables of testimony in the ark.

Day 5. Ex. xxvi and xxvii.

(1) xxvi. What four layers of curtains covered the tabernacle? What appearance would it have from without and what from within? Compare the contrast between Christ seen from without (Is. liii. 2) and seen from within (Phil. iii. 8).

(2) What was the purpose of the veil (spoken of in verses 31-33), and what is its typical significance? See Heb. ix. 7, 8, x. 19; Mk. xv. 38.

Note.—It will be helpful to draw a ground plan of the tabernacle so far as it has been described in these two chapters, with the court, the holy place, and the most holy place, and the altar, table of shewbread, candlestick and ark in their proper positions.

Day 6. Ex. xxviii. The priest's garments.

(1) (a) Who may minister in this tabernacle? Any Israelite? See verse 1 and Heb. v. 4. (b) Notice the phrase 'Aaron and his sons with him . . . that *he* may minister' (verse 1). Of what is this family priesthood, united in one head—he ministering and the rest only assistants—a type? See 1 Pet. ii. 5. (c) Aaron must wear 'holy garments' (verse 2). Why? See the word 'sanctify' (i.e. 'set apart') in verse 3, R.V., also verse 41.

(2) A description of the high priest's garments is given in this portion. For the order in which they were put on, see Lv. viii. 7-9. Each is significant—the coat of pure linen (verse 39) indicating the high priest as a righteous man; the blue robe (verses 31-35) as a heavenly man; the ephod with the names of the tribes (verses 3-29) as a representative man; the mitre with its golden plate (verses 36-38) as a holy man. Reflect how in all these ways the high priest of Israel in his priestly garments was a type of Christ.

Notes.—(1) The Ephod was a shoulder garment, covering breast and back.
(2) The breastplate was probably a bag or pouch fastened to the front of the Ephod, and called 'the breastplate of judgment' because it contained the Urim and Thummim, which were used to ascertain the divine will. See Nu. xxvii. 21 and Ezr. ii. 63. Their exact form and use is not now known.
(3) Aaron bore the names of the tribes upon his shoulder (the place of strength) and upon his heart (the place of affection).

Day 7. Ex. xxix. The dedication of the priests.

It was not sufficient for Aaron and his sons simply to wear the holy garments. They must be solemnly consecrated to their office.

(1) Distinguish the various parts of the ceremony—the cleansing, the robing, the anointing, and the sacrifices.

(2) How does our High Priest stand out in marked contrast to Aaron? See Heb. vii. 26-28.

Notes.—(1) This chapter is repeated very largely in Lv. viii. The sacrifices offered may be further considered then.
(2) The word translated 'consecrate' in this chapter is different from that in xxviii. 3, which should rather be rendered 'sanctify' as in R.V. The word here means dedication to special service.

Week 27. EXODUS XXX–XXXVIII

Day 1. Ex. xxx and xxxi.

(1) (a) xxx. What two articles of furniture are here added to those already mentioned, and what is their position? (b) What does incense stand for? See Ps. cxli. 2; Rev. viii. 3, 4, v. 8 (R.V.).

What is suggested by the word 'perpetual' in verse 8? Cf. 1 Thes. v. 17. What is the significance of verse 10? (c) At his consecration the priest's whole body was washed (Ex. xxix. 4), but thereafter, before engaging in any priestly ministry, he had to wash his own hands and feet. What is the meaning of this for our own service of God? See Jn. xiii. 10; 2 Cor. vii. 1; 1 Jn. i. 8, 9.

(2) xxxi. What was God's part and what man's in the designing and making of the tabernacle (see verses 1-11 and cf. xxv. 2, 9)?

Day 2. Ex. xxxii.

(1) The people. How does the narrative show the strength of the people's reaction towards idolatry? In verses 4-6 what four acts constituted their idolatry, and which is selected for mention by Paul in 1 Cor. x. 7?

(2) Aaron. Whom did Aaron profess still to worship? But how did God view it? And how Moses? What was Aaron's unworthy excuse? On whom, and on what, did he seek to throw the responsibility for his own action?

(3) Moses. What features of his character stand out in this whole incident?

Day 3. Ex. xxxiii.

There now follows a period of suspense, during which the people mourned, and Moses set up a tent outside the camp. Here God came in the pillar of cloud to speak with him.

(1) Verses 1-11. What was God's attitude at this time (a) towards the people, (b) towards Moses?

(2) Verses 12-23. What were Moses' three petitions, and what answers did God give? How does this series of petitions and answers show on the one hand the growth of desire and faith on Moses' part, and the richness of God's grace on the other?

Notes.—(1) Verses 1-3. The cause of mourning seems to be that God threatens to revoke the promise of xxv. 8, xxix. 45, 46 and return to the earlier method of guidance by His angels (see xiv. 19, xxiii. 20-23).

(2) Verse 7. This tent of meeting cannot be the tabernacle (although that also was sometimes called by that name, see xxix. 42-44, xxxv. 21), because it was not built yet. It was apparently an ordinary tent pitched outside the camp during the period of suspense.

(3) Verses 14, 15. The words 'with thee' are not in the Hebrew. It would seem that Moses understood verse 14 to mean that God would be with him personally, and in verses 15, 16 he asks that God will go with the people also (see xxxiv. 9). Notice the change from 'thee' in verse 14 to 'us' in verses 15, 16, and the emphatic phrase 'I and Thy people'.

Day 4. Ex. xxxiv.

(1) Show how fully God fulfilled to Moses the promise of xxxiii. 19, and answered Moses' request. Against what, however, was Moses, as representative of the people, sternly warned?

(2) What result followed Moses' prolonged communion with God, of which others, but not himself, were conscious? What, in the case of Christians, issues from the contemplation of the glory of Christ? See 2 Cor. iii. 18; Lk. xi. 36.

Day 5. Ex. xxxv–xxxvi. 7.

(1) Note all the different kinds of person mentioned as contributing by work or gifts to the making of the tabernacle. What illustration do we find in this portion of the way in which the service of God in His Church calls for the help of all His people, whatever may be their talents, rank or age? See 1 Cor. xv. 58.

(2) What example for ourselves may be found in the spirit in which the people wrought or brought gifts, and also in the value and abundance of their giving? Cf. 2 Cor. viii. 1-5.

Day 6. Ex. xxxvi. 8–xxxvii. 9.

(1) Try to picture the holy place, as seen from within. What would the sides consist of, what the roof, what the ends, and what the floor?

(2) In Heb. x. 20 the veil is said to typify Christ's flesh. But the veil was of the same texture and appearance as the inner curtain and the curtains that formed the entrance to the holy place (see xxxvi. 8, 35, 37). Many therefore see in the holy place, as viewed thus from within, a picture of Christ as He appeared on earth: the wood of the boards representing His human nature; the gold His divine nature; the white of the fine linen representing His righteousness; the blue, His heavenly origin; the purple, His kingship; the scarlet, His sacrifice; and the floor, which was the sand of the desert, His sharing of our human lot. Ponder this picture in symbol of our Saviour.

(3) xxxvii. 1-9. How do the ark and the mercy seat also speak of Christ?

Note.—The pronoun 'he' in xxxvi. 10, 11, etc., does not represent any particular individual, but is like the French '*on*'. It might be better rendered 'they', as in Moffatt's translation. But the ark (xxxvii. 1) was Bezaleel's own work.

Day 7. Ex. xxxvii. 10–xxxviii.

(1) The tabernacle signified both God's approach to man and also man's way of drawing near to God. In the light of this fact,

what do you find signified by the table of shew-bread, the candle-stick or lamp-stand, and the altar of incense? Consider how in these symbols God offers to man communion, light, and a place for prayer, intending him to share in this communion, to receive and tend the light, and to pray continually. How are these things fulfilled to us in Christ? See Jn. vi. 57, viii. 12; Heb. iv. 16.

(2) Whence came the brass for the laver? Consider the part played by women in the making of the sanctuary. Whence came the silver for the sockets of the sanctuary? See also xxx. 11-16. What typical significance is there in the fact that the tabernacle was founded on atonement money?

Week 28. EXODUS XXXIX–LEVITICUS X

Day 1. Ex. xxxix and xl.

(1) Try to make a complete ground plan of the tabernacle, with its outer court and all its furniture in position. Then try to visualize the tabernacle, set up as here described, and the high priest and the priests in their vestments. Beautiful as it all was, what does the Epistle to the Hebrews say about it (Heb. viii. 4, 5, ix. 8-10)?

(2) What phrase occurs repeatedly in these chapters concerning the making of the tabernacle? What thoughts does this stir in our minds concerning our own service to God? Cf. Jn. v. 19, 20 and 1 Jn. ii. 6. With xl. 33b cf. Jn. xix. 30; Acts xx. 24; 2 Tim. iv. 7.

Note.—xl. 26. 'The golden altar', i.e. the altar of incense, called 'golden' to distinguish it from the brazen altar of burnt offering in the outer court (xl. 29).

Day 2. Lv. i. The burnt offering.

God is now dwelling in the midst of His people, and gives them directions concerning their worship of and communion with Him. Notice how throughout this book God is the speaker, through Moses.

(1) Verse 1. From where does God speak? See Ex. xxv. 22 and contrast Ex. xix. 3.

(2) The burnt offering. It signifies (a) that God requires entire devotion from His people (see 'burn *all*' in verses 9, 13, and of Dt. vi. 5, 6); and (b) that as the worshipper, being sinful, cannot offer such entire devotion in his own person, God has appointed a way whereby, through the death of a perfect animal ('without blemish', verse 3) offered in his stead, he may be accepted. Consider how these two features of the burnt offering, atonement (verse 4), and consecration, are fulfilled for us in Christ (see Heb. ix. 14), thereby making acceptable our own consecration of ourselves (Rom. xii. 1).

Day 3. Lv. ii and iii. The meat ('meal', R.V.) offering and the peace offering.

(1) God requires in His people, also, a blameless life (see Ps. xxiv. 3, 4; Mt. v. 48), represented by the meal offering, the *purity* of whose ingredients is emphasized (see ii. 1, 'fine flour'; ii. 11, 'no leaven'). The worshipper, unable to offer a blameless life in himself, draws near, by God's appointment, with acceptance (see ii. 2, 9, etc., 'a sweet savour') in the power of an offering possessing the perfection which he lacks. Consider how the Lord Jesus is the perfect meal-offering (Heb. vii. 26), and how in union with Him we also are called to walk after His example (1 Jn. ii. 6). With ii. 10 cf. Jn. vi. 57.

Note.—The peace offering speaks of communion, based on the blood of atonement (iii. 1, 2). See further Day 5 (2).

Day 4. Lv. iv–vi. 7. The sin and trespass (or 'guilt', R.V.) offerings.

(1) The burnt, meal, and peace offerings were offered by worshippers who were living in communion with God. But what if they have committed some sin or trespass, and communion has to be *restored*? The answer is given in today's portion: see iv. 2.

(2) With regard to the sin offering, note particularly what was done with the *blood* and with the *body* of the sacrifice (iv. 6, 7 and 11, 12). How do these solemn ordinances indicate God's hatred of sin and even suggest that sin endangers the very covenant relationship itself, which must therefore be openly re-established? Reflect on what it cost the Saviour to be our sin offering. See Is. liii. 6; Heb. xiii. 12.

Note.—The sin and trespass offerings have much in common, but the sin offering had reference rather to the *person* of the offender in his guilt Godwards, whereas the trespass offering was an atonement for the offence especially in its relation manwards. Hence the sin offering differed for different classes of persons (iv. 3, 13, 22, 27); and in the trespass offering the transgressor, in addition to his offering, had also to make amends for the wrong done (v. 16, vi. 4, 5).

Day 5. Lv. vi. 8–vii. Further instruction about the offerings, with special reference to the priests.

Distinction must be made between public and private offerings. In addition to the private burnt offerings of the people, there was a daily, public burnt offering morning and evening. See Ex. xxix. 38-42. It is this daily sacrifice that is referred to in vi. 9, 12, with directions that the fire must not be allowed to go out upon the altar.

(1) Neither the sacrifice that represented the people's consecration of themselves to God, nor the fire—which was the symbol

of Jehovah's acceptance of it—must be allowed to fail, even as He Himself fails not. What lesson does that carry for us? Cf. Heb. vi. 11, 12.

(2) vii. 11-21. In the peace offering the people offered to God the spontaneous gifts of their love. What, according to vii. 15, 16, were the three kinds of private peace offerings which individuals might bring? And what corresponding offerings are we encouraged to bring to God in Heb. xiii. 15, based, as always, on the ground of atoning blood ('*By Him* let us offer')? What corresponds in our Christian experience to the eating by the worshipper of part of the sacrifice? Cf. Ps. xxii. 26; Jn. vi. 56. With vii. 20, 21 cf. 1 Cor. xi. 27, 28.

Note.—A 'wave offering' (vii. 30) means an offering or part of an offering presented to the Lord by waving it towards Him, before receiving it back from Him. In a 'heave offering' (vii. 32) the word 'heave' does not mean to throw, but to lift or take off, and indicates the part of the offering taken off for the priests.

Day 6. Lv. viii. Dedication of the priests and tabernacle.

See Ex. xxix. 44. The directions for the ceremony were given in Ex. xxviii, xxix; this chapter gives the account of it.

(1) After the washing and the robing and the anointing came the sacrifices. Note what these latter consisted of. The anointing oil typifies the Holy Spirit. Cf. 2 Cor. i. 21; Lk. iv. 18.

(2) In the sacrifice of the ram of consecration (i.e. of dedication to special service), what special use was made of the blood? And what does this symbolism signify regarding those who are thus set apart for the service of God? What do ear, hand, and foot represent? Cf. Rom. vi. 13.

Day 7. Lv. ix and x. Aaron's entry upon his office, and the sin of his sons.

The tabernacle and priests having been sanctified and dedicated, all was now ready for the normal work of the priesthood to begin.

(1) What was Aaron's first offering in beginning his ministry? Though pardoned, anointed, and consecrated, he still needed mercy through atoning blood. But when all was duly offered, how did the Lord show in full measure His acceptance of His people's worship? With ix. 22a cf. Nu. vi. 22-27.

(2) In all the seven days of the ceremonies of dedication no incense had been offered. Whether on this account or for some other cause, what did Nadab and Abihu do? And what happened? Consider some reasons why God acted thus, and the error, or errors, against which the incident is a warning.

Notes.—(1) x. 1. 'Strange fire'. This may mean fire not taken from the altar, but the central thought is that it was fire which God had not authorized.

(2) x. 8-11. It has long been thought that Nadab and Abihu may have been indulging in wine—hence this prohibition.

(3) The significance of chapter x. 16-20 seems to be that Aaron realized that Nadab and Abihu had taken part in the offering of the sin-offering and that this rendered it unacceptable and unclean. This is a touching story of Aaron's full acceptance of God's verdict upon his own sons.

Week 29. LEVITICUS XI–XVIII

Day 1. Lv. xi. Distinction between clean and unclean.

(1) Divide the animals mentioned into the four categories of verse 46.

(2) What would these distinctions teach Israel regarding God and His worship? See verses 44, 45. Reflect also what great changes in their habits the coming of God to dwell among them brought about. Cf. 1 Pet. i. 14-16; Eph. iv. 22-24.

(3) How did our Lord show that these distinctions are not now binding? What constitutes defilement in God's sight? See Mk. vii. 14-23 (R.V.).

Day 2. Lv. xii–xiii. 46. Born unclean (xii); the plague of sin (xiii).

(1) Did the mere fact of being born a Jew give a child a place in the covenant? See verse 3 and note (1) below. How does this illustrate such passages as Ps. li. 5; Eph. ii. 3b; Jn. iii. 5?

(2) How does chapter xiii show, under the figure of leprosy, that sin is not merely acts of transgression, but something evil in men's *nature*? What parallels can you trace between the plague of sin and leprosy? Consider, for example, how marks that were outwardly small gave evidence of inward corruption. Cf. Je. xvii. 9.

Notes.—(1) Circumcision had a twofold significance, namely, identification with God's covenant people and purification from unfitness to be such.

(2) xii. 8. See Lk. ii. 22.

(3) xiii. 2. 'A bright spot'. It is said that the bright spot is often so small that it is like pustules made by the pricking of a pin.

Day 3. Lv. xiii. 47–xiv. 32.

(1) If leprosy be regarded as a type of sin, what is the general lesson enforced in xiii. 47-59 regarding sin-contaminated habits and practices? Cf. Jude 23; Rev. iii. 4.

(2) What is the significance of the fact that the leper had to be healed before he was cleansed from the defilement of his leprosy? Can a man who is not saved be sanctified?

(3) Read xiv. 4-7 in the light of Rom. vi. 3-7. Observe how washing, robing, sacrifices, consecration to God, and anointing were all required before the leper was restored to the full privilege of drawing near to God. How are all these provided for us in Christ?

Day 4. Lv. xiv. 33–xv.

(1) How does this portion show that sin, wherever found and in whatever form, is defiling in God's sight, and prevents acceptance before Him?

(2) Chapter xv is usually taken to represent the defilement of secret sin. Observe how it pollutes the whole life and all around and how this kind of defilement needs the blood of atonement no less than other forms of sin. Cf. Ps. li. 6; Mt. i. 21.

Day 5. Lv. xvi. The day of atonement.

(1) Sketch out the order of the ceremony.

(2) In what respects was the ritual of the day of atonement different from that of any other sacrifices?

(3) What do you learn from this chapter (a) regarding the conditions of approach into God's presence; (b) the defilement and need of cleansing even of the tabernacle itself; (c) the complete removal of sin's guilt through substitution; (d) the necessity on man's part of submission in penitence and faith to God's way of salvation?

Day 6. Lv. xvii.

There are two main instructions in this portion: first, that all domestic animals which are killed shall be brought to the tabernacle (verses 3-9); and second, that no blood must be eaten (verses 10-16). The former of these instructions points to a time when animals were not killed except in connection with worship of some kind.

(1) What would this first instruction (verse 3-9) teach the Israelites about God? See Dt. vi. 4. Where do you find in these verses that this instruction is directed against idolatrous worship?

(2) Why was the eating of blood so strictly forbidden? See verse 11, R.V. What clear proof is given in this verse that the idea of substitution of one life for another underlies these Old Testament sacrifices?

Day 7. Lv. xviii.

In xviii-xx the Lord passes from the worship to the *walk* of His people. Chapter xviii prohibits unlawful marriage, unchastity, and Moloch worship but the last is dealt with more fully in xx. 2-5.

(1) What reasons are given for Israel's obedience to these laws? See verses 1-5 and 24-30. Cf. Eph. iv. 17.

(2) What application does the apostle Paul make of verse 5 in Rom. x. 5-10 and Gal. iii. 11-14? If, in Christ, 'life' is obtained through faith, are we thereby excused from obedience?

(3) What light is thrown by this chapter upon God's command for the extermination of the Canaanites?

Week 30. LEVITICUS XIX–XXVII

Day 1. Lv. xix and xx.

Chapter xix lays down a number of miscellaneous precepts relating to a holy walk. Chapter xx deals with the subject of chapter xviii.

(1) What is the special attribute of God that receives emphasis in these chapters as a ground of obedience to His commands? Cf. 1 Pet. i. 14-17.

(2) Notice how many of the commands of chapter xix centre on the thought of love to one's neighbour (verse 18b; cf. Mk. xii. 31).

(3) Why was God's anger so kindled against those who worshipped Moloch or had sympathy with such worship? See Ex. xx. 3; Je. xliv. 3, 4; Jas. iv. 4, 5 (R.V.).

Note.—Moloch was the national god of Ammon, and worship of him seems to have been associated with great cruelty. Children were offered in sacrifice and burned with fire.

Day 2. Lv. xxi and xxii. Laws concerning priests and offerings.

(1) How many separate sections do you find in these regulations?

(2) What words and expressions occur repeatedly, giving the reason why these instructions are imposed?

(3) How may we learn from this portion that things which are apparently small in themselves but which are spiritually unclean may mar our Christian life? See 2 Tim. ii. 20-22.

Day 3. Lv. xxiii. The public feasts or holy convocations of Israel.

These, as outlined in this chapter, were seven in number, including the weekly sabbath.

(1) Make a list of the feasts and note what was the general character of each. What did they have in common and what were their differences?

(2) Consider the typical significance of the three main feasts: (a) the passover (see 1 Cor. v. 7, 8); (b) the feast of weeks or pentecost (see Acts ii. 1-4); (c) the feast of tabernacles, the final ingathering of the harvest (see Rev. vii. 9). If we know the fulfil-

ment of the passover in redemption, and of pentecost in the indwelling of the Spirit, ought we not also to be looking forward to
the fulfilment of the feast of tabernacles when the Lord comes
again?

Notes.—(1) Verse 11. The sheaf of the first fruits of the barley harvest
waved on the morrow after the sabbath points to Christ's resurrection. Cf.
1 Cor. xv. 23.

(2) Verses 16, 17. 'Fifty days'—hence the name pentecost.

(3) 'Two wave loaves'—the first fruits of the wheat harvest, representing
the church of Christ in its first beginnings (Jn. xii. 24).

Day 4. Lv. xxiv.

(1) What may we learn from the word 'pure' found four times
in verses 1-9? (In the Hebrew there are two words used twice
each, but the meaning is similar.) Also, what may we learn from
the word 'continually', also used four times? Apply these words
to your own worship and service in Christ.

(2) 'Behold the goodness and the severity of God' in this
chapter. Cf. Heb. x. 19-31, where the same attributes of God are
set forth side by side.

Day 5. Lv. xxv.

(1) How was the year of jubilee reckoned, and what was its
general purpose? Cf. Gal. v. 1.

(2) What principles are set forth in verses 17, 23, 36, 38, 42,
55 which throw light upon our own relationship to God and to
one another in Christ? Cf. 1 Cor. vi. 19b, 20; Rom. vi. 14.

Day 6. Lv. xxvi.

(1) What spiritual blessings, corresponding to those promised
here to an obedient Israel, are promised us in Christ? See 1 Tim.
i. 14; Jn. xiv. 27; Rom. viii. 35-39; 2 Cor. vi. 16-18.

(2) The punishments fall into five groups: (a) punishments
upon their persons; (b) punishments upon their possessions; (c)
upon children and cattle; (d) the sword, pestilence, and famine;
(e) the overthrow and exile of the nation. To what extent have
they fallen upon the Jewish nation?

(3) What conditions of restoration are mentioned in verses 40-
46? Cf. Dn. ix. 3-19; 2 Ch. vii. 14.

Day 7. Lv. xxvii.

Instruction as to what is to be done where an offering has been made to
the Lord and the giver wants to redeem it; and also a regulation about tithes.

(1) What different cases are dealt with in this chapter?

(2) What does the chapter show of the Lord's character?

THE EPISTLE TO THE HEBREWS

INTRODUCTION

(See New Bible Handbook, pp. 389-393)

THE Epistle is an exhortation and warning to Jewish believers to continue in the faith of Christ and not to fall back into Judaism. Christ is set forth as the fulfilment of Old Testament type and prophecy, and the faith and endurance of the Old Testament saints are held up as examples to believers. Needless to say, the teaching of the Epistle has a scope and value far beyond what is of immediate concern to Jewish believers of the first century. It shows the new covenant, of which Jesus, the Son of God, is Mediator, to be not only far superior to the first covenant, but the final and perfect religion, both as regards revelation (i. 1–ii. 18) and redemption (iii. 1–x. 18). The Epistle contains also practical teaching concerning life under the new covenant. It constitutes a divine call to all who have professed themselves Christians to see that their faith is a reality, and to continue in it. It does not omit a very definite gospel message to the unsaved. It sets forth Christ very fully in His capacity as our High Priest, magnifies His divine nature, and yet points out the reality of His humility and suffering as no other book does in the whole Bible, the Gospels not excepted.

AUTHORSHIP

The Epistle is anonymous. The preponderating opinion till recently was that it was the work of the apostle Paul, but this was by no means universally held. Guesses had been made at authorship, the names of Apollos and of Priscilla, wife of Aquila, having been brought up in this connection. We need not doubt that the Epistle is Pauline in the sense that, if not written by the apostle himself, it was written by one who was familiar with, and influenced by, his teaching. The expression 'they of Italy salute you' (xiii. 24) provides a clue to the destination of the Epistle. The literal meaning is 'from Italy', and the expression suggests that the Epistle was written to a congregation of Jewish believers in Italy, and possibly in Rome.

ANALYSIS

i–ii. 18. Christ the perfect Revealer, better than angels (a) as the Son of God (i. 5-14); and (b) as the Son of Man (ii. 5-15).

iii–x. 18.   Christ the perfect Redeemer, better than Moses
             (iii. 1-6) and better than Aaron (a) in His person
             and character (iv. 14–v. 10); (b) in the 'order'
             of His priesthood (vii. 1-25); and (c) in His
             ministry (viii. 1–ix. 12) and in His offering (ix.
             13–x. 18).

x. 19–xii. 29.   Practical teaching.

xiii. 1-25.   Final counsels and greetings.

Within this outline are contained five passages of solemn warning:

ii. 1-4.   Against the danger of drifting.

iii. 7–iv. 13. Against the danger of missing God's promised rest.

v. 11–vi. 20.   Against the danger of losing salvation.

x. 26-39.   Against the danger of drawing back.

xii. 25-29.   Against the danger of refusing to hear God's final
                word.

Week 31.   HEBREWS I–VI

Day 1. Heb. i.

(1) What seven statements are made about Christ in verses 2b
and 3? And how do these show the salvation which is through
Him to be better than all that went before?

(2) How do the Scriptures, quoted in verses 5-14, confirm the
statement of verse 4? Show how differently God speaks of Christ,
as compared with what He says of angels.

Notes.—(1) The emphasis laid upon Christ's superiority to angels, which to
us seems obvious, is explained by the fact that, to the Jews, one of the chief
glories of the Old Testament revelation was that it was given through angels.

(2) Verse 7. Angels are created beings; they are God's servants; and their
form and appearance suffer change and transformation at God's pleasure.
Contrast the royal dominion and unchanging being of the Son (verses 8-12).

Day 2. Heb. ii.

(1) Verses 1-4. What is the argument used in this warning,
and against what danger is it directed? Verse 1 should be read
in R.V.

(2) Verses 5-10. What, according to the Scriptures, is man's
destiny? And how do we see God's purpose for man being fulfilled
in Christ?

(3) Verses 11-18. In what respects is Christ *one* with us, and
because of this, what three things is He able to do for us?

Note.—In this profound passage the writer is answering an implied objection,
namely, 'Granted that the *heavenly* Christ is better than the angels, what of
Christ in the lowliness and suffering of His human life?' Cf. 1 Cor. i. 23. To

this the answer here given is threefold: (a) in God's purpose man is superior to angels; (b) under the old dispensation, while God and man drew nearer to each other, the two remained essentially separate (cf. Heb. ix. 8), but in Christ they become one; (c) hence Christ is able to redeem man and lift him up to glory, through His cross and resurrection.

Day 3. Heb. iii. 1-6.

Verse 1 is introductory to this whole section (iii. 1–x. 18); see *Analysis*. The background of the writer's thought is the redemption of Israel from Egypt and their journey to the promised land.

(1) Israel had an apostle, Moses (see note below), and a high priest, Aaron. How, in this respect, does the new covenant differ from the old? Consider the significance of the words 'holy', 'brethren', 'heavenly calling' in their practical application to our lives.

(2) Verses 2-6. See Nu. xii. 7. Can you find three points in these verses in which Christ excels Moses?

Notes.—(1) Verse 1. 'Apostle'—used here as meaning one sent upon a special mission. Cf. Ex. iii. 10; Jn. xx. 21.

(2) Verse 2. 'His house', that is, the people of God, in the midst of whom God dwells as in a house or household.

(3) Verse 6. The word 'hope' is one of the important words of the Epistle, expressing the glorious future to be ushered in at the second coming of Christ. See vi. 11, 18, vii. 19, x. 23 (R.V.).

Day 4. Heb. iii. 7–iv. 13.

The R.V. should be used throughout this portion.

(1) What passage of Scripture is expounded in iii. 7-19, and what warning do we receive from it? Observe specially the description of the danger given in verses 12 and 13 and how it may be averted; also *who it was* that sinned and perished in this way. See verses 16-19, R.V.

(2) By what argument is it shown in iv. 3-9 that the rest of God ('My rest'), which Israel lost by unbelief, remains still to be possessed? How is it defined, and what is the condition of obtaining it? See verses 1, 2, and 9.

(3) What fivefold description is given in iv. 12 of God's word, one portion of which the writer has just been expounding? How should these characteristics of God's word, together with the fact that He knows all our heart (iv. 13), stir us to diligence (iv. 11)?

Day 5. Heb. iv. 14–v. 10. Jesus the perfect High Priest in His person and character.

The writer has now reached the beginning of the central and most important part of the Epistle (see *Analysis*), in which he shows that the Christian faith, as a religion of redemption, is the final religion, having achieved *eternal* redemption (ix. 12).

(1) iv. 14-16. What two things are we told to do, and on what grounds?

(2) v. 1-10. What characteristics of a true priest are set forth in verses 1-4 concerning (a) his function; (b) his disposition; and (c) his appointment to office? And how do verses 5-10 show that, in Jesus, these characteristics are found in perfection? See Note (2) below.

Notes.—(1) 'Profession' or 'confession' (R.V.), another important word in this Epistle. The open confession of our faith is throughout insisted upon (see x. 23, xi. 13, xiii. 13).

(2) In verses 5-10 the writer reverses the order of treatment, taking first, appointment to office (verses 5, 6); second, disposition (verses 7, 8); and third, function (verses 9, 10).

(3) Verses 7-10 give us a very sacred and very amazing insight into the earthly humility and human nature of our Lord.

Day 6. Heb. v. 11–vi. 8.

As the writer is about to begin his exposition of the Melchisedec priesthood of Christ, he is arrested by a sense of the difficulty of expounding it to people, the ears of whose minds have become dulled.

(1) v. 11-14. What is the writer's complaint about his readers? How is it with ourselves? Have we been growing in spiritual knowledge or are we still feeding upon elementary Christian teaching?

(2) vi. 1-3. What teaching constitutes the foundation of the gospel? See Acts ii. 38, viii. 37, xvii. 31, xix. 3-6, xx. 21, xxiv. 25.

(3) vi. 4-8. What reason is given here for not laying again this foundation?

Notes.—(1) 'Perfection', that is, the perfection offered in Christ. Cf. Col. i. 28.

(2) The solemn warning in verses 4-6 (cf. x. 26-31) is a difficulty to some. It is best taken as referring to professors, who have 'tasted' and then rejected without assimilating.

Day 7. Heb. vi. 9-20.

(1) What gives the writer confidence as to his readers' final salvation (verses 9-10)? But what does he desire concerning them (verses 11, 12)?

(2) Verses 13-20. What unshakable grounds of assurance have we that, if we have made our refuge in Christ, our hope will not be put to shame? Yet what qualities does a true 'laying hold' demand? See verses 12, 15, and cf. iii. 6, x. 36; Lk. xxi. 19 (R.V.).

Week 32. HEBREWS VII–X

Day 1. Heb. vii. 1-14. Christ as High Priest superior in the 'order' of His priesthood.

(1) What characteristics of Melchisedec, as he stands portrayed in Scripture (Gn. xiv. 18-20), does the writer mention in verses 1-3?

(2) On what grounds is Melchisedec shown in verses 4-10 to be superior to the Levitical priesthood?

(3) What evidence is adduced in verses 11-14 to show that the Aaronic priesthood was essentially defective and not intended to be permanent, and that this carried with it a change also in regard to *the law*?

Note.—The writer does not stay to expound all the characteristics of Melchisedec which he mentions in verses 1-3, but concentrates on those which depict him as abiding a priest in perpetuity, and thus being a type of the Son of God.

Day 2. Heb. vii. 15-28.

(1) Verses 15-19. See Ps. cx. 4 ('for ever'). What double contrast is here brought out between the Levitical and Melchisedec orders of priesthood? How does this show that the two orders are incompatible, and that the introduction of the second implies the abrogation of the first?

(2) Verses 20-22. See Ps. cx. 4 ('The Lord hath sworn'). What is the significance of God's oath? Notice particularly the words 'will not repent', and cf. vi. 17.

(3) Verses 23-28. How do these verses show that in Jesus we have a perfect High Priest, and that He perfectly meets the sinner's need?

Notes.—(1) Verse 16. 'The law of a carnal commandment', that is, a legal code moving in the sphere of physical qualifications, and therefore within the limitations of mortality. Contrast 'the power of an indissoluble life' in Christ. See R.V. mg.

(2) Verse 25. 'To the uttermost', both of time and of degree.

Day 3. Heb. viii.

The writer is now about to enter upon a new aspect of Christ's Priesthood, namely, His High Priestly ministry. In this chapter he shows that this ministry is exercised (a) in a better sanctuary, not on earth but in heaven (verses 1-5); and (b) in connection with a better covenant (verses 6-13). Cf. Je. xxxi. 31-34; Mt. xxvi. 28.

(1) Verses 1-5. Some hearts perhaps craved that Christ might be on earth, ministering in the earthly sanctuary. What twofold answer is given in these verses?

(2) Verses 6-13. What is said here about the first covenant? And what four particulars are given of the new covenant, showing its superiority? Are these things known to you in glad experience?

Day 4. Heb. ix. 1-14. Christ the High Priest of a better sanctuary.

(1) Verses 1-8. In this description of the furnishings and service of the earthly sanctuary, to what feature is attention specially drawn? And what does the Holy Spirit teach us by it?

(2) Verses 9-10. In what respect did the gifts and sacrifices of the earthly sanctuary fail of effect, and for what reason?

(3) Verses 11-14. How do the service and sacrifice of Christ, both in their essential character and in their result, stand out in contrast to the service and sacrifices of the first covenant?

Notes.—(1) Verse 4. 'The golden censer'. The Greek word may also mean 'the golden altar of incense' (see R.V. mg.). Some take the reference to be the censer used on the day of atonement (Lv. xvi. 12, 13). The altar of incense was not in the holy of holies (Ex. xl. 26).

(2) Verses 6 and 8. 'The first tabernacle' here means 'the holy place', as distinct from the holy of holies.

(3) Verse 9. 'As touching the conscience make the worshipper perfect' (R.V.), that is, free the conscience from guilt and defilement. See also verse 14.

Day 5. Heb. ix. 15-28.

Further instances are here given of the preciousness and power of the blood of Christ: first, in relation to the new covenant (verses 15-23); and second, as being a single sacrifice, offered once for all (verses 24-28).

(1) What was the one thing necessary for making a covenant?

(2) How does the fact that Christ offered one sacrifice prove its abiding efficacy? See verses 24-26.

(3) Observe the contrast in verses 27 and 28 between (a) sinful man—appointed to death—going to judgment; and (b) the Saviour—dying for our sins—returning in salvation. Are you among those who 'look for Him'?

Note.—It is best, as in R.V., to read 'covenant' throughout this passage, except in verses 16 and 17, where the meaning seems to be 'testament' or 'will'. The Greek word has both meanings.

Day 6. Heb. x. 1-18. Final exposition of Christ's sacrifice.

(1) Verses 1-4. In what three ways were the sacrifices of the tabernacle inadequate?

(2) Verses 5-10. What is the new and different sacrifice offered by Christ, and what is its efficacy (verse 10)? 'Sanctified' here means brought into a relationship of acceptance and service with God for ever.

(3) Verses 11-18. The difference between the two systems is here summed up. Write down as many contrasts as you can find. How has the abiding validity of Christ's sacrifice been attested by the Holy Ghost?

Notes.—(1) Verse 5. The writer here, as elsewhere, quotes from the Greek version of the Old Testament.

(2) Verse 14. 'Perfected' etc. The meaning is that by the one sacrifice of Christ everything that hinders our access to God is removed.

Day 7. Heb. x. 19-39.

Having finished his doctrinal exposition, the writer proceeds to give practical counsel for the life we are to live under the new covenant (see *Analysis*).

(1) Verses 19-25. What is to be (a) the believer's relation to God; (b) his witness in the world; and (c) his responsibility to his fellow believers?

(2) Verses 26-39. Consider the terrible doom of the apostate in contrast to the blessedness described in **x.** 19-22. What various reasons for steadfast endurance does the writer urge in verses 32-39? Cf. Gal. iii. 4.

Notes.—(1) Verse 22. As the high priest and his sons at their consecration for service in the earthly sanctuary were washed with water and sprinkled with the blood of sacrifice (Ex. xxix. 4, 21), so we in 'heart' and 'body', that is, inwardly and outwardly, in our whole being, have been made clean in Christ.

(2) Verses 22, 23 (R.V.), 24. Note the combination of faith, hope, and love, as in 1 Cor. xiii. 13; 1 Thes. i. 3.

Week 33. HEBREWS XI-XIII

Day 1. Heb. xi. 1-22. The importance of faith. See also vi. 12 and x. 38.

(1) In how many different ways is faith manifested in this portion? In what way or ways is faith manifested in your life?

(2) What changes were brought into the lives of the people here mentioned, and what results did faith effect?

(3) What is the ultimate end of those who live by faith?

Day 2. Heb. xi. 23-40.

(1) Verses 24-27. How did Moses by faith overcome (a) the allurements of the world; and (b) the threats of the world? Observe the emphasis laid in both cases upon the *vision* that faith gives. Cf. 1 Jn. v. 4; 2 Cor. iv. 18.

(2) Verses 28-31. Consider in these four instances of faith how difficult it must have been to exercise faith, and the great results that followed.

(3) Verses 32-38. A summary of the achievements (verses 32-35a) and the sufferings (verses 35b-38) of faith. What challenge is presented to us by the fact that these men and women lived *before Christ?*

Day 3. Heb. xii. 1-17.

(1) Verses 1-4. What three conditions must be fulfilled if the Christian race is to be run and the prize attained? Cf. 1 Cor. ix. 24-26; Phil. iii. 13, 14.

(2) Verses 5-11. How are we to look upon suffering, if it befall us, and what is to be our attitude under it?

(3) Verses 12-17 set forth what should be our attitude towards others in times of trial. What is said here about helping the weak, about pursuing high aims (verse 14), and about mutual responsibility and watchful oversight? Cf. x. 24, 25; Gn. iv. 9.

Day 4. Heb. xii. 18-29.

(1) Verses 18-24. Final contrast between the two covenants. In what respects does the heavenly Mount Zion of the new covenant excel in glory the earthly mountain Sinai of the first covenant? Cf. 2 Cor. iii. 7-11.

(2) Verses 25-29. What is the danger against which warning is here given? Try to state in your own words the two main points of the argument.

Note.—Verses 22 and 23. The central words of these two verses may be interpreted either as applying solely to angels (the word 'church' meaning 'convocation') or as indicating two separate companies: the angels, and the Church. The first of these alternatives is probably to be preferred. This Epistle does not elsewhere speak of the Church as signifying the whole body of the redeemed in Christ, nor does the writer conceive of the Church as being, at the time he wrote, in heaven. The only human beings he sees there, as a separate company, are the Old Testament saints, now made perfect through Christ's sacrifice. But he does see the angels, gathered there in festal assembly, a convocation of the firstborn of heaven's citizens. His purpose is to show that whereas at Sinai the people saw only a temporary manifestation of angels, we, through the new covenant, are brought into abiding fellowship with them in their life and worship in the eternal city.

Day 5. Heb. xiii. 1-8.

(1) What various aspects of Christian duty are set forth in these verses? What gracious promise is quoted? What should be our response?

(2) In what two ways should Christian leaders, whose life on earth has ended, be remembered (verse 7, R.V.)? What is the connection between verses 7 and 8?

Note.—Verse 1. 'Continue'. Cf. vi. 10, x. 33, 34.

Day 6. Heb. xiii. 9-25.

(1) If, because of our confession of Christ, we must suffer the loss of former earthly fellowships, what two sources of comfort are here brought before us? See verses 12-14 and note below.

(2) What sacrifices has the Christian to offer?

(3) What is the difference between the two petitions of the great prayer of verses 20, 21? And on what massive foundations are they based?

Notes.—(1) Verse 9. It would appear that the readers of the Epistle were being urged to partake of sacrificial meals, such as were common under the law, to maintain fellowship with the non-Christian Jewish community. The writer reminds them (a) that grace, not food, strengthens the soul; (b) that the sacrifice of Christ was essentially a sin offering, in connection with which, under the law, there was no sacrificial meal (verses 10, 11; cf. Lv. iv. 11, 12, 20, 21); (c) if they would have fellowship, therefore, with Christ, it will not be by staying within the camp of Judaism, but by going forth to Him 'without the camp'.

(2) Verse 21. 'Make you perfect', that is, repair and equip, putting into a fit condition to serve him.

Day 7. Revision.

Consider the two covenants. (a) How was the first covenant defective in its sanctuary, its priesthood, and its sacrifices? (b) How in all these things is the second covenant perfect? Are we availing ourselves, as we should, of our privileges in Christ Jesus?

PSALMS I—XLI

INTRODUCTION

(See New Bible Handbook, pp. 186, 187, 191-198)

THE Book of Psalms may be regarded as the inspired hymn-book of the Jewish Church, containing psalms for both public and private worship. Those with the superscription (or subscription)[1] 'To the chief musician' seem specially intended for public worship. Others were, perhaps, originally personal meditations which were taken over for use in the service of the sanctuary and in family worship at home. There are also didactic poems and historical recitals. The book stood at the head of the third section of the

---

[1] A reference to Hab. iii. 19 (last clause) suggests the probability that, in those of the psalms which have headings or titles, the musical part of the title, including words 'To the Chief musician', should really be attached to the end of the preceding psalm.

Hebrew Scriptures, to which it often gave its name.[1] This section followed the books of the prophets.

The contents of the book were composed at various periods during the whole of Israelite history from the exodus to the Babylonian captivity. One psalm at least is the work of Moses (Ps. xc). Many are by David, one or two by Solomon, a few by certain of the Temple singers, and many again are anonymous. Some have a title and others have none. The psalms divide into five divisions, as follows: i–xli, xlii–lxxii, lxxiii–lxxxix, xc–cvi, cvii–cl. The end of each division except the last is marked by the word 'Amen'.

This third section of the Old Testament Scriptures, at the beginning of which the psalms stand, may be said to strike, on the whole, a more individual note than the preceding ones. While the prophets write largely (though not, of course, entirely) from the point of view of the outward and national life, the psalms deal largely with personal spiritual matters. It is needless to say that they look forward, as do the prophets, to the Person and work of our Lord Jesus Christ.

The R.V. should be used throughout the study of the psalms.

Week 34. Psalms i–xii

Day 1. Pss. i and ii.

(1) Sum up in two headings, one negative, the other positive, the characteristics of the righteous as given in Ps. i. 1, 2. Have we proved for ourselves the blessedness (as pictured in verse 3) of conforming to this standard? In the light of the gospel, who are 'the righteous'?

(2) Contrast in i. 4-6 the final end of the righteous, as compared with that of the 'ungodly' (r.v. 'wicked').

(3) What reasons are given in Ps. ii why rebellion against the Lord and His anointed king is, and must be, 'a vain thing'? Cf. Acts iv. 25-28.

Notes.—(1) i. 2. 'The law of the Lord'; i.e. the revealed will of Jehovah.

(2) i. 3. 'Planted'; better 'transplanted'. The picture is that of a tree selected by the owner of an orchard, and transplanted near to the irrigation channels by which the garden was watered.

(3) i. 6. 'Knoweth'; in the sense of 'careth for'. Cf. Na. i. 7.

(4) Ps. ii is the first of what are known as messianic psalms, that is, psalms which prophesy the sufferings and glory of the coming Messiah.

Day 2. Pss. iii and iv.

For the circumstances in which these psalms were written see 2 Sa. xv-xvii.

[1] See, e.g. Lk. xxiv. 44.

(1) Ps. iii is a morning psalm. As David wakes, what adverse conditions confront him (see verses 1, 2)? How does he strengthen his faith (verses 2-5), until it rises into confident assurance of victory (verses 6-8)? What may we learn from his example in our own conflicts?

(2) Ps. iv is an evening psalm. In verses 2-5 David addresses his adversaries. What counsel does he give them? and in what does he find his own strength, joy, and security?

Notes.—(1) iii. 5. If this psalm was written, as seems likely, on the second morning after David's flight from Jerusalem, it was a great encouragement to him that the night had passed without an attack. Cf. 2 Sa. xvii. 1, 16.

(2) iv. 3. 'Him that is godly.' A reference to David himself; see R.V. mg. and 2 Sa. v. 2; Ps. lxxviii. 70, 71.

(3) iv. 4. 'Stand in awe'; the Hebrew word literally means 'tremble', whether with fear or anger. The LXX takes it to mean 'tremble with anger' (cf. R.V. mg.) and Paul follows this in Eph. iv. 26. If it be taken as 'tremble with fear', the meaning is 'stand in awe' of God who is my avenger, and 'sin not', i.e. desist from your rebellion.

Day 3. Ps. v.

(1) What does this psalm reveal about God?

(2) Study the psalm as an example of prayer. When, how, for what, and why does David pray?

(3) Do we also pray much, hate evil, and rejoice greatly?

Day 4. Ps. vi.

Another example of prayer. Note the divisions, first an anguished cry (verses 1-3), second, calmer pleading, with reasons why God should answer (verses 4-7), third, the victory of faith (verses 8-10).

(1) Do you know in experience how thus to 'fight the good fight of faith', rising from a sense of overwhelming need to an assurance of answered prayer and certain deliverance? Cf. Ps. lxii. 8.

Note.—David seems to have suffered both from sickness and from the taunts of his enemies. His sickness gave them occasion to point to him as one 'smitten of God'.

Day 5. Pss. vii and viii.

(1) Ps. vii falls into two parts. The first part (verses 1-10) consists of an impassioned protestation of innocence in the face of ruthless persecution, and an appeal to God for judgment. On what grounds is David's confidence based?

(2) The second part of the psalm (verses 11-17) consists of reflections on the certain doom of the wicked, followed by an ascription of praise to God. In what two ways does judgment

overtake the wicked? See verses 11-13 and 14-16, and compare
Ps. xxxiv. 16; Pr. xxvi. 26, 27.

(3) What light is thrown upon Ps. viii (a) by our Lord's reference to it in Mt. xxi. 16, and (b) by Heb. ii. 5-9?

Notes.—(1) Ps. vii probably belongs to the period in David's life when he
was being hunted by Saul. It is not known who Cush was, except that he was
a man of Saul's tribe.

(2) vii. 7. The word 'return' is difficult to explain. It is possible that the
word should be rendered 'sit'. Verses 6-9 are a picture of God seated in judgment.

Day 6. Pss. ix and x.

These psalms were probably originally one, as is shown by the fact of their
common 'alphabetic' structure. In the LXX they are one psalm. The contents
are, however, different. Ps. ix is mainly a song of praise, celebrating victory
over foreign nations; but Ps. x consists mainly of prayer, pleading for the overthrow of the wicked within Israel.

(1) What does David say about the Lord, especially in Ps. ix?
To how much of what he says can you say 'Amen' from your own
experience?

(2) What is said in these two psalms, and especially in Ps. x,
about the wicked man—his thoughts, his actions, and his final
end?

Notes.—(1) ix. 8. 'People'; better, 'peoples' (R.V.), and so also in verse 11.
The whole psalm has to do with God's judgment upon the surrounding nations.

(2) ix. 17. 'Hell'; not the place of torment, but 'Sheol' (R.V.), the place of
the dead. The meaning is that through the judgments which God is executing,
the life of the wicked will be cut short by death.

Day 7. Pss. xi and xii.

(1) Why did not David follow the counsel given him to flee in
the hour of peril? What vision did he see that gave him confidence? Cf. Ne. vi. 10-13; Heb. xi. 27. But is it always wrong
to flee in face of danger? Cf. Jn. x. 39, 40; Acts ix. 24-26; Mt. x.
23.

(2) How are the word of man and the Word of God contrasted
in Ps. xii?

Notes.—(1) xi. 3. Better, perhaps, as in R.V. mg. The righteous have not
been able to effect any change for the better; why then remain in the midst of
danger?

(2) xii. 3 may be rendered as a prayer. 'May the Lord cut off', etc.

(3) xii. 5. God's answer to the prayer.

Week 35. PSALMS XIII–XXI

Day 1. Pss. xiii and xiv.

(1) Notice the delay in the answer to David's prayer. How did
he act in the face of it? Cf. Lk. xviii. 1.

(2) Have we known what it is thus to experience delay in receiving an answer from God, until circumstances became, humanly speaking, almost desperate (xiii. 3, 4); and yet, like David, to rise through faith to a triumphant assurance of coming blessing? Cf. Mk. xi. 24 (R.V.).

(3) What do we learn from Ps. xiv about the extent of the corruption that has befallen man, and about the reason for it?

Notes.—(1) Ps. xiv is most probably a national psalm. Verses 1-3 refer to mankind in general and verses 4-6 to some cruel oppression of Israel, such as that of Pharaoh, and God's deliverance of His people.

(2) xiv. 5. 'There were they in great fear'; a reference perhaps to the destruction of the Egyptians (Ex. xiv. 30).

(3) xiv. 7. 'Bringeth back the captivity'; better, perhaps, 'restores the ortunes of'. It is not necessarily an allusion to the Exile, for the same phrase is used by the pre-exilic prophets, see Ho. vi. 11; Am. ix. 14.

Day 2. Pss. xv and xvi.

(1) As you read Ps. xv are you not impressed by two facts, (1) that clause by clause the Psalmist's description is fulfilled in Christ, and (2) that clause by clause, *we* have come short? What has the gospel to say to us in this situation? See Heb. x. 19-22, xiii. 20, 21; Jude 24, 25.

(2) What, according to Ps. xvi, are the marks of the believing man (verses 1-4), what his privileges (verses 5-8), and what his prospects (verses 9-11)?

Notes.—(1) xv. 5a. See Lv. xxv. 35-37. 'The positive rule of the Old Testament has become obsolete under the circumstances of modern society, but the principle which underlies it is still of obligation' (*Camb. Bible*).

(2) xvi. 2 and 3. It is important here to follow the R.V. (as also in verses 4, 9, 10). Note also the distinction between LORD (Jehovah) and Lord (sovereign Master).

(3) xvi. 7. 'My reins'; literally 'kidneys', used figuratively as representing the inward feelings.

(4) xvi. 10. Quoted by Peter (Acts ii. 27) and by Paul (Acts xiii. 35) with reference to Christ. As with Ps. xv, the psalm is fulfilled in Him, and in us through Him.

Day 3. Ps. xvii.

The background of the psalm is a situation of extreme peril (verses 9, 11) arising from the attacks of evil men. The R.V. is of special value here.

(1) In verses 1-7 on what two grounds does David base his plea? Cf. Jn. xvi. 27; 1 Jn. iii. 21, 22.

(2) How are his enemies described (a) in their inward character, (b) in their attitude towards the Psalmist, (c) in their aims and outlook?

(3) What kept David from being corrupted by his evil environment, and what contrast is set forth between his own desires and those of his enemies? Are we like him in this?

Notes.—(1) Verse 4. 'The ways of the violent'; cf. xxxiv. 10, lxii. 10.
(2) Verse 9. 'My deadly enemies'; i.e. enemies who seek my death.
(3) Verse 10a. See R.V. mg. and cf. 1 Jn. iii. 17.

Day 4. Ps. xviii. 1-27.

This great psalm must be read in the light of David's life-story as described in 1 Sa. xvi–2 Sa. viii. King of a united nation, victorious over surrounding peoples, blessed with the great promise of the continuance of his royal line, David magnifies the power and goodness of his God.

(1) Verses 1-3. Cliff, fortress, rock, shield—these had been David's places of refuge; but God, he says, was more to him than them all. What are the defences and securities in which men trust today? Is God to you all that these can give, and more? Cf. Hab. iii. 17, 18; Phil. iv. 12, 13.

(2) Verses 12-19. To what does David bear testimony in these verses and how do they encourage us to bring our own need to God, however dark the outlook? Cf. Ps. lxii. 8.

(3) Verses 20-27. David declares that his deliverance is a reward for his righteousness, and that God's dealings with men are according to their moral character. Is this the case and, if so, what hope is there for sinners?

Note.—Verses 9-16 are probably not intended to be taken literally, but as a poetic description in vivid imagery of the strength and majesty with which God came to David's aid. There is no record of God's scattering David's enemies by an actual storm.

Day 5. Ps. xviii. 28-50.

(1) Make a list of all that God did for David, as set forth in these verses. What corresponding help may we expect from Him in spiritual service? Cf. 1 Cor. xv. 10; Eph. i. 19.

(2) According to Rom. xv. 9 (where verse 49 of the psalm is applied to Christ) the psalm may be regarded as a prophetic anticipation of the final triumph of Christ over all His enemies and of His universal reign. Have you ever pondered this glorious consummation and given thanks?

Notes.—(1) Verse 29. 'Through a troop'; better, 'after a troop'; a probable allusion to 1 Sa. xxx. 8. The next clause may allude to 2 Sa. v. 6, 7.
(2) Verse 35. 'Gentleness' or 'condescension' (R.V. mg.). Literally 'humbleness of mind'. Cf. Ps. cxiii. 5-8; Is. lvii. 15; Mt. xi. 29; Phil. ii. 5-8.

Day 6. Ps. xix.

(1) Describe in your own words what the heavens, the firmament, day and night, the sun, tell us of God (verses 1-6). Cf. Jb. xxxviii. 31-35; Pss. lxxiv. 16, cxlviii. 3-6; Mt. v. 45.

(2) Contrast with this the revelation given in the law (verses 7-11) showing how great is the advance, both in clearness, and fulness of effect.

(3) Do we share the Psalmist's deep desire for deliverance from sin, and for acceptance with God? How does the gospel provide a better solution for the problem of sin? See Note (2) below, also Acts xiii. 38, 39; Rom. viii. 1-4.

Notes.—(1) Verse 4. 'Their line'; i.e. their 'measuring line'. Cf. Je. xxxi. 39. The boundary of their message is earth's farthest limit.

(2) Verses 11-13. The law provided an atonement for sins of ignorance (here called 'hidden faults'), but not for deliberate wilful sinning (here called 'presumptuous sins'). See Lv. iv. 2; Nu. xv. 30, 31. Therefore the Psalmist prays that he may not be held guilty for the former (it being assumed that the sacrifices have been offered), and that he may be withheld from the latter.

Day 7. Pss. xx and xxi.

These two psalms are closely linked together. In Ps. xx a battle is about to take place between the king of Israel at the head of his people, and his foes. Sacrifices have been offered, and the king with his people commit their cause in faith to God. In Ps. xxi the battle is won, and the people give thanks to God for their king, and look forward to further victories.

(1) Ps. xx falls into two parts, verses 1-5 and 6-8, with a concluding prayer. What is the keynote of the first part, and what of the second? Observe the threefold mention of the Name of God.

(2) Ps. xxi also falls into two parts, verses 1-7 and 8-12, with a concluding prayer. To whom is the first part addressed, and to whom the second? Show how what is said of the king finds its fulfilment in Christ.

(3) What is the secret of the king's joy? Do we know the same secret? Cf. Ne. viii. 10 (last clause).

Week 36. PSALMS XXII–XXIX

Day 1. Ps. xxii. 1-21.

This is a prophetic psalm 'testifying beforehand the sufferings of Christ, and the glory that should follow' (1 Pet. i. 11). It falls into four sections or strophes, of which today we study the first three.

(1) Verses 1-10. In this strophe faith wrestles to hold fast to the fact that Jehovah is '*my* God', and wins the victory. What did the sufferer's enemies say, and on what, in face of these taunts, did his faith stay itself? With verses 6-8 cf. Mt. xxvii. 39-43, and with verse 1 cf. Mt. xxvii. 46.

(2) Verses 11-18. The sufferer pours out his heart before the Lord. Consider what an exact picture is given here of the Passion scenes in the Gospels. With verse 18, for example, cf. Mt. xxvii. 35; Jn. xix. 23, 24.

(3) Verses 19-21. Faith wins the victory. This third strophe is cut short by the shout of assurance that God has heard and answered. See Note (4) below.

Notes.—(1) Verse 3. 'Inhabitest'; better, 'art enthroned upon' as in R.V. mg.—a beautiful picture of the praises of Israel rising as a cloud to form a throne, on which God sits.

(2) Verse 14. 'Wax', 'melted'; a symbol of faintness. See Jos. ii. 11.

(3) Verse 20. 'My darling'; literally 'my only one', that is, 'my one precious life'.

(4) Verse 21. This verse might be written thus:
> 'Save me from the lion's mouth
> From the wild oxen's horns. . .
> *Thou hast answered me.*'

Contrast this with verse 2, 'Thou answerest not'.

Day 2. Ps. xxii. 22-31.

In this fourth strophe of the psalm we are in a different world, a world of praise, worship, and vision of divine triumph.

(1) Trace in these verses some of the happy results of the sufferings described in verses 1-21.

(2) This closing strophe might have been thought exaggerated before Jesus came. How could the deliverance of one sufferer be the cause of all nations and classes worshipping the Lord, and be the theme of unending story from generation to generation? Yet in the light of the New Testament, how is the prophecy seen not only to have been fulfilled, but far exceeded?

Notes.—(1) Verse 22. This is applied to Christ in Heb. ii. 12.

(2) Verse 25. 'I will pay my vows'; i.e. by sacrifice. Cf. Pss. lxvi. 13, cxvi. 17, 18. At such sacrifices others gathered round, and shared in the feast (Dt. xii. 18, xvi. 11, 14). The Psalmist sees a great company gathered—'the meek', 'all the ends of the earth', 'rich and poor', 'from generation to generation'.

Day 3. Pss. xxiii and xxiv.

(1) How does Ps. xxiii show that he who trusts in the Lord lacks for nothing? In other words, what good things did David find under the care of his Shepherd? Make a list of them, verse by verse.

(2) What may be learned about the King of glory from verses 1 and 2 of Ps. xxiv, and what from verses 3-5? What is required of His worshippers in hand, heart, soul, and lips?

Note.—Ps. xxiv. There is little doubt that this psalm was composed to be sung when David brought the ark of God to Jerusalem (see 2 Sa. vi). In the worship of the Christian Church, verses 7-10 have been interpreted of Christ's ascension. They are rather a prophecy of the return of the Lord Jesus as the King of glory to set up His kingdom on Mount Zion. Cf. Is. xxiv. 23.

Day 4. Ps. xxv.

This is one of the so-called alphabetic psalms. In the Hebrew text each two lines (with one or two exceptions) begin with a fresh letter of the Hebrew alphabet, in order. The Psalm begins and ends with a series of petitions (verses 1-7 and 15-21), and in the centre is a section consisting of reflections on the character and ways of God (verses 8-14). Verse 22 seems to have been added later.

(1) What three main petitions does the Psalmist make in verses 1-7, and what in verses 15-21? What light do the petitions throw upon his circumstances and spiritual experience? Are the last two lines of verse 5 true of you also?

(2) What in verses 8-14 is said about God, and what He does for those who fear Him? Do you believe these things; and if so, what effect should they have upon your life?

Day 5. Ps. xxvi.

The psalm centres in the prayer of verse 9, where David prays that he may not share the fate of the wicked. Often in his early life must it have seemed that he was about to be cut off.

(1) On what grounds in verses 1-8 does he base his plea?

(2) Describe in your own words the main trend of David's life as he describes it here? Can you make a similar claim for yourself?

(3) How does the closing verse show that David has reached the assurance that his prayer is answered? Compare Week 34, Day 4 (1).

Notes.—(1) Verse 2. 'Examine . . . prove . . . try'; a searching test both of outward conduct and of inward thought.

(2) Verse 6. Cf. xxiv. 3, 4; Ex. xxx. 19, 20.

(3) Verse 8. 'Thine honour'; better, as in R.V., 'Thy glory'. Cf. Ex. xl. 34.

(4) Verse 12. 'An even place'; i.e. a place of safety and ease, where he can fulfil the promises of verses 6 and 7.

Day 6. Ps. xxvii.

The psalm falls into two parts, which are very different in character. In the first part David's heart is full of confidence and praise (verses 1-6); in the second his spirit is oppressed, and he pleads anxiously for help (verses 7-14).

(1) Does Christian experience also know such variations of

mood? Cf., e.g., Lk. x. 17-24 with xxii. 39-46, and Rom. viii. 35-39 with 2 Cor. vii. 5, 6.

(2) In verses 1-6 what does David say the Lord is to him, and will do for him, and what is David's chief desire? Cf. Ps. xci. 1, 2.

(3) In verses 7-14 what are David's seven petitions? How does he address God, and how does he encourage himself to continue in prayer? Cf. 1 Sa. xxx. 6 (last clause).

Note.—Verse 10. The first clause is probably a proverbial expression indicating great need, such as that of a deserted child.

Day 7. Pss. xxviii and xxix.

(1) Many have thought that the circumstances portrayed in Ps. xxviii correspond to David's situation at the time of his flight from Absalom. What points of correspondence can you discern?

(2) On what attributes of God does David rely in presenting his petition? How rich and full also his thanksgiving for God's answer to his cry! Can you say verse 7 as the witness and resolve of your own heart?

(3) Ps. xxix is the description of a thunderstorm viewed as a manifestation of God's glory. What spiritual lessons does it teach regarding God and regarding our duties and privileges as His people? Notice how verses 1 and 11 are combined in the angels' song in Lk. ii. 14.

Notes.—(1) xxix. 3. 'The voice of the Lord'; i.e. thunder, and so throughout the psalm. Cf. xviii. 13.

(2) Verse 6. 'Sirion'; an old name for Hermon. See Dt. iii. 9.

(3) Verse 7. 'Divideth (or 'cleaveth', R.V.) the flames of fire'. A reference to flashes of lightning.

(4) Verses 9 and 10 should be read as in the R.V.

Week 37. PSALMS XXX–XXXVI

Day 1. Ps. xxx.

(1) From what danger had God delivered David, and what indications are there that the danger had been very great? This gave rise to reflections in his mind, first, about sorrow in general, and second, about his own life. What does he say about sorrow (verse 5)?

(2) In regard to his own life, to what conclusions does David come as to (a) the salutary effects of the affliction, (b) the purpose for which he had been delivered?

Notes.—(1) Verse 3. See R.V. mg. David was already, as it were, among the dead.

(2) Verse 5. See R.V. It is a beautiful picture. Weeping, like a passing traveller, lodges for the night only: the morning light brings Joy to abide. Cf. verse 11.

(3) Verse 12. 'My glory'; i.e., my soul.

Day 2. Ps. xxxi.

In this psalm David, beginning with an urgent sense of need, and rising by the exercise of faith to the heights of praise (verses 1-8), is suddenly cast down to deeper depths than before, and has to fight the fight of faith anew (verses 9-18) until at last he stands triumphantly upon the uplands of song (verses 19-24).

(1) Notice in verse 2 the words 'Be Thou', and in verse 3 'Thou art'. 'It is the logic', says Delitzsch, 'of every believing prayer'. In prayer do you stop at 'Be Thou', or go on to say by faith 'Thou art'?

(2) What would you pick out as the most bitter ingredient in David's cup of sorrow (verses 9-18)? What would you do if you were in like case? What did David do?

(3) In verses 19-24 what witness does David bear to God, and what message does he bring to fellow-believers everywhere? If we accept and act on the message, what will follow? Shall not we also prove the witness true, and thus be able to encourage others?

Notes.—(1) Verse 5a. See Lk. xxiii. 46, an evidence that this psalm was in our Lord's mind upon the cross.

(2) Verse 8. 'In a large place' (R.V.); with liberty of movement, in contrast to being 'shut up' (verse 8a).

(3) Verse 10. 'Iniquity'; the LXX reads here 'affliction'.

(4) Verse 12. Is this a reference to David's time of exile? Cf. 1 Sa. xxvi. 19.

(5) Verse 23c. 'And richly requite arrogant men' (Moffatt).

Day 3. Ps. xxxii.

David's account of his spiritual experience after his great sin.

(1) How does David describe the miseries of a guilty conscience? See verses 3, 4.

(2) What is the indispensable condition of forgiveness? Cf. Pr. xxviii. 13.

(3) What three great blessings does the forgiven soul receive, filling the heart with joy? But what two conditions of their enjoyment are laid down? See verses 5-11.

Notes.—(1) Verses 1, 2. See Rom. iv. 6-8.

(2) Verse 3. 'When I kept silence'; i.e. about my sin.

(3) Note the R.V. readings in verses 6 and 9.

Day 4. Ps. xxxiii.

This psalm begins where Ps. xxxii left off. The Hebrew word translated 'rejoice' in verse 1 is the same as that translated 'shout for joy' in xxxii. 11. The structure of the psalm is as follows: verses 1-3, introductory call to praise; verses 4-19, reasons why the Lord is to be praised; verses 20-22, concluding response of faith.

(1) How many reasons can you find in verses 4-11 why the Lord should be praised?

(2) Verse 12 is the central verse of the psalm. What reasons are given in verses 13-19 why the nation whose God is the Lord is blessed above other nations?

(3) In view of all that is said in verses 4-19 does your heart join in the call to praise of verses 1-3 and the declaration and prayer of verses 20-22?

Note.—Verse 3. 'A new song'; the song of the redeemed. See Ps. xl. 3. 'Play skilfully'. *Verb. sap.* for all who aspire to lead the praises of God's people.

Day 5. Ps. xxxiv.

This is an alphabetic psalm like Ps. xxv. For the circumstances, see the psalm title or heading and also 1 Sa. xxi. 12–xxii. 2. The psalm shines with a new light when regarded as composed in the cave of Adullam for the instruction of David's followers. The analysis is as follows: verses 1-3, call to praise; verses 4-7, four instances of Jehovah's deliverance; verses 8-10, an invitation to make personal trial of the way of faith; verses 11-14, what life in the fear of Jehovah means; verses 15-17, the principles underlying this philosophy of life; verses 18-21, the question of afflictions raised and answered. Verse 22 sums up the teaching of the psalm and points forward to the New Testament.

(1) Who are those who may expect the Lord's blessings? Note the various ways in which they are described. Are we ourselves entitled to claim blessing on the same grounds?

(2) Make a numbered list (avoiding repetition) of the blessings God gives to His people, as stated in this psalm.

Day 6. Ps. xxxv.

(1) The psalm falls into three divisions, each ending with a promise to give God thanks. Discover these sections, and give to each an appropriate heading, summarizing its contents.

(2) David gives a vivid picture of the vigour, subtlety and malice of his persecutors and reacts against them with equal vigour. What is the main cry of his heart, and on what grounds does he plead? In what respects is he an example to us?

Notes.—(1) Verses 4-6. Concerning this and similar prayers in the Psalms, see the *New Bible Handbook*, p. 196.

(2) Verses 11 and 12. See R.V. Malicious insinuations were made against David, which had never even entered his mind. Cf. 1 Sa. xxiv. 9, 17.

(3) Verse 13 (last clause). A difficult phrase of uncertain meaning. It seems to indicate heartfelt prayer, possibly repeated prayer.

Day 7. Ps. xxxvi.

(1) What are the principles of ungodly living and what its fruits? See verses 1-4.

(2) How different the character of God! Which of His attributes are here extolled, and what blessings flow from them? Are we living in the enjoyment of these blessings? See verses 5-9.

(3) To what twofold prayer do the Psalmist's reflections give rise and what vision is given him of the final end of those who work iniquity?

Note.—Verses 1 and 2. It seems best to regard transgression as personified, and as speaking in the heart of the evil man. The verses may then be translated as follows:

'Transgression uttereth its oracle to the wicked within his heart,
For it flattereth him in his eyes
That his iniquity shall not be found out and be hated'.

See R.V. and R.V. mg.

Week 38. PSALMS XXXVII–XLI

Day 1. Ps. xxxvii. 1-20.

The psalm is alphabetic, each two successive lines commencing with a new letter, except that in three instances (verses 7, 20, 34) three lines are grouped under one letter, and in three instances (verses 14, 15; 25, 26; 39, 40) five lines. 'The same fundamental ideas recur throughout; but four symmetrical divisions of 11, 9, 11, and 9 verses respectively, in each of which a particular thought is prominent, may be observed' (*Camb. Bible*). These divisions are verses 1-11, 12-20, 21-31, 32-40. The first two form today's portion.

(1) Verses 1-11. What counsels are given in these verses? Under what two main heads may they be summed up, and what promises are made if these counsels be observed?

(2) Verses 12-20. How does this section amplify verses 2, 9, and 10 of the first section? Though the wicked seem to prosper, and the righteous seem to suffer loss, how have the righteous the advantage in the end?

Notes.—(1) Verses 3 and 4. There is some uncertainty in these two verses as to what is counsel, and what is promise. But it seems best to follow the R.V. in verse 3, and the R.V. mg. in verse 4.

(2) Note the changes in the R.V., especially in verses 10 and 20.

Day 2. Ps. xxxvii. 21-40.

(1) Verses 21-31. This third section of the psalm expands in fuller measure what was said of the reward of the righteous in the first section in verses 4, 6, 9, 11. What does this third section say about the righteous?

(2) Verses 32-40. How would you state in your own words the contrast between the righteous and the wicked, as summed up in this closing section?

(3) Why *must* there be this difference in the destiny of the two classes? See e.g. verses 22, 23, 24, 28, 39, 40; and cf. Ps. xxxiv. 15, 16.

Notes.—(1) Note the R.V. changes, especially in verses 35, 36 and 40.

(2) Verses 37 and 38. The word translated 'end' may be rendered 'posterity' (see R.V. mg.) and this was probably the thought in the Psalmist's mind. His vision was limited to life on earth; but in the light of the New Testament our eyes look beyond life here to the final 'end' in the life to come.

Day 3. Ps. xxxviii.

(1) The three divisions of the psalm are marked by the fact that they all begin with an address to God. Do you discern a progress in faith from one section to the next?

(2) If this psalm was written when David's great sin first came to light and struck dismay and horror into the hearts of his friends, can we wonder that its tone is so subdued? How great the contrast with Ps. xxxv! What light does the psalm throw upon the effects of discovered sin in the life of a believer?

Notes.—(1) Verse 5. 'My wounds'; i.e. my stripes, a poetic description of God's scourging.

(2) Verse 11. 'My sore'; better as in R.V., 'my plague'. His friends regard him with horror as if he were a leper.

(3) Verse 14. 'Reproofs'; better, 'arguments' as in R.V. mg., i.e. arguments in self-defence.

(4) Verse 20b. 'Because, etc.'; better, 'for my following of good'. The meaning is 'although I have sought to do good to them'. Cf. Ps. xxxv. 12-14.

Day 4. Ps. xxxix.

(1) Why was the Psalmist at first silent, and why did he break silence and speak? When he gave utterance to his thoughts, to whom did he speak? What may we learn from him in this? Cf. Ps. lxii. 8b; Jas. iii. 5, 6.

(2) What truths had been revealed to the Psalmist about our life on earth, and about man? Would you say that a realization of these same truths is very much needed in our land today? Cf. Mt. vi. 31-33; Lk. xii. 13-21.

(3) What does the psalm reveal as to the only safe place for confidence, and on what special ground does the Psalmist come to this conclusion?

Notes.—(1) Verse 6. See R.V. mg.

(2) Verse 8. Behind all that is said in the psalm lay the consciousness of transgressions. God used David's fall to open his eyes to many things.

(3) Verse 11. 'Like a moth'; read as in R.V. mg. It is God who is compared to a moth (cf. Ho. v. 12).

(4) Verse 12. 'As the strangers and sojourners among them were specially commended to the care of Israel (Ex. xxii. 21, etc.), he would plead to be treated by God with a corresponding clemency' (*Camb. Bible*).

Day 5. Ps. xl. 1-10.

This psalm, like Ps. xxvii, consists of two parts, which differ widely in their content. The first part is full of joyous thanksgiving for recent deliverance; the second pleads for help in the midst of distress and danger.

(1) What five things does David say in verses 1-3 that God did for him, and what effect did his deliverance have upon those who witnessed it? Cf. Acts ix. 35, 42.

(2) To what reflections, resolve, and actions did his deliverance give rise in David's own heart and life? See verses 4-10.

(3) Reading the psalm in the light of the New Testament compare especially verses 1-3 with Eph. ii. 1-10, and verses 6-8 with Heb. x. 4-10.

Notes.—(1) Verses 6-8 are quoted in Heb. x. 5-7, but from the LXX version, which has a different reading in the second line of verse 6. The general meaning is not, however, essentially different. 'As the ear is the instrument for receiving the divine command, so the body is the instrument for fulfilling it' (*Camb. Bible*).

(2) Verse 9. 'Righteousness'; i.e. God's righteousness. Cf. verse 10.

Day 6. Ps. xl. 11-17.

(1) How would you describe in your own words the vivid picture of his condition given by the Psalmist in verse 12 (R.V.)?

(2) What does he do in his dire need, and with what result? What vision of victory does he see by faith? See verses 13-16.

(3) The vision gives place to the consciousness of present need (verse 17). But a great change has taken place. Contrast verse 17 with verse 12. What has caused the Psalmist's soul thus to find rest and peace?

Notes.—(1) Verse 11. Some make this verse the conclusion of the first part of the psalm, translating it thus: 'Thou, O Lord, wilt not restrain . . . shall continually, etc. . . .'

(2) Verses 13-17 are found again in the Psalter in Ps. lxx.

Day 7. Ps. xli.

This psalm seems to belong to the time of Absalom's rebellion (see verse 9 and 2 Sam. xvii. 1-3). If so, it would appear that David suffered from a severe illness at this time.

(1) What gives David cause for hope in verses 1-3? Cf. Pr. xiv. 21. Are we thus generous? Cf. Jas. ii. 14-16; 1 Jn. iii. 16-22.

(2) On the other hand, what reasons has he for anxiety? See verses 4-9.

(3) Amid 'fighting without and fear within' (2 Cor. vii. 5), how did his faith finally gain the victory?

Notes.—(1) Verse 1. David is here referring to himself though speaking in general terms.

(2) Verse 3b. Moffatt translates 'and brings him back to health', which is probably the right meaning. The Heb. text literally means 'Thou changest his lying down' (see R.V. mg.).

(3) Verse 11. This may allude to the failure of Ahitophel's counsel. See 2 Sa. xvii. 14, and Ps. iii. 5 (Note on p. 81).

I and II THESSALONIANS

INTRODUCTION

(See New Bible Handbook, pp. 377-381)

THESE two Epistles were written in Corinth during Paul's second missionary journey, and not long after the church in Thessalonica had been founded (Acts xvii. 1-10). The first was written upon Timothy's return from a visit to Thessalonica, and the second a few months later. They are among the most personal of the apostle's letters in the New Testament, and present a vivid picture both of himself and of his readers, while revealing also the marvellous results of his missionary work in the great heathen city, the capital of Macedonia.

The apostle was greatly encouraged by the report, which Timothy brought, of the church's steadfastness under persecution and of continued progress. But there were some matters that gave him concern, in particular the prevalence of erroneous views about the second advent. The chief theme of the two Epistles, therefore, is the second coming of Christ, which is shown to be a comfort in bereavement, a motive to patience, an inspiration to hope, a safeguard in temptation, a help to purity, a challenge to watchfulness, a ground of rejoicing, and a separating and sanctifying power. The apostle's great aim is summed up in 1 Thes. iii. 13.

ANALYSIS

1 Thessalonians

i. The founding of the church.
ii. Service for Christ.
iii–iv. 12. Sanctification and the daily walk.
iv. 13–v. The second coming and Christian behaviour.

2 Thessalonians

i–ii. 12. Further teaching about the second coming.
ii. 13–iii. Final exhortations.

Week 39. 1 AND 2 THESSALONIANS

Day 1. 1 Thes. i.

(1) Verse 1. A new society had come into being in Thessalonica. How is it here described, what was its bond of union, and what its inestimable wealth?

(2) What light is thrown by this chapter upon the fact and meaning of conversion? How were the Thessalonians converted? What was the nature of the preaching, and what the character of the response?

(3) Gather out the outstanding features of the Christian life and character of these converts. Making all allowance for the difference in circumstances, is the Christian life of today of this character?

Notes.—(1) Verse 3. Their faith issued in good works, their love toiled on for others' good, their hope of Christ's return endured, as they lived in communion with Him who had become their God and Father. Cf. Heb. xi. 27b.

(2) Verse 5. 'In much assurance'; better, 'with full conviction' (R.S.V.), that is, complete conviction on the part of the preachers as to the truth of their message.

Day 2. 1 Thes. ii.

(1) Verses 1-12. The real Paul. What does he here say of the aim, method, and spirit of his life and service? Make a list of the various points, those that show what he was not, and those which show what he was. As you ponder the list, what strikes you most forcibly?

(2) Verses 13, 14. What further light is here thrown upon the conversion of the Thessalonians, and upon conversion in general? Many hear the word of the gospel without being converted. What made the difference in the case of these Thessalonians?

(3) Verses 15-20. What two attitudes to missionary preaching are here set in contrast? Are you seeking to win others, and can you enter at all in experience into what Paul speaks of in verse 20?

Notes.—(1) Verse 2. Cf. Acts xvi. 19-24. 'Bold in our God'—note the source of their courage. 'With much contention.' Better, 'in the face of great opposition' (R.S.V.).

(2) Verse 7. Read as in R.V.

(3) Verse 18. He who engages in the work of the gospel will meet the opposition of Satan. Cf. Mk. iv. 15; 1 Thes. iii. 5.

Day 3. 1 Thes. iii.

(1) How is persecution regarded in this chapter (a) in relation to its inevitability (cf. Jn. xvi. 33), and (b) in relation to the spiritual peril which accompanies it (cf. 1 Pet. v. 8, 9)?

(2) It had been no easy thing for Paul to let Timothy go to Thessalonica (verses 1, 2), but now he had his reward. What two facts reported by Timothy gave him special comfort and joy? See verses 6-8 and cf. 3 Jn. 4.

(3) What twofold prayer, for himself and for his converts, did Paul pray? Note its intensity, and urgency, and, as regards his converts, what things he desires for them and the fulness of his prayer. Note, too, how it was accompanied with thanksgiving (verse 9; Phil. iv. 6; Col. iv. 2). What lessons may we learn from it about our own praying?

Notes.—(1) Verse 1. Cf. Acts xvii. 15.

(2) Verse 6. 'But now when Timotheus came'; better, as in R.V., 'But when Timothy came even now.' Paul wrote immediately.

Day 4. 1 Thes. iv.

(1) What three aspects of Christian living are emphasized in verses 1-12, and on what grounds?

(2) Why does the apostle go on reiterating the charge not only to practise mutual love and holiness, but to *increase* 'and *abound*' in these things? See iii. 12, iv. 1, 10, and compare Phil. iii. 12-14. Is not this counsel most necessary also today? Have we progressed in sanctification since our conversion?

(3) Verses 13-18. What practical use does Paul make here of the fact of the Lord's return (cf. iv. 18, v. 11) and what revelation does he give regarding it? State in your own words just what he says will happen.

Notes.—(1) Verse 8. 'Who hath also given unto us his holy Spirit'; better, as in R.V., 'Who giveth his Holy Spirit unto you'. The indwelling Holy Spirit is the seal of God's ownership, the evidence that we are His. See Eph. i. 13; Rom. viii. 9b. It is by the power of the Spirit that we overcome the flesh. See Gal. v. 16.

(2) Verses 11, 12. Read 'to aspire to live quietly, to mind your own affairs, and to work with your hands, as we charged you; so that you may command the respect of outsiders, and be dependent on nobody' (R.S.V.). Cf. 2 Thes. iii. 10-12; Eph. iv. 28.

Day 5. 1 Thes. v.

(1) Verses 1-11. How will the 'day of the Lord' break upon the world, and what will it mean (a) for men in general, and (b) for the people of Christ? Cf. Mt. xxiv. 32-44; Lk. xxi. 28.

(2) What is the difference between Christians and non-Christians as described in these verses? In view of the Lord's return, and the coming of 'the day of the Lord', how should Christians live?

(3) Make your own list of the injunctions in v. 12-22. If we say, 'Who is sufficient for these things', what is Paul's answer?

Notes.—(1) Verse 2. 'The day of the Lord'; an Old Testament phrase, signifying God's future intervention in history in salvation and judgment (Is. ii. 12, xiii. 6; Zp. i. 14, iii. 11, 16), and applied in the New Testament to the second coming of Christ (Lk. xvii. 24; 1 Cor. i. 8, etc.).

(2) Verse 6. 'Let us not sleep'; the word 'sleep' is used in this passage in three meanings; in this verse in the sense of spiritual insensibility, in verse 7 in the meaning of natural sleep, and in verse 10 in the sense of physical death, as in iv. 14, 15 (cf. iv. 16, 'the dead in Christ').

(3) Verse 12. 'Know'; in the sense of 'hold in respect', 'appreciate'.

(4) Verse 22. 'Appearance'; better, 'form', as in R.V.

Day 6. 2 Thes. i–ii. 12.

(1) Compare and contrast chapter i of this Epistle with chapter i of the first Epistle. What resemblances do you find and what differences?

(2) How is Christ's coming a comfort to persecuted Christians, and a terror to the unconverted? Contrast what is said by the apostle as to the final end of those who do not, and those who do, obey the gospel. What is his prayer for the latter? Are you seeking that this prayer may be fulfilled in you?

(3) Without going into the complicated question as to who 'the man of sin' is, consider his methods, his motives, his influences, and power, and his end, that we may see sin in its full manifestation in a human life, and realize how hateful it is. Observe also who are deceived by 'the man of sin'.

Notes.—(1) i. 5. 'A manifest token of the righteous judgment of God'. The reference is to their faith and patience, which is a clear indication of what the righteous judgment of God will be, namely, that they will be accounted worthy. Cf. Lk. xx. 35.

(2) i. 6. 'If so be that' (R.V.); better, 'since indeed' (R.S.V.).

(3) i. 7, 8. Cf. Mk. viii. 38; Is. lxvi. 15; Je. x. 25.

(4) ii. 1. 'By the coming'; better, 'concerning the coming' (R.S.V.).

(5) ii. 2. 'Spirit'; prophetic utterance: 'word'; reasoned discourse (cf. verse 15). 'The day of Christ is at hand'; better, 'has come' (R.S.V.).

(6) ii. 12. 'Damned'; better, 'condemned' (R.S.V.).

Day 7. 2 Thes. ii. 13–iii.

(1) Consider how in ii. 13, 14 the whole work of salvation is summarized. What is its origin, what are the means God uses, what is man's part and what the final end?

(2) What three prayers does Paul pray in this portion, and what prayer does he ask for himself? With iii. 16 cf. Jn. xiv. 27, xvi. 33; Phil. iv. 6, 7.

(3) What defect in the church's life does Paul rebuke, and what directions does he give to remedy it?

Notes.—(1) iii. 2, 3. From the unbelief of men the apostle turns to the faithfulness of the Lord.

(2) iii. 5. 'Patient waiting'; better, 'patience' (R.V.) or 'steadfastness' (R.S.V.). The heart is apt to wander. May the Lord guide it into the abiding place of God's love and Christ's patience!

JOB

INTRODUCTION

(See New Bible Handbook, pp. 186-191)

THE book of Job shows us a good man overwhelmed by appalling calamities and physical suffering, struggling to reconcile his own experience and his honest observation of human life in general with faith in God's justice.

The author of the book is unknown, and even the date is uncertain. But the entire absence of any reference to Israel and the patriarchal civilization described favour an early date. It is possible that the book is an inspired drama rather than a literal history, but it is certain from Ezk. xiv. 14 and Jas. v. 11 that it was at least founded on historical fact.

This book is valuable for its warnings and its positive teaching. It warns us, by the example of the friends of Job, how not to deal with those in sorrow or in intellectual or spiritual difficulty. It emphasizes the necessity of honesty in defence of truth (xiii. 4-12; xlii. 7). It displays an unparalleled example of faith in God against all appearances; for, despite a few temporary lapses, Job does maintain his faith, appealing from the seeming injustice of God's dealings to the just God who must exist somewhere, if only He could be found.

In the speeches of Elihu, but still more in the preface and ending, the book suggests reasons why God's own people may have to pass through suffering. Job himself has a momentary glimpse of the answer to this problem (xxiii. 10). The divine speeches and Job's reaction to them reveal to us that the true solution to all difficulties about the ways of God is not argument, but contact with the Lord Himself. Jehovah does not enter into argument with Job, but simply displays Himself, and Job is wholly satisfied.

The book is also remarkable in its prophetic aspect. Job, in his pathetic gropings after God, cries out for an Arbitrator between God and himself, who might lay His hand on both. And though the very heart of his problem was the absence of belief in a future life which would redress the inequalities of the present, he is first led to wish that there might be another life (xiv. 13-15) and later he rises on the wings of faith and inspiration to a positive statement that one day his Redeemer would stand upon the earth, and that after his own body had been destroyed he would see God (xix. 25-27).

ANALYSIS

i, ii.	The origin and nature of Job's calamities.
iii.	Job's patience breaks, and he curses the day of his birth.
iv–xiv.	The first cycle of speeches.
xv–xxi.	The second cycle of speeches.
xxii–xxxi.	The third cycle of speeches.
xxxii–xxxvii.	The speeches of Elihu.
xxxviii–xli.	The Lord answers Job out of the storm.
xlii.	Job completely submits, and is commended by God and restored to double prosperity after he has interceded for his friends.

N.B.—It is particularly important in studying the book of Job to use the Revised Version. The translation is much clearer, and the following notes and questions are based upon it.

Week 40.   Job i–xiv

Day 1. Job i–iii.

(1) i–ii. 10.   What does this portion reveal concerning (a) Job's character; (b) the measure of his calamities; and (c) the reason why such a man was permitted to suffer so greatly?

(2) ii. 11–iii.   What caused Job, who had hitherto maintained a faith undismayed (i. 21; ii. 10), to break out in the anguished cry of chapter iii?

THE FIRST CYCLE OF SPEECHES (IV–XIV)

Job's terrible sufferings, which his friends had now watched in silence for seven days, produced in him, and in them, a very different reaction. Holding firmly to the current doctrine that suffering is inflicted by God because of sin (and in proportion to the sin), they concluded that Job must have committed grievous sins, though they believed also that by confessing and forsaking these he might be restored to the divine favour. They therefore urged him to repent. Job resented their attitude. Conscious of his integrity, he found in his sufferings an insoluble enigma; and under the torment of his pain, made bitter complaint against God's treatment of him.

Day 2. Job iv and v.   First speech of Eliphaz.

(1) iv. 1-11.   Eliphaz expresses surprise at Job's despair.   What, in his view, should Job have remembered?

(2) iv. 12–v. 7.   What truth was brought home to Eliphaz in a vision?   And how did it show him that suffering is inevitable for weak, sinful, man (iv. 19–v. 1), and that murmuring is foolish (v. 2-5)?

(3) v. 8-27.   What course does Eliphaz recommend to Job (see v. 8 and 17), and what does he promise to Job if he will follow it?

Notes.—(1) iv. 10, 11 are an illustration of the fate of the wicked.

(2) v. 6, 7.   The meaning is that affliction does not come without cause. Man's nature, being prone to evil, draws trouble upon him.   Cf. iv. 8.

Day 3. Job vi and vii.   Job's reply to Eliphaz.

Job draws attention first to the greatness of his sufferings (vi. 1-13), then he expresses keen disappointment at the attitude of his friends (vi. 14-30). Finally, swept away by the contemplation of his misery, he flings question after question upon God (vii).

(1) What insight do we get in Job's words into the intensity of longing which one who is undergoing great suffering has for understanding and sympathy?   Have you ever disappointed a friend because of a lack of this?   See especially vi. 14.

(2) By what four images does Job in vii. 1-10 describe his life?

(3) How do Job's questions addressed to God in vii. 12-21 help us to understand his problem?

Notes.—(1) vi. 13. 'No, there is no help, none; and all aid has abandoned me' (Moffatt).

(2) vi. 27. Job accuses his friends of being as heartless as those who would cast lots for a fatherless child or bargain over a friend.

Day 4. Job viii–ix. 24. First speech of Bildad and Job's reply.

(1) Bildad gives essentially the same view of God and the same counsel as Eliphaz did. To whom does he appeal for confirmation of his teaching?

(2) Bildad's harsh cocksureness drives Job almost to distraction. Bildad had said that if Job were pure and upright surely God would awake for him (viii. 6), but Job's whole problem is that he is pure and upright, and God, on the contrary, attacked him. How, he asks, can man get his rights in such a case (ix. 2, see note below)? To what very different conception of God does Job give expression in ix. 3-24?

Notes.—(1) viii. 11-13. As the papyrus and reed grass (R.V. mg.) wither when deprived of soil and water, so the wicked, losing God's favour, will suddenly perish. Other images of the downfall of the wicked are given in verses 14b-15, and 16-19.

(2) ix. 2. The meaning here is, How will man establish his righteousness before God?

(3) ix. 13, 14. Rahab is here probably another name for 'dragon' (cf. Is. i. 9). The argument is, If the dragon fought in vain against God, how much ess shall I prevail?

Day 5. Job ix. 25–x. Job's reply (continued).

Obsessed with the idea that God is determined to hold him guilty, Job is unable to rise above his misery (ix. 25-31), and longs that God were human like himself, or that there were some umpire between them (ix. 33, R.V. mg.). In chapter x he again seeks to discover why God treats him thus, and comes to the desperate conclusion that this is God's real nature (x. 13).

(1) How has Job's longing, expressed in ix. 32-35, been met in the Lord Jesus? See 1 Tim. ii. 5; Heb. iv. 15.

(2) Do you think God was displeased by Job's boldness? See xxxviii. 2; xl. 8, but also xlii. 7. Cf. Ps. lxii. 8b; 1 Sa. i. 9-18.

Notes.—(1) ix. 35. 'Inwardly I have no guilty fears' (Moffatt).

(2) x. 10-15. Job's conception of God, under the pressure of his sufferings, becomes temporarily distorted. He conceives that all God's care of him from his birth onwards was but a mask to hide His real purposes. God was such that if he sinned it would be marked against him; if he became a wicked man, woe betide him; and even if he were righteous, he must still hang his head.

Day 6. Job xi and xii. First speech of Zophar, and Job's reply.

To Zophar Job's words seemed boastful and impious, and he administers a sharp reproof (xi. 1-6). Then, after a eulogy of God's wisdom (xi. 5-12), he urges Job to repent that he may be restored (xi. 13-20). His speech, however, only stirs Job to indignant remonstrances (xii. 1-10). How easy it is to try to improve an occasion without really understanding it! True doctrine, mistakenly applied, may exasperate rather than heal.

(1) What four steps in repentance does Zophar counsel Job to take? See xi. 13, 14. Consider also the beautiful picture which he draws of the blessings which will come to Job in consequence of repentance (xi. 15-19).

(2) In xii. 11-25 Job discourses on the wisdom and strength of God far more profoundly than Zophar had done. What examples of God's action does he cite?

Notes.—(1) xii. 4, 5. Job declares that it is only because he has .allen into misfortune that men dare to hold him in such contempt.

(2) xii. 12, 13. Verse 12 may be read as a question, 'With the aged wisdom?' meaning 'Do you say that wisdom is with the aged?' 'No! with *God* is wisdom.'

(3) xii. 18. 'He dismantles royalty, and drives kings off in chains' (Moffatt).

(4) xii. 22. No darkness is impenetrable to Him!

Day 7. Job xiii and xiv. Job's reply (continued).

After a further rebuke to his friends (xiii. 1-12), Job, as before in chapter vii, turns from them to God (xiii. 13-22), and pleads his cause before Him (xiii. 23–xiv). He mourns his desperate condition and approaching death (xiii. 23–xiv. 12), and then, suddenly, the arresting thought breaks upon him that there may be a life hereafter, in which he will be restored to God and fellowship. If it were so, he says, how patiently would he await that happy day! How joyfully respond to God's call! (xiv. 13-15). But the vision fades, and he bemoans again his hopeless outlook (xiv. 16-22).

(1) What may we learn from Job's rebuke to his friends of the responsibility of speaking to men on God's behalf? See xiii. 7-12 and xlii. 7, 8. Are we sufficiently watchful about this?

(2) Contrast the fleeting vision of a future life in xiv. 13-16 with the light and certainty of our Lord's word in Jn. xi. 25, 26. How does this whole chapter help us to understand the difference the gospel has made? See Rom. viii. 18; 2 Cor. iv. 17, 18.

Week 41. JOB XV–XXXI

SECOND CYCLE OF SPEECHES (XV–XXI)

Job's friends had failed to persuade him to take the only course that seemed to them to offer a hope of his restoration. Their speeches, therefore, in this second cycle assume a harsher tone and contain no appeal to acknowledge his sin, but dwell on the character and fate of the wicked. Job at first is greatly oppressed by this fresh evidence that God and man alike are against him, but finally, in chapter xxi, he denies the accuracy of his friends' observations and arguments.

Day 1. Job xv–xvii. The second speech of Eliphaz, and Job's reply.

(1) Observe the severity of the words of Eliphaz as compared with his first speech. He was angry because Job did not behave as Eliphaz thought he ought to behave. Have you sometimes found yourself losing sympathy with those you seek to win, because they will not accept what seems to you so clear?

(2) Job's agony of mind is pitiful, yet he cleaves in spite of everything to God. What verses in chapters xvi and xvii show particularly the light of an unquenchable faith shining through Job's deep darkness?

Notes.—(1) xv. 4. Job's attitude, Eliphaz says, injures true religion.

(2) xv. 11b. A reference probably to his previous speech.

(3) xv. 12. 'Wink', i.e. flash in wrath.

(4) xv. 18, 19. Eliphaz claims that his doctrine is ancient and pure, untainted by foreign heresies.

(5) xvii. 2, 3. Turning from his friends, whom he calls 'mockers' (verse 2), Job pleads with God to undertake for him, for there is no one else who can do so.

(6) xvii. 13-16. Sheol is the place of the dead, conceived as a kind of prison under the earth with gates (xxxviii. 17), bars (xvii. 16), and keys (Rev. i. 18). Job affirms that the worm and corruption of the grave are now as near to him as his nearest relatives.

Day 2. Job xviii and xix. Second speech of Bildad, and Job's reply.

(1) Bildad tells Job that the fixed order of the world will not be overturned because he, Job, is angry (xviii. 1-4). In what five stages is the sinner's downfall described? See verses 5-6, 7-10, 11-14, 15-19, 20-21.

(2) Job is completely broken by the persistent assumption of his friends that he is wicked (xix. 1-5). Set upon by God (6-12) and forsaken by man (13-20), ought he not to be pitied by his friends (21, 22)? But in this darkest hour, to what grand assurance does his faith triumphantly rise?

Notes.—(1) xix. 23, 24. Job desires that his plea might be indelibly recorded, so that it might never be lost to sight. But even as he speaks, his faith grasps something far better (25-27).

(2) xix. 26. 'In my flesh' or 'without my flesh' (R.V. mg.).

(3) xix. 28, 29. Job warns his friends that if they persist in persecuting him, and in asserting that the cause of his sufferings is in himself (i.e. in his sins), they will suffer divine judgment.

Day 3. Job xx and xxi. Second speech of Zophar, and Job's reply.

(1) Zophar, hot with anger, makes known to Job truth old as time (xx. 1-4). What does he say about the sinner's prosperity

(5-11), the punishment that sin brings (12-22), and God's final judgments (23-29)?

(2) Zophar's speech stirs Job to give utterance to thoughts that fill his own mind with fear (xxi. 5, 6). The facts of life, he says, present a very different picture from that which Zophar has drawn. What, in fact, happens to the wicked in this life (7-34)?

(3) What charges does Job bring against his friends? See xxi. 22, 27, 34. What lay at the root of the difference between him and them?

Notes.—(1) xx. 11. 'When manly vigour fills his frame, he and his manly vigour go to dust' (Moffatt).

(2) xx. 23. See R.V. mg. The meaning seems to be that God will rain wrath upon the wicked as his food. Cf. Ps. xi. 6.

(3) xxi. 2. Job, in sarcasm, tells his friends that the best comfort they can give him is to listen to what he has to say.

(4) xxi. 13b. The wicked have no long, painful illness at death.

(5) xxi. 30. Read as in R.V. mg.

(6) xxi. 31. 'Whoever tells him plainly what he is? Whoever punishes him for his crimes?'

THIRD CYCLE OF SPEECHES (XXII–XXXI)

In this third cycle there is no speech from Zophar (see, however, xxvii. 7-23, note), and the speech of Bildad is very brief. Eliphaz first charges Job with specific sins—which Job later vehemently denies (xxxi)—and then makes a final appeal to him to 'return to the Almighty', who will forgive and bless.

Day 4. Job xxii–xxiv. Third speech of Eliphaz, and Job's reply.

(1) What blessings does Eliphaz say will come to the man who walks in God's favour? There are at least seven blessings enumerated. With verse 29 cf. Pr. xxiv. 16; Mt. xxiii. 12, and with verse 30, Jas. v. 16.

(2) Job insists upon his integrity, and longs that he might be able to lay his case before God (xxiii). What strange anomalies does he see, as he looks out upon the world? See xxiv. He can see no solution to the mystery. What light shines upon it for us in the New Testament? See Jn. v. 28, 29; Rom. ii. 4-11; Rev. xx. 11-15.

Notes.—(1) xxii. 2-4. The argument of Eliphaz is that God's treatment of men is not with a view to any gain or advantage to Himself, but for man's sake. Since we cannot suppose that He punishes them for piety (verse 4), it must be because of their sin.

(2) xxiii. 10. 'Yet He knows how I live; when He tests me, I shall prove sterling gold' (Moffatt).

(3) xxiv. 1. 'Times', 'days', i.e. times and days of judgment. Job's complaint is that the wicked seem to act unchecked.

(4) xxiv. 4b-17. Descriptions of (a) the sufferings of the outcast and op-

pressed people, and (b) those who work evil under cover of darkness (13-17).

(5) xxiv. 18-24. In verses 18-21 Job gives the orthodox view of what happens to the wicked, and in verses 22-24 he gives, in contrast, the true facts, as he himself sees them. Verse 22 should be read as in R.V. mg. Verse 24 has the same meaning as xxi. 13b; see note there.

Day 5. Job xxv–xxvii. 6. Third speech of Bildad, and Job's reply.

(1) What is Bildad's answer to Job's plea of personal uprightness? Would Job have dissented from the general fact of man's sinfulness? With verse 4 compare Job's words in xiii. 26, xiv. 4.

(2) Job knows God's greatness as well as Bildad. How does he describe it here, as it operates in the underworld of Sheol (xxvi. 5, 6) and in the heavens and the earth (xxvi. 7-13)? And how finally does he show how immeasurable God's greatness is? See verse 14.

(3) The knowledge of God's greatness does not, however, answer Job's problem—why the Almighty was dealing with him thus. What one thing is Job resolved to hold fast? See xxvii. 1-6. Was he right in this?

Day 6. Job xxvii. 7–xxviii.

(1) In what four ways is the wicked man's fate described in xxvii. 7-23? See verses 13-15, 16-18, 19-22, 23.

(2) What two kinds of wisdom are distinguished in chapter xxviii—the first known to God alone, the second belonging to man?

(3) How does the chapter show that the first kind of wisdom is not discoverable by man? And how is this conclusion modified in the New Testament? See 1 Cor. i. 30, ii. 7-16; Eph. i. 8-10.

Notes.—(1) xxvii. 7-23. These verses contradict what Job has just been saying in xxi and xxiv. They would be much more appropriate in the mouths of Job's friends, and are thought by some to be the third speech of Zophar which has become displaced.

(2) xxviii. 1-11. This is a description of mining operations. Miners open up the dark depths (verse 3), burrow underground and are forgotten by those who walk above them, and swing suspended in cages or on ropes (verse 4). Verse 5 gives a vivid contrast between agricultural operations on the surface of the earth and the work of miners underground. For verse 10 see R.V. mg.

(3) 'Wisdom in this passage, as in other parts of Scripture where it is spoken of, is properly the idea or conception lying behind or under the order of the universe—the world plan' (A. B. Davidson).

Day 7. Job xxix–xxxi. Final speech of Job.

(1) How does Job describe the contrast between his past and his present condition?

(2) Of what sins, secret and public, does Job here declare himself innocent? Make a list and use it for self-examination.

Notes.—(1) xxix. 7. The 'gate' and the 'street' (or 'broad place', R.V. mg.) signify the place of assembly of the city council.

(2) xxix. 24. See R.V. mg. The meaning is that Job encouraged others, who had lost confidence, while never losing his own joyousness.

(3) xxx. 2-15. Even the least and lowest of men now held Job in derision.

Week 42.   JOB XXXII–XLII

Day 1.   Job xxxii and xxxiii. Introduction of Elihu, and his first speech.

Elihu was a younger man than Job's three friends, and appears to have been a silent listener to their discussions. Stirred by their failure to find an answer to Job, and still more by Job's own attitude, he essays to take speech himself. He has a profound reverence for God, and has been pained by Job's utterances. He emphasizes mainly two points: that God being what He is, He cannot be unjust nor can man contend with Him; and that the purpose of affliction is often to preserve men from sinning.

(1) On what grounds does Elihu, as a younger man, claim the right to speak? And in what spirit does he enter upon the discussion?

(2) In chapter xxxiii Elihu takes up the assertions that Job has made: the first, that God counted him as an enemy, though he was innocent (8-11); and the second, that God refused to hear and answer his appeal (13, see note). Elihu's answer to the first assertion is given in verse 12 and to the second in verses 13-20, where he argues that God does speak to man. In what ways does he say God speaks, and for what purpose?

Notes.—(1) xxxii. 13, 14. Elihu says the friends of Job must not ride away on the excuse that they had found an unlooked-for wisdom in Job, which God alone could overcome; Elihu believes that there is a reply to Job, and that he can give it.

(2) xxxiii. 6, 7. An allusion to Job's words in ix. 34, 35, xiii. 21.

(3) xxxiii. 13. 'Now why do you complain of Him for never answering your cry?' (Moffatt).

(4) xxxiii. 23, 24. 'One among a thousand', i.e. one of God's many angels. 'He' in verse 24 refers to God.

Day 2.   Job xxxiv and xxxv. Elihu's second and third speeches.

These two chapters are closely connected, giving an answer to two further assertions which Job had made: first, that God was wronging him (xxxiv. 5, 6); and second, that there is no profit in drawing near to God (xxxiv. 9). The first assertion Elihu answers in chapter xxxiv, and the second in chapter xxxv. His first answer is that God, just because He is God, cannot be unjust (xxxiv. 10-12, cf. Gn. xviii. 25; Rom. iii. 5). He then develops this thought, viewing God first as Creator (verses 13-15) and second as Ruler (verses 17-30); and finally gives counsel to Job (verses 31-33, see note below) and condemns his attitude (verses 34-37) In regard to Job's second assertion, Elihu answers that man's conduct cannot affect God; it can affect only man (xxxv. 2-8).

(1) What do you think of Elihu's discourse in chapter xxxiv? If he was right in regard to God, was he not too severe in regard to Job? See especially verses 7, 8 and 35-37.

(2) God does deliver those who cry to Him, giving them songs in the night (xxxv. 10); if not, there is a reason. What reason does Elihu here suggest why the oppressed may cry for help in vain?

Notes.—(1) xxxiv. 14. The first clause may be rendered 'If He set his heart upon Himself'. The thought of verses 13-15 seems to be that God as Creator has no motive for injustice, and that the existence and preservation of the universe is an evidence of God's interest in His creatures.

(2) xxxiv. 17-19. 'Can any one opposed to justice govern? Would you denounce the strong God and the just, who tells a king he is a knave, tells nobles they are villains, who never favours princes, never prefers rich men to poor?' (Moffatt).

(3) xxxiv. 23-30. There is no need for God to act as men do by process of trial and judgment—an allusion to Job's words in xxiii. 3, 4. God knows all, and acts at once.

(4) xxxiv. 31a. 'No, tell God' (Moffatt)—an advice to Job to confess his error.

Day 3. Job xxxvi and xxxvii. Fourth speech of Elihu.

(1) xxxvi. 1-25. In this first part of his speech Elihu gives further description of God's just and beneficent rule, and urges Job to humble himself before Him ere it be too late. What does Elihu say as to the purpose of affliction?

(2) xxxvi. 26–xxxvii. To what manifestation of God's greatness does Elihu here draw attention? And to what conclusion does he seek to lead Job?

Notes.—(1) xxxvii. 7. 'That keep men within doors . . . to let all mortals feel His power' (Moffatt). Verse 6 should end with a comma, not a full stop.

(2) xxxvii. 20. Elihu expresses dread at the thought of contending with God.

Day 4. Job xxxviii–xl. 5. God answers Job out of the storm.

With much of what Elihu said Job was no doubt in agreement, though his problem had not been solved, and his mind was not quieted to listen to the voice of God Himself, as He comes to deliver and bless His tried and faithful servant. God first challenges Job to stand up to Him, as Job had often said he wished to do (xxxviii. 3, cf. xiii. 3, xxiii. 3, 4, xxxi. 37).

(1) God presents before Job a picture of some of the wonders of earth and sky (xxxviii. 1-38) and then a picture of some of the marvels of animal life, accompanied throughout by humbling

questions bringing out Job's littleness in comparison with God. Why did God speak thus rather than remove Job's perplexities? Was it because Job *needed* to be humbled? Cf. xxxviii. 2.

(2) What was the effect upon Job? See xl. 3-5.

Notes.—(1) xxxviii. 13. Cf. xxiv. 16, 17.
(2) xl. 5. 'Once . . . twice'. 'Hebrew idiom for a number of times'.

Day 5. Job xl. 6–xli. God answers Job out of the storm a second time.

In His first revelation God had rebuked Job for his presumption in desiring to contend with Him; but Job had gone further, and, in upholding his own righteousness had cast doubt upon God's righteousness, both in regard to himself as an individual and in His governance of the world. God now speaks to Job on this point, ironically inviting Job to act as God and show that his own right hand can save him (xl. 6-14).

(1) Having called upon Job to array himself with honour and majesty (xl. 10), He brings before him two powerful wild creatures —the hippopotamus (xl. 15-24) and the crocodile (xli)—and bids him observe them closely. Try to picture them as here described.

(2) What does God intend that Job should learn from these animals? What questions does He ask Job?

Notes.—(1) xl. 19b. See R.V. mg. The 'sword' may refer to the tusks.
(2) xli. 9. 'The hope of him', i.e. the hope of catching him.
(3) xli. 13. 'His outer garment', i.e. his scaly armour. 'His double bridle' may refer to the two corners of his jaws.

Day 6. Job xlii.

(1) What brought Job to the deep humbling and self-abasement described in verses 1-6? Was it the argument which God used, or was it rather just the fact that God had appeared and had spoken with him? Unbelief vanished in the light of God's countenance, and Job's heart found rest, even though the *reason* of his sufferings had not yet been explained to him.

(2) How do Job's friends show themselves to have been true men of God, though bound by doctrinal prejudice? Read the closing verses of the book in the light of Jas. v. 11 and 16.

Day 7. Revision.

Note down the main lessons which you have learned from the reading of the book of Job. What, in particular, does it teach about suffering in its purpose and in its effects?

PROVERBS

INTRODUCTION

(See New Bible Handbook, pp. 186, 198-200)

PROVERBS i. 7 provides the key to the Book and to the whole of
the Wisdom Literature (Job, Proverbs, Ecclesiastes). It all starts
from the creed of one God—Jehovah—and wisdom is to know
and do His will. The term 'proverb' has the double meaning of
a short parable and a pithy saying.

The Proverbs are all intensely practical, covering the human
race and the whole of its activity, aiming at giving 'knowledge and
discretion', or the building up of the 'perfect man', by fixing truth
in the memory. As expressing eternal spiritual principles many of
them can receive their full meaning only when applied to the
believer in Christ.

ANALYSIS

i–ix.	The appeal of wisdom.
x–xxii. 16.	Proverbs (grouped in various ways).
xxii. 17–xxiv.	Second collection, headed 'Words of the Wise.'
xxv–xxix.	Third collection, ascribed to Solomon.
xxx, xxxi.	Words of Agur and Lemuel.

Week 43. PROVERBS I–XI. 13.

Day 1. Pr. i.

(1) From the expressed purpose of the book in verses 1-6, what
personal profit may we expect from studying it?

(2) Contrast the enticement of sinners with the call of wisdom.
What will be the end in each case of following the one and rejecting
the other?

(3) How may we apply the words of wisdom in verses 22-33 to
our Lord Jesus Christ? See, e.g., Mt. vii. 13-27; Lk. xix. 41-44.

Note.—The word translated 'simple' is used in Proverbs in the sense of
inexperienced and credulous, and hence unwary and easily led astray. Cf.
xiv. 15.

Day 2. Pr. ii and iii.

(1) What directions are given in these chapters for the attaining
of wisdom? Make a list of them as a guide to your own life.

(2) What benefits does wisdom bring us, and from what evils
does it preserve us? How far have we proved this in our own
experience?

(3) 'My son'. What application does the writer of the Epistle to the Hebrews give to these words? See Heb. xii. 5-10.

Day 3. Pr. iv and v.

(1) What are the main lessons that the speaker seeks in these chapters to impress upon us? What measure of heed have we given and are we giving to these most urgent counsels? Cf. Lk. viii. 18.

(2) iv. 23-27 provide an admirable guide to successful living. Cf. verse 18. Heart, lips, eyes, feet; what directions are given concerning each?

(3) What is the end of those who neglect this way of wisdom? See iv. 19, v. 9-14, v. 21-23.

Notes.—(1) iv. 24. 'Froward' means twisted, crooked, and perverse—forsaking the paths of truth.

(2) v. 6 and 14. The meaning in both verses is obscure. Verse 6 is translated by Moffatt thus: 'The high road of life is not for her, shifty and slippery are her tracks.' Verse 14 may mean, 'I had well-nigh come to complete grief in the congregation and assembly.'

Day 4. Pr. vi and vii.

(1) Verses 1-5 give warning against foolish financial commitments and pledges. What other warnings are given in these chapters?

(2) In what forms do the sins here spoken of manifest themselves at the present day?

(3) Test your life in the light of vi. 16-19.

Notes.—(1) vi. 1. 'Stricken thy hand'; a method of giving a pledge, cf. 2 Ki. x. 15. Suretyship, frequently condemned in Proverbs, held grave dangers, because of the responsibility resting upon the surety, and the penalties to which he was liable. Cf. Gn. xliii. 9.

(2) vi. 13 describes the secret, clandestine ways of the evil-minded man.

Day 5. Pr. viii. 1-31.

This passage should be read in the R.V., especially verses 22, 23.

(1) Contrast the description of wisdom with that of the woman in vii. 5-27. How do they differ in speech, in conduct, in what they offer, and the goal to which they lead their followers?

(2) What is said of wisdom in verses 22-31 concerning (a) her existence from the beginning; (b) her part in creation; (c) her communion with God; (d) her interest in man? Consider how in all these respects there is here a dim foreshadowing of Christ. See, e.g. (a) Jn. xvii. 5; (b) Jn. i. 1-3; Col. i. 15-17; (c) Mt. xi. 27; (d) Heb. ii. 17, 18.

(3) What sayings in this portion grip you most strongly?

Day 6. Pr. viii. 32–ix.

(1) What similar but still greater gifts than those which wisdom offers in viii. 32-36 are offered in Christ? See, e.g., Mt. xi. 29; Lk. xi. 28; Jn. xiv. 21, xvii. 2, 3, iii. 36.

(2) Set ix. 1-6 and ix. 13-1? side by side. In what respects are wisdom and folly (ix. 13, R.V. mg.) alike, and wherein do they differ?

Day 7. Pr. x–xi. 13.

(1) In x. 2-6 there are four conditions of wellbeing in circumstances, mind, and character. What are they?

(2) In the light of Jas. iii. 10, what uses of the faculty of speech in this chapter are (a) commended, (b) to be avoided?

(3) What will the possession of integrity secure for a man (xi. 1-13)?

Week 44. PROVERBS XI. 14–XXII. 16.

Day 1. Pr. xi. 14–xii.

(1) What two kinds of sin or sinners are said in this passage to be an abomination unto the Lord?

(2) What other sins are here condemned? In what verses are they traced to their origin in the *heart*? Cf. iv. 23; Mt. xii. 34, 35, xv. 18, 19.

(3) Apply to yourself the five principles for the using of money expressed in xi. 24-28.

Day 2. Pr. xiii–xiv. 21.

(1) 'Considering the issue of their life' (Heb. xiii. 7, R.V.). What is said in today's portion concerning the issues of their life in the case of the righteous and of the wicked respectively?

(2) Gather out what is taught about 'fools' and 'folly'. What, in contrast, should the manner of our life, if we are wise, be (a) in relation to the Word, (b) in relation to our neighbours, and (c) in conduct and speech?

Day 3. Pr. xiv. 22–xv. 23.

(1) What is said in today's portion about the beneficent effects of right words?

(2) What is said about 'the Lord'? How may we discern the fear of the Lord in our own hearts?

(3) Can we claim to have the five things making for satisfaction which are enumerated in xv. 13-17?

Day 4. Pr. xv. 24–xvi.

(1) How does xv. 24-33 illustrate what has been called 'the sanity of religion'?

(2) Gather out what is said in today's portion about the Lord, and about man's proper attitude to Him.

(3) Consider in xvi. 27-30 the multiplied evil wrought by evil men. Cf. Ps. xcvii. 10.

Day 5. Pr. xvii and xviii.

(1) Gather out the sins condemned in chapter xvii.

(2) What reasons are given in chapter xviii why we should 'watch the door of our lips'?

(3) Consider the two fortresses in xviii. 10, 11; and compare Jn. x. 27, 28; Lk. xii. 15-21.

Note.—xviii. 10. 'The Name of the Lord' denotes the character of God Himself, as revealed to us in the Scriptures. See, e.g., Ex. xxxiv. 5, 7. For us it is summed up in 'Jesus'.

Day 6. Pr. xix–xx. 13.

(1) Make a list of the varied conditions and circumstances in respect to which counsel is given in today's portion. Which of them apply more particularly to yourself?

(2) What is said about the Lord? Show how the fact of His presence forms the foundation on which the writer's counsels are based.

(3) Have you found a 'faithful man' (xx. 6)? Do others find such a man in you? Cf. Rev. xvii. 14.

Day 7. Pr. xx. 14–xxii. 16.

(1) In xx. 17-25 what different kinds of action are to be avoided?

(2) xx. 24 speaks of God's sovereignty, and xx. 27 of man's responsibility. What other verses in today's portion touch on these two complementary truths?

(3) Gather out from today's portion those principles for wise living that most impress you.

Notes.—(1) xx. 27. 'The spirit of man'; here a synonym for 'the conscience'. 'All the innermost parts of the belly' is a Hebrew idiom for the whole inward being. Cf. verse 30.

(2) xxi. 4. The meaning of the word 'plowing' (R.V. 'lamp') is uncertain.

(3) xxii. 16. 'He that giveth to the rich'; that is, to gain favour.

Week 45. PROVERBS XXII. 17–XXXI

Day 1. Pr. xxii. 17–xxiii.

A new series of aphorisms begins here, extending to the end of chapter xxiv and divided into two parts (xxii. 17–xxiv. 22 and xxiv. 23–34).

(1) What counsels already given in earlier chapters are repeated in today's portion?

(2) What are the marks of a wise 'son' (xxiii. 15)? What will he avoid, and what will he practise?

(3) What, according to xxiii. 29-35, are the effects of too much indulgence in wine?

Notes.—(1) xxiii. 6-8. 'Him that hath an evil eye'; that is, a niggard. The meaning of verse 7a is not clear. A possible rendering is 'For as he dealeth (stingily) with himself, so he deals with thee.'

(2) Verse 14. 'From hell'; better, as in R.V., 'from Sheol'; i.e. from an early death.

Day 2. Pr. xxiv.

(1) What missionary call is heard in verses 11, 12? Are we saying concerning those who are going down to death, 'Behold, we knew it not'?

(2) What other instructions are given? Make a list of them.

(3) What did the wise (verse 23) learn from the field of the sluggard? What references have been made to slothfulness in earlier chapters? See also xxii. 13, xxvi. 16.

Notes.—(1) Verse 26. 'He kisseth the lips'; the meaning is, 'He shows love'. Moffatt translates: 'He is a true friend who is honest with you.'

(2) Verse 27. First acquire the means to set up house, and then marry and build.

Day 3. Pr. xxv–xxvi. 12.

(1) How does our Lord in one of His parables adapt the teaching of xxv. 6, 7?

(2) Observe in xxv. 8-25 how many illustrations are given of the power and influence of words both to do good and to do harm. Are we sufficiently careful in this matter?

(3) In what ways does the passage xxvi. 1-12 enforce the familiar injunction 'Don't be a fool'? Among whom did Christ find 'fools'? See Mt. vii. 26, xxiii. 17, xxv. 2; Lk. xi. 40, xii. 20, xxiv. 25.

Note.—The 'fool' is one who is wilfully unresponsive to the teaching of divine wisdom, and going his own self-chosen way, hurts himself and others.

Day 4. Pr. xxvi. 13–xxvii.

(1) What various kinds of wrong speech are exposed in xxvi. 18–xxvii. 2?

(2) 'My son, be wise' (xxvii. 11). What directions for wise living do you find in xxvii. 5-22, especially in regard to friendship?

(3) What, according to xxvii. 23-27, is the reward of diligence? See also xxvii. 18, xxviii. 19; Rom. xii. 11 (R.V.).

Notes.—(1) xxvii. 16. The meaning is uncertain. The LXX has a different rendering: 'The north wind is a harsh wind, but it has an auspicious name' (Moffatt).

(2) xxvii. 21. See R.V. 'By his praise', i.e. by the praise he receives. The judgment of those in the midst of whom a man lives discovers his true worth. Cf. xxxi. 31.

(3) xxvii. 25, 26 should more probably read, 'When the hay is removed and the after-growth appears, and the grass of the mountains is gathered, then thy lambs will supply thee with clothing, and thy goats furnish the price of a field' (I.C.C.).

Day 5. Pr. xxviii and xxix.

(1) Gather out in these chapters the verses which present a contrast between the righteous and the wicked. How do these differ in character and conduct? Consider also their influence for good or evil upon society, especially if they hold positions of authority.

(2) What is said about the importance of keeping the law, and what about a right attitude to the poor? There are four references to the first, and at least five to the second.

(3) Put a mark against verses in these two chapters that you feel to be specially incisive and memorable.

Day 6. Pr. xxx.

The last two chapters of Proverbs are appendices. Chapter xxx gives the words of Agur, of whom nothing further is known. The chapter should be read in the R.V., where the different sections of which it is composed are clearly shown. Agur first looks Godward, and is humbled by the mystery of the divine being and power. Later he looks out upon the world of men and animals and notes a number of striking facts, which he records.

(1) Notice the definiteness, urgency, content and motive of Agur's prayer. Compare with it the prayer which our Lord taught His disciples to pray.

(2) Are the 'generations' or classes of men mentioned in verses 11-14 still present? State in four words the sins of which they were guilty.

(3) What four lessons may the four animals mentioned in verses 24-28 teach us?

Day 7. Pr. xxxi.

(1) What three virtues did King Lemuel's mother urge upon her royal son? Are they any less necessary for all who will occupy positions of responsibility?

(2) Does verse 7 convey that what is wrong as a rule may be right as an exception?

(3) Make a list of the qualities of the ideal housewife as depicted in verses 10-31.

Notes.—(1) Verse 10. 'Virtuous'; the Hebrew word includes both moral worth and practical efficiency. Cf. xii. 4, xiv. 1. Ruth was such an one. See Ru. iii. 11.

(2) Verse 18b. This does not mean that she worked all night, but that her house was well ordered, and ready against emergencies. Cf. xiii. 9.

ROMANS

INTRODUCTION

(See New Bible Handbook, pp. 354-358)

THE Epistle to the Romans was written from Corinth during three months which Paul spent in the province of Achaia, as described in Acts xx. 2, 3 (R.V.). Its purpose is to present to the church in Rome (which he had not founded, but which he hoped soon to visit) a reasoned statement of the gospel which he preached, together with a discussion of the great problem of Jewish unbelief and of the relation of both Jews and Gentiles to Jesus Christ and His salvation. From xv. 23, 24 it would seem that the apostle to the Gentiles felt that he had done everything possible to carry out his task in the east. The time had now come to put into operation his plans for extending his work westwards. In such a task it would no doubt be advantageous to have the prayerful support and practical fellowship of the church in the metropolis. Rome was a strategic centre and the church there would seem to have been as cosmopolitan as the city. A clear statement of the gospel which he would be preaching would be the best means of clearing up any misunderstandings which might arise through Jewish-Gentile tensions or through other causes, and of gaining for Paul the fellowship and co-operation he desired.

At the outset Paul declares that the gospel is the power of God unto salvation to every one that believes, because in it is revealed a righteousness which comes from God, and is obtained and maintained through faith (see i. 16-17, R.V., the key verses of the Epistle). Then the great themes of human guilt—of free grace and the righteousness which comes from God, of justification by faith, the new life in Christ Jesus, the work of the Holy Spirit, the divine sovereignty, and the inclusion of 'the nations' in God's purposes of love—are unrolled one by one, making the Epistle to many the most marvellous book in the Bible.

ANALYSIS

i. 1-17.	Introduction: the theme of the Epistle stated.
i. 18–iii. 20.	The failure of human righteousness.
iii. 21–v.	God's way of salvation expounded, illustrated, and its excellence displayed.
vi–viii.	Justification by faith in relation to holiness.
ix–xi.	The problem of Israel; God has *not* broken His promise, but will gloriously fulfil it.
xii–xv. 13.	Holiness in practical life.
xv. 14–xvi.	Concluding personal messages.

Week 46. ROMANS I–IV. 15

Day 1. Rom. i. 1-17.

(1) What does the apostle say in these verses about himself? See verses 1, 5, and each verse from 9 to 16. With i. 14 cf. 1 Cor. iv. 1, ix. 16, 17.

(2) What does he say about the gospel, its origin, theme, content, and power?

Note.—Verse 17. The phrase 'a righteousness of God', here and in iii. 21, means a righteousness provided for man in Christ, and has to be distinguished from the phrase 'the righteousness of God' or 'His righteousness' in iii. 5 and iii. 25, 26, which means God's character as righteous.

Day 2. Rom. i. 18-32. Human sin and God's wrath.

(1) How does Paul show the sin of man to be (a) deliberate, and (b) inexcusable? How did it begin, and how result in blindness of heart and in moral degeneration?

(2) How does God's wrath manifest itself? Notice the three stages in verses 24, 26 and 28. Cf. Ps. lxxxi. 12; Acts vii. 42. A

picture of God's wrath at work is seen in the book of Judges (see Second Year, Weeks 19-21). Do you see it at work in the world of today?

Note.—Verse 18. 'Hold', better as in R.V., 'hold down'.

Day 3. Rom. ii. 1-16. Principles of divine judgment.

(1) What four things are said about God's judgment in verses 2, 6, 11 and 16? Can you find in the passage any other characteristics of it?

(2) What will be the decisive test in the judgment? See verses 7-10. How will this bring under condemnation the self-righteous person who, while condemning others, himself also sins? See verses 1, 3 and 4.

Notes.—(1) Verses 7 and 10 in no way contradict the truth that salvation cannot be earned by works. Paul is not dealing at this point with the method of salvation, but with the nature of the test in the day of judgment. The test is righteousness (cf. 1 Jn. iii. 7, 10). If a man is not righteous in heart and life, he will be condemned. Later Paul will show that the only way to become righteous is through faith in Christ.

(2) Verses 12-15. The meaning is that men will be judged by the light they have had. If they have been under the law of Moses they will be judged by that; if not, they will be judged by the standards they possess by nature through reason and conscience.

Day 4. Rom. ii. 17-29. The sin of the Jews—pride and formalism.

(1) What ten points does Paul enumerate in verses 17-20, upon which the Jews of his day were inclined to congratulate themselves? But is racial and religious pride, accompanied by moral shortcomings, confined only to Jews? If 'Christian' were substituted for 'Jew', and 'the word' for 'the law', how far would the argument apply to professing Christians today?

(2) The Jews rested upon circumcision as the seal of God's covenant with them. But what else does Paul here show to be required without which the outward sign ceases to have value? Cf. 1 Sa. xvi. 7. How would you frame the argument in relation to *Christian* ordinances?

Day 5. Rom. iii. 1-20. Objections answered, and sin and guilt shown to be universal.

(1) In verses 1-8 the apostle answers questions and objections which he found that men raised against the gospel. They are stated in a very condensed form and, if found difficult, may be passed over. Notice, however, how Paul describes the Old Testa-

ment Scriptures, to what two attributes of God he holds fast, and what kind of conduct he strenuously repudiates.

(2) In verses 10-18 Paul gives the general verdict of Scripture upon man in his fallen condition. What does Scripture say (a) about the general trend of human life (verses 10-12, cf. Is. liii. 6a); (b) about man's speech (verses 13, 14); and (c) about his conduct and inner attitude to God (verses 15-18)? How does this witness confirm the verdict of experience already given in i. 18-32 and ii. 17-29, and lead to the conclusion of iii. 19, 20?

(3) Do you assent to the truth that it is impossible for any child of man, by his own efforts, to escape condemnation at the bar of God's judgment?

Notes.—(1) Verse 20. 'The works of the law'; a phrase which occurs also in verse 28, and denotes conduct such as may be attained by man's own effort in obedience to a divinely-given statute. Cf. Gal. iii. 10-12.

(2) 'Justified' means 'declared, or pronounced, righteous'.

Day 6. Rom. iii. 21-31. The one way of salvation, revealed in the gospel.

(1) The answer to the question how guilty man can be saved is found in the revelation of a righteousness of God; that is, a righteousness provided by God (see Day 1, Note). It will help greatly to clarify what is said about this righteousness in this all-important paragraph of the Epistle (verses 21-26) if the various points are written down one by one. There are fifteen in all.

(2) What two inferences follow? See verses 27, 28 and verses 29, 30, and cf. 1 Cor. i. 29-31; Gal. iii. 28. And what is Paul's answer to an objector who might say that the gospel of salvation by faith, which Paul preached, made the law of no account?

Notes.—(1) The whole of this passage should be read in the R.V., which makes many points clearer.

(2) Verse 27. The term 'law' (*nomos*) is used in this verse in rather a different sense from that which it has elsewhere in this passage. Perhaps the nearest equivalent word in English to the meaning here is 'principle' (see R.S.V.).

Day 7. Rom. iv. 1-15. The witness of Scripture.

Paul has made three statements which were directly opposite to the Jewish interpretation of Scripture. The first was in iii. 20, that by the works of the law shall no flesh be justified; the second in iii. 30, that God would justify Gentiles through faith without circumcision; and the third in iii. 19 and 28, that salvation is given independently of the law. Paul proceeds, therefore, in chapter iv to show that Scripture supports these propositions. He bases his argument mainly on Gn. xv.

(1) Abraham, and David also, were men pre-eminently in the favour of God (see, e.g. Is. xli. 8; Acts xiii. 22). On what basis, then, according to Scripture, was righteousness reckoned to them? See verses 1-8.

(2) At what *time* in Abraham's life was his faith reckoned to him as righteousness? Was it before or after his circumcision? How does this vitally affect the question at issue regarding the admission of Gentiles? See verses 9-12.

(3) The Jews thought that the promise to Abraham and his seed was bound up with the observance of the law. How does Paul show that the very opposite must be true, in the nature of the case? See verses 13-15.

Week 47. ROMANS IV. 16–VIII. 17

Day 1. Rom. iv. 16-25. The correspondence between Abraham's faith and ours.

(1) Consider, for example,

    (a) The promise to Abraham (Gn. xv. 5-7) and the corresponding promise to us (Gal. iv. 5-7).

    (b) The inability of Abraham in himself (verses 18, 19) and our corresponding inability. See iii. 20.

    (c) The God in whom Abraham believed (verse 17) and the God in whom we believe (verse 24).

    (d) The result to Abraham (verse 22) and to us (verses 23, 24a).

(2) In what sense are our sins and our justification the cause of Christ's death and resurrection, as stated in verse 25? Cf. Is. liii. 4-6, 8b, 11; 1 Pet. ii. 24; 1 Cor. xv. 17.

Day 2. Rom. v. 1-11. Is justification by faith real and lasting?

(1) What immediate blessings does it bring? See verses 1 and 2. Can you say 'Amen' to these in your own experience?

(2) Someone, however, may say: 'But what of the tribulations attending the Christian life? Do they not detract from its blessedness?' What is Paul's answer to this? See verses 3-5.

(3) Verses 6-10 expand the latter part of verse 5. What is the proof of God's love? And what assurance does this give respecting the future?

Notes.—(1) The A.V. is to be preferred in verses 1-5, but in verse 11 read the reconciliation' as in R.V.

(2) The whole argument of the passage turns upon the words 'and not only so' in verses 3 and 11. It shows that the Christian has three grounds of confidence regarding his salvation: (a) present experience; (b) God's love meeting us in tribulation; and (c) God Himself (verse 11). The argument of verse 11 is similar to that of viii. 31, 32. Notice the thrice-repeated 'Rejoice' in verses 2, 3, 11 (R.V.).

Day 3. Rom. v. 12-21. The universality of sin and death more than met by the universality of salvation in Christ.

(1) In what respects does Paul show God's salvation in Christ to be far mightier for good than man's fall in Adam was for evil?

(2) What four 'reigns' are spoken of in this passage? Two of them are known to all in sad experience. Are we beginning now to know the other two in glad experience through Jesus Christ our Lord?

Note.—The passage should be read in the R.V.

Day 4. Rom. vi. 1-14.

The Christian has died to sin in Christ's death and lives now to God through union with Christ in His resurrection. Paul here regards sin under another aspect—as a tyrant power holding men in bondage. The only way of escape from sin as a tyrant master is to die to it, and this has been made possible for us in Christ.

(1) For those who are spiritually united with Christ, what is now their position (a) in relation to sin, and (b) in relation to God? And how has this change been effected?

(2) This being our position in Christ Jesus, how are we to abide in it so as to live in daily experience a life of victory over sin? See verses 11-14, noting particularly the expressions 'reckon', 'let not', and 'present' (R.V.).

Notes.—(1) The passage should be read in the R.V. The question in verse 1 arises out of what Paul has said in chapter v. 20b.

(2) Verses 3-10 are an exposition of verse 2.

(3) Verse 6. 'Our old man' means 'the man we were of old', subject to sin. 'The body of sin' means 'the body in which sin ruled', whose members were employed in sin's service (see verses 13 and 19).

(4) Verse 7. A statement of the general principle that death ends all obligation and relationships (cf. vii. 1, 2), here applied to our former relationship to sin. 'Justified from sin' (R.V.) means 'acquitted from any claim sin makes upon us as its slave'.

Day 5. Rom. vi. 15–vii. 6. Not under law, but under grace.

Two questions may arise out of the statement of vi. 14: the first, 'Shall we then continue to sin?' and the second, 'How is it possible to be not under law?' The first is answered in vi. 15-23, and the second in vii. 1-6.

(1) In vi. 15-23 what two masters are contrasted? What kinds of service do they respectively demand, and with what result? In view of all these things, what is the only possible answer to the question whether we should continue in sin?

(2) To answer the second question (How is it possible to be not under law?) Paul finds in the marriage tie an illustration of a person being subject to law and subsequently set free from it (verse 1-3), and applies it to the case of the Christian (verse 4). In the case of the Christian, by whose death is his old position under law brought to an end? Who is the new husband? And what are the fruits of this new union, as contrasted with those of the old (see verses 5, 6)?

Notes.—(1) vi. 23. Read '*In* Christ Jesus our Lord' as in r.v. Cf. 1 Jn. v. 11.

(2) vii. 4. When Christ's body was broken in death, He passed to a life free from all subjection to legal ordinances and we, having died with Him, are also set free. Joined to Him in His resurrection life, life henceforth is to be lived, not in legal bondage, but in the glad obedience of love.

Day 6. Rom. vii. 7-25. Life under the law—its inevitable failure and misery.

(1) Verses 7-13. The phrase 'the sinful passions which were through the law' in vii. 5 (r.v.) might suggest that *the law itself is sinful*. What evidence does Paul give in these verses to show that the law is holy and good, and yet (a) reveals sin; (b) provokes sin; (c) results in death; and (d) thereby brings to light the exceeding sinfulness of sin?

(2) Verses 14-25. Which is the stronger force in a man's life, the law or sin? What, then, is the inevitable result of life 'under the law', even at its best?

Note.—In verses 14-25 the apostle expands what he means by the phrase 'the oldness of the letter' (vii. 6). The law of God commands from without, but sin as a power *within* compels obedience to its own dictates. Two things are needed. (a) deliverance from the condemnation which the law of God pronounces, and (b) a power within greater than that of sin to enable us to do God's will. Both are provided in Christ, as Paul shows in chapter viii, expounding the meaning of his words 'newness of the spirit' (vii. 6).

Day 7. Rom. viii. 1-17. Life in the spirit—its sure victory.

(1) Verses 1-4. What is the happy condition of those who are 'in (union with) Christ Jesus'? Paul explains in verses 3 and 4 (a) how their deliverance has been brought about; (b) what God's purpose is in effecting it; and (c) how those must walk who would experience it.

(2) Verses 5-11. Life according to the flesh, and life according to the Spirit, are here contrasted in tendency and in result (verses 5-8). What is it that effects the change from life in the flesh to life in the Spirit? And how does life in the Spirit carry with it also ultimate victory over death?

(3) Verses 12-17. What, then, is our duty? And what are our privileges?

Notes.—(1) The passage should be read in the R.V.

(2) Verse 2. The Spirit, sin, and death are regarded as powers exercising authority, and the Spirit proves the stronger. Cf. Gal. v. 16, 17.

(3) Verse 3. 'In the death of His own Son, who has come in our nature to make atonement for sin, God has pronounced the doom of sin, and brought its claims and its authority over man to an end' (Denney).

(4) 'Flesh' here denotes our corrupt human nature. To 'walk after the flesh' is to follow its cravings. The flesh is not destroyed in us, but the deeds which it would do can be 'mortified' or made dead (verse 13).

Week 48. ROMANS VIII. 18–XI

Day 1. Rom. viii. 18-39. Present sufferings the prelude to glory.

The apostle comes back to the fact of present suffering and expounds more fully chapter v. 3-5.

(1) What threefold ground of confidence does Paul give in verses 18-27 that the present time of suffering will issue in glory? See verses 18-22, 23-25 and 26-27, noting the three occurrences of the word 'groan' or 'groanings'. Cf. Ex. ii. 23-25.

(2) In verses 28-39 how many distinct reasons does Paul give for the Christian to rejoice, though everything in this world should seem against him?

Day 2. Rom. ix. 1-13. God's word has not failed.

In chapters ix–xi Paul deals with the great problem of the rejection of their Messiah by the bulk of the Jewish nation, and God's consequent rejection of them. Two questions arise: (a) Has God broken His promises? and (b) If not, how are they to be fulfilled? Paul answers the first question in chapters ix, x, and the second in chapter xi.

(1) Chapter viii is full of triumphant joy. How, then, can Paul speak of having great sorrow and unceasing pain in his heart? What made him sorrowful? How much of this Christian joy and how much of this Christian sorrow do we ourselves know?

(2) Verses 6-13. The question with which Paul is here dealing is: If God rejects those Jews who reject Jesus as Messiah, has not His word come to nought? For were not the promises (verse 4) made to the Jews? How does Paul answer this question? And

what two principles of God's election does he find in the Old Testament stories of the births of Isaac and of Jacob and Esau respectively?

Day 3. Rom. ix. 14-29. The sovereignty of God.

(1) How does Paul show that in His election of men God retains absolute liberty of action (a) without compromising His own righteousness, and (b) without giving man any just ground of complaint? See verses 14-22. At the same time observe how Paul lays emphasis upon God's *mercy*. See verses 15, 16, 23-26.

(2) Applying these principles, what Scriptures does Paul cite to show that what was happening, both in regard to the exclusion of the bulk of the Jews and also in regard to the admission of the Gentiles to become the people of God, was nothing new in God's dealings, and therefore need not be a stumbling-block to faith?

Day 4. Rom. ix. 30-x.

The cause of Israel's failure is shown to be their refusal to accept God's way of righteousness.

(1) What are the two ways of seeking acceptance with God which are here contrasted? And how are they shown to be mutually exclusive? See ix. 30-x. 9.

(2) Righteousness by faith (verses 8-15). What does the apostle say regarding (a) its simplicity; (b) its universal application; and (c) the necessity of proclaiming it?

(3) What light do verses 16-21 throw upon man's responsibility in hearing the gospel? Observe also with what skill the apostle shows that the faith of the Gentiles and the disobedience of Israel are all foretold in the Scriptures. The word of God, therefore, far from coming to nought (ix. 6), was actually finding fulfilment in what was taking place.

Day 5. Rom. xi. 1-10.

The rejection of Israel is in part only, not total.

(1) What three reasons are given in this portion to show that God has not cast Israel wholly away?

(2) How have the remnant who have been saved come into that blessedness? And how have the others failed to obtain salvation? What has been God's part in the result, and what man's?

Day 6. Rom. xi. 11-24.

The rejection of Israel is for a time, not final.

(1) If a man trips and stumbles he may either rise again or

fall and perish. What reasons does Paul give here for his confidence that Israel's rejection is not final?

(2) Against what spirit does he warn Gentile believers? What lessons ought we to learn for ourselves from God's dealings with Israel?

(3) How does this passage encourage the vigorous prosecution of missions to the Jews?

Notes.—(1) Verses 11, 12. The noun 'fall' in these verses might be better translated 'lapse'. It is from a different root from the verb translated 'fall'.

(2) Verse 16. See Nu. xv. 17-21. As the offering of the first fruits was regarded as consecrating the whole harvest, so in the choice of the patriarchs the whole nation became set apart for God. Cf. verse 28.

Day 7. Rom. xi. 25-36.

(1) By what Scriptures does Paul confirm that Israel shall yet be saved?

(2) Consider the plan of God as here revealed. By what successive steps has God already acted, and will still act, to bring about the result stated in verse 32? Test your insight into the marvel of God's plan by the measure in which you spontaneously enter into the doxology in verses 33-36.

Notes.—(1) Verse 25 (last clause). Cf. Mk. xiii. 10; Lk. xxi. 24.

(2) Verses 26 and 27. The quotation up to verse 27a is from the LXX of Is. lix. 20, 21; that of verse 27b is from Is. xxvii. 9. Cf. also Zc. xii. 10, xiii. 1.

Week 49. ROMANS XII–XVI

Day 1. Rom. xii. Practical Christian living—in the Church.

Chapters xii and xiii form a new section of the Epistle, in which the apostle sets forth the practical life of the believer: first, in the religious sphere as a member of the Church (xii); and second, in the secular sphere as a member of the state (xiii). The starting-point is the dedication of our bodies to God, to live, not according to the practices of the world, but to do His will (xii. 1, 2). The goal is the return of the Lord (xiii. 11-14).

(1) Fundamentally, what should be the believer's conscious and deliberate attitude (a) to God, and (b) to the world? What will be the result?

(2) It has been suggested that the teaching of verses 3-8 might be summed up in the word 'humility', and that of verses 9-21 in the word 'love'. How far is this true?

(3) Take one by one the precepts of this chapter, and ask yourself of each—Am I living thus?

Notes.—(1) Verse 1. 'The mercies of God'. The reference is partly to the latter part of chapter xi, but also to the whole promise for deliverance from the guilt and power of sin, as expounded in chapters iii–viii.

'Your reasonable service'. Cf. 2 Cor. v. 14, 15 ('We thus judge' means 'We have come to the considered judgment').

(2) Verse 20. 'Coals of fire'. A figurative emblem of severe pain, here the pain of shame and contrition.

(3) The whole passage should be read in the R.V. and from a Bible with references.

Day 2. Rom. xiii. Practical Christian living—in the world.

(1) What three main reasons does Paul give in verses 1-5 why it is right to submit to the civil power? And how will this submission express itself in practice?

(2) What single guiding principle should control the Christian's life in society? See verses 8-10.

(3) Verses 11-14 (forming the close of the section xii–xiii). Paul gave in xii. 1 one powerful motive to live the life set forth in these chapters, namely, 'the mercies of God'. What further motive does he present here? What will wearing the 'armour of light' mean in practice, negatively and positively? Am I so living?

Day 3. Rom. xiv. Mutual consideration.

There seems to have been in the church in Rome a minority who felt themselves bound in conscience by religious scruples, which those of a more robust faith did not share. The apostle addresses both classes in verses 1-12, and then in verses 13-23 addresses himself specially to 'the strong'.

(1) What rules does Paul lay down in verses 1-12? Can you find four reasons why it is wrong to judge other Christians in such matters?

(2) Verses 13-23. What should 'the strong' be concerned about most in their relation to their weaker brethren? What danger arises if 'the strong' act with a high hand? What are the most important things to be preserved at all costs in a Christian community?

(3) If in doubt ourselves about the lawfulness of a thing, can we do it because we see other keen people doing it? If not, why not?

Notes.—(1) Verse 1. The meaning seems to be that the Church should make the weaker brethren welcome, but avoid argument in their presence.

(2) Verse 5. There is no need to suppose that Paul was thinking of the weekly sabbath here at all, but rather of Jewish holy days.

(3) Verse 6. There is an important principle here, akin to that of verse 23b. It is that if we can *thank God* in what we do, receiving it as His gift, it is right to do it; otherwise not.

Day 4. Rom. xv. 1-13. True brotherhood.

(1) The counsel given in verses 1-2 is by no means easy to

follow. What three sources of help and encouragement are suggested in verses 3-5? And what glad result will follow if success is achieved (verse 6)?

(2) What Scriptures does Paul select to show that it was God's purpose from the beginning to save both Jews and Gentiles in Christ?

(3) Why the emphasis on 'hope' in this passage? See verses 4, 12, 13. Does division among believers tend to increase depression? What, in contrast, ought to be the life of Christians, as expressed in verse 13?

Day 5. Rom. xv. 14-33. Paul's work and plans.

The Epistle from i. 16 onwards has been more like a treatise than a letter. Now Paul resumes the epistolary form, and there are many links between this closing section (xv. 14 to end) and i. 1-15.

(1) How does Paul in verses 15-21 describe his work—in relation to its nature, scope, power, and results? How far is this description applicable to our own work in connection with the gospel?

(2) What matters lay nearest to Paul's heart at this time, as shown in verses 20-29? Also, what may we learn about the importance which he attached to intercessory prayer? Have we a kindred spirit and outlook?

Notes.—(1) Verse 16. The figure here is that of the sacrifices of the Old Testament ritual. Paul's work was to bring Gentiles to God as an offering, sanctified by the Holy Ghost. See R.V. mg.

(2) The contributions of the Gentile churches to the poor of the church in Jerusalem were the result of much labour on Paul's part, and he looked for important results in the closer drawing together of Jewish and Gentile believers. See 2 Cor. viii and ix, especially ix. 12-15.

Day 6. Rom. xvi. 1-16. A glimpse of some early Christians.

(1) What may we learn about Phœbe from her name and the place where she lived (see notes below), from the description of her as 'sister' and 'servant of the church', and from the service which she rendered? What did Paul ask for her from the Christians at Rome, and on what grounds?

(2) Looking down the list of names, note the references to (a) diligent service; (b) sufferings borne for Christ; and (c) Christian character. Cf. 2 Cor. v. 9, 10 (R.V.).

(3) How often do you find the phrase 'in the Lord' or 'in Christ Jesus' or 'in Christ'? Notice also the different connections in which it is used. Have we not here the inner secret of the Christian life, service, and fellowship of the early Church?

Notes.—(1) Verse 1. The name Phœbe, being that of a goddess, suggests that Phœbe had a heathen background. But now she is a 'sister' in the Lord, one of the household of faith (cf. Eph. ii. 19). 'A servant of the church', not necessarily in any official capacity, but a church worker. 'Succourer of many' (cf. xii. 13). Cenchrea, the eastern part of Corinth, was not an easy place in which to live as a Christian.

(2) Verse 7. 'My kinsmen'. This probably means 'fellow countrymen'. 'Fellow-prisoners'. They may at the time have been imprisoned with Paul for the gospel's sake. 'Of note among the apostles'. Outstanding Christians, holding apostolic office.

(3) Verse 10. 'The approved' (R.V.). One whose life had stood the test.

(4) Verse 13. Rufus. Possibly the same as the Rufus of Mk. xv. 21. 'Chosen in the Lord', that is, a choice Christian, one of special quality.

Day 7. Rom. xvi. 17-27.

(1) (a) How may perverters of the gospel be recognized? See 1 Tim. vi. 3; Mt. vii. 15-20. (b) How may we be safeguarded from them? Cf. 2 Jn. 10; 2 Tim. ii. 14-16; 1 Thes. v. 22. (c) What encouragement have we in the conflict?

(2) Verses 25-27. How is God described? How does the present age differ from all that went before? What is the one all-important end to be achieved? Cf. i. 5. What is the method to be adopted?

Note.—The 'mystery' spoken of in verse 25 is fully expounded in the Epistle to the Ephesians. See e.g. Eph. iii. 3-6.

ECCLESIASTES

INTRODUCTION

(See *New Bible Handbook, pp. 201-203*)

THIS book speaks through the mouth of Solomon, but does not in any way build on his authority. In the earlier part the writer describes human life as seen by a shrewd observer, who controverts the arguments of those who find a satisfactory aim in life either in intellectual labour, or in the gathering of riches, or in pleasure, or even in the attainment of an ethical ideal, seeing that death terminates all, and comes to all alike.

Man cannot by searching find out the deep things of God (iii. 11) but must bow before His sovereignty (iii. 14). Whatever appearances may indicate, God judges righteously, though judgment be long delayed (viii. 12, 13).

The recurring phrase 'under the sun' may be regarded as indicating the purely human standpoint adopted by the writer in the earlier chapters, and as roughly equivalent to 'in the world as man sees it'. It is most helpful for the Christian to contrast the vanity of this world, its business and pleasures, as set forth in Ecclesiastes, with our glorious heritage in Christ as set forth in the New Testament. For the great glory of the Lord Jesus is that he fills life with meaning, and makes abundantly worth while all that is done along the lines of His will, so that life is the very opposite of 'vanity'.

The book is the inspired record of a spiritual pilgrimage, reaching its culmination in chapter xii (cf. xii. 13, 14 with Rom. ii. 16). In Ecclesiastes, perhaps more than in any other book of the Old Testament, the standpoint of the writer should be borne in mind, and particularly the fact that he saw nothing for man beyond death save judgment. His attention is concentrated upon this life, for 'our Saviour Jesus Christ, who abolished death, and brought life and incorruption to light through the gospel' (2 Tim. i. 10, R.V.), had not yet appeared.

ANALYSIS

i. 1.	The title.
i. 2–11.	The endless monotony of human life on earth.
i. 12–ii.	The Preacher's experiences—wisdom, pleasure, labour alike fail to satisfy. 'There is nothing better for a man than to eat and drink and enjoy himself, as he does his work' (ii. 24, Moffatt's translation).
iii–vi.	Further illustration of the vanity of man's striving. His life is hemmed in by divine control, and ends in death. Various counsels. Riches do not satisfy.
vii–xi. 8.	The kind of life men should lead. Wisdom is better than folly. The fear of God brings a sure reward. God's works are unsearchable. Various counsels.
xi. 9–xii.	Childhood and youth pass; old age and death draw near. The ultimate conclusion; fear God and keep His commandments.

Week 50. ECCLESIASTES

Day 1. Ec. i and ii.

The book opens (i. 2, 3) with a statement of one of its main themes, namely, the futility and unprofitableness of human life and labour 'under the sun'. See *Introduction*.

(1) i. 4–11. How is the unchanging *sameness* of man's experience from age to age brought out in these verses? Contrast the Chris-

tian's outlook as given in such scriptures as Lk. i. 78, 79; 2 Cor. iv. 6, v. 17.

(2) How did the Preacher discover by personal experience that neither the pursuit of wisdom (i. 12-18), nor the enjoyment of pleasure (ii. 1-11), can satisfy man's heart?

(3) Though wisdom is better than folly (ii. 13, 14a), what three facts rob even wisdom of its power to satisfy? See verses 14b-17, 18 and 23, 24-26.

Notes.—(1) i. 2. 'Vanity of vanities'; i.e. vanity in the highest degree; 'utterly vain' (Moffatt).

(2) i. 3. 'Under the sun'; a phrase occurring 29 times in the book.

(3) i. 7, 8. The R.V. is clearer here, as also in i. 11, ii. 3, 8, 21, 26.

(4) i. 14. 'Vexation of spirit'; better, 'a striving after wind', as in R.V.; i.e. something quite futile.

(5) ii. 25. 'More than I'; read as in R.V. mg., 'apart from Him', i.e. from God.

Day 2. Ec. iii–iv. 8.

(1) iii. 1-15. The Preacher here elaborates the truth, already expressed in ii. 24-26, that everything is in the hand of God. What instances does he give to show that the sovereign control of God extends over all human life? Cf. Mt. x. 29, 30.

(2) What in the light of this does the Preacher declare to be the best use of life? See verses 12, 13. The Preacher comes back repeatedly to the same conclusion; see, e.g., ii. 24, iii. 22, v. 18, viii. 15, ix. 7-9. But what other note is sounded in verse 14, which also is heard throughout the book? Cf. v. 7, vii. 18, viii. 13, xii. 13.

(3) In iii. 16–iv. 8 what four instances does the Preacher give of the futility of life, and what reflections did they awaken in his mind?

Notes.—(1) iii. 1. 'Season . . . time'; the two words express two thoughts, (a) that everything happens at an appointed time, and (b) that the time is appropriate in relation to the working out of God's purpose. Cf. Ps. xviii. 30a.

(2) iii. 11. Read as in R.V. The meaning of this difficult verse seems to be that while God has placed in man's heart desires that go beyond the temporal, yet man cannot grasp His plan. This also is a thought repeated in later chapters. See vi. 12, viii. 16, 17.

(3) iii. 16. Wickedness and iniquity in the seat of law and government.

(4) iv. 4-6. 'Also I saw that human toil and skill mean jealousy between man and man. . . . He is a fool who folds his hands, and lets life go to ruin. Still, one handful of content is better than two hands full of toil and futile effort' (Moffatt).

(5) iv. 7, 8. The picture of a miser.

Day 3. Ec. iv. 9–vi.

(1) What are the advantages of companionship, as described in iv. 9-12? How does this apply in the spiritual life? See, e.g., Mt. xviii. 19; Mk. vi. 7; Lk. x. 1; Acts xiii. 2, xv. 12.

(2) What does the passage v. 1-7 teach concerning worship, in respect to (a) the right attitude of spirit, (b) words spoken in God's presence, (c) the importance of carrying out promises made?

(3) What does the Preacher say in v. 8–vi concerning riches and rich people?

Notes.—(1) The R.V. is clearer n many verses. See especially iv. 12, 14-16, v. 14.

(2) iv. 13-16. The picture of a youth rising by wisdom to be king, though born poor and in prison. At first all the people were with him, hailing him as ruler (verses 15, 16a); yet the next generation did not favour him (verse 16b). The persons alluded to in these verses are quite unknown.

(3) v. 1. 'Keep thy foot'; that is, 'never enter God's house carelessly' (Moffatt).

(4) v. 3. As cares and labours cause a man to dream, so do many words in worship give rise to folly.

(5) v. 8, 9. The meaning here is obscure.

(6) v. 20. 'Then he will never brood over the fewness of his days' (Moffatt).

(7) vi. 10, 11. 'Whatever happens has been determined long ago, and what man is has been ordained of old; he cannot argue with One mightier than himself' (Moffatt). In verse 11 read as in R.V. mg. The meaning is that much talking against God's dealings is profitless.

Day 4. Ec. vii and viii.

The Preacher has declared several times that man's best course in this present world is to enjoy the portion in life which God has given him, and the fruit of his labour. See Day 2 (2). In these later chapters, while still holding to this view, he enquires more closely into the kind and quality of life which men hould lead.

(1) What does he commend, and what discountenance in vii. 1-10?

(2) Gather out the varied counsels given in vii. 11–viii. 5. See notes below, and with vii. 16 compare Lk. xiv. 25-27.

(3) In spite of life's anomalies (viii. 10, 14) and the insoluble riddle of it all (viii. 17), of what one thing is the writer sure concerning the final end of the righteous and the wicked?

Notes.—(1) The R.V. should be read in vii. 7, 11-12, 21, viii. 1, 10.

(2) vii. 14. 'Anything that shall be after him'; i.e. what is to happen. Cf. vi. 12.

(3) vii. 18. 'Shall come forth of them all'. Moffatt translates: 'shall avoid both extremes'.

Day 5. Ec. ix–x. 7.

(1) What two facts govern man's life on earth (see ix. 1 and ix. 2-6)? In view of these facts the Preacher can reach no other conclusion than what he has said before. See ix. 7-10 and Day 2 (2). In what does it fall short of New Testament standards?

(2) What illustration is used in ix. 13–x. 3 to show the value of wisdom? Yet how little is it honoured (ix. 16), and how easily marred (ix. 18b–x. 1)!

(3) What two faults to which rulers are prone are mentioned in x. 4-7?

Notes.—(1) The R.V. is clearer in ix. 1, 7, 12, 17, x. 1, 4.
(2) x. 2. 'A wise man's sense will keep him right; a fool's mind leads him wrong' (Moffatt).

Day 6. Ec. x. 8–xi. 8.

(1) Today's portion gives counsel on various matters. Make a list of these. The main thought is that men should be diligent in work in spite of possible danger or loss.

(2) x. 8-15. How is it shown in these verses (a) that no useful work can be done without the possibility of unexpected danger (see Note 1 below); and (b) that wisdom is needed?

(3) When human life and activity is thus beset by many limitations and uncertainties, ought we to do nothing? What is the Preacher's answer in xi. 1-8? Cf. Day 2, Note (4).

Notes.—(1) x. 8-10. The word 'shall' in these verses is better rendered 'may'.
(2) x. 11, 19. Read as in R.V. The last clause of verse 19 seems to mean that where there is money, there is full supply.
(3) xi. 1, 2. 'Trust your goods far and wide at sea, till you get good returns after a while. Take shares in several ventures; you never know what will go wrong in this world' (Moffatt).
(4) xi. 8. 'The days of darkness'; i.e. which follow death. Cf. ix. 5, 10.

Day 7. Ec. xi. 9–xii.

(1) In the Preacher's counsel to youth (a) in what is youth to rejoice? (b) to what all-important fact are they to give heed? and (c) whom are they to remember? What further summons does the New Testament give? See Mk. i. 15; 2 Tim. ii. 1. With xii. 1a cf. Pss. ciii. 2, cxix. 55.

(2) Contrast with the picture of old age and death the joyful

hope to which we are begotten by the resurrection of our Lord. Cf. 2 Cor. iv. 16-18; 2 Tim. iv. 6-8; 1 Pet. i. 3-5.

(3) In summing up man's duty, what place does the Preacher give to God? How was this perfectly exemplified in Jesus (cf. Jn. xiv. 31), and in Him made possible for us all? See Mt. v. 48; Rom. viii. 3, 4; Heb. xiii. 20, 21.

Notes.—(1) xi. 10. 'Vanity' has here the meaning of 'transitory' or 'passing'.

(2) xii. 2. Old age compared to winter weather, when storm succeeds storm.

(3) xii. 3-6. A series of pictures of the failure of man's various bodily faculties in old age, such as strength of limb, number of teeth, keenness of sight, etc. 'When old age fears a height, and even a walk has its terrors, when his hair is almond white, and he drags his limbs along, as the spirit flags and fades' (Moffatt's translation of verse 5).

(4) xii. 11. See R.V. Both A.V. and R.V. renderings probably refer to inspired scriptures, which, whether they are goads to prick the conscience, or strong nails or pegs (typifying trustworthiness), are alike from the one Shepherd.

GALATIANS

INTRODUCTION

(See New Bible Handbook, pp. 364-368)

THE particular situation with which the Epistle deals must be kept in mind if its great argument is to be understood. Paul had preached the gospel of salvation by faith in Jesus Christ to the Galatians, who were of Gentile race. They had welcomed him with enthusiasm, and many had believed (iv. 14, 15). But they had later been visited by Jewish-minded Christian teachers who had told them that it was not enough simply to believe on Jesus Christ: they must also be circumcised, and keep the Law of Moses. These teachers had further cast doubts upon Paul's apostleship, and had sought to undermine his authority. We can understand with what mingled sorrow, indignation and deep concern Paul refutes the teaching of the legalists, and defends both his own position and the truth of the gospel, which he had proclaimed.

The question at issue assumes a different form today, but is none the less vital. Is acceptance with God to be obtained by any effort of ours, or is it, as the gospel declares, the free gift of God's

grace through the redemptive work of Christ, to be obtained by
faith alone? The enduring value of this Epistle lies in the answer
given by Paul, under the inspiration of the Spirit, to this question.

ANALYSIS

i. 1–10.	Introduction.
i. 11–ii. 21.	Paul declares that the gospel which he preached is not of human origin, but came to him by the revelation of Christ.
iii. 1–v. 1.	Acceptance with God is not obtained by doing what the law commands, but by faith in Jesus Christ.
iii. 1–9.	The facts of their own experience confirmed by the case of Abraham.
iii. 10–14.	The hopeless position of those under the law, from which the death of Christ alone delivers.
iii. 15–18.	The original covenant of promise is not superseded by the law.
iii. 19–24.	The true function of the law.
iii. 25–iv. 7.	The blessedness of those who have believed in Christ.
iv. 8–20.	Appeal not to backslide.
iv. 21–v. 1.	The spiritual freedom of the believer illustrated from 'the law' itself.
v. 2–vi. 10.	The life of the Christian: (a) faith, hope, love; (b) walking in the Spirit.
vi. 11–18.	Conclusion.

Week 51. GALATIANS
Day 1. Gal. i.

(1) What does Paul say in verses 1-10 (a) about God, (b) about
Christ, (c) about himself, (d) about the gospel? Note these things
carefully, for they lay the foundation on which the Epistle rests.

(2) What four statements about the gospel are made in verses
11 and 12? Paul demonstrates the truth of these statements in the
rest of chapters i and ii, by giving a review of his life-story.

(3) What five periods in his life are described in verses 13-24?
Are there any points where his experience touches yours?

Note.—Verse 10 is parenthetical. Paul appears to have been charged by his opponents with being a man-pleaser, and interjects after writing verses 8-9, 'Am I now seeking the favour of men or of God?' (R.S.V.) that is, 'words such as I have just written do not look like man-pleasing, do they?'

Day 2. Gal. ii.

(1) What two further incidents in his life does Paul refer to in this chapter and how do they help to demonstrate the truth of i. 11-12?

(2) Observe Paul's courage. What does he say twice over was his chief motive in taking so firm a stand? See verses 5 and 14. What may we learn from this?

(3) Consider in verses 16 and 20 how clearly Paul states, first, the sole ground of acceptance with God, and second, the inward principle of the Christian's life. Can you give the assent of your experience to each clause of these two verses?

Notes.—(1) Verses 1-10. In this visit of Paul and Barnabas to Jerusalem, Paul in a private talk with the leaders of the church laid before them the gospel which he was preaching among the Gentiles (verse 2), with the result that they acknowledged his call to the apostleship of the Gentiles, and gave him the right hand of fellowship (verses 6-10). An effort was made during the visit, by some in the church, to insist on Titus, a Gentile believer who was with Paul, being circumcised, but Paul did not yield (verses 3-5).

(2) Verses 15-18. Jews generally regarded uncircumcised Gentiles as 'sinners' and unclean, and there were some even within the church who thought that by eating with uncircumcised Gentiles, they made themselves 'sinners' (cf. Acts x. 28). Paul's contention was that the real transgressor was the man who having accepted justification by faith, sought to rebuild the barrier of the Law (verse 18).

Day 3. Gal. iii. 1-18.

These verses are a fourfold argument in proof of ii. 16. (a) Verses 1-5, an argument from experience, (b) verses 6-9, an argument from Scripture teaching about Abraham, (c) verses 10-14, an argument from the meaning of Christ's death, and (d) verses 15-18, an argument from the fact that the covenant of promise was long prior to the giving of the law.

(1) Try to state the substance of these arguments in your own words.

(2) Consider the phrases 'by the works of the law' and 'they that are of the works of the law' on the one hand, and 'by the hearing of faith' and 'they that be of faith' on the other. Show how they express radically different principles.

(3) How does Paul show that faith in Christ has from the very beginning been God's plan, and the only way of salvation?

Notes.—(1) Verses 1-5. Paul in his visit to Galatia had set clearly before his hearers Christ crucified, and they, through believing, had received the Spirit (cf. Acts xiii. 52), and suffered persecution in consequence. 'By the hearing of faith' (verses 2 and 5) is an abbreviated expression for hearing the Word of the gospel, and receiving it with faith. Cf. Rom. x. 8-17.

(2) Verse 7. 'The children of Abraham'; in the sense of spiritual likeness. Cf. Jn. viii. 39.

(3) Verses 8, 9. Paul interprets the promise of Gn. xii. 3b to mean that just as Abraham received the blessing of justification by faith (Gn. xv. 6), so a time would come when men of all nations would 'in Abraham', i.e. through his seed, which is Christ (verses 14, 16), receive the same blessing in the same way.

(4) Verse 15. 'I speak after the manner of men'; i.e. I take an illustration from human life. Some translate 'covenant' here, by 'will', but it makes no difference to Paul's point. Even a human covenant or will, if once ratified, stands, and cannot be altered. How much more then must God's covenant stand firm! Cf. Heb. vi. 13-18.

(5) Verse 16. It is not by chance, Paul says, that Scripture speaks of 'Abraham and his seed'. For God all through had looked forward to Christ as the one in whom His promise was to be fulfilled. Cf. 2 Cor. i. 20.

Day 4. Gal. iii. 19–iv. 7.

(1) iii. 19-24. See *Analysis*. Paul has seemed to make light of the law, and his opponents might ask, 'Wherefore then serveth the law?' Can you find in these verses five purposes which the law serves?

(2) iii. 25-29. What are the privileges of believers as here set forth? Write them down in your own words.

(3) What, according to iv. 5, is the purpose of our redemption, and what amazing privilege is said in iv. 6 to flow from our filial relationship to God in Christ?

Notes.—(1) iii. 19, 20. 'Added because of transgressions'; i.e. the law gave to sin the form of transgression and so made men conscious of guilt before God when they sinned. Cf. Rom. iii. 19, 20, v. 20, vii. 7, 13.

'It was ordained by angels by the hand of a Mediator' ('intermediary,' R.S.V.). Paul introduces these words to show that the promise is superior to the Law even in the very manner of its promulgation. In the case of Abraham God Himself spoke the promises directly, whereas the giving of the law was through intermediaries on both sides—God being represented by angels (cf. Dt. xxxiii. 2 (LXX); Acts vii. 53; Heb. ii. 2), and the people by Moses.

(2) iii. 24. 'Schoolmaster'; better, 'custodian', as in R.S.V. The Greek word denotes a guardian attendant, appointed to watch over the sons of a household when young.

(3) iii. 26. Read 'sons' as in R.V., not 'children'.

(4) iii. 27. 'Put on' here means 'take the standing or position of', i.e. to have the standing of Christ before God.

(5) iv. 3. 'The elements of the world'; R.V., 'rudiments'; R.S.V., 'elemental spirits'. The meaning is uncertain. It seems best to take it as meaning rudimentary teachings that do not rise above this world, and are merely types and

shadows of heavenly realities (cf. Heb. viii. 5, ix. 1, x. 1). Paul calls them in verse 9 'weak and beggarly', i.e. without power, and without resources, unable to deliver men from the world (cf. i. 4) and give them the position of sons and heirs of God.

Day 5. Gal. iv. 8–v. 1.

(1) iv. 8-20. Paul pleads with the Galatians not to backslide. What plea does he use in verses 8-11, and what in verses 12-20?

(2) What indications are there in these verses that Paul regarded the situation with the utmost gravity and with great distress of heart? Are we beginning to know something of a concern for souls such as Paul had? See 2 Cor. xi. 28, 29; 1 Thes. iii. 6-8.

(3) iv. 20–v. 1. Paul suddenly decides to present the teaching he has been giving in the form of a *picture*, taken from Gn. xvi, from a part of the Scriptures which the Jews specially called 'the law'. In this picture, what is the position of those who are 'under the law', and what in contrast is the portion of believers? Cf. Eph. ii. 18, 19.

Notes.—(1) iv. 12. The meaning seems to be: 'I, a Jew, have become as you, a sinner trusting alone in Christ for salvation. Do you, then, become as I am', i.e. hold fast to the same position. The last clause of the verse is best taken with what follows, and should be translated, 'In nothing did you wrong me'.

(2) iv. 17, 18. 'They zealously seek you in no good way' (R.V.). A reference to the new teachers, who were eager to win the favour of the Galatian believers in order to cut them off from Paul and his gospel so that they would have no one to turn to but themselves. If these teachers had really come to do good, Paul would have raised no objection (verse 18).

(3) iv. 20. 'I stand in doubt of you'; better, 'I am perplexed about you', as in R.V.

(4) iv. 26. 'Jerusalem, which is above'; cf. Heb. xii. 22.

(5) iv. 27, 30. Paul quotes two Scriptures to show that the future lies with believers, and not with the party of the law.

Day 6. Gal. v. 2–24.

Spiritual freedom may be lost in two ways, (a) by false teaching, in this case the teaching of the necessity of circumcision (verses 2-12), and (b) by living to please self (verses 13-15). The secret of victory is to give the Holy Spirit full sway within us; He will subdue the flesh, and bring forth in us the fruit of holiness (verses 16-25).

(1) To be circumcised meant taking the way of the law. What four results would follow if they did so? What in contrast is the way of the gospel (verses 5-6)?

(2) Verses 13-15. How should the Christian use his freedom? Cf. Jn. xiii. 12-17; Lk. xxii. 26.

(3) Verses 16-24. The Christian has within him 'the flesh', i.e. his fallen sinful nature, and the Spirit, and he must take sides in the conflict between them. What must be his attitude to the flesh (verses 16, 24) and what to the Spirit (verses 16, 18); and how will this be manifested in his life and character (verses 22-24)? Observe the simplicity of the gospel way of holiness. Are you proving it in experience?

Notes.—(1) Verse 5. 'The hope of righteousness'; i.e. the hope of future glory that springs from justification through believing on Jesus Christ. Cf. Rom. v. 1, 2; 1 Pet. i. 3. Notice in verses 5-6 the collocation of faith, hope and love, as in 1 Cor. xiii. 13; 1 Thes. i. 3.

(2) Verses 16, 17. Life for the Christian is not, as it were, an open way, in which he can walk where and as he pleases. It is a battlefield. But if he 'walk in the Spirit', i.e. let the Spirit rule and regulate his inner life, there will be victory over the flesh.

(3) Verse 18. The Christian is free from the law as a rule of life, yet, led by the Spirit, he does that which the law approves (verses 22, 23).

(4) Verse 24. The self-life, condemned, is nailed to Christ's cross. Cf. ii. 20; Rom. vi. 6.

Day 7. Gal. v. 25–vi.

(1) In v. 16-24 the apostle has spoken of the life of the Christian in his individual character; in v. 25–vi. 10 he speaks of the Christian's life in his social relationships. What will the result of walking in the Spirit be in that sphere? Make a list of what you find, and test your own relation to fellow-Christians by it.

(2) vi. 11-18. If we would be Christians after the pattern of Paul, what will be our attitude to the cross? Gather up what is said about the cross in this Epistle. What reasons can you discover why Paul esteemed the cross so highly?

Notes.—(1) vi. 2. 'The law of Christ'; cf. Jn. xiii. 34; 1 Jn. iv. 21.

(2) vi. 3-5. It is not good to compare oneself with another, and to glory over him. For that is to glory only in respect of another's shortcomings. In the judgment each will have to bear his own burden—the things he himself has done. Cf. 2 Cor. v. 10.

(3) vi. 8. 'Soweth to the flesh'; acts of self pleasing: 'Soweth to the Spirit'; acts of obedience to the Spirit.

(4) vi. 11. 'How large a letter'; better, 'with how large letters', as in R.V. Usually, it would seem Paul wrote the closing salutation in his own writing (1 Cor. xvi. 21; 2 Thes. iii. 17), but in this case he wrote more, possibly the whole letter.

(5) vi. 12, 13. Paul's opponents gloried in new additions of circumcised believers, because this gave them favour in the eyes of fellow-Jews.

THE SONG OF SOLOMON

INTRODUCTION

(See New Bible Handbook, pp. 203-206)

THE Song of Solomon is beloved of Christians not so much because of its exquisite literary charm, its rich appreciation of the beauty of nature and its deep insight into the human heart, as because they find in it a parable of heavenly realities. It speaks to them of the love of Christ for His Church, and gives to them words in which to utter their hearts' devotion to Him.

It is uncertain who wrote it. The phrase 'which is Solomon's' in i. 1 may equally mean 'which is for Solomon' (as in the title of Ps. lxxii) or 'which is about Solomon'; and there is no other clue to its authorship.

According to the earlier and more usual interpretation, there are only two main characters—Solomon and his bride. Many commentaries of great devotional beauty and insight have made this interpretation familiar, in which the bride is regarded as a type of the Church, and Solomon of Christ. An analysis of the Song, based upon this view of it, will be found in the *New Bible Handbook*.

Others, however, discern in the background of the story another figure, the figure of a shepherd, who is the bride's true lover. It is he whom she called 'my beloved'. A maid from the village of Shulem, she had gone one day to visit her garden, when she fell in unexpectedly with some of Solomon's retinue, who took her captive to the palace (vi. 11-13). There the king visits her, and struck by her great beauty seeks to win her for himself. But she has a shepherd lover to whom her heart is pledged, and to whom she remains faithful. Three times the king visits her, wooing her with growing ardour, until at last, finding all his efforts of no avail, he sets her free. At the close of the book she is seen leaning on the arm of her beloved, returning to her village home, where she is received by her family and friends as the shepherd lover's acknowledged bride.

An analysis of the book, based on this interpretation, is given below. It will be seen that, in this view, much of the book consists of reveries in which the bride communes in thought with her beloved, and of incidents and dreams connected with him, which with artless simplicity she tells to the ladies of the court. In this view of the book the shepherd lover is a type of Christ, and Solomon a type of the world, against whose enticements the soul remains faithful to Him to whom its love is pledged.

We must form our own views on these questions from the study of the book. But whichever interpretation be adopted, the book remains a spiritual picture of the mutual love of Christ and His people, and a precious treasure to His own.

ANALYSIS

SECTION I. i. 2–ii. 7. *Scene in the private apartments of Solomon's palace.*

  i. 2–8.   The maid, soliloquizing, expresses her longing for her absent lover (2-4). Then, seeing the ladies of the court eyeing her, she explains to them the darkness of her complexion (5, 6), and breaks out into a cry that she might know exactly where her lover is (7), to which the ladies of the court reply that she should go to seek him (8).

  i. 9–11.   The king enters, praises her beauty, and promises to adorn her with jewels.

  i. 12–ii. 6.   The king having gone to his repast, the maid falls into a reverie, in which, in imagination, she communes with her beloved in some forest glade.

  ii. 7.   She bids the ladies of the court not to seek to arouse love by artificial means.

SECTION II. ii. 8–iii. 5. *The bride relates an incident of the past.*

  ii. 8–14.   Her beloved came one morning to call her to go with him.

  ii. 15.   She is sent instead by her brothers into the vineyard. Cf. i. 6.

  ii. 16, 17.   She bids her beloved return at the end of the day.

  iii. 1–4.   When he did not return, she could not rest, but went out into the night to seek him.

  iii. 5.   The same charge as in ii. 7.

SECTION III.   iii. 6–viii. 4. *The struggle is intensified, but ends in victory.*

iii. 6–iv. 7.   Solomon, appearing in royal splendour, makes a determined attempt to capture the maid's affections.

iv. 8–v. 1.   Alarmed, she flees in thought to her beloved, whose voice she hears, bidding her escape with him from the dangers of the palace (8). He pours out his love for her in words far excelling the conventional tributes paid to her by the king (9-16a). Her heart opens to him, and she sees their marriage day as if already come (16b–v. 1).

v. 2–16.   The bride relates a disturbing dream which she has had; and in answer to a question from the ladies of the court gives an impassioned description of her beloved.

vi. 1–3.   The ladies of the court ask where he is, that they, too, may seek him, a suggestion that leads the bride to declare that no other can share her privilege of possession.

vi. 4–10.   The king enters, and tells her in words of admiring praise that there is none who can compare with her, and that even his queens have sung her praises.

vi. 11–13.   The bride interrupts to explain how she came to be in the king's palace.

vii. 1–9.   The king continues to urge his desire.

vii. 10–viii. 3.   The bride, refusing, turns in heart to her beloved.

viii. 4.   The same charge as in ii. 7 and iii. 5.

SECTION IV.   viii. 5–14. *The scene is the bride's village home.*

viii. 5.   The bride, released, returns with her beloved to her home.

viii. 6, 7.   The bride's panegyric on true love.

viii. 8–12.   She recalls her brothers' words, and declares her faithfulness.

viii. 13, 14.   Her lover bids her speak and in the presence of his friends she calls him her beloved.

Week 52. SONG OF SOLOMON.

N.B.—*The questions below are based upon the Revised Version.*

Day 1. Ct. i. 2–ii. 7. See *Analysis*.

(1) i. 2-8. 'Thy love is better than wine', 'Draw me, we will run after thee', 'We will be glad and rejoice in thee', 'O thou whom my soul loveth'. Does our heart speak thus of Christ?

(2) ii. 3, 4. Consider the two figures by which the bride expresses the bliss of communion. See notes 5 and 6 below. Have we experienced that Christ gives comfort, rest and refreshment, and that he leads us into a place of delight, protected by love? Cf. Ps. lxiii. 3-5.

Notes.—(1) i. 5, 6. The bride's brothers in the heat of anger sent her to the vineyards.

(2) i. 12-14. Women wore small bags of myrrh, suspended from the neck under their dress. To the bride, her beloved was as the costliest perfume.

(3) i. 15, the shepherd speaks; i. 16–ii. 1, the bride; ii. 2, the shepherd; ii. 3-7, the bride.

(4) ii. 1. The bride describes herself as an ordinary wild flower of the meadow (see R.V. mg.).

(5) ii. 3. 'Apple-tree'; giving shade (3b-4) and fruit (3b).

(6) ii. 4. 'Banqueting house'; literally 'house of wine' (R.V. mg.), signifying 'a place of delight'.

(7) ii. 7. A difficult verse, which seems to mean that love should awake or come to life of itself, and not by artificial stimulation.

Day 2. Ct. ii. 8–iii. 5.

(1) How does this portion illustrate the trial of being prevented from enjoying some anticipated opportunity of communion with Christ by the opposition of others? See *Analysis*, and compare the position of the Psalmist in Pss. xlii and xliii.

(2) iii. 1-4. What characteristics of true love are seen in these verses? Cf. Ps. cxix. 2, 10; Je. xxix. 13; Lk. xv. 4 ('until he find'). Notice, too, the name by which four times she describes her lover. Is this our own attitude to Christ?

Note.—ii. 17. A picture of evening, not (as A.V.) of early morning. The shadows flee away, when the sun that causes them sets. The bride hoped for a meeting with her beloved in the cool of the evening, when he returned from the 'mountains of separation' (R.V. mg.), but was disappointed. Night came, and her heart still sought him (iii. 1).

Day 3. Ct. iii. 6–v. 1.

(1) iii. 6–iv. 7. See *Analysis*. A picture of the glory and allurement of the world. Cf. Ec. ii. 4-8; Phil. iii. 8; Gal. vi. 14; 1 Jn.

ii. 15, 16. Are you like the bride of the song, faithful to the Lover of your soul, or like Demas? See 2 Tim. iv. 10, and in contrast, Phil. i. 20, 21.

(2) iv. 8-15. Is it possible that Christ should find such delight in His people? Yet see Pss. cxlvii. 11, cxlix. 4; Is. lxii. 5b; Jn. xv. 9, 10; Eph. i. 18 (last clause), v. 25-27.

(3) iv. 16b. Are we willing to open the garden of our inner life to Christ, to do there what He will? Is our heart reserved for Him alone (iv. 12)? Cf. Is. xxvi. 13.

Notes.—(1) iii. 6. 'Pillars of smoke'; fragrant columns of smoke arising from burning incense.

(2) iii. 7. 'Litter'; in verse 9 'Palanquin', a couch covered by a canopy borne by four or more men.

(3) iv. 4. The neck, decked with ornaments, is compared to a battlemented tower, hung with shields.

(4) iv. 8. The bride hears the voice of her beloved, calling her to himself. The verse seems to be a poetic description of the dangers to which she is exposed in the palace.

Day 4. Ct. v. 2–vi. 3.

(1) v. 2-8. This dream (see note 1 below) may teach important lessons. Why did the bride not respond to her beloved (verse 3)? and what did she suffer in consequence? How may we apply these things to ourselves? Cf. Ho. v. 15; Rev. iii. 20.

(2) What is the answer in our hearts to the question of v. 9? Do we rejoice to tell of Christ? Is He to us the chiefest among ten thousands and 'the altogether lovely One'? Cf. the doxology in Rev. i. 5, 6 and the description of Rev. i. 12-16.

Notes.—(1) v. 2. The words 'I was asleep' indicate that the bride is relating a dream.

(2) v. 4. The door was bolted, see verse 5.

(3) v. 10. 'The chiefest among ten thousand'; literally, 'marked out by a banner' (see R.V. mg.); i.e. distinguished from all others as a standard bearer is distinguished, and hence 'pre-eminent'.

Day 5. Ct. vi. 4–viii. 4. See *Analysis*.

(1) The glowing intensity and purity of the bride's love for her beloved gave her a look that inspired a sense of awe in the beholder. Ought not the qualities mentioned in vi. 4 and 10 to be also found in Christ's Church? Cf. Acts ii. 43a, iv. 13, 33, v. 11.

(2) Compare together the three similar utterances of the bride in ii. 16, vi. 3 and vii. 10. Would you say that in Christian experience the order is as follows: (a) Christ's love, 'His desire is towards

me' (vii. 10; cf. 1 Jn. iv. 19); (b) our acceptance of Him, 'my beloved is mine' (ii. 16, vi. 3); (c) the yielding of ourselves to be His, 'I am my beloved's' (ii. 16, vi. 3, vii. 10)? Have we made this surrender?

(3) vii. 13. What fruit are we laying up for our Lord? Cf. Rom. xv. 16-17; Phil. ii. 16.

Notes.—(1) vi. 4. 'Tirzah'; the name (meaning 'delight') of a beautiful town, which later became the royal residence of the kings of northern Israel. 'Comely as Jerusalem'; cf. Ps. xlviii. 2.

(2) vi. 9. 'Choice'; or 'pure' (R.V. mg.); in verse 10 translated 'clear'.

(3) vi. 12, 13. A possible translation is 'My soul has unwittingly brought me to the chariots of the companions of my prince'; i.e. she fell in with some of Solomon's retinue. She fled, but they called her back, and gazed upon her, as she put it, as if she were a company of dancers.

(4) vii. 1-6. These verses may be part of the song composed by the women (vi. 9b and 10), or may be spoken by Solomon. In verses 7-9 he is certainly the speaker.

(5) vii. 11–viii. 3. The bride's refuge from Solomon's advances is always to commune in spirit with her beloved. Cf. i. 12–ii. 6, iv. 8 ff.

(6) viii. 4. Cf. ii. 7, iii. 5.

Day 6. Ct. viii. 5-14.

(1) 'Leaning upon her beloved'. Are you learning this secret of blessedness in relation to Christ? Cf. Jn. xv. 4, 5; Phil. iv. 13.

(2) viii. 6, 7. If this be true of human love, how much more must it be so of the love of God! Cf. Rom. viii. 35-39. Is our love to Christ of this pattern?

(3) viii. 10. The bride of the story was as a wall in her constancy. Are we thus loyal to Christ, willing to let the world and all it offers go its way if we may but possess Him? Cf. Phil. iii. 8; Rev. iii. 4, 5.

Notes.—(1) viii. 5. 'Under the apple-tree I awakened thee'; that is, the apple-tree overshadowing the bride's home had been their trysting-place; as also the place of the bride's birth.

(2) viii. 6. 'Set me as a seal', etc.; in ancient times men carried their seal fastened to breast or wrist for safe preservation. The bride would ain be thus held fast on the heai iand arm of her beloved.

'Jealousy is cruel as the grave'; better, 'ardent love is unyielding as Sheol'.

(3) viii. 8-10. The bride's brothers had waited to see if she would be as a wall against temptation, or as an open door to give it entrance. Now she claims that she has shown herself as a wall.

(4) viii. 11, 12. Solomon appears to have offered her a vineyard of great wealth; but she put it aside in favour of the vineyard which was hers in her beloved.

(5) viii. 13. The beloved speaks. 'Thou that dwellest in the gardens'; cf. i. 6, viii. 11. 'Companions'; cf. i. 7.

Day 7. Revision.

How did the bride of the story remain faithful under such great temptation as met her in Solomon's palace? It has been said that it was by the exercise of four things:

    (a) Memory—thinking constantly of her beloved.
    (b) Fear—the fear of losing him.
    (c) The practice of his presence.
    (d) Hope—the hope of being reunited with him.

Does your study of the book confirm this, and if so, what application has it to ourselves in relation to our Lord?

SECOND YEAR

SECOND YEAR

MARK

INTRODUCTION

(See New Bible Handbook, pp. 319-322, 328-333)

IT is generally held that this Gospel was written by John Mark, the nephew of Barnabas, and is the earliest of the four Gospels. According to tradition it is based upon the teaching of the apostle Peter, whose interpreter Mark became (cf. 1 Pet. v. 13), and was written in Rome for the church there. It begins with a short preliminary statement of John the Baptist's ministry, and of the baptism and temptation of Jesus, and then passes on to His public ministry in Galilee. In common with the other Gospels, it devotes a comparatively large space to His sufferings, death and resurrection.

The story centres in the confession of Peter, 'Thou art the Christ' (viii. 27-29). Up to that time it tells of our Lord's activity in preaching and healing; but after the confession of Peter, Jesus makes known to the Twelve that He must suffer and die, and be raised the third day, and His face is turned towards the cross. The disciples failed to understand, and the work of Jesus in this latter half of the Gospel consists largely in teaching His disciples, and seeking to wean them from the false ideas of the kingdom which possessed their minds.

The closing verses of the Gospel (xvi. 9-20) do not appear to be the original ending. Some ancient MSS. end at xvi. 8, and others have a different paragraph at the close (see xvi. 9, R.V. mg.). But these verses contain the great missionary commission and are a part of Scripture.

ANALYSIS

147

Week 1. MARK I–III

Day 1. Mk. i. 1-13.

(1) In what two ways did John the Baptist 'prepare the way of, the Lord'?

(2) Observe how Father, Son and Holy Spirit are all active in the events recorded—and Satan also. What can we learn from this portion of the powers of good and evil contending for the spirit of man today? Cf. Eph. vi. 11-13.

Notes.—(1) Verses 2 and 3. See Mal. iii. 1 and Is. xl. 3. Why, in some MSS. the words are all ascribed to Isaiah (see R.V.) cannot now be known.
(2) Verse 13. 'He was with the wild beasts'; a fact which brought comfort to the early Christians under persecution. Cf. Heb. ii. 18, iv. 15.

Day 2. Mk. i. 14-34.

Opening of Jesus' ministry in Galilee.

(1) Verse 15. When it is remembered with what intense eagerness all Israel looked for the coming of God's kingdom (cf. Acts xxvi. 6, 7), consider what a thrill of excited expectancy the message of Jesus would arouse. What new demand did Jesus add to John's summons to repent?

(2) Try to put yourself in the place of the four disciples whom Jesus called to follow Him, and to re-live their experiences as described in verses 16-34. Have you had any comparable experience in your own life?

Notes.—(1) Verse 22. 'Authority'; like that of a king. Cf. Ec. viii. 4a.
(2) Verses 32, 33. See note on Lk. iv. 40 (Vol. 1, p. 19).

Day 3. Mk. i. 35–ii. 12.

Tour in Galilee.

(1) After the astonishing events of the preceding day Jesus had to consider what He should do next. How did He arrive at a decision, and to what decision did He come? What bearing has this (a) upon our prayer life and (b) upon the Church's missionary duty? Cf. Jn. xx. 21; Mk. xvi. 15.

(2) Consider how the healed leper, by disobedience, interrupted

the Lord's plan (see note below). Have we been guilty of like heedlessness?

(3) Had you been present when the sick man was laid before Jesus (ii. 4), what do you think you would have noticed most? What did Jesus see, and what other evidences do you find in the story of His powers of discernment? Cf. Jn. ii. 24, 25; Acts i. 24.

Notes.—(1) i. 45. For 'the city' read 'any city' (Moffatt). The leper's disobedience interrupted the Lord's tour.

(2) ii. 4. The house would have a flat roof, which could be reached by an outside staircase (cf. xiii. 15).

√ **Day 4.** Mk. ii. 13–iii. 6.
Beginnings of opposition.

(1) Levi or Matthew (Mt. ix. 9; Mk. iii. 18), who was a publican or tax collector, was sitting in his tax office when Jesus called him. In what ways did he show the reality of his faith, and how is he an example to us?

(2) If Jesus did not come to call the righteous, how can the righteous enter His kingdom? See Paul's answer in Phil. iii. 4-9.

(3) What evidence is there that even at this early stage of His ministry Jesus foresaw His violent death?

Notes.—(1) ii. 15-17. The words 'righteous' and 'sinner' signified in current speech those on the one hand who followed the rules of the scribes concerning observance of the law, and those on the other who had cast off 'the yoke of the law' and lived irreligious lives. Tax collectors were classed along with 'sinners'.

(2) ii. 18. The Jews of this time looked upon fasting as an indispensable part of a truly religious life, as important as prayer and almsgiving. Strict Pharisees fasted twice a week (Lk. xviii. 12).

(3) ii. 23, 24 and iii. 2. The scribes taught that to pluck ears of corn was a form of *reaping*, which the law did not allow on the sabbath (Ex. xxxiv. 21); also that it was unlawful to do the work of healing on the sabbath, *unless life was in danger*.

√ **Day 5.** Mk. iii. 7-19a.
The calling of the Twelve.

(1) In what two ways does Mark indicate that the crowds were greater than ever? Do you think that this, coupled with what is said in verse 6, had anything to do with the new step Jesus took in appointing the Twelve?

(2) What, according to verses 14 and 15, was the purpose of their appointment? How were they chosen, and what was their response?

(3) Consider these twelve men. What is it that is conspicuous about them?

Day 6. Mk. iii. 19b-35.

Attempts to stop Jesus' work.

(1) The first attempt was made by Jesus' family (see note below). How did they regard Him (verse 21), and how did He regard them (verse 33)? Did He mean to disown them, or was it only that He was distinguishing between the natural sphere, in which they were His kinsfolk, and the kingdom of God, where kinship rests on grounds other than that of blood-relationship?

(2) The second attempt was made by the scribes from Jerusalem. How did they seek to discredit Him? Jesus' reply falls into three parts. He disproves their assertion, sets forth the true explanation of His power over evil spirits, and gives a solemn warning. State His argument in your own words.

Note.—The new paragraph begins with 19b (see R.V.) and verses 19b-21 are connected with verses 31-35. The words 'His friends' in verse 21 mean literally 'they from His home', and might be translated 'His family'.

Day 7. Revision.

(1) Looking back over the first three chapters, what evidences are there of Jesus' popularity, and what of growing opposition? Who were for Him and who were against Him, and on what grounds? How also did Jesus deal with the criticism and opposition directed against Him?

(2) What indications do you find that already an inner circle of disciples was forming round Jesus, and that He encouraged this development? What strikes you most about Jesus in Mark's picture of Him at the beginning of His ministry?

Week 2. MARK IV-VII. 23

Day 1. Mk. iv. 1-20.

Illustration of Jesus' teaching by parable.

(1) What does this parable teach concerning (a) the reasons why even the teaching of Jesus failed to produce fruit in the lives of many of the hearers: (b) the criterion by which true success is measured in gospel preaching: and (c) the method by which the kingdom comes in this present age?

(2) 'He that hath ears to hear, let him hear.' Is the Word finding entrance into your heart (verse 15)? Is it taking deep root (verses 16, 17)? Are you allowing some other crop to mature in your heart (verses 18, 19)? What measure of fruit is being produced in your life (verse 20)?

Day 2. Mk. iv. 21-34.

Further illustrations of Jesus' teaching by parables.

(1) How is the responsibility of the hearer brought out in verses 21-25, first, for what he does with his knowledge, and second, for his attitude to what he hears?

(2) The parable in verses 26-29 is peculiar to this Gospel. Assuming that the casting in of the seed represents the ministry of Jesus, that the seed and the soil represent the Word and the mind of man respectively, and that the harvest represents the Lord's return, what may we learn (a) as to the significance of Jesus' first coming; (b) as to the vitality of the Word as it works in the human heart; and (c) as to what will take place at the end of the present age?

(3) How does our Lord in the parable of the mustard seed describe the beginnings of the kingdom, and how its final end? Do we share His magnificent confidence as to the final issue of His work?

Day 3. Mk. iv. 35–v. 20.

Instances of Jesus' mighty works.

(1) In the story of the storm, what were the disciples surprised at in Jesus, and what was He surprised at in them? Do you find a lesson here for ourselves?

(2) Contrast what men had attempted, without success, to do for the demoniac, with what Jesus did for him. Reflect on this as an illustration of the difference between man's way of curbing evil by restraint and the Saviour's way of inward transformation.

(3) Notice the instructions given by the Lord to the healed man (verse 19). What bearing has this on our own witness? Contrast these instructions with i. 44. How do you account for the difference?

Notes.—(1) v. 1. 'The country of the Gadarenes'; more probably, as in R.V., 'the Gerasenes'. This district lay on the east side of the Lake of Galilee, where there was a mixed population of Jews and Gentiles.

(2) v. 6-13. The cure was not immediate. Notice the remarkable use by the demoniac of the singular and plural in the pronouns 'my', 'we', 'he', 'them'. In what way the swine were acted upon, as indeed the nature of demon-possession in general, is not explained. The point to hold fast is that the man was restored to health and sanity, to home and friends, and made a witness to God's mercy.

Day 4. Mk. v. 21-vi. 6a.

Further instances of Jesus' mighty works.

(1) What brought the woman to Jesus? Why did she come, as

it were, by stealth? Why did the Lord not allow her to slip away unobserved? What additional benefit did she gain from speaking with Him face to face? What may we learn from these things?

(2) What traits in our Lord's character are revealed in this section?

(3) How does the passage vi. 1-6a illustrate the importance of our Lord's words in i. 15—'*Believe* the good news'? What kept the people of Nazareth from believing, and what impoverishment did they suffer in consequence?

Day 5. Mk. vi. 6b-29.

The first mission of the Twelve.

(1) In the sending out of the Twelve, observe the contrast between the greatness of their commission and authority (verses 7 and 11) and their entire simplicity of life. Is there a lesson here for today? What evidence do you find that their mission caused a great stir?

(2) How would you sum up Herod's character? What were the causes of his failure?

Day 6. Mk. vi. 30-56.

Crisis and culmination of the Galilean ministry. Cf. Jn. vi. 14, 15.

(1) What is the significance for His followers today of the Lord's command to His disciples in verse 37 and of the whole miracle? Cf. xvi. 15.

(2) Picture the situation described in verses 45-53—the disciples acting in obedience to the Lord's command, yet in distress because of an opposing wind, and Jesus, so it seemed, far away. Have you known any such experience? What light does the story throw upon the life of discipleship, upon its trials and its deliverances?

Notes.—(1) Verses 31-33. A scene of great excitement is here depicted.
(2) Verse 48. 'The fourth watch', i.e. the last watch beginning about 3 a.m.

Day 7. Mk. vii. 1-23.

Conflict with the Pharisees, and scribes from Jerusalem. In answering the question of verse 5 Jesus divides His reply into two parts, dealing first with the general question of observing the tradition of the elders (verses 6-13), and then with the question of defilement (verses 14-23). In answering the latter question, He lays down in verse 15 a general principle, and develops it in its two parts, the first in verses 18-19, and the second in verses 20-23.

(1) What did Jesus say of 'the tradition of the elders', and what example did He give of its anti-scriptural teaching?

(2) Note how verse 21 destroys the illusion that thoughts do not

matter if they never take shape in acts. Are we seeking deliverance from the uncleanness of an evil *heart*, or, like the Pharisees, content with a fair appearance outwardly?

Note.—Verse 3. 'The tradition of the elders'; that is, rules and regulations drawn up by past generations of scribes to guide people how to act. The Pharisees were those who made it their aim to walk strictly according to this 'tradition'. They regarded themselves, and were regarded by others, as 'the righteous'.

Week 3. MARK VII. 24–X. 31

Day 1. Mk. vii. 24-37.

Ministry to the north and east of the Lake of Galilee.

(1) Why did Jesus at first seem to refuse the woman's petition (cf. Mt. xv. 24), and how did she finally obtain her request? What may we learn from her concerning faith?

(2) Can you see any reasons why the healing of the deaf and dumb man should have been effected in a way which appears difficult and laborious? Consider how this man may have known little or nothing about Jesus by reason of his limitations. Put yourself in his place, and reflect what the actions of Jesus would suggest to him, thus quickening his expectancy. Cf. Mt. ix. 29.

Day 2. Mk. viii. 1-26.

(1) What two characteristic features in the Lord Jesus stand out in the miracle of viii. 1-9? Why was it that the Pharisees did not believe in Him?

(2) Verses 14-21 show that discipleship involves thought and reflection on our Christian experience, leading to growth in spiritual understanding. Cf. 1 Sa. xvii. 37. Are you growing spiritually?

(3) Consider the story of verses 22-26 as an illustration of Phil. i. 6. Compare also Paul's prayer for those to whom he was writing in Eph. i. 17-19.

Note.—The miracle of viii. 1-9 differs from that of vi. 35-44 in a number of respects; in its location, in the number of people, in the number of loaves, in a different word for 'baskets' (see Greek text), and in other ways.

Day 3. Mk. viii. 27-38.

Confession of Jesus as the Christ. See *Introduction*.

(1) What lay behind Peter's protest in verse 32, and why did the Lord rebuke him so severely?

(2) What implications for the Christian are here involved with

regard (a) to self, (b) to Christ, and (c) to the world? Two alternative courses are presented in verses 35-37, and each must make his choice between them. What does Jesus declare will be the final result of choosing wrongly?

Note.—Verse 34. For the meaning of the word 'deny', see Lk. xii. 9, xxii. 34. Here it means to disown self, to refuse to recognize the claims of self as against those of Christ.

✓Day 4. Mk. ix. 1-29.

(1) In the transfiguration scene we see Elijah and Moses representing the first Covenant, the three disciples representing the New Covenant, Jesus in the midst in heavenly glory, and around the whole the cloud, symbolic of the presence of God. Contemplate this picture of eternal realities. Have you a part in it?

(2) What question did the scene raise in the minds of the three disciples who witnessed it? And how did Jesus reply? Consider how closely John the Baptist resembled Elijah.

(3) The scene at the foot of the mount. Why was Jesus so disappointed at what He found? What does the story teach concerning (a) the importance of faith, and (b) the necessity of prayer? Verses 23 and 29 should be read as in R.V.

✓Day 5. Mk. ix. 30-50.

(1) 'If any man desire to be first' in the kingdom of God, what must he be?

(2) What three reasons does Jesus give in verses 39-41 why the disciples should *not* have acted as they did?

(3) Jesus urges in verses 43-48 the amputation of a limb that the life may be saved. Did He mean the literal amputation of a limb and, if not, what did He mean?

Notes.—(1) Verses 44, 46, 48. A reference to the Valley of Hinnom outside Jerusalem, where the refuse of the city was cast, and which had become a synonym for hell. The meaning is that the ruin of a soul in hell is final.

(2) Verse 49. 'Salted with fire'; subjected to a fiery process of discipline (cf. 1 Pet. i. 7) to purge out corruption.

✓Day 6. Mk. x. 1-16.

(1) What is the considered judgment of Christ regarding divorce, and on what grounds does He base it?

(2) How does the incident of the children support and encourage every effort to bring children everywhere to Jesus?

(3) What is it to receive the kingdom of God 'as a little child'? How does a little child receive the good things of this life?

Day 7. Mk. x. 17-31. The rich young ruler.

(1) Jesus here applies the general principle of viii. 34 to a particular case. There is often some particular hindrance that holds people back. What was it in the case of this man?

(2) What lessons did Jesus draw from the incident for the benefit of His disciples?

(3) What may those who leave all to follow Christ expect (a) in this world, and (b) in the world to come? But what is the meaning of the warning in verse 31? Cf. 1 Cor. xiii. 3.

Week 4. MARK x. 32-XIII

Day 1. Mk. x. 32-52.

Going up towards Jerusalem.

(1) How many times has Jesus spoken of His sufferings, according to Mark's record, and what effect had it upon His disciples? Are *our* hearts responsive to this aspect of His teaching? Cf. Gal. vi. 14.

(2) What is the difference between greatness in the world, and greatness in the kingdom of God? How is this exemplified in the Lord Himself?

(3) Would Bartimaeus have received his sight if he had not cried out? Cf. Mt. vii. 7, 8; Jas. iv. 2 (last clause). If we mourn our spiritual poverty and barrenness, may not the reason lie here? How would you characterize Bartimaeus' prayer?

Day 2. Mk. xi. 1-19.

The public entry into Jerusalem.

(1) Jesus had hitherto refrained from publicly declaring His Messiahship. See iii. 11, 12, viii. 30, ix. 9. Why did He declare it now?

(2) Assuming that the fig-tree was to our Lord a symbol of Jerusalem, what lesson does His act of judgment upon it teach? Cf. Lk. xiii. 6-9.

(3) What features of our Lord's character are specially exhibited in the incidents of today's portion?

Notes.—(1) Verse 13. It was not the season of figs, but Jesus drew near to see if a tree, which made such a profession of richness, had perhaps also fruit.

(2) Verses 15 and 16. These things cannot have been done without confusion and disorder.

(3) Verse 17. See Is. lvi. 7 and Je. vii. 11.

Day 3. Mk. xi. 20-33.

(1) Reflect on the situation in which the Lord found Himself at this time. How many and strong, humanly speaking, were the forces against Him, and yet how quiet and confident He was in His faith in God! What does He tell us are the essential conditions of prevailing prayer?

(2) 'Neither do I tell you', Jesus said. Why did Jesus refuse to give an answer? How had these men shown that they had not the capacity to judge the point at issue?

Day 4. Mk. xii. 1-27.

(1) Observe in the parable of the vineyard and our Lord's comment upon it (a) His connection with and yet difference from the prophets, and (b) how the Scriptures foretell His rejection and yet assign to Him the highest place.

(2) The representatives of the Pharisees and Herodians came in the guise of honest inquirers, but their purpose was to lay a trap for the Lord. If, as One who claimed to be the Messiah, He said it was right to pay tribute, they could discredit Him with the people; if He said it was wrong, they could accuse Him to the Roman governor. How did Jesus escape the snare, and what important truth is taught by His reply?

(3) With regard to the future life what do we learn from these verses concerning (a) change of nature, and (b) continuity of identity? Cf. 1 Cor. xv. 37, 38. On what ground does Jesus base the certainty of resurrection?

Note.—Verse 26. Jesus refers to Ex. iii. 1-6. He thus draws His argument from that part of the Scriptures, which the Sadducees regarded as alone authoritative.

Day 5. Mk. xii. 28-44.

(1) Jesus pronounced this scribe to be 'not far from the kingdom of God'. What would he have needed to do to enter in?

(2) What is the difference in meaning between the phrases 'with all thy heart', 'with all thy soul', etc., in verse 30?

(3) Contrast the scribes and the widow, as described in verses 38-44. What, in the case of the former, elicited censure, and in the case of the latter praise from our Lord? Examine your own conduct and motives in the light of these verses.

Day 6. Mk. xiii. 1-23.

Teaching about the future. Notice carefully what gave rise to it, and especially the questions put to the Lord. See verses 1-4.

(1) The Lord first gives a general forecast of what His disciples would meet with. Against what three dangers in particular does He warn them? See verses 1-13.

(2) In verses 14-23 Jesus discloses the sign of the destruction of the Temple, about which the four disciples had asked (verse 4). What four vivid illustrations does He give of the need of hasty departure when the sign appeared?

(3) What injunction is repeated three times in verses 5-23 and what other counsels are given which are applicable to ourselves?

Notes.—(1) Verse 14. 'The abomination of desolation' (Dn. ix. 27, xi. 31, xii. 11) is a Jewish expression for the violation of the holy city by a foreign army. Cf. Lk. xxi. 20.

(2) Verse 15. 'Him that is on the housetop.' The flat roofs of houses in Palestine were used for places of rest and social intercourse. Cf. Acts x. 9.

Day 7. Mk. xiii. 24-37.

The prophecy continues, rapidly unfolding successive events—'after that tribulation (24) . . . and then (26) . . . and then (27)'.

(1) Would you say that Jesus' picture is bright or dark?

(2) How shall we practically fulfil the command to 'watch'? Are we sufficiently awake to the fact that the day of Christ is not past, but is to come? Does our manner of life attest our faith in Christ's ultimate and possibly imminent triumphant return; or, if He came, would He find us sleeping?

Notes.—(1) Verses 24, 25. According to Lk. xxi. 24 the tribulation is still continuing. If so, then the events of these two verses will mark the close of the present age. The phraseology may perhaps, as in the Old Testament, symbolize national and international upheavals, cf. e.g. Is. xiii. 10, xxxiv. 4; Ezk. xxxii. 7, etc.

(2) Verse 26. Cf. viii. 38; Dn. vii. 13, 14.

(3) Verse 27. Cf. 1 Thes. iv. 17; 2 Thes. ii. 1; Mt. xiii. 41, 49.

(4) Verses 33-37. 'Watch', i.e. be wakeful, and alert.

Week 5. Mark xiv-xvi

Day 1. Mk. xiv. 1-25.

(1) What various attitudes towards Jesus are found in this section? How are these surprising reactions to be accounted for?

(2) On what four grounds did Jesus praise Mary?

(3) In the words 'This is my body', Jesus was speaking, as the words 'blood . . . shed' in verse 24 show more clearly, of His death (cf. Gn. ix. 6; Ps. lxxix. 3). Ponder the words 'bread', 'blood', 'gave', 'take', 'eat', 'the new covenant', as throwing light

on the nature and method of salvation. Cf. 1 Pet. i. 18-19; Jn. i. 12 ('received' is the same word as 'take'), vi. 32, 33, 51, 56.

Note.—The expression 'This is my body' corresponds to the Passover formula 'This is the bread of affliction which our fathers ate in the land of affliction.' To deduce the doctrine of transubstantiation from this passage, we should require different words, and a different historical context.

Day 2. Mk. xiv. 26-52.

(1) In speaking as he did in verse 29, how did Peter display a wrong attitude both towards Christ and towards the Scriptures? Wherein lay the mistake of Peter and the rest? Are you contradicting the Lord in anything that He is saying to you?

(2) What is meant by 'the hour' and 'the cup' in verses 35, 36? What exactly was our Lord's petition? Was it answered and, if so, how? Cf. Heb. v. 7, 8.

(3) In the hour of betrayal and arrest where did our Lord find support and guidance? What may we learn from His example? Cf. Ps. cxix. 50, 92, 105.

Day 3. Mk. xiv. 53-72.

The object of the Jewish Council was to find legal ground for putting Jesus to death. It had been previously decided that He must die (xiv. 1), but some ground must be sought, which would justify their action in condemning Him, and enable them to secure Pilate's confirmation of the verdict.

(1) Consider Jesus' situation from a human standpoint, and then place in contrast the claim He makes. It has been said that we cannot escape from the inexorable trilemma that either Christ deceived mankind by conscious fraud, or He was Himself deluded and self-deceived, or He was divine. Do you agree?

(2) Observe the varying moods through which Peter passed on this eventful night (see xiv. 19, xiv. 29, 31, and here). Where was Peter when temptation assailed him and how did temptation come? Is it not a scene often repeated—a follower of Jesus among non-Christians, not having prayed, out of touch with his Lord, faced by a sudden question giving opportunity to confess Christ, and instead of confession, denial?

Day 4. Mk. xv. 1-23.

The main concern of the Jewish leaders now was to get their verdict carried into effect. For this they required the Roman governor's consent, for the Romans reserved to themselves the right of capital punishment.

(1) What three wrong steps did Pilate take? We look back upon the scene from a distance and with condemnation. But when

people today choose expediency instead of truth and justice, are they not acting as Pilate did? Cf. Rom. ii. 1.

(2) Try to picture the mocking of the soldiers, remembering that Jesus had just been scourged, a punishment of brutal severity.

(3) The insertion of the words 'father of Alexander and Rufus' seem to imply that Simon became a Christian, and that his sons were well-known in the church. Assuming that his son Rufus is the Rufus of Rom. xvi. 13, let your imagination weave together the probable life story of Simon from its beginning to its end.

Day 5. Mk. xv. 24-41.

(1) Mark gives one Old Testament Scripture which was fulfilled in the cross (verse 28). Can you think of others?

(2) What is the answer to the question in verse 34?

(3) What is the spiritual significance of the rending of the veil? Cf. Heb. ix. 8, x. 19, 20; Eph. ii. 18.

Day 6. Mk. xv. 42–xvi. 8.

(1) What seven distinct acts are mentioned as having been done by Joseph of Arimathea? Considering who he was and the situation at the time, what qualities of character are shown by his behaviour?

(2) What reflections are suggested by the fact that though God did not intervene to save His Son from dying on the cross, yet He rescued His body from the unworthy burial ordinarily given to those who had been crucified?

(3) What is involved in the fact that Jesus lives? Cf. Rev. i. 17, 18.

Day 7. Mk. xvi. 9-20.

(1) What three appearances of the risen Jesus are recorded in these verses? How came these mourning, weeping, unbelieving men to believe in the resurrection with a strength of conviction which neither the lapse of time nor any after circumstances could weaken—unless, in fact, Jesus did rise from the dead and appear to them (cf. Acts i. 3)?

(2) 'The gospel' (verse 15 cf. i. 1). What is the significance of Jesus' coming into the world? and what duty does this impose upon those who are His followers?

(3) If we truly believe in what is recorded in verse 19, ought not verse 20 to become true of us also?

PSALMS XLII—LXXII

(See page 164 and New Bible Handbook, pp. 186, 187, 191-198)

Week 6. PSALMS XLII–LI

✓ **Day 1.** Pss. xlii and xliii.

These two psalms were probably originally one. Notice the thrice-repeated refrain (xlii. 5, xlii. 11, xliii. 5).

(1) What word occurs four times, expressing the Psalmist's spiritual condition at this time?

(2) What were the chief causes of his sorrow, and what his chief desire? Does God's presence and favour mean as much to us?

(3) What means did the Psalmist use to find support and deliverance?

Notes.—(1) Ps. xlii. 2. 'Appear before God'; i.e. in His temple. Cf. Ps. lxxxiv. 7.

(2) Verse 4. See R.V. It had been the Psalmist's privilege to lead the pilgrim procession to 'the house of God'.

(3) Verse 11. 'Health of my countenance'; i.e. 'my salvation'.

Day 2. Ps. xliv.

A national appeal to God in a time of great suffering.

(1) What does faith say concerning God in the light (a) of past experience; (b) of His relationship to His people? See verses 1-8.

(2) Yet what were the facts of the situation, as seen by the natural eye? See verses 9-22.

(3) When faith and circumstances seem thus to be in conflict, and we are at a loss to understand God's dealings, what does the psalm teach us to do? Cf. Is. l. 10; Lk. xviii. 1.

Day 3. Ps. xlv.

A marriage song of a king. If the king be a type of Christ (see Heb. i. 8, 9), the bride may symbolize the Church.

(1) What features in Christ's character are here portrayed?

(2) What counsel is given to the bride if she would win the king's favour? What does this mean in its application to ourselves?

Notes.—(1) The R.V. is better in verses 1, 5, 6, 7, 8, 13, 14.

(2) Verse 14, 15. 'Brought'; better, 'conducted', i.e. in procession, with attendant maidens and every mark of rejoicing.

Day 4. Pss. xlvi–xlviii.

These psalms are a trilogy of praise in memory of a great deliverance, most probably that of Jerusalem from the king of Assyria. They should be read in the light of 2 Ki. xviii–xix.

(1) Gather out what is said about *God* in these psalms—His power, His character, His relation to the world, and His relation to His own people.

(2) How would you express the leading thought of each of the three psalms?

(3) What should be the response of God's people to such a manifestation of His power and love? See, e.g., xlvi. 2, 4, 8, 10; xlvii. 6, etc. Consider how much greater cause we have thus to make response, who have seen God's salvation manifested in the victory of Christ.

Notes.—(1) xlvi. 5. 'Right early'; better, 'when the morning dawns', i.e. the morning of deliverance. See R.V. mg. and cf. Mk. vi. 48, 51.

(2) xlvii. 1. 'People'; better, 'peoples' as in R.V., and so also in verses 3 and 9a. The nations of the world are here addressed.

(3) xlvii. 2. 'A great king'; i.e. the true 'great king' in contrast to the Assyrian monarch, who bore this title. See Is. xxxvi. 4. Cf. also xlviii. 2.

(4) xlvii. 9. 'Shields'; meaning 'rulers'. The verse is prophetic of Christ's final victory. See 1 Cor. xv. 24, 25; Rev. xv. 3, 4.

Day 5. Ps. xlix.

An inspired meditation (see Note (2) below), addressed to all men, on the vanity of riches. It anticipates our Lord's teaching in Lk. xii. 13-21.

(1) How do men in general regard wealth? See verses 6, 13, 18.

(2) But what are the facts? What can wealth *not* do (verses 7-9), and what is the end of the rich man (verses 10-14, 17-20)?

(3) Why is it better to trust in God than in riches (see verses 14, 15), and what is the Psalmist's counsel to himself and to us? See verses 5 and 16.

Notes.—(1) Verse 1. 'People'; better, 'peoples' as in R.V.

(2) Verse 4. 'I will incline mine ear'. Cf. Ps. lxxxv. 8; Heb. ii. 1. The word 'parable' here might perhaps be better rendered as 'poem'. The word 'dark saying' means a perplexing question.

(3) Verses 5, 6. Read as in R.V.

(4) Verses 7 and 9 should be read together, verse 8 being parenthetical. With verse 7 cf. Ex. xxi. 30. There were cases where, in human relationships, life could be redeemed with money; but it is not so when God summons the soul.

Day 6. Ps. l.

A picture of God's judgment of His people, in four sections: (a) Introduction (verses 1-6); (b) God speaks to His people (verses 7-15); (c) God speaks to the wicked (verses 16-21); (d) Epilogue (verses 22, 23).

(1) What three attributes of God in His capacity as Judge are stressed in verses 1-6? Who are being tried (verse 5), and who

are called to be witnesses of the trial (verses 4a and 6)? Cf. 2 Cor. v. 10; 1 Pet. iv. 17.

(2) What does God condemn in His people, and what does He ask from them?

(3) Contrast the conduct and secret thought of the wicked, and his end, with the conduct of those who please God, and their end.

Day 7. Ps. li.

Note the occasion of the psalm, as given in the title.

(1) On what two grounds, in verses 1-4, does David plead for forgiveness? Cf. Dn. ix. 9; Pr. xxviii. 13.

(2) David realizes that his whole nature is sinful, and that God requires sincerity and integrity in the innermost part of his being (verse 6; cf. 1 Sa. xvi. 7). What, therefore, in verses 7-12, does he plead for in *addition to forgiveness*? Cf. Ezk. xxxvi. 25-27.

(3) What does David promise shall be the outcome of God's answer to his prayer? See verses 13-17.

Notes.—(1) Verse 4. This does not mean that David had not also sinned against man (cf. verse 14, 'bloodguiltiness'), but that he now saw his sin in this one outstanding aspect of it, as being a sin against God. Cf. Gn. xxxix. 9; 2 Sa. xii. 13.

(2) Verse 12. 'Thy free spirit'; better, 'a willing spirit' (see R.V. mg.); i.e. a spirit *inclined* to do God's will. Cf. Ezk. xi. 19, 20; Gal. v. 16.

Week 7. Psalms LII–LXIII

Day 1. Pss. lii–liv.

Of these three psalms the second (Ps. liii) is a duplicate (with slight variations) of Ps. xiv. For the occasion of Pss. lii and liv see their titles and cf. 1 Sa. xxii. 9; xxiii. 19.

(1) Ps. lii presents the picture of a successful godless man strutting through the world in his pride. How is he described, and how is it shown that in the end he *cannot* prosper? Cf. Ps. xxxiv. 15, 16; Jas. iii. 4-8.

(2) What has Ps. liii to say of the extent of man's sin? Cf. Rom. i. 18-32, iii. 10-12.

(3) What may we learn from Ps. liv (a) of the severity of faith's trial; (b) of the ground of faith's confidence; (c) of faith's assurance of triumph? Consider how all this is perfectly exemplified in our Lord's life, and especially in its closing days.

Notes.—(1) Ps. lii. 9, read as in R.V.

(2) Ps. liii. 5. Possibly a reference to the destruction of Sennacherib's army (2 Ki. xix. 35).

(3) Ps. liii. 6. 'Bringeth back the captivity'; more probably 'turneth the fortunes' (*Camb. Bible*).

Day 2. Ps. lv.

(1) Of the two ways of meeting trouble, in verses 6-7 and 22 respectively, which is the better, and why? Have you been tempted to be an 'escapist'?

(2) What was the bitterest element in the Psalmist's grief? See verses 12-14, 21 and cf. 2 Sa. xv. 31; Jn. xiii. 21. Observe, however, the difference between David's cry in verse 15, and our Lord's word concerning Judas (Mk. xiv. 21).

Notes.—(1) The meaning of the psalm is clearer in the R.V.

(2) Verses 9-11. Violence, strife, iniquity, mischief, wickedness, oppression, deceit, seem to be personified as walking on the walls and in the streets of the city.

(3) Verse 15. 'Among them'; better, 'in their inward part' as in R.V. mg. The R.V. mg. should be followed also in verse 18.

(4) Verse 22. 'Thy burden'; the Hebrew word translated 'burden' means literally 'that which He hath given thee'; see R.V. mg. The thought seems to be, Take back to God, and cast upon Him the burden He has laid upon you, and He will sustain you under it.

Day 3. Pss. lvi and lvii.

These two psalms are closely connected, and, according to their titles, should be read against the background of 1 Sa. xxi. 10–xxii. 1.

(1) In Ps. lvi notice the refrain, in verses 3-4, and 10-11. What links are revealed here between prayer, God's Word and faith?

(2) What purpose did David cherish if his life were spared? See verse 13. This verse shines for us with deeper meaning in the light of Christ. See, e.g., Eph. ii. 4-10.

(3) Consider in Ps. lvii (a) the trials by which David was surrounded; (b) the assurance of faith, compelling him to songs of praise; (c) his pure desire for God's glory.

Notes.—(1) Ps. lvi should be read in the R.V., and the R.V. mg. in verses 2, 6 and 13. In Ps. lvii the R.V. is better in verses 3, 4 and 9, and the R.V. mg. in verse 8.

(2) Ps. lvi. 8. God counts David's days of wandering, and treasures up his tears. Cf. Mt. x. 30.

Day 4. Pss. lviii and lix.

(1) Ps. lviii. Contrast the description of God as the righteous Judge with the wicked judges spoken of in verses 1-5. Notice also the many vivid images, especially in verses 4-9.

(2) Ps. lix. In how many ways does David address God, and what encouragement in time of trouble may be found in each?

(3) How does the psalm reveal David's confidence in God, and

the place of faith in a life of victory? Cf. Mk. xi. 22; Jn. xi. 40; 1 Jn. v. 4.

Notes.—(1) Both psalms should be read in the R.V.

(2) lix. 5 and 8.   The reference to heathen nations, as if they were the enemies spoken of, is an argument against the Davidic authorship. It is possible that an original psalm of David was later adapted for national use in the temple.

(3) Verse 6. The wicked are compared to the fierce dogs that roam in an eastern city. The figure changes in verse 7. Cf. Pr. xv. 28b.

Day 5. Ps. lx.

For the occasion of this psalm see the title and 2 Sa. viii. 3, 13, 14. The circumstances are not wholly clear. It would seem that while David was engaged in a campaign against Syria (Aram), the Edomites invaded Judah from the south, creating a situation of grave danger. The psalm was written when David first heard the news.

(1) The psalm should be read in these divisions: (a) David pours out his heart before God (verses 1-4); (b) prayer based upon God's promises, and His purpose of good towards Israel (verses 5-8); (c) faith triumphs (verses 9-12).

(2) What may we learn from David's example as to how to meet bad tidings?

Notes.—(1) Verse 4. Read as in R.V. mg. David's words are grimly sarcastic. 'Hast thou given thy worshippers a flag, only that they might fly from the archers?' (Moffatt).

(2) Verse 6. Shechem west of the Jordan, Succoth east of it, thus representing the whole land.

(3) Verse 8. 'Upon Edom'; better, 'to Edom', as in R.V. mg. Moab and Edom were to have a menial place in God's household, as compared with Israel. Even proud Philistia must shout cries of homage.

Day 6. Pss. lxi and lxii.

Psalms lxi-lxiii form another trilogy, like xlvi-xlviii. They were all most probably written shortly after David's flight from Absalom (see lxiii title), and should be read against the background of the story in 2 Sa. xv-xvii. Today we study the first two.

(1) Ps. lxi. Consider David's circumstances—a fugitive, his throne occupied by another, his life sought. What were his heart's chief desires, as expressed in his prayers (verses 1-4, see Note (1) below)? Observe also his confident hope, and his wholehearted devotion (verses 5-8). Is he not in this a type of our Lord?

(2) Ps. lxii. How did David's situation appear in the eyes of his enemies (verse 3 R.V. and Note (3) below), and how to the eye of faith (verses 6-7)?

(3) Out of the fulness of his own joyous confidence in God,

what message was David able to give to his followers? See verses 8-12. Have you also found that faith leads to testimony?

Notes.—(1) lxi. 4. Better taken as a prayer, 'Let me sojourn in Thy tent for ever; let me take refuge in the hiding-place of Thy wings' (*Camb. Bible*).

(2) lxi. 5b. Read, with LXX, 'Thou hast given (their) possession to them that fear Thy name', i.e. the rebellion has been crushed. Cf. R.V. mg.

(3) lxii. 3. See R.V. David appeared to his enemies as a falling wall, and tottering fence: one more blow and he would be down.

(4) lxii. 11, 12. 'Once, twice'; a Hebrew idiom for 'repeatedly', here signifying that the truth David sets forth in these verses had sunk deep into his heart.

Day 7. Ps. lxiii.

The title of the psalm assigns it to the time when David was crossing the wilderness of Judah, that is, from Jerusalem to Jordan, in his flight from Absalom, as described in 2 Sa. xvi. The psalm begins in a mournful way, but suddenly, at verse 2 (R.V.), the note changes, and the psalm becomes one of joyous praise. The most satisfactory explanation of the change, and of David's words, '*So* have I seen Thee in the sanctuary' (R.V.), is that there in the wilderness David was given a vision of Jehovah as vivid and glorious as ever he had seen Him in the sanctuary, and it transformed for him the whole outlook.

(1) Consider how full of sorrow David's heart must have been at leaving Jerusalem, and especially the sanctuary of God. See verse 1 and cf. 2 Sa. xv. 24-30.

(2) What, however, did the vision of God in the wilderness do for him? (a) Though he had lost all—kingdom, throne, capital—he felt that to have God's lovingkindness was better than all that life could offer (verse 3). (b) Even the hours of the coming night, full of peril as they might be (see 2 Sa. xvii. 16), would be filled with praise (verses 5-6). (c) With God beside him, victory was assured (verses 7-11).

Week 8. PSALMS LXIV–LXXII
Day 1. Pss. lxiv and lxv.

Psalm lxiv, like lviii and lix, has for its theme the certainty of God's judgment upon the wicked. Ps. lxv, on the other hand, is a psalm of praise to God, as the God of the whole earth, the only Saviour from sin, and the giver of fruitful harvests.

(1) Ps. lxiv. Comparing this psalm with lix, what do you find the same, and what different (a) in the description of the wicked, and (b) in the purpose, method, and result of God's judgment?

(2) Ps. lxv. What attributes of God are revealed respectively in the three divisions of the psalm? See verses 1-4, 5-8, 9-13.

(3) What special blessedness is the portion of those who dwell in His presence? Can you bear witness to this in your own experience?

Notes.—(1) lxiv. 6. The meaning is that they seek out new kinds of iniquity, and lay deep and crafty plans.

(2) lxv. 9. 'The river of God'; a poetical expression for an abundant rain.

Day 2. Pss. lxvi and lxvii.

Psalm lxvi is a summons to the nations to join in praise to God for a great deliverance which He has wrought for His people, such as the deliverance of Jerusalem from Sennacherib. If this was the occasion, the speaker in verses 13-20 may well be king Hezekiah himself, speaking as the representative of the nation. Ps. lxvii may belong to the same time. See Is. xxxvii.

(1) Ps. lxvi. What aspect of God's character is emphasized in the opening verses of the psalm and how does the Psalmist describe the trouble from which the people were delivered?

(2) What response does the speaker in verses 13-20 make in gratitude for God's mercies, and to what does he attribute God's answer to his prayer?

(3) Ps. lxvii. Do we share the longing of the Psalmist that all nations might know God and His salvation? By what means did the Psalmist think it would be achieved, and what further method has been taught us by Christ? See Mt. xxviii. 19; Mk. xvi. 15; Jn. xv. 26, 27, xvi. 7, 8; Acts i. 8.

Notes.—(1) Ps. lxvi. 6. A reference to the Exodus.

(2) Verse 8. 'People'; better, 'peoples' as in R.V., and so in lxvii. 3 and 5. The R.V. is better also in lxvii. 6.

(3) Verse 9. 'Holdeth our soul in life'; i.e. has not suffered us to perish.

(4) Verse 17. 'He was extolled'; better, 'high praise was under my tongue', as in R.V. mg. His faith anticipated an answer, and his lips were already forming words of praise.

(5) Ps. lxvii. 2. 'Thy saving health'; i.e. Thy salvation.

Day 3. Ps. lxviii. 1-18.

This splendid psalm describes the onward march of God through history to His final triumph. The threefold reference to the sanctuary in verses 17, 24, 35 (see Note (4) of Day 4 below), suggests that like Ps. xxiv it was written to celebrate the bringing of the ark to Jerusalem. See 2 Sa. vi. 15, 17, 18.

(1) What attributes of God are set forth in verses 1-6, and what should be His people's response to His appearing? See verses 3, 4. Cf. Lk. i. 68, ii. 10.

(2) What periods in Israel's history are specially referred to in the historical retrospect in verses 7-18; and what aspects of God's character are revealed? As you look back upon your own life-story since Christ appeared to you to bring you out of bondage, what special manifestations of His power and grace stand out in your memory?

Notes.—(1) Verse 1. See Nu. x. 35.

(2) Verses 4 and 6. Read as in R.V., and in 6a cf. R.V. mg.

(3) Verse 7. See Jdg. v. 4, 5.

(4) Verse 9. 'Thine inheritance'; i.e. the land of promise, as the word 'therein' (verse 10) makes clear. The plentiful rain, with which God blessed the land (cf. Ps. lxv. 9), may perhaps symbolize all His good gifts. Cf. Ho. vi. 3.

(5) Verse 11. Read as in R.V. and cf. Ex. xv. 20; 1 Sa. xviii. 6.

(6) Verses 13, 14. See R.V. The meaning is uncertain. Verse 14 may be a picture of the kings and their armies fleeing as snowflakes driven before a storm.

(7) Verses 15, 16. The high hills are represented as envious because God has chosen Zion.

(8) Verses 17, 18. Read as in R.V. God enters Zion with His heavenly hosts. Cf. Ps. xxiv. 7-10; Eph. iv. 8.

Day 4. Ps. lxviii. 19-35.

(1) Verses 19-27. How is the blessedness of God's people described? See verses 19-23. Have you known Him in your own experience as here set forth, and offered to Him the grateful worship of your whole heart, as Israel offered the united worship of their tribes (verse 27; cf. Eph. v. 18-20)?

(2) Verses 28-35. What God has done (verses 7-18) and is doing (verses 19-27) is but the prelude to greater triumphs. What vision does the Psalmist see of a world-wide homage paid to God, and how is this confirmed by other Scriptures? See, e.g., 1 Cor. xv. 24, 25; Rev. xi. 15.

(3) What verse or verses in this psalm have most gripped your heart? Make a note of them that your heart may say with the Psalmist 'blessed be God' (verse 35).

Notes.—(1) Verses 19-23. Read as in R.V. 'But', in verse 21, might perhaps be better rendered 'Yea', for verses 21-23 are connected with verse 20 as showing how God is a God of deliverances. Verse 22 refers to the enemy. Though they hide in Bashan, or even in the depths of the sea, God can reach them there.

(2) Verse 25. 'Among them were the damsels'; better, 'In the midst of the damsels', as in R.V. It is a vivid picture of a procession, with singers and players on instruments, and on either side maidens with tambourines.

(3) Verse 30. Read as in R.V. 'The wild beast of the reeds' represents Egypt, and the 'bulls' followed by their 'calves' other kings and their peoples.

(4) Verse 35. Read as in R.V. mg. 'Thy holy places'; better, 'Thy sanctuary' (*Camb. Bible*).

Day 5. Ps. lxix.

This psalm is notable, first because the New Testament quotes from it more than from any other psalm, except perhaps xxii, and second, because amidst prayers of humble supplication the Psalmist suddenly breaks into cries of passionate imprecation (verses 22-28). See Jn. xv. 25, ii. 17; Rom. xv. 3, xi. 9, 10; Acts i. 20; quoting verses 4, 9, 22, 23, 25 of the psalm.

(1) What features in the Psalmist's sufferings most closely pre-figure those of our Lord, helping us to understand how deeply He tasted of human woe? Cf. Heb. iv. 15.

(2) Verses 20, 21 take us specially to Gethsemane and the cross (cf. Mt. xxvi. 37, xxvii. 34, 48), but at the point of deepest suffering when the Psalmist breaks out in imprecatory prayer, what did our Lord pray? See Lk. xxii. 42, xxiii. 34, and cf. Mt. v. 44; Acts vii. 60.

(3) Yet in what respects do verses 22-28 foreshadow the judg-ment that has fallen upon the Jewish people? Cf., for example with verses 22, 23, Mt. xiii. 14; 1 Thes. v. 3, R.V., and with verse 25, Mt. xxiii. 38. Is the lesson for ourselves to be found in Rom. xii. 19, 20?

Note.—The R.V. should be read in verses 6, 11, 22, 26 and 32.

Day 6. Pss. lxx and lxxi.

These psalms are alike in being reminiscent of other psalms. Ps. lxx is taken bodily from Ps. xl, and Ps. lxxi. 1-3 from xxxi. 1-3; and the rest of Ps. lxxi is largely made up of fragments of other psalms.

(1) Observe the triple movement in Ps. lxxi: (a) faith, pray-ing, rises to hope and praise (verses 1-8); (b) faith, under a renewed sense of urgent need, falls back into prayer, and again rises to hope and praise (verses 9-16); (c) faith, for the third time driven to prayer, rises quickly to assurance, praise and witness, and there abides (verses 20, 22-24). Cf. our Lord's threefold prayer in Gethsemane. See also 2 Cor. xii. 8.

(2) What does the Psalmist pray for in verses 1-4, what in verses 9-13, and what in verses 17, 18, 21 (R.V.)?

(3) Note the recurring 'Thou art' in verses 3, 5, 6 (R.V. mg.), 7. What else does the Psalmist say of God? Can you echo his words?

Notes.—(1) lxxi. 7. 'I am as a wonder'; with reference to his sufferings. Cf. Is. lii. 14.

(2) Verses 10, 11. Read as in R.V. 'Soul' in verse 10 means 'life'.

(3) Verse 15. 'The numbers thereof'; i.e. of God's mercies. Cf. Ps. xl. 5.

(4) Verses 16-18. Read as in R.V. Note the double 'declared'.

(5) Verses 20, 21. See R.V. and cf. 2 Cor. i. 9, 10.

Day 7. Ps. lxxii.

This is a prophetic psalm, in which Christ is typified by Solomon, whose name means 'Peace'.

(1) What are the two outstanding personal characteristics of Christ as King, as seen in this psalm? See verses 1, 2 and 12-14, and cf. Ps. cxvi. 5.

(2) What does the psalm say will be (a) the results; (b) the extent of His rule? See especially as regards (a) verses 3-7, 12-14, 16, 17, and as regards (b) verses 8-11.

(3) Does not this psalm give a perfect picture of that happy earth which men are vainly trying to bring into being by their own wisdom and work? But, according to Scripture, who alone can bring it to pass, and to whom, therefore, should men look for its accomplishment? See verses 1, 17, 18, 19.

Notes.—(1) Verse 6. 'The mown grass'; i.e. meadows that have been mown, and need fresh rain. Cf. Am. vii. 1.

(2) Verses 7, 8. Read as in R.V. 'The river' is the Euphrates.

(3) Verse 16. 'An handful'; better, 'abundance', as in R.V. 'Earth'; better, 'land', as in R.V. mg.

(4) Verses 18, 19. This doxology is not part of the original psalm, but is added as the close of Book ii.

NUMBERS

INTRODUCTION

(See New Bible Handbook, pp. 115-123, 143-146)

In the book of Numbers the narrative of Israel's journey from Egypt, interrupted at the foot of Sinai (Ex. xix) for the giving of the law, is resumed. The history, however, is throughout the book alternated with further laws and enactments. The book is a story of failure. The people are brought to the edge of the promised land, but owing to unbelief and disobedience are prevented from entering in. Then follows the long forty years of wandering in the wilderness, passed over almost in silence except for one or two incidents. Finally, the people come again to Kadesh-barnea, the whole generation that came out of Egypt as adults being dead, with three exceptions. Their first conquests are recounted, and their destiny foretold in the mysterious prophecies of Balaam.

ANALYSIS

Week 9. NUMBERS I–XI

Day 1. Nu. i and ii. The numbering and position of the tribes.

(1) Who exactly were numbered, and what light does this throw upon the nature of Christian service? Cf. 2 Cor. x. 3-6; Eph. vi. 10-13. What tribe was not included, and why? Yet see x. 8, 9, xxxi. 6; Dt. xx. 2.

(2) Draw a sketch of the ground plan of the camp, showing how the tribes were grouped round the tabernacle. Cf. 1 Cor. xiv. 33, 40; Col. ii. 5. But did the safety of the tabernacle lie in the numbers and organization of the tribes? And if not, where did it lie? See Zp. iii. 17.

(3) What bound this great multitude together into one? And how far is there a parallel here to the oneness of believers in Christ? Cf. Eph. iv. 4-6.

Day 2. Nu. iii.

(1) What work was assigned to the Levites, and how was it divided among the three 'families' of the tribe? What location in the camp was given to each of these families and what to Moses

and Aaron? If the family of Merari should be tempted to feel that their work was less honourable than that of the Kohathites, what fact would still every murmur? See verses 5, 36, and 45 (last clause).

(2) How did the tribe of Levi come to occupy this official position? And how was the difficulty that there were 273 more 'first-born' than there were Levites, adjusted? Notice that as the question of sin was not present, there was no need for the shedding of blood. Contrast Eph. i. 7; 1 Pet. i. 18, 19.

Day 3. Nu. iv.

(1) How do the instructions of verses 1-20 bring out in a specially impressive way the holiness of God? Cf. Is. vi. 2, 3; Rev. iv. 8.

(2) Each Levite had his appointed task. Does this hold also in Christian service? Cf. Mk. xiii. 34; Eph. iv. 7. What was the reason for the age limits for the Levites' service? Need we fear that the Lord will expect of us service beyond our experience, or that we have not strength to bear?

Day 4. Nu. v–vi. 21.

(1) v. 1-4. What three kinds of person were to be excluded from the camp, and why? What was this meant to teach concerning the nature of God?

(2) v. 11-31. Consider this, to us, strange enactment from the point of view of the protection it afforded to the innocent woman who was unjustly suspected. Water is often used as typical of the word of God. Do you see any parallel here with Heb. iv. 12, 13?

(3) In what ways did the Nazirite's separation to the Lord find expression? Cf. Heb. ix. 10 (R.V.), and for a New Testament parallel, see Rom. xii. 1, 2. What may the fact that even the very separation of the Nazirite had to be cleansed by a sin-offering teach us as to our constant dependence upon the sacrifice of Christ, if our service is to be accepted of God? Cf. Heb. ix. 13, 14.

Day 5. Nu. vi. 22–viii. 4.

(1) vi. 22-27. What is the significance of Jehovah's 'name' being put upon the children of Israel? See Dt. xxviii. 10; Dn. ix. 18, 19.

(2) With the threefold blessing of Aaron cf. 2 Cor. xiii. 14. What blessings would the person thus blessed enjoy?

(3) How does chapter vii show the spirit both of brotherliness, unity, and also of liberality prevailing at this time among the

princes of Israel? What was the reason for their gifts, and what example is given by them for our instruction? Cf. 2 Cor. v. 14, 15, ix. 15.

Day 6. Nu. viii. 5–x. 10.

(1) viii. 5-26. What was the relation of the Levites to God, to Aaron and his sons, and to the people? What may the solemn and elaborate ceremonies required for their purification and consecration to God's service in outward things teach us concerning our own need of inward purification, who are called to render spiritual service before God? Cf. Rom. vi. 13; Tit. ii. 14; 2 Cor. vi. 17–vii. 1.

(2) What principles concerning guidance may be found in ix. 15-23 which are applicable also to us?

Notes.—(1) ix. 1-14 describes how provision was made for those prevented from observing the passover at the proper time.

(2) x. 1-10. The trumpets had a message manwards (verses 1-8) and a message Godwards (verses 9, 10).

Day 7. Nu. x. 11–xi.

The second section of the book begins here. The Israelites leave Mount Sinai, and the order of the tribes, when marching, is outlined.

(1) How may Moses' argument in the case of Hobab be adapted for our own use in inviting others to live the life of pilgrimage?

(2) Who were they that led the Israelites into discontent? See xi. 4 and cf. Ex. xii. 38. Why was the Lord's anger kindled greatly? See Ps. lxxviii. 18-20. What is the spiritual counterpart of 'the fleshpots of Egypt', and do we hanker after them? Are we looking backwards or forwards in our following of Christ? See 1 Cor. x. 6; Eph. v. 3-10.

(3) What different aspects of God's character are revealed in chapter xi?

Week 10.　Numbers xii–xx

Day 1. Nu. xii and xiii.

(1) What moved Miriam and Aaron to criticize Moses? Cf. Ex. xviii. 6. How did the meekness of Moses, spoken of in xii. 3, manifest itself on this occasion, and what testimony did God bear to him? Cf. Heb. iii. 1-6; 1 Pet. ii. 23.

(2) How are faith and unbelief illustrated in the story of the spies? What is our own attitude towards Canaan, the land of God's promises? Is it that of xiii. 30, or that of xiii. 31? Cf. Phil. iii. 13, 14; Acts xx. 22-24.

Day 2. Nu. xiv.

(1) Contrast the faithless 'many' (note the frequent occurrence of the word 'all' in this chapter) with the faithful few. How does this chapter show that unbelief is not only sin, but folly? Cf. Lk. ix. 23, 24; Heb. iii. 12, 13.

(2) What life-long disqualification did the sin of the people, though pardoned, bring upon them—and this though they had all been numbered at the beginning as 'able to go forth to war' (Nu. i. 3)? See 1 Cor. ix. 27, x. 1-6.

Day 3. Nu. xv.

Verses 1-31 give regulations to be observed after entering Canaan.

(1) Verses 1-12. The size of the meat ('meal', R.V.) offering accompanying a blood sacrifice was to be in proportion to the value of the sacrificial animal. May we not learn something about God's character from this, that He desires to see balance and becomingness in our service of Him? Cf. Rom. xvi. 2; Phil. i. 27; 1 Tim. ii. 10; Tit. ii. 1, 3; Phm. 8 (R.V.).

(2) There were some kinds of sin for which the law provided no atonement. What were these? Contrast Acts xiii. 39.

Note.—Verse 38. 'Fringes' or 'tassels' (R.V. mg.) made of twisted thread and attached by a blue ribbon to the robe, to remind the wearer of the commandments of the Lord and of his obligation, as one who is 'holy', to keep them. Cf. Dt. xxii. 12; Mt. xxiii. 5 ('border' or 'tassels').

Day 4. Nu. xvi. 1-35.

(1) What evidence do you find that there was a double revolt: one against Moses and Aaron by Korah and other *Levites*, with 250 leading men of the tribes; and the other by Dathan and Abiram, of the tribe of *Reuben*, against Moses? What was the ground of complaint in each case, and wherein was it wrong? Cf. Heb. v. 4; 2 Cor. x. 18.

(2) Try to picture the double judgment in verses 32-35. Why was it of such severity? In answering this question, reflect upon what might have happened to Israel if the revolt had succeeded.

Day 5. Nu. xvi. 36–xviii. 7.

(1) In what three ways in this portion did God strengthen and confirm the position and privileges of Aaron? This was essential for the time being, until He should come who should be the perfect High Priest. See Heb. vii. 11, 18, 19.

(2) Reflect on Aaron's character, how strong his actions were *when with Moses* (Ex. xi. 10; Nu. xiv. 5, xvi. 46-50), and how weak

when left by himself (Ex. xxxii. 1-6, 21-24). Was the difference between the two men simply one of natural character or had it a deeper ground? Where did Moses find his strength? See Heb. xi. 27b.

Day 6. Nu. xviii. 8–xix.

(1) What assurance may we find in xviii. 8-32 that God will make all needful provision for the needs of those whom He calls to special service? Cf. Mt. vi. 33, 34; Phil. iv. 19; Heb. xiii. 5, 6.

(2) What are the special features of the sacrifice described in xix? Note the animal, the place of sacrifice, and the ritual. For what purpose were the ashes used?

(3) What corresponds in Christian experience to defilement arising from contact with death? See Eph. ii. 1; Heb. ix. 14 ('dead works'); Rom. vi. 16, 21. Consider how this sacrifice is a type of the sacrifice of Christ (a) in its abiding efficacy and constant accessibility; (b) in its cleansing power; and (c) in its absolute necessity (verses 13 and 20).

Notes.—(1) xix. 9. 'Purification for sin'; better, as in R.V., 'sin offering'.

(2) As the efficacy of the sacrifice was stored up, as it were, in the ashes, so the efficacy of the blood of Christ is stored up in the word of the gospel, and exerts its cleansing power when the believer whose conscience is defiled by sin submits to the gospel as applied by the Holy Spirit. See Heb. ix. 13-14; 1 Jn. i. 9.

Day 7. Nu. xx.

(1) Note the place—Kadesh (verse 1), and recall what had happened there (see xiii. 26) forty years before. Do you think that the memory of this, and the discovery of the same spirit as of old in the new generation, together with sorrow over the death of Miriam, may all have combined to make Moses less ready to meet this new test?

(2) What was Moses' sin in this instance? See verses 10, 12, and 24; also Dt. xxxii. 51 and Ps. cvi. 32, 33.

(3) Reflect upon the life of Miriam. See Ex. ii. 7, xv. 20, 21; Nu. xii; Mi. vi. 4.

Note.—Verse 14. 'Thy brother Israel'; see Gn. xxxvi. 1.

Week 11. NUMBERS XXI–XXIX

Day 1. Nu. xxi.

(1) In our Lord's application of the story of the brazen serpent to Himself in Jn. iii. 14, 15, what parallels do you find (a) between the condition of the Israelites bitten by serpents and man's

condition as a sinner, and (b) between the method of salvation in each case? Why was a serpent chosen as the object to be set upon the pole? See 2 Cor. v. 21.

(2) What evidence is there in this chapter that the new generation, of which Israel was now composed, were being disciplined to form a powerful fighting force? To what various forms of discipline were they subjected (see verses 2, 6, and 28) and what campaigns did they fight? Cf. Rom. v. 1-5.

Notes.—(1) Verse 4. This part of the journey was not only circuitous, but through specially arid desert. Hence the people's discouragement.

(2) Verses 16-18. In this case the Israelites did not receive water out of a rock, but had to dig for it under the sand.

Day 2. Nu. xxii.

(1) In approaching the story of Balaam, a clue to his real character and motives is given in three New Testament passages. See 2 Pet. ii. 15, 16; Jude 11; Rev. ii. 14.

(2) What was God's first command to Balaam? When it was so plain and unequivocal, why did Balaam later ask God again (verse 19)?

(3) What command did God give Balaam the second time? How would the incident of the angel in the way tend to keep Balaam in obedience?

Day 3. Nu. xxiii.

(1) The Israelites probably knew nothing of this attempt to injure them. How then does this chapter show God's protective care over His people and His power to turn intended evil into blessing? Cf. Is. liv. 17; Mi. vi. 5.

(2) In what respects was the last claim of verse 9 true of Israel? Cf. Ex. xxxiii. 16, xix. 5, 6; 1 Ki. viii. 53.

(3) In Balaam's second prophecy (verses 18-24), on what grounds is the certainty of Israel's success based? Compare with this the grounds on which the assurance of salvation for the believer is based in Rom. viii. 28-39.

Note.—With xxiii. 10b cf. xxxi. 8.

Day 4. Nu. xxiv and xxv.

(1) In what ways, according to Balaam's prophecies, would God bless Israel? Where do we find in his words a distant vision of the Messiah?

(2) With xxv. 1-5 cf. xxxi. 16. In spite of Balaam's knowledge of God and professions of virtue, what were the dominant motives of his character? Cf. 2 Cor. xi. 14; 2 Tim. ii. 19; Mt. vii. 18-20.

Note.—xxv. 13. 'Made an atonement'. The Hebrew word literally means 'cover up'. The normal method of atonement was by a substitutionary blood sacrifice (cf. Heb. ix. 22), but there are some instances, as in this case, where the sin was sufficiently covered by other means. See also Ex. xxxii. 30; Nu. xvi. 46.

Day 5. Nu. xxvi.

(1) A new generation had arisen (see verses 64, 65), and a comparison with chapter i shows that while the total number remained nearly the same, some tribes had increased in number and some decreased. How did this affect their inheritance in the land? Is our own strength increased or diminished since first we followed Jesus Christ?

(2) What lessons may we learn from the fact that those who were numbered at the first census perished in the wilderness? See 1 Cor. x. 1-5; Heb. iii. 17-19; and with verse 65 cf. Heb. xii. 25.

Day 6. Nu. xxvii.

(1) What was commendable in the action of the daughters of Zelophehad? And to what result, larger than the mere granting of their request, did it lead? Cf. Ex. xx. 12; Nu. xxxvi.

(2) What was Moses' request when commanded to prepare for death? What light does this throw upon his character?

(3) In what important respect was Joshua's commission, as here described, inferior to that of Moses'? Cf. Eph. iv. 7.

Note.—Verse 21. 'Urim'; see note on Ex. xxviii. 30 (Vol. 1, p. 61).

Day 7. Nu. xxviii and xxix. Review of the sacrifices of Israel.

(1) Distinguish between the daily sacrifice throughout the year offered every morning and evening (xxviii. 3-8) and the additional sacrifices (a) on the sabbath (xxviii. 9, 10); (b) at the new moon each month (xxviii. 11-15); (c) throughout the feast of unleavened bread (xxviii. 17-25, see note below); (d) at the feast of weeks (xxviii. 26-31); (e) at the blowing of trumpets (xxix. 1-6); (f) on the day of atonement (xxix. 7-11); (g) at the feast of tabernacles (xxix. 12-38).

(2) What was the purpose of all these sacrifices? See xxviii. 2. What takes their place under the new covenant? See Heb. x. 1-18.

Notes.—(1) xxviii. 24. The meaning is that the sacrifices prescribed above in verses 19-22 are to be offered daily throughout the feast. The word 'meat' in the Hebrew is 'bread' as in verse 2. See R.V. mg.

(2) xxix. 39. In addition to the regular public sacrifices, the people offered private sacrifices, such as are prescribed in Lv. i-xii.

Week 12. NUMBERS XXX–DEUTERONOMY III

Day 1. Nu. xxx and xxxi.

(1) What is the teaching of chapter xxx upon responsibility in speech? Cf. Ec. v. 2, 4-6; Mt. v. 33-37. Observe that our Lord extends the responsibility to *every* kind of utterance (Mt. xii. 36).

(2) What may we learn from chapter xxxi concerning the relentless severity with which we must put to death the sins which, if indulged, will weaken and destroy our fitness in God's service? Cf. Col. iii. 5-11, R.V.

(3) Observe the recognition given to the Lord in the hour of victory.

Day 2. Nu. xxxii.

(1) What called forth from Moses so stern a rejoinder to the request of the two and a half tribes, and on what condition was their request granted? Are we playing our part in the winning of Christ's inheritance, or are we more concerned to secure the best for ourselves?

(2) What great principle with regard to sin is revealed in verse 23 of this chapter? Can you think of any instances in Scripture which illustrate its working?

Day 3. Nu. xxxiii and xxxiv.

(1) Many of the places on the journey cannot now be identified, but the fact remains that the miracle was wrought and Israel was brought out of Egypt to the borders of the promised land. What corresponding experience of God's saving power have you known?

(2) What policy was to be pursued towards the Canaanites, and what would be the consequences of its neglect? If Canaan represents the spiritual inheritance into which Jesus, here typified by Joshua, leads us, what attitude towards spiritual enemies is here set before us? Cf. Eph. v. 3-14.

(3) Chapter xxxiv. What are the boundaries of our inheritance in Christ? If knowledge of the promised inheritance and careful preparation for entering were thus required of Israel, what stimulus should this bring to ourselves? See Heb. iv. 11, vi. 11, 12.

Day 4. Nu. xxxv and xxxvi.

(1) For what purposes were the cities of refuge established, and what were the conditions on which security in a city of refuge was

available? See note below. Observe the gravity in God's sight of the crime of murder.

(2) Picture in imagination the anxious flight of the manslayer until the city of refuge was reached. Of what stage in a sinner's salvation may this be taken as an illustration? Cf. Heb. vi. 18b.

Notes.—(1) xxxv. 12. 'Avenger' (Heb.). 'He that acts as kinsman'. It was an understood principle in primitive times that if a man took the life of another, he himself must be slain by the dead man's nearest relative. The establishment of cities of refuge provided safeguards against injustice (a) by distinguishing between accidental and intended manslaughter; and (b) by giving the manslayer, if he had acted unintentionally, a place of refuge.

(2) xxxvi. The previous decision about the inheritance of Zelophehad (see xxvii. 1-11) gave rise to the danger that the land of one tribe might pass into the possession of men of another tribe. Hence the further law was promulgated that daughters who received an inheritance must marry within their own tribe.

DEUTERONOMY

INTRODUCTION

(See New Bible Handbook, pp. 115-123, 146-153)

THE book of Deuteronomy finds the people again on the threshold of the land after the forty years of wandering. Moses, who is about to lay down his great task, addresses them before his death. The book consists chiefly of his addresses. Naturally, there is much matter repeated from earlier portions of the Pentateuch and, as naturally, it is generally in a rather different form. Laws that were promulgated in the wilderness are adapted for use in the land. New matter, such as that relating to the central sanctuary and the setting up of the kingdom, is introduced. Finally, Moses, after solemn warnings to the people, appoints his successor, and ascends Mount Nebo to be laid to rest by God.

ANALYSIS

i–iv. Moses' first address. Theme: God's blessing and guidance in the past.

v–xxvi. Moses' second address. He reminds the people of the law, and repeats many criminal, civil, and religious instructions, varying them when necessary in view of the coming settled life in the land.

xxvii, xxviii. Blessings and curses, and the conditions on which each would come on the people.

xxix, xxx. The covenant. Foreshadowings of God's purpose in the gospel.

Day 5. Dt. i.

(1) The burden of this chapter is the people's sin in refusing to go forward to the promised land. How is the sin described (see verses 26, 27, 32), and what made the guilt of it greater (see note below on verses 9-18; also verses 31, 33)?

(2) What solemn lesson is taught in verses 40-45? Cf. Is. lix. 1, 2; Je. xi. 14; Heb. xii. 17.

Note.—Verses 9-18. These verses seem to be introduced to show that the people were both numerous and well organized when they reached Kadesh, and therefore fully ready to enter the land if their eyes had been upon the Lord.

Day 6. Dt. ii.

(1) What do we learn from this chapter of the sovereignty of God over the nations? Cf. Acts xvii. 26. Why were Edom, Moab, and Ammon spared? See verses 4, 9, 19.

(2) What phrase, twice repeated, shows the necessary link between God's gift of the inheritance and His people's enjoyment of it? See verses 24 and 31 and Jos. i. 3. Does not failure here account for much of the poverty of our Christian experience?

Notes.—(1) Verses 4-8. This is not the same incident as that of Nu. xx. 14-21, but a later instruction when Israel had reached the eastern border of Edom.

(2) Verses 10-12 and 20-23 are parenthetical notes on ancient history.

Day 7. Dt. iii.

(1) How did the conquest of Sihon and of Og disprove the faithless fears of forty years before? Cf. i. 28 with ii. 36 and iii. 4-6.

(2) In verse 22 Moses passes on to Joshua the word that God had previously given to himself (see verse 2). What general principle is here illustrated? Cf. Jn. xv. 15b; 1 Jn. i. 3; Mt. xxviii. 20a.

(3) Try to imagine the intensity of Moses' desire in verses 24, 25. What insight are we given into prayer and its answer by this incident? Cf. Nu. xx. 12; Ps. cvi. 32, 33 (R.V.).

Notes.—(1) Verse 11. 'Bedstead' or possibly 'sarcophagus'. It was eleven feet long and six broad.

(2) Verse 26. 'For your sakes' or 'because of you'. The people's rebellion led to Moses' sin.

Week 13.   DEUTERONOMY IV–XI

Day 1. Dt. iv. 1-40.

This is the second part of Moses' first discourse, and consists of an exhortation based upon God's gracious dealings, as described in chapters i to iii.

(1) What is said about God in this portion, and about His relation to Israel?

(2) What is said about the word of God, spoken by Moses?

(3) Against what sin in particular are the people warned, and by what arguments is the warning reinforced?

Note.—Verses 1, 2, etc. 'Statutes, judgments, commandments, testimonies' (verse 45). These are all words describing the law in its different aspects.

Day 2. Dt. iv. 41–v.

With chapter v begins Moses' second discourse, extending to chapter xxvi. Chapter iv. 44-49 is the introductory superscription.

(1) What is the significance of the pronouns 'thy' and 'thou' which occur throughout the ten commandments? Cf. Lv. xix. 3; Ps. lxii. 12; Je. xvii. 10 ('every man').

(2) What is taught us in this portion of God's respect for human choice?

(3) What was it in the temper of the people that drew from God the words of commendation in verse 28, and the expression of His desire that it might so continue always (verse 29, R.V. mg.)?

Note.—v. 3. 'Our fathers', i.e. 'our forefathers', viz. the patriarchs. Cf. iv. 37; vii. 8.

Day 3. Dt. vi.

(1) What was God's purpose in giving the law? And what was the primary duty of the Israelite?   What was he to do, and what was he to beware of and not do?

(2) What insight is given in this chapter into the necessity and method of family religion?

Day 4. Dt. vii.

(1) Is there anything in the Christian's warfare corresponding to the uncompromising attitude to the peoples of the land which God required of Israel? See Mk. ix. 43-50; Eph. v. 11, 12.

(2) What reasons are given why Israel should be whole-heartedly obedient? And what application have they to ourselves?

(3) What picture is given in this chapter of God (a) in His love and willingness to bless His people, and (b) in His faithfulness and power?

Notes.—(1) Verse 2. 'Utterly destroy'. The Hebrew word means to separate to a deity (see R.V. mg.) and hence to put to death or destroy, as here and in verses 25, 26.

(2) Verse 20. 'The hornet', a powerful insect, whose attack in large numbers is dangerous and may prove fatal. Some take it, however, here and in Ex. xxiii. 28 and Jos. xxiv. 12 in a figurative sense, as meaning some plague or terror that spreads dismay.

Day 5. Dt. viii.

(1) What threefold purpose did God have in leading Israel through the experiences of the wilderness? How did our Lord apply verse 3b to His own case in Mt. iv. 4? With verse 5 cf. also Heb. xii. 7, 10, 11.

(2) In days of prosperity what subtle danger would beset them? And how were they to guard against it? Compare the advice which Barnabas gave to the church in Antioch (Acts xi. 23b).

Day 6. Dt. ix–x. 11.

(1) What further danger would follow on the heels of victory after they conquered the promised land? And how does Moses in this passage seek to safeguard them against it? Cf. Lk. xviii. 9-14.

(2) What does the example of Moses teach as to the responsibility and power of intercessory prayer? Note the costly nature of his prayer and the uncompromising dealing with sin that accompanied it. On what grounds did Moses base his plea for the people? And what was the outcome? Cf. Jas. v. 16.

Note.—x. 6-10 are a parenthesis. See R.V.

Day 7. Dt. x. 12–xi.

(1) What nine or more commandments are found in x. 12–xi. 1? Consider the particular meaning of each, and ask yourself: 'Am I thus living?' Cf. Rom. viii. 4 (R.V.).

(2) What three main arguments does Moses use in chapter xi to lead the people to give heed to God's commands, and to teach them to their children? See verses 2-9, 10-17, 22-25.

Week 14. DEUTERONOMY XII–XXV
Day 1. Dt. xii and xiii.

In this second part of the long discourse extending from v to xxvi, Moses sets forth in greater detail the statutes and laws which God commanded him to teach.

(1) What provisions and safeguards against the practice of idolatry are found in these chapters, and what judgments upon those who do this evil? See also xvii. 2-7.

(2) What application may such commands as are given in xii. 2 and 3 and xiii. 5, 8-10, 12-18 have in the life of a Christian? See Lk. xiv. 26; 2 Cor. vi. 14–vii. 1.

Note.—The provision of one sanctuary, to which all sacrifices must be brought, was a safeguard against idolatrous worship at ancient shrines of the Canaanites. Cf. 2 Ki. xvii. 10-12.

Day 2. Dt. xiv and xv.

These two chapters contain laws concerning (a) clean and unclean foods (xiv. 5-21); (b) tithing (xiv. 22-29); (c) the seventh year or year of release (xv. 1-18); and (d) firstling males of the herd or flock (xv. 19-23).

(1) What seven reasons are given for obedience to these laws, one of them being repeated several times? How far are these reasons applicable to ourselves? Cf. Jn. xv. 10.

(2) What light do these laws throw upon God's character? Do you find in the words of xv. 16 the expression of your own heart's resolve towards Christ? Cf. 2 Cor. v. 14, 15.

Notes.—(1) xiv. 1b. A reference to heathen mourning practices, signifying excessive grief. Cf. 1 Thes. iv. 13.

(2) xv. 1. 'Make a release', that is, let the debtor off.

Day 3. Dt. xvi and xvii.

(1) In connection with the feast of weeks and the feast of tabernacles, what two requirements are made of the worshipper, and why? With regard to free-will offerings, on what principle is the amount of the gift to be determined? Cf. 1 Cor. xvi. 2; 2 Cor. viii. 12; 1 Pet. i. 8.

(2) What was to be the character of Israel's king if one were appointed? And what was to be the source of his wisdom? Cf. 2 Tim. iii. 15-17.

Notes.—(1) xvi. 21. See R.V. and R.V. mg. The Ashera appears to have been a pole, planted by an altar, as a symbol of the god worshipped there.

(2) xvii. 8-13. If a case is too difficult for the local judge to handle (see xvi. 18-20) it is to be brought to the central sanctuary.

(3) xvii. 16, 17. Notice the word 'multiply' three times. Horses (power), wives, and wealth were coveted by kings of the time. See 1 Ki. x. 26-28, xi. 3, 4.

Day 4. Dt. xviii and xix.

(1) What were the special ministries of priests and prophets? Observe in chapter xviii how both alike were God's provision for His people's need. Of what kind of person in heathen religion did the prophets in Israel take the place?

(2) In whom was the prophecy of xviii. 18, 19 finally fulfilled? See Acts iii. 22, 23; vii. 37. Do we listen to Him as we should? Cf. Mk. ix. 7.

(3) In what way· do the regulations concerning cities of refuge both protect against injustice and at the same time enforce just penalty? See further Nu. xxxv.

Note.—xix. 14. This law is intended to guard the inheritance of the poor against the greed of wealthy neighbours. Cf. xxvii. 17; Pr. xxiii. 10, 11.

Day 5. Dt. xx and xxi.

These chapters contain laws designed to check savage cruelty in war and to make the Israelite armies an effective fighting force.

(1) Upon whom was their reliance in all their undertakings to be placed?

(2) What illustration do these chapters give both of the compassion and of the severity of God?

(3) What application do the writers of the New Testament make of xxi. 22, 23? See Jn. xix. 31; Gal. iii. 13; 1 Pet. ii. 24.

Day 6. Dt. xxii and xxiii.

(1) Compare xxii. 1-4 with our Lord's teaching in Mt. v. 43-48. How did He extend and deepen the law of brotherly compassion?

(2) What failures in moral behaviour are condemned in these chapters? Observe how the eye of God penetrates into every part of each man's soul and personal life. See xxiii. 14 and cf. Ps. cxxxix. 1-5, 23, 24.

Notes.—(1) xxii. 5. A practice associated with certain forms of heathen worship and therefore sternly forbidden.

(2) xxii. 9-11. Applied spiritually, these laws forbid the association of things morally incompatible. Cf. 2 Cor. vi. 14-16.

(3) xxiii. 15, 16. The reference appears to be to a slave fleeing from a foreign country and taking refuge in a city of Israel.

Day 7. Dt. xxiv and xxv.

(1) In the various laws in chapter xxiv inculcating kindly behaviour, to what motive is appeal twice made? Cf. Mt. xviii. 32, 33; Eph. v. 2.

(2) What application does Paul make of xxv. 4? See 1 Cor. ix. 9; 1 Tim. v. 18.

(3) Taking Amalek, grandson of Esau (Gn. xxxvi. 12), as a type of 'the flesh', that is, of our fallen carnal nature, compare what is said here with Gal. v. 17 and 24.

Week 15. DEUTERONOMY XXVI–XXXIV

Day 1. Dt. xxvi.

(1) In what way did the law require each Israelite to reflect upon and give thanks for national mercies? And for what mercies

was he specially to give thanks? Have not we far greater cause to do this? Cf. Ps. ciii. 1-5; Col. i. 12-14.

(2) Verses 16-19 are the closing exhortation of the discourse begun in chapter v. What covenant obligations did God and Israel respectively undertake? Under the new covenant what has God promised and what do we undertake?

Note.—Verses 12-15. See Dt. xiv. 28, 29. The Israelite, who has paid his third-year tithe, is to declare openly that he has obeyed God's command, and to pray for God's blessing.

Day 2. Dt. xxvii–xxviii. 14.

(1) What was Israel commanded to do after passing over Jordan? For the historical fulfilment, see Jos. viii. 30-35. How does this portion reveal God's desire for His people's happiness? Cf. xii. 7, 12, 18, xiv. 26, xvi. 11, 14, xxvi. 11.

(2) The offences mentioned in xxvii. 15-26 are mainly such as might escape the detection and punishment of courts of law. How does this fact add to the importance of these curses, solemnly and publicly declared, and assented to by the people?

(3) Contrast the blessings of xxviii. 1-14 in their nature with the New Testament phrase 'every spiritual blessing in heavenly places' (Eph. i. 3, R.V.). What difference between the old and new covenants is here indicated?

Day 3. Dt. xxviii. 15-68.

Verses 15-19 are in direct contrast to verses 1-6. Thereafter the curses are described in five paragraphs, which are somewhat similar in content. These are (1) verses 20-26; (2) verses 27-37; (3) verses 38-44; (4) verses 49-57; (5) verses 58-68.

(1) Examine these five paragraphs, noting their similarities. What are the evils contained in these curses?

(2) Verses 45-48. What attitude of heart would bring these curses upon them? Cf. Heb. x. 26-31, xii. 25-29.

Note.—Verse 46. 'For a sign and for a wonder'; a sign of divine judgment, and a wonder causing astonishment.

Day 4. Dt. xxix and xxx.

(1) Picture the moving scene described in xxix. 1, 2, 10, 11, and consider what strong reasons the people had for being loyal to Jehovah. Why, then, did Moses fear that they would not prove steadfast? See xxix. 4, 18, 19; Acts xx. 29, 30.

(2) For what purpose is revelation given, according to xxix. 29? Cf. Jas. i. 22.

(3) What is God's character as revealed in chapter xxx? And

what is man's responsibility? If the words of xxx. 11-14 could be spoken of the commandment given through Moses, how does Paul show that they are still more abundantly true of the gospel? See Rom. x. 6-9.

Note.—xxix. 19. 'To add drunkenness to thirst'. Read as in R.V. 'to destroy the moist with the dry', a proverbial expression meaning to destroy *all*. It expresses here that the outcome of the idolater's attitude and action is utter destruction.

Day 5. Dt. xxxi.

(1) What made it possible for Israel, and what makes it possible for us, to be 'strong and of a good courage' and 'to fear not, nor be affrighted', even when great human leaders pass away? See verses 1-8 and Heb. xiii. 7, 8 (R.V.).

(2) Notice in how many different ways the Lord, through Moses, sought to safeguard Israel against the backsliding which He knew, nevertheless, would take place. What alone can keep us steadfast? See 1 Pet. i. 5; Gal. v. 16. Cf. also Dt. xxxii. 46, 47.

Day 6. Dt. xxxii. 1-47.

The analysis of this magnificent poem is as follows:
(a) The writer's purpose and hope, verses 1-3 (see note below).
(b) God's perfections, and Israel's perversity, verses 4-6.
(c) God's goodness to Israel, verses 7-14.
(d) Israel's backsliding, verses 15-18.
(e) Divine judgment upon Israel, verses 19-29.
(f) The victory of heathen nations over Israel is of God's permitting, verses 30-35.
(g) But He will finally avenge His people and show them His mercy, verses 36-43.

(1) What is said of God in His essential attributes? And what, in contrast, of the nature of Israel?

(2) What did God do for Israel (at least seven things are mentioned in verses 7-14), and how did Israel requite His loving-kindness?

(3) What is God's purpose in His judgments, and what shall be the final outcome?

Notes.—(1) Verse 2. Better 'Let my teaching drop as the rain'—an expression of the writer's hope that his words may act upon the hearts of men as the rain and dew upon the soil.

(2) Verse 4. 'The Rock' (see also verses 15, 18, 30, 31, 37), a figure expressing the thought of a refuge and place of defence.

(3) Verse 8. 'According to the number', etc., that is, He reserved for Israel an inheritance adequate to their numbers.

(4) Verses 11 and 12. Read as in R.V.

(5) Verse 14. 'Fat of kidneys of wheat', that is, the choicest wheat.

(6) Verse 15. 'Jeshurun', a poetical name for Israel, signifying 'the upright one'. See Dt. xxxiii. 5, 26; Is. xliv. 2.

(7) Verse 29. 'Consider their latter end', that is, discern whither their perversity must lead.

(8) Verse 34. God is not unmindful of the sins of Israel's enemies.

Day. 7   Dt. xxxii. 48–xxxiv.

Chapter xxxiii, like Gn. xlix, requires for its full study much research.

(1) In the light of such words as verses 3, 7 (last clause, R.V.), 12, 16b, 23b, 25, 27, etc., consider how great were Israel's blessings. Yet are not our blessings in Christ much greater still?

(2) Ponder the death of Moses (xxxii. 48-52, xxxiv).   What lessons may it teach us?

I PETER

INTRODUCTION

(See New Bible Handbook, pp. 397-400)

THE Epistle is attested by very early external evidence as a genuine writing of the apostle Peter. It was written from 'Babylon' (v. 13) between A.D. 64 and 67; but it is impossible to be certain whether this was the literal Babylon, or Rome under this figurative title (cf. Rev. xiv. 8), or a district so named in Egypt (today Old Cairo) where a Jewish colony existed.

The Epistle is addressed to the 'sojourners of the dispersion' in Asia Minor. But though Peter was the apostle of the circumcision, and the term 'dispersion' was ordinarily applied to the Jews scattered among the nations, the Epistle itself contains clear evidence that its readers at least included converted heathen (i. 14, ii. 9, 10, iv. 3, 4), who were addressed as the spiritual Israel dispersed among the heathen.

The Epistle had a double purpose: to comfort and encourage the Christians in a time of persecution actual or threatened, and to exhort them, all the more on account of this danger, to holiness of living. The problem of suffering, especially the suffering of God's people, was the main subject of the Book of Job, and we have met with contributions to its solution again and again in Isaiah and in the Gospel of John. In this Epistle, as in Job, it is of primary importance, and here we find a noble and satisfying answer to Job's despairing questionings. Compare, for example, Jb. x. with 1 Pet. i. 6-9. Peter has a key to the problem which Job had not. He knew that a Sinless One had suffered and died, bearing our sins in His body on the tree; so that undeserved suffering has the halo of His glory round it, and to bear it aright is to follow in the steps of the Redeemer.

ANALYSIS

Week 16. 1 Peter

Day 1. 1 Pet. i. 1–12.

(1) By what means and for what purposes does God choose His elect? Notice the mention of both these purposes in Ex. xxiv. 7, 8, and see note below.

(2) How can the Christian 'rejoice with joy unspeakable' (verse 8) while he is 'in heaviness through manifold temptations' (verse 6)? What causes of joy does Peter enumerate in verses 3-9? Cf. Is. lxi. 3.

(3) What light is thrown in verses 10-12 upon the work of the prophets? Notice how they were looking forward to the coming of Christ, and contrast this with our looking forward to His second coming.

Note.—Verse 2. 'Sprinkling of the blood of Jesus Christ.' The sprinkling of the blood signifies the acceptance and ratification of the new covenant and all that it entails. See Ex. xxiv. 7, 8 and Heb. xii. 24, xiii. 20, 21.

Day 2. 1 Pet. i. 13–ii. 3.

(1) What instructions are given to the Christian? What kind of life should he be living and why?

(2) What is the place of fear in the Christian life? Cf. Heb. x. 18-31, and contrast Rom. viii. 15. Is there any contradiction with the latter verse?

(3) By what means are we born again? and what, according to ii. 1, 2, are the negative and positive conditions of spiritual growth? Consider these closely.

Day 3. 1 Pet. ii. 4-17.

(1) Under what figures does Peter speak of the Christian Church? See the *Analysis* above. Each figure suggests special blessings and responsibilities conveyed to the individual by membership therein; can you identify these?

(2) When Peter thinks of Christians in the world, how does he address them? What qualities of citizenship should the Christian show? See verses 13-17.

Notes.—(1) Verses 4-8. Peter justifies his comparison of Christ to a stone from three Old Testament passages, Ps. cxviii. 22; Is. viii. 14, xxviii. 16. To the believer Christ is the corner stone on which the whole building rests; to the unbeliever He is a cause of stumbling.

(2) Verse 16. 'A cloke of maliciousness'; i.e. 'an excuse for base conduct' (Weymouth). Cf. Gal. v. 13.

Day 4. 1 Pet. ii. 18–iii. 12.

(1) If a Christian has to work under someone who is unreasonable or perhaps hates him for being a Christian, what encouragements and warnings are there for him in this section? For what purpose, according to verse 24, did the Lord Jesus Christ die for us, and are we realizing this purpose in our lives? With ii. 22-25 compare Is. liii. 4-12.

(2) What qualities in wife and husband make for a happy and harmonious wedded life?

(3) What seven characteristics are mentioned in verses 8 and 9, which should make Christians in their mutual relationships? How does the quotation from Ps. xxxiv confirm that this is the way of blessing?

Day 5. 1 Pet. iii. 13–iv. 7.

Peter returns here to the subject of suffering. Cf. i. 6, 7, ii. 19-21. The passage should be read in the R.V.

(1) In what spirit should the Christian explain his faith to a hostile questioner? Seven points are mentioned in verses 14-16.

(2) The Christian should not suffer for *evil* doing, but he may suffer, if God so will, because of well doing. What was the experience of the Lord Himself in this respect? How does Peter describe here the nature, purpose and issue of His sufferings? Cf. Heb. ii. 10, xii. 2.

(3) With what, then, are we to arm ourselves for the conflict? And what incentives to a life of holiness in an unfriendly world are set before us? See iv. 1-5.

Notes.—(1) iii. 19, 20. Two main interpretations have been given of these obscure verses. The earlier, which prevailed up to the time of the Reformation, and to which many still adhere, regard the word 'spirit' in verse 18 as referring to the human spirit of our Lord, and takes the meaning of verse 19 to be that between His death and resurrection Christ preached to certain spirits in prison in the nether world. The later interpretation, widely held after the Reformation, regards the word 'spirit' as referring to the Holy Spirit and takes the meaning to be that Christ in the Spirit preached through Noah to the spirits of the wicked of that day. Neither interpretation is without difficulty.

(2) iii. 21. The reference to baptism is in a sense a digression. The meaning is that as Noah and his family were saved through water by means of the ark, so believers are saved through the waters of baptism by Christ our Saviour. Baptism denotes not an outward, but an inward cleansing.

(3) iv. 6. Here again interpreters differ as to whether 'the dead' spoken of were alive or dead at the time of hearing. The main teaching of the passage is not affected, whichever view is taken.

Day 6. 1 Pet. iv. 8-19.

(1) In the Christian community what should be common to all, and how is the individuality of each member rightly expressed? Cf. Jn. xiv. 10; Rom. xii. 4-8; 2 Cor. iii. 5, 6.

(2) In verses 12-19 Peter touches on a subject that must have pressed sorely upon those to whom he was writing, namely, the imminent prospect of a much severer trial than they had yet experienced. What grounds for comfort and courage does he give? Observe his insistence here and throughout the Epistle upon the avoidance of evil. Cf. i. 14, ii. 11, 12, 16, iii. 10, 11, 16, 17, iv. 2.

Day 7. 1 Pet. v.

(1) What qualities of Christian leadership are emphasized in verses 1-4? What light does the answer to this question throw upon the claim of the pope to be Peter's successor?

(2) Peter has spoken of *love* more than once (i. 22, iii. 8, iv. 8). What other grace does he emphasize here, and how is it to be manifested both manwards and Godwards?

(3) Who is our chief adversary, and how is he to be resisted? If suffering be in the foreground of the apostle's picture what lies beyond as the final goal?

JOSHUA

INTRODUCTION

(See New Bible Handbook, pp. 90-93, 154-160)

THE book of Joshua tells us nothing about its authorship, but in Jos. xv. 63 we have a clear indication that it was written before David's capture of Jerusalem.

The book tells the story of the crossing of Jordan, the conquest of the promised land and its division among the tribes, ending with the death of Joshua after he had obtained from the whole people a solemn promise (soon to be broken) that they would be faithful to Jehovah.

The apparent discrepancy between the seemingly universal conquest of Palestine (in ix–xi) and the stubborn, and often unsuccessful fighting referred to in the latter part of the book and in the early part of Judges, is explained by the fact that in ix–xi the united army of Israel was meeting and crushing organized resistance. But after the division of the land, the Israelite army broke up into its component tribes, each of which attempted to possess its own lot, meeting with a stubborn resistance from those who had fled from the united army or had not come in its way. The 'discrepancy' is further explained by (1) the spiritual declension of the people; (2) the ruling geographical factor of Palestine, the division into the hill country and the coastal plain. The latter remained unconquered until David's time.

This book, especially in its early chapters, is full of most valuable spiritual teaching. The land of Canaan is to be regarded, not as a type of heaven, but rather as symbolizing *God's promised blessings in Christ.* The entry of the Israelites into the land thus becomes for us a picture of the life of victory over our spiritual enemies, and of the Christian's appropriation, through the fight of faith, of all God's blessings. Viewed in this light the story of Rahab and the spies, the crossing of Jordan into the promised land, the circumcision at Gilgal, the vision of the captain of the Lord's host, the fall of the walls of Jericho, the consequences of Achan's sin, the destruction of the Canaanites—all these incidents have a meaning which goes far beyond the historical facts, telling us of the conditions under which God's greatest spiritual blessings are gained or forfeited.

ANALYSIS

i.	Introductory.
ii–v.	Preparations for the conquest: Rahab and the spies; Jordan crossed; the people circumcised.
vi–viii.	The first victories; Jericho and Ai taken; the fall of the latter delayed by Achan's sin.
ix.	Gibeon makes peace by a trick.
x, xi.	The crushing of organized resistance first in the south, then in the north.
xii.	The list of the conquered kings.
xiii–xix.	The division of the land: the tribes attempt to take possession of their lots.
xx, xxi.	The cities of refuge and the Levitical cities.
xxii.	The altar of witness beyond Jordan.
xxiii, xxiv.	Closing scenes in the life of Joshua; the people's promise.

Week 17. JOSHUA I–IX

Day 1. Jos. i.

(1) What promises did God give to Joshua, and on what conditions did they depend?

(2) What do you learn here about the importance of Bible study and the blessing attached to obedience, both for the individual and for the nation?

Note.—In meditating on this passage, remember the spiritual significance of Canaan (see *Introduction*, last paragraph). With verse 8 cf. Ps. i. 2. With verses 13 and 15 cf. Heb. iv. 8-11.

Day 2. Jos. ii.

(1) How does the story in this chapter justify the statement in Hebrews that Rahab's action was due to faith? Compare her words with the actual position of the Israelites at the time, and note especially verse 11. See also vi. 22-25; Heb. xi. 31.

(2) What parallel is suggested to you by the house protected by the scarlet thread? With verse 19 cf. Ex. xii. 22.

(3) Observe how Rahab's faith kindled the faith of Joshua (cf. carefully verses 24 and 9). What stimulus does this give us in the life of faith?

Day 3. Jos. iii and iv.

The symmetrical arrangement of these chapters is striking. There is an introduction (iii. 1-6) and a conclusion (iv. 19-24); and in between are three sections (iii. 7-17, iv. 1-14, iv. 15-18), each of which begins with a command of God to Joshua, then goes on to state Joshua's communication of it to the people, and finally relates its fulfilment in act.

(1) Compare the attitude of the people here with that of their fathers in Nu. xiv. 1-4. Were not the dangers the same, and God's presence the same (cf. verse 10, 'the living God is among you', with Nu. xiv. 9, 'the Lord is with us')? Why, then, this difference in attitude and action? Are *we* willing now to go forward to 'possess our possessions' in Christ?

(2) Notice the various stages in the crossing of the Jordan as given in iii. 5, 6, 15, 16 and iv. 1, noting the parts played by God and by the people. Is there any counterpart to these stages in the spiritual life in entering into God's blessings? Cf. 2 Cor. vii. 1; Rom. xiii. 14; Heb. xi. 29; Jas. ii. 20; Lk. ix. 62. With iii. 4 cf. Is. xxviii. 16, last clause.

(3) The way through the Jordan was opened by the ark (iv. 7), which typifies Christ. Read the incident of the twelve stones buried in Jordan, and the twelve stones taken out of Jordan and set up in Canaan, in the light of Rom. vi. 4.

Day 4. Jos. v and vi.

(1) Circumcision was the sign of covenant relationship (see Gn. xvii. 9-14). What is the spiritual significance of it for us at the beginning of life in Canaan? See Dt. xxx. 6; Je. iv. 4; Col. ii. 11.

(2) Have you taken up the position that Joshua took in relation to the Lord? See v. 14, 15, and cf. Ps. xvi. 2 (R.V.).

(3) What lessons on Christian service does the story of the fall of Jericho teach us? See especially vi. 2, vi. 14, 15, vi. 16 and vi. 19. Cf. also 2 Cor. x. 4; Heb. xi. 30.

Note.— With vi. 25 cf. Mt. i. 5. Salmon may have been one of the spies.

Day 5. Jos. vii.

(1) Why was prayer alone of no avail on this occasion? What had to be done first? See Is. lix. 1-2.

(2) What do verses 11 and 12 teach us about the power of one man's sin to infect a whole community? When God looked at this one sin, how many sins did He see in it? Reflect on the evil and folly of disobedience.

Day 6. Jos. viii.

(1) Why do you think God bade Joshua take all the people of war, and set an ambush in addition, for the capture of so small a place? Cf. viii. 3, 4.

(2) With verses 34, 35 cf. i. 7-8; Acts xx. 27; 2 Tim. iii. 16-17. What do these verses teach us about our duty as Christians in relation to the Scriptures?

Day 7. Jos. ix.

(1) Wherein exactly lay the subtlety of the plan of the people of Gibeon? Cf. verse 1 with Dt. vii. 1-2, and then cf. Jos. ix. 9. How did the leaders of Israel come to fall into the trap?

(2) What further mistake did Joshua and the princes *avoid*? Can you find a clause in Ps. xv referring to it?

Week 18. JOSHUA X–XXII

Day 1. Jos. x.

(1) When a man publicly allies himself to the Christian cause he must expect opposition from the enemy; but what has this chapter to say about the responsibility of Christians towards each other in such a case?

(2) How does Joshua use experience to deepen faith? With verse 26 cf. Col. iii. 5, R.V.mg.

Note.—Verses 12-14. R.V. mg.: 'Sun, be silent'. It would seem that a miracle of some kind is here described, but it is not necessary to assume that this involved the stoppage of the earth's diurnal motion, nor is much gained by speculation as to what secondary causes God used to work His ends.

Day 2. Jos. xi and xii.

(1) Follow the story of chapters x–xii on a map, and note how chapter x refers to the southern half of the country and xi. 1-15 to the northern half. In what respect did Joshua's conquest follow a similar course in the north as in the south? To what causes was his final victory due?

(2) What is the spiritual value of making a list of battles fought and won? Cf. xiii. 1-8 and xxiii. 14.

Notes.—(1) xi. 20. See Dt. ix. 4, 5 and Gn. xv. 16, and cf. Ex. ix. 12. The Canaanites, like Pharaoh, were sentenced to go their own way—the way of destruction—because they had already chosen evil rather than good.

(2) In xi. 21 we read that Joshua cut off the Anakim from Hebron, Debir, and other places; in chapters xiv and xv it is Caleb and Othniel who take Hebron and Debir; while in x. 36-39 we have read that at a still earlier time Joshua took Hebron and Debir, and 'destroyed all the souls that were therein'. The explanation is that those whom Joshua is said to have killed on the earlier occasion were those whom he captured in the cities when he took them the first time; a considerable part of the population must have fled before he attacked the cities, and must have returned and reoccupied them while he was away in the north. xi. 21 describes in summary form operations which covered a long time, and attributes to Joshua as commander-in-chief what was done by Caleb and others under his orders.

(3) xi. 13; R.V. is important in this verse.

Day 3. Jos. xiii–xv. 12.

(1) God tells Joshua exactly what territories remain to be possessed. Are there in your life blessings promised to us in Christ which are not yet possessed, and remaining enemies to be subdued? Ask Him to reveal them to you with like precision.

(2) With xiv. 6-13 cf. Nu. xiii. 30 and xiv. 6-9. How does Caleb show that his faith has not wavered during the forty-five years of waiting? And what reason is here given for the reward that God gives him?

Day 4. Jos. xv. 13–xvii.

(1) 'South land' in xv. 19 implies land with little water. Is your environment similarly unpromising? If so, what message is there for you in Achsah's request to her father and his response? In chapter xiv Caleb is seen as the strong and steadfast warrior; here he is seen as a bountiful father, true type of our Father God. See Lk. xi. 13; Phil. iv. 19.

(2) Contrast the spirit shown by Manasseh, Ephraim, and even Judah with that of Caleb (xiv. 12). What was Joshua's answer to Ephraim's complaints? Is there any excuse for tolerated sin in the Christian's life? Cf. Rom. vi. 12-14; 1 Jn. iii. 6-10.

Note.—The R.V. should be read in xvi. 10 and xvii. 13, 18.

Day 5. Jos. xviii and xix.

(1) With chapter xviii. 3 cf. Eph. i. 3 and Rom. viii. 32. What wrong attitude is Joshua's pointed question designed to correct? See Heb. vi. 11, 12.

(2) What evidence do you find in these chapters that God's promised blessings in Christ, though ours already by God's gift, become ours in actual possession and experience only through the fight of faith and through resolute action? Cf. 2 Pet. i. 4-11; 1 Tim. iv. 13-16.

Day 6. Jos. xx and xxi.

(1) Find the cities of refuge on a map. On what geographical plan were they chosen, and how does this plan correspond to one of the chief attributes of the Lord Jesus—*our* refuge?

(2) The tribes were required to give from their inheritance a certain portion for the use of those who were set apart for God's service. In what ways does this principle apply today? See 1 Cor. ix. 13, 14; Gal. vi. 6.

Note.—xxi. 20, 23. 'Gibbethon'. See also 1 Ki. xv. 27 and 2 Ch. xi. 14. The references in Joshua and 1 Kings taken together confirm the statement of 2 Chronicles.

Day 7. Jos. xxii.

(1) What was Joshua able to commend in the conduct of these tribes? And what charge did he give them? With verse 5 cf. i. 8.

(2) What roused the remaining tribes to anger? Was their anger justified? How does the story warn us against passing hasty judgment?

Note.—R.V. is better in verses 24 and 33.

Week 19. JOSHUA XXIII–JUDGES IV

Day 1. Jos. xxiii. Joshua's charge to the leaders of the tribes.

(1) On what three conditions does the fulfilment of the promise in verse 5 depend? See verses 6-13.

(2) What declaration of the faithfulness of God does this chapter contain? Cf. xxi. 43-45. Can you endorse Joshua's testimony?

Day 2. Jos. xxiv. The national covenant at Shechem.

(1) Consider what pains Joshua took to make the occasion as impressive and as effectual in result as possible, as, for example, the choice of the place of assembly, so rich in national memories (Gn. xii. 6, xxxiii. 19, xxxv. 2, 4; Jos. viii. 32-35; Acts vii. 16); his recital of God's mercies in the past (cf. Rom. xii. 1); his refusal to accept the people's first, too-lightly-spoken response to his chal-

lenge; the writing of the covenant; and erection of the memorial.

(2) What evidence is there in this chapter, notwithstanding all that God had done, of the superficiality and instability of the Israelites' religious life? Cf. Ho. vi. 4. On what points in the character of God does Joshua lay stress? Is this emphasis needed today?

Day 3. Revision.

JUDGES

INTRODUCTION

(See New Bible Handbook, pp. 93, 94, 160-165)

THE author of the book of Judges is not known. It seems to have been written during the reign of Saul, or early in that of David. See xix. 1, xxi. 25, i. 21.

The book opens with an introductory section in two parts. The first (i. 1–ii. 5) gives an account of some of the attempts made by the tribes to possess their 'lots', and tells how they were rebuked by the angel of Jehovah. The second (ii. 6–iii. 7) shows the falling away after Joshua's death, and sums up the salient features of the period about to be described. The main portion of the book (iii. 8–xvi. 31) gives the history of the judges, of whom twelve in all are mentioned, namely, Othniel, Ehud, Shamgar, Deborah and Barak, Gideon, Tola, Jair, Jephthah, Ibzan, Elon, Abdon, Samson. In this list Deborah and Barak are reckoned as one and Abimelech is excluded. Of the twelve, six (namely, Othniel, Ehud, Deborah and Barak, Gideon, Jephthah, and Samson) are given extended mention, the others being little more than named. The last five chapters of the book (xvii. 1–xxi) narrate two instances of the religious declension and wickedness that prevailed in Israel at the beginning of this period. The authority of the priesthood seems to have lapsed, tending to loss of national unity and moral deterioration.

The book bears testimony to the faithfulness of God, showing both His righteous judgments and His enduring mercy. It contains some memorable examples of faith, and reveals also the hideous blackness of human sin. There is also much instructive teaching in it on the workings of God's providence, especially in regard to the instruments that He can use in the working out of His holy purposes.

ANALYSIS

Day 4. Jdg. i–ii. 5.

An account of the efforts of the tribes of Israel to possess their allotted inheritance. Verses 1-20 relate the doings of Judah and Simeon, and verses 22-29 the doings of Ephraim and Manasseh ('the house of Joseph').

(1) Judah began well. Why did they fail to complete their task? Ought their advance to have been checked by 'chariots of war'? See Dt. xx. 1; Jos. xvii. 16-18; Jdg. iv. 13-15; Mt. ix. 29; Heb. xi. 33.

(2) What charge did the angel of the Lord bring against Israel? And what consequence followed upon their failure? What may we learn from this as to the folly of the least compromise with evil? Cf. Heb. xii. 14-17; Rom. vi. 16.

Note.—i. 10-15. These verses are found also in Jos. xv. 13-19, and refer probably to an earlier period.

Day 5. Jdg. ii. 6–iii. 6.

(1) Backsliding, judgment, deliverance, renewed backsliding— trace this unvarying cycle in the history of the period, as summed up in this portion. What sort of spiritual life corresponds to this in the life of the individual? Cf. Col. iii. 5, 6; Rev. iii. 1-3.

(2) What may we learn from ii. 10 and iii. 6 as to the importance (a) of Christian teaching of the young, and (b) of Christian marriage? See Dt. vi. 6, 7; Eph. vi. 4; 1 Cor. vii. 39 (last clause); 2 Cor. vi. 14.

Day 6. Jdg. iii. 7-31.

(1) Observe what the Lord did *against* Israel (verses 8 and 12) and what He did *for* Israel (verses 9 and 15). What caused Him to do the first, and what caused Him to do the second? What insight does this give into the principles of God's dealings with His people? See Ps. xxxiv. 12-18; 2 Ch. vii. 13, 14.

(2) Compare and contrast Othniel, Ehud, and Shamgar, both in what they did and in their method of doing it. What quality was present in all three that enabled God to use them? See 2 Ch. xvi. 9.

Day 7. Jdg. iv.

(1) In Heb. xi. 32, 33 Barak's faith is extolled. How did his faith manifest itself?

(2) Why do you think Barak was unwilling to undertake the campaign without Deborah? In what respect did it show a defect in his faith? What insight does this incident give into God's willingness to bear with and make concession for human weakness? Cf. Ex. iv. 13-16; Ps. ciii. 13, 14.

Week 20. JUDGES V–XII

Day 1. Jdg. v.

The story falls into three parts: (a) verses 1-11, the situation before the deliverance; (b) verses 12-18, the rallying of the tribes, and rebuke of the irresolute; (c) verses 19-31, the victory, and the death of Sisera.

(1) Observe to what dire straits backsliding had reduced the tribes (verses 6-8, cf. iii. 31; 1 Sa. xiii. 19, 22). What parallel spiritual consequences are found in the life of the backsliding Christian?

(2) What qualities are praised in the story, and what kind of conduct is condemned? What does this mean as applied to ourselves in the circumstances of today? See Lk. viii. 14, ix. 62; Acts xv. 26.

Notes.—(1) Deborah approves of Jael's deed; did God approve? The act of Jael seems to be on much the same footing as that of Jacob when he deceived his father. Both deeds were in themselves treacherous (the original gives no ground for the notion that Sisera intruded into a forbidden part of the tent), and God never approves of treachery. Yet in both deeds there was another element which He did approve—Jacob's earnest desire for the blessing, and Jael's zeal for her people against their oppressor. We know that Jacob's treachery was severely punished, while his desire was granted; if we knew Jael's subsequent history we might find God dealing with her on similar lines.

(2) R.V. is important in verses 2, 10-17, 22, 26, 29 (mg.).

Day 2. Jdg. vi.

The oppression by the Midianites took the form of an annual invasion of the land by immense hordes of nomads from across the Jordan, who possessed themselves of everything. The effect is described in verses 4 and 6.

(1) When the people cried unto the Lord, what was His first answer? See verses 7-10, and cf. ii. 1, 2; Ps. lxxxi. 8-11.

(2) How did God answer Gideon's question in verse 13? What promises did He give to him? And what public act of confession and witness did He require from him? What is the application of all this to ourselves? Cf. 2 Tim. ii. 19, 21.

(3) By what three visible signs did God strengthen Gideon's faith? Consider what these signs would teach Gideon.

Day 3. Jdg. vii. 1-23.

(1) What further principle, in addition to that expressly stated in vii. 2, appears in the choice of few out of many to be God's instrument for victory? In answering, observe the defects in the character of those rejected in the two tests; and as regards the second, consider which type of drinker would be more alert against a possible surprise attack. Cf. 1 Cor. ix. 27, x. 12.

(2) What does the story of the victory (note especially the words of the shout in verse 18) teach us about Christian service and warfare as co-operation with God—God working through chosen men? 'Christ alone can save the world, but He cannot save the world alone.' Cf. 1 Cor. iii. 5-9.

(3) Observe how Gideon's faith, by divine encouragement (verses 9-14), rose under seemingly hopeless prospects (verse 12) to complete assurance of victory (verse 15). Do you know anything of such confident assurance, leading to daring and victorious action?

Day 4. Jdg. vii. 24–viii.

(1) Note Gideon's dealing with the complaints of Ephraim, with the insults of the elders of Succoth and Penuel, the vigour of his pursuit and capture of Zebah and Zalmunna, and the respect which these princes showed to him. What various qualities

of character are here revealed? Consider the description in verse
18 as that which should apply to a Christian as a child of the King.

(2) What temptation did Gideon overcome? Contrast, however, the frequent reference to God's guidance in chapters vi and
vii with the entire absence of this in viii. 24-27. Was this the
reason of Gideon's going astray? See Jos. ix. 14; Ps. cvi. 13b;
also Dt. xvii. 17.

Note.—Verses 24-27. The ephod of the high priest (as described in Ex.
xxviii) was a shoulder garment covering breast and back, ornamented with
gems and gold, and having in front the breastplate containing the Urim and
Thummim, which were used in discovering God's will. Gideon's ephod was
probably a similar article, used to obtain answers from God; but the people
came to regard it as a kind of idol.

Day 5. Jdg. ix–x. 5.

(1) Consider in this story

    (a) The sin of Gideon in associating with a Shechemite (that
        is, a Canaanite woman) and having a son by her. See
        viii. 31; Dt. vii. 3.

    (b) The sin of the people of Shechem (ix. 16-18).

    (c) The sin of Abimelech (ix. 1-5).

Compare verses 56 and 57 and consider how in each case the
words of Nu. xxxii. 23b were fulfilled.

(2) What may we learn from the life of Jotham? Consider the
circumstances in which he found himself (ix. 5, 6). What did he
do, and what did he not do? What kind of man do you picture
him to be?

Notes.—(1) Verses 7-15. The first part of the parable contains a reference
to viii. 22, 23. Verse 15 presents the ironical picture of great trees seeking to
shelter under a bramble, and being destroyed in a forest fire which started
from the very thorn bush whose shade they had sought.

(2) Verses 23, 24. The facts are (a) that discord arose between the Sche-
chemites and Abimelech; (b) that this was a punishment from God for the sin
of both parties; (c) that the immediate agent in producing the discord was an
evil spirit. God overruled the malice of the demon for His righteous ends. He
'sent' n the sense that He permitted to go.

Day 6. Jdg. x. 6–xi. 28.

(1) What was the extent of Israel's backsliding at this time, and
of their ensuing misery? Cf. Je. ii. 12, 13, 19. By what successive
steps were they restored? And what evidence is given that their
repentance was sincere and true? Cf. Mt. iii. 8.

(2) What shows that there was in Jephthah true piety and faith, in spite of his origin and upbringing? Cf. Heb. xi. 32; Lk. xiv. 26-30.

(3) Summarize Jephthah's answer to the Amorite claim. Are you giving an equally uncompromising answer to Satan's claim on any part of the territory in your life?

Note.—R.V. is clearer in x. 8 and xi. 26.

Day 7. Jdg. xi. 29–xii.

(1) Read the story of Jephthah's vow in the light of Ec. v. 2-6; Dt. xxiii. 21-23, and see also note below. What does this story teach about (a) the sacredness of a promise to God, and (b) the necessity of first considering what this promise may involve?

(2) What light does Jephthah's action against Ephraim throw upon his character? Contrast Gideon's way of answering the pride of Ephraim. See viii. 1-3, and cf. Pr. xv. 1; Eph. iv. 2, 3.

Note.—Opinion is sharply divided as to whether Jephthah did or did not put his daughter to death. Some think that she became dedicated to God as a kind of religious recluse. But was Jephthah the kind of man, who, having made a solemn vow, would later modify it to something less costly? Cf. 1 Sa. xiv. 39-46, when Jonathan's life was saved from a like fate only by the people's intervention.

Week 21. JUDGES XIII–XXI

Day 1. Jdg. xiii.

(1) Picture the thrill in the hearts of Manoah and his wife at the angel's message. A son, and a saviour for Israel!

(2) What was required of the mother? How was the child's Nazirite calling to be different from that of the ordinary Nazirite vow? See Nu. vi. 1-5, 13-18.

(3) What evidences of faith do you find in Manoah and his wife? And how did the wife's faith show itself to be greater than that of her husband? How may her argument in verse 23 be applied in our own case?

Note.—Verse 16. The angel refused to take food as a man. Manoah is brought gradually to recognize that the visitor was divine (verse 22).

Day 2. Jdg. xiv and xv.

(1) Note the contradictory elements in Samson's character: for example (a) his profession of consecration and his living to please himself, (b) his abstaining from wine and his indulgence in lust. How many more such contrasts can you discover? Is your life marred by similar inconsistencies? See 2 Cor. vi. 14.

(2) What does the incident of xv. 18, 19 teach regarding God's ability to supply every need of His servants? Cf. Phil. iv. 19.

Day 3. Jdg. xvi.

(1) What may we learn from this chapter (a) of the folly and fruit of sin; (b) of the exultation of God's enemies when His servants fail; and (c) of God's enduring mercy to the penitent?

(2) Looking back upon Samson's life from its bright dawn to its dark but victorious close, what is it that gives him a place among the true soldiers of 'the good fight of faith'? See Heb. xi. 32.

Day 4. Jdg. xvii and xviii.

This story belongs to the time described in chapter i. The Levite spoken of appears to have been a grandson of Moses (xviii. 30, R.V.). The tribe of Dan, having failed to take possession of their original allotment (see Jos. xix. 40-48; Jdg. i. 34-36), made the raid to the north which is related here. The story shows the decline of true religion and the lawless condition of the times.

(1) How would you describe the religion of the man Micah and of the Danites? Whom did they worship, and after what manner? And upon what did they rely to secure God's favour? Wherein did they fall short of true religion?

(2) The Levite was recognized by all as a man who stood in a special relationship to God. What impression does he make upon you? Did he walk worthily of his profession? What may we learn from him? Cf. Is. lxi. 8a; 1 Jn. ii. 4-6.

Notes.—(1) xvii. 7. 'Of the family of Judah'. The words refer to the place Bethlehem, not to the Levite, who was only a 'sojourner' in Judah. There was another Bethlehem in the land of Zebulun. See Jos. xix. 15.

(2) The R.V. should be read in xviii. 2, 7, 16, 17, 21.

Day 5. Jdg. xix–xxi.

This story belongs to the period shortly after Joshua's death; Phinehas, the grandson of Aaron, was still alive. See xx. 28.

(1) How does this story show the evil consequences of sin? Trace, for example, how the initial wrongdoing of the woman in xix. 2 set in train a series of events which led to her death.

(2) Observe also how the wickedness of the men of Gibeah brought destruction upon almost their whole tribe.

Day 6. Jdg. xix–xxi (continued).

(1) Note the various indications of the profound effect upon the tribes of the sin of the men of Gibeah. See, e.g. xix. 30, xx. 1, xx. 8, 11. The sin was aggravated in their eyes by being a breach

of hospitality (xix. 23; cf. Gn. xix. 8) and committed against a Levite.

(2) How is the fact to be accounted for that the tribes, moved thus by a common horror and indignation, were twice defeated by the single tribe of Benjamin, even though they had asked counsel of the Lord? What do you gather from xx. 23 about their attitude? Was it strong or weak?

Day 7. Jdg. xix–xxi (continued).

(1) The tribes recognized after their victory that in the heat of passion they had gone to excess (xxi. 1-4), and then sought to remedy matters by further excesses. They had made two oaths (see xxi. 1 and 5), and proceeded to keep one and break the other. Which did they keep and which did they break? What does the whole story suggest with regard to vows and oaths? See Mt. v. 33-37.

(2) To what does the writer attribute this weak and unhappy condition of things in Israel? See xxi. 25, xvii. 6; cf. Rom. xiii. 3, 4. It is assumed that the king would rule in God's fear and according to His law. See 2 Sa. xxiii. 3; Dt. xvii. 19-20.

I CORINTHIANS

INTRODUCTION

(See New Bible Handbook, pp. 351-354, 359-362)

THIS Epistle was written by Paul from Ephesus (xvi. 8, 9, 19) during his third missionary journey (Acts xix. 1-10) about A.D. 56 or 57. It is well to have in view, in reading the Epistle, the great Greek city of Corinth, with its pride of intellect, its idolatries and immoralities, and its busy commerce and thronging life. The purpose of the Epistle was partly to answer questions sent to Paul by the Corinthians (vii. 1, viii. 1, xii. 1), partly to deal with distressing news which had come to him from Corinth about factions and other abuses in the church (i. 11, v. 1, vi. 1, xi. 18, 20). Paul had already written at least one letter to the Corinthians (v. 9), of which perhaps a fragment is imbedded in 2 Corinthians (2 Cor. vi. 14–vii. 1).

It will be seen from the analysis that the Epistle is very largely concerned with questions of practical morality, and as such it has a deep interest for our own as for every age. But these questions

are not dealt with on a basis of psychological analysis, but on the
ground of the relation of the soul to God. For example, the factious spirit is wrong, because a saving relation with God is not
obtained by intellectual brilliance but by humble faith, and
because the ministers of God's gospel are simply His servants,
responsible to Him. Again, immorality is a defiling of the temple
of the Holy Ghost, a misuse of the blood-bought property of the
Redeemer. The ruling principles which Paul lays down in the
problem of meats offered to idols are first, that our liberty must
not hurt the brother for whom Christ died, and secondly, that we
cannot partake of the table of the Lord and the table of demons.
Thus in morals, as in doctrine, the great truth prevails that
Christianity is Christ.

The Epistle contains two of the grandest passages in the New
Testament, the beautiful description of Christian love in chapter
xiii, and the defence and explanation of the doctrine of the resurrection in chapter xv.

ANALYSIS

i. 1–9.   Introduction.

i. 10–iv.   Factions in the Church.

> i. 10–ii.   The spirit of factions rests on intellectual
> pride, which is contrary to the essence of the
> gospel. There is a heavenly wisdom, but the
> natural man cannot understand it.
>
> iii-iv. 8.   Ministers of the gospel are not leaders of
> parties, but servants of God: to Him they are
> responsible and their work must pass His tests.
>
> iv. 9–21.   The apostolic example of humility and
> patience: but there is also apostolic authority.

v and vi.   Moral disorders in the Church.

> v. A great offender judged, and disciplinary rules
> laid down.
>
> vi. Litigation between Christians in heathen courts
> forbidden; the spiritual basis of purity of life.

vii.   Marriage and celibacy.

viii–xi. 1.   Meat offered to idols.

> viii. Liberty must be restrained by love.
>
> ix. Paul's example.
>
> x–xi. 1. Above all, no compromise with idolatry.

Week 22.   1 Corinthians i–xi. 1

Day 1.   1 Cor. i. 1-17.

(1) What are the essential marks of a Christian as given in verses 1-9? In view of these, in what particulars is his outlook on life likely to differ from that of an unbeliever?

(2) What was the cause of the divisions in the church at Corinth? See verse 12, also iii. 4. How might it arise in our own times, and even in our own Christian circle?

(3) How does Paul in verse 13 emphasize the uniqueness of Christ? Is Christ to you someone apart from and far above all human teachers? Cf. Mt. xvi. 13-18; Jn. iii. 30, 31.

Day 2.   1 Cor. i. 18-ii.

(1) If the preaching of Christ crucified was to the Jews a stumbling block, and to the Greeks foolishness, why did Paul preach the cross, and in doing so eschew the 'wisdom of words', which the Greeks loved? See i. 18-ii. 5.

(2) What wisdom did Paul teach among believers? Whence did he receive it, and by whom alone was it understood? See ii. 6-iii. 2.

(3) Looking back over the passage, pick out the work of God the Father, Son, and Holy Spirit respectively in man's salvation. Is the Lord Jesus Christ to you all that Paul speaks of in i. 30?

Notes.—(1) ii. 6. 'Them that are perfect'; that is, mature believers as contrasted with 'babes' (iii. 1), equivalent to 'he that is spiritual' (ii. 15) as contrasted with 'carnal' (iii. 3).

(2) ii. 13. 'Comparing, etc.'; 'interpreting what is spiritual in spiritual language' (Moffatt), that is, thought and words alike spiritual.

(3) Verse 14. 'The natural man'; i.e. the unconverted man.

Day 3. 1 Cor. iii and iv.

(1) Two similes are used in chapter iii in regard to the growth of the Church, namely, husbandry and building. What is God's part, and what man's? What is the responsibility of the Christian teacher?

(2) How does glorying in men obscure the real glory of the Christian's position in Christ? See iii. 21-23.

(3) In chapter iv Paul sets forth the true picture of himself and his fellow-apostles. What is their relation to Christ? See verses 1-7. What is their lot in the world? See verses 8-13.

Notes.—(1) iii. 12, 13. The different materials here mentioned are by some taken to represent the teachings of those who are building the Church, the gold, silver and precious stones being the doctrines of the cross, and the wood, hay and stubble the wisdom of the world.

(2) iv. 4. 'By myself'; better as in R.V., 'against myself'.

(3) iv. 8-13. Paul sarcastically compares the Corinthians, according to their own estimate of themselves, with the actual circumstances of the apostles, in an endeavour to show them their danger. Cf. verse 16.

Day 4. 1 Cor. v and vi.

(1) What should be the attitude of the Church when serious evil finds its way into its midst? How does Paul enforce this by a reference to the Passover? Notice in chapter v the distinction between sinning Christians and non-Christians, and the Church's action towards them respectively.

(2) What reasons does Paul give in chapter vi against Christians bringing their disagreements before the world? What light do these throw upon the high calling of the Church, and upon the conduct of Christians one towards another?

(3) What is said in vi. 15-20 about the Christian's body in relation (a) to the Lord, and (b) to the Holy Spirit, and what teaching does the apostle draw from this? Cf. Rom. xii. 1, 2.

Notes.—(1) v. 5. Probably implies a punitive physical affliction in addition to excommunication.

(2) vi. 2. 'The saints shall judge the world'; sharing with Christ in the rule of His messianic kingdom.

Day 5. I Cor. vii.

In this chapter Paul is answering specific questions regarding marriage which had been addressed to him. He is not dealing with the subject in all its bearings. For another aspect, not touched on here, see Eph. v. 22-33. The chapter, which should be read in the R.V., may be divided as follows: (a) some general instructions, 1b-7; (b) counsel to the unmarried, 8-9; (c) divorce forbidden in Christian marriage, 10-11; (d) counsel in cases where one partner has become a Christian and the other not, 12-16; (e) a fundamental rule for Christians, 17-24; (f) some reasons for abstaining from marriage, 25-35; (g) counsel to fathers, 36-37; (h) counsel to widows, 38-39. Notice that Paul does not dictate whether a Christian should or should not marry. He shows that marriage and the single life are equally permissible, and leaves each free to decide which is best in his own case. As regards marriage, however, a condition is laid down in the last clause of verse 39.

(1) Paul himself preferred to abstain from marrying (verses 7 and 8). On what grounds did he choose this for himself, and commend it to others, if they were able for it? See especially verses 29-35.

(2) What rule for a Christian is laid down three times in verses 17-24? Has it any application, do you think, under present-day conditions?

Notes.—(1) Verses 7 and 8. 'Even as I'; that is, abstaining from marriage.

(2) Verses 10 and 12. 'Unto the married'; that is, Christian married couples. 'Unto the rest', that is, couples married when non-Christian, and one of whom has been converted.

(3) Verse 14. A difficult verse. There seems to have been a fear in some minds that continued union with an unbeliever might be defiling to the Christian partner. 'No!' says the apostle, 'it works the other way.'

(4) Verse 17. 'Distributed'; or 'allotted'.

(5) Verse 20. The word 'calling' does not mean secular vocation, but God's call in Christ. That divine calling finds each in a particular environment and setting. Let him not be in haste to alter it!

Day 6. I Cor. viii–ix. 23.

Liberty and self-denial. The church in Corinth had asked the apostle about the eating of food which had been offered before an idol. Picture yourself as a Christian in Corinth, invited to a social banquet in a temple, or seated as a guest in the house of a non-Christian friend, and offered food which had been presented in sacrifice to an idol. What should you do—eat or not eat? Paul, in chapter viii, gives two guiding principles—truth and love.

(1) Using the knowledge of truth alone as guide—such truth, for example, as is stated in verses 4-6, the answer to many of the Christians in Corinth seemed quite clear. They were prepared to aet and had no scruples at all in the matter—and the apostle agreed with them. See verse 8.

(2) But knowledge alone, without the other guiding principle of love, may lead astray. To what grievous results may it lead, according to Paul's teaching here?

(3) The Christian, then, must curtail his liberty in love to his weaker neighbour and for the gospel's sake. How does Paul show in viii. 13–ix. 23 that this is his practice all the time and in everything?

Notes.—(1) Verse 1. The church in Corinth was rich in knowledge: see i. 5.

(2) Verse 6. In the light of these truths, there is no room for other gods.

(3) Verse 7. 'With conscience of the idol'; better, as in R.V., 'being used until now to the idol'. Heathen converts, recently converted, might feel that food sacrificed to idols was tainted, and consequently their conscience rebuked them if they ate it.

(4) ix. 22. 'To the weak'; that is, those whose grasp of Christian truth was feeble, and who were timid in exercising their liberty in Christ.

Day 7. 1 Cor. ix. 24–xi. 1.

The need of self-discipline, and final conclusions on the subject of eating food offered to idols.

(1) To what does the apostle in ix. 24-27 compare the Christian life? How did he discipline himself and to what end?

(2) Paul has shown the need of self-discipline. What example does he bring forward to show the results of failure in discipline? See x. 1-13. What warning is contained for us in these verses?

(3) In x. 14-33 the apostle sums up the discussion begun in chapter viii. Observe that he distinguishes sharply between eating meats that have been offered before an idol, and eating in an idol temple. Why does he express disapproval of the latter, but permit the former (except in the special circumstances of verse 28)? What two principles does he lay down in conclusion to guide Christians in such matters?

Notes.—(1) ix. 27. 'I maul and master my body, in case, after preaching to other people, I am disqualified myself' (Moffatt).

(2) x. 1-4. The people of Israel who came out of Egypt enjoyed similar privileges to those of Christians. Hence we may learn from their example (verse 11).

(3) x. 29, 30. The meaning seems to be that to eat in such a case is to bring oneself needlessly under the condemnation of another's conscience, and even to be evil spoken of.

Week 23. 1 CORINTHIANS XI. 2–XVI

Day 1. 1 Cor. xi. 2-34.

This chapter deals with two irregularities in public worship. The first concerned the part played by women in the worship of the church in Corinth. It would appear that they had begun to pray and prophesy with the veil, which at that time was a distinctive feature of women's dress, laid aside. The second had to do with unseemly behaviour at the social meal preceding the observance of the Lord's Supper, and connected with it.

(1) Paul's judgment regarding the first irregularity is based upon principles that lie deep in God's creative purpose, and even in His own nature. How does he show that God has given as between men and women (he seems to be speaking particularly of the marriage relationship, see Eph. v. 23) a position of headship to men, which remains within the Christian society, and therefore extends to matters of church order?

(2) What, according to verses 23-26, is the central significance of the Lord's Supper?

(3) What light do verses 20-22 throw upon the meaning of the phrase 'eat (or drink) *unworthily*'? What is the penalty of such eating, and how is it to be avoided?

Notes.—(1) Verse 10. 'Because of the angels'; they are regarded as spectators.

(2) Verses 20-22 are clearer in R.V. The Lord's Supper was partaken of during, or at the close of, a social meal, to which each brought a contribution. In Corinth some brought much, and ate to excess, others who in their poverty had little to bring, went hungry. It was a wholly unworthy way of eating the Lord's Supper.

(3) Verse 29. 'Damnation'; better, as in R.V., 'judgment'. What is meant is temporal judgment, or chastening, with a view to escaping final condemnation (verse 32).

Day 2. 1 Cor. xii.

(1) How many different kinds of gift and of service does Paul mention in this chapter? Can you find twelve? On what principle are they given, and for what purpose?

(2) Consider how the figure of the human body illustrates both the unity and the diversity of the Church. What gives to the body of Christ and to each of His members *life*?

(3) What other lessons does the apostle draw from this illustration of Christians being the body of Christ? See verses 15-31.

Notes.—(1) Verses 1-3. The test of the presence of the Spirit of God is loyalty to Jesus as Lord.

(2) Verse 28. 'Helps, governments'; that is, 'gifts for helping the weak, gifts for church administration' (Way).

Day 3. 1 Cor. xiii.

The apostle had urged the believers at Corinth to be zealous to possess the more excellent of the gifts (xii. 31), but before going on to explain what he means by this (chapter xiv) he pauses to point out that spiritual gifts are of no profit without love (chapter xiii).

(1) Why is love so all-important? Cf. 1 Jn. iv. 8. Has the truth of it so gripped you as to be moulding your life?

(2) In verses 4-7 there are fifteen clauses describing love. Write them in a column and then try to put opposite each a single word summarizing it. Then ask yourself: Is this found in me?

(3) In what way does Paul show further in verses 8-13 that love is greater than all?

Day 4. 1 Cor. xiv.

(1) Try to form a mental picture of the church's worship in Corinth. In what ways did it differ from the church's worship today?

(2) What two principles should govern the conduct of public worship and of church gatherings? See verses 26 (last clause) and 40. How did Paul apply these principles in his directions about public worship in Corinth?

(3) Is it right to desire and seek to obtain spiritual gifts for oneself? Many in the church at Corinth seem to have coveted to speak with tongues. To what gift, however, does Paul give a far higher place, both for the edification of believers (verses 2-19) and the conversion of non-Christians (verses 20-25); and on what grounds?

Note.—Verses 2 and 3. The 'tongues' appear to have been ecstatic cries, arising from inward exaltation of spirit, and uttered in sounds which were distinct from ordinary speech, and not intelligible except through interpretation. Prophecy, on the other hand, was the delivery of a God-given message, which might be a foretelling of what was to come to pass (cf. Acts xi. 28), but ordinarily was for 'edification and exhortation and comfort'.

Day 5. 1 Cor. xv. 1-34.

(1) What does Paul's summary of the gospel suggest as to where the emphasis should be placed in Christian preaching, and as to the importance he attached to the written Word? What does the gospel bring to men and on what condition? See verses 1-5, and cf. Mt. i. 21; 1 Tim. i. 15.

(2) Make a list of the positive evidences which Paul gives in verses 5-11 for the resurrection of Christ, including the changes wrought in himself. Also what negative evidence does he adduce —that is to say, if Christ be *not* risen, what fivefold catastrophe follows? See verses 15-19.

(3) What light does Christ's resurrection throw upon the future? As the full harvest follows the first fruits, so must Christ's resur-

rection lead to certain developments. What are they and what bearing should this have upon the kind of life we live?

Notes.—(1) Verse 28. No change in the eternal relations between the persons of the Trinity is meant here. It is the Son's willing subjection in love. Cf. xi. 3 (last clause).

(2) Verse 29. The best explanation of this much discussed verse is that Paul refers to relatives and friends of departed believers, who have turned to Christ and been baptized for their sakes, that is, through their witness. Their baptism has been useless if the dead do not rise.

Day 6. 1 Cor. xv. 35-58.

(1) What does the analogy of the seed suggest as to the relation between the natural body and the spiritual body that shall be? What four adjectives does Paul use of the present earthly body? In contrast, what words does he use to describe the heavenly body?

(2) 'The image of the heavenly' in verse 49 signifies likeness to Christ in His glorified body, as in Rom. viii. 29; Phil. iii. 21. But in the light of Col. iii. 9, 10, and 2 Cor. iii. 18, in what ways and by what means is the image of Christ already being formed in believers?

(3) What will take place when Christ comes again? Cf. 1 Thes. iv. 13-18. In view of this what should be the character of our present life and service?

Notes.—(1) Verse 36. See R.V. Resurrection in Paul's view is not a strange thing, but is embedded in the heart of God's creative plan, in grace as in nature.

(2) Verse 51. 'We' means 'we Christians'. Some will be alive when Christ comes.

Day 7. 1 Cor. xvi.

(1) Paul was concerned about a fund which he had initiated among the Gentile churches to aid the poor of the church in Jerusalem. What directions does he give here for the ingathering of the money and its despatch, and what may we learn from his practical wisdom?

(2) In verses 13 and 14 Paul views the church in Corinth as an army encamped in hostile territory. What fivefold direction does he give?

(3) What traits in Paul's Christian character shine out in this chapter, and in the whole book?

Notes.—(1) Verse 7. 'By the way'; that is, in passing. Paul felt that a *brief* visit would be unsatisfactory.

(2) Verse 17b. Another rendering is 'They have fully made up for my deprivation of you' (Way).

II CORINTHIANS

INTRODUCTION

(See New Bible Handbook, pp. 351-354, 362-364)

THIS Epistle was written from Macedonia (ii. 13, vii. 5, viii. 1, ix. 2-4) after Paul had left Ephesus (Acts xx. 1, 2). Paul had met Titus on his return from a mission to Corinth, and the report which Titus gave greatly relieved Paul's anxieties, especially in regard to the church's favourable reception of, and action upon, a severe letter which Paul had written to them (ii. 3, 4, vii. 5-16). But there were still other matters which gave Paul much concern. There was a minority in the church opposed to him, and their influence had been strengthened by the arrival of Jewish Christians who claimed apostolic rank, and sought to undermine Paul's authority by making false insinuations against him.

The whole Epistle vibrates with strong feeling, now glowing with love, now weighed down with sorrow, now burning with indignation. It is the most personal of Paul's Epistles to the churches, for he had been deeply wounded by the doubts cast upon his personal integrity, his love for those whom he had won for Christ, and upon the validity of his apostolic commission. He knew well also that in their attacks upon him his enemies were really striking at his gospel (xi. 1-5). Hence the vehemence of his defence.

The Epistle falls into three main sections, chapters i-vii, viii-ix, x-xiii. The chief theme of the first is the nature of Paul's Christian ministry—its divine glory and power (ii. 12-iv. 6); its human weakness and final reward (iv. 7-v. 10); its motive, message and methods (v. 11-vi. 10). The theme of chapters viii and ix is the collection which Paul is organizing, with the motives for and blessedness of Christian giving. In the closing chapters Paul feels himself reluctantly compelled to declare what manner of man he is, that his readers may know how far from the truth the slanders of his enemies are. These chapters give an insight into the apostle's character such as we find nowhere else. They also contain promises for the weak, and a much-needed warning against the crafty disguises of Satan.

ANALYSIS

i. 1-11.   After salutation, Paul rejoices in the heavenly comfort which he has received in his sore trouble.

i. 12–ii. 11.   Paul vindicates himself from the charge of fickle-
                 ness and states why he did not come to
                 Corinth; he urges them to forgive the offender.

ii. 12–iv. 6.   How God blesses Paul's labours in the gospel, as
                 He did at Corinth; the glory of the new
                 covenant is greater than that of the old.

iv. 7–vi. 10.   Paul's sufferings in the cause of Christ are great,
                 but abundantly worth while, both in view of
                 the glorious future, and of the grandeur of the
                 gospel message which he pleads with his
                 readers to accept.

vi. 11–vii. 4.   He pleads with the Corinthians more fully to
                 reciprocate his affection, interrupting the plea
                 with a solemn warning to be separate from the
                 world.

vii. 5-16.   Paul's joy at the good news brought by Titus.

viii and ix.   Concerning the collection for the poor Christians
                 of Judaea.

x.   Paul warns the Corinthians against resisting his
                 authority.

xi–xii. 13.   With great reluctance he contrasts his own gifts,
                 labours and sufferings, with those of his tra-
                 ducers, concluding with his heavenly visions
                 and their results.

xii. 14–xiii. 10. He is coming with love in his heart, and he begs
                 that they will not force him to use severity.

xiii. 11-14.   Conclusion.

The Revised Version should be used in the study of this Epistle.

Week 24. 2 Corinthians I–VII

Day 1. 2 Cor. i. 1-11.

(1) On what ground does Paul rest his claim to apostleship?
Cf. Gal. i. 1. How does he describe the church in Corinth in spite
of its defects? What blessings does he ask for its members? How
far are these blessings real to you?

(2) Paul, in the service of Christ, has been passing through
times of great suffering (verse 5)—*how* great is described in verses
8-10. What spiritual gain has come (a) to Paul himself, (b) to
others, through his sufferings?

(3) Observe how Paul counts upon the prayers of others. Are we thus supporting those who are in the front line of the battle? If prayer fails, what double loss ensues (verse 11)?

Notes.—(1) Verse 6. Observe the changes in the R.V.

(2) Verses 8-10. 'Have you ignorant'; in the sense of 'underrate'. The Corinthians knew of the affliction, but not of its gravity. 'I absolutely despaired of life. Yes, and when I asked, What shall be the end? the whispered answer of my heart was, Death. This taught me to rely no more on my own strength but upon God alone, for He can raise up men actually dead' (Way).

Day 2. 2 Cor. i. 12-22.

(1) To what does Paul's conscience bear witness regarding his relations (a) with the world, (b) with fellow-believers? Can you say the same?

(2) Paul acknowledges that he had altered his original plan, but denies that it was due to fickleness (see *Introduction*). What remarkable argument does he use to prove this in verses 18-22?

(3) What three functions of the Holy Spirit are referred to in verses 21, 22, and what do you understand by each? Cf. 1 Jn. ii. 20, 27; Eph. i. 13, 14.

Notes.—(1) Verse 12. 'Not with fleshly wisdom'; cf. 1 Cor. ii. 6; Jas. iii. 13-18.

(2) Verse 13. 'It is simply untrue that I send any private communications. The only letters which I write are those which you read out to the congregation —ay, and which you do recognize as the expression of my mind, and will never cease, I hope, to recognize as such' (Way).

(3) Verses 17-19. Paul was the messenger of God whose word in the gospel was true and stedfast; therefore Paul's words must be true and stedfast also.

(4) Verse 20. 'He, who has God's Son, Jesus Christ, has all God has promised' (Denney). When we believe this and utter with thankful hearts an appropriating Amen, we glorify God.

Day 3. 2 Cor. i. 23–ii.

There had been a gross case of immorality in the church in Corinth (1 Cor. v. 1) and Paul had written strongly about it. This was the reason for his altering his plans. He did not wish to come with a rod (i. 23, ii. 1) and postponed his visit in the hope that his letter would achieve its purpose. This had been the case, and Paul now counselled that the offender be forgiven (ii. 5-11).

(1) What may we learn from the spirit in which Paul administered discipline? Notice with what depth of feeling he entered into the matter (ii. 4, 12, 13) and how he defines his relation to the believers in Corinth (i. 24).

(2) Paul was ever conscious of the malignant activity of the great enemy. In what ways can a scandal in church life give Satan an advantage?

(3) Does the Word of God promise that faithful preaching of the gospel will win all who hear it? How does Paul describe his own experience in this regard? Cf. iv. 4.

Notes.—(1) i. 24. Paul wanted their faith to be between them and God directly. Cf. Rom. xi. 20; 1 Cor. ii. 5.

(2) ii. 5. 'As for him who was the cause of all this grief, it is not I whom he has grieved, but all of you—in some measure, that is, for I do not wish to be too severe' (Way).

(3) Verse 14. 'Causeth us to triumph'; better, 'leadeth us in triumph', as in R.V. In an ancient Roman triumphal procession the captives used to carry censers of incense that diffused their scent far and wide on either side. Paul likens himself to a captive in Christ's train, diffusing the fragrance of the knowledge of Him.

Day 4. 2 Cor. iii–iv. 6.

(1) The intruders at Corinth (see *Introduction*) made much, we may gather, of letters of recommendation which they carried (cf. Acts xviii. 27), and may have said, or implied, that Paul did not possess such, though he was very ready to commend himself (iii. 1). What striking answer does Paul make? Is there anyone on whose heart through your agency Christ has written by His life-transforming Spirit, a message which others can read of His saving power?

(2) In iii. 6-11 the old and new covenants are contrasted. In what three respects is the new covenant here shown to excel in glory?

(3) In the great passage iv. 1-6 how is Christ described, how the gospel, how Satan, how conversion, and how the true preacher?

Notes.—(1) iii. 6. 'The letter killeth, but the spirit giveth life'; Paul has condensed into these few words the teaching about the law and the gospel, which is expounded fully in Rom. vii-viii.

(2) iii. 18. 'With unveiled face'; that is, with face turned to the Lord in faith (verse 16). Jews who reject Christ still do not realize that the old covenant is transitory. See verses 12-16 (R.V.) and cf. Ex. xxxiv. 29-35 (R.V.).

Day 5. 2 Cor. iv. 7–v. 10.

(1) Why has God placed the treasure of iv. 6 in a weak vessel—the earthen vessel of man's frail human nature? And how does this arrangement work out in actual experience? See iv. 7-12.

(2) 'A miserable life', does someone say, with an emphasis on the 'dying'? And Paul answers: 'Not to the believing heart'. Viewed by faith (cf. Heb. xi. 1), how do present afflictions appear, and what prospect is seen at the end? See verses 13-18.

(3) In v. 1-4 Paul defines one aspect of the future prospect more closely. What awaits him after death or, if Christ should come first, as would be Paul's desire (verse 4), at His coming? How is Paul sure that this prospect is no mirage (cf. Is. xxxv. 7a, R.V. ing.), and what effect has it upon his present aim (see verses 5-10, R.V.)?

Notes.—(1) iv. 10-12. Cf. i. 8-10, vi. 9.

(2) v. 3, 4. 'Not be found naked'; a reference to the unclothing that takes place at death, when the spirit leaves its earthly body. Paul's desire was, as verse 4 shows, that he might live to see the second coming, and so escape death. Cf. 1 Cor. xv. 53.

(3) v. 10. The issues of the judgment here spoken of are not eternal life or death; but praise or blame, glory or disgrace. Cf. 1 Jn. ii. 28.

Day 6. 2 Cor. v. 11–vi. 10.

(1) What great motive dominated Paul's life, and to what conclusion did it lead him? See verses 14-17. How far are we like Paul in this matter?

(2) What was the central fact which Paul was sent to proclaim and at what infinite cost was it brought to pass?

(3) In vi. 3-10 Paul describes in twenty-eight particulars the kind of life and experience into which his acceptance of Christ and of Christ's commission had led him. Unless we receive the grace of God in vain, shall we not also be led in some measure into a similar life experience? Are any of these points true of yourself?

Notes.—(1) v. 12. An allusion to the intruders who were undermining Paul's influence in Corinth (see *Introduction*). Paul's purpose in these verses (11-13) is to assure his readers that however he may appear to some, whether mad or sane, in heart he is true to God and to them.

(2) Verse 16. 'Know we no man after the flesh'; that is, we do not regard people merely according to their natural human gifts and qualifications.

(3) Verse 21. 'The sin is laid by God upon the sinless One. . . . His death is the execution of the divine sentence upon it . . . and there is henceforth no condemnation to them that are in Christ' (Denney).

Day 7. 2 Cor. vi. 11–vii.

(1) In what five ways does Paul show in vi. 14-16 that Christians must be a separated people? What arguments does he use in vi. 16–vii. 1 to lead us to complete separation from all that defiles, and to wholehearted endeavour to make holiness perfect? Are you willing to test your friendships and your inmost purposes by this passage? Cf. Ps. cxxxix. 23, 24.

(2) How does Paul describe his state of mind while waiting for Titus? Paul was hindered in other work for God by the anxiety

which the sin of the Corinthians laid upon him. Cf. ii. 12, 13; Heb. xiii. 17.

(3) What two kinds of sorrow for sin are here distinguished (a) in their nature, and (b) in their result? By what signs did the Corinthians show that they were genuinely penitent?

Notes.—(1) vi. 11-13. Paul's loving heart overflows towards the Corinthians and he yearns for a corresponding large-hearted affection from them towards him. Verse 12 means that any sense of constraint they might feel towards Paul arose not from any lack of love in him, but from the narrowness of their own affections.

(2) vi. 14–vii. 1. This is a parenthesis, introduced to make clear that when Paul bids his readers to be broadened in their affections, he does not mean increased tolerance of *evil*. 'Belial' is here a name for Satan.

(3) vii. 10. 'Godly sorrow'; that is, sorrow towards God, regarding the sin as an offence against Him. Cf. Ps. i. 6. 'The sorrow of the world', on the other hand, is such sorrow as the worldling feels, concerned only with the painful consequences of the sin, and not leading to repentance.

Week 25. 2 CORINTHIANS VIII–XIII

Day 1. 2 Cor. viii. 1-15.

Chapters viii and ix form the second section of the Epistle (see *Introduction*), which relates to the fund that Paul was collecting from the Gentile churches for the poor in the church at Jerusalem. It lay very near to his heart, and had great importance in his eyes, as a demonstration of the oneness of all believers as members of one body in Christ.

(1) In what condition were the churches of Macedonia at this time in regard to their circumstances? Yet what was their spiritual attitude, and in what four ways did it show itself? To what does Paul ascribe it?

(2) What is the chief point in the appeal which Paul makes in verses 7-15? Gather out the other points which he makes, and consider them in their application to our own giving.

Notes.—(1) Verse 2. 'Trial'; better, 'test'.

(2) Verse 4. 'Begging us earnestly for the favour of taking part in the relief of the saints' (R.S.V.).

(3) Verse 5. 'Gave their own selves'; that is, for any personal service the Lord might require of them.

(4) Verse 15. The story of the manna indicates God's purpose that in material things His people should neither have surplus nor want. They should, therefore, mutually help one another.

Day 2. 2 Cor. viii. 16–ix.

Today's portion falls into two parts. First, in viii. 16-24, Paul explains why he is sending Titus and two others to Corinth, and gives them his warm commendation. Second, in chapter ix, he shows the blessings of cheerful and generous giving.

(1) What may we learn from Paul's example of the duty of praise where praise is due? See viii. 18, 19, 22, 23.

(2) What lesson is taught here of the importance of being business-like in dealing with the Lord's money? Cf. Rom. xii. 17; 2 Cor. vi. 3, xii. 16-18.

(3) What kind of giving does God value, and what reward does He give? What four blessings are mentioned in verses 12-14 as arising from such ministry?

Notes.—(1) viii. 19. 'This grace'; that is, 'this gracious work' (R.S.V.). Cf. verse 6.

(2) ix. 15. 'His unspeakable gift'; that is, the gift of Christ, so great as to be beyond expression, the spring and pattern of our giving.

Day 3. 2 Cor. x.

In this third section of the Epistle (see *Introduction*) Paul has specially in view the disaffected minority, who were being led astray by visiting preachers, who were enemies of Paul and of the gospel. His desire is to destroy the influence of these men, so that his visit, when it comes, may not be one of strife and conflict. In this chapter he twice refers to a charge, which his enemies made against him (x. 1b, 10), that while he might be able to write vigorous letters from a distance, he was weak and ineffective when present in person. Paul answers that he has powerful weapons at his command, and that the church in Corinth falls within the sphere of his God-given authority.

(1) Consider Paul's description of his ministry as a warfare (verses 3-6). What is the aim he has in view? What fortresses have to be captured, and how is victory achieved? Have you known in your own experience (a) of lawless elements in your own thought-life brought into captivity to the obedience of Christ, and (b) of winning such victories for Christ in the thought-life of others?

(2) What does Paul claim for himself in verses 7-16, and what hope for future service does he express? Cf. Rom. xii. 3, xv. 18-24.

(3) What principle does Paul insist on with regard to 'glorying', that is, taking credit for work accomplished?

Notes.—(1) Verses 2, 3. 'Walk in the flesh' means to live a human life on earth; 'walk after the flesh' means to be actuated by private and selfish interests; 'war after the flesh' means to fight in the energy and wisdom of self, and of the world.

(2) Verse 9. This is perhaps best rendered in English as a separate sentence: 'Do not let it be imagined that I am trying to scare you by hectoring letters' (Way).

(3) Verse 12. Cf. Pr. xxvi. 12.

(4) Verse 16. 'In another's province, etc.' (R.V.); an allusion to those who came to a church already founded by someone else, to make mischief there.

Day 4. 2 Cor. xi. 1-29.

(1) Why was Paul so concerned? What did he fear? See verses 1-4 and compare Gal. i. 6-10, iv. 19.

(2) On what two grounds, especially, was Paul amazed that the Corinthians should so readily tolerate these false teachers? See verse 4 and verses 19-20. But see also verses 13-15. What warning for our own day can be drawn from what Paul says about the false teachers, their methods, and their message? Is 'another Jesus' preached today?

(3) Let the imagination dwell clause by clause upon the list of sufferings in verses 23-29.

Notes.—(1) Verse 3. Notice the change in R.V. The believer's mind should be undivided and open towards Christ.

(2) Verse 5. R.S.V. renders: 'these superlative apostles'. An ironical reference to the intruders at Corinth who exalted themselves so highly.

(3) Verses 7-12. Paul refused to take money from the church in Corinth, and says that he will continue so to do, one reason being that his enemies who, it is implied, did receive support from the church, would have liked to see Paul doing the same.

(4) Verse 16. Paul feels ashamed to be engaged in self-praise; but in the circumstances he can do no other. Cf. xii. 11. He will do even this for the church's sake. It is to be noted, however, that he speaks less of what he has done than of what he has suffered. Cf. verse 30.

Day 5. 2 Cor. xi. 30–xii. 10.

(1) How would you describe the danger to avert which the 'thorn in the flesh' was sent to Paul? Under what circumstances do we need to be specially on our guard against this danger? What light does this throw on Satan's strategy?

(2) What did Paul do about this 'thorn' (cf. Mt. xxvi. 44), and how was his prayer answered? Notice the force of the present tense in the Lord's reply.

(3) What lessons did Paul learn that changed his whole attitude to trial? Have we begun to understand these things? Cf. Rom. v. 3-5; 1 Pet. iv. 14.

Notes.—(1) xii. 5. Paul contrasts himself, as a passive recipient of divine revelations, with himself in other capacities.

(2) Verse 7. The 'thorn in the flesh' seems to have been severe bodily suffering of some kind, but its exact nature is not disclosed.

(3) Verse 9. 'He said'; better, as in R.V., 'He hath said'—a word of abiding application. 'My strength' should be rendered 'My power', to correspond with 'the power of Christ'. It is the same word in the Greek text.

Day 6. 2 Cor. xii. 11-21.

(1) In verses 11-15 Paul summarizes his past ministry in Corinth, and his attitude towards them. Of all that he says in these verses what impresses you most as showing the measure of his Christlikeness? In answering this question bear in mind how deeply he has been wronged by the ingratitude and suspicion of the church.

(2) In verses 16-18 Paul anticipates and answers a possible thrust of malice from his enemies: 'Be it so', they might say, 'you did not receive support directly, but you organized a collection'. How does Paul answer, and what high commendation does he give to Titus?

(3) In verses 19-21 Paul answers another thought that may arise in their minds, namely, that he has been on his defence before *them*, and has thereby admitted some ground for the accusations made against him. What two-fold reply does Paul make?

Notes.—(1) Verse 11. 'The very chiefest apostles'; see xi. 5, note.
(2) Verse 13. 'Forgive me this wrong'; spoken in irony.
(3) Verse 14. 'We seek not yours, but you'; cf. iv. 5, 15, v. 13, xiii. 9.

Day 7. 2 Cor. xiii.

(1) What effect has Paul's love for the Corinthians on his attitude to their sin? In answering consider the evidence of both verses 1-6 and verses 7-10. See also xii. 20, 21.

(2) Consider how closely related the exhortations and promises of verse 11 are to the teaching of the whole Epistle.

(3) Consider how the prayer of verse 14 sums up our Christian heritage, and gives the complete solution to our threefold need— our sin, sorrow, and weakness.

Notes.—(1) Verse 1. When Paul comes he will hold a judicial enquiry. Cf. Mt. xviii. 16; 1 Tim. v. 19.
(2) Verses 2-4. Christ crucified through weakness is not the whole gospel. He also lives by the power of God, and that power will be manifested also in His servant Paul.
(3) Verses 5, 6. 'Reprobate'; that is, fail to meet the test.
(4) Verses 7-10. Paul would rather that the Corinthians should act rightly, and so make it needless for him to rebuke them, than that he should gain prestige by the demonstration of his apostolic authority.
(5) Verse 11. 'Be perfect, etc.'; better, 'mend your ways, heed my appeal, agree with one another, live in peace' (R.S.V.).

RUTH

INTRODUCTION

(See New Bible Handbook, pp. 165-167)

THE general tone shows the setting of the story to be that of the time of the Judges. The book was read at the time of the Feast of Pentecost. The outstanding lesson of the book is the way in which the hand of God is seen guiding the faithful in the details of everyday life, as also in the events through which the way was prepared for the birth of the Son of David (see Mt. i. 5).

ANALYSIS

i.	Ruth's faithfulness to Naomi.
ii–iv. 12.	Ruth's contact with Boaz.
iv. 13-22.	Ruth's marriage.

I and II SAMUEL

INTRODUCTION

(See New Bible Handbook, pp. 167-172)

THE two books of Samuel formed a single work known as 'Samuel' in the Hebrew Canon. The Septuagint translators made the division. They grouped 1 and 2 Samuel with the two books of Kings to form the four 'Books of the Kingdoms'. The story is that of the development of the nation from the state described at the end of Judges to the established monarchy under David, and the events of David's reign.

The chief religious theme is that Israel are the people of Jehovah, who alone is their true Ruler. First, they are rebuked for their decadence and sin by Samuel, who accedes to their demands for a king. But he warns them fully of the consequences. Saul, a king much to the people's mind, is anointed at God's command and his history proves the danger of a self-willed leader. Finally, David is appointed and leads the people with the one aim of pursuing the will of God, until in his turn he falls into sin. The incidental events are all evidences of the inherent sinfulness of the natural man and proof of the enabling power of God granted to those who go forward in faith, as David and Samuel did. The underlying history is a continuation of that of the Pentateuch and Judges with the theme—'a people for My Name'.

ANALYSIS

1 Samuel

i–vi.   Eli's high-priesthood and its failure.

vii–xv.   Samuel as judge; the first king rejected.

xvi–xxxi.   David during the reign of Saul.

2 Samuel

i–viii.   David consolidates his position and takes Jerusalem.

ix–xii.   David the king, to the time of his great sin.

xiii–xx.   The punishment of sin—Absalom's rebellion.

xxi–xxiv.   An appendix containing other historical incidents and summaries, and David's last words.

Week 26. RUTH AND 1 SAMUEL I–VII. 2

Day 1. Ru. i and ii.

(1) Put yourself in Ruth's place, and consider the cost of her decision to follow Naomi into the land of Israel. Orpah, too, had been a good daughter (verse 8), but what difference was there between her attitude and that of Ruth? What lessons may Ruth teach us in regard to our following of Christ? Are we as resolute as she was? See Lk. ix. 23, 57-62, xiv. 25-33.

(2) In chapter ii what qualities are outstanding (a) in Boaz, and (b) in Ruth?

(3) Notice how what seemed to be a chance happening was overruled by God for blessing. Cf. ii. 3 and 20. Can you recall similar experiences?

Day 2. Ru. iii and iv.

(1) How does the whole story show forth the Lord's lovingkindness to those that trust in Him? Cf. La. iii. 22-26, 31-33; Na. i. 7; Rom. viii. 28.

(2) What example are we given in chapter iv in regard to matters which affect the rights of others?

(3) In what respects is Boaz a type of Christ? See note below.

Note.—iii. 12. 'Near kinsman'; the Hebrew word (*goel*, meaning 'next of kin') has a technical meaning in Hebrew law. The next of kin had certain duties and privileges, among them being that of redeeming the land or person of a kinsman who had been compelled to sell his land or himself through poverty (cf. Lv. xxv. 25, 47-49). To draw a portion of a kinsman's mantle over oneself (iii. 9) was the legal way of claiming protection and redemption. A kinsman-redeemer must be able and willing to redeem and pay the redemption price in full. Cf. iv. 4-6; Gal. iii. 13, 14.

Day 3. 1 Sa. i.

(1) Do you find any indication that Hannah made any retort or retaliation against her tormentor? What rather did she do with her grief, and how in this is she an example to us? Cf. Ps. lxii. 8; 1 Pet. ii. 23.

(2) Why was Hannah's countenance no more sad (verse 18)? Had the situation altered in any way? Cf. Mk. xi. 24 (R.V.); 1 Jn. v. 15.

(3) With verses 26-28 compare Ps. cxvi. 12-14; Ec. v. 4, 5.

Day 4. 1 Sa. ii. 1-10.

Hannah's prayer merits careful study. She is inspired to see in her own experience the principles of God's dealing with the world, and to declare His glory and His universal reign through His anointed king. The passage should be read in the R.V.

(1) Contrast verse 1 with i. 7-10, noting the change wrought in Hannah. Are we joyful in our God; and if not, why not? Cf. Ps. lxxxix. 15-17; Is. lxi. 10; 1 Pet. i. 6-8.

(2) What does Hannah say (a) of God, (b) of His works? What illustration of these things can you recall in Scripture story, e.g. in the lives of Gideon, David, etc.?

(3) What shall be the final end, as described in verses 9, 10? Cf. 2 Thes. i. 6-10.

Notes.—(1) Verse 1. 'Mine horn'; the horn symbolizes strength and honour; cf. verse 10; Ps. lxxxix. 17. 'My mouth is enlarged'; i.e. instead of being put to silence.

(2) Verse 5. 'Ceased'; see R.V. mg.

Day 5. 1 Sa. ii. 11–iv. 1a.

(1) What two aspects of the sin of Hophni and Phinehas made it specially grievous in God's sight? See ii. 17, 29, 30, and compare verse 24.

(2) In chapters i–iii what do you find to commend in Eli? Wherein then did he fail, and how is this a lesson to all parents? Cf. Pr. xxix. 17; Mt. x. 37.

(3) Notice the expressions used about Samuel in ii. 18, 21, iii. 1, 7, 19. What new thing came into Samuel's life in the experience described in iii. 1-14?

Notes.—(1) ii. 15, 16. Hophni and Phinehas insisted on receiving their share of the sacrifices before the fat, which was the Lord's portion (Lv. iii. 3-5), was burned upon the altar.

(2) Verse 18. 'Ephod'; see Ex. xxviii. 4, note.

(3) Verse 22. Read as in R.V.

(4) Verse 29. Read as in R.V. mg.

(5) The first clause of chapter iv belongs to today's section.

Day 6. 1 Sa. iv. 1b-22.

(1) Try to picture what a crushing blow the events related in this chapter were for Israel. What is the answer to the question in verse 3?

(2) The ark was the visible symbol of Jehovah's presence. Why, then, did the Israelites' use of it prove unavailing? In what ways may Christians today make a similar mistake?

(3) Of what central truth had the Israelites lost sight? See 1 Pet. i. 15, 16.

Day 7. 1 Sa. v–vii. 2.

(1) Read the story of v. 1-5 in the light of Is. ii. 18, xliii. 8-11; Je. x. 10, 11.

(2) Trace the thoughts in the minds of the Philistine leaders which led up to the action described in vi. 10, 11. Wherein were their thoughts right, and wherein defective? What was their only motive?

(3) For what transgression did judgment fall upon the men of Beth-shemesh? Cf. Ex. xix. 21; Heb. xii. 28, 29; and see note below.

Notes.—(1) It would appear that there was an outbreak of bubonic plague of great violence. 'Emerods' in verse 6, etc., should be translated 'tumours', as in R.V. Bubonic plague is characterized by boils or tumours, and is carried by rats.

(2) vi. 19. The ark, according to God's command, was to be kept closely covered when not in the Holy of Holies. See Nu. iv. 5, 6, 15, 20 (R.V. mg.).

Week 27. 1 SAMUEL VII. 3–XV

Day 1. 1 Sa. vii. 3–viii.

(1) How does the story of chapter vii reveal the conditions of victory, even on the field of former defeats? Have you had some such experience?

(2) Why did God, while granting their request for a king, at the same time rebuke them for making it? In answering this question, consider the situation as described in viii. 1-3. Some change seemed required, and to ask for a king was not necessarily a wrong request (see Dt. vii. 14). How then did the people err?

(3) Contrast Samuel's prayerfulness, faith and obedience with the attitude of the people.

Notes.—(1) viii. 7. 'They have rejected me'; God read in their hearts a turning away from Himself.

(2) viii. 10-18. A graphic picture of the tyrannies of an eastern king.

Day 2. 1 Sa. ix–x. 16.

This section describes the private anointing and choice of Saul to be king, the next section his public election, and xi. 14-16 his crowning.

(1) In ix. 1-14 observe how the free actions of men are over-ruled to bring about God's purposes; also God's active interest in and direction of the affairs of His people. How may this give us hope in dark hours?

(2) What three confirmatory signs were given to Saul? How would they give him assurance that Samuel's words in x. 1 were indeed true?

(3) How does this section show that when God calls, He also equips?

Notes.—(1) x. 3, 4. The three men were going up to the sanctuary to offer sacrifice. It was very remarkable that they should give to Saul part of the intended offering.

(2) x. 8. See xiii. 8-14.

Day 3. 1 Sa. x. 17–xi. 13.

(1) What may we learn from x. 17-24 of the forbearance of God? See especially verse 19. Cf. Pss. ciii. 14, 15, lxxviii. 37-39; Rom. ii. 4.

(2) To what does Scripture attribute Saul's vigorous action, and his success? Had it not been for this would he not have remained as one of the helpless, weeping multitude of verse 4? Cf. Acts i. 8.

(3) What two noble qualities shine forth in Saul's words in xi. 13?

Day 4. 1 Sa. xi. 14–xii.

(1) How did Samuel show the people that, though the form of government had changed, the basic principles on which their prosperity depended remained unaltered?

(2) What were the outstanding features in Samuel's character as seen in this chapter?

(3) Summarize the counsels and warnings of verses 20-25. Observe the place Samuel gives to prayer. Yet if the people turn not from their wicked ways, will prayer avail? See verse 25 and cf. Je. xv. 1.

Note.—xi. 14. 'Gilgal'; see Jos. iv. 15-24.

Day 5. 1 Sa. xiii.

(1) How did Saul's attack upon the Philistines begin and what was their reaction?

(2) Consider in the light of verses 5, 6 and 19-22 the danger in which the Israelites were placed.

(3) How did Saul show his unfitness to be king of the people of the Lord? Had he not pressing reasons for taking action? Yet see xii. 14, 15. How does this incident illustrate the principle that God proves man by specific tests, and that one sinful act may have irreparable consequences?

Notes.—Verse 1. This is a usual form of words to record the age of a king at his accession and the length of his reign (cf. 2 Sa. ii. 10, v. 4, etc.); but here the numbers seem to have been lost, and the verse should read 'Saul was . . . old when he began to reign, and reigned . . . and two years over Israel'. For the number 30 in R.V., see R.V. mg.

Verse 2. Some years must have elapsed between chapters xii and xiii, for Jonathan here appears as a grown man.

Day 6. 1 Sa. xiv.

(1) Whence came Jonathan's great courage?

(2) What indications do you find of Saul's impatience and how did it lead him to hasty and wrong decisions?

(3) Yet what evidence is there that with all his self-will Saul was anxious not to offend the Lord? How do you account for this?

Notes.—(1) Verse 18. See R.V. mg.

(2) Verse 24. Saul's purpose was probably religious, viz., by fasting to obtain God's favour.

(3) Verses 33, 34. Cf. Lv. iii. 17.

Day 7. 1 Sa. xv.

(1) How far was Saul obedient?

(2) Was God satisfied? Contrast verse 11 with verse 13. See also Dt. vi. 4, 5 ('all').

(3) What excuse did Saul make, and how did Samuel answer him? What may we learn from his words of the value which God attaches to obedience?

Notes.—(1) Verse 15. Cf. Jos. vii. 1.

(2) Saul was religious in outward observance (cf. xiv. 33, xxviii. 3), but not obedient in heart. This, Samuel says, is as heinous as idolatry or witchcraft.

(3) Verse 24. Cf. Ex. xxxii. 22, 23.

(4) Verse 32. 'Delicately'; see R.V. mg.

Week 28. I Samuel XVI–XXVI

Day 1. I Sa. xvi.

(1) How is true obedience illustrated in Samuel's behaviour?

(2) What great truth was brought home to Samuel at Bethlehem? Consider how this truth is emphasized in our Lord's teaching. See Mt. vi. 1, vii. 15, etc.

(3) Study the beautiful picture in verses 14-23 of the love and service with which Saul was surrounded. How does the story show that human means may do much to alleviate spiritual trouble, but cannot cure it?

Day 2. I Sa. xvii. 1-54.

(1) What was it that gave David courage and confidence when all others were dismayed? Cf. 1 Jn. v. 5.

(2) How did David's earlier victories over the lion and the bear prepare the way for slaying a giant? Are we making full use of our present opportunities that we may be prepared for greater emergencies in the future?

(3) Was Saul's reasoning in verse 33 sound? If not, what was lacking? Are we meeting life's challenges as Saul advised in this instance, or after the example of David?

Notes.—(1) Verse 4. 'Six cubits and a span'; about ten feet.
(2) Verse 18. 'Take their pledge'; i.e. bring back a token that they are well.
(3) Verse 22. 'Carriage'; i.e. 'baggage', as in r.v.
(4) Verse 29. See r.v. mg.

Day 3. I Sa. xvii. 55–xix.

(1) What were the causes of Saul's enmity against David and in what ways did it express itself?

(2) By what means were Saul's attempts to destroy David foiled?

(3) How did Jonathan and Michal show their love for David? Compare Paul's love for Christ, Phil. i. 20, 21, iii. 8.

Notes.—(1) xviii. 10. 'Prophesied'; the word is used of an ecstatic condition excited either by good or evil spiritual inspiration. Here it is the latter. See r.v. mg.
(2) xix. 13. 'An image'; in Heb. 'the teraphim' (see r.v.). These were household images, such as Rachel had used long before, and to which her descendants still clung. In this case a single image is meant, apparently life size. See Gn. xxxi. 19; Jdg. xvii. 5, xviii. 14; 2 Ki. xxiii. 24.
(3) xix. 23, 24. 'Naked'; i.e. with his outer garment laid aside. Carried away by religious excitement, he fell into a kind of trance, and lay on the ground for a day and a night.

Day 4. 1 Sa. xx–xxi. 9.

(1) What was David's purpose in seeking Jonathan? What request did Jonathan in turn make of David?

(2) Consider how much Jonathan gave up and was willing to suffer for David's sake. What characteristics of the love which Paul describes in 1 Cor. xiii are found here?

(3) When human need and ceremonial obligations come into conflict as in xxi. 6, what guidance do we find here as to the right course to take? Cf. Mt. xii. 3-8.

Notes.—(1) xx. 6. Such were the standards of morality that even the best of the people seemed to have no scruple in using lies and deception to save life. Cf. xix. 17, xx. 28, 29, xxi. 2.

(2) xx. 26. 'He is not clean'; i.e. ceremonially not clean, and, therefore, not fit to take part in a sacrificial feast. Cf. Lv. vii. 19, 20.

(3) xxi. 1, 'afraid'; R.V. 'trembling'. Another instance of the fear in which people lived in those days. Cf. xvi. 2, 4.

(4) xxi. 7. 'Detained before the Lord'; perhaps in fulfilment of a vow.

Day 5. 1 Sa. xxi. 10–xxii.

(1) Do you gather from xxi. 10-15 and xxii. 3-5 that David's flights out of the holy land were done without God's guidance, and were not in God's will for him? What motive is twice mentioned in the former passage as determining his actions? Cf. Pr. xxix. 25.

(2) What new kind of life now begins for David? What three classes of persons turned to him as their leader?

(3) Read the story of xxii. 7-19 in the light of Pr. vi. 34, xiv. 30 (R.V. mg.), xxvii. 4. What should be the Christian's attitude to jealousy? See Rom. xiii. 13, 14; 1 Cor. xiii. 4.

Notes.—(1) xxii. 5. 'In the hold.' A reference probably to the Moabite fortress mentioned in verse 3. What finally happened to David's parents is not known. A Jewish tradition, however, says that they were murdered by the king of Moab, and hence David's severity towards Moab in 2 Sa. viii. 2.

(2) xxii. 8. It would seem that Saul had somehow heard of Jonathan's covenant with David and was filled with fury.

Day 6. 1 Sa. xxiii and xxiv.

(1) In what ways did God's protecting hand cover David and what special encouragements did he receive? Cf. Ps. xxxvii. 23, 24, xci. 4.

(2) What held David back from killing Saul when it was in his power to do it, and his followers were urging him on? What virtues shine forth in his self-restraint, and what lessons may we learn from him? Cf. Rom. xii. 19, 20.

(3) Consider the effect of David's magnanimity upon Saul. Saul saw the evil of his way and wept; yet did not turn from it. What lessons are here taught us? Cf. Ho. vi. 4.

Notes.—(1) xxiii. 1. 'Keilah'; a city of Judah, not far from Adullam on the edge of the Philistine plain.

(2) xxiii. 26. Note David's desperate plight.

(3) xxiv. 14. 'A dead dog . . . a flea'. 'As harmless as the one, as hard to catch as the other, as little important as either' (Maclaren).

(4) xxiv. 20. Saul knew what God purposed, yet continued to fight against it, seeking to avert its worst consequences.

Day 7. 1 Sa. xxv and xxvi.

(1) Describe Nabal's character. Why did he act as he did, and what was it that he lacked?

(2) What, in contrast, were the outstanding features in Abigail's character? and in what ways is she an example to us?

(3) In chapter xxvi Saul and David stand out clearly. David, as we have seen, was not without fault, and Saul had many fine qualities. What was the essential difference between them that caused Saul to be rejected of the Lord and David favoured?

Notes.—(1) xxv. 17. 'Such a son of Belial.' See R.V. mg., also ii. 12 (R.V. mg.).

(2) xxvi. 19. 'This day'; emphatic. David means that he is about to flee out of the country (cf. xxvii. 1), where other gods are worshipped.

Week 29. 1 SAMUEL XXVII–2 SAMUEL VI

Day 1. 1 Sa. xxvii and xxviii.

(1) Contrast David's words in xxvii. 1 with xvii. 37. What did he gain by becoming the servant of a heathen king? and what price had he to pay for it? Cf. 2 Ch. xix. 2; Jas. iv. 4.

(2) What brought Saul to consult the witch of Endor?

(3) Looking back over Saul's story, what was the root cause of his rejection and fall? In what ways is he a warning to us? Cf. 1 Cor. ix. 24-27.

Day 2. 1 Sa. xxix–xxxi.

(1) Into what great difficulty had David brought himself, and how was he delivered? Do we ever give the world cause to say, 'What is that Christian doing here?'?

(2) Try to picture the scene of desolation upon which David and his followers looked. What effect did it have upon David?

(3) Chapter xxxi recalls the disaster of chapter iv. How may we learn from these defeats the reasons for failure in the conflict against the enemies of God's kingdom?

Day 3. Revision.

(1) What illustrations of Gal. vi. 7 do you find in this book?

(2) Consider Samuel as prophet, intercessor, and servant of God.

(3) How did David's experiences, as recorded in this book, all serve to train him for his future life-work? Cf. Rom. viii. 28.

Day 4. 2 Sa. i.

(1) How does this incident of the Amalekite set forth the great guilt of those who crucified the Lord Jesus? Cf. 1 Thes. ii. 15, 16.

(2) Consider David's position. His adversary and persecutor was dead, and the way to the throne open. Yet what filled his mind in that hour, as we see from his elegy? What is the one reference to himself? Cf. Rom. xii. 10, 14, 15.

Notes.—(1) Verses 9 and 10. 'Stand upon me'; better 'beside me', as in R.V. Saul was still upright; see verse 6.

(2) The Amalekite's story is at variance with 1 Sa. xxxi and is doubtless made up in the hope of gaining a reward from David. He probably came across Saul's dead body and stripped it.

(3) Verse 18. Read as in R.V. 'The Bow' is the title of the song. The Book of Jasher may have been a collection of historical songs.

(4) Verse 21. 'Fields of offerings', i.e. fertile fields, providing produce for offerings.

Day 5. 2 Sa. ii and iii.

(1) In this somewhat long portion trace what is said about three men. (a) *David.* Do you find, along with the story of David's growing power, any evidence that in one direction he was treading a wrong and dangerous path, and laying seeds of future trouble for himself and his family? See Dt. xvii. 17. (b) *Abner*, a man of many gifts, who, though he knew God's will (iii. 18), did not do it. What was the outcome of his attempt to serve his own ends? Cf. Je. x. 21, R.V. (c) *Joab.* What relation was Joab to David? See 1 Ch. ii. 16. What light does this portion throw upon his character? Was it only to avenge Asahel that he slew Abner? and why did not David punish him?

Note.—iii. 33, 34. Read as in R.V. The word 'fool' here means a wicked person, one guilty of crime.

Day 6. 2 Sa. iv–v. 16.

(1) Consider how long David had to wait before the promise made to him by Samuel (1 Sa. xvi. 13) was fulfilled. Compare Hab. ii. 3; Heb. vi. 12, 15.

(2) What did David learn in this waiting time that made him more fit to be king?

(3) What lessons may be deduced from the fact that the capture of Jebus was accomplished only after the nation became *united*? Cf. Mk. iii. 24; Ps. cxxxiii. 3.

Notes.—(1) v. 6-8. Read as in R.V.

(2) v. 9. 'Millo'; or, more literally, 'the Millo'. The meaning is uncertain, but it is probably the name of an ancient citadel in the city.

Day 7. 2 Sa. v. 17–vi.

(1) In his conflict with the Philistines, as described in v. 17-25, David enquired of the Lord twice. Did he receive the same answer in each case? Is this also your experience in prayer, that God answers in different ways? Compare, for example, Jn. iv. 50 with Jn. xi. 11.

(2) Why did Uzzah die? See 1 Sa. vi. 19; Nu. iv. 15; Lv. x. 1, 2. If God attached such importance to reverence in the case of what was but a symbol of His presence, with what reverence should we draw near, who have to do not with symbols and shadows, but with divine realities? Cf. Heb. x. 28, 29, xii. 28, 29.

(3) What may we learn from David's attitude regarding the relative importance of himself and of the affairs of God? Is our attitude in this respect at all comparable to his? Notice that in this case God was displeased, not with David, but with Michal.

Notes.—(1) vi. 3. 'Drave the new cart'; but see Nu. iii. 29-31, viii. 9-22 and verse 13 below. This was the inauguration of fully constituted worship in the new capital of the kingdom, and therefore neglect of God's ordinances could not pass unrebuked.

(2) vi. 14. 'David danced'; such religious dances were usually performed by women only. David not only danced, but put off his kingly robes, and attired himself in the dress of a priest.

Week 30. 2 SAMUEL VII–XVII
Day 1. 2 Sa. vii.

(1) How does the chapter illustrate Is. lv. 8, 9?

(2) What promises did God make to David, and how are they fulfilled in Christ?

(3) What may we learn from David's example here, about praise and prayer, and, in particular, about the relation of petition to promise? See verses 18-29.

Notes.—(1) Verses 3-5. Notice how human judgment was overruled by divine revelation.

(2) Verse 19. 'Is this the manner of men?'; better, 'And this is a law or men' (*Camb. Bible*). The words express David's astonishment that a promise so far-reaching should be made to weak human beings.

Day 2. 2 Sa. viii and ix.

(1) Chapter viii describes a series of wars with surrounding nations. Where a strong stand is taken for the Lord, opposition is aroused. What is referred to twice as the secret of David's success, and what did David do with the spoil he won in these wars? What application have these things to ourselves?

(2) In what respects may the story of Mephibosheth, blessed for Jonathan's sake, be used to illustrate God's dealings with us, who are 'accepted in the Beloved' (Eph. i. 6)? For further references to Mephibosheth see iv. 4, xix. 24-30.

Notes.—(1) viii. 1. See R.V.
(2) viii. 6, 14. 'Preserved'; see R.V. The Heb. word means 'saved'.
(3) viii. 13. See R.V. mg.
(4) viii. 18. 'The Cherethites and Pelethites'; probably a bodyguard of foreign (Philistine) troops. See 1 Sa. xxx. 14; 2 Sa. xv. 18, xx. 7; 1 Ki. i. 38.

Day 3. 2 Sa. x and xi.

(1) What lessons may be drawn from chapter x in regard to the warfare in which as soldiers of Christ we are engaged? How did this particular fighting begin, what was its progress, and how did it end? Note especially how it involved the whole strength of the nation. With x. 9 compare 2 Cor. i. 8-10, and with x. 12 compare 1 Cor. xvi. 13.

(2) What was the beginning of David's sin, and how did one wrong step lead on to another? Cf. Jas. i. 14, 15. Note, too, that it happened when David was at the height of his success. Cf. 1 Cor. x. 12.

Notes.—(1) The blow struck David from a quarter from which he expected only kindness, and was of the greatest severity, both in the grossness of the insult, and the strength of the subsequent attack.
(2) xi. 1. 'David tarried still at Jerusalem': contrast Uriah's attitude, verse 11.
(3) xi. 27, last clause. Cf. 2 Cor. v. 9, R.V.

Day 4. 2 Sa. xii–xiii. 37.

(1) Sin had partially blinded David. He could see sin in others, but not his own sin. How were his eyes opened? Note that God requires fearless men for His service. Cf. Mi. iii. 8.

(2) What may we learn from chapter xii about (a) penitence, (b) pardon, and (c) chastening? Cf. Ps. xxxii. 3-5; Heb. xii. 6, 11.

(3) What warning does chapter xiii give against evil friendships, and of the consequences of allowing sin to have dominion in the heart? Cf. Rom. vi. 12, vii. 5.

Notes.—(1) xii. 9. 'Despised the word of the Lord'. This was the most grievous feature of David's sin. Cf. 1 Sa. xv. 23, 26; Ps. li. 4.

(2) xii. 31. David was a child of his age, and when insulted could inflict a terrible revenge. Cf. 1 Sa. xxv. 32-34.

(3) xiii. 20. 'Absalom her brother'. Absalom was Tamar's full brother (verse 4b), and, therefore, according to eastern custom, had a duty to avenge her wrongs.

(4) Verse 37. 'For his son'; i.e. for Amnon.

Day 5. 2 Sa. xiii. 38–xiv.

A new section begins here, leading up to Absalom's rebellion.

(1) Try to visualize the situation. Absalom—since Amnon's death heir to the throne—was in exile, and had been absent about three years. David was both father and king. His heart yearned for Absalom; his sense of justice held him inactive. How did Joab seek to break the impasse?

(2) In verse 14 the woman, whom Joab had sent to David, applies her parable to God, declaring that He does not take away life, but devises means to restore the sinner (R.V.). The woman may be alluding here to David's own case, but her words shine with new depths of meaning in the light of the gospel. Work this out with the help of such verses as Ezk. xxxiii. 11; Is. liii. 6; 1 Jn. ii. 1, 2.

(3) Joab's ruse was only partially successful (verse 24). Why was this?

Notes.—(1) xiii. 38, 39. The meaning seems to be that the lapse of time assuaged David's anger and grief about Amnon, and caused his affections to flow out towards his still living son, Absalom.

(2) xiv. 7. Those who demanded the murderer's death had justification according to the law (see Dt. xix. 11-13). The woman based her plea on the ground of her own great need.

(3) xiv. 13. The woman's argument was that the judgment which the king had just pronounced was not in agreement with his conduct towards Absalom.

Day 6. 2 Sa. xv–xvi. 14.

(1) What factors contributed to Absalom's initial success? and by what means was he frustrated?

(2) Contrast Absalom, David's son, with Ittai, the foreign soldier, in their attitude to David. What is the measure of my loyalty to Christ? Can I say what David's servants said (verse 15) and what Ittai said? See La. iii. 40.

(3) What characteristics stand out in David in this, perhaps the darkest, hour of his life?

Notes.—(1) xv. 7. 'Forty'. See R.V. mg.
(2) xv. 11. This verse shows how closely Absalom's treacherous purpose had been guarded.

Day 7. 2 Sa. xvi. 15–xvii.

(1) Hushai is twice called 'David's friend'. What other friends had David in Jerusalem at this time? Are we as active for our absent king as Hushai and his companions were for theirs?

(2) Chapter xvii describes a period of imminent peril for David; for if Absalom had followed Ahithophel's counsel, David could hardly, humanly speaking, have survived. To what does the story ascribe the fact that Ahithophel's counsel did not prevail? Cf. xv. 31; 2 Ch. xxv. 16b; Ps. xxxiv. 16.

(3) When Hushai saw that his counsel had prevailed, what *action* did he take, and why? Consider the importance in the service of Christ of following up an initial gain by appropriate action. Have we sometimes failed just here?

Notes.—(1) xvi. 23. See R.V. mg. The reference is to the Urim and Thummim by which God's will was made known. Ahithophel's counsel was popularly regarded as almost equally unerring.
(2) xvii. 16. See R.V. David was awaiting word at some ford of the Jordan, ready to cross, if need be (xv. 28). See also verses 21, 22.

Week 31. 2 SAMUEL XVIII–XXIV

Day 1. 2 Sa. xviii–xix. 8.

(1) What evidences do you find in verses 1-5 of David's active leadership and of his assurance of victory? David himself describes the renewal of his faith and courage in Ps. iii.

(2) What lessons may we learn from the two memorials to Absalom spoken of in verses 17, 18? See Jos. vii. 26, viii. 29; Pr. xxix. 23; 1 Jn. ii. 16.

(3) What illustrations of David's tender affection for his children have we already met? See e.g. 2 Sa. xii. 16-18, xiii. 36, 37, xviii. 5. What worthy elements are to be found in his great grief over Absalom's death, and what unworthy? With xix. 5-7 compare Pr. xxvii. 6a.

Day 2. 2 Sa. xix. 9-39.

(1) Consider the situation as depicted in verses 9-15—a reaction in favour of David among the northern tribes; the tribe of Judah

holding itself aloof; David's urgent message to the elders of Judah, and his promise to Amasa, and the immediate effect of his appeal. But was his appointment of Amasa the fruit of wisdom, or was it the hasty act of an angry spirit? Cf. Pr. xiv. 29b; Ec. vii. 9.

(2) What qualities in David stand out in his treatment respectively of Shimei, Mephibosheth, and Barzillai?

(3) How does the passage illustrate 1 Cor. iii. 12-15. When our King returns, what will He say to us His servants?

Notes.—(1) Verse 11. The fact that Absalom's rebellion centred in Hebron (xv. 7-12) shows how deeply the tribe of Judah was implicated in it.

(2) Verse 13. 'Amasa, son of Abigail'; she was David's sister (xvii. 25; 1 Ch. ii. 16): he was therefore David's nephew and Joab's cousin.

Day 3. 2 Sa. xix. 40–xx.

(1) What insight is given here into jealousies between the tribes —Judah, the northern tribes, and Benjamin all claiming precedence? To what calamitous consequences did these jealousies threaten to lead the nation? Cf. Mk. x. 35-45; Gal. v. 15.

(2) How was the threatened disaster arrested? What part was played respectively by David, by Joab, and by the wise woman in the town of Abel? Cf. Ec. ix. 14-16.

(3) How would you describe Joab in his character and gifts?

Notes.—(1) xix. 40, 41. Instead of seeking to make the king's return a national event the tribe of Judah slipped in first.

(2) xx. 1. Sheba's hope was to recover the leadership for the tribe of Benjamin, Saul's tribe.

(3) xx. 6. David already seems to have begun to repent of his appointment of Amasa. He did not reinstate Joab directly, but did so through Joab's younger brother, Abishai.

Day 4. 2 Sa. xxi.

(1) What lesson does the story of verses 1-10 enforce in regard to God's attitude towards a breach of promise? Cf. Ps. xv. 1, 4b. Observe, too, how seriously David regarded it, and to what lengths he was willing to go to make amends.

(2) What other instances of rash zeal are found in Saul's life? See 1 Sa. xiii. 11, 12, xiv. 24, 29. Consider how much suffering may be brought upon others by unwise impetuosity.

(3) Verses 15-21 afford a further illustration of the strength of Israel's enemies. See Week 30, Day 3 (1) above, and cf. Eph. vi. 12. What special message, however, do these verses bring to us as *individuals*? Have we defeated any giant, or wrought any great victory? With verses 15-17 compare Rom. xvi. 4.

Notes.—(1) For the story of Israel's promise to Gibeon, see Jos. ix. 15, 19. There is no other mention in Scripture of Saul's having broken this promise.

(2) Verse 8. See R.V. Michal seems to be written wrongly here for Merab. See 1 Sa. xviii. 19.

(3) Verse 10. Rizpah; see iii. 7. Her act of extraordinary devotion and courage is not elsewhere spoken of in the Bible.

(4) Verse 17. 'Light'; better 'lamp' as in R.V.

(5) Verse 19. Cf. 1 Ch. xx. 5 which seems to have preserved more accurately the original text.

Day 5. 2 Sa. xxii.

(1) We have already met the psalm in the Psalter (Ps. xviii.). It may be sufficient, therefore, today, to ask ourselves as we read it, How much of the psalm can I affirm to be true also in my experience?

Notes.—(1) Verse 6. 'The sorrows of hell'; better, as in R.V., 'the cords of Sheol', Sheol being pictured as a hunter with cords and snares to catch his victim.

(2) Verse 19. See R.V.

Day 6. 2 Sa. xxiii.

(1) Consider in verses 1-7:

  (a) How David is described, and the direct claim that is made for the divine inspiration of the words that follow

  (b) The vision of the king that shall be (verses 3b-4, R.V. mg.) in His character (verse 3b) and in the issues of His reign (verse 4).

  (c) The basis upon which David's hopes of this glorious future rest (verse 5). Do you find here a much deeper note struck than in xxii. 20-25?

  (d) The judgment upon the wicked.

(2) Ponder the exploits of David's mighty men. What followers David had! We have a far greater Leader. What sort of followers are we?

Note.—Verse 5. The verse may be translated thus:
'For is not my house thus with God?
for an eternal covenant hath He made for me,
ordered in all and secured;
for all my salvation and all good pleasure
shall He not cause it to spring forth?' (*Camb. Bible*)
Because of God's covenant, the salvation promised to David, and all God's good pleasure, shall certainly come to pass.

Day 7. 2 Sa. xxiv.

The taking of a census was permitted by the law (Ex. xxx. 12; Nu. i. 2, 3). It is also evident that God's anger was kindled against the nation before David commanded the census to be made. It was not, therefore, the taking of a census in itself that was displeasing to God. It was rather the growth in the nation of a spirit of pride and vainglory, because of great victories won; and David himself yielded to this temptation, in commanding that the people be numbered. Cf. Pr. xvi. 5.

(1) How did David become aware that he had erred, and what did he do?

(2) How did God overrule the sin and the suffering for good? See Note 2 below, and compare Gn. l. 20.

Notes.—(1) Verse 1. 'Again'; an allusion probably to the famine in chapter xxi.

(2) We learn from 2 Ch. iii. 1 that Araunah's threshing floor was on Mount Moriah, which became the site of the temple.

JOHN

INTRODUCTION

(See New Bible Handbook, pp. 319-322, 338-344)

THE author of this Gospel claims to have been an eye-witness of the scenes that he records (i. 14, xix. 35; cf. 1 Jn. i. 1-3), and in xxi. 24 his identity with 'the disciple whom Jesus loved' is asserted. Among the many reasons for identifying this disciple with John the son of Zebedee, one of the most striking is the evangelist's habit of referring to the Baptist as 'John' only, and never mentioning the son of Zebedee by name.

The other three Gospels are chiefly concerned with our Lord's ministry in Galilee; a bare hint is all that they give us that He so much as visited Jerusalem between His baptism and the final Passover (Mt. xxiii. 37; Lk. xiii. 34; and perhaps Lk. iv. 44; see R.V. mg.). John, on the other hand, has little to say about our Lord's work in Galilee (ii. 1-12, iv. 43-54, vi); for the most part the scene of his narrative is Judaea, and especially Jerusalem, where almost from the first the Lord was rejected (i. 11, iv. 43, 44, v, etc.).

It is important to observe that in the record of Jesus' ministry up to His death, seven miracles are recorded in this Gospel. These are (1) The turning of water into wine (ii. 1-11); (2) The healing of the nobleman's son (iv. 46-54); (3) The healing of the impotent man (v. 2-9); (4) The feeding of the five thousand (vi. 4-13);

(5) The walking on the water (vi. 16-21); (6) The healing of the man born blind (ix. 1-7); (7) The raising of Lazarus from the dead (xi. 1-44). John calls these miracles 'signs' (a fact brought out more clearly in the R.V.), by which he means that they have a meaning beyond themselves, and point to corresponding works in the spiritual realm, such as the raising of the spiritually dead, the opening of the eyes of the spiritually blind, etc.

The purpose of the Gospel is clearly stated, 'that ye might believe that Jesus is the Christ, the Son of God, and that believing ye might have life through His name' (xx. 31). It shows the divine Word coming to His own people, revealing the Father to them both by teaching and by 'signs', and yet rejected and persecuted to the death. To the world this Gospel reveals the tremendous claims of the Lord Jesus and the awfulness of rejecting Him. To the disciple it reveals the implications of accepting Him, showing the interdependence of love and obedience, of life and feeding upon the Lord, of fruit-bearing and abiding in Him.

The section vii. 53–viii. 11 is omitted by all the oldest Greek MSS. now existing, with one exception, and its style and vocabulary are more like those of Luke (in whose Gospel four MSS. insert it) than those of John. But though this section was probably not written by John, it bears every evidence of truth, and we may thankfully accept it as part of the inspired Word of God.

ANALYSIS

viii. 12–59. Jesus is the light of the world, and the
     I AM.

ix. Blindness cured, and blindness intensified.

x. Jesus is the Good Shepherd, and He is One with
    the Father.

xi. Jesus is the resurrection and the life.

xii. Jesus is about to be glorified through death.
    Summary of the effect of His ministry.

xiii–xvii. Jesus reveals Himself to His disciples in the farewell
              discourses and the High-Priestly prayer.

xviii–xxi. Jesus is glorified in His arrest, His trial, His passion
             and His resurrection.

Week 32. JOHN I–IV. 26

Day 1. Jn. i. 1-18.

(1) What facts do we learn here about our Lord before He was
born on earth? See the whole passage, including verse 18, and
compare Heb. i. 1-3 and Col. i. 15-17.

(2) What was the difference between John the Baptist and
Jesus, and for what purposes did each come into the world?

(3) Contrast the tragedy of those who reject Christ, with the
privileges given to those who receive Him. See especially verses
10-14, 16. Have you begun to know these privileges?

Notes.—(1) Verses 3, 10, 17. For 'by' read 'through' as in R.V. mg. The
Greek word is the same as in verse 7.

(2) Verse 5. The light of Christ is like a beam, piercing the darkness of the
world, not wholly dispelling it, but also not overcome by it. See R.V. mg.

(3) Verse 9. Read as in R.V. mg.

(4) Verse 16. 'Grace for grace'; i.e. one grace succeeding another.

Day 2. Jn. i. 19-34.

(1) What do we learn here about (a) the character, and (b) the
work of John the Baptist. See also iii. 28-30.

(2) What fourfold testimony does John the Baptist bear to
Jesus in verses 26-34? Is Jesus all this to you?

Notes.—(1) Verse 29. 'Seeth Jesus coming'; probably after the forty days
in the wilderness, when He was tempted of Satan. That Jesus' baptism had
already taken place is shown by verse 32. Cf. Lk. iii. 21, 22.

(2) Verse 30. 'Who is preferred before me'; i.e. is of higher rank than I.
This clause should be omitted in verse 27, see R.V.

Day 3. Jn. i. 35-51.

(1) John, Andrew, Simon Peter, Nathanael—how did these men become followers of Jesus? Philip's call was different. What lessons may we learn (a) of the value, and (b) of the great results of personal work?

(2) How did Jesus deal with each of these men, especially with Simon and with Nathanael, and how does this illustrate the truth of what is said of Jesus in ii. 25? Do you believe He can change you into something you could never become of yourself, as He did Simon, and that He can show you greater things than you have yet experienced, as He promised to do for Nathanael?

Notes.—(1) Verse 40. 'One of the two . . . was Andrew.' The other, we may assume, was John.

(2) Verse 42. 'Thou art . . . thou shalt be'; cf. 2 Cor. v. 17. 'A stone'; Letter 'rock'.

(3) Verse 47. An allusion to the story of Jacob in Gn. xxxii. 24-29. Nathanael may have been wrestling under the fig-tree, as Jacob did at the ford Jabbok.

(4) Verse 51. This word, as shown by the plural 'you', was spoken not to Nathanael only, but to all the disciples. It is another allusion to the story of Jacob, see Gn. xxviii. 12, 13. Jesus brings God nearer to men than did the ladder Jacob saw in his dream. 'Son of Man', a name chosen to supplement the titles Nathanael had used. Jesus is Son of God and King of Israel, but also Son of Man.

Day 4. Jn. ii. 1-22.

(1) Verses 1-11 contain the story of the first of the seven 'signs' (see *Introduction* and verse 11 R.V.) which symbolize the spiritual blessings that Jesus brings to men. What does He do in human lives, in response to faith and obedience (verse 5) that is like the changing of water into wine? Cf. Acts viii. 8, 39 (last clause), xiii. 52.

(2) Try to picture the Temple court, with its market in full activity, that you may better appreciate the tremendous energy and the courage of Jesus in doing what He did.

(3) How does the whole incident show our Lord's consciousness of His divine mission, and of what the Jews' rejection of His claim would entail? Cf. Mal. iii. 1-3; Mk. ii. 20.

Notes.—(1) Verses 1-3. The narrative suggests that the marriage was in the home of near relatives of Jesus, for Mary had authority to give orders to the servants; also that the coming of Jesus and His disciples was unexpected, and was the cause of the shortage of wine.

(2) **Verse 4.** Behind the almost abrupt reply of Jesus lies the consciousness that the old life in the home with His mother had ended, and was not to be resumed.

(3) **Verse 14.** The High Priests permitted the outer court of the Temple to be used for the sale of animals needed for sacrifice, and the exchange of Roman money into Jewish coinage. Note our Lord's use of the words 'my Father'; see v. 18.

Day 5. Jn. ii. 23–iii. 21.

(1) Why was Jesus not satisfied with the faith spoken of in ii. 23? Cf. iv. 48, vi. 30; Mk. viii. 11, 12; Acts viii. 13.

(2) What three things at least are involved in being 'born again', or 'born from above' (R.V. mg.)? See Mt. xviii. 3; Jn i. 12, 13; 2 Cor. v. 17. Why will nothing short of the new birth suffice?

(3) What does this section teach regarding (a) the cost of redemption; (b) why that price was paid; (c) the terms on which salvation is offered; (d) the result of rejecting it; (e) why so many do reject it?

Notes.—(1) Verse 5. 'Born of water'; a reference to John's baptism, which the Pharisees refused (Lk. vii. 30). 'Born of the Spirit'; an experience found through receiving Jesus (i. 12).

(2) Verse 8. As with the wind, so with the movement of the Spirit: the effect is real and recognizable, though the process is hidden.

(3) Verses 13, 14. The gospel speaks of heavenly things, of which Christ is the sole revealer; cf. iii. 31, 32; Mt. xi. 27.

Day 6. Jn. iii. 22-36.

When the feast was ended the people dispersed, and it seemed as if the visit to Jerusalem had been without abiding result (cf. i. 11). Jesus then withdrew with His disciples into the country districts of Judaea, and there engaged in similar work to that which John the Baptist was doing. See verses 22, 23.

(1) What was John's reply to those of his followers who complained to him that Jesus was attracting more people than John was, and what was John's consolation in thus effacing himself? Is verse 30 the motto also of your life?

(2) What seven things are said about Jesus in verses 31, 32, 34, 35, which set Him apart from and above all others?

(3) In what two ways is man's acceptance or rejection of Jesus described, and what is the consequence that follows in each case? See verses 32, 33, 36.

Notes.—(1) Verse 29. 'The friend of the bridegroom'; one whose function it was to ask the hand of the bride for the bridegroom, and to arrange the marriage.

(2) Verse 32. 'No man' is not to be taken literally (see verse 33), but as meaning men in general.

(3) Verse 33. 'Set to his seal'; i.e. 'solemnly declared' (Weymouth).

(4) Verse 36. 'Believeth not'; better, as in R.V., 'obeyeth not'. What is meant is refusal to obey the call to believe and live.

Day 7. Jn. iv. 1-26.

(1) What did our Lord mean by 'living' water, and why, when He had awakened in the woman a desire for it, did He not at once grant her request? What was necessary before He could do so?

(2) Trace the successive steps by which Jesus brought the woman to feel her need of salvation, and pointed her to Himself.

(3) What kind of worship does God desire, and why? With verses 25, 26, compare xiv. 6.

Notes.—(1) Verses 1-3. In the hostility of the Pharisees Jesus seems to have recognized His Father's signal to leave Judaea.

(2) Verse 4. 'He must needs go'; i.e. He was urged by an inward constraint.

(3) Verses 7-9. Jesus did two things which strict Jews of the time would not have done, viz. to speak to a woman thus in a public place (cf. verse 27), to ask a favour of a Samaritan. Cf. also verse 40.

(4) Verse 20. 'This mountain'; i.e. Mount Gerizim, where the Samaritans had built a temple. The temple had been destroyed, but the Samaritans regarded the place as holy.

Week 33. JOHN IV. 27–VII. 24

Day 1. Jn. iv. 27-54.

(1) What is the refreshment of which our Lord speaks in verse 32, and how were the things that had just happened an illustration of it? See verses 34-38 and compare verses 6, 7. Have you tasted such refreshment in work for the Lord?

(2) Observe the two grounds of faith in verses 39-42. How far does our faith rest upon what we have been told by others, and how far on our own personal experience of the Lord?

(3) The story of verses 46-54 is the second of the seven signs (see *Introduction*). What spiritual blessing does the Lord bring to men which may be likened to the healing of fever? Cf. xiv. 27. Observe the necessity of *faith* (verse 50).

Notes.—(1) Verse 28. 'Men'; better, 'people' (R.S.V.).

(2) Verses 35-38. In the natural world there were yet four months till harvest; but in the spiritual sphere in this instance reaping followed close upon the sowing.

(3) Verse 44. Jesus, it would seem, did not expect much honour among His own people (cf. Lk. iv. 24). The Galileans welcomed Him, however, as a

wonder worker, with the same disappointing kind of faith as had been shown in Jerusalem (ii. 23-25), and this accounts for Jesus' seemingly harsh word in verse 48.

Day 2. Jn. v. 1-29.

(1) Verses 2-9, the third of the seven 'signs' (see *Introduction*). What spiritual blessing does Jesus bring to men corresponding to the healing of a long-continued infirmity? The danger in such a case is that there is no longer the *will* to be healed. Cf. verse 6, '*Wilt* thou?'

(2) In verses 17-29 what does Jesus say of Himself (a) in relation to God and (b) in relation to men? Make a list of and ponder what He says under each of these heads.

(3) What assurance have we in these verses that everyone who truly believes on Jesus is immediately made partaker of eternal life? Cf. iii. 36a. How is faith here defined?

Notes.—(1) Notice the changes in r.v. in verses 3, 4, 24, 29.

(2) Verse 8. 'Bed'; better, 'pallet' (r.s.v.).

(3) Verse 10. The scribes stressed such statements as Je. xvii. 21, 22; Ne. xiii. 19, and forbade the carrying of anything out of doors on the Sabbath.

(4) Verse 25. What is meant here is spiritual resurrection from the death of sin. Contrast verse 38.

Day 3. Jn. v. 30-47.

(1) To what four different testimonies to Himself does Jesus appeal? Which does He himself regard as of least importance?

(2) Is it still possible to study the Bible without finding life; and, if so, what is lacking? What reasons does Jesus give for the Jews' failure? Cf. 2 Cor. iii. 14-16.

Notes.—(1) Verse 31. The Lord seems to be answering an unspoken objection in the minds of his hearers, as if they said, 'You have no one but yourself to speak for you. Why should we believe?'

(2) Verse 39. 'Search the scriptures'; better, as in r.v., 'Ye search the scriptures.'

Day 4. Jn. vi. 1-21. With verse 2 compare ii. 23, iv. 45, 48.

(1) Verses 4-13. The fourth of the seven 'signs' (see *Introduction*). Trace the stages by which God's supply reached the hungry people, noting especially the part played by the disciples. What does this teach us as to how we, with our feeble resources,

may satisfy the spiritual need of the hungry multitudes around us? Cf. 2 Cor. iii. 5, 6.

(2) Why do you think Jesus, after this great miracle, which had so stirred the people, departed again into a mountain Himself alone? Cf. Mk. i. 35; Lk. v. 16, vi. 12. What may we learn from this?

(3) Verses 16-21. The fifth of the seven 'signs'. What spiritual blessing does Jesus bring to His people that may be likened to walking upon the sea? Is it the power to rise above adverse conditions, and not to be submerged and defeated by them? Cf. 2 Cor. iv. 8, 9.

Notes.—(1) Verse 7. 'Two hundred pennyworth'; see Mt. xviii. 28 (R.V. mg.); about £7.

(2) Verse 14. 'That prophet that should come'; cf. Dt. xviii. 15; Mt. xi. 3, here identified by the people with the Messiah, as verse 15 shows.

Day 5. Jn. vi. 22-40.

Today's portion consists mainly of a dialogue between Jesus and the people, who had seen the miracle of the multiplied loaves, and were eagerly seeking Him. It will help to clarify the section to note down the three questions the people asked and the request they made (see verses 25, 28, 30, 34), and to consider Jesus' reply in each case.

(1) With what motive were the people seeking Jesus, and what did they seek from Him? What in contrast had Jesus come to give, and how was it to be obtained? See verses 27-29.

(2) The people wanted Jesus to outdo Moses. Jesus immediately lifts their thoughts to God, who in His Son has something far better to give than the manna of old. How do verses 32-35 amplify verses 27-29, making clearer what the gift is, which is offered through Jesus, and how it is to be obtained?

(3) Verses 36-40 are a kind of soliloquy on the part of Jesus. Although these to whom He is speaking believe not, yet God's purpose will not fail. What is the guarantee (a) of the final complete success of Jesus' mission, and (b) of the security of him who believes in Jesus?

Notes.—(1) Verses 22-25 explain the astonishment of the crowd to find Jesus next day on the Capernaum side of the lake. They had noticed that He had not gone with the disciples.

(2) Verse 26. 'Miracles'; better, 'signs', as in R.V. The people should have discerned in the miracle a sign of the kingdom of God, but they saw only a miraculously provided meal. 'This gives the measure of their messianic expectation. He was the true Messiah who could maintain them in life without toil' (Dodds).

Day 6. Jn. vi. 41-71.

Today's portion falls into four parts: (*a*) verses 41-51, Jesus' reply to murmurings of the Jews; (*b*) verses 52-59, Jesus' answers to the wranglings of the Jews; (*c*) verses 60-65, Jesus' reply to murmurings of His disciples; (*d*) verses 66-71, Jesus asks the Twelve, 'Will ye also go away?'

(1) Verses 44 and 45 are an expansion of verse 37a. God gives souls to His Son by *drawing* them through His Word. Cf. i. 23, v. 46, 47. But what must *man* do if he is to be saved? See verses 45 ('cometh'), 47 ('believeth'), 51 ('eat').

(2) What new point did Jesus introduce in verse 51 that caused His hearers to strive among themselves? How does He expand this thought in verses 53-58? Try to state what He says in your own words, showing what saving faith is.

(3) The closing verses 60-71 make clear that what Jesus offers to men is not fleshly or material gain (cf. verse 27) but spiritual life through union with Himself. What three reasons does Peter give why he and his fellow disciples remained faithful when many others went back? See verses 68, 69 (R.V.).

Notes.—(1) Verse 62. When Jesus has ascended to heaven, it will become clear that He has not been speaking of a literal eating of His flesh and blood, but of something that is spiritual and life-giving. Cf. Lv. xvii. 10-12.

(2) The approaching Passover Feast was clearly in our Lord's thought as He spoke, and there may be anticipatory allusions to the Lord's Supper; but Jesus is speaking in this discourse, not of the sacrament itself, but of the truths of which the sacrament is the expression.

Day 7. Jn. vii. 1-24.

Chapters vii–x. 21 give an account of Jesus' visit to Jerusalem at the Feast of Tabernacles six months before His death. The story vividly portrays the various attitudes towards Jesus among different groups. These groups fall into two main classes, one, 'the Jews', who included the chief priests, Pharisees, rulers and 'them of Jerusalem', and the other, 'the people', that is, the general multitude from all parts, who were attending the feast. The first of these two classes was, in the main, hostile to Jesus.

(1) What advice did His brethren give Him, and how did Jesus reply? See verses 3-8. How does this incident reveal how difficult Jesus' path was? Can we, His disciples, if faithful, expect an easy path? See xv. 18-21. Has verse 13 any reproach for you?

(2) What two tests (one affecting the enquirer, and one concerning Himself) does our Lord suggest whereby the source of His teaching can be known?

(3) In verses 19-24 Jesus defends Himself from the charge of Sabbath-breaking on account of the miracle He had wrought on

His previous visit (see v. 16). What argument does He use, and how does it penetrate beneath the outward appearance to the essential rightness of His action? See verse 24 and Note (3) below.

Notes.—(1) Verse 3. 'His brethren'; see ii. 12.

(2) Verse 15. 'How is it that this man has learning, when he has never studied?' (R.S.V.).

(3) Verses 21-24. The law of Moses commanded circumcision on the eighth day after birth (Gn. xvii. 12; Lv. xii. 3), and it was the practice of the Jews to perform the rite on that day, *even if it fell upon the Sabbath*. Jesus argued that to make a man every whit whole on the Sabbath had even more justification than to circumcise him.

Week 34. JOHN VII. 25–XI. 27

Day 1. Jn. vii. 25-52.

(1) What illustrations are found in these verses (a) of the deep impression made by the Lord Jesus upon many, and yet (b) how their incipient faith was checked by ignorance, or prejudice, or pride?

(2) The chief priests and the Pharisees by no means saw eye to eye in most matters, but they were united against Jesus. What action did they take at this time, and how was it unsuccessful? It is often said, 'No thinking person now believes that. . . .' Do you find a precedent for this attitude in this passage?

(3) In what way is the promise of verses 37, 38 an advance on that of Jn. iv. 13, 14, and how does it bring out the fact that we are saved to serve? Cf. Acts i. 8.

Notes.—(1) Verse 38. 'Out of his belly'; i.e., as we should express it, 'out of his heart'. Jesus seems to be alluding to the rock in the wilderness (Nu. xx. 11). He Himself is that Rock (cf. 1 Cor. x. 4), and those who believe on Him become in their turn transformed into a rock from which living water flows.

(2) Verse 51. It was a bold act on the part of Nicodemus to say to those who had just uttered words of contempt for the common people who knew not the law, 'Are you not showing ignorance of the law yourselves in acting as you are doing?'

(3) Verse 52. There had been one or two Galilean prophets, such as Jonah and Hosea, but the meaning is that Galilee was not a country where one would look for a prophet, still less for the Messiah.

Day 2. Jn. vii. 53–viii. 29.

(1) For the passage vii. 53–viii. 11 see *Introduction*. It has perhaps been introduced here as an illustration of viii. 15. What may we learn from it about our attitude to the sinner? Cf. Lk. xviii. 9-14. Verse 7 is sometimes used as an argument for condoning

sin; but are not Jesus' words rather a summons to judge ourselves with the same severity with which we would judge others?

(2) How does Jesus set forth in verses 13-29 His relationship to His Father, and of the Father to Him? Note down carefully the separate ways in which that relationship is shown. It is a marvellous unfolding of His inner life.

(3) What promise is given to those who follow Him, and what on the other hand is said to be the consequence of persistent unbelief?

Notes.—(1) viii. 12. An allusion to the pillar of fire, which guided the children of Israel on their journey through the wilderness (cf. Nu. ix. 15-23) and which was commemorated during the Feast of Tabernacles by brilliant lighting of the Temple.

(2) Verses 13, 14. There is no contradiction with v. 31. There Jesus says that if He had been the sole witness in His own cause, His witness would not have been true. But in both passages He goes on to point out that He is not alone in His witness. See verses 17, 18.

(3) Verse 24. Cf. vi. 53.

Day 3. Jn. viii. 30-59.

The conflict between Jesus and the Jews grows sterner, until it culminates in an open breach. Cf. vi. 66.

(1) What is necessary if a profession of faith (verse 30) is to lead to true discipleship, and to the full freedom of sonship? Cf. Lk. viii. 15; Gal. iv. 1-7. What shows that those who believed at this time were only 'stony-ground hearers' (Lk. viii. 13)? See verse 37, note.

(2) What does Jesus reveal to be their true condition? By physical descent 'the seed of Abraham', and therefore in that sense 'children of the kingdom' (cf. Mt. viii. 12), what were they spiritually in relation (a) to sin, (b) to the devil, and (c) to God?

(3) What do we learn in this passage about (a) the Person and (b) the character of Christ?

Notes.—(1) Verse 33. Jesus had touched their pride. As Abraham's seed, they considered themselves the free people of God.

(2) Verses 34, 35. 'Servant'; better, 'slave' (R.S.V.). As sinners, we are not free, but are slaves in bondage.

(3) Verse 37. 'Has no place'; better, 'gains no ground' (Weymouth). Cf. R.V.

(4) Verse 51. 'Shall never see death'; i.e. in its full horror as the wages of sin. Cf. vi. 50, xi. 26; 1 Cor. xv. 55-57; 2 Tim. i. 10.

(5) Verse 56. 'My day'; i.e. the day of my triumph; cf. Heb. xi. 13.

(6) Verse 58. 'I am'; i.e. eternally existent.

Day 4. Jn. ix. 1-38.

(1) Picture in imagination the successive scenes of this vivid and beautiful story.

(2) This is the sixth of the seven 'signs' (see *Introduction*). Of what spiritual blessing that Jesus brings to men is it a type? Cf. Acts xxvi. 18. How does the story show that in this case the spiritual miracle of which the physical was a symbol also took place? See especially verses 11, 17, 31-33, 35-37.

(3) What motive for zeal in the Lord's service is given us in verses 1-5? With verse 5 compare Mt. v. 14.

Notes.—(1) Verse 6. The Jews believed that saliva had curative value. Jesus in using it wished to quicken the man's faith.

(2) Verse 7. 'He went his way'; an instance of the obedience of faith. Cf. iv. 50.

(3) Verses 24, 25. In seeking to silence the man's testimony they only made him more resolute.

Day 5. Jn. ix. 39–x. 21.

The teaching of ix. 39-41 is similar in meaning to that of Lk. x. 21. There follow three parables (x. 1-6, 7-10, 11-18), which expound in pictorial form the significance of what was taking place, namely, that the fold of Israel has fallen into the hands of self-seeking men, but the true shepherd is drawing to Himself His own sheep.

(1) Read verses 1-6 in the light of the blind man's story. The false shepherds had cast him out (ix. 35), but the true shepherd had found him. How do the flock know the shepherd, and what does he do for them? Have you experienced the comfort of the words 'He goeth before'?

(2) What are the privileges and blessings of those who enter in through Christ as the door, and what the sorrows and miseries of those who remain under self-seeking shepherds? See verses 7-10.

(3) What are the marks of the good shepherd? Can you find in verses 11-18 (a) proof that our Lord's death was not a mere martyrdom, (b) the purpose of His life and death, and (c) an incentive to missionary work? Cf. Rev. vii. 9, 10, 15-17.

Notes.—(1) x. 1-6. Jesus the Shepherd, John the Baptist the porter, the Pharisees the thieves and robbers who had usurped authority in the fold of Israel.

(2) Verse 16. 'One fold'; better,' one flock', as in R.V.

Day 6. Jn. x. 22-42.

The Feast of the Dedication was held at the close of December, and, therefore, only about two months had elapsed since the incidents of ix–x. 21.

(1) When the Jews found Jesus among them again, they gathered round Him, and asked Him to declare plainly if He were the Christ. Why did Jesus not give them the answer they desired, but pointed them to His teaching and His works? Cf. Mt. xvi. 20.

(2) In the six statements of verses 27 and 28, how is the sheep's relation to the shepherd described, and how the shepherd's relation to the sheep? What is the doubly sure ground of the flock's security?

(3) Ponder the argument from the Scriptures, which Jesus uses to refute the charge of blasphemy made against Him. He claims a far more intimate relation to God, and a far higher mission (verses 36, 38), than the judges, spoken of in Ps. lxxxii, whom the Scripture calls 'gods' and 'sons of the most High'. Why, then, should He be called a blasphemer if He says, 'I am the Son of God'?

Notes.—(1) Verse 23. 'Solomon's porch'; a cloister along the eastern side of the outer court of the Temple (Acts iii. 11, v. 12.)

(2) Verse 30. The word 'one' is neuter in the Greek: 'a unity', not 'One Person'.

Day 7. Jn. xi. 1-27.

(1) Verses 1-16. Picture the scene. In Bethany, the two sisters wait for Jesus to come; in Peraea, Jesus receives the message. Two questions arise: (a) should He go at once? (b) should He go at all? Show how, in each case, the action of Jesus is different from that which human love and wisdom might have dictated. What was the ground of His action, and what lessons may we find here for our own comfort and use?

(2) Verses 17-27. In what ways do these verses comfort the bereaved Christian, even though he cannot look for a miracle such as this chapter describes?

Notes.—(1) Verse 3. Jesus was in Peraea, 'beyond Jordan' (x. 40).

(2) Verses 9, 10. To each of His servants God appoints a life day, in which he may walk freely, without stumbling, in the light of God's will; but if he seeks to prolong his day selfishly by evading duty, he falls into darkness.

(3) Verse 26. 'Shall never die.' For the believer death is no more death. Jesus calls it 'sleep', which is a state of life. Cf. Jn. viii. 51, note.

Week 35. JOHN XI. 28–XIV. 14

Day 1. Jn. xi. 28-44.

(1) Why did Jesus not speak to Mary words of faith, as He had done to Martha? Was it that she was completely crushed under

her sorrow, and had no faith that even Jesus could now do anything? Was it this submission to the victory of death, this collapse
of faith, that caused Jesus such disturbance in spirit? See note
below.

(2) What do we learn here about our Lord's prayer life, and
the way in which His miracles were wrought? Cf. Jn. v. 19, 20,
xiv. 10. Consider the confidence of His faith in thus publicly giving
thanks that God had heard Him *before* the miracle was wrought.
Cf. 1 Ki. xviii. 30-39; Mk. xi. 24 (R.V.).

(3) This is the seventh 'sign' (see *Introduction*). Of what spiritual
blessing, which Jesus brings to men, is it a type? See v. 25; Eph. ii.
5.

Notes.—(1) Verses 33-38. The word 'weep' in verse 33 is the wailing of
mourners (see R.V. mg.); that in verse 35 implies silent tears of sympathy.
Jesus' 'groaning in spirit' was something deeper, and seems to have been caused
by the wailing and by the unbelieving comment of verse 37. His spirit was
moved to indignation by these manifestations of unbelief. Cf. Mk. v. 38, 39;
Mk. viii. 12, ix. 19; Lk. vii. 13.

(2) Verse 40. 'Believe . . . see'; cf. Mk. xv. 32, 'see and believe'. The
world says 'see and believe', but Jesus says 'believe and see'.

Day 2. Jn. xi. 45–xii. 19.

(1) Observe the varied effects of the miracle. See especially
xi. 45, 46, 47-53, 54, xii. 10, 11, 17-19, and cf. Lk. xvi. 31. How
is it that the same act quickens faith in some, and hatred in
others? Cf. xi. 47, 48, xii. 11, 19; Mt. xxvii. 18.

(2) How does the story of xii. 1-8 show that Jesus values highly
the devotion of a loving heart, even if expressed in unconventional
ways?

(3) What twofold illustration have we in this passage that God
overrules men's purposes and actions for the fulfilling of His own
designs? See especially xi. 47-53, xii. 12-16.

Notes.—(1) xi. 48. The Jewish leaders feared that Jesus might lead a revolt
for which the Romans would exact severe punishment. Caiaphas said openly
that there was only one solution—the death of Jesus, and the others agreed.
Note the step they took in verse 57.

(2) xii. 2. 'They made him a supper'; a public banquet in recognition of
what Jesus had done in the raising of Lazarus.

Day 3. Jn. xii. 20-36.

In this chapter John completes his record of Jesus' revelation of Himself to
the world (see *Analysis*). That revelation has been given to the Jews, but in
this incident an indication appears that the great Gentile world beyond is
seeking to 'see Jesus'. This moved the Lord profoundly, for the world was in

His heart (cf. iii. 16, x. 16); but He knew that between Him and the fulfilment of His heart's desire lay the necessity of His atoning death, and of His return to His Father. The coming of the Greeks, therefore, took His thoughts at once to the cross.

(1) What is the difference between a grain in the granary, and a grain sown? How does this illustrate the differences between two ways of spending our life? Which did Jesus choose, and what does He promise to all who will follow Him in this choice?

(2) What threefold consequence is stated in verses 31, 32 as issuing from the Lord's choice? Has this threefold result taken place in your life?

(3) Verses 35, 36 give Jesus' last appeal to the nation. What may we learn from it as to our own immediate duty? Cf. viii. 12; Eph. v. 7-14; 1 Thes. v. 4-6.

Notes.—(1) Verse 25. The word 'life' occurs three times. In the first two cases it means our natural earthly life, in the third the life which Jesus is, and gives.

(2) Verses 31, 32. We are approaching the trial of Jesus before the Jewish Council and Pilate; it is not He that was judged and condemned, however, but they. 'Two rulers are represented here as contending for possession. . . . The ruler in possession, Satan, shall be rejected . . . but Jesus by the cross shall acquire an irresistibly attractive power' (Dods).

Day 4. Jn. xii. 37-50.

The problem of Jewish unbelief was one of great perplexity to many in the beginning of the gospel. Paul devotes three chapters to it in his Epistle to the Romans, and John deals with it here.

(1) Verses 37-43. The problem is stated in verse 37, and the answer is given in verses 38-40. What twofold explanation of Jewish unbelief does John give? What other hindrance also entered in to prevent those who had begun to believe from making open confession?

(2) The *seriousness* of rejecting Jesus is the subject of verses 44-50, in which John summarizes the teaching of Jesus on this matter. Why is it so serious to reject Jesus? See especially verses 45, 46, 50 and compare Pr. i. 20-33.

Notes.—(1) Verse 42. 'Put out of the synagogue'; cf. ix. 22. This was a very severe punishment, involving separation from public worship and from social intercourse.

(2) Verse 45. 'Seeth'; better, 'beholdeth', as in R.V. The word is used in the spiritual sense as in vi. 40.

Day 5. Jn. xiii. 1-20.

Jesus' ministry of teaching to the world without is finished (xii. 36). In this chapter begins His final teaching to His own disciples. See *Analysis.*

(1) How do the statements in verses 1-3 enhance the grace and wonder of Jesus' action in washing the feet of His disciples at this time?

(2) What important lesson did Jesus teach in response to Peter's interruptions? See verses 8 and 10. See Note 2 below, and cf. Tit. iii. 5; 1 Jn. i. 7.

(3) What further application did Jesus make of His action as an example to His followers? Cf. Lk. xxii. 22-27; 1 Pet. v. 5. Are we giving sufficient heed to this matter? See verse 17.

Notes.—(1) Verse 2. 'Supper being ended'; better, 'during supper', as in R.V.

(2) Verse 10. 'Washed'; better, 'bathed', as in R.V., that is, has been in the bath. The disciples had been cleansed, all except Judas. Cf. xv. 3.

(3) Verse 20. To be connected with verse 16, giving the other side of the disciples' position.

Day 6. Jn. xiii. 21-32.

(1) What evidence do you find that the eleven had not hitherto suspected Judas in any way, and what light does this throw upon Judas, as to his outward behaviour? As to what he really was in heart, see vi. 70, xii. 6, xiii. 2, 27, and cf. 1 Sa. xvi. 7; Pr. iv. 23.

(2) The giving of a sop, or morsel of bread dipped in gravy, was a mark of friendship. Ponder the depth of Jesus' love in acting thus towards Judas at this time. What was the effect of this last appeal? See verse 27.

(3) In verses 31, 32, two glorifyings of the Son of Man are spoken of, one present, the other future, and the second is said to depend upon the first. What are these two glorifyings? For the first see i. 14, xi. 4, xii. 23, xvii. 4, and for the second xvii. 1, 5.

Note.—Verses 25, 26. Jesus and His disciples were reclining, Jewish fashion, on couches round the table. It would appear that Judas was on the Lord's left, the place of honour, and John on the Lord's right. John's question and Jesus' answer would be whispered.

Day 7. Jn. xiii. 33–xiv. 14.

The institution of the Lord's Supper, recorded by the other Gospels, probably took place between verses 32 and 33. Then Jesus began to speak about His going away, a theme that occupies the remainder of His talk that evening. Having introduced it, He went on to urge the duty of mutual love, but Peter interrupted, and Jesus does not return to the subject of mutual love until xv. 12.

(1) How do verses 37 and 38 enforce Paul's warning in 1 Cor. x. 12? xiv. 1-3 are an expansion of the last words of verse 36. The separation, though necessary, is not final, but rather full of a bright hope.

(2) What claims does Jesus make for Himself in verses 4-11, (a) in regard to man's approach to God; (b) in regard to man's knowledge of God; and (c) in regard to the source and origin of His own words and works?

(3) What prospect does He set before His disciples as a consequence of His return to the Father? See verses 12-14. Do you know anything of this in your experience?

Notes.—(1) xiii. 33. 'Little children'; a term of special affection. Cf. verse 1b.

(2) xiv. 1b. Many prefer the rendering 'Believe in God, believe also in Me'. See R.V. mg. and cf. Mk. xi. 22.

(3) Verse 2. 'Mansions'; better, 'abiding-places' (R.V. mg.), or 'rooms' (R.S.V.). The word is the same as that rendered 'abode' in verse 23.

(4) Verse 12. 'The works that I do'; i.e. from heaven. Christ dwelling in the believing disciple will do His works. Cf. verse 10, last clause.

'Greater works'. Greater because wrought in the spiritual sphere, the raising of the spiritually dead, etc. See *Introduction.*

Week 36. JOHN XIV. 15–XVII

Day 1. Jn. xiv. 15-24.

(1) When the Spirit comes, what threefold relationship will He have to the disciples? See the three prepositions in verses 16, 17 and Note (2) below.

(2) When the Spirit comes, what five marvellous things will happen in the experience of the disciples? See (a) verse 18, (b) verse 19, (c) verse 20, (d) verse 21, (e) verse 23.

(3) On the disciples' side what is the necessary condition on which these things can be known?

Notes.—(1) Verse 16. 'Comforter'; literally one called to one's side, to give help or counsel.

(2) Verse 17. 'He dwelleth with you'; the preposition here is not the same in the original Greek as that of verse 16. The 'with' of verse 16 expresses companionship, that of verse 17 the idea of a stand-by.

(3) Verse 18. 'Comfortless'; better, 'desolate', as in R.V. The literal meaning is 'orphans'.

(4) Verse 22. The disciples thought that the Messiah, when He manifested Himself, would come in visible power and glory to set up His kingdom. Cf. Acts i. 6.

Day 2. Jn. xiv. 25–xv. 8.

(1) Jesus had said He was going away, and the disciples' hearts were troubled (cf. xvi. 6). He had just spoken also of the importance of keeping His words (verses 15, 21, 23); but if He were going

away, His teaching would cease, and much of what He had said
had slipped from their memory (cf. Mk. viii. 18). How does Jesus
in verses 25-29 answer these fears? Do you know in experience the
reality of what is promised in verses 26 and 27?

(2) What do we learn in verses 30 and 31 about (a) the Father,
(b) Christ, (c) Satan, (d) the world?

(3) What does the parable of the vine teach about (a) the
purpose for which the branches exist, (b) the husbandman's
dealing with the branches, (c) the dependence of the branches
upon the vine? How does Jesus apply these things to His disciples?
With verses 3 and 7 compare xiv. 15, 21, 23; see also viii. 31, 32;
Heb. iv. 12.

Notes.—(1) xiv. 26. 'In my Name'; notice the central position of Jesus in
the gospel economy. The Holy Spirit is sent in His Name; we, His disciples,
pray in His Name (verses 13, 14).

(2) Verse 28. 'My Father is greater than I'; cf. x. 29, 30; Heb. x. 12, 13.

(3) Verse 30. 'The prince of this world'; cf. xii. 31, xvi. 11; 2 Cor. iv. 4;
Eph. ii. 2; 1 Jn. v. 19.

'Hath nothing in me'; no inch of territory in my life.

Day 3. Jn. xv. 9-25.

Jesus is going away, and the disciples will be left in the world. In today's
portion Jesus speaks (a) about their life among themselves (verses 9-17); and
(b) about their life in the world (verses 18-25).

(1) What five privileges does Jesus say will be the portion o
His people (see verses 9, 11, 15, 16), and what are the essentia
conditions for the enjoyment of them (see verses 10, 11, 12, 14,
17)?

(2) What seven reasons does Jesus give in verses 18-25 why His
disciples may expect to meet hatred in the world?

(3) Putting verses 9 and 12 together consider (a) how the
Father loved Christ, that is, in what ways His love for Christ was
manifested (cf. iii. 35, v. 20; but also Mt. xxvi. 39), (b) how Christ
has loved us, and (c) how we ought to love one another. Cf. Eph.
v. 1, 2; 1 Jn. iii. 16-18.

Day 4. Jn. xv. 26–xvi. 15.

The last two verses of chapter xv connect with xvi. 7-11. The opening verses
of chapter xvi are a parenthesis, spoken because of the effect upon the disciples
of His words about the hatred they would encounter from the world.

(1) What evidence do you find in xvi. 1-7 that the disciples
were cast down by Jesus' words? Why did He say that He had
not spoken of these things before, and why did He speak of them

now? Notice, however, that He did not lighten in any way the dark picture He had drawn, but rather shaded it more deeply (xvi. 2).

(2) What new force, however, would be brought to bear upon the world (see xv. 26, 27) and what threefold result will follow (xvi. 8-11)? How would this make Jesus' departure an advantage instead of a loss?

(3) What further will the Spirit of truth do for the disciples, to their great gain? See verses 12-15.

Notes.—(1) xvi. 1. 'Offended'; better, 'made to stumble', as in R.V.

(2) Verse 2. 'Put out of the synagogue'; see xii. 42, note.

(3) Verse 4b. Jesus had spoken of persecution, but not in connection with His own departure. See Mt. x; Lk. xii. 4, etc.

(4) Verse 5. Peter had asked this very question, but with the thought in his mind that he might go with Christ, xiii. 36, 37. They had not given willing acceptance to Jesus' statement of His departure, nor sought to enquire into what it meant, but were crushed under it.

(5) Verses 8-11. 'Reprove'; better, 'convict', as in R.V., or 'convince', as in R.S.V. There is no single English word which exactly expresses the meaning of the Greek word. In Mt. xviii. 15 (R.V.) it is translated 'show him his fault'. The Holy Spirit will convince men of their false standards of sin, righteousness and judgment (Is. lv. 8, 9). He will show them that the essence of sin is unbelief in Christ; that true righteousness is not that of the Pharisees (works of the law) but the righteousness exhibited in Christ, and declared in the gospel; and that judgment awaits all who follow the prince of the world. At Pentecost the hearers were convinced by the Spirit's witness through the apostles, exactly as Jesus here says (verses 9-11).

(6) Verse 13. 'Things to come'; better, 'the things that are to come', as in R.V.; for example, the significance of the cross, into which Jesus does not here enter.

Day 5. Jn. 16-33.xvi.

(1) To Jesus, the events that would happen between the present moment and the coming of the Spirit were clear, but to the disciples all was dark. On what points does Jesus lay emphasis as He tries to prepare them for what they must pass through? See verses 16, 20, 21.

(2) In verses 22-27 He looked beyond 'the little while' of events immediately ahead to the time when the Spirit has come. What blessings and privileges does He say the disciples will then enjoy? He mentions at least four in these verses. What in particular does He say about prayer, and what light do His words throw upon the meaning of 'in my Name'? Cf. xiv. 13, 14, xv. 16.

(3) In verse 33 Jesus sums up the situation. In what two opposing spheres would the disciples live? What would be their

experience in the one and in the other? What was to be the ground of their courage and confidence?

Notes.—(1) Verse 16. 'See . . . see'; the first 'see' is in the Greek a different word from the second: cf. R.V. The second 'see' refers to the spiritual vision at Pentecost (cf. xiv. 19), and so also in verses 17 and 19.

(2) Verse 23. 'Ye shall ask me nothing'; better, 'ask me no question', as in R.V. mg. The meaning is that they will be taught of the Spirit. Cf. xiv. 26, xvi. 13, 14; 1 Jn. ii. 27.

(3) Verse 25. 'Proverbs'; better, 'figures', as in R.S.V.

Day 6. Jn. xvii.

(1) Taking the chapter as a whole, what seven things does our Lord say He has done during His earthly ministry? Two of the seven are each mentioned twice. Are we availing ourselves as we should of the results of this sevenfold ministry of our Lord? For example, are the latter portions of verses 8 and 11 true of us?

(2) The prayer falls into three divisions, (a) verses 1-5, for Himself, (b) verses 6-19, for the immediate circle of disciples, (c) verses 20-26, for the great company who should afterwards believe. Throughout the prayer, how is God addressed?

(3) Looking more closely at the first part of the prayer (verses 1-5), we notice that Jesus manifests His consciousness that His earthly ministry is ended (verse 4). There is, however, a further work opening before Him (verse 2; cf. x. 28), and for this further work He needs new and larger powers. What, therefore, does He ask for Himself? See verses 1 and 5.

Notes.—(1) Verse 2. 'Power'; better, 'authority', as in R.V. The whole of humanity lies within the sphere of Christ's commission. Cf. Ps. ii. 8; Mt. xxviii. 18, 19 (R.V.); 1 Tim. ii. 5.

(2) Verse 5. A prayer that the glory of which for a time He had 'emptied Himself' (Phil. ii. 6, 7) may be restored to Him. Could any but the eternal Son thus speak? Cf. i. 18.

Day 7. Jn. xvii (continued).

(1) In the second division of the prayer (verses 6-19) what does Jesus say have been the results of His ministry thus far in the lives of His disciples? See verses 6 (last clause), 7, 8, 10, 12, 14, 16. What does He pray concerning them?

(2) In the third division of the prayer (verses 20-26) what two longings of the Saviour's heart find repeated expression, one concerning His own, and one concerning the world? How is the fulfilment of the second made dependent upon the realization of the first?

(3) What evidence of our Lord's deep love for us is given by His petitions, especially in verses 22-26? If these things are His desire for us, should it not also be our desire to know them to the uttermost? Cf. Phil. iii. 12.

Notes.—(1) Verse 6. 'The men which Thou gavest me'. Observe how often in this prayer the disciple company is thus described. See verses 2, 7, 9, 11, 12 especially and cf. vi. 37, 39, 44.

(2) Verse 15. 'From the evil'; better, 'from the evil one', as in r.v.

(3) Verse 17. 'Sanctify'; the root meaning is to consecrate, or set apart for God, but the term includes also the practice in daily life of what such consecration involves.

Week 37. JOHN XVIII-XXI

Day 1. Jn. xviii. 1-27.

(1) What qualities stand out in our Lord's character, as seen in today's portion? Consider especially His submission to arrest (verse 4), and the reason for it (verse 11), His successful intervention to prevent the arrest of His disciples (verse 8), the effect of His presence and words upon those who came to take Him captive (verses 5, 6), and His bearing before the high priest (verses 19-24).

(2) How did Peter's own actions contribute to his fall? The first denial was quite uncalled for (verse 17), and must have struck a chill to the heart of John. Was it not a result of Peter's fear that he would be recognized as the man who had attacked the high priest's servant? One denial led to another, and so to another.

Notes.—(1) Verse 1. 'A garden'; John does not mention the agony in Gethsemane, but alludes to it in verse 11.

(2) Verse 3. 'A band of men'; better, 'the band of soldiers', as in r.v. These would be soldiers from the Roman garrison. 'Officers' would be temple guards. The Jewish rulers sent a strong force equipped with lanterns, etc. (in spite of the Paschal moon) to ensure capture.

(3) Verse 9. The story of Peter shows how easily the disciples, had they been arrested, might have fallen away

(4) Verse 20. The pronoun 'I' is emphatic. Jesus' answer shows His scorn for the secret intrigues of Annas and his accomplices.

Day 2. Jn. xviii. 28–xix. 16.

Today's portion describes the trial of Jesus before Pilate, at the latter's headquarters in Jerusalem, called the Praetorium. See Note (1) below. The Jews would not enter within the building (xviii. 28) so Pilate had to go out to them, which must have been galling to his pride.

(1) The story is broken up into a number of scenes, some without the Praetorium, and some within. Those without the building

are xviii. 28-32, 38-40, xix. 4-7, 12-16, and those within the building are xviii. 33-37, xix. 1-3, 8-11. It is worth while to take time to grasp the exact course of the trial.

(2) What light is thrown upon the Jewish leaders, as to their character and purpose, and what upon Pilate? Pilate's action in scourging Jesus after pronouncing Him innocent, and finally handing Him over to the Jews to be crucified, may horrify us most. But who did Jesus say had the greater sin?

(3) Over against these men contemplate the figure of the Lord; note His calmness, His confidence, and the inexhaustible depth of His words. What claims did He make for Himself, and what does He declare to be the purpose of His coming into the world?

Notes.—(1) xviii. 28. 'Hall of judgment'; the Greek word is Praetorium (see R.V. mg.), that is, the headquarters of the Roman governor, probably at this time Herod's palace, hence R.V. rendering 'palace'.

(2) Verse 31b. The Romans had deprived the Jews of the right of capital punishment.

Day 3. Jn. xix. 17-37.

(1) The story of the crucifixion is told in seven incidents, namely, verses 17-18, 19-22, 23-24, 25-27, 28-29, 30, 31-37. How does each incident manifest some fresh aspect of the glory of the suffering Saviour?

(2) What Scriptures are quoted in this portion as having found fulfilment in this hour? How does their fulfilment confirm that Jesus is the Christ?

Day 4. Jn. xix. 38–xx. 10.

(1) What do you find remarkable about the burial of Jesus (a) in the men who supervised it, (b) in the manner in which they did it, and (c) in the fact that God, who had not intervened to save His Son from the cross, now arranges for Him a burial worthy of a king?

(2) Nicodemus is mentioned three times in this Gospel; see iii. 1-15, vii. 45-52, and here. What evidence do you find in him of a growing faith in Jesus and courage in confessing Him? Cf. vii. 51 (note).

(3) xx. 1-10. How do these verses show that the disciples were not expecting the resurrection of the Lord? What was Mary Magdalene's interpretation of the moving of the stone? Peter was obviously perplexed to know what to think. Only John grasped the truth. What was it that convinced John? See Note 3 below.

Notes.—(1) **xix. 38.** Joseph . . . Nicodemus. Both these men were members of the Sanhedrin, the council that had condemned Jesus. See iii. 1, vii. 50; Lk. xxiii. 50, 51.

(2) **xix. 39.** 'About an hundred pound weight.' A truly lavish supply.

(3) **xx. 6, 7.** The clothes were lying undisturbed in the position they had occupied when wrapped round the body; and the napkin that had been round the head lay by itself where the head of Jesus had lain.

Day 5. Jn. xx. 11-31.

Today's portion contains cumulative evidence of the resurrection of Jesus.

(1) By what thought was Mary obsessed when she saw the tomb empty? See verses 13 and 15. Neither the vision of angels nor of the Lord Himself availed to turn her from it. What at last convinced her?

(2) What shows that up to the evening of that day the disciples were still unconvinced? See verse 19. What convinced them? Consider not only His appearance among them, but also His words (verses 21-23). Who could have spoken such words but Jesus?

(3) What finally convinced Thomas? We, unlike him, are among those 'who have *not* seen'. Are we also among those whom the Lord calls blessed, because, having not seen, they have nevertheless believed (verse 29), and who, believing, have 'life through His Name' (verse 31)?

Notes.—(1) Verse 17. Note the distinction, 'My Father and your Father.' Jesus never said of Himself and His disciples 'Our Father'. He is the only begotten Son; we are sons 'in Him'.

(2) Verses 21-23. The risen Lord reverts to the subject which had occupied His mind in the upper room, how His work was to be carried on after His return to the Father (see esp. xiv. 12-27). He tells His disciples plainly that His work is to be continued through them. He speaks to them not as a privileged class among believers, but as disciples, that is, as representing believers in general, and describes the *nature* (verse 21), the *power* (verse 22), and the *authority* (verse 23) of their commission. Its nature is that it is after the pattern of His own commission from the Father; its power is to be that of the Holy Spirit; and its authority is to declare and convey to men the divine forgiveness, where the conditions are fulfilled, and to withold it, where the conditions are not fulfilled. Such is the high vocation of all believers who are in spiritual union with the Son, and through the Son with the Father, by the indwelling of the Holy Spirit. This is the true preaching of the gospel (see Lk. xxiv. 47; Acts ii. 37, 38, x. 43, xxvi. 17, 18).

Day 6. Jn. xxi. 1-14.

(1) Consider the situation. The disciples, in obedience to the Lord's instruction, had returned to Galilee (see Mk. xvi. 7), but Jesus had not yet appeared to them there (verse 14, see Note 6).

They were restless, perplexed, not knowing what to do, and Peter said, 'I go a-fishing'. What danger was there in this return to their old way of life?

(2) How did the Lord remind them of their true calling, and of their dependence upon Him for success? Cf. Lk. v. 1-11; Mk. i. 17, 18.

(3) What other lessons of spiritual value do you find in this story?

Notes.—(1) Verse 3. 'That night they caught nothing'; self-willed and self-chosen activity is unfruitful. Contrast verse 6.

(2) Verse 5. 'Children, have ye any meat?'; better, 'Lads, have you any fish?' Jesus used an ordinary term of address to men at work.

(3) Verse 7. John, the man of spiritual insight; Peter, the man of impulsive action; cf. xx. 6-8.

(4) Verse 8. 'Two hundred cubits'; i.e. about 100 yards.

(5) Verse 12. 'Come and dine'; better, 'Come and have breakfast' (R.S.V.).

(6) Verse 14. 'The third time'; first time, xx. 19-23; second time, xx. 24-29; third time, now in Galilee.

Day 7. Jn. xxi. 15-25.

(1) What is the significance (a) of the name Jesus used in addressing Peter (cf. i. 42); (b) of the phrase 'more than these' (cf. Mk. xiv. 29); (c) of Jesus' asking Peter three times, 'Lovest thou Me?' (cf. xiii. 38)?

(2) Though Peter had failed, Jesus re-commissioned him. What does this incident teach us (a) as to the possibility of restoration after backsliding, (b) as to the test Jesus applies to those to whom He gives oversight over His flock? Can we say to the Lord what Peter said in verse 17?

(3) What may we learn from verses 18-23 about (a) the Lord's direction of each disciple's life; (b) the possible wide differences in His plan for one disciple and another; and (c) the necessity of each making sure that he himself is following the Lord, no matter how others may be led?

Notes.—(1) Verse 19. Peter, according to tradition, died a martyr's death in Rome.

(2) Verse 23. A verse introduced to correct a current misunderstanding of what the Lord had said concerning John.

I and II KINGS

INTRODUCTION

(See New Bible Handbook, pp. 172-175)

THE two books form a single unit, the present somewhat arbitrary division having originated in the Vulgate. They give an account and complete history of the kings and the kingdoms ('of the kingdoms' is the probable literal rendering of the titles). The account bears marks of being the work of a single author using as his sources various documents (see 1 Kings xi. 41, xiv. 29, xiv. 19, etc.) including prophetic memoirs. It is important to remember that the whole is written from the religious and prophetic point of view, not from that of the secular historian. As *The New Bible Commentary* remarks: 'This is the explanation why certain of the kings who were most important for their contemporaries, e.g. Omri (1 Ki. xvi. 23-28), Azariah or Uzziah (2 Ki. xv. 1-7), Jeroboam II (2 Ki. xiv. 23-29), are passed over in virtual silence. It is spiritual, not political, lessons that we are to learn. That is why the two periods of crisis, the reigns of Ahab for the north and of Hezekiah for the south, are given at special length.'

Expressed concisely, the theme of the Book is that of Israel as the redeemed people of Jehovah, bearing His Name, and the kings as His representatives. Thus a wicked king is a paradox, as well as historically evil, and a good king by righteous acts is setting forth the rule of God. The sin of the people inevitably leads to the captivities, and throughout, political incidents are shown to be the effect of the fidelity or idolatry of the people. One proof of this is that prophetic activity is marked in the reigns of wicked kings.

ANALYSIS

1 Kings

i–xi.	The last days of the United Kingdom.
	i–ii. 11. David's last days and charge to Solomon.
	ii. 12–iv. Solomon, his character and wisdom.
	v–viii. The Temple.
	ix–xi. Solomon's magnificence and failure.
xii–xvi.	The division and the divided kingdoms to the accession of Ahab.
xvii–xxii.	Elijah.

2 Kings

  i–ii. 11.   Elijah (continued).
  ii. 12–xiii.   Elisha.
  xiv–xvii.   The course of events leading to the captivity of
         Israel.
  xviii–xx.   Hezekiah (and Isaiah).
    xxi.   Manasseh's evil reign.
  xxii, xxiii.   Josiah's reformation.
  xxiv, xxv.   The captivity of Judah.

Week 38. 1 Kings i–viii

Day 1. 1 Ki. i.

(1) Get hold of the story. Who supported Adonijah, and who supported Solomon, and by what means was Adonijah's attempt to seize the throne frustrated?

(2) This is the last mention of Nathan in Scripture. In his actions here and also in 2 Sa. vii and xii how does he exemplify by his faithful and disinterested conduct our duty as servants of God?

(3) With verse 5 compare Lk. xiv. 11; and with verse 6 compare Pr. xiii. 24, xix. 18, xxix. 17.

Notes.—(1) Verse 5. Adonijah, as David's eldest surviving son (see 2 Sa. iii. 4), had a claim to recognition (see 1 Ki. ii. 15). At the same time this might be overruled by the king (verses 20 and 27).

(2) Verses 52, 53. Solomon spares Adonijah on certain conditions, but commands him to withdraw from public affairs.

Day 2. 1 Ki. ii.

(1) How and why were Adonijah, Joab and Shimei put to death? Solomon's own reaction was to let bygones be bygones, but David counselled against this, and Solomon acted accordingly. What do you think was David's motive in giving the counsel he did? Was it on personal grounds of revenge, or for Solomon's sake, or a sense that justice had not been done? Cf. 2 Sa. iii. 38, 39.

(2) In what is said about Joab in chapters i and ii do you find confirmation of your answer to question 3 in Week 31, Day 3? Why did Joab support Adonijah?

(3) What lessons may we learn from Adonijah's life-story?

Day 3. 1 Ki. iii and iv.

(1) Solomon's request was pleasing to God (iii. 10), but was it the highest gift he could have asked? Compare Ex. xxxiii. 13; Phil. iii. 8, 10. What do you put first in prayer?

(2) In iii. 16-26 what three sins did the mother of the dead child progressively commit? How does this illustrate the saying that one sin leads to another?

(3) What good things are said about Solomon in these two chapters, and what benefits did his rule bring to his people? What, according to the writer, was the deepest ground of his prosperity?

Notes.—(1) iv. 4b. This was true only at the very beginning of Solomon's reign. See ii. 35.

(2) In iv. 5 and 26 read as in R.V. mg.

(3) iv. 29. 'Largeness of heart'; i.e. 'breadth of mind' (Moffatt).

Day 4. 1 Ki. v.

(1) To what great task did Solomon first set his hand, and what motives moved him to undertake it? Are we as ready to speak to a non-Christian friend of the goodness of God and of our desire to serve Him, as Solomon was to speak to Hiram?

(2) What may we learn from the fact that even in the arrangements which Solomon made with Hiram for materials and skilled labour, he acted *according to the wisdom given him by God*? Cf. Eph. v. 15-17; Jas. i. 5, iii. 17.

(3) Besides the labourers who were not Israelites, workers were needed also from Israel. Solomon, however, exempted the latter from the heaviest work (see ix. 22; 2 Ch. ii. 17, 18). What is the position in the kingdom of Christ in this respect? Cf. Mt. xxv. 15 ('to every man'); Mk. xiii. 34; Jn. xiii. 14, xx. 21.

Note.—Verse 11. 'Twenty measures' should probably be 'twenty thousand measures', as in LXX.

Day 5. 1 Ki. vi–vii. 12.

(1) Try to form a mental picture of 'the house of the Lord'. What was its length, its breadth, its height? What the size of the porch, and what of the inner sanctuary, here called 'the most holy place' or 'the oracle'? Notice, too, the side rooms, arranged in three stories round the sides and back of the house. These would take away from the long narrow appearance of the building, and provide space for storage, etc.

(2) Of what material were the walls made, with what were they lined on the inner side, and how adorned? Observe also the care expended upon the design and workmanship of the two sets of doors. What may we learn from these things? See 1 Ch. xxii. 5, 14-16; 1 Cor. iii. 12-15.

(3) 'The house of the Lord' was surrounded by both an inner court (vi. 36) and a great outer court (vii. 12). What five buildings were in this outer court? See vii. 1-12.

Notes.—(1) vi. 2. 'Cubits'; a cubit was about eighteen inches.

(2) vii. 2. 'The House of the Forest of Lebanon'; so called because of the number of pillars made from cedars of Lebanon. It was a Hall of Assembly.

(3) vii. 6. 'The porch of Pillars'; better, 'The Hall of Pillars'. Its use is not known.

(4) vii. 7. 'The Porch of the Throne'; better, 'Throne room' or 'Hall of Judgment'.

Day 6. 1 Ki. vii. 13–viii. 11.

Today's portion describes (a) the making of the brass furnishings and implements for the temple court, vii. 13-47; (b) the golden furniture and utensils for the house itself, vii. 48-50. Many of the details are difficult to grasp, but it is possible to distinguish the two great pillars, with their ornamented capitals, the great basin resting upon twelve oxen, and the ten carriages with wheels, richly ornamented, and carrying lavers; and also within the house, the golden altar of incense, the table of shew bread, and ten candlesticks or lamp stands. There was also a brazen altar in the temple court, which is mentioned later (see viii. 64).

(1) What may we learn concerning our own service for Christ from the spirit and aim that animated Solomon (cf. 2 Cor. ix. 7; Rom. xii. 11), and from the fact that he pursued the task through seven years until it was *finished* (cf. Acts xiv. 26, xx. 24; 2 Tim. iv. 7; Lk. xiv. 28, 29)?

(2) Finally, when all was prepared, the ark was brought in to the place reserved for it under the wings of the cherubim in the most holy place. Is the Lord Christ thus enthroned in you, His temple? Cf. Eph. iii. 16, 17.

(3) How did the Lord show His pleasure in Solomon's work? In what ways is His indwelling manifested in your life?

Day. 7 1 Ki. viii. 12-66.

(1) Verses 14-21. What promise is here spoken of as having been fulfilled? Are there experiences in your life of which you can say 'God spake with His mouth . . . and hath with His hand fulfilled it'?

(2) **Verses 22-53.** Observe how thanksgiving for the fulfilment of the promise stimulated further prayer. What general petition and what particular petitions (there are seven in all) did Solomon make? On what grounds did he base his prayer?

(3) **Verses 54-62.** In this 'blessing', how did Solomon sum up Israel's story? What two petitions did he offer, and to what ends? and what charge did he give the people? Consider how applicable his words are to ourselves.

Notes.—(1) Verse 12. 'The thick darkness'; there was no light in the most holy place, to symbolize the inscrutable mystery of the divine nature. Cf. Jb. xxvi. 14. The ark symbolized His presence in the midst of His people.

(2) Verse 16. 'My name'; a phrase used frequently in this chapter as signifying God in the fulness of His self-revelation.

(3) Verse 38. 'The plague of his own heart'; i.e. 'what plagues himself' (Moffatt).

(4) Verse 51. 'The furnace of iron'; i.e. in which iron is smelted.

(5) Verse 65. 'Seven days and seven days'; i.e. seven for the dedication of the altar, and seven for the feast, as explained in 2 Ch. vii. 8, 9.

Week 39.   1 KINGS IX–XVI

Day 1. 1 Ki. ix–x. 13.

(1) Comparing ix. 3 carefully with viii. 29, in what two respects did God exceed Solomon's request? Observe also the close relation between God's promise and His commands, and between His fulfilment of His promise and obedience. Cf. Jn. xiv. 14, 15, 21, xv. 7 1 Jn. iii. 22.

(2) What light does today's portion (from ix. 10 onwards) throw upon Solomon's interests and activities, his relations with other rulers, and the fulfilment to him of God's promise in iii. 12, 13?

(3) In what ways is the Queen of Sheba an example to us? Consider the purpose of her visit, the difficulties of it, and her reward.

Notes.—(1) ix. 14. A talent of gold, it is reckoned, would be the equivalent of £6,150, but would in those days have far higher purchasing power.

(2) ix. 25. See 2 Ch. viii. 13, 14.

Day 2. 1 Ki. x. 14–xi.

(1) Solomon was outwardly at the height of his power, wealth and fame (see x. 14-29). But what was going on within his heart in respect (a) of his affections, and (b) of his relation to God (see xi. 1-8)? Read Pr. iv. 23-27 (R.V.).

(2) What was the gravamen of God's charge against Solomon? With xi. 11 compare xiv. 8, 9 and 1 Sa. xiii. 13. Contrast what is said concerning Christ in Jn. xiv. 31; Phil. ii. 8; Heb. v. 8, 9.

(3) How does the account of the events of xi. 14-40 bring out God's overruling hand? Cf. Dn. iv. 34, 35; Ps. cxxxv. 5, 6. What effect should this truth have upon a believing heart? See Acts iv. 23-30.

Notes.—(1) x. 16. 'Targets'; long, oblong shields covering the whole body. The shields of verse 17 were small round shields.
(2) x. 28. See R.V.
(3) xi. 1. 'Strange'; i.e. 'foreign'.
(4) xi. 28. Jeroboam owed his promotion to Solomon himself.

Day 3. 1 Ki. xii. 1-32.

(1) To what causes was the division of the kingdom due?

(2) Comparing the two kings Rehoboam and Jeroboam, how would you summarize the character of each?

(3) What four actions of Jeroboam are spoken of in verses 25-32, and what was their purpose? Clever as they were politically and according to human judgment, wherein lay their fatal error? See verse 30; xiii. 33, 34; 2 Ki. xvii. 21.

Day 4. 1 Ki. xii. 33–xiii.

(1) What was the root fault in Jeroboam's character, and how did God in His mercy seek to show him the folly of the course he was pursuing? See xii. 33–xiii. 10.

(2) What punishment fell upon 'the man of God out of Judah' and why? Cf. xx. 36, and contrast our Lord's firmness in Mt. xvi. 22, 23.

Day 5. 1 Ki. xiv.

(1) Jeroboam and Ahijah had both been called of God, the one to be king (xi. 31), and the other as a prophet. What was the difference between them in their carrying out of their office, and how does this show what qualities are required in a servant of God?

(2) How were the seeds of the destruction of the kingdom of Israel sown at its very inception?

(3) What two pictures of Rehoboam's reign are given in verses 21-31? What light do they throw upon the state of the kingdom of Judah, and upon Rehoboam's character?

Notes.—(1) The name, Abijah, given by Jeroboam to his son, shows that Jeroboam still worshipped Jehovah, for Abijah means 'my father is Jah'.

(2) Verse 17. 'Tirzah' was the residence of the kings of the northern kingdom. Cf. xv. 21, xvi. 15, etc.

(3) Verses 23, 24. All that is mentioned in these verses was associated with idolatry. Cf. Je. ii. 20.

Day 6. 1 Ki. xv–xvi. 7.

(1) In this portion two kings of Judah are mentioned, and two of Israel. Who were they, and how long did each reign?

(2) What is the one standard by which these men are judged in Scripture? In relation to this standard, which of them were disapproved, and why, and which of them was approved, and why?

(3) When life on earth is ended, what will be the thing that matters? 'He was a great scholar, he made a huge fortune, he rose to be a peer: she was a noted beauty, a leader of fashion, a queen of society—what will all such epitaphs be worth, if God's finger carves silently below them, "He did that which was evil in the sight of the Lord"?' (Maclaren).

Notes.—(1) xv. 10. 'His mother's name'; strictly his grandmother (see verses 2 and 8). Maachah apparently continued to be officially 'queen mother', see verse 13 (R.V. mg.).

(2) xv. 17. 'Ramah' was only 5 miles from Jerusalem to the north.

(3) xvi. 7. 'Because he smote him'; cf. xv. 27, 29.

Day 7. 1 Ki. xvi. 8-34.

(1) In the northern kingdom the dynasties of Jeroboam and Baasha were utterly destroyed. So it was also with the dynasty of Omri; see xxi. 22. Yet the royal line of David continued in the kingdom of Judah. Why this difference? In answering the question take into account what is said in xi. 36 and xv. 4.

(2) How does the story of the northern kingdom show that the people departed farther and farther from God until the climax was reached with Omri (verse 25) and Ahab (verse 30)? What may this teach us as to the self-propagating power of sin?

(3) What was the special sin of Ahab, by which he provoked the Lord to anger? How did he go beyond what previous kings of Israel had done, and what led him to do it?

Notes.—(1) Verse 24. Omri was an able and powerful ruler, whose name is mentioned in the ancient Assyrian records and in the Moabite stone of Mesha. His selection of Samaria as the capital was an important event in Israel's history.

(2) Verses 31, 32. The calves set up by Jeroboam (see xii. 28) were supposed to represent the God of Israel. Ahab's sin was greater in that he worshipped Baal, the god of Tyre, and built in Samaria a 'house of Baal'.

Week 40. 1 Kings xvii–2 Kings iv. 7

Day 1. 1 Ki. xvii and xviii.

(1) What was the supreme issue at stake that drew forth Elijah, as the servant of Jehovah, to face King Ahab?

(2) How was the prophet, after his first encounter with the king, still further trained in faith and obedience, that he might be prepared for the supreme struggle on Mount Carmel? What did his experiences at the brook Cherith—and in Zarephath teach him?

(3) What was the secret of Elijah's strength and victory? See xviii. 41-45; Jas. v. 17, 18, and cf. xvii. 1 with Heb. xi. 27b.

Note.—xviii. 45, 46. 'To Jezreel'; about seventeen or eighteen miles. This extraordinary feat of endurance indicates that the prophet was keyed up to a high degree of nervous tension.

Day 2. 1 Ki. xix.

Prophets among the people of Israel were held in high regard. Elijah therefore supposed that after so great a moral victory as that won at Carmel, king and nation would return to Jehovah. But Jezebel had no such awe in her heart, and Elijah found himself faced by her wrathful fury. It was a rude shock to all his hopes.

(1) What difference do you notice between the account of Elijah's flight at this time and that of his previous flights to Cherith and Zarephath? What causes for his deep depression and sense o failure can you think of?

(2) Read the story of verses 5-18 in the light of Ps. ciii. 13, 14. How did God comfort, teach and restore Elijah?

(3) When God's call came to Elisha, how did he respond? Are you thus ready to do God's will, in whatever sphere of service He may appoint? Cf. Mk. i. 15-18.

Notes.—(1) Verse 4. 'Under a juniper tree'; 'under a broom bush' (Moffatt), a shrub affording only scanty shelter.

(2) Verse 8. 'Into Horeb, the mount of God'; the site of God's covenant with Israel (see Dt. iv. 9-20). This was probably the object of Elijah's journey from the first.

(3) Verses 15, 16. It was not God's plan that Elijah should complete the work of reformation in his own person.

(4) Verse 19. 'Twelve yoke of oxen'; indicates a wealthy farm.

Day 3. 1 Ki. xx.

The reappearance of true prophets of Jehovah in this chapter is striking. It seems to indicate that Elijah's ministry had effected a change in the whole attitude of public opinion, and even in Ahab himself.

(1) What was the difference between Ben-hadad's two demands,

which made Ahab reject the second, though he had yielded to the first? What threat did Ben-hadad then make, and what was Ahab's answer?

(2) How many times in this chapter is the intervention of a prophet recorded? What may we ourselves learn from the messages these men were sent of God to deliver?

(3) In what ways does this chapter reveal weakness in Ahab and what warning is hereby given us concerning our own character and actions? Cf. Mt. vi. 24; Jas. i. 8.

Notes.—(1) Verse 14. 'The young men of the princes of the provinces'; that is, attendants of the provincial governors, probably all picked men.

(2) Verse 27. A graphic simile.

Day 4. 1 Ki. xxi.

(1) Consider the parts played by Ahab, Jezebel, and the elders of Jezreel respectively in the murder of Naboth. What was the special guilt of each?

(2) What was it that distinguished Elijah from all these? Does God find in us those whom He can use to do His work, and who are willing to speak His message without reckoning the cost?

(3) How does Scripture sum up Ahab's character? Observe especially the expression which is twice used in these verses concerning him.

Notes.—(1) Verses 2 and 3. Ahab's offer was fair in itself, but when he failed to gain his desire, he was displeased. Yet Naboth, according to the law, had the right to refuse. See Lv. xxv. 23; Nu. xxxvi. 7.

(2) Verse 15. We learn from 2 Ki. ix. 26 that Naboth's sons also were put to death, that there might be no surviving heir.

Day 5. 1 Ki. xxii.

(1) Verse 3. Is there some part of our God-given inheritance in Christ (as, e.g., Rom. vi. 12-14) which we do not possess, 'because we be still, and take it not'?

(2) Compare the attitude of the two kings in regard to asking counsel of the Lord. Did they not both err—Ahab because he would not have done it at all but for Jehoshaphat, and Jehoshaphat because he did it *after* the decision was made? Do we sometimes find ourselves committing both these errors?

(3) What may we learn from Ahab's foolish hatred of Micaiah? What was the reason of it and to what end did it lead? Cf. Jn. viii. 40.

Notes.—(1) Verse 3. 'Ramoth in Gilead'; possibly one of the towns mentioned in xx. 34.

(2) Verse 6. These prophets were probably prophets of the calf worship which Jeroboam had established (xii. 28, 29). In name they may have been prophets of Jehovah, God of Israel, but they were not true prophets as Micaiah was.

(3) Verses 19-23. An allegorical picture, not to be taken literally.

(4) Verse 31. An ungrateful return for Ahab's clemency, see xx. 31-34.

Day 6. 2 Ki. i and ii.

These two chapters contain the last two stories about Elijah.

(1) Contrast the end of King Ahaziah with Elijah's end. What was the fundamental difference between these two men? See 1 Jn. ii. 15-17, v. 4.

(2) In what three ways was Elisha tested (see ii. 1-15) and what qualities in him does his conduct reveal? Have we the same resolute spirit to do 'my utmost for His highest'? See Note 2 below.

(3) Elisha's miracles are parables of spiritual truths. What does ii. 19-22 teach concerning our great Elisha, Jesus Christ, and His cleansing of the corrupted springs of human life? Cf. Ezk. xlvii. 9; Zc. xiii. 1; Rev. xxi. 6, xxii. 1-3.

Notes.—(1) i. 17. 'Because he had no son'; a reference to Ahaziah. The new king Jehoram was Ahaziah's brother. See iii. 1.

(2) ii. 9. See note in R.V. mg. Elisha wanted to be fully equipped for the high service to which he was called.

(3) ii. 23-25. 'Little children'; better, 'young lads', as in R.V. mg. These were youths of Bethel, whose attitude reflected the spirit of the place. Coming out to meet Elisha in a large band, they mocked the prophet, who was bald in mourning for his master (cf. Jb. i. 20), and said 'Go up', that is, 'Ascend to heaven as you say your master did'. It was a grievous insult, and Elisha, righteously angry, invoked the judgment of God upon them. Shaken by the whole episode, he did not enter Bethel but made his way to Carmel.

Day 7. 2 Ki. iii–iv. 7.

Today's portion contains two further stories of Elisha.

(1) What was the cause of the attack upon Moab, and how was Elisha brought into the situation? A map should be used to show the route taken by the attacking armies, and the place where the miracle was wrought.

(2) Contrast the kings, who sought God's help only in the hour of extreme peril, and Elisha, who walked in communion with God, and was engaged in His service. How does the story show what one man of faith can do to save a multitude?

(3) How does the story of iv. 1-7 illustrate the working of faith? Was it easy for the woman to do what Elisha bade her do? Yet if

she had not believed and acted upon his word, could she have been delivered?

Notes.—(1) iii. 11. 'Which poured water, etc.'; that is, he was Elijah's attendant.

(2) iii. 20. Travellers report that in that region there is water under the sand.

Week 41. 2 KINGS IV. 8–XIV

Day 1. 2 Ki. iv. 8-44.

There are in these verses three miraculous works wrought by Elisha, each them rich in spiritual instruction.

(1) Verses 8-37. In what ways is the lady of Shunem an example to us and what may we learn also from these verses regarding the character and conduct of a servant of God? What lessons are to be drawn from Gehazi's failure?

(2) Verses 38-41. Do you find a parallel between this scene and the story of Mk. iv. 35-39? Why does God permit these sudden perils to beat upon His servants, bringing them almost down to death? Cf. 2 Cor. i. 9.

(3) Verses 42-44. What features in Elisha's character does this beautiful incident bring out? Cf. Mk. vi. 37-44; 2 Cor. viii. 9.

Note.—Verse 42. The present was for Elisha; and if there was still scarcity of food (verse 38), the gift would be the more precious. But Elisha shared it with all who were with him.

Day 2. 2 Ki. v–vi. 7.

Two more miracles wrought by Elisha.

(1) Chapter v. There are four important figures in this chapter —the captive maid, Naaman, Elisha and Gehazi. What lessons may we learn from each?

(2) vi. 1-7. Regarding Elisha as a type of Christ and 'the sons of the prophets' as representing ourselves, what is suggested by the phrases '*every man* a beam' (verse 2), and 'go with thy servants' (verse 3). Also how do verses 5-7 show (a) that Christ can meet our every need, and restore to us, if we have lost it, the power of effective service; but (b) that we must ourselves lay hold of His provision, if it is to be of value to us?

Notes.—(1) v. 17. The idea in Naaman's mind was that Jehovah, the God of Israel, could not be rightly worshipped except on Israelitish soil. His faith was still very imperfect, as verse 18 also shows.

(2) v. 22. 'A talent of silver'; that is, 'four hundred pounds' (Moffatt), a very large sum to be asked for two young men of the sons of the prophets.

Day 3. 2 Ki. vi. 8–vii.

Two more stories of Elisha, in which he is seen in close relation with the king of Israel. The king is unnamed in both stories. He relies upon Elisha (vi. 21), but later turns against him (vi. 31; see note 2 below).

(1) vi. 8–23. Why was the young man afraid, and why was the prophet not afraid? Have we learned the secret of the conquest of fear? See Heb. xi. 27.

(2) Observe the severity of the siege, and the greatness of the faith that enabled Elisha to speak as he did in vii. 1. How does the judgment that fell upon the unbelieving officer illustrate the punishment that will follow all wilful unbelief? Cf. Mk. xvi. 16b; Jn. iii. 36.

(3) How do the four lepers condemn by their example those who, knowing the glad news of the gospel, fail to make it known? Are you a silent Christian?

Notes.—(1) vi. 25. 'Ten pounds in silver was paid for the head of an ass, and twelve shillings for a pint of dove's dung' (Moffatt).

(2) vi. 31. Elisha appears to have been sustaining the hopes of king and people by the promise of divine deliverance. The king's faith now gave way, and he burned with anger against the prophet.

(3) vii. 1. 'A shekel'; 'half a crown' (Moffatt).

Day 4. 2 Ki. viii and ix.

Today's portion contains (a) two incidents connected with Elisha's ministry; (b) a brief summary of the reigns of two kings of Judah; (c) the story of the revolution under Jehu, through which the house of Ahab was destroyed.

(1) viii. 1–15. How does the first of these two incidents illustrate God's watchful care over His own? Cf. Ps. xxxiii. 18–22; Rom. viii. 28. In the second incident why did Elisha weep? Cf. Je. viii. 16–ix. 1; Lk. xix. 41–44.

(2) What is the ground of the judgment pronounced upon the two kings Jehoram and Ahaziah, and what lessons do their lives teach regarding the baneful results of marriage alliances with those who are the enemies of God?

(3) Ponder the vivid story of the revolution, as given in chapter ix, noticing especially how it began, and the references to the word of God and its fulfilment. Cf. Heb. x. 31, xii. 29; 2 Ki. x. 30.

Notes.—(1) viii. 10. The sickness in itself was not fatal, but Elisha was given a vision of other things that would happen, which filled him with horror. Moffatt translates verse 11 thus: 'The man of God's face became rigid with horror.'

(2) Verse 13. Read as in R.V Hazael was elated at the prospect of doing such deeds.

(3) Verse 16. It is important to distinguish between Jehoram, son of Jehoshaphat, king of Judah, and Jehoram (or Joram), son of Ahab, king of Israel. Their reigns were in great measure contemporaneous.

(4) Verse 26. Athaliah was the daughter of Ahab and Jezebel, and, therefore, the granddaughter of Omri. See 1 Ki. xvi. 29, 31. She married Jehoram, king of Judah (verse 18).

Day 5. 2 Ki. x.

(1) Trace the course of Jehu's rise to power. Looking back to chapter ix, where was he first anointed, and acclaimed as king? Whither did he then go, striking down in swift succession Jehoram, Ahaziah and Jezebel? Whom did he further slay, as recorded in x. 1-14; and by what means?

(2) How does the story go on to show that Jehu had another aim in view, not at first revealed? What was that aim, and how was it accomplished? See x. 15-28.

(3) As you ponder the story, how would you describe Jehu (a) in his natural character, (b) in his religious attitude?

Notes.—(1) Verse 1. The word 'Jezreel' must be a copyist's error, for Jehu's letters were sent from Jezreel, where Jehu still was, to Samaria. The LXX translates 'sent to the rulers of the city, and to the elders', i.e. the city of Samaria.

(2) Verses 9, 10. Jehu quiets the people of Samaria, by reminding them that all that was happening was but the fulfilment of God's word through Elijah. See 1 Ki. xxi. 21, 23, 24.

Day 6. 2 Ki. xi and xii.

In today's portion we pass from the history of the northern kingdom to the re-establishment in Judah of the worship of Jehovah.

(1) What was Athaliah's purpose, and by what two persons, under God, was it brought to nought? What new light does 2 Ch. xxii. 11 throw upon the story? Compare with the faith and courage of Jehoshabeath and Jehoiada that of Moses' parents, Heb. xi. 23.

(2) What signs of healthy moral and spiritual life do you find in these chapters, and in what respect shortcoming? Examining our own life in the light of these chapters we may ask, Have I made a covenant (xi. 17)? Do I deal faithfully (xii. 15)?

(3) What light is thrown upon the character of Jehoash? See further 2 Ch. xxiv. 17-24.

Day 7. 2 Ki. xiii and xiv.

This is another composite portion, containing first a brief account of two kings of Israel, Jehoahaz, and Jehoash or Joash (to be distinguished from the king of Judah of the same name); then two incidents connected with Elisha;

and finally an account of the reigns of Amaziah, king of Judah, and Jeroboam II of Israel.

(1) What evidence is there that in the reign of Jehoahaz Israel was greatly impoverished? Also what reason is assigned for this state of things?

(2) Under Jehoash the strength of Israel again increased, but Elisha nevertheless rebuked Jehoash. Why? Are we inclined, as Jehoash was, to stop short of claiming full salvation?

(3) How did Amaziah fail? Cf. Pr. xvi. 18, xxix. 23.

Notes.—(1) xiii. 5. A reference to Jeroboam II, see xiv. 27.

(2) xiv. 13. 'Four hundred cubits'; about 200 yards.

(3) xiv. 23. Jeroboam II had a long and successful reign, during which the northern kingdom of Israel was greatly extended. See verse 25.

(4) Verse 25. 'The entering in of Hamath' may refer to the pass between Hermon and Lebanon in the north; 'the sea of the Arabah' is the Dead Sea. There is no other reference in Scripture to this particular prophecy of Jonah.

(5) Verse 28. 'Which had belonged to Judah'; the meaning is obscure.

Week 42. 2 KINGS XV–XXV

Day 1. 2 Ki. xv and xvi.

These two chapters cover a period of about eighty years. It is helpful to make a list in parallel columns of the kings of Judah and Israel respectively, mentioned in today's portion, with the length of their reigns.

(1) Taking first the kings of Judah, how does Ahaz stand out in sharp contrast to his father Jotham, and his grandfather Azariah (Uzziah)? What two particular acts of folly, one political, the other religious are recorded of him? Cf. Ps. cxlvi. 3-5; Is. vii. 1-9.

(2) With regard to the northern kingdom of Israel, how long did the dynasty of Jehu continue? See x. 30 and cf. Ho. i. 4, which indicates that notwithstanding his religious zeal, Jehu's revolution sowed seeds of destruction, not only for his own house, but also for the kingdom.

(3) What happened after Jehu's dynasty came to an end? What great loss did the northern kingdom suffer in the reign of Pekah? Do you find any good thing recorded of any of the kings of the northern kingdom in these two chapters? Cf. Ho. vii. 7, viii. 4, xiii. 11.

Day 2. 2 Ki. xvii.

This chapter tells of the end of the northern kingdom of Israel, with the causes of its downfall, and what followed after it.

(1) Can you trace a progressive deterioration in Israel's moral and spiritual condition in verses 9-18? Compare the phrase 'did

secretly, etc.' in verse 9 with 'sold themselves, etc.' in verse 17. What are the modern counterparts of the sins which Israel committed? See Col. iii. 5 (last clause); Heb. xii. 25.

(2) Consider what great events had taken place in Israel's history in the territory of the northern kingdom, which had brought glory to God, and deliverance to the people. To what condition was it now reduced? Cf. 2 Tim. iii. 5; Is. xxix. 13.

Notes.—(1) Verse 2. In what way Hoshea sinned less grievously than preceding kings is not explained.

(2) Verses 33, 34. The word 'fear' is used here in two senses, in verse 33 of outward worship, and in verse 34 of heart reverence.

Day 3. 2 Ki. xviii–xix. 7.

(1) What four points about Hezekiah's attitude and conduct with reference to God are mentioned in xviii. 3, 5 and 6? Are these things true of us? How did Hezekiah's faith manifest itself in action, and what evidence had he of God's favour and blessing? See verses 4, 7 and 8.

(2) Imagine yourself an inhabitant of Jerusalem listening to the Assyrian speaker, Rabshakeh. There were two directions from which people at that time thought that help might be expected— from Egypt and from Jehovah. How does Rabshakeh seek to show that neither is of any avail?

(3) What was the prophet Isaiah's answer to the Assyrian challenge? Cf. Ex. xiv. 13; 1 Sa. xvii. 44, 45; Dn. iii. 15-18. Are you able to encourage others by your faith, or are you among those that fear and need encouragement?

Notes.—(1) xviii. 22. Hezekiah's reforming zeal was no doubt unpopular with many. Rabshakeh knew this, and sought to turn it to advantage for his own ends.

(2) xix. 3b. A figure of speech denoting a crisis of extreme gravity.

Day 4. 2 Ki. xix. 8-37.

(1) Comparing Hezekiah's action and words in verses 14-19 with those of the earlier crisis in verses 3, 4, what evidence do you find that Hezekiah's faith had grown stronger?

(2) How did Sennacherib appear to merely human judgment? How did he appear as seen by Isaiah with the eyes of faith? Are we learning to look at the world situation today in relation to God? Cf. Jn. xiv. 1.

(3) What does the whole story teach as to the difference which faith in God makes in individual and national life?

Notes.—(1) Verse 25. God is the speaker from this point.

(2) Verse 29. The meaning is that only in the third year from the time at which the words were spoken would there be normal sowing and reaping. The fulfilment of the prophet's pronouncement would attest his divinely given authority.

Day 5. 2 Ki. xx and xxi.

The events described in chapter xx happened in the earlier part of Hezekiah's reign before the invasion of Sennacherib (see verses 6 and 13, and also xviii. 15, 16), and are introduced here as a kind of appendix to the story of Hezekiah.

(1) Put yourself in Hezekiah's place, and try to picture the effect upon him of Isaiah's announcement. What did he do (cf. Ps. cii. 24) and what did God then do? How would these experiences help to prepare Hezekiah for the greater tests of faith that he was to meet when Sennacherib attacked him?

(2) Hezekiah was vehemently opposed to idolatry, but not immune against flattery. Cf. Pr. xxix. 5. How did Isaiah view the incident, and what word of judgment was given him to speak? For its fulfilment over a century later see chapter xxv.

(3) Summarize in your own words Manasseh's flagrant idolatry. What judgments did God declare through His prophets? Do you think it can have been easy for the prophets to speak thus? Cf. Mi. iii. 8.

Notes.—(1) xx. 12. 'Berodach-baladan'; better, 'Merodach-baladan' (see Is. xxxix. 1), a northern chieftain, who had seized Babylon and was looking round for every possible means of strengthening his position. His reign did not last long, and it would have been folly for Hezekiah to enter into alliance with him.

(2) xxi. 13. The first half of the verse means that Jerusalem shall receive the same measure of judgment as Samaria and the house of Ahab. The metaphor in the second half of the verse is a very strong and vivid one.

Day 6. 2 Ki. xxii and xxiii.

(1) 'Huldah the prophetess.' What other instances have we had in recent studies of the influence which one woman can exercise for good or evil?

(2) Make out a list of all that Josiah did both positively to promote true religion, and negatively to destroy the false. Are our lives marked by a similar eagerness to depart from iniquity and to live in covenant with God? Cf. 2 Cor. vi. 14–vii. 1.

(3) What was the mainspring of Josiah's reforming zeal? Cf. Ps. cxix. 161b; Is. lxvi. 2; see also xxiii. 25, and contrast the behaviour of Jehoiakim in Je. xxxvi. 23-25.

Day 7. 2 Ki. xxiv and xxv.

(1) Looking back to xxiii. 31, what four kings reigned between Josiah's death and the fall of Jerusalem? What was the length of their reigns, and what was their record, as described in these chapters?

(2) In what ways was Nebuchadnezzar's treatment of Jerusalem after his second capture of it much more severe than when he captured it the first time?

(3) What reasons are given in chapter xxiv for the captivity? Cf. xxiii. 26, 27; Je. xv. 1-4; Dt. iv. 26, 27. What does this teach us about the end of persistent sinning? Yet what star of hope is seen shining in the closing verses of the book? Cf. 2 Sa. vii. 14, 15.

Notes.—(1) xxv. 19. 'Them that were in the king's presence'; literally, 'them that saw the king's face' (R.V.); i.e. men who were of the king's more intimate circle.

(2) xxv. 22. 'Gedaliah the son of Ahikam'; see xxii. 12; Je. xxvi. 24. The story of his assassination is told more fully in Je. xl-xli. 10.

ISAIAH

INTRODUCTION

(See New Bible Handbook, pp. 211-219)

ISAIAH, the 'evangelical Prophet', began his ministry at the end of Uzziah's reign, and continued through the reigns of Jotham, Ahaz, and Hezekiah. A Jewish tradition, to which allusion is perhaps made in Heb. xi. 37, states that he was slain in the reign of Manasseh by being sawn asunder. He was a man of outstanding faith in God, and came to exercise a large influence upon his fellow-countrymen. He had to contend with many difficulties, for the moral and spiritual condition of the people was corrupt. The rich oppressed the poor, and revelled in wanton luxury; justice was shamelessly bought and sold. When in distress, men turned to idols; and when in danger, they sought alliances with heathen powers. Isaiah urged a quiet trust in Jehovah, as the only sure path of safety; and when, in the supreme crisis of the Assyrian invasion, his counsel was followed, it was triumphantly vindicated in the destruction of the Assyrian army.

Isaiah spoke much of impending judgment; but he foresaw also the coming of the Messiah, and the establishment of His kingdom. His interest was not confined to his own nation of Judah only. He prophesied also concerning the northern kingdom of Israel (whose overthrow he witnessed), and the heathen nations surrounding Palestine.

The last twenty-seven chapters (xl–lxvi) contain a very remarkable group of prophecies, spoken primarily for the comfort and warning of those who lived in the period of the Jewish captivity in Babylon after the destruction of Jerusalem by Nebuchadnezzar about 150 years after Isaiah's time. It is not possible here to discuss the modern contention that chapters xl–lxvi are not the work of Isaiah, but of one or more prophets who lived in the period of the exile, or later. The problem is dealt with quite fully in the Introduction to Isaiah in *The New Bible Commentary*, where the arguments adduced in favour of and against the unity of the book are carefully set down and analysed. Suffice it to say here that these studies are based upon the view, not lightly held, and supported by ancient Jewish tradition, and by the writers of the New Testament, that Isaiah was the author of the whole book. He had already foreseen in the vision of xiii–xiv. 23 (to which his name is attached; see xiii. 1) and in other visions (e.g., xxi. 1-10, xxxv, xxxix. 6) the rise of Babylon to power and glory, and then her downfall, and the release of her Jewish captives. But in these later prophecies the glad message of redemption is revealed to him in far greater fulness. He takes his stand in prophetic vision in that later age, and declares the messages which God puts into his heart and upon his lips.

The chapters fall into three main sections (see *Analysis*), each ending with a statement of the doom of the wicked (xlviii. 22, lvii. 20, 21, lxvi. 24). Embedded in these chapters are four prophecies, usually known as the 'Servant' passages (see *Analysis*), in which the prophet describes God's ideal Servant, and, in so doing, draws a perfect picture of the Lord Jesus Christ. This is an illustration of a notable feature of the prophecies of these chapters, that they look far beyond the period of the return under Cyrus to the coming of Jesus Christ, and the final events of this present age. While spoken primarily to and of Israel, they have a message to all who belong to Christ. The triumphant faith in God, the revelation of God's character, and of the principles of His working, the insight into the human heart in its sin and weakness, the 'exceeding great and precious promises', with which these chapters abound, these and other features make this part of Scripture a veritable mine of wealth to the believing heart.

ANALYSIS

i. Introductory. God's controversy with His people.

ii–iv. Prophecies of judgment, lying between two messianic oracles.

v. The Song of the Vineyard. A series of woes. Vision of an invading army.

vi. Isaiah's Call.

vii–x. 4. Events connected with the alliance of Ephraim (i.e. northern Israel) and Syria against Judah, and prophecies arising out of them, some Messianic.

x. 5-33. Assyrian invasion of Judah, and its results (a) for Assyria, (b) for Judah.

xi–xii. Messianic prophecies.

xiii–xxiii. Prophecies against the nations, except xxii. 1-14 (Jerusalem) and xxii. 15-25 (Shebna and Eliakim).

xxiv–xxvii. Prophecies of the Day of the Lord, in its twofold aspect of world judgment, and deliverance for Israel.

xxviii–xxxiii. Prophecies connected with a proposed alliance with Egypt. Some speak of judgment, others of deliverance, and of Messiah's coming.

xxxiv–xxxv. Vengeance upon Edom, contrasted with the salvation of the redeemed of the Lord, as they return from exile.

xxxvi–xxxix. Historical.

xl–xlviii. The glad tidings of Israel's redemption from captivity through the agency of Cyrus. The supremacy of Jehovah over the nations and their gods.
xlii. 1-7. The first of the 'Servant' passages.

xlix–lvii. Messages of encouragement and comfort, with rebuke of those who practise evil.
xlix. 1-9 ⎱
l. 4-9   ⎰ The second, third and fourth of the
lii. 13-liii ⎰ 'Servant' passages.

lviii–lxvi. Rebuke of sin. Visions of Zion's glory. Prayer for God's intervention, and God's answer, that the people will be sifted. The true Israel will

inherit 'the new heaven and the new earth',
and those who refuse to turn to God will be
destroyed.

*N.B.—The questions below are throughout based upon the R.V. text. It
is assumed that the student will use this in his reading of the Book of Isaiah.*

Week 43. ISAIAH I–X

Day 1. Is. i.

Today's portion is cast in the form of a trial at law, which has been called
'The Great Arraignment'. God accuses His people (verses 1-9 and 21-23), and
passes sentence upon them (verses 18-20 and 24-31). The defence is quashed
(verses 10-17).

(1) How far does God's accusation of His rebellious people
apply to the Christian backslider today?

(2) What is God's attitude to formal worship unaccompanied
by righteousness of life? See verses 10-17, also Ps. xl. 8, 9; Am. v.
21-24; Mi. vi. 6-8.

(3) What is the double purpose of God's judgment revealed in
verses 24-31? Can you link it with verses 19 and 20?

Notes.—(1) Verses 2-4. Israel's sin was the more grievous because of her
special privileges.

(2) Verses 5, 6. Sinful Israel is pictured as a body suffering all over from
sword wounds, scourge bruises, and abscesses.

(3) Verse 10. In God's sight His people are as depraved as Sodom and
Gomorrah. Cf. iii. 9; Mt. xi. 23, 24.

(4) Verse 22. Silver and wine are probably metaphors for the leaders of the
nation.

Day 2. Is. ii–iv.

The prophet's lofty vision of future possibility in ii. 2-5 gives way to a picture
of coming judgment in ii. 6-22, made inevitable by man's failure. From a
description of the anarchy (iii. 1-8) which will result from the prevalent sins
of the ruling class, both men and women (iii. 9–iv. 1), he turns to a more confident expectation of the glory which will follow the judgment (iv. 2-6).

(1) Try to build a comprehensive picture of the hope for the
future given in ii. 2-5 and iv. 2-6. What is said about the Word of
the Lord, the peace of the world, the holiness of God's people, and
their blessedness under His protecting care?

(2) Can you detect from these chapters what Isaiah regarded
as the greatest sin, and why it is so abominable?

Notes.—(1) ii. 2-4. A prophecy almost identical with Mi. iv. 1-4, and probably borrowed by Micah from Isaiah.

(2) ii. 6. The striking of hands may refer not only to friendship but to trade bargaining. Commercial greed is further condemned in verse 7a.

(3) ii.10-21. The day of the Lord is likened to a devastating storm.

(4) iii. 12. A reference to the childishness and effeminacy of King Ahaz.

(5) iv. 5, 6. The symbolism seems to be based upon Israel's experience in the wilderness. See Ex. xiii. 21, 22, xl. 34, 35, 38.

Day 3. Is. v.

God directly and publicly accuses His people of sin, and warns them of judgment, first by the Song of the Vineyard (verses 1-7), then by a series of 'Woes' (verses 8-23), and finally by a description of the judgment (verses 24-30).

(1) Compare Isaiah's song of the Vineyard with Christ's parables of the Wicked Husbandmen (Mk. xii. 1-9) and the Barren Fig Tree (Lk. xiii. 6-9). Note the differences, and then work out the one great lesson taught in all three passages. How can it be applied to our lives today?

(2) Make a list of the six 'Woes' in verses 8-24, finding twentieth century words to describe each sin denounced.

Notes.—(1) Verse 10. A warning of barrenness. Ten acres of vineyard will yield only one bath (eight gallons) of wine, instead of about 500. Also the land will yield only one-tenth of the seed sown, for an ephah is the tenth part of a homer.

(2) Verse 13. 'Are gone.' An example of 'the perfect tense of prophetic certainty', that is, an event still future is spoken of in the vision of faith as having already happened.

(3) Verse 14. 'Hell'; i.e. Sheol (Greek 'Hades'), the place where all the dead go, considered as a dim and shadowy underworld.

(4) Verse 26, 'Ensign'; better, 'signal'. Cf. xi. 10, 12, xiii. 2, xviii. 3, xxx. 17. It was a signal post, set up on a hill.

Day 4. Is. vi.

The brilliant reign of King Uzziah, whose glory was excelled only by that of Solomon, ended in ignominy (see 2 Ch. xxvi). The words 'in the year that King Uzziah died' suggest that it was while meditating on the transitoriness of human kingships that Isaiah saw this vision.

(1) Isaiah's sense of sin followed his vision of God in His holiness. What may this teach us as to how we may see ourselves as we really are?

(2) Observe the sequence—vision, repentance, cleansing, commission. Is it possible to have the last without experiencing those that precede?

(3) What other main lessons are taught in this chapter? Make a list of them, that you may observe in future studies how all Isaiah's later teaching was coloured by this vision.

Notes.—(1) Verse 7. 'Purged', or 'expiated' (R.V. mg.). The word is the technical term for expiation by sacrifice. Cf. verse 6, 'from off the *altar*', and 1 Pet. i. 16-20.

(2) Verses 9, 10. In seeking to understand these verses (with which cf. Mk. iv. 10-12, where Jesus quotes them), remember these two facts:

(a) Although the Word is preached in order to bring salvation to those who will hear, it inevitably brings condemnation to those who will not. Cf. Jn. iii. 16-21.

(b) The Old Testament, with its unshakable faith in God's sovereignty, often refuses to distinguish between intention and inevitable result, between God's permissive and directive will. Thus, to say 'Preach to them and they will not respond' could equally well be expressed, 'Preach to them in order that they may not respond'.

(3) Verse 13. A much reduced remnant will survive the judgment, like the stump of a felled tree.

Day 5. Is. vii. 1–viii. 15.

Isaiah now turns his attention from the internal condition of Judah to the realm of international politics. The historical background of chapters vii–x. 4 is the so-called Syro-Ephraimitic confederacy, when King Rezin of Syria and King Pekah of Israel conspired against Judah (735 B.C.). Ahaz of Judah, overcome with panic (vii. 2), rejected the counsel of Isaiah that he should trust in God (vii. 3-4), and appealed to King Tiglath-Pileser of Assyria, an act which Isaiah predicted would have disastrous consequences in the end, even though at first apparently successful (vii. 17–viii. 4).

(1) Isaiah's advice to Ahaz is the first occurrence in the book of his characteristic message about quiet confidence in God. To the material mind of Ahaz it seemed suicidal. What connection has Isaiah's attitude with the vision of chapter vi? Cf. Heb. xi. 27b.

(2) How could the Lord be both a sanctuary and a stone of stumbling (viii. 13-15); and how may He be to us the former and not the latter? Cf. 1 Pet. ii. 7, 8.

(3) What great prophecy of Christ is found in today's portion? See Mt. i. 21-23. In daily experience do you know Christ as 'Immanuel'?

Notes.—(1) The two names 'Shear-jashub' ('A remnant shall return') and Maher-shalal-hash-baz ('Speed, spoil, haste, prey') sum up Isaiah's double message of doom and hope.

(2) vii. 3. Ahaz was probably making preparation for the siege when Isaiah met him.

(3) vii. 6. 'The son of Tabeel'; or 'Ben-tabeel'. Almost certainly a Syrian name, and doubtless a man whose sympathies were strongly anti-Assyrian.

(4) vii. 14. The primary meaning seems to be that before a certain child (as yet unborn) emerges from infancy, his diet will have to be limited to curds and honey, since the devastated land will yield no better food (vii. 21, 22). But the child's remarkable name indicates a prophetic reference to the Messiah. The

ravages of war are depicted further in vii. 18-20 and 23-25. The land will be infested with swarms of Egyptian flies and Assyrian bees, and shorn by an Assyrian razor. Even the best vineyards, worth 1,000 shekels, will become a wilderness.

(5) viii. 6. 'The waters of Shiloah'; i.e. the water supplies of Jerusalem, dependent on subterranean springs and reservoirs under the Temple area, here used symbolically of God's providence. The phrase 'this people' must refer either to Israel or a pro-Syrian party in Judah, unless, as some think, the verb Isaiah used was not the word 'rejoice', but a word of similar letters meaning 'faint before'.

Day 6. Is. viii. 16–x. 4.

The prophet will withdraw his disciples, and the elect remnant will thus take shape (viii. 16-18). The dark days (viii. 19-22) will end in the coming of a great light, the advent of the Messiah (ix. 1-7). The remainder of chapter ix is a prophecy of judgment upon the northern kingdom of Israel. Let Judah then beware (x. 1-4)!

(1) When disaster comes, and God seems to have hidden His face, what is man tempted to do (viii. 19)? Cf. Lv. xix. 31; 1 Sa. xxviii. 6, 7. What must the child of God do in such a case? What test does Isaiah propose for spiritist teachings?

(2) Contrast the condition of things under God's anger (viii. 21, 22, ix. 8–x. 4) with Isaiah's picture of Messiah's reign (ix. 1-7).

(3) What names are given to the coming king? Does He so reign in your heart?

Notes.—(1) viii. 19-22. Until the people abandon their resort to spiritism, and turn to God and His revelation, there will be no dawn for them, but only darkness.

(2) ix. 1. The anguish of the northern kingdom 'in the former time' no doubt refers to Tiglath-Pileser's invasion mentioned in 2 Ki. xv. 29. 'The latter time', though future to the prophet, is described with the past tense of prophetic certainty (cf. v. 13 note). For the fulfilment, in part, of the prophecy, see Mt. iv. 15, 16.

(2) ix. 6. 'Wonderful, Counsellor'; better, 'Wonderful counsellor', as in R.V. mg. Cf. xxviii. 29. 'Everlasting Father'; i.e. one who is unceasingly a father to His people.

(3) ix. 12b. Notice how this solemn statement recurs as a refrain in verses 17, 21 and x. 4.

Day 7. Is. x. 5-34.

A prophecy of the Assyrian invasion of Judah.

(1) Contrast the invasion as seen in the mind of the Assyrian king (verses 7-10, 13, 14), and as seen in the purpose of God (verses 5, 6, 12, 16-19). How does this passage help us to understand how the holy God can use evil men or nations to carry out His purposes?

(2) In the stress of the trial it might have seemed that God had cast off His people. But was it so (verses 20-23)? Cf. Rom. ix. 27-29. What was the purpose of God's chastening?

(3) How does today's portion make more clear the two predictions implied in the names of the prophet's two sons? See Day 5, Note (1).

Notes.—(1) Verse 17. 'The light of Israel' and 'his Holy One' are names for God.

(2) Verse 20. 'Him that smote them'; i.e. the king of Assyria. The 'remnant' will have learned the lesson Ahaz had failed to learn.

(3) Verses 24, 26. 'After the manner of Egypt'; i.e. similar to the bondage and the Exodus. 'His rod' in verse 26 is God's rod; cf. Ex. iv. 20.

(4) Verses 28-32. A vivid picture of the approach of the enemy, checked only at the very walls of Jerusalem.

Week 44. ISAIAH XI–XXV

Day 1. Is. xi and xii.

The Assyrian cedar would be irrevocably felled, but out of the stump of the pollarded Judæan tree will come forth a shoot—the Messiah, in whom Isaiah's hope for the future is centred. His glorious reign is considered (1) in relation to human society (xi. 2-5); (2) in relation to the brute creation (xi. 6-9); and (3) in relation to world history (xi. 10-16). There follows a song of thanksgiving to God for His forgiveness, together with a vision of a united Israel (cf. xi. 13) enjoying the blessings of salvation, and engaging in missionary activity among the nations.

(1) What are the characteristics of the Messiah as here portrayed? Should they not also be characteristics of His people, and are they so in your case?

(2) Compare this picture of the Messiah's reign with ix. 1-7. What new truths are here set forth?

(3) Chapter xii is the song of those who have discovered that God's anger is turned away from them. What results of salvation are mentioned here, and are you experiencing them all?

Notes.—(1) xi. 1. 'Jesse'; i.e. David's father (1 Sa. xvii. 58). The Messiah would not only sit on David's throne (ix. 7), but be Himself descended from David.

(2) xi. 10-16. Gentile nations (verse 10) and repatriated Jews (verses 11-16) will both be attracted by the Messiah's ensign (for the meaning of 'ensign' see v. 26, note) and will share together in the Messiah's kingdom. In these verses are the germ of predictions which are further elaborated in xl–lv.

Day 2. Is. xiii-xiv. 23.

In today's portion we leave the Book of Immanuel, and enter what has been called the 'jungle of prophecy' (xiii–xxiii). See *Analysis*. It contains 'the burdens of the Lord', oracles concerning foreign nations, many parts of which are now obscure. The first oracle concerns Babylon, and is directed first against the city (xiii. 1–xiv. 2), and second, against the king (xiv. 3-23). Its predictions have been literally fulfilled.

(1) For what sin was Babylon chiefly condemned? Was it for her wickedness, or for her oppression of God's people, or for her attitude to God? Notice that it is God who administers judgment (xiii. 4-6, 10, 21, etc.), though He acted through human agents.

(2) In what respects may Babylon be regarded as a picture of the world in opposition to God (as Jerusalem or Zion is a picture of God's people), and the king of Babylon a picture of Satan, the prince of this world? Cf. Gn. xi. 1-9; 2 Thes. ii. 4; Rev. xviii. 2, 3.

Notes.—(1) xiii. 2-6. 'The day of the Lord' is the day of His manifestation, and here denotes the day of His vengeance upon Babylon.

(2) xiii. 12. The population will be so reduced, that men will be scarcer than gold.

(3) xiv. 3, 4. The oracle is in the form of a satirical ode, which the exiles are to sing on their release.

(4) xiv. 9-17. The departed spirits in Sheol assemble, surprised and scornful, to greet the arrival of the king whose pomp is now stripped from him.

(5) xiv. 18-20. In contrast with other kings, who received a royal burial, each in his own tomb, the body of the king of Babylon will be left where it falls in battle.

Day 3. Is. xiv. 24–xvi.

A series of denunciatory oracles directed against Assyria (xiv. 24-27), Philistia (xiv. 28-32), and Moab (xv–xvi).

(1) xiv. 24-27. What two attributes of God are emphasized in these verses? How do they encourage us to trust in His Word?

(2) In the prophecy against Moab consider (a) the severity of the judgment, (b) the sympathy of the prophet with Moab in her sufferings, and (c) the reason why her doom is inevitable. Does our heart go out in compassion to proud sinners as we reflect on the judgment awaiting them if they reject Christ?

Notes.—(1) xiv. 29, 'the rod that smote thee is broken'. A reference probably to the death of Tiglath-Pileser of Assyria who died just before Ahaz. However, it was no use rejoicing at this, for the power of Assyria would be revived in a form more deadly than ever.

(2) xiv. 30-32. The meaning is that while even the poorest in Judah shall be secure (verses 30a and 32), Philistia shall be destroyed.

(3) xv. The proper names are Moabite towns, known and unknown. On the signs of grief and mourning in verses 2 and 3, cf. xxii. 12; Mi. i. 16.

(4) xvi. 1-5. The Moabites are advised to send tribute in the form of lambs (cf. 2 Ki. iii. 4) to the king of Judah. Verses 3-5 is the Moabites' plea for refuge.

(5) xvi. 14. 'As the years of an hireling.' An expression denoting the full appointed period, in this case three full years.

Day 4. Is. xvii–xix.

Oracles concerning Damascus (i.e. Syria) and Ephraim, Ethiopia, and Egypt, with a short oracle (xvii. 12-14) prophesying the overthrow of the Assyrian hosts.

(1) How is Ephraim's sin described in xvii. 10, together with its inevitable issue? Cf. Dt. viii. 19, 20; Je. xviii. 15; Ho. viii. 14.

(2) Contrast in chapter xviii man's scheming and planning (see Note (3) below) with God's attitude of quiet watchfulness, knowing what He will do (verses 4-6). Cf. Ps. ii. 1-5.

(3) Gather out from today's portion what is said of the results of God's judgments in causing men to turn unto Him. What encouragements for missionary work, especially in certain countries, may be derived from these chapters?

Notes.—(1) xvii. 4-6. Ephraim's judgment is described under three figures, sickness, reaping and fruit gathering. Verse 4 shows that the phrase, 'the glory of the children of Israel' in verse 3 is used ironically.

(2) xvii. 12-14. The onward advance of the Assyrian armies (verses 12, 13a) is vividly contrasted with their sudden destruction. Cf. xxxvii. 36, 37.

(3) xviii. 1, 2. A description of Ethiopia, whose ambassadors have come to consult with Judah about plans to resist Assyria. 'The rustling of wings' is probably an allusion to the swarms of insects which infest the land. Isaiah gives the ambassadors a message to take back (verses 2b-7), that God is watching, and will shortly deal with the Assyrian menace.

Day 5. Is. xx–xxii. 14.

The story of an acted prophecy on the futility of reliance upon Egypt (xx) is followed by four oracles concerning Babylon (xxi. 1-10), Edom (xxi. 11, 12), Arabia (xxi. 13-17), and Jerusalem (xxii. 1-14).

(1) In what ways does today's portion teach us that God is behind the events of history, knowing all beforehand, and carrying out His purposes?

(2) Taking xxi. 12 to mean that impending events will bring morning to some, and night to others, what great event is impending of which this is true? Cf. 2 Thes. i. 6-10. What lesson may we learn from the prophet's counsel to the Edomites?

(3) In what two respects does Isaiah in xxii. 1-14 find fault with the people of Jerusalem? Do you find the same spirit prevalent today?

Notes.—(1) Chapter xx. It was not unusual for prophets to enforce their teaching by symbolic action, see, e.g., Je. xiii. 1-7; Ezk. iv. 1-3; Mt. xviii. 1-6.

(2) xxi. 2-5. 'The treacherous dealer. . . .' Perhaps better, 'the violent man uses violence'. The vision of the Medo-Elamite troops taking Babylon by storm overwhelms the prophet; yet while *he* is so distressed, the people of Babylon are feasting in unconcern.

(3) xxi. 6-9. Isaiah is bidden in his vision to appoint a watchman to look out for the approach to Babylon of the attacking army. He grows impatient at the delay, when suddenly the storm-troops arrive.

(4) xxi. 10. Israel under Babylon's tyranny had been as corn under the threshing machine.

(5) xxi. 11. The reference to Seir, the great Edomite mountain, indicates that the oracle concerns Edom. 'Dumah' seems to be an anagram of Edom.

(6) xxi. 13-17. Dedanites were travelling Arabian merchantmen. Tema is probably Taima, an important oasis on the caravan route between the Persian Gulf and Egypt. The merchantmen, driven from the main routes, were succoured by the inhabitants of Tema.

(7) xxii. 2, 3. The prophet bewails the conduct of the people, thronging the house-tops, shouting and rejoicing, when calamity was near. 'They were bound by the archers'; better, 'Without bow (which had been cast aside) they were taken prisoner.'

Day 6, Is. xxii. 15–xxiii.

In xxii. 15-25 Isaiah predicts that Shebna, the palace steward, will be ousted by Eliakim, and will end his days in exile and shame, while Eliakim and his house will be exalted. Chapter xxiii is a prophecy concerning Tyre, and is the last of the series of oracles which began in xiii.

(1) Behind the deposition of Shebna, and the promotion of Eliakim, was the divine purpose (notice the repeated 'I' in these verses). Do you detect God's hand in everyday affairs, and believe that He has a purpose of good for everyone whom He can call 'my servant' (verse 20)? Cf. Jn. xv. 16.

(2) Compare the pride of Assyrian militarism (x. 5-34) with the pride of Phœnician materialism. Both are alike hateful to God. What forms does pride assume today and what is our defence against it? See 1 Pet. v. 5-7.

(3) Isaiah foresees a day when Tyre's riches will no longer be hoarded for her own selfish enjoyment, but will be lavished upon Jehovah and His people. If then he is not condemning wealth in itself as evil, what is he attacking in the earlier part of the chapter?

Notes.—(1) xxii. 15. 'Treasurer; better, 'steward' (R.V. mg.). The office of palace steward was one of great influence. Shebna, however, was a foreigner, who had no relatives in Jerusalem ('Whom hast thou here?') and so really no place there ('What hast thou here?'). In preparing a costly tomb for himself, he showed an arrogance of spirit which drew down upon him God's stern judgment.

(2) xxii. 25. If this refers to Eliakim, it seems to foretell his future fall from office through the number of unworthy relatives depending upon him.

(3) xxiii. 1. Tarshish is probably Tartessus in Spain. 'Ships of Tarshish' originally denoted cargo boats bound for Tartessus, but the name came to be applied to any large trading vessels. 'Kittim' is almost certainly Cyprus.

(4) xxiii. 3. 'Shihor.' A name for the Nile; see Je. ii. 18 (R.V. mg.).

(5) xxiii. 15. 'After 70 years.' Usually interpreted as symbolic of a long period. 'As in the song of the harlot'—a reference to a popular song of that title, part of which is quoted in verse 16.

(6) xxiii. 18. Cf. Ps. xlv. 12, lxxxvii. 4. God, in His power and mercy, can transform even the acquisitive spirit, which was embodied in Tyre.

Day 7. Is. xxiv and xxv.

Chapter xxiv begins the long apocalyptic vision of the Day of the Lord which continues until xxvii. It seems impossible to give it any certain historical background, and it was probably intended to be an ideal description of the last great judgment which will engulf the whole world. The horizon is very black except for the bright gleam of light which appears in verse 23, and which leads on to the burst of praise in xxv, just as chapter xii follows chapter xi. First in his own name (xxv), and then in the name of the redeemed community (xxvi), the prophet gives thanks for their certain deliverance from the final judgment and for their everlasting bliss and security.

(1) Consider how inevitably xxiv. 6 follows xxiv. 5. The principle is stated clearly in Gal. iii. 10. Do you see the logical connection with Gal. iii. 13?

(2) The deliverance of the righteous remnant (see Note (1) below) will bring glory to God (xxiv. 15) and to themselves (xxiv. 16) at the same time. How is this possible? Cf. 2 Thes. i. 10, 12.

Notes.—(1) xxiv. 13-16. Within the universal calamity the tiny remnant will still lift up their voice in worship, they alone will survive (verse 16) and share in the new kingdom which will be established in Jerusalem (verse 23) after the powers of darkness and the wicked kings of the earth have been 'shut up in prison' (verses 21, 22).

(2) xxv. 2, 3. In this verse, as in xxiv. 10, 12 and xxvi. 5, 6, 'the city' refers to no special town, but to any stronghold of opposition to God, in contrast to God's 'strong city', Zion (xxvi. 1, 2). The former will be 'made an heap' (xxv. 2), but the latter fortified with impregnable bulwarks (xxvi. 1).

(3) xxv. 7. The 'covering' or 'veil' may be a picture of mortality and death (cf. verse 8), or of ignorance and prejudice, or of sorrow (cf. verse 8 again).

Week 45. Isaiah xxvi–xxxix
Day 1. Is. xxvi and xxvii.

In chapter xxvi Isaiah puts into the mouth of the redeemed a song of praise similar to that which he had himself sung in xxv. Chapter xxvii is a fitting conclusion to the series of prophecies which began in xxiv. After declaring judgment upon three world powers (verse 1), it promises ultimate restoration to Judah (verses 2-6, 12-13). There must be chastening, but not such as Israel's enemies have suffered (verses 7-11).

(1) Consider the safety of those whom God calls 'my people' when the storm of His judgment breaks (xxvi. 20, 21). In what ways does the prophet's picture of salvation in chapter xxvi resemble, and in what ways differ from that in xxv?

(2) What is the response of God's people in chapter xxvi to His mercy and judgment? Do our hearts also speak thus?

(3) How does chapter xxvii express the principle underlying God's chastisement of His people, and also His ultimate purpose?

Notes.—(1) xxvi. 16-18. 'They' (verse 16) and 'we' (verses 17, 18) both refer to the redeemed people, who realize how futile their own efforts were until they called earnestly upon God.

(2) xxvi. 19. The prophet's answer to the people's plaint is the promise of resurrection. His words here and in xxv. 8 are among the clearest utterances of the Old Testament upon that subject.

(3) xxvii. 1. The three monsters represent three world powers, probably Assyria, Babylon and Egypt.

(4) xxvii. 4, 5. God's fury will be directed no longer against His people (the vineyard) but against their enemies (the thorns and briars). Verse 5 means that the enemies will be consumed unless they sue for peace with Him.

(5) xxvii. 7-11. God will not smite Judah as sorely as He will her smiters (verse 7). His judgment will indeed fall (verses 10, 11), but it will be restrained ('in measure', verse 8). By bearing punishment Judah's guilt will be expiated, and the happy result will be a rejection of idolatry for ever (verse 9).

Day 2. Is. xxviii.

This is the first of four chapters of warning to Judah. Their main theme is the folly of seeking help from Egypt. Warnings of terrible judgment (observe the recurrence of the word 'woe', see xxviii. 1, xxix. 1, 15, xxx. 1, xxxi. 1) intermingle with assurances of God's intervention in mercy. The divisions of xxviii are as follows: verses 1-4, judgment upon Samaria; verses 5, 6, after the judgment; verses 7-13, the drunken rulers of Judah rebuked; verses 14-23, the coming storm of God's judgment will sweep away all man-made policies; verses 23-29, if the farmer acts with wisdom, how much more God?

(1) How many consequences of intemperance can you discern in verses 1-4 and 7, 8?

(2) Straightforward preaching of God's Word is always criticized. What was the protest which Isaiah received (verses 9, 10)? and what was the real cause of his opponents' antagonism (verses 12, 14, 15)?

(3) How do verses 16-22 show (a) that God has a plan; (b) the futility of unbelief and rebellion? How may we apply the parable in verses 23-29 for our own comfort?

Notes.—(1) Verses 9-13 describe an encounter which Isaiah had with the licentious priests and prophets of his day. Verses 9, 10 give their protest, and verses 11-13 the prophet's reply.

(2) Verses 15-18. Isaiah calls the proposed alliance with Egypt 'a covenant with death'. 'The overflowing scourge' is Assyria. Verse 16 is applied in the New Testament to Christ, see Rom. ix. 33, x. 11; 1 Pet. ii. 6-8.

(3) Verses 23-29 are a parable illustrating the fact that God, like the farmer, acts with wise method and purpose. Note the renderings in R.V. mg.

Day 3. Is. xxix–xxx. 17.

Though Jerusalem ('Ariel') shall be brought very low, yet shall the besieging army be routed (xxix. 1-8). The people are without discernment (xxix. 9-13); therefore God will reveal Himself in an act of judgment that will cause them to marvel (xxix. 15, 16). Then shall come an era of joy, righteousness, worship and instruction (xxix. 19-24). In chapter xxx the prophet returns to the alliance with Egypt, and foretells its direful consequences.

(1) Observe the contrast between the extreme distress of Jerusalem in xxix. 2-4, and her complete triumph in xxix. 5-8. How may this encourage us in time of severe trial?

(2) Can you find in xxx. 8-12 the explanation for the people's blindness in xxix. 9-12, as also for their discernment in xxix. 18? What may this teach us in regard to our own understanding of the things of God?

(3) On what various grounds does Isaiah urge upon his hearers that they should rely upon God rather than upon Egypt? Trace out in xxx. 8-17 the respective issues of the two ways.

Notes.—(1) xxix. 1-8. 'Ariel'; a name for Jerusalem which may mean 'lion of God' or, as is more probable here, 'hearth of God'. (Cf. Ezk. xliii. 15, R.V. mg.) Jerusalem will become an altar hearth, soaked with the blood of many victims. For a similar metaphor see xxxiii, *note*, xxxiv. 6, *note*.

(2) xxx. 1. 'Cover with a covering', or 'weave a web' (R.V. mg.), in the general sense of devising a plan.

(3) xxx. 4-6. Hezekiah's ambassadors are pictured in verse 6 as crossing the desert, risking its dangers, and laden with treasure. In verse 5 they are seen negotiating with the Egyptians at Zoan and Hanes, which were probably cities of the Nile delta. All would prove profitless.

(4) xxx. 7. 'Rahab', a nickname for Egypt. The prophet adds an epithet, and dubs Egypt 'Rahab sit still'.

(5) xxx. 13, 14. Two vivid metaphors are used to describe Judah's peril—a wall bulging and about to crash in ruins, and a pitcher shattered into useless fragments.

Day 4. Is. xxx. 18–xxxii.

In these chapters the prophet repeats three themes: (1) *God will judge* the faithless who turn to Egypt for help (xxxi. 1-3), and the self-satisfied women who leave God out of account (xxxii. 9-14); (2) *God will protect* Zion (xxx. 27-33 and xxxi. 4-9); (3) *God will establish* the Messianic kingdom in Zion (xxxii. 1, 2).

(1) In xxx. 20 the word 'teachers' may be plural, in which case the reference is to the prophets, whose teaching will keep the people on the right road; but it more probably should be read as 'teacher' (as in R.V. mg.) referring to one Teacher, namely, the Holy Spirit. How has this promise been fulfilled to us in Christ? See Jn. xiv. 26, xvi. 13. How important to be sensitive to the voice of this teacher, and prompt to obey it!

(2) Many trusted in Egypt because she *seemed* strong (xxxi. 1). How does Isaiah here show the folly of this, as compared with trusting in Jehovah?

(3) Consider how the description of the royal 'man' of xxxii. 1, 2 has been fulfilled in Christ. See, e.g., Jn. xvii. 12, iv. 14, xiv. 27. What are the characteristics of His kingdom as given in xxxii. 5-7, 15-20? Cf. also xxx. 19-22.

Notes.—(1) xxx. 20. Scanty siege rations shall give place to the rich food of God's revelation.

(2) xxx. 25, 26. A poetic description of the blessings of the new age, to be interpreted symbolically as showing the abundance of God's provision. For the phrase 'when the towers fall', cf. ii. 11-17.

(3) xxx. 27-33. Notice the wealth of imaginative metaphor—the storm, the flood, the bridle. The meaning of verse 32 is not fully clear. Moffatt renders 'He clubs them down to peals of music'. 'Tophet' was a name given to the valley of Hinnom outside Jerusalem, where the foul rites of human sacrifice were practised in honour of the god Molech. Its original meaning seems to have been 'fire place', and Isaiah declares that God has prepared such a place for a great holocaust in honour of the king (of Assyria). There is a play upon words in the Hebrew, for the word for 'king' is *melek* (=Molech).

(4) xxxii. 15. When judgment is complete, there will come a new era of blessing through the outpouring of 'spirit from on high'.

(5) xxxii. 19. Across the prophet's vision of the Messiah's reign there breaks a furious hailstorm, perhaps in remembrance of the imminent Assyrian invasion. Cf. xxviii. 2, 17, xxvi. 5.

Day 5. Is. xxxiii–xxxv.

The opening verses of xxxiii reflect the excitement and panic which preceded Sennacherib's approach (verses 7-9) and the prophet's triumphant faith that the proud Assyrian would suffer defeat (verses 1-6, 10-12). The remainder of the chapter shows the profound effects of this deliverance, and paints a glowing picture of the coming kingdom. Chapters xxxiv and xxxv present a striking contrast between the fearful doom of God's enemies, symbolized by Edom (xxxiv), and the glorious future which awaits God's redeemed people (xxxv).

(1) In the picture of the Messiah's kingdom given in xxxiii. 14-24 (a) what are the characteristics of His people, (b) what will the Lord be to them, and (c) what blessings will they enjoy?

(2) Applied spiritually, what blessings are spoken of in chapter xxxv which are available to believers now? In particular, can you discover in verses 8-10 four or five characteristics of the 'high way', i.e. the Christian life?

Notes.—(1) xxxiii. 10-12. God's answer to His people's prayer (verse 2). Verse 11 is addressed to the enemy, 'breath' here meaning 'fury'. 'Your fury shall consume yourselves' (Moffatt).

(2) xxxiii. 14. The ungodly are afraid, and ask, How shall any man dwell in the presence of such a God? The following verses give the answer.

(3) xxxiii. 17. Words that look forward to the Messiah, cf. Ps. lxxii. 8.

(4) xxxiii. 18, 19. The things that before affrighted them, such as Assyrian officials counting the tribute, Assyrian engineers surveying the fortifications, the barbarian Assyrian armies, will all belong to the past.

(5) xxxiii. 20, 21. Zion likened to a well-erected tent, and then to a city surrounded by broad waters, where no man of war is seen. How different Zion's present plight (verse 23)! But suddenly ('then' is emphatic) the tables are turned, and Assyria becomes a spoil and a prey.

(6) xxxiv. 6, 7. God's judgment of Edom pictured as a sacrifice in Bozrah, an Edomite city.

(7) xxxiv. 16. 'The book of the Lord.' Probably refers to some collection of Isaiah's previous prophecies. None of them shall fail. The spirit of God will accomplish in history what the mouth of His servant has commanded in prophecy. Cf. lv. 11; Je. i. 9, 10.

(8) xxxv. 7, 8. See R.V. mg.

Day 6. Is. xxxvi and xxxvii.

We have now reached 701 B.C., the year of Sennacherib's siege of Jerusalem, so long predicted. Chapters xxxvi–xxxix repeat, with a few omissions and additions, the history recorded in 2 Ki. xviii. 13-xx. The course of events seems to have been as follows: (1) After receiving the tribute demanded (2 Ki. xviii. 14-16), Sennacherib sent three envoys with an army to demand further the surrender of Jerusalem (xxxvi. 1-xxxvii. 7). (2) This was refused and the Assyrian troops withdrew, but Sennacherib sent a letter to Hezekiah renewing his demands (xxxvii. 8-35). This also was rejected, and the chapter concludes with a brief account of how God fulfilled His word (xxxvii. 36-38).

(1) The Rabshakeh (see Note 2 below) tried to undermine the defenders' morale by exaggerating the Assyrian might (xxxvi. 8, 9, 14) and minimizing that of Jehovah (xxxvi. 15, 18-20). He also gave a misleading picture of the people's plight if they did not surrender, and of their prosperity if they did (xxxvi. 12, 16, 17). Does the tempter use similar tactics with you?

(2) Wherein lies the falsity of the argument in xxxvi. 18-20 and xxxvii. 10-13? Cf. xxxvii. 18-20, 23-29.

(3) Both Hezekiah and Isaiah recognized in Sennacherib's challenge a blasphemous insult to the living God (xxxvii. 6, 7, 17, 23). How did this give them confidence? Cf. 1 Sa. xvii. 26, 36, 45-47.

Notes.—(1) xxxvi. 1. The chronological note is wrong, for 701 B.C. was Hezekiah's twenty-sixth year. Possibly the note belongs properly to xxxviii. 1, and has become misplaced. See *Note* (1), Day 7, below.

(2) xxxvi. 2, 3. Rabshakeh was the title of the Assyrian chief-captain, second to the Tartan or commander-in-chief. As there were three envoys (2 Ki. xviii. 17), so three Jewish high officials were sent to meet them.

(3) xxxvi. 7. Whether in ignorance or in subtlety, the Rabshakeh spoke of Hezekiah's religious reformation (2 Ki. xviii. 4), as if it had been an act of

disrespect towards Jehovah. Possibly to a heathen mind it appeared in that
light.

(4) xxxvii. 30. Isaiah promises Hezekiah that by the third year the Assyrian
menace would have been so completely removed that they could sow and reap
in peace.

(5) xxxvii. 37, 38. An interval of about twenty years lies between the events
recorded in these two verses.

Day 7. Is. xxxviii and xxxix.

(1) How does chapter xxxviii show forth (a) the power of
prayer (cf. Jas. v. 16b), (b) a loving purpose behind suffering
(cf. Ps. cxix. 71, 75), (c) the completeness of God's forgiveness
(cf. Ps. ciii. 12; Mi. vii. 19), (d) the duty of praise (cf. Ps. xiii. 6)?

(2) What evidence is there in this chapter that true faith in
God does not preclude the use of human means?

(3) Wherein lay Hezekiah's sin in displaying his royal treasures
and military might to the envoys of Merodach-baladan? Cf. 2 Ch.
xxxii. 25, 31. How does the incident reveal what was in his heart?

Notes.—(1) The events of these chapters preceded Sennacherib's invasion,
Hezekiah reigned 29 years (2 Ki. xviii. 2), so that he fell ill in the fourteenth
year of his reign.

(2) xxxviii. 7, 8. The sign was a miraculous alteration of the shadow on the
sun-dial, and not necessarily of the sun in the sky. It may have been caused
by eclipse or reflection, and appears to have been a local phenomenon only
(cf. 2 Ch. xxxii. 31).

(3) xxxviii. 12, 13. Note the metaphors. His body ('my habitation', R.V.
mg.) will be removed like a shepherd's tent. His life will resemble a piece of
unfinished cloth on a loom, carefully rolled up by the weaver (himself), but
abruptly cut off from the loom by God. All day long and the following night
he expected God to end his life as a lion crushes its prey.

(4) xxxviii. 15. With this verse his words change from complaint to praise,
and he pledges himself to live the rest of his life in humility, and in praise
(verses 19, 20).

(5) xxxviii. 11 and 18. The thought that death cut them off from God made
it a cause of dread to Old Testament believers. Contrast 1 Cor. xv. 20, 55, 56.

(6) xxxix. 1. Merodach-baladan made himself king of Babylon in defiance
of Assyria in 721 B.C., but was taken captive by the Assyrian king Sargon in
709. Before his downfall he sought to secure himself against Assyria by foreign
alliances, one of which was with Judah in 714. Hezekiah's sickness and remarkable recovery gave him occasion to make a first approach. Cf. 2 Ch. xxxii. 31.

Week 46. ISAIAH XL–XLVIII
Day 1. Is. xl.

The prophecies of these chapters have as their main theme the proclamation
that God is about to restore the exiled Jews in Babylon to their own land. See
Introduction. They refer to a time when the words spoken to Hezekiah in xxxix.

5-7 have been fulfilled (cf. also xiii–xiv and xxi. 1-9). The first eleven verses are a prologue in which the prophet hears heavenly voices declaring to Jerusalem the glad message of redemption.

(1) What are the four or five great facts announced by the various voices in verses 1-11? Imagine yourself one of the exiled captives in Babylon, and with what thrilling power they would fall upon your ear. Would you not say, Can it ever be? (Cf. verse 27.)

(2) The prophet's answer is given in verses 12-26. It can be because of what God is, supreme over all. Follow his argument as he shows God's supremacy (a) in creation (verse 12); (b) in His wisdom (verses 13, 14); (c) by comparison with nations (verses 15-17); (d) by comparison with idols (verses 18-20); (e) by comparison with the great of the earth (verses 21-24); (f) in His control of the stars (verses 25, 26).

(3) Do you feel the thrill of the appeal in verses 27-31? Is it not equally applicable to ourselves? What then is the response of *your* heart?

Notes.—(1) Verse 2, 'comfortably'. Literally 'speak to the heart' (R.V. mg.). 'Warfare', meaning a term of conscripted military service, used here of the period of the exile. Render 'term of service', as in R.V. mg. Cf. Jb. vii. 1, xiv. 14. The phrase, 'double for all her sins', means that the penalty paid is amply sufficient (cf. chapter liii and Rom. v. 20).

(2) Verse 10. 'His arm shall rule for Him'; i.e. He shall rule by the might of His arm. Cf. Ps. lxvi. 7.

(3) Verse 15. 'Isles'. Used generally in Old Testament of the islands and coastlands of the Mediterranean, but here and elsewhere in these chapters is almost equivalent to 'lands', with the implied thought of remoteness.

(4) Verse 22. 'Upon the circle of the earth'; better, 'above', as in R.V. mg. God sits high above the earth. Cf. Ps. cxiii. 5, 6.

(5) Verse 24. Read as in R.V. mg.

(6) Verse 27. 'My judgment, etc.' 'My rights are unregarded by my God' (Moffatt).

(7) Verse 31. 'Renew'; i.e. receive a new kind of strength (literally, exchange or better) by which they will fly, run without wearying, walk without fainting.

Day 2. Is. xli.

In this magnificent chapter the supremacy of Jehovah, the God of Israel, is further demonstrated. First the nations (verses 1, 2), and then their gods (verses 21-29) are summoned before Him, and challenged as to what counsel they can give, and what control they can exercise in regard to the world-shaking onward march of Cyrus. They know nothing and can do nothing. It is Jehovah who alone can predict the future, for He has planned all, and brought it to pass. Let Israel lift up his head, for he is God's elect and for him He has great purposes in view (verses 8-20).

(1) The reference in verses 2 and 25 is to Cyrus. The nations in their fear make new idols (verses 5-7), but the idols are nothing (verses 23-24, 28-29). What, in contrast, is Jehovah's relation to this mighty conqueror, and to the events of history in general (verses 2-4, 25-27)?

(2) Tabulate the promises made to Israel in verses 8-20. How far and in what sense are they true for us today? Cf. 2 Cor. i. 20. In what measure have we tried and proved them?

Notes.—(1) Verses 2, 3. In verse 2 God is the subject, in verse 3 Cyrus. Verse 3b seems to refer to the speed of Cyrus' advance, 'swiftly with feet that never touch the ground' (Moffatt). Cf. Dn. viii. 5.

(2) Verse 4. 'Who hath wrought and done it? He that calleth the generations from the beginning.' The reference is to God's eternal being, 'I, the Lord, the First.'

(3) Verse 14. 'Thou worm Jacob'. The Jews, so helpless, as it seemed, in exile, liable to be crushed under foot as a worm, are to be made a powerful threshing instrument. Cf. Ps. xxii. 6, 7.

(4) Verse 21. The idols are now summoned before Jehovah (see verse 23). 'Strong reasons' might be better rendered 'proofs', i.e. of what they can do.

(5) Verses 22, 23. God challenges them to make known past events in their issues, and what the future has in store. 'Do good or do evil', i.e. 'Do something or other, that we may marvel at the sight' (Moffatt).

(6) Verse 26. 'He is righteous'; better, 'It is right', i.e. a true prophecy. Cf. xliii. 9.

Day 3. Is. xlii–xliii. 13.

In xli Isaiah has shown that God has great purposes for Israel, His servant. That purpose is now declared. It is a purpose of blessing to all nations (xlii. 1-4 and 5-9; cf. Gn. xii. 3b). In order to accomplish it, God will redeem His people from their present plight (xlii. 13-16), confounding those that trust in idols (xlii. 17), and calling forth from far and near a pæon of praise to His Name (xlii. 10-12). Israel's present condition, under God's chastisement for her sins, is indeed pitiable (xlii. 18-25), but God will ransom His people, letting other nations suffer subjection in their stead (xliii. 1-7), and Israel shall then bear witness before the assembled nations to Jehovah's sovereign might and glory (xliii. 8-13).

(1) xlii. 1-4. The prophet, in this picture of God's ideal Servant, perfectly portrays the Lord Jesus. See Mt. xii. 18-21. What is said concerning (a) His relation to God; (b) His equipment for His task; (c) the purpose and scope of His mission; (d) the qualities that characterize Him; (e) the method of His ministry; (f) His endurance; (g) the final fulfilment of His work?

(2) It might seem impossible, in view of Israel's present distressful condition, that such a people could ever serve God (xlii. 18-25). But how does Isaiah show that what is impossible with men is

possible with God? What does God promise to do? See xlii. 13-16, xliii. 1-7.

(3) What witness will Israel, when redeemed, bear to Jehovah (xliii. 8-13)? Have we a like witness to give to the world of the reality of God's saving power?

Notes.—(1) xlii. 1-4. This is the first of the 'Servant' passages (see *Introduction* and *Analysis*). The word 'judgment' means here the whole system of divine ordinances, and is almost equivalent to 'true religion'. So also in verse 4.

(2) xlii. 4a. See R.V. mg. The words 'fail' and 'be discouraged' are the same in Hebrew as 'smoking' (i.e. burning dimly) and 'break' in verse 3.

(3) xlii. 11. 'Sela.' The name of the chief town of Edom, meaning 'rock'. It is better, perhaps, to retain here the A.V. rendering, 'the inhabitants of the rock'. The first half of the verse will then refer to the wilderness with its townships and villages, and the second half to dwellers in the rocks and hills. Kedar is the name of a desert tribe.

(4) xlii. 13-16. Jehovah describes Himself as a mighty conqueror, leading forth His people. Cf. lix. 17.

(5) xlii. 19. 'Blind'; i.e. to destiny and mission.

(6) xliii. 3, 4. The meaning seems to be that God will give to Cyrus other peoples to serve him in payment for setting the Jews free.

(7) xliii. 8-13. Once again, as in xli. 1-7, the nations are summoned before Jehovah, and Israel stands forth as witness to His absolute supremacy.

Day 4. Is. xliii. 14–xliv. 23.

Today's portion is in two parts. In the first part (xliii. 14–xliv. 5) God declares His invincible power and forgiving grace. In making reference to Babylon's impending downfall (xliii. 14, 15) He answers an unspoken objection that such a thing is incredible. 'Do you not remember what I did at the Red Sea?' He asks (xliii. 16, 17). 'Yet what I am about to do now is greater still' (xliii. 18-21). He answers, too, a deeper cause of their unbelief, namely, a guilty conscience (xliii. 21-24). 'I know it all', He says, 'but I will pardon all' (xliii. 25). If I were strict to mark iniquity, you could not stand (xliii. 26-28). But my purpose toward you is one of blessing (xliv. 1-5).

The second part of today's portion contrasts Jehovah with the idols (xliv. 6-20) and renews His promise of full forgiveness (xliv. 21-23).

(1) What was the new thing that God was about to do, greater even than His deliverance of Israel at the Red Sea? Cf. chapter xxxv. What application has it to ourselves?

(2) How does xliii. 22-28 show that Israel was not justified by works, but only by free grace? Cf. Rom. iii. 23, 24. What further gift had God in store for His redeemed people, and what blessings will it bring (xliv. 3-5)? Cf. Jn. vii. 37-39.

(3) What is the effect of idolatry on the mind of the worshipper? See xliv. 18-20. Have you realized the greatness of our privilege in knowing the true God? See xliv. 6-8

Notes.—(1) xliii. 14. 'The ships of their rejoicing' or 'pleasure-boats' (Moffatt). The meaning is that the people of Babylon will flee down the river in panic.

(2) xliii. 22-24. During the exile, God had not burdened them with demands for sacrifice and offering. But they had burdened Him with their sins.

(3) xliii. 27, 28. 'Thy first father'. A reference probably to Jacob, cf. xlviii. 1. 'Thine interpreters' may refer to priests and prophets; cf. Je. ii. 8. 'I will profane'; better, as in A.V. and R.V. mg., 'I have profaned.' The original reading, however, may possibly have been, 'Thy princes profaned my sanctuary, therefore I have made Jacob, etc.'

(4) xliv. 2. 'Jeshurun.' A name for Israel, meaning 'upright'. Cf. Dt. xxxii. 15, xxxiii. 5, 26.

(5) xliv. 5. Not only will Israel's offspring increase (verse 4), but foreigners also will attach themselves to Jehovah as His people.

Day 5. Is. xliv. 24–xlv.

Allusion has already been made to Cyrus, but not by name (xli. 2, 25). Now he is directly and personally addressed, as one whom God has chosen as an instrument of His purpose of good towards Israel, and the purpose for which he has been raised up is declared (xliv. 24–xlv. 8). Those who object to this view of God's relation to Cyrus are rebuked (xlv. 9-13), and there follows a remarkable prophecy of universal acknowledgment of Jehovah as the one God, in whom alone is salvation (xlv. 14-25).

(1) What is said in xliv. 24–xlv. 8 concerning (a) God's power in creation and in human history; (b) Cyrus and what God will do for him and through him; (c) God's purpose in all this for Israel and the world? Consider the fulfilment of these prophecies in history.

(2) What twofold answer is given to those who challenge God's word of revelation, and cavil at His ways? See xlv. 9-13.

(3) Where do you find in today's portion (a) a gospel for the whole world, and (b) a further teaching about justification?

Notes.—(1) xliv. 25. 'The tokens of the liars' or 'boasters' (R.V. mg.). The people referred to are the diviners and soothsayers of Babylon, who had great influence. Cf. xlvii. 13.

(2) xliv. 28. 'Shepherd'; used frequently in the meaning of 'ruler'.

(3) xlv. 3. 'The treasures of darkness'; i.e. treasures concealed from sight.

(4) xlv. 7. 'Evil' here means 'misfortune'.

(5) xlv. 11. It is possible that the true reading should be 'will ye question Me . . . and lay commands upon Me?'

(6) xlv. 13. 'Not for price or reward.' This seems to contradict xliii. 3, 4, but that passage speaks of the reward God gave, this of Cyrus' motive.

(7) xlv. 14-17. Spoken to Israel. Verses 14b, 15 are the confession of the nations mentioned in 14.

Day 6. Is. xlvi and xlvii.

These two chapters concern Babylon, the first showing the impotence of Babylon's gods and the folly of worshipping them (verses 1-7), and rebuking those Jews who would not receive God's revelation of His purposes (verses 8-13); and the second depicting Babylon as a proud queen humbled to the position of a menial slave, with none to help her.

(1) Observe the difference in xlvi. 1-4 between the gods of Babylon that have to be borne by beasts, and carried away by their worshippers, and Jehovah who bears His people throughout their history. Is your religion one that is a burden to you or one that bears you even to old age?

(2) What sins brought about Babylon's downfall, and God's judgment upon her?

(3) What is the attitude of the word of God to all forms of fortune-telling, crystal-gazing, and the like? What may we learn from chapter xlvii about what will happen in the hour of judgment if we have been trusting in any other than in God?

Notes.—(1) xlvi. 1, 2. The inhabitants of Babylon laid their chief idols (Bel and Nebo) on beasts, and carried them away in their flight.

(2) xlvi. 5-7. A passage very similar to xl. 18-20.

(3) xlvii. 3, 4. 'Accept no man.' The expression, as it stands, is obscure. By a slight emendation, supported by one or two LXX manuscripts, the meaning is as follows: 'I will take vengeance and will not be entreated, saith our Redeemer, the Lord of Hosts is His Name, the Holy One of Israel' (*Camb. Bible*).

(4) xlvii. 6. 'I polluted mine inheritance'; i.e. allowed the holy land to be defiled by foreign conquerors.

Day 7. Is. xlviii.

There seems to have been a party among the exiles which received God's message concerning Cyrus with disfavour. God has already rebuked them more than once (xlv. 9-13, xlvi. 12, 13); and now in verses 1-11 of this chapter He answers an objection they seem to have raised that the teaching was novel, and not in accord with God's usual procedure. He tells them that in spite of their rebellious attitude, He will carry out His plans. There follows in verses 12-16 a further confirmation of this, and then a divine lament that Israel had so often frustrated God's gracious purposes by their refusal to listen to His voice (verses 17-19). The chapter ends with a summons to go forth from Babylon with joy and singing, for the hour of their deliverance had come, and God would lead them safely through the desert (verses 20, 21).

(1) How slow the people were to give glory to God! If He did not make known beforehand what He was about to do, the people would say that some other god had done it (verse 5); if He did make it known, they would say, It is what we knew already (verse 7). Do we thus grieve God by failing to acknowledge Him, and to give Him glory?

(2) Is your life like that depicted in verses 17-19, bringing disappointment to God's loving heart, or does it bear glad testi-

mony to the richness of His grace, as the prophet bids us do in verses 20, 21?

Notes.—(1) Verse 1. 'Out of the waters of Judah'; cf. Ps. lxviii. 26, R.V.

(2) Verses 3-6a. 'The former things.' A reference to prophecies long foretold and now fulfilled; see also verse 5a. In verse 6b God acknowledges that He has now used a different method, keeping back the revelation of His intended action until just before it happened, but in this also He had a purpose (verse 7).

(3) Verse 10. 'But not as silver.' A phrase that seems to express the divine sorrow that the refining process had not given a better result, such as happens when silver is refined. Cf. Je. vi. 29, 30. The word 'chosen' should be read 'tried', as in R.V. mg.

(4) Verse 14. 'All ye' refers to Israel, 'which among them' to the nations, and 'the Lord hath loved him' to Cyrus (cf. R.V. mg.).

(5) Verse 16. In the first part of the verse God speaks; cf. xlv. 19. The last clause seems to be an isolated fragment.

Week 47. ISAIAH XLIX–LVII

Day 1. Is. xlix–l. 3.

In chapters xl–xlviii the prophet has been concerned to show the supremacy of Jehovah over the nations and their gods, and that God's purpose is to be accomplished through Cyrus. These two themes now disappear, and attention is turned to Israel's glorious future. Much of the section xlix–lv consists of words of encouragement, spoken to overcome the doubts, hesitations and difficulties which the message of the preceding chapters had aroused in many minds. It contains also three of the 'Servant' passages in which the mission, the sufferings, and the atoning death of the Lord's Servant are set forth. (See *Analysis.*)

(1) Verses 1-6. The 'Servant' speaks to the nations. What does he say concerning (a) his call; (b) his equipment; (c) his initial non-success, and his attitude in face of this; (d) the new task which God gave him to do? Although the passage applies to the Lord Jesus Christ, Paul uses part of it of himself and Barnabas. See Acts xiii. 47. How is this? Have we then a share in the Servant's task? See Jn. xx. 21.

(2) Try to put yourself in the position of Israel in exile, as described in verse 7a (cf. xli. 14, 'worm'), and then contemplate the faith that could see and declare the transformation announced in verses 7b-13. On what is the prophet's faith founded? With verse 7 compare Ps. xxii. 6 and 27-29a.

(3) How does the Lord answer Zion's doubts, first that the Lord has forsaken her (verse 14); second, that her children are taken from her and lost to her (verse 21); third, that Babylon was too strong to give up its prey (verse 14); and fourth, that her covenant relation with Jehovah is broken (l. 1)?

Notes.—(1) Verse 8. 'In an acceptable time'; i.e. in a time of favour. Cf. lxi. 2 (R.V. mg.).

(2) Verse 9. 'Saying.' It is Jehovah who here speaks to the captives of Babylon.

(3) Verse 12. 'From the land of Sinim.' This might well be China, if it could be shown that Jewish exiles had reached so far at that time. Cf. lxvi. 19, 20.

(4) Verses 14-21. Zion is here pictured as a bereaved mother.

(5) Verse 17. Zion's children hasten homewards; and the enemies who are in the city depart out of it. Cf. verse 19, last clause.

(6) l. 1, 2. 'What writ of divorce did I ever hand to your mother?' (Moffatt). The meaning is that the breach between Jehovah and Zion and her children is not irreparable.

Day 2. Is. l. 4–li. 16.

Another portrait of the 'Servant' (l. 4-9), with some words of encouragement and warning based on it, is followed by a message of comfort in three parts (each beginning with the word 'hearken') to those among the exiles who 'follow after righteousness' (li. 1-8). A cry to Jehovah to make bare His arm (li. 9-11) receives a gracious answer, rebuking the fears of His people (li. 12-16).

(1) What qualities are revealed in this picture of the Servant? Let your own life be searched thereby, for is not all that is here said of the Servant, though it applies first to Christ, true also in Him of His people?

(2) What comfort and encouragement for your own faith do you find in li. 1-8? The passage bids us look *back* (verses 1-3), *on* (verses 4-6), and *up* (verses 7, 8).

(3) Are you among those to whom the rebuke of li. 12, 13 applies? Claim then the comfort which the Lord gives to all such in these verses.

Notes.—(1) l. 4-7. Notice what is said of the servant's tongue, ear, back, cheek, face. The hair refers to the hair of the beard, the tampering with which was accounted a great insult. Cf. 2 Sa. x. 4.

(2) l. 11. The evil designs of those who planned mischief would recoil upon themselves.

(3) li. 2. Cf. Rom. iv. 16-21; Heb. xi. 8-12. The people are bidden to recall the supernatural character of the beginning of their national history. The same Lord is with them still. The perfect tenses in verse 3 ('hath comforted', etc.) are expressions of certainty, things still future being spoken of as already accomplished.

(4) li. 5. 'Righteousness . . . salvation.' Cf. the use of the same two words in verses 6 and 8, and other verses in these chapters: see, e.g., xlvi. 13, lvi. 1. The righteousness here spoken of is not so much an attribute of God's character as the 'justifying righteousness' which He manifested in coming to Israel's deliverance, and which is therefore equivalent to His salvation. The terms acquire a deeper meaning in the light of the gospel. Cf. Rom. i. 16, iii. 21, 22, x. 10.

Day 3. Is. li. 17–lii. 12.

Today's portion consists of further messages of encouragement, the first two of which are addressed to Zion, pictured as a queen mother prostrate on the ground, drunk with the wine of God's wrath. She is told that the cup is now to pass to her oppressors, and is bidden to arise and be strong (li. 17–lii. 6). The third oracle (lii. 7-12) pictures the joy when news that the exiles are returning reaches Zion, and then, addressing the exiles, bids them hasten to set out upon the journey.

(1) What message have verses li. 17–lii. 6 for a backslider who is in bondage under the power of the world, and feels himself the object of God's chastisement? (a) Are salvation and holiness still possible for him? Consider in this connection the seeming hopelessness of Zion's condition (li. 18-20, 23; cf. La. ii 13). (b) If such a backslider is to be saved, what must he himself do? See lii. 1, 2. Consider in this connection God's strong words of promise and reassurance in lii. 3-6.

(2) Let your imagination picture the joy of Zion described in lii. 7-12. What application does the apostle Paul make of this passage in Rom. x. 14, 15 and 2 Cor. vi. 17?

Notes.—(1) The prophecy here concerning Zion is the reverse of what is said of Babylon in xlvii. 'The cup of staggering' means the cup that causes staggering.

(2) li. 23. An allusion to the practice of making captives lie face downward on the ground, and using their backs as a road.

(3) lii. 8. 'Eye to eye'; i.e. face to face. They shall see the Lord face to face when He returns to Zion.

Day 4. Is. lii. 13–liii.

This is the fourth of the 'Servant' passages, which portray with such marvellous accuracy the mission, character, and redemptive work of the Lord Jesus Christ. (See *Introduction* and *Analysis*.) Today's portion falls into three parts: (1) an introductory summary, announcing the Servant's exaltation after extreme suffering, and the effect of this upon surrounding nations and kings (lii. 13-15); (2) the story of His life and suffering unto death, told by His now penitent fellow-countrymen (liii. 1-9); and (3) the glorious issue, both for Himself and others, of His sufferings and redemptive work (liii. 10-12).

(1) Let our eyes rest upon the Lord Jesus as He is depicted in lii. 13-15. Note the outstanding characteristic of His service, the depth of His suffering, the height to which He is exalted, and the effect of this upon the nations. Cf. xlix. 7; Ps. lxxii. 11; Jn. xix. 1-5; Eph. i. 20, 21.

(2) Work out in detail the many close parallels between liii. 1-9 and the actual life of the Lord Jesus, as, for example, (a) the form of His manifestation to the world; (b) the reception accorded Him; (c) His sufferings and the meaning of them; (d) His beha-

viour when arrested; (e) the manner of His death and of His burial.

(3) Who are the 'seed' spoken of in liii. 10, and what benefits are shown in this whole passage to have been procured for them by the Servant's substitutionary death? Cf. Heb. ii. 10.

Notes.—(1) lii.15. 'Sprinkle.' A word used in connection with purification (Lv. xiv. 7; Nu. xix. 18) and with expiation (Lv. xvi. 14). This idea, however, comes in a little strangely here, and the R.V. mg. 'startle' agrees better with the word 'astonish' in verse 14.

(2) liii. 1. 'Our report'; better, 'that which we heard', as in R.V. mg. The nations had not heard (lii. 15); but Israel, hearing, had not believed.

(3) liii. 5. 'Bruised'; i.e. crushed; so also in verse 10.

(4) liii. 8. 'Considered'; or possibly 'complained', in the sense of making an appeal against the sentence. All were indifferent. Cf. Mt. xxvii. 39-44.

(5) liii. 9. The introduction of the word 'rich' here is very remarkable in view of Mt. xxvii. 57-60.

(6) liii. 11. 'By his knowledge' may mean 'by means of His knowledge' or 'by the knowledge of Him' (on the part of others). Cf. Jn. xvii. 3.

Day 5. Is. liv.

A glowing picture of the blessedness of Zion and her children in the full love of Jehovah. In verses 1-10 the figure is that of a wife, in verses 11-17 that of a city.

(1) Carey applied verses 2 and 3 to the missionary enterprise, and summoned the Church to reach out to the unevangelized nations. What does this chapter mean for you? In what direction does it summon you to 'lengthen your cords and strengthen your stakes'? Have you grasped how great your God is, how far-reaching His purposes of blessing?

(2) The word 'for' occurs as a conjunction seven times in verses 4-10. Tabulate the reasons given why God's reconciled people should not fear.

(3) 'This is the heritage', says the prophet, 'of the servants o the Lord' (verse 17). He is referring to what is said above in verses 11-16. What are the contents, and what is the security of their inheritance?

Notes.—(1) Verses 1-3. Zion, desolate and solitary, shall find herself full of people. Cf. xlix. 18-21. But she must believe, and sing, and work.

(2) Verse 4. 'Be ashamed', 'be confounded', 'be put to shame'. Three separate verbs are used in the Hebrew, which may be translated 'shamed', 'abashed', 'humiliated'.

(3) Verse 16. They need not fear the smith who fashions a weapon of war, nor the destroying power that will use it, for both are God's creatures and under His control.

Day 6. Is. lv.

An urgent appeal to those who are seeking satisfaction in the world, and to those who walk in wickedness and unrighteousness. God's offered blessings are free; they give life, and satisfy the heart, and endure for ever. Seize then the present opportunity, for the Lord's thoughts of salvation are high beyond man's conceiving, and His purposes will surely be accomplished.

(1) Is the appeal in this chapter any less applicable or less urgent in our day than it was to the Jews living in Babylon? Are you then sounding it forth to those around you? Try to state its argument in present-day language.

(2) Verses 8, 9. Is this our conception of God, that He is far better than we imagine? Consider, for example, how much higher the Lord's thoughts for Simon Peter's life were than Peter had any conception of when he first came to Him. Cf. Mt. xvi. 17, 18; Lk. v. 10b; Jn. i. 42; 1 Pet. v. 1. Is it not so also in your case? Cf. 1 Cor. ii. 9, 10.

(3) Verses 10-13. Hudson Taylor said, 'There is a living God, He has spoken in the Bible, He means what He says, and will do all that He has promised'. Is that not the teaching of these verses? Do you believe?

Notes.—(1) Verse 1. Cf. Jn. vii. 37; Rev. xxii. 17b.

(2) Verse 3. 'Incline your ear . . . come . . . hear'—how simple the way! Cf. Jn. v. 24; vi. 37.

(3) Verses 3-5. 'The sure mercies of David'; i.e. the mercies surely promised to David. Cf. Ps. lxxxix. 28. The meaning seems to be that as David was a leader of many nations, and a witness to them of Jehovah (cf. Ps. xviii. 43), so Israel shall be a leader and witness to the world. Cf. xliii. 12; also Acts xiii. 34.

Day 7. Is. lvi and lvii.

The good tidings of Jehovah's purpose to bring back the exiles and to restore Jerusalem produced many repercussions among different classes of hearers. In the opening verses of today's portion the prophet replies to the questionings of two special groups: (1) non-Jews, who had joined themselves to Israel (lvi. 3a, 6-8), and (2) eunuchs, who feared God (lvi. 3b-5). Might they also participate in the promised deliverance? The Lord's answer is that if they fulfilled the conditions of the covenant, they would be welcome to a full share in its blessings. In lvi. 9–lvii. 14 the prophet rebukes two other groups: the leaders of the community in Jerusalem (lvi. 9-12), and those who were openly practising idolatry (lvii. 1-14). There follows a striking description of the kind of persons with whom God will dwell, and of His purposes of grace towards His people (lvii. 15-21).

(1) In what ways does lvi. 1-8, with all its width of outlook, still fall short of the offer of the gospel? The mystery of which Paul speaks in Eph. iii. 5, 6 was not yet revealed, though we who live

in the light of Christ can see its glory shining through the prophet's words. With verse 7 cf. Mt. xxi. 13, and with verse 8 Jn. x. 16.

(2) Consider the sad picture in lvi. 9–lvii. 14 of a community whose leaders were unworthy, and whose members were forsaking the Lord for idols. What warnings for ourselves may be found in it?

(3) What do these two chapters and more particularly lvii. 15-21 teach us about God?

Notes.—(1) lvi. 3b-5. In the new community physical and racial disabilities would no longer be a ground of exclusion. Cf. Dt. xxiii. 1, 3-8.

(2) lvi. 9. 'All ye beasts of the field'; i.e. surrounding nations.

(3) lvi. 10. 'Watchmen'; i.e. the leaders of the community, also called 'shepherds' (verse 11). They loved ease, gain, and drunken carnivals.

(4) lvii. 3. A reference to their idolatrous practices; so also in verses 7, 8.

(5) lvii. 6. 'The smooth stones in the valley.' The meaning is uncertain.

(6) lvii. 9. 'The king', or rather 'Molech'. Cf. xxx. 33, note.

(7) lvii. 10. 'Thy way'; i.e. the journey to the idol of their choice.

(8) lvii. 11. 'You went on fearlessly, in faithlessness, giving no thought to me, in your indifference. Is it not so? I said no word, I hid my face from you, and on you went, fearing me not.' (Moffatt.)

(9) lvii. 12. 'Declare thy righteousness'; spoken ironically and meaning 'thy lack of righteousness'.

(10) lvii. 18, 19. Connect the last words of verse 18 with verse 19, and read 'To his mourners I create the fruit of the lips' (that is, praise). Cf. lxi. 3; Ho. xiv. 2, R.V. mg. 'Far off' and 'near', i.e. those in exile, and those in or near Jerusalem.

Week 48. ISAIAH LVIII–LXVI

Day 1. Is. lviii.

Two prophecies, one about fasting, the other about observing the Sabbath. This chapter, as also lix, seems to be addressed to the Jews living in Jerusalem. That they practised fasting during the period of the exile is confirmed in Zc. vii. 3-5.

(1) Has fasting in itself any value in God's sight? What does He look for in His people? and why is such conduct called 'fasting'?

(2) What promises does God make in verses 8-12? Each one of them suggests a blessed experience. What, therefore, must be the joy and heavenly beauty of a life in which all of them are finding fulfilment? Is such a life possible to us, and if so, what are the conditions?

(3) Under Babylonian rule the attitude of the Jews towards the Sabbath was a severe test of their loyalty to Jehovah. The same is true in many mission fields today in regard to the observance of Sunday. But in regard to Sabbath keeping, as with fasting, it

is not the mere observance of it that is pleasing to God, but the attitude of the heart. How is this brought out in verses 13 and 14?

Notes.—(1) Verse 3. 'Exact all your labours'; better, 'oppress all your labourers' as in R.V. mg.

(2) Verse 4. 'Ye fast for strife and debate and to smite, etc.' Fasting, if not done in the right spirit, is apt to make men irritable and contentious, quick to use their fist.

(3) Verse 5. Other outward signs of fasting are mentioned by our Lord in Mt. vi. 16.

(4) Verse 9. 'The putting forth of the finger'; probably a gesture of haughty contempt.

(5) Verse 13. 'If thou turn away thy foot from the Sabbath.' That is, regard it as holy ground, not to be profaned by common business. Cf. lvi. 2; Ne. xiii. 15-21.

Day 2. Is. lix.

This chapter in its opening verses is an exposure of the sins that separate from God (verses 1-8). It is thus closely linked with the preceding chapter (cf. lviii. 1), but deals not only with one or two particular matters, as does lviii, but with the whole sinful condition into which the people had fallen. In verses 9-15a the people describe their sorrowful state, and make confession. But they feel that if action on God's part is to be for ever restrained by their sinfulness the position seems hopeless indeed (see notes on 'judgment' below). Then in the closing verses of the chapter comes the triumphant divine answer (verses 15b-21). God is not baffled, and when there is no human help He Himself comes to the rescue, in judgment upon evil-doers on the one hand, and in redemption for the penitent on the other. His covenant with the latter is described in verse 21.

(1) If salvation tarry, and God seems to do nothing, our natural tendency is to assume that He is unable, or unwilling, to help. But what, according to the opening verses of this chapter, is the true reason for His silence? Cf. i. 15-17; Mi. iii. 4.

(2) Verses 3-15. How many kinds of sinning can you find in these verses, and how are the consequences in the personal and social life of the people described?

(3) What is the motive of God's intervention, as described in verses 15b-21? What is its twofold purpose, and what its world-wide issue? When does St. Paul look for this to be fulfilled to Israel (Rom. xi. 25, 26)? Yet, for us who believe on Jesus Christ, is it not in part fulfilled to us now, and not least verse 21? Cf. Jn. xiv. 16, 26.

Notes.—(1) Verse 3. 'Blood'; cf. verse 7; 2 Ki. xxiv. 4; Ps. cvi. 37, 38; Pr. i. 11.

(2) Verse 4. No regard for righteousness and truth in the processes of law.

(3) Verses 5, 6. The plan and plots of evil-doers working fresh evil, and giving no useful result.

(4) Verse 8. Cf. Pr. iv. 12-15; Is. lvii. 20, 21.

(5) Verse 9. The word 'judgment' is used in these verses in two senses (a) as right done by man (verse 8, R.V. mg., 15b), and (b) divine judgment, exercised on behalf of Israel against her oppressors (verses 9, 11, 14). The people's lament was that the latter was withheld, because the former was lacking.

(6) Verse 16. 'No intercessor.' Better, 'none to interpose', as in R.V. mg.

Day 3. Is. lx.

An inspired vision of Zion, when God shall have fulfilled towards her all His purpose, and clothed her with His glory. Like other prophecies in these chapters, it was in part fulfilled in the historical return of the Jews under Cyrus, and in the rebuilding of Jerusalem under Nehemiah, but its final fulfilment is not yet. Meanwhile it is full of instruction for the people of Christ, who are the children of the spiritual Zion, which is above (Gal. iv. 26).

(1) Try to picture it in imagination—the world in darkness, a light breaking on Zion, the nations and their kings attracted (verses 1-3); Zion's son's returning, and wealth pouring in from east and west (verses 4-9); open gates, and constant traffic, and the Temple beautified (verses 10-16); the city wealthy, peaceful, righteous, strong, illumined by God as her light (verses 17-22).

(2) Gather out the references to God in this chapter, and observe carefully the place which He occupies in the Zion here described. Has He this central place in your life, in your Christian fellowship? As Zion would have been no different from other cities, so neither can any life shine with true splendour, save through God's indwelling and reign. Cf. 1 Cor. xv. 10.

(3) Consider how many of the features of beauty and glory in the Zion of this chapter are to be found, in their spiritual counterpart, in a life dwelling in the fulness of the Holy Spirit. See especially verses 2, 5, 7 (last clause), 13 (last clause), 16b, and 17-21, and compare 2 Cor. iii. 18, iv. 6, vi. 16, Eph. iii. 14-21.

Notes.—(1) Verses 6, 7. 'Ephah', a Midianite tribe; 'Kedar' and 'Nebaioth', tribes of N. Arabia.

(2) Verses 8, 9. The ships coming rom the west, with their white sails, looking like a flock of doves.

(3) Verse 13. 'The place of my sanctuary'; i.e. the Temple, called also 'the place of my feet'.

(4) Verse 17. 'I will appoint Peace as your governor, and Justice as your ruler' (Moffatt).

(5) Verse 21. 'That I may be glorified'. Compare 'He hath glorified thee' (verse 9) and 'I will glorify the house of my glory' (verse 7, so also verse 13). Where God is glorified, all else is glorified in Him. Cf. 2 Thes. i. 12.

Day 4. Is. lxi–lxiii. 6.

Chapter lxi and lxii contain further prophecies of the restoration and future glory of Zion, after the manner of chapter lx, but showing also the necessity of faith and prayer on the part of the people, and readiness to take action. The closing verses of today's portion (lxiii. 1-6) present a striking picture of God's judgment upon the nations.

(1) How would you summarize the teaching of chapters lxi and lxii regarding the Lord's purpose of good for Zion? In Lk. iv. 17-21 our Lord says that the opening words of lxi were spiritually fulfilled in His own ministry. We may therefore interpret the promises of these chapters as applicable in a spiritual sense to ourselves. What may we learn, for example, about the condition of the unsaved soul (lxi. 1), the offer made to him (lxi. 3, 4), the relation to God into which he is brought (lxi. 6, 8, 9, lxii. 4, 12), and, in general, the thought and purpose of God for His redeemed people?

(2) In lxi. 10, 11 the voice of the people is heard, responding with the glad anticipation of faith to God's call, and accepting with joy the promised salvation. Is this your attitude also towards the salvation given us in Christ?

(3) In lxi the coming salvation is proclaimed, in lxii it is prayed for (verses 1, 6, 7). If the gospel is to prevail on earth, are not both the proclamation of it and prayer concerning it still necessary? See Rom. x. 14, 15; 2 Thes. iii. 1. What characteristic of prevailing prayer is here emphasized?

Notes.—(1) lxi. 6. 'The priests of the Lord'; i.e. having access to Him. Cf. Ex. xix. 6; Rev. i. 6, R.V.

(2) lxi. 7. Cf. Jb. xlii. 10.

(3) lxi. 8. 'I hate robbery with iniquity'; a reference to the treatment Israel received from her oppressors.

(4) lxii. 2. 'A new name.' 'The symbol both of a new character, and a new relation to God' (*Camb. Bible*). Cf. Rev. ii. 17, iii. 12.

(5) lxii. 8. The intercessors (verses 6, 7) may rest upon the word and oath of Jehovah; cf. 2 Sa. vii. 25; Heb. vi. 18.

(6) lxiii. 4. The day of redemption is also a day of judgment. These verses describe 'the day of vengeance of our God' (lxi. 2).

Day 5. Is. lxiii. 7–lxiv.

In lxii. 6, 7 the need of intercessors is mentioned. Today's portion is a prayer such as these intercessors might have used. The order of thought is as follows: (1) Contemplation of God's lovingkindness in the early days of the nation's history (lxiii. 7-9); (2) the nation's rebellious spirit and God's chastisements, and the nation's wistful longings after the days that were past (lxiii. 10-14); (3) earnest prayer, based on Jehovah's relation to Israel, and the shame of the nation's present plight (lxiii. 15-19); (4) intensified prayer for God's intervention (lxiv. 1-5a); (5) confession of sin and the consciousness that the nation can plead no merit or righteousness before God (lxiv. 5b-7); (6) return to the pleas of lxiii. 15-19 (lxiv. 8-12).

The prayer contains three elements:

(1) Thanksgiving. Though the circumstances were desperate, the need so urgent, yet the suppliant begins his prayer with the contemplation of God's mercies. Is there not a lesson here? Do we rush into petition when we pray, or do we first recall God's past mercies? Cf. Paul's practice, Eph. i. 16; Phil. i. 3, iv. 6; Col. i. 3.

(2) Petition. What five pleas are found in lxiii. 15-19? Do you use arguments with God in prayer why He should grant your petition? In lxiv. 4, 5 the suppliant begins to advance another plea. What is it, and why is he unable to continue it, but breaking down in confession, returns to the pleas already used?

(3) Confession. See lxiii. 10 and lxiv. 5-7. Regarding the place and importance of confession in prayer see Lk. xv. 21, xviii. 13, 14; 1 Jn. i. 9.

Notes.—(1) lxiii. 10. 'His holy spirit.' The references to the spirit in this prayer are strikingly clear and full.

(2) lxiii. 11. 'Then he remembered'; i.e. Israel remembered. Cf. R.V. mg.

(3) lxiii. 13. 'As a horse in the wilderness'; better, 'pasture-land'. Cf. Ps cvi, 9, R.V. mg. The meaning is that they had no difficulty in keeping their footing.

(4) lxiii. 16. The argument is the same as in xlix. 15.

(5) lxiii. 17a. The prolonging of the suffering was tending to more ungodliness.

(6) lxiii. 18. 'But a little while'; a difficult phrase. Some amend verse 18a to read 'Why should ungodly men scoff at thy sanctuary?' (Moffatt).

(7) lxiv. 6. As the faded leaf is swept away by the wind, so their iniquities carry them to ruin.

Day 6. Is. lxv.

This and the following chapter give the answer to the prayer of lxiii. 7–lxiv. It falls, so far as this chapter is concerned, into three parts. First, God says that He has always been willing to hear their cry (verses 1, 2, see *Note* below), but they have not called upon Him. Their hearts have been rebellious, and their lives a provocation (verses 3-7). Second, the whole nation is not like that, for within it are God's chosen. Therefore He will sift the elect from among the wicked (verses 8-12). Third, when the sifting is over, the true Israel will enjoy the fulness of God's blessing in a renovated universe (verses 13-25).

(1) What picture of God is unfolded in verses 1, 2? Cf. Mt. vii. 11, xxiii. 37. It is a supplementary picture to that in lix. 1, 2.

(2) Contrast the life and end of those that forsake God, as described in verses 8-16, with the lot of God's chosen. Are you proving in experience the blessedness of the latter?

(3) What seven outstanding features characterize the life of the

people in Jerusalem in the new age that is to dawn? See verses 17-25.

Notes.—(1) Verse 1. 'I am enquired of'; better, 'I was to be enquired of'; m.e'I was willing to be enquired of'. 'Ready was I to answer men who never ·iasmd e, ready to be found by men who never sought me. I cried out, Here I, aketo folk who never called to me' (Moffatt). Cf. lxiv. 7a.

(2) Verses 3-7. A condemnation of various idolatrous practices.

(3) Verse 8. 'When a bunch of grapes holds some good wine, men say, Destroy it not, it holds a blessing' (Moffatt). So God will save the good in Israel.

(4) Verse 11. 'Fortune' and 'Destiny'. The Hebrew words are Gad and Meni, the names of two gods; see R.V. mg.

(5) Verse 15. The names of the ungodly shall be used only as an imprecation. God will give His elect a new name. Cf. lxii. 2.

(6) Verse 16. 'The God of truth'; i.e. the God of Amen (R.V. mg.). 'The faithful God, who has kept His word, and fulfilled it.'

(7) Verse 20. 'He who dies youngest lives 100 years; anyone dying under 100 years must be accursed by God' (Moffatt).

Day 7. Is. lxvi.

The distinction between those who are disobedient to, and those who fear, Jehovah is maintained, and the final destiny of the two classes is made clear. In the new age, God will be glorified and the true Israel exalted. 'All flesh' will worship Jehovah, and transgressors will be forever destroyed. The chapter may be analysed as follows: (1) Temple worship is not all that God desires. Those in whom He takes pleasure are contrasted with those whom He will punish (verses 1-4); (2) a message of comfort to the faithful (verses 5, 6); (3) Zion's children multiplied (verses 7-9); (4) the future glory of Jerusalem (verses 10-14); (5) God's enemies overwhelmed (verses 15-18a); (6) God's glory declared among the Gentiles, who will restore exiled Jews (verses 18-20); (7) final picture of the new age (verses 21-24).

(1) When God looks down upon men's worship, what is it that He values? Is it the building? Is it the outward form of worship or what is it? See verses 1-4, and compare note below.

(2) What is the end of those who, having heard God's voice, will not give heed? See especially verses 4, 5, 6, 17, 24. What, on the other hand, is promised to Zion and her children? See verses 7-14, 20-22. While these promises are made primarily to Jerusalem and are yet to be fulfilled, they also declare the spiritual good things, which God has provided for us in His Son, and which we may claim for ourselves in Him. Cf. Rom. viii. 16, 17, 32; 1 Cor. iii. 22; 2 Cor. i. 20.

(3) How does the prophet's vision of God's purpose for the nations fall short of the glory of the full revelation of this 'mystery' in the New Testament?

Notes.—(1) Verse 2. 'Contrite'; literally 'broken'. The Hebrew word is different from that used in lvii. 15, which means 'crushed', but the thought is much the same, that there is no inward rebellion against God. 'Trembleth at His Word'; i.e. in awe and reverence.

(2) Verse 3. The meaning probably is that the people referred to combined the worship of Jehovah with gross idolatry. 'Oxen some sacrifice and also human lives; they offer lambs and also dogs in worship. Oblations due and swine's blood in their rites; incense, and yet they reverence an idol' (Moffatt).

(3) Verse 4. Cf. Pr. i. 24-31.

(4) Verse 19. 'I will set a sign among them'; i.e. 'do something that shall be a sign of My power'. Cf. Is. vii. 11. 'Tarshish', etc., are names of distant lands. See Ezk. xxvii. 10, 13. 'Pul' should probably be 'Phut' as in Ezekiel.

(5) Verse 21. 'Of them also'; i.e. of the restored Jewish exiles.

THE EPISTLES OF JOHN

INTRODUCTION

(See New Bible Handbook, pp. 403-5)

1 John

THIS Epistle has no name attached to it by the author himself. But it was certainly written by one who personally knew the Lord Jesus while He was on earth (i. 1-4; iv. 14), and internal evidence amply supports the witness of the early Christians that the apostle John was its author.

The Epistle was written to guard the churches from threatening danger. Men had arisen who were teaching and practising error. While using Christian language and professing to know God in a special way, they neither held the truth with regard to Christ's Person, nor did they manifest in their lives a character corresponding to their lofty profession. John in this Epistle sets forth three marks of a real knowledge of and fellowship with God, lacking which all claims to possess these high privileges were false. These marks are, first, righteousness of life, second, brotherly love, and third, faith in Jesus as God incarnate. The teaching of the Epistle has an abiding value, because it deals with facts and principles that do not change with the passing years, but remain true for every generation of Christians.

2 and 3 John

If 1 John was written by John the apostle, so also were these two short letters, which resemble it so closely in general outlook and even in phraseology. They cast an interesting light upon conditions prevailing in the Christian Church at the end of the first century. Prophets, teachers and evangelists exercised an itinerant ministry among the churches and received hospitality in the homes of believers. But when teachers of error began to appear and sought hospitality with the rest, the question arose, should such be received or not? If not, by what test might the true be distinguished from the false? It is with different aspects of this question that these two letters mainly deal. Nothing is known with certainty as to who 'the elect lady and her children' in 2 John are, whether a Christian family or, as some think, a Christian church: nor is anything known of the three persons mentioned by name in 3 John, beyond what is said of them in the Epistle itself.

ANALYSIS OF I JOHN

i. 1–4. Introduction. The apostolic witness—its authority, content and aim.

i. 5–ii. 27. *God is Light,* and the test of true fellowship with Him is threefold.

> i. 5–ii. 6. Confession of and cleansing from sin, and obedience to Christ.
>
> ii. 7-11. Brotherly love.
>
> ii. 18-27. Confession that Jesus Christ is come in the flesh.
>
> *Note.*—ii. 12-17 is a digression, an outflow of the apostle's affection.

ii. 28–iv. 6. *God is Love,* and the test of true sonship to Him is, as before, the threefold evidence of:

> ii. 28–iii. 10. Practical righteousness.
>
> iii. 11-18. Brotherly love.
>
> iv. 1-6. Confession that Jesus Christ is come in the flesh.
>
> *Note.*—iii. 19-24 is a digression on the subject of assurance.

iv. 7–v. 12. *God is Love,* and the test of our dwelling in Him, and His dwelling in us is, as before:

> iv. 7-21. Mutual love.
>
> v. 1-3. The keeping of God's commandments.
>
> v. 4-12. Belief that Jesus is the Son of God.

v. 13-21. Conclusion. Five Christian certainties.

ANALYSIS OF 2 JOHN

1-3.   Opening salutation.
4.   The joy of finding Christians who are true.
5-11.   Counsel and warning.
12, 13.   Ending.

ANALYSIS OF 3 JOHN

1, 2.   Opening salutation.
3, 4.   The joy of hearing good news of Gaius.
5-8.   Gaius praised for his hospitality.
9, 10.   Diotrephes condemned.
11, 12.   Demetrius approved.
13, 14.   Ending.

Week 49. THE EPISTLES OF JOHN

Day 1. 1 Jn. i–ii. 2.

(1) To what unique experience in his life is the writer referring in verses 1-4? How does he describe it? To what inestimable privilege did it lead him, and why does he want to make it known? Cf. Jn. i. 14; 1 Thes. iii. 8, 9.

(2) 'God is Light.' Consider how high above the ideas of heathenism this conception rises. Cf. Rom. i. 23; 1 Cor. x. 7, 20. Do we ourselves sometimes fall short of it and think of God as less than perfectly good? See Note (2) below.

(3) The nature of God determines the conditions of fellowship with Him. How has He made fellowship with Himself possible for sinful man and what is His provision to enable fellowship to be maintained and to meet failure if it should occur? If men deny in one way or another their need of this provision, what may we conclude concerning them? See verses 6, 8, 10.

Notes.—(1) i. 4. 'Your joy'; more probably 'our joy', see R.V.

(2) i. 5. 'Light'; used in Scripture in various meanings, as signifying truth, goodness, joy, safety, life, just as 'darkness', on the contrary, denotes falsehood, evil, sorrow, peril, death. Here it signifies perfect truth and goodness, without any vestige of evil.

'No darkness at all'; lit.—'Darkness there is not in Him, no, not in any way.' (Westcott.)

Day 2. 1 Jn. ii. 3-27. See *Analysis*.

(1) Verses 3-11. If a man claim to know God, to abide in Christ and to be in the light, what must be his attitude to (a) Christ's word and commandment; (b) the example of Christ's life on earth; and (c) fellow-Christians?

(2) Verses 12-17. It seems best in verses 12, 13 to regard the term 'little children' as including all to whom John is writing (cf. ii. 1, 18, 28, etc.). He then divides them into the two groups of 'fathers' and 'young men'. Ponder what is said to each group in turn and the solemn warning in verses 15-17.

(3) Verses 18-29. Amidst false teaching and defection, what three safeguards for our continuance in the faith does John give? See especially verses 24-27. If a professing Christian falls away from the truth, what is proved thereby, which before the falling away may not have been at all obvious?

Notes.—(1) Verse 7. Cf. Jn. xiii. 34, 35, xv. 12.

(2) Verse 8. John calls the old commandment new in the sense that with the passing of the years the light has grown clearer and he sees familiar truths shining in a new light.

(3) Verse 15. 'The world.' This denotes here human society as governed by selfishness, covetousness and vainglory. To the world in this sense we must not let our affections become attached. Cf. Jas. iv. 4.

Day 3. 1 Jn. ii. 28–iii. 10.

We enter today upon the second section of the Epistle (see *Analysis*). John has been speaking up to this point of the Christian life as a life of *fellowship with God, who is Light*. Now he speaks of it as a life of *sonship to God, who is Love,* and shows that the evidences that we are really living it are, as before, righteousness, love and belief.

(1) ii. 28–iii. 3. The apostle, having begun in verse 29 to show that the test of sonship is righteousness of life, is carried away by the marvel of the new birth into a rapturous outburst of wonder and joy. Whence comes our sonship? How does the world regard it? What will be its future glory? How should this affect us now? Cf. Col. iii. 4, 5.

(2) iii. 4-9. These verses resume and expand the truth of ii. 29. What five reasons are given to show that sinning is utterly incompatible with being a child of God?

Notes.—(1) ii. 28. This verse gives clear proof that John, no less than Paul and Peter, believed in the Lord's second coming. See also iii. 2, iv. 17.

(2, ii. 29. 'Born of Him'; the first reference to sonship in the Epistle.

(3) iii. 1 and 4. Read as in R.V.

(4) iii. 9. 'Seed'; rendered 'nature' in R.S.V.

'He cannot sin'; cf. Mt. vii. 18. The apostle is contending against men who taught that sonship to God could be combined with sinning. John calls all such 'children of the devil'.

Day 4. 1 Jn. iii. 11–iv. 6.

(1) iii. 11-18. By what various arguments does John show in verses 11-15, that mutual love is the essential mark of the children of God and that hatred is inadmissible? After what *manner* should we love? See verses 16-18 and cf. Jn. xv. 12; Eph. v. 1, 2.

(2) iii. 19-24. A digression on the subject of assurance before God. The apostle first considers the case of a Christian whose heart condemns him. What will the consciousness of having shown love to others do for such an one? See verses 19, 20 R.V. and cf. iv. 17; Heb. vi. 9, 10. Next the apostle considers the case of a Christian whose heart does not condemn him because he is practising all the characteristics of a truly Christian life—obedience, love and faith. What blessings does this man enjoy? See verses 21-24.

(3) What two tests are here given by which to know whether a prophet is or is not speaking by the Spirit of God? See especially iv. 2 and 6, and Note 3 below.

Notes.—(1) The R.V. is clearer throughout this passage, especially in iii. 16, 19, 20, iv. 3, 5.

(2) iii. 14. Cf. Jn. v. 24. This gives the practical test whether a professed aith in Christ is genuine. Cf. Gal. v. 6b; Jas. ii. 15-17.

(3) iv. 6. 'We are of God.' The pronoun 'we' in the first half of this verse refers primarily, as in i. 1-3, to John as representing the apostles, while not excluding those who, following after them, base their teaching upon the apostolic foundation.

Day 5. 1 Jn. iv. 7–v. 3.

We are now beginning the third section of the Epistle, in which the apostle speaks of the Christian life as a life in which God, who is Love, dwells in us and we in Him (see *Analysis*). The same three evidences of righteousness, love and faith are again emphasized, but especially love and faith. Righteousness, under the aspect of obedience (as in ii. 3-5), is touched upon in v. 2, 3.

(1) iv. 7-10. What arguments are used in verses 7 and 8 to show that true Christians must love one another? In verses 9 and 10 the apostle speaks of the manifestation of God's love in Christ. How does he describe the gift? What does he say of its purpose? By what means was this purpose achieved? and for whom did God do this?

(2) iv. 11-18. The apostle goes over the same ground as before, but at a higher level. How does he here describe the Christian's relation to God and how does he show that no higher or closer relationship can be conceived? Out of the depths of that relationship, the believer bears his testimony through the Spirit (verses 13-16; cf. Jn. xv. 26, 27).

(3) iv. 19-v. 3. In view of Mt. xxii. 36, 37 why does not the apostle say in verse 11, 'Beloved, if God so loved us, we ought also to love God'? Why does John say, 'We ought also to love *one another*'? What other test of our love for God is also mentioned?

Notes.—(1) iv. 17, 18. 'Because as He is, etc.'; cf. Jn. iii. 35a with xvi. 27. Those who are loved of the Father need not look forward with dread. If we are still afraid, the remedy is to dwell more in love. Cf. Rom. viii. 15.

(2) iv. 19. 'We love Him'; read 'We love', as in R.V.

(3) v. 1. Faith in Jesus as the Christ implies *receiving* Him as such, and to receive Him is to be born of God (Jn. i. 12, 13).

Day 6. 1 Jn. v. 4-21.

As chapter iv deals mainly with love, so this chapter (especially verses 4-13), deals mainly with faith.

(1) The apostle has already given a warning against the subtle attraction of the world (see ii. 15-17). Now he reveals how the world may be conquered. Who does he say will overcome the world and by what means? See verses 4-6 (R.V.) and Note (1) below.

(2) A faith that can effect such great results must be well attested. What fivefold witness is given in verses 7-10 (R.V.), and what marvellous fact does the witness attest?

(3) Verses 13-20. There are here five great certainties concerning which John says, 'We know'. Are you building your life upon this foundation?

Notes.—(1) Verse 6. This verse probably refers to our Lord's baptism and death, not to Jn. xix. 34. He came not only to call us to repentance by the witness of His baptism, but also to wash away our sins with His blood. The two sacraments of the Christian Church are the standing memorials of these things.

(2) Verse 7 should be omitted and also the words 'in earth' in verse 8. See R.V.

(3) Verses 9, 10. God has spoken to man in Jesus with the utmost clarity and finality. He that believes has an inward witness: he that believes not makes God a liar.

(4) Verse 16. 'A sin unto death'; i.e. the open final choice of darkness in preference to light.

(5) Verse 18. Read as in R.V. 'He that was begotten of God' means the Lord Jesus.

(6) Verse 19. 'Lieth in wickedness'; better 'in the evil one', as in R.V.

(7) Verse 21. Idols; anyone professing to worship God, who denies that Jesus is the Son of God, is worshipping a false God. Be on your guard against all such idols, is John's final word.

Day 7. 2 and 3 Jn.

(1) Compare the tests of a true Christian found in 2 John, with those given in 1 John.

(2) What dangers arise from listening to false teaching and what is John's answer to the claims of 'advanced thought'? See Note (1) below.

(3) Consider the three men mentioned in 3 John, all professing Christians. What does the apostle praise in Gaius, what faults does he find in Diotrephes, and what threefold witness does he give in praise of Demetrius?

Notes.—(1) 'Truth' . . . 'the Truth'. In 2 and 3 John, the R.V. gives more accurately than does the A.V. the places where the definite article is or is not present. If not present, the word 'truth' has the meaning of sincerity, integrity, reality: where the definite articles is present, the word denotes the truth as revealed in the gospel.

(2) 2 Jn. 2. 'For the truth's sake.' The clause is to be attached to 'whom I love, etc'. 'Truly I love you all . . . for the sake of the truth, etc.' (Weymouth). Those who hold the truth of the gospel cannot but truly love one another.

(3) Verse 4. 'Walking in truth, etc.', i.e. living true Christian lives in obedience to the command which we have received from the Father (Weymouth).

(4) Read verse 8 and especially verse 9 in the R.V. The apostle does not condemn progress towards a fuller understanding of the revelation given us in Christ, but teachings which, in the name of progress, go beyond the revealed Word.

(5) Verse 10. 'Into your house'; better, 'into the house '(R.S.V.).

(6) 3 Jn. 5. 'Beloved, it is a loyal thing you do when you render any service to the brethren, especially to strangers' (R.S.V.). 'Strangers' means Christians not personally known to them; cf. Heb. xiii. 2.

(7) Verse 6. 'After a godly sort', lit. 'worthily of God' (R.V.), i.e. 'as befits God's service' (R.S.V.).

(8) Verse 9. 'Receiveth us not'; i.e. does not acknowledge our authority (R.S.V.).

AMOS AND HOSEA

INTRODUCTION

(See New Bible Handbook, pp. 239-241, 243-246)

THESE two prophets are linked together in that both prophesied to the northern kingdom of Israel about the same time.

Amos was the earlier by a few years. His ministry took place in the latter part of the reign of Jeroboam II. He himself belonged to Judah, and was a herdsman when called of God to prophesy to northern Israel (Am. vii. 14, 15). The kingdom was at that time outwardly prosperous, but all kinds of evil were rife in the land, and the people, thinking themselves secure in Jehovah's favour, resented any reproof (Am. v. 10). They did not realize that they were not worshipping Him in the way that He desired, and that their sins were bringing judgment near. Amos, filled with a vision of the majesty and righteousness of God, denounced the sins of the land, and the false worship that was offered. Let them not imagine that because they were the people of Jehovah, therefore they would escape punishment (Am. iii. 2).

The first three chapters of Hosea also belong to the closing years of the reign of Jeroboam II, but the remaining chapters reflect the chaotic conditions of the period that followed Jeroboam's death. Hosea was a native of the northern kingdom, and had been deeply taught in the school of sorrow. His own sad history was used by the Holy Spirit to fit him in a unique way to see into the heart of God, and to depict the sorrow which His people's ingratitude and unfaithfulness cause to Him. No prophet so clearly shows us the love of God, without in any way weakening the claims of His holiness; and thus he prepares the way for the perfect revelation of God's love and holiness given in our Lord Jesus Christ.

ANALYSES

Amos

i. 1, 2. Introduction.

i. 3–ii. Oracles against surrounding nations, ending with Judah and Israel.

iii–vi. 'A series of addresses, three of which begin *"Hear ye this word"* (iii. 1, iv. 1, v. 1) and end with a threat introduced by *"therefore"* (iii. 11, iv. 12, v. 11, 16); and two begin with *"Woe"* (v. 18,

vi. 1).   In these the crimes and impending
punishment of Israel are set forth at length'.
(Kirkpatrick, *The Doctrine of the Prophets*, p.
105.)

vii. 1-9.   Three visions.
vii. 10-17.   Amos expelled from Bethel.
viii–ix. 10.   Two more visions of coming doom.
ix. 11-15.   The ultimate restoration.

Hosea

i–iii.   Hosea's personal history a type of God's relation
with Israel.
iv–viii.   Israel's guilt and the corruption of the nation.
ix–xi. 11.   Israel's doom is necessary and inevitable.
xi. 12–xiii.   Israel's ingratitude and unfaithfulness deserve
destruction, yet Jehovah yearns over His
people.
xiv.   One day, after the punishment, Israel will repent
and be restored.

Week 50. Amos–Hosea III

Day 1. Am. i and ii.

(1) Trace upon a map the position of the countries upon which
the Lord pronounces judgment, and notice the skill with which
Amos first mentions surrounding nations, and finally swoops down
upon Israel herself.

(2) What are the particular sins that call forth God's judgment,
and what may we learn from this as to the things God hates?
Notice the difference in tone and pleading when He speaks of
Judah and Israel.

(3) What attributes of God are revealed in today's portion?

Notes.—(1) i. 2. 'Habitations'; better 'pastures', as in R.V. The whole verse
summarizes Amos' message of impending judgment.

(2) Verse 3. 'Threshing instruments of iron'; heavy machines for threshing
grain, here used as instruments of torture upon the people of Gilead.

(3) The R.V. should be read in i. 5, 9 and ii. 8, 13.

(4) ii. 1. Desecration of the dead was considered specially wicked.

(5) Verse 7a. 'They trample down the poor like dust' (Moffatt).

(6) Verse 8. See Ex. xxii. 26. The verse means that the judges demanded
unjust fines (R.V.), accepting payment in clothing and wine, and then made
use of these at their sacrificial feasts.

Day 2. Am. iii and iv.

(1) iii. 1-8. In the opening two verses Amos makes a statement that must have been very startling to his hearers. Therefore in verses 3-8 he shows that he is not prophesying without good reason.

When the Lord speaks to you, is it as inevitable that you should speak out as it was to Amos? Notice how this necessity (verses 7, 8) is compared with the necessary sequences of cause and effect in the preceding verses. Cf. 1 Cor. ix. 16.

(2) iii. 9-15. What is the significance of the invitation to the Philistines and Egyptians to come and see the evil done in the city of Samaria? Cf. 2 Ki. xxi. 9. Does this explain why the threatened judgment is so severe?

(3) Does God use similar methods to those described in iv. 6-11 to draw an individual sinner or backslider to Him? Cf. 1 Cor. xi. 30-32; Heb. xii. 6-11. Notice the refrain five times repeated, and the solemn conclusion in verse 12 (cf. Pr. xxix. 1).

Notes.—(1) iii. 2. 'Known'; in the sense of acknowledging and caring for in a special way. Cf. Ps. i. 6; Na. i. 7.

(2) The R.V. is important in iii. 3 (mg.), 5, 6, 12; and in iv. 2, 3, 4.

(3) iv. 1. 'Ye kine of Bashan'; a reference to the noble and wealthy women of Samaria. The cattle of Bashan were noted for their quality.

(4) iv. 2. 'Your posterity'; better, 'your residue' (R.V.), i.e. the very last one of you.

(5) iv. 4, 5. These verses are ironical in tone. Let the people multiply their sacrifices and their worship; in God's sight it is only multiplying transgression.

Day 3. Am. v and vi.

There are three addresses in today's portion; see *Analysis*.

(1) v. 1-17. Contrasting these verses with chapter iv observe the different methods which God uses to draw men to Him—first through natural calamities and then by a passionate plea for right living. What sins are rebuked in these verses, and what is the one way of escape?

(2) v. 18-27. What is necessary to make our worship acceptable to God? How did Israel fail, and is any of our worship in danger of falling under the same judgment?

(3) vi. What was the difference between Amos and the rulers of Israel, that made him see judgment approaching, and made them 'put far away the evil day'? Cf. Lk. xii. 54-57.

Notes.—(1) v. 3. 'That went forth'; i.e. to war. Ninety per cent casualties.

(2) v. 9. Read as in R.V.

(3) Verses 25, 26. See R.V. and cf. Acts vii. 42, 43. These verses are obscure, but seem to mean that the idolatrous tendency in Israel found expression in the days of the wandering in the desert, as it was doing now in Amos' day.

(4) vi. 1, 2. Read as in R.V. The leaders of Israel regarded themselves as at the head of the chief nation of all. Verse 2 is obscure, but the argument is not affected by its omission.

(5) Verse 10. 'Uncle'; better, 'kinsman', as in R.V. mg. The reference to 'burning' indicates a time of emergency; cf. 1 Sa. xxxi. 12.

Day 4. Am. vii–viii. 3.

(1) What four separate visions did Amos see, as recorded in vii. 1-9 and viii. 1-3? Try to picture each, and what it signified.

(2) How did the first two visions differ from the last two in their ending, and how does this show the inward attitude of Amos towards the people and their doom, that lay behind his stern denunciation of sin? Cf. Je. ix. 1, xiv. 11, 12.

(3) How does today's portion reveal the fearless courage of the prophet, and the danger to which his obedience to God's call exposed him? Cf. Acts xx. 24; Phil. i. 20, 21.

Notes.—(1) vii. 1. 'Grasshoppers'; better 'locusts'.

(2) Verse 4. Read as in R.V. 'The great deep' probably means the underground depths that supplied water from below; cf. Gn. vii. 11. Springs and streams were drying up and the land was suffering.

(3) Verse 10. Bethel was the chief sanctuary of the northern kingdom; see 1 Ki. xii. 26-33.

Day 5. Am. viii. 4–ix.

(1) What injustices are exposed in chapter viii and what motive lay behind them? What, therefore, will God do? There are seven distinct kinds of judgment in viii. 7-14.

(2) ix. 1-10. This is the fifth and last vision which Amos saw. How does it show that (a) God is no respecter of persons; (b) mere outward religion does not save; (c) Jehovah is God of the whole earth; and (d) none can escape from His hand? Cf. Ps. cxxxix. 7-12.

(3) The closing verses of the book show that God's ultimate purpose is not judgment but mercy. What use did James make of ix. 11-12 at the Council in Jerusalem (see Acts xv. 15-17)?

Notes.—(1) The R.V. is important in viii. 8, ix. 1, 5, 6, and 12.

(2) viii. 11. 'A famine'; cf. Ps. lxxiv. 9; Mi. iii. 7; Is. viii. 20, 21.

(3) ix. 2. 'Hell'; i.e. Sheol, the place of the dead; see R.V. mg.

Day 6. Ho. i and iii.

Hosea's life story is outlined in these two chapters. Tomorrow we shall study the parallel story of Jehovah's relations with Israel, as described in chapter ii.

(1) i. 2. What evidence do you find (a) that at the time of his marriage Hosea was already conscious of his prophetic calling, and did all things, including his marriage, with his eyes upon the Lord; (b) that he was not aware, when he married Gomer, that she would prove unfaithful; and (c) that on looking back later upon the whole matter, he recognized that God had brought him through this bitter experience in order that he might understand what Israel's unfaithfulness meant to Him? Is there sorrow or difficulty in your life which should be similarly interpreted? Cf. Gn. l. 20.

(2) What other prophet used his children's names to make known God's message?

(3) iii. Gomer, having proved unfaithful, appears to have forsaken Hosea and sunk to the position of a slave. Hosea, loving her still, redeemed her, but placed her for a time under discipline. How does the prophet use this to illustrate God's love and Israel's future (verses 1, 4, 5)?

Notes.—(1) i. 4. See 2 Ki. x. 11, 30. Jehu did right in executing sentence upon the house of Ahab, but the spirit of cruelty and self-seeking in which he did it were displeasing to God.

(2) The passage i. 10–ii. 1 is a prophecy of the future, in which the divine love interrupts the message of doom. It is characteristic of Hosea that prophecies of judgment are followed by messages of loving mercy, even at the cost of seeming contradiction.

(3) iii. 4, 5 is a reference to the exile; cf. La. i. 3, ii. 9.

Day 7. Ho. ii.

(1) The adulterer seeks satisfaction in unlawful relationships; the harlot debases high possessions for material gain. How does Hosea show that this is what Israel has done in relation to Jehovah? See especially verses 5, 8, 13.

(2) Does this apply also to a *Christian* backslider, and is the guilt of such an one less grievous than that of Israel? Cf. Jas. iv. 4, 5, R.V.

(3) What promise is given in verses 14-23 of the final complete triumph of God's love? Cf. Is. xi. 7-9, ii. 4, 5; Rom. viii. 18-21.

Notes.—(1) Verse 5. 'My lovers'; a reference to the local gods of the land (or 'Baalim', verse 13) whom the Israelites in their backsliding conceived to be the givers of nourishment (bread and water'), clothing ('wool and clothing') and joy ('oil and drink'), and to whom accordingly they offered worship (verse 13).

(2) Verses 14, 15. The Israelites, after leaving Egypt, wandered in the wilderness, and entered the promised land by the valley of Achor. Now they shall again be brought into the wilderness (i.e. the exile), but after this time of affliction, they shall return to Canaan, and will find the valley of Achor, not, as at the first, a place of trouble (Jos. vii. 24), but a door of hope. Cf. Is. lxv. 10.

(3) Verses 18-23. A beautiful picture of peace (verse 18), communion with the Lord (verses 19, 20), and abounding blessing (verses 21-23). Jezreel, which means 'God sows', is used in verse 22 as a name for Israel.

Week 51. Hosea iv–Joel

Day 1. Ho. iv–v. 14.

(1) Note down in chapter iv. 1-14 (a) the outward sins which caused the Lord to have a controversy with His people, and (b) the inward heart condition of which these sins were the outcome. To what extent might the description be applied to our land today?

(2) iv. 15-19. This passage may be interpreted as a warning to the southern kingdom of Judah not to ally herself with Israel (here called Ephraim; see Note 5 below). Why this warning, and what message has it for us? Cf. Mt. xv. 14; 2 Cor. vi. 14-16.

(3) What in chapter v are shown to be the real obstacles that separate the people from God, and God from the people? Observe in these chapters the responsibility of the priests and rulers (iv. 4-9, 18, v. 1, 10), and by what vivid images Hosea describes God's judgment upon the nation (v. 8-14).

Notes.—(1) iv. 4. 'But none protests, no man complains, for my people are no better than their priestlings' (Moffatt).

(2) Verse 14. 'They themselves'; i.e. the men, the fathers of families, and heads of households. In these verses the spiritual and literal meanings of 'whoredom' intertwine; the Canaanite worship was full of immorality at the shrines.

(3) Verse 15. 'Beth-aven'; 'house of vanity', used ironically for 'Bethel', house of God.

(4) Verse 16. The second half of the verse is best taken as a question: 'How now can the Lord feed them like a lamb in a broad meadow?'

(5) Verse 17. 'Ephraim'; the leading tribe of the northern kingdom, and therefore frequently used by Hosea as a name for the people of that kingdom. Only in chapter xiii does it refer to the tribe.

(6) v. 7. 'The new moon'; i.e. the *next* new moon: within a month ruin may be upon them. See r.v. mg.

(7) Verse 10. 'Like them that remove the landmark'—common thieves.

(8) Verse 13. 'King Jareb'; i.e. 'king Combative, king Pick Quarrel, a nickname for the Assyrian monarch' (G. A. Smith). See r.v. mg.

Day 2. Ho. v. 15–viii.

(1) The passage v. 15–vi. 6 is a dialogue between God and the people, in which after God has expressed His purpose to withdraw His presence (v. 15), the people lightheartedly profess repentance, and their confidence in God's restored favour (vi. 1-3); but the true situation is far otherwise than the people think (vi. 4-6). Has God ever met your cry of repentance with 'What shall I do unto thee?' and, if so, why? What does God desire to find in His people? Cf. Mt. ix. 13, xii. 7, xxiii. 23-26.

(2) The remainder of today's portion consists of descriptions of the state of the nation—the sinfulness of priests, kings and people (vi. 7–vii. 7); their instability and folly (vii. 8–viii. 3); God's anger against both their rulers and their idols—all alike man made (viii. 4-13). What do you find here (a) about the sins that abounded; (b) about false alliances that blinded their eyes; (c) about the real causes of their perilous condition?

(3) What sentences or phrases strike you most, and speak most forcibly to yourself?

Notes.—(1) vi. 5 and 7. The R.V. mg. is clearer in these verses.

(2) vi. 6. 'The knowledge of God'; one of the key words of the book. The absence of this knowledge was Israel's fatal defect; see ii. 8, iv. 6, etc.

(3) vii. 1. The LXX links the last clause of chapter vi with this verse, thus: 'When I would turn the fortunes of My people, when I would heal Israel, etc.' The R.V. should be read in verses 5 and 15. 'On the day of our king' must refer to some great day in the king's life, perhaps a birthday. 'Baker' (verse 6) should rather be rendered as 'anger' (see R.V. mg.).

(4) viii. The R.V. is better in verses 6, 8, 10 and 12.

Day 3. Ho. ix and x.

These chapters are prophecies of coming judgment, and show how the people's sin will bring upon them (a) exile (ix. 1-8); (b) a diminished population (ix. 9-17); and (c) the destruction of both the sanctuaries and the throne, and the reducing of the nation to servitude (x. 1-15).

(1) ix. 1-8. This passage was perhaps spoken at a religious festival, when the people were making merry after the manner of the heathen at their festivals (see verse 1). Rejoice not thus, the prophet says, for exile is at hand. How does he describe the changes that exile will bring?

(2) ix. 9-17. God Himself speaks. He sees lust prevalent in the nation, as in the most shameful days of Israel's history (verses 9, 10, cf. Jdg. xix; Nu. xxv). To what results would it lead? Cf. I Thes. iv. 3-8.

(3) What different kinds of sin are spoken of in chapter x? Give
to each a name. What counsel does the prophet give as to the one
way of escape from the coming judgment? Cf. Je. iv. 3, 4.

Notes.—(1) The R.V. is clearer throughout these chapters.
(2) ix. 7b, 8. The meaning is obscure. Many think that the words 'the
prophet is a fool, etc.' are the words of the people; cf. Je. vi. 10; Jn. viii. 48;
Acts xxvi. 24.
(3) x. 1. 'Pillars' (R.V.). A common feature of a Canaanitish shrine, imitated
by the Israelites in their worship.
(4) Verses 5 and 6. 'The calves of Beth-aven'. See iv. 15, note, and 1 Ki.
xii. 28. For the meaning of 'king Jareb' see v. 13, note.
(5) Verse 9. See R.V. mg.
(6) Verse 10. 'Their two transgressions'. Perhaps meaning the sins of the
throne (cf. ix. 15, last clause), and of the worship.
(7) Verse 11. The position of Israel is to be changed from that of the heifer
treading the threshing floor and eating freely (Dt. xxv. 4) to the heavy labour
of the yoke.
(8) Verse 14. 'As Shalman spoiled Beth-arbel.' The reference is uncertain.
Shalman is probably the same as Shalmaneser, 2 Ki. xvii. 3.

Day 4. Ho. xi and xii.

In chapter xi another aspect of God's dealings with Israel breaks into clear
view—His persistent *love*. Judgment there must be (verses 5-8) but God will
not make a final end of His sinning people. Cf. La. iii. 22; Rom. xi. 1.

(1) How was God's love manifested in Israel's beginnings? See
xi. 1-4, and compare Dt. vi. 6-8. How was this love still manifested,
in spite of all His people's backsliding? See xi. 8-11.

(2) In chapter xi God has spoken of His attitude to Israel; now
in xi. 12–xii. 2 He speaks of Israel's attitude to Himself. Then the
prophet reminds the people of the very different history of their
ancestor Jacob (xii. 3, 4). What is the attitude to Himself which
God desires? See xii. 6 and cf. vi. 6, x. 12.

(3) What, alas, was Israel's response to all God's pleadings
(xii. 7-14)? It is for this that judgment is near. Cf. Mt. xxiii.
32-39.

Notes.—(1) xi. 8. 'Repentings'; better, 'compassions', as in R.V.
(2) Verses 9 and 12 are clearer in R.V. mg.
(3) xii. 12. Cf. verse 9 and ii. 14, 15.
(4) Verse 7. 'Merchant'; see R.V. mg. Israel, who had been sent to cleanse
Canaan (Lv. xx. 22-24), had become as Canaan.

Day 5. Ho. xiii and xiv.

(1) In what four ways is the coming judgment described in
xiii? See verses 3, 7-8, 15, 16. And what four reasons are given

for this judgment? See verses 1-2, 4-6, 9, 16. What may we learn
from this as to what sin in essence is? Cf. Jn. xvi. 9.

(2) Chapter xiv describes the final triumph of God's love; cf.
ii. 14-23. What, according to this chapter, does repentance involve
(see verses 1-3, 8), and what is the divine response? Notice the
three 'I wills' of verses 4, 5a, and cf. Lk. xv. 22-24.

(3) What kind of life is symbolized by the emblems used in
verses 5b-7—the lily, Lebanon, the olive tree, corn, and wine? Cf.
Jude 24, 25.

Notes.—(1) Verse 2. 'The calves of our lips'; see R.V. and R.V. mg. and cf.
Heb. xiii. 15.

(2) Verse 3. Cf. v. 13, vii. 11, viii. 9, xii. 1; Is. xxx. 16, xxxi. 1.

JOEL

INTRODUCTION

(See New Bible Handbook, pp. 242-3)

NOTHING is known of this prophet beyond what is stated in the
first verse of his book, and the evident fact that he prophesied to
Judah. It is generally agreed that he was either one of the earliest
of the prophets, or one of the latest. The date is not important
for the study of his message.

The occasion of his prophecy was an unprecedented plague of
locusts, apparently accompanied by drought (i. 18-20). He summoned the people to national repentance and self-humbling, and
on their doing this, he was authorized to declare the speedy departure of the locusts and the restoration of the land.

But the prophet was given also a more distant vision. The
plague of locusts was a symbol of the approaching Day of the Lord,
and Joel foresees the outpouring of the Spirit, and the gathering
of the nations to answer for their misdeeds towards Israel. Jehovah
will triumph, and Israel be blessed.

ANALYSIS

i. 1–ii. 17.   The plague of locusts and a national summons to
                repentance.

ii. 18–27.   The locusts will be destroyed, and the land wil
                recover its fertility.

ii. 28–32.   The outpouring of the Holy Spirit.

iii. 1–21.   The day of the Lord; the judgment of the nations,
                and blessings upon Judah and Jerusalem.

Day 6. Joel i–ii. 17.

Today's portion contains two addresses on the plague of locusts, both describing in different ways its severity, and summoning the people to repent.

(1) Consider in chapter i the destructiveness of the locust scourge, affecting all classes, so that they had nothing for themselves, nothing for others, nothing to offer to God. In what ways does sin produce a similar waste in the life of the individual? Cf. Lk. xv. 14-16.

(2) What are the essentials of true repentance, as given in ii. 12-13 and what pleas does the prophet put into the lips of the priests, as they make intercession? Cf. Dn. ix. 15-17. What two thoughts, one of rebuke, and one of encouragement, are implied in the words 'even now' in ii. 12 (R.V.)?

Notes.—(1) i. 4. It is probable that the four insects mentioned in this verse were all locusts of different kinds. See R.V. mg.

(2) ii. 6-8. Read as in R.V.

Day 7. Joel ii. 18–iii.

(1) Reading ii. 18 as in R.V., verses 19-27 become God's answer to His people's prayer. What picture of God's heart is here given, and what does He promise His people? Cf. Ho. xiv. 4-7; Ps. xxxii. 5-7. How may this be applied spiritually to the case of a Christian who has backslidden and has repented? See Lk. xv. 20, 22-24.

(2) How has the prophecy of ii. 28-29 already been fulfilled far more wonderfully than Joel foresaw? Have we received the Spirit? Cf. Acts xix. 2 (R.V.).

(3) Chapter iii is a vision of mercy upon Israel, and judgment upon her enemies. In what ways had the nations angered God by their treatment of Israel, and what judgment would fall upon them? Cf. Zc. xiv. What, according to iii. 17, 21 is the supreme blessedness of God's people?

Notes.—(1) ii. 18, 19. Read as in R.V. The prayer has been answered.

(2) iii. 1. 'When I shall bring again, etc.' may be rendered 'When I turn again the fortunes of'; cf. Ps. xiv. 7; Jb. xlii. 10.

OBADIAH

INTRODUCTION

(See New Bible Handbook, pp. 246-7)

OBADIAH'S message is almost entirely a denunciation of Edom for unbrotherly conduct to Israel, and a prophecy of the destruction of that proud kingdom and people. But the prophet associates Edom's fall with the day of Jehovah, and foresees Israel's recovery of their promised possessions, and the universal triumph of God's reign and kingdom.

The Edomites as the descendants of Esau, and the Israelites, as the descendants of Jacob, were enemies from the time that Israel took possession of Canaan (see Nu. xx. 14-21), and there are many references in the historical and prophetic books to Edom, which show the antipathy between Edom and Israel, and the difference in their destinies. See, e.g., 2 Sa. viii. 14; 2 Ki. xiv. 7; Je. xlix. 7-22; Ezk. xxv. 12-17; Am. i. 11-12; Mal. i. 1-5.

ANALYSIS

1-9. The doom of Edom, despite his confidence in his impregnable strongholds.

10-14. The sin for which Edom is to be punished.

15-21. The day of Jehovah is at hand when Edom shall be punished and Israel shall triumph.

Week 52. OBADIAH, JONAH AND MICAH

Day 1. Obadiah.

(1) For what sins is Edom to be punished? What counterpart have these sins in the spiritual life? See, e.g., Lk. xviii. 14, xxiii. 35; 1 Cor. x. 12, xiii. 6; 1 Jn. iii. 17.

(2) Verse 17. Is not this verse true in a spiritual sense also of us, who belong to Christ? How far then are we experiencing deliverance from our spiritual enemies, living holy lives, and possessing our possessions in Christ?

(3) What does this short book reveal of God's character and attributes? Profound and far-reaching as Obadiah's vision of God is, yet in what respects does it fall short of the New Testament revelation in Christ Jesus?

Notes.—(1) Verse 1. 'The vision of Obadiah.' 'This is what the Lord Eternal has to say of Edom—the tidings we heard from the Eternal, as an envoy went through the nations with his summons to rise and make war on her' (Moffatt).

(2) Verses 5 and 6. The spoiling of Edom would be more thorough than that of robbers or grape gatherers.

(3) Verses 7 and 8. Edom, bereft of understanding, would be deceived and driven out (see R.V. mg.) by her own allies.

(4) Verses 10-14. See 2 Ki. xxv. 10-14; La. ii. 15, 16.

(5) Verse 16. Cf. Je. xxv. 27, 28.

JONAH

INTRODUCTION

(See New Bible Handbook, pp. 247-8)

JONAH is mentioned in 2 Ki. xiv. 25 as having predicted the victories of Jeroboam II by which the borders of the kingdom of Israel were greatly enlarged. If Jonah prophesied at the beginning of Jeroboam's reign, he would precede Amos by about twenty years only. At that time Assyria was already a great power, and had begun to reach out westwards: in fact, Jeroboam's victories were partly due to Assyrian raids upon Damascus and neighbouring states, which weakened these kingdoms. It would seem that Jonah was afraid of Assyria, whose cruelties were well known, and whose power was dreaded.

To this man came the commission to go to Nineveh and cry against it. One might have thought that such a commission would not be unwelcome, but to Jonah it was so hateful that he resolved rather to resign his prophetic office than obey it. The book is the story of what happened. It is one of the most remarkable books in the Bible, and rich in spiritual teaching.

ANALYSIS

  i.   Jonah's disobedience and deliverance from death.
 ii.   His prayer of penitence, and thanksgiving.
iii.   His fulfilment of his commission, resulting in Nineveh's repentance.
 iv.   Jonah's anger, and God's reproof.

Day 2. Jon. i and ii.

The key to Jonah's flight is found in iv. 2. If he went to Nineveh as commanded, Nineveh might repent, and be spared to become later the destroyer of Israel. If he did not go God's judgment would fall upon Nineveh, and Israel be saved.

(1) In his dilemma what did Jonah do, and what did God do?

(2) Though Jonah would not go to Nineveh, he was willing to give his life for the heathen sailors on board the ship. How do you reconcile these two things?

(3) Can you trace in Jonah's prayer the steps by which he was restored from backsliding?

Notes.—(1) i. 3. 'Flee . . . from the presence of the Lord'; i.e. abandon God's service. Cf. 1 Ki. xvii. 1 ('before whom I stand').

(2) Verse 5. 'Fast asleep'; showing what a strain he had been through.

(3) Verse 17. 'Three days and three nights'; cf. Mt. xii. 40. According to Jewish reckoning this may mean one full day with the night before and the night after.

(4) ii. 10. 'Upon the dry land'; probably upon the shore of Palestine.

Day 3. Jon. iii and iv.

(1) What lessons does our Lord draw from the story of chapter iii? See Mt. xii. 38-41.

(2) Comparing iii. 10 with Joel iii. 18 (R.V.) what illustration do we find of the truth stated by Peter in Acts x. 34, 35?

(3) What picture of God is given us in chapter iv as a whole?

Notes.—(1) iii. 3. 'An exceeding great city'; Nineveh, in its full extent, consisted of four cities, making an irregular quadrangle of about 60 miles in circuit.

(2) iv. 6. 'Gourd'; fast-growing, trailing or climbing plant with broad leaves.

MICAH

INTRODUCTION

(See New Bible Handbook, pp. 248-251)

MICAH was a contemporary of Isaiah, but whereas Isaiah was a prophet of the court and of the city, Micah came from Moresheth-gath (i. 1, 14), a country town near the western border of Judah. Notice, e.g., how often he uses the image of a flock and its shepherd (ii. 12, iii. 2, 3, iv. 6, iv. 8, v. 4, R.V., v. 8, vii. 14). His prophetic ministry began only a few years after that of Hosea, and there are many traces in his book of the influence upon him both of Hosea and of Isaiah. See, e.g., Mi. i. 7 and Ho. ii. 13, viii. 6, ix. 1; and again Mi. vi. 5 and Is. x. 5; Mi. vii. 1 and Is. xxiv. 13, etc. Mi. iv. 1-4 and Is. ii. 2-9 are almost verbally the same. Yet Micah was no plagiarist. He had his own message, and exercised a profound influence, as is seen from the reference to him in Je. xxvi. 16-19. As Jonah's prophetic word moved the king of Nineveh to repent, so Micah's similar prophecy moved king Hezekiah; and so deep was the impression Micah made that these things were remembered about him a century later, and were instrumental in saving the life of the prophet Jeremiah.

Micah's word still lives, because the Spirit of God is in it, and he has important lessons to teach us for our own day.

ANALYSIS

i and ii. Judgment must come, but in the end there will be blessing.

    i. 1-16. A vision of Jehovah come in judgment; Samaria falls and country towns in the lowland of Judah will be overwhelmed.

    ii. 1-11. The sins of the wealthy and powerful which brought the judgment.

    ii. 12, 13. A prophecy of restoration.

iii–v. Further prophecies of coming judgment, and further blessing.

    iii–iv. 8. The sins of rulers, prophets and priests will bring destruction upon Jerusalem; yet in the latter days it will be restored and the rule of Jehovah established.

    iv. 9-13. Zion must suffer exile, but later will be victorious.

    v. 1-15. Temporary humiliation will lead to future triumph.

vi and vii. Jehovah in controversy with His people states His real demands; then denounces Judah's sin and gives warning of the consequences. The prophet speaking in the name of a penitent people, laments the terrible condition of social family life, but waits for God in confidence and hope, and is assured of the final fulfilment of all God's promises.

Day 4. Mi. i and ii.

(1) Try to imagine the effect of the prophet's words in chapter i. if you had been living in the district specially threatened. See notes below.

(2) What classes of the community, and what sins, are rebuked in chapter ii?

(3) With ii. 13 cf. 2 Cor. ii. 14 (R.V.). Are we in Christ's triumphal march? Do we know Him as 'the Breaker' who has broken our bands in sunder (Ps. cvii. 14) and set us at liberty (Lk. iv. 18), and broken our (spiritual) enemies before us (2 Sa. v. 20 R.V.)?

Notes.—(1) i. 5. 'The high places of Judah.' The LXX renders 'the sin of the house of Judah'. The prophet sees the capital cities of the kingdoms of both Israel and Judah as the main sources of the corruption of the whole country.
(2) Verses 10-12. There is a play upon the names of these towns. Moffatt translates thus: 'Grovel in the dust at Dust-town (Bethophrah); fare forth stripped, O Fair-town (Saphir); Stir-town (Zaanan) dare not stir. . . .' See also R.V. mg.
(3) Verse 13. 'The beginning of sin.' Lachish was the border town at which chariots and horses purchased in Egypt would be received in Judah. See v. 10 and Is. xxxi. 1, xxxvi. 9.
(4) Verses 14 and 15 are clearer in the R.V.
(5) ii. 4, 5. The wealthy landowners lament that the lands they have acquired pass to the enemy.
(6) Verses 6 and 7. The prophet recites the protests with which his words are received. See Moffatt's translation and cf. iii. 11.

Day 5. Mi. iii–iv. 8. See *Analysis.*

(1) In chapter iii Micah again denounces the leaders of the nation, rulers, prophets and priests, for their grievous sins. (a) What was the sin of the rulers? See iii. 1-3, 9-11a. (b) What are the marks of the true prophet as contrasted with the false? Can you see why the true prophet was unpopular? Is there a modern counterpart to iii. 11b? Cf. ii. 6, 7, notes.

(2) Under what conditions does the Word of God predict the establishment of peace and the end of war? See iv. 1-8.

Notes.—(1) iii. 2, 3. Those whose office it was to administer justice crushed and devoured the poor by their evil and heartless exactions.
(2) Verse 5. 'That bite with their teeth, etc.'; 'who cry "All's well" if they get food to eat' (Moffatt).
(3) Verse 10. Jerusalem was being adorned with fine buildings at the cost of the lives of the people.
(4) iv. 1. Zion pre-eminent as the seat of God's revelation and rule. Read as in R.V. mg.
(5) Verse 8. Read as in R.V.

Day 6. Mi. iv. 9–v.

Two prophecies, iv. 9-13 and v. 1-15. See *Analysis*.

(1) iv. 9-13. Zion must suffer chastisement (verses 9, 10), but what remarkable contrast is set forth between men's thoughts concerning Zion and God's purpose for her (verses 11-13)? Cf. Ps. ii. and also Mt. v. 11, 12, where our Lord applies a similar contrast to the individual Christian.

(2) v. 1-6. Micah was one of the earliest of the prophets to see in vision the figure of the Messiah. How does Micah picture Him in these verses? What great significance had the prophecy of verse 2 in the life of our Lord? See Mt. ii.

(3) v. 7-9 and 10-15 seem to be two detached fragments, the first giving a picture of Israel among the nations in the days of her restoration, and the second a vision of God's purifying of His people. Cf. Ho. xiv. 1-3. What may we learn by comparing verse 7 with Ho. xiv. 5, and how may the lesson be applied to our lives?

Notes.—(1) iv. 10. 'Even to Babylon.' A remarkable instance of prophetic prevision, because at the time the great enemy was Assyria, not Babylon. But see Is. xxxix. 6, 7.

(2) In iv. 11 and 13 the R.V. is clearer; as also in v. 2-5 and 15.

(3) v. 1. The meaning of the opening words is obscure.

(4) Verse 5. 'Seven shepherds, etc.'; the meaning may be that there will be an ample supply of leaders.

Day 7. Mi. vi and vii.

(1) What is the controversy of the Lord with His people (vi. 1-8)? In how many ways does it illustrate the relationship between the wayward Christian and his Lord? Is your life exemplifying verse 8?

(2) How are the sins of the city described in vi. 9–vii. 6? Make a list of them. Are they to be found also today? How is it shown that sin brings sorrow?

(3) In chapter vii Micah seems to speak on behalf of a penitent people. As he waits upon the Lord, what is his attitude, and what promise is given him (verses 7-13)? What is his prayer, and what God's answer (verses 14-17)? What vision is finally given him verses 18-20)?

Notes.—(1) vi. 13 and 14 are clearer in the R.V.; so also is vii. 3.

(2) vii. 11. 'The day comes for your walls to be mended, the day for frontiers to be far extended' (Moffatt). Cf. R.V. mg. and Zc. ii. 1-5.;

THIRD YEAR

MATTHEW

INTRODUCTION

(See New Bible Handbook, pp. 322-328)

IT is customary to see in Matthew's Gospel the 'lineaments of the Davidic King' (Westcott), thereby signifying that this Gospel sets forth Jesus as the Christ, the promised Son of David. This is true, but it also declares that He is the Saviour from sin (i. 21) and the Son of God (i. 23, iii. 17, xvi. 16, 17); and although the writer was obviously a Jew to the core, and wrote primarily for Jewish Christians, yet he recognizes that Jesus is the Saviour, not of the Jews only, but of all nations (ii. 1, 11, xxviii. 19, 20).

Nevertheless, this is the most Jewish of the Gospels. It is significant that our Lord's genealogy is traced back, not to Adam, as in Luke's account, but to Abraham, 'the father of the Jewish race'. If Mark shows us Christ as Servant, Luke as Man, John as God 'manifest in the flesh', Matthew presents us with Christ the King of Israel.

The story of the birth of Christ shows distinct signs of being derived from Joseph's side, as the story given by Luke would seem to come from Mary's.

The Gospel is characterized by the larger place it gives to the teaching of our Lord, and in particular to His teaching in parables and about 'things to come'.

ANALYSIS

i. 1–iv. 11. Early days of the Messiah.

    i and ii. Genealogy, birth and childhood incidents.

    iii. 1-12. The herald proclaims His coming ministry.

    iii. 13–iv. 11. His baptism and temptation.

iv. 12–xvi. 12. The ministry in Galilee.

    iv. 12-25. Preaching, and call of disciples.

    v–vii. The Sermon on the Mount—the kingdom expounded.

    viii–xvi. 12. Teaching, preaching and healing, mainly in Galilee. Commissioning and sending forth of the Twelve. Increasing opposition.

Week 1. MATTHEW I–V. 16

Day 1. Mt. i.

(1) Run your eye over the names in this genealogy, and consider how sinful some of them were. How did God provide that
Jesus should be 'son of Abraham', and 'son of David' (i. 1), born
of a sinful race, and yet 'without sin' (Heb. iv. 15)?

(2) 'He shall save His people from their sins.' Can you testify
that He does so, taking into account sin's power as well as its
guilt? If not, what is lacking?

(3) How do these verses indicate that the coming of Jesus was
in God's plan from the beginning, and that in Him Old Testament
prophecy finds its fulfilment?

Notes.—(1) Verse 1. 'The book', etc.; cf. Gn. v. It is probable that this
title covers only the following genealogy. The words 'Now the birth', etc.
(verse 18) begin a new section.

(2) Verse 17. This arrangement into three periods of fourteen generations
each is not exact, some generations being omitted. It is not certain why it is
thus arranged; possibly that it may be more easily memorized.

(3) Verse 19. According to Jewish law, Mary being betrothed to Joseph was
already regarded as his wife.

Day 2. Mt. ii. 1-12.

(1) Consider the significance of the coming of the wise men
from the East in the light of such passages as Is. xlii. 6; Lk. ii. 32;
Jn. x. 16.

(2) Their gifts (verse 11) were only the outward and visible
signs of heart worship and adoration (verses 2 and 11). What
relation do the former bear to the latter in our lives?

(3) How are our Lord's words in Jn. xviii. 37 (last clause) illustrated in the differing reactions of the wise men and of Herod to

the advent of the king? Consider and contrast these reactions in detail.

Day 3. Mt. ii. 13-23.

(1) Notice how accurately the words of prophecy, which Matthew quotes, were fulfilled in the events of our Lord's infancy (verses 15, 17-18, 23). What light does this throw upon the nature of prophecy (cf. verse 15, R.V., 'spoken by the Lord'; Heb. i. 1; 1 Pet. i. 11; 2 Pet. i. 21)?

(2) What features in the life and character of Joseph stand out in this and the preceding chapter? Try to put yourself in his place. What may we learn, for example, from his implicit obedience to the guidance given him of God, remembering how this affected not only himself, but also Mary and 'the young child'?

Notes.—(1) Verse 18. Quoted from Je. xxxi. 15-17, where the words are followed by a message of comfort.

(2) Verse 23. The general thought seems to be that the obscurity and lowliness of our Lord's upbringing in the despised town of Nazareth (cf. Jn. i. 46) was foreshadowed by the prophets (cf., e.g. Is. liii. 2). The difficulty is that no known word of prophecy speaks of the Messiah as a Nazarene. Some have thought that there is an allusion to the prophecies which speak of Him as a 'branch' (e.g. Is. xi. 1), which in Hebrew is *netzer*, but this is doubtful.

Day 4. Mt. iii.

Thirty years have passed since the coming of the wise men. Now, in fulfilment of another prophecy, John appears, and Jesus, grown to mature manhood, comes forth from Nazareth.

(1) Picture John's appearance, summarize his message, try to realize the amazing influence he exerted, and then consider what lessons are to be learned from his life and from his teaching. With verse 9, cf. Jn. viii. 39; Rom. ii. 28, 29, ix. 6-8; Gal. iii. 6, 7.

(2) What evidence is there in verses 13-15 that Jesus regarded His baptism by John as an act of profound significance? Ponder His words in verse 15 in the light of Ps. xl. 7, 8; Jn. vii. 18; Is. liii. 11; 1 Pet. ii. 24, 25; 1 Jn. ii. 2; 2 Cor. v. 21.

Day 5. Mt. iv. 1-11.

(1) From a study of verses 1-11, show how Jas. iv. 7 was illustrated in the experience of Jesus.

(2) 1 Jn. ii. 16, with its threefold division, is a good commentary on the threefold temptation of our Lord. What was the special point of the appeal in each temptation?

(3) Can you think of specific temptations in your own Christian experience along similar lines? By the use of what weapon did Christ prevail? See verses 4, 7, 10 ('it is written').

Day 6. Mt. iv. 12-25.

(1) What is the nature of the 'darkness' spoken of in verse 16? Cf. Lk. i. 79; Jn. i. 5, xii. 45, 46. How did the light manifest itself, and how is it manifested today? Cf. Jn. i. 4, 14, viii. 12; Mt. v. 14.

(2) What demand did Jesus make upon those who would enter the kingdom of heaven? Cf. iii. 2; Acts ii. 38, xx. 21. Give in one sentence the best definition you can of repentance. The following references will be helpful: Lk. xv. 18; Mt. xxi. 28-32; and Mt. iii. 8 with Acts xxvi. 20.

(3) What was the first response to Christ's appearing? Is your attitude towards Him like that of the multitudes in verses 24, 25 (cf. Jn. ii. 24, vi. 14, 26), or like that of the men in viii. 19-22, or like that of Peter, Andrew, James and John (verses 18-22)?

Notes.—(1) Verses 12-14. The incidents recorded in Jn. i. 29-iv. 3 happened between verses 11-12 of this chapter.

(2) Verse 18. The word 'net' here is a casting-net of circular shape and thrown by a single person. Fishermen on the Lake of Galilee also used a drag-net, referred to in xiii. 47, 48. In verses 20-22 the word 'nets' is a general word, denoting any kind of net. The only reference in the Gospels to fishing with line and hook is in xvii. 27.

Day 7. Mt. v. 1-16.

The three chapters v-vii, commonly known as 'The Sermon on the Mount', expound the gospel of the kingdom, answering questions that must have arisen in the minds of those who heard the proclamation, first of John, and now of Jesus: 'The kingdom of heaven is at hand' (iii. 2, iv. 17).

(1) Consider in detail the personal disposition and character of those who belong to the kingdom and to whom the kingdom belongs.

(2) What blessings are offered to them? Make a list of these.

(3) Verses 13-16. By what two similes does our Lord describe the relation to the world of those who belong to the kingdom? And in what two ways does He warn them that they may fail to exercise their proper function?

Notes.—(1) Verse 3. 'Poor in spirit', i.e. conscious of their spiritual poverty and need of divine help. Cf. Lk. xviii. 13, 17; Rom. vii. 18; 1 Cor. xv. 10.

(2) Verse 4. 'Mourn', i.e. mourn concerning sin. Cf. Ps. cxix. 136; Ezk. ix. 4; Lk. xix. 41, 42.

(3) Verse 5. Cf. Ps. xxii. 26, cxlvii. 6; Mt. xxi. 5; 1 Pet. iii. 4.

Week 2. MATTHEW v. 17–IX. 17

Day 1. Mt. v. 17-48.

(1) In view of our Lord's respect for the law and the Old Testament (see verses 17, 18 and the story of the temptation in chapter iv), what inferences do you draw from the fact that He proceeds to add to it?

(2) How often, and in relation to what subjects, does our Lord say, 'But I say unto you'? What is the nature of the modification of former teaching which He makes in each case? Cf. xv. 18-20; Pr. iv. 23; 1 Sa. xvi. 7.

(3) If this is the standard of righteousness required in the kingdom of heaven (verse 20), how shall men be saved? Cf. Rom. iii. 20-26, viii. 1-4.

Notes.—(1) Verse 18. 'One jot or one tittle'; better 'not an iota, not a dot', as in R.S.V. The meaning is 'no smallest particle'.

(2) Verses 21, 22. 'In danger of the judgment'; that is, liable to the verdict of the court, i.e. condemned to death. '*Raca*' is a word of contempt, rendered in R.S.V. by 'whoever insults his brother'. The general meaning is that anger without a cause and abuse are as deserving of the death penalty as is the act of murder. Cf. 1 Jn. iii. 15.

(3) Verses 23-26 give two practical applications of the above teaching.

Day 2. Mt. vi. 1-18.

(1) What was wrong with the religion of the scribes and Pharisees, here called 'hypocrites', and what kind of religion does our Lord commend in contrast? Cf. Je. xvii. 10. Is your religious life, in regard to almsgiving, prayer and fasting, characterized by reality?

(2) In the Lord's Prayer, what may we learn (a) from the order of the petitions, and (b) from the lowly position He gives us (i) as God's children (verse 9) and subjects of His kingdom (verse 10), and (ii) as beggars, debtors, weaklings, and slaves (verses 11-13a)?

(3) What does our Lord lay down as a condition of our receiving divine forgiveness, and why is this condition essential (verses 12, 14, 15, v. 24)?

Notes.—(1) Verse 1. 'Alms'; better, as in R.V., 'righteousness'. The term includes all the three practices mentioned in today's portion—almsgiving, prayer and fasting.

(2) Verses 2, 5, 16. The word 'hypocrite' means one who plays a part, and hence, a pretender.

Day 3. Mt. vi. 19-34.

These verses deal with the relation of the subjects of the kingdom to the material things of our earthly life, and especially to money. Verses 19-24 are addressed to those who are rich, and verses 25-34 to those who are poor.

(1) What should be the rich disciple's attitude to his wealth? How may he best use it, and why should he use it thus?

(2) What should be the needy disciple's attitude to the material necessities of life? What should he do, and what should he not do, and on what grounds?

Notes.—(1) Verses 22, 23. An 'evil' eye, according to Jewish thought, signifies a covetous or niggardly disposition; see e.g. Dt. xv. 9; Pr. xxviii. 22 (R.V.). A 'single' or 'sound' eye (R.S.V.) here betokens a generous disposition; cf. Pr. xxii. 9.

(2) Verses 25, 27, 28, 31, 34. 'Take no thought'; better, as in R.V., 'be not anxious'.

Day 4. Mt. vii.

(1) Compare verse 1 with verse 16 and see Jn. vii. 24. If judging is not always wrong, what does our Lord here condemn?

(2) In verses 13-23 what threefold responsibility does Christ lay upon those who would enter His kingdom (a) as to a right choice at the beginning (verses 13, 14), (b) as to a right discrimination between the false and the true (verses 15-20), and (c) as to the condition of being acknowledged by Him at the last (verses 21-23)?

(3) What is the difference between the two builders of verses 24-27? How do the two houses differ? Is the house of your life secure?

Notes.—(1) Verse 2. A censorious person is sharply judged by others.

(2) Verse 15. 'Beware of false *prophets*'. Christ is thinking here not of false teaching, but of false men—men who may be orthodox in their doctrine, but are wolves in sheep's clothing.

Day 5. Mt. viii. 1-17.

In chapters viii and ix are nine examples of our Lord's deeds of power. To-day's portion contains the first three.

(1) Consider how different the persons were who received healing and the different methods which our Lord used. In each case He triumphed. What may we learn from these things regarding His power as Saviour?

(2) What in the centurion's faith was so remarkable that it drew forth Christ's word of strong approval? Notice also how Paul in Gal. iii. 7-9 teaches the same truth.

Day 6. Mt. viii. 18-34.

(1) In verses 18-22 it is recorded that our Lord (a) when He saw great multitudes, left them, and (b) checked two would-be disciples who desired to follow Him. Why did He act thus? Was He afraid of too great popular excitement, and of people following Him too easily? Cf. Lk. xiv. 25-27. In what practical ways is the following of Christ a costly thing to you?

(2) How did the disciples in the storm show that they had faith in the Lord, and in what ways did they reveal that their faith was as yet but 'little'? When Christ is with us, ought not faith to dispel fear, however violent the storm? Cf. Ps. xxiii. 4; Jn. xiv. 1, 27.

Notes.—(1) Verses 21, 22. The man probably wished to stay at home until his father died. For the phrase 'the dead', see Jn. v. 25.

(2) Verse 29. For other instances of the recognition of our Lord by the devil and his demons and our Lord's attitude to it, see iv. 3, 6; Mk. i. 24, iii. 11, 12; and cf. Acts xvi. 16-18.

Day 7. Mt. ix. 1-17.

(1) Instances have been given to show our Lord's power to heal disease. How, in verses 2-8, does He show that He can deal also with the deeper trouble of sin? Consider how much greater reason we have for believing in His saving power. (See e.g. Is. liii. 5, 6; Mt. xxvi. 28; Eph. i. 7.) And yet *do* we believe?

(2) The gospel is good news for sinners. Notice how 'at home' sinners were in Christ's presence. Is our religion of the same quality or does it 'put people off'?

(3) Show how our Lord's quotation in verse 13 reveals in a word the fundamental difference between God as He is and God as the Pharisees conceived Him to be. Cf. v. 7, xii. 7, xxiii. 23; Mk. xii. 33; also Is. i. 11-17; Mi. vi. 6-8.

Week 3. MATTHEW IX. 18–XIII. 23

Day 1. Mt. ix. 18-35.

(1) Consider the various incidents as symbolizing what our Lord can do for men in the spiritual sphere, removing some long-standing moral weakness, giving life to the spiritually dead, and vision, and ability to speak. Have you seen these miracles happen?

(2) What drew these diverse persons to Jesus? Are you conscious of any need—in your own life, or in some other life? Is Jesus able to meet it? If so, what should you do?

Day 2. Mt. ix. 36–x. 23.

(1) Chapter ix. 36-38. Have you seen the multitudes with the eyes of Jesus? Have you felt His compassion? Have you heard His summons to pray? Are you praying?

(2) In the instructions of x. 5-23 those of verses 5-15 seem to refer specially to the work they were to do before the Lord's death, and those of verses 16-23 to the time between His ascension and the fall of Jerusalem. In verses 5-15 some of the instructions are plainly temporary. Do you find among them any principles that are still applicable in evangelistic and missionary work? Cf. e.g. Mk. xvi. 15; Acts i. 8; Lk. xxiv. 47.

(3) In verses 16-23 what does Christ say that His disciples may expect from men, and what may they expect as His ambassadors from God? Also, what is to be their own attitude and disposition?

Note.—Verse 23. This difficult verse has been interpreted in various ways. The most appropriate meaning in this context seems to be that our Lord is referring not to His final advent, but His coming in judgment in the fall of Jerusalem.

Day 3. Mt. x. 24–xi. 1.

Further instructions, more general in character.

(1) Verses 24-33. Why were the disciples not to fear in the face of such conditions as are here described? Write down the reasons given for courage and confidence.

(2) How do you reconcile verses 34-36 with the title of our Lord at the close of Is. ix. 6? Cf. Heb. vii. 2.

(3) Verses 37-39. Are we worthy followers of such a Leader? If we are losing our life for His sake, what shall we find? Cf. Jn. xii. 25, 26.

Notes.—Verses 40-42 stand in contrast to verses 14, 15, which speak of those who do not receive Christ's messengers.

'These little ones'; i.e. Christ's messengers. See Mk. ix. 41.

'A cup of cold water'; in a hot country a greatly valued gift.

Day 4. Mt. xi. 2-30.

(1) What is John the Baptist's unique place in Bible history? What was his relation to the era of 'the prophets and the law', now ending, and what was his relation to the new era of 'the kingdom of heaven', now opening?

(2) How many different attitudes towards Jesus do you find recorded in this chapter? What is the attitude *He* commends? Is it yours?

(3) Yet observe how confident He is, and what claims He makes for Himself, and what He commands and offers.

Notes.—(1) Verse 12 seems to point to the tremendous dynamic of John's movement, stirring men to lay hold of the kingdom.

(2) Verse 19. 'Of her children'; better 'by her works', as in R.V. The wisdom of God's ways is justified by results.

(3) Verse 23. 'Exalted unto heaven . . . brought down to hell.' Metaphors for prosperity and ruin.

(4) Verse 29. 'Take my yoke' means 'become my disciple'.

Day 5. Mt. xii. 1-21.

(1) In our Lord's teaching in verses 1-13, what three main principles are set forth with regard to the true observance of the sabbath? What answer do these give also against those who would either abolish or secularize the day of rest?

(2) Note the anger of the Pharisees at His claims. Cf. Jn. v. 16-18. What did Jesus do in the face of their hostility?

Day 6. Mt. xii. 22-50.

(1) Consider the solemnity of the warnings which the Lord addressed to the Pharisees in reply to their attempts to discredit Him, and the further high claims which He continued to make for Himself.

(2) From verses 43-45 show that the doctrine of Christ *for* us cannot be separated from that of Christ *in* us.

(3) How does the whole of today's portion illustrate and enforce the teaching of Pr. iv. 23?

Notes.—(1) Verse 31. 'The blasphemy against the Holy Ghost'; the Pharisees were filled with such hatred and prejudice that they attributed a manifestly good work to the activity of Satan.

(2) Verse 36. 'Every idle word': because it comes from the heart; see verse 34.

(3) Verses 49, 50. Cf. vii. 21; Lk. xi. 27, 28.

Day 7. Mt. xiii. 1-23.

(1) Study the prepositions used in the parable of the sower: *by* (verse 4); *upon* (verse 5); *among* (verse 7); *into* (verse 8). How does this continue the main teaching of yesterday's portion? Note question (1) of yesterday.

(2) Study our Lord's teaching on *endurance* in this Gospel. With verses 5-6 and 20-21 compare x. 22 and xxiv. 13 with their contexts. Note Col. ii. 6, 7, and especially the word 'rooted'.

(3) What is the principle lying behind the method of teaching by parables? See verses 10-17 and note below.

Note.—Our Lord found two kinds of hearers, those that were unreceptive, and those that heard and received. The latter would have been able to receive direct instruction without parable, but the former would have been hardened or would have turned away. So the Lord concealed the instruction in a story, and unreceptive hearers, carrying away the story, might perhaps one day awaken to realize the spiritual truth within it. Thus the parabolic method was a method of love, having a twofold aim, to carry those who heard and believed forward in their knowledge, and at the same time not to lose touch with those who at present did not understand.

Week 4. MATTHEW XIII. 24–XVII. 13

Day 1. Mt. xiii. 24-52.

(1) Today's portion consists of six parables. Note how they fall into three pairs, each pair illustrating different aspects of the kingdom.

(2) What facts about the judgment and the future life can you gather from our Lord's words?

(3) Verses 44-46 reveal two different types of entry into the kingdom. In what respects are they alike and in what different? Can you think of any people in Scripture who illustrate each type?

Notes.—(1) Verse 24. 'His field'; the field of the world belongs to the Son of Man. Cf. verse 37.

(2) Verse 25. 'Tares'; more exactly 'darnel' (R.V. mg.), which in the early stages of its growth closely resembles wheat. Cf. vii. 15.

(3) Verse 44. In ancient times men often hid their treasure in the earth, hoping to recover it later. Cf. Je. xli. 8. But circumstances might prevent their return and the treasure might lie undiscovered for a long time.

Day 2. Mt. xiii. 53–xiv. 12.

(1) What do we learn from the closing verses of chapter xiii of the nature and of the folly of prejudice? How does prejudice cause unbelief?

(2) How does the story of Herod enforce the teaching of such verses as v. 33-37 and xii. 34-37?

(3) Contrast Herod and John. What was the fundamental difference between the two men?

Day 3. Mt. xiv. 13-36.

(1) 'Love suffers long, and is kind', says St. Paul. How were these two qualities manifested by our Lord in today's portion: first towards the multitude, and then towards the disciples?

(2) Draw as many lessons as you can for the Christian life from verses 22-33 and, more especially, from Peter's walking upon the water. What was the reason for Peter's failure?

Day 4. Mt. xv. 1-20.

(1) In what three principal ways had the Pharisees gone wrong in their religion?

(2) Observe what stress our Lord lays upon the importance of the heart rather than the teaching or the outward actions of a man. Cf. v. 8, 28, xi. 29, xii. 34, xviii. 35, xxii. 37.

(3) According to the Lord's teaching the heart of man is defiled. How, then, can he be cleansed? Cf. Acts xv. 9; Heb. ix. 13, 14; 1 Jn. i. 7.

Day 5. Mt. xv. 21-39.

(1) What was outstanding in this woman's faith that Christ should call it 'great' (verse 28; cf. viii. 10)?

(2) The story is an illustration of the testing of faith. Is the Lord testing your faith in regard to some petition? If so, what should you do? Cf. Lk. xi. 8, xviii. 1; Heb. vi. 15, x. 36; 1 Pet. i. 7.

(3) From the fact that the people who saw the miracle of verses 30 and 31 'glorified the God of *Israel*' it would appear that they were, at least in the main, Gentiles. Cf. Mk. vii. 31, R.V. ('through the midst of the borders of Decapolis'). How could Jesus thus act in the light of verse 24? Does the answer lie in the word 'compassion' (verse 32)? Cf. Lk. xv. 20.

Notes.—(1) Verse 22. 'A woman of Canaan'; and therefore a Gentile.

(2) Verse 22. 'O Lord, thou Son of David.' Contrast the simple 'Lord' of verse 25. The woman had no claim upon Him as Son of David.

(3) Verse 29. Into a mountain; i.e. the high ground above the shore of the lake.

Day 6. Mt. xvi. 1-20.

(1) Verses 1-4. Notice the word 'tempting'. Does the incident not recall iv. 5-7? The near presence of Satan at this time is indicated also in verse 23. In the view of Jesus, what did this demand for signs reveal as to the spiritual condition of His critics?

(2) Comparing Peter's confession concerning Jesus with the general opinion about Him among the people, how would you bring out the vast difference between these two conceptions of Him?

(3) What three things does the Lord say to Peter in verses 17-

19? With verse 17, cf. Jn. vi. 37; 1 Cor. xii. 3; with verse 18, cf. 1 Cor. iii. 11; 1 Pet. ii. 4-6; and with verse 19, cf. xviii. 18; Jn. xx. 23. See also Notes (3) and (4) below.

Notes.—(1) Verse 1. 'The Pharisees . . . with the Sadducees.' Representatives of the two chief parties in the nation. The Pharisees were led by the scribes, and the Sadducees by the chief priests.

(2) Verse 4. 'Adulterous'; i.e. unfaithful to God. Cf. xii. 39; Mk. viii. 38.

(3) Verse 18. The view that Peter is the rock on which Christ said He would build His Church is in conflict with other Scriptures. Peter himself says that *Christ* is the foundation upon whom all who believe are built as living stones to form a spiritual house (1 Pet. ii. 4-6). The Roman Catholic church has erred here, as in the words 'This is My body', by a too literal and narrow interpretation. Our Lord did not say 'Thou art Peter, and upon thee will I build My church'. His meaning rather is 'Thou art well named Peter (=rock) because in the fact that I truly am what you have just declared Me to be, and because, by My Father's revealing of this to you, you have been brought to know and declare it, in this I find the rock upon which I will build My church —Myself the foundation, and you the first living stone to be built upon it'.

'The gates of hell.' That is, of Hades. This union between Christ and the living stones that form His Church will not be destroyed by death, but continue for ever; cf. Rev. i. 17, 18.

(4) Verse 19. The expressions 'the keys', 'binding', and 'loosing' were all commonly used among the Jews to signify the possession of authority. Jesus promises to Peter authority in the development of the kingdom of heaven upon earth, and the fulfilment of the promise is amply attested in the book of Acts and in the Epistles of Peter. See e.g. Acts ii. 37-39, v. 1-11, x. 46-48, xv. 7; 1 Pet. v. 1-4, etc. That this authority was not given to Peter only is clearly shown by xviii. 18. See Note there.

Day 7. Mt. xvi. 21–xvii. 13.

(1) Chapter xvi. 21-23. What had happened which made this new revelation possible? But notice how different still were the thoughts of Jesus from the thoughts of His followers. Contrast His 'must' with Peter's 'Be it far from thee, Lord'. Note, too, that the Lord detected in Peter's words the presence of Satan.

(2) Chapter xvi. 24-28. What does Jesus say about Himself in these verses, and what about the life of discipleship?

(3) Chapter xvii. 1-13. What evidences are there in these verses that Jesus was pursuing the path of God's will?

Week 5. MATTHEW XVII. 14–XXI. 22

Day 1. Mt. xvii. 14-27.

(1) What were the reasons for the powerlessness in the lives of the disciples? Do the same sins as theirs play a part in your spiritual life?

(2) Verses 24-27. 'Lest we should offend them.' What is the principle underlying Jesus' action? See note below; also 1 Cor. x. 32, xiii. 5b; 1 Pet. ii. 13, 14.

Notes.—(1) Verse 15. 'Lunatick'; literally 'moonstruck', that is, 'epileptic'; epilepsy being supposed to be caused by the moon. But there was in this case also demon possession.

(2) Verses 24, 25. See Ex. xxx. 11-16. The half shekel became in later times a yearly tax paid to the temple. Jesus' argument is that rulers do not take tax from their children, and therefore He and His followers, as the sons of God, were free; but it was better to waive personal rights rather than give offence.

Day 2. Mt. xviii. 1-14.

(1) Verses 1-5. What three important principles does Christ set forth in these verses in answer to the question of the disciples? State them in your own words.

(2) Verses 6-9. In verse 6 the Lord seems to pass from the actual child to think of weak and immature believers. How does He bring out in verses 6 and 7 the responsibility of those who cause such little ones to stumble?

(3) Verses 10-14. In these verses 'little ones' seems still to refer to believers. In what three ways does Christ show the value that each one of them has in the sight of God?

Notes.—(1) Verse 3. 'Be converted'; better 'turn', as in R.V. The meaning is 'turn from the ambition to be great'.

(2) Verse 10. In Jewish belief only the chiefest angels beheld the face of God. Our Lord's meaning is, therefore, that the 'little ones' of whom He speaks have powerful protectors.

Day 3. Mt. xviii. 15-35.

(1) In most quarrels there is wrong on both sides. In such a quarrel, one's duty is to seek reconciliation by confessing one's own fault (Jas. v. 16). But if, as is presupposed here, the wrong is done to us, and we are blameless, what course ought we, as Christians, to take? And for what end?

(2) In verses 18-20 the Lord is looking into the future, when He has returned to the Father. His disciples, He says, will be in such communion with Himself that their prayer and their action in His name shall be confirmed in heaven. Cf. Jn. xiv. 12-14. Do we really believe that God has given such authority and such promises to His children?

(3) How does the parable in verses 23-35 answer Peter's question in verse 21? What other lessons does it teach?

Note.—Verse 18. 'Binding' and 'loosing' mean 'forbidding' and 'allowing'. The Lord on earth exercised this power in regard to His kingdom, and He here promises to His disciples that when He has left them they, too, will have authority, as they speak and act in His name. The promise implies communion between Him in heaven and them on earth through the coming of the Holy Spirit (verse 20; Jn. xx. 22, 23).

Day 4. Mt. xix. 1-22.

(1) 1-12. Two questions concerning marriage are answered in these verses: (a) Is marriage a temporary arrangement which can be ended by divorce, or is it a relationship so close as to be, in God's intention, indissoluble, except, of course, by death? (b) Is the celibate life preferable to married life? What are the answers given by Jesus?

(2) How slow the disciples were to grasp their Master's outlook! Cf. xviii. 1-5. If the kingdom of heaven is composed of the childlike, what, in consequence, must be the King's attitude towards children?

(3) Ponder the incident of verses 16-21 in the light of vi. 24. In turning away from the counsel of Jesus, how did the young enquirer show the choice of his heart? What is your choice? Cf. Is. xxvi. 13.

Note.—Verse 17. Read as in R.V.

Day 5. Mt. xix. 23–xx. 16.

(1) xix. 23-26. Why are riches so great a hindrance to entering into the kingdom of God? See Lk. vi. 24, viii. 14, xii. 13-21, xvi. 19-31; 1 Tim. vi. 9, 10, 17; Jas. v. 1-6.

(2) What may we learn from xix. 27-30 (a) as to the *quality* of service that Christ approves, and (b) as to the generosity with which such service is rewarded? Cf. Jn. xii. 26.

(3) Peter's question in xix. 27 suggests that he was looking at the question of service and reward in too legal a spirit—so much service, so much reward. How does the Lord show in the parable of the householder, and in xix. 30 and xx. 16, that the legalistic spirit is not the spirit of the kingdom of heaven?

Notes.—(1) xix. 25, 26. The disciples still conceived salvation to rest on a basis of fulfilment of the law. If the rich, who had leisure and means to fulfil the law's requirements, did not succeed, who could be saved? Jesus' reply is that no one can be saved by his own efforts, but by God alone. Cf. Eph. ii. 8, 9.

(2) xix. 28. The regeneration, that is, when all things have been restored. Cf. Acts iii. 21; Rom. viii. 21.

(3) xx. 2. 'A penny a day'; the usual wage at the time.

(4) xx. 15. 'Is thine eye evil?' See vi. 22, 23, note.

Day 6. Mt. xx. 17-34.

(1) Look closely at this picture of Jesus, with the burden of the cross resting upon mind and heart, and yet meeting triumphantly every call and claim upon Him.

(2) What, in contrast, filled the hearts and minds of the disciples? See verses 20 and 21, and compare verse 24 and xviii. 1, xix. 27. How patiently the Lord deals with them! When and how was verse 23 actually fulfilled in the lives of the sons of Zebedee?

(3) With verse 28 compare Jn. xiii. 3-5; Phil. ii. 7; 1 Pet. i. 18, 19. What are the characteristics of greatness in the kingdom of God?

Notes.—(1) Verse 21. Cf. xix. 28.
(2) Verse 22. 'The cup'; cf. xxvi. 39.
(3) Verse 24. 'Moved with indignation'; indignant anger. The same word comes in xxvi. 8.

Day 7. Mt. xxi. 1-22.

(1) Discover from the narrative what we may learn of the thoughts (a) of the multitude, (b) of the disciples, (c) of the chief priests and scribes, and (d) of Jesus Himself on the day of His public entry into the city. What was the purpose and value of what He did that day?

(2) Contemplate the supreme courage of Jesus in taking action to cleanse the temple of the abuses that had become entrenched there under the patronage of the priests.

(3) Verses 18-22. Jerusalem with its unbelief was, on the one hand, like a barren fig tree, having a profession of religion, without its fruit, and, on the other hand, it was like a mountain, standing in Christ's way. What does Christ say can be done by the prayer of faith in regard to both these difficulties? Are we beginning to realize 'the exceeding greatness of His power to us-ward who believe' (Eph. i. 19) given us in Christ? Cf. xviii. 18, 19; Jn. xiv. 13, 14.

Week 6. MATTHEW XXI. 23–XXV

Day 1. Mt. xxi. 23-46.

(1) Men continually say they need more light (compare the continual demand for a sign in Christ's day). What do we learn in verses 23-27 about the conditions of illumination? Cf. Lk. xvi. 29, 30; Jn. vii. 17.

(2) What would you say from the parable in verses 28-32 are the essentials of repentance? Cf. iii. 8; 2 Cor. vii. 10, 11.

(3) What does the parable of verses 33-44 teach regarding (a) the motives of the husbandmen (i.e. the chief priests and scribes), and (b) the outcome and consequence of rejecting Christ?

Notes.—(1) Verse 42. The quotation is from the same Psalm as the Hosanna cries of xxi. 9, 15.

(2) Verse 43. 'A nation bringing forth the fruits thereof.' Some interpret this as referring to the Gentiles, others to the church. Cf. xvi. 18, 19; 1 Pet. ii. 8, 9.

(3) Verse 44. 'The distinction is between men who believe not in the Christ through misunderstanding, and those who reject Him through an evil heart of unbelief.' (*Exp. Gk. Test.*)

(4) Verse 46. 'Took Him for a prophet'; cf. xvi. 14, xxi. 11.

Day 2. Mt. xxii. 1-14.

The prophetic mood was upon Jesus in high degree in these days. In to-day's parable He describes the present and foresees the future progress of His kingdom.

(1) Verses 2 and 3 plainly refer to the time of His earthly ministry. What was God's purpose in sending His Son? Yet how was it requited by that generation? Cf. Jn. i. 11, iii. 19, v. 40.

(2) Verses 4-7 look forward to the period which culminated in the destruction of Jerusalem. In what two ways did those who received the invitation react towards it? Cf. Jn. xvi. 1-3.

(3) Verses 8-14 look forward further still to the ingathering of the Gentiles. How does the parable bring out that, while the invitation is now made free to all, God's demand for holiness is no less stringent under the gospel than under the law? Cf. Ps. xciii. 5; Zc. xiv. 20, 21; Rev. xix. 7, 8.

Day 3. Mt. xxii. 15-46.

(1) In verses 15-40 three questions are asked, and over against each is set our Lord's reply. Do you not marvel at His wisdom and insight into Scripture? Are we persevering in our own study of God's Word?

(2) Consider our Lord's teaching upon (a) our duty to the state, (b) the resurrection and the life to come, and (c) our duty towards God.

(3) Jesus Himself then put a question which His critics and enemies could not answer. What is the answer? See Rev. xxii. 16 ('the root and the offspring of David').

Day 4. Mt. xxiii.

(1) In verses 1-12 what things does Jesus condemn in the Pharisees and scribes, and what, in contrast, is to be the behaviour and disposition of His own followers? 1 Cor. xiii. 4, 5, clause by clause, is a commentary on our Lord's words. How does your life stand this test?

(2) What word does our Lord use seven times (in R.V. six times, see Note (2) below) in the seven woes which He pronounces upon the scribes and Pharisees to describe their character? By what other terms, also, does He describe them? Try to work out in detail why He spoke of them thus. Remembering that the scribes and Pharisees were the most religious people in the land, consider whether in our religious circle, or in our own life, we may not be in danger of coming under a like condemnation.

(3) Contemplate the revelation given in these verses of 'the wrath of the Lamb'. The judgment which Jerusalem had brought on herself was irrevocable, in spite of the love of Christ.

Notes.—(1) Verse 5. 'Make broad their phylacteries'; these were small boxes of leather, fastened to forehead or wrist, and containing passages of Scripture. 'Enlarge the borders.' That is, the tassels, four in number, attached to the foot of the outer robe. Our Lord did not condemn these practices, but only the exaggeration of them as a token of greater piety.

(2) Verse 14 is omitted in the R.V.

(3) Verse 23. Scrupulosity in tithing to the smallest herb combined with indifference in regard to judgment (or justice), mercy and faith.

(4) Verse 35. Zacharias, son of Barachias, should probably be 'son of Jehoiada' (2 Ch. xxiv. 20). Barachias is probably a scribal error. Luke's record says that our Lord said simply Zacharias. (See Lk. xi. 51.)

Day 5. Mt. xxiv. 1-42.

The teaching of this chapter was given in answer to the questions of the disciples, who, astonished at Jesus' statement of the coming destruction of the temple (verse 2), ask Him (a) when shall these things be? and (b) what shall be the sign of Thy coming, and of the end of the world (or age)? The disciples conceived all these events to be contemporaneous, but to the Lord it was not so. The chapter may be divided as follows: (a) verses 4-14; Jesus speaks of 'the end' (verses 6, 14) and what will lead up to it. His eye ranges over the whole course of history up to the end of the age. (b) Verses 15-28; Jesus speaks of the siege and destruction of Jerusalem, describing first its terrors (verses 15-22) and then distinguishing His coming from it (verses 23-28). There will be great religious excitement, with false Christs and prophets appearing, but His coming will not take place thus. (c) Verses 29-31; His coming is described. (d) Verses 32-42; Jesus speaks of the time of these events. First (verses 32-35) He speaks of the time of the destruction of Jerusalem. It will happen within that generation. Second (verses 36-42) He speaks of the time of His coming.

No one knows, save God the Father, when it will be; but it will be when men are not expecting it, and it will be sudden; therefore He says 'watch'.

(1) Make a list of what the Lord foresees will happen between the end of His life on earth and the end of this age (see verses 4-14). Notice especially verses 12, 13 and 14. How do they apply to the present time?

(2) What are to be the characteristics of the Christian, in view of his Lord's return, as depicted in today's portion?

Notes.—(1) Verse 15. The meaning is given more clearly in Lk. xxi. 20.

(2) Verse 27. 'The coming.' The Greek word Parousia is used four times in the chapter in verses 3, 27, 37, 39. The coming will not be in the wilderness or secret chamber (verse 26), but in the clouds of heaven (verse 30).

(3) Verses 29-31. Luke's Gospel shows that a period intervenes between the fall of Jerusalem and the second coming. See Lk. xxi. 24. Possibly Matthew regards the tribulation of the Jewish people as still continuing. The language of verse 29 is probably to be taken symbolically, as signifying great political commotions on the earth. Cf. Is. xiii. 9-11, xxxiv. 4, etc.

(4) Verses 40, 41. Illustrations of the suddenness of the coming.

Day 6. Mt. xxiv. 42–xxv. 13.

(1) In regard to the Lord's return, what do we know with certainty and what is left uncertain? In this situation, what should the believer's attitude be? Gather out the different words which the Lord uses to describe this.

(2) Does it matter what the believer's attitude is? See especially xxiv. 47, 51, xxv. 10-12.

(3) What caused the undoing of the foolish virgins, and wherein lay their failure? 'They that were ready went in' (verse 10, cf. xxiv. 44). What does the parable teach about the impossibility of repairing unreadiness at the last minute?

Notes.—(1) The 'house' in xxiv. 43 is a small dwelling with mud walls, which can be dug through; verse 45, however, refers to a large household with numerous servants.

(2) xxiv. 51. Mark the severity of the punishment, showing the importance which the Lord attaches to faithfulness.

(3) xxv. 3, 4. The 'lamps' were oil-holding receptacles with a wick, and were fastened to the top of a long pole. After burning for some hours the flame had burned low. The wise virgins had brought flasks of oil from which they could replenish their lamps.

Day 7. Mt. xxv. 14-46.

(1) In the parable of the talents what does the Lord commend in the first two of the three servants mentioned? The two men were not of equal capacity; but in what were they alike?

(2) The third servant, on the other hand, though bearing the name of servant and having some of his master's property in his care, showed no interest whatsoever in advancing his master's cause. How, therefore, was he treated on his master's return? What application has this to ourselves? See verse 29.

(3) What conclusion must we come to regarding the person of One who claims for Himself the right to decide the final destiny of men?

Notes.—(1) Verse 15. The 'talents' are often taken to represent natural gifts and abilities, but they are here distinguished from the natural ability of the servants. What 'goods' did the Lord entrust to His servants at His ascension? Cf. 1 Cor. xii. 4-7.

(2) Verse 26. The master might have contested the servant's conception of him, but instead of that he shows that even if that were his true character the servant ought to have done something to further his interests. He was thus condemned as unfaithful by his own confession.

(3) Verses 31-46. Many different views are taken of this majestic prophecy. The simplest and most straightforward is that it refers to Christ's return in glory (cf. verse 31 with xvi. 27), and that 'all the nations' means 'the whole world', who shall be gathered before Him in judgment. Compare also x. 40-42, xii. 48-50.

Week 7. MATTHEW XXVI–XXVIII

Day 1. Mt. xxvi. 1-19.

(1) 'He said' (verse 1) . . . 'but they said' (verse 5). Humanly speaking, whose word seemed likely to prevail? Yet whose word did prevail? Cf. Acts iv. 27, 28; Ps. xxxiii. 10, 11.

(2) Read verses 6-16 in the light of Lk. ii. 35b. What thoughts are in your heart towards Jesus as you consider the events of this week?

(3) 'My time is at hand' (verse 18; cf. verse 45; Jn. vii. 6, 8, 30, viii. 20, xiii. 1, xvii. 1). How far would you say it is true that 'He lived in order that He might die'?

Day 2. Mt. xxvi. 20-35.

(1) When Jesus said 'One of you shall betray me', what made the disciples say each in turn 'Is it I'? And when later He said 'All ye shall be offended in me this night', what made them answer in effect 'Not I'? Do we know such sudden changes of mood, and have we learned the difference between living by feelings and by faith?

(2) What was the purpose of the outward symbols in the institution of the Lord's Supper?

Day 3. Mt. xxvi. 36-56.

(1) The writer of the Epistle to the Hebrews connects our Lord's sufferings in Gethsemane with His appointment as High Priest (Heb. v. 5-9). What was the sacrifice which, as High Priest, He must offer? Cf. our Lord's prayer in verses 39 and 42 with Heb. x. 4-10.

(2) Consider in how many ways the disciples failed Jesus on the night of His betrayal. To what did the Lord Himself attribute their failure? Note what light and comfort our Lord found in Scripture (verses 31, 54, 56). Was not the disciples' failure in part due to their ignorance of Scripture, and if so, what lesson lies here for us?

Notes.—(1) Verse 38. The word 'watch' here and in the following verses means 'keep awake' (R.S.V. mg.).

(2) Verse 45. 'Sleep on now', etc.; better 'Are you still sleeping and taking your rest?' (R.S.V.).

(3) Verse 56. Cf. Ps. lxix. 20.

Day 4. Mt. xxvi. 57-75.

(1) Consider the thoughts of the disciples concerning Jesus (see e.g. verse 58, 'to see THE END') and the thoughts of the chief priests and elders (verses 65-68). Against this background contemplate the greatness of the prisoner in His whole bearing and in His declaration concerning Himself.

(2) Comparing verse 61 with Jn. ii. 19, 21, in what respects was the evidence of these two witnesses 'false'?

(3) In what ways did the downfall of Peter differ from that of Judas? See also xxvii. 3-5.

Notes.—(1) Verse 63. The High Priest put Jesus on oath, thus compelling a reply.

(2) Verse 64. 'Thou hast said'; cf. xxvii. 11 ('Thou sayest'). The words mean 'yes' (cf. Mk. xiv. 62), but they are probably intended to indicate that the sense which Jesus attached to the words was not that which the High Priest had in mind. Jesus was not a political Christ, and hence He goes on to speak of the manner in which He would reign, expressing Himself in Scripture language (see Ps. cx. 1; Dn. vii. 13).

'Nevertheless'; more simply, 'but', as in R.S.V.

'Hereafter'; better 'henceforth', as in R.V.

Day 5. Mt. xxvii. 1-31.

(1) Comparing these verses with 1 Pet. ii. 7, 8, what was the effect of contact with our Lord on (a) Judas, (b) Pilate?

(2) Consider also the powerful influences which were brought

to bear upon Pilate, and still more upon Judas, not to do to Jesus what they did do. What is it that leads men to act thus against their conscience and their better judgment?

(3) Read today's portion anew in the light of Is. liii. 3. What is our answer to the great question in verse 22?

Day 6. Mt. xxvii. 32-61.

(1) The story of our Lord's sufferings inevitably raises the question, Why did not God intervene? The chief priests' answer was that Jesus was not what He claimed to be, that He was a deceiver (verses 41-43, 63, cf. Jn. vii. 12), and therefore God would have nothing to do with Him. What, in your judgment, makes this answer untenable?

(2) On the other hand, the Christian answer is igiven in such passages as Is. liii. 5, 6. Do you believe that th s is the right answer? If so, what should be our response? Cf. Rom. xii. 1.

(3) Is it entirely true to say that God did not intervene? What evidences can you find that God was at work all through?

Note.—Verses 32-37. In these verses the pronoun 'they' refers to the soldiers in charge of the execution.

Day 7. Mt. xxvii. 62–xxviii.

(1) What was the reason for the great care which the chief priests and Pharisees took in making the sepulchre sure? How true was the word of Jesus in Lk. xvi. 30, 31!

(2) Note the foremost place taken by the women disciples in the story of the resurrection. They were the first to see the risen Lord and to worship Him. Was this because they were women or because they loved more? Cf. Gal. iii. 28; Jn. xiv. 21.

(3) xxviii. 18-20. Notice the word 'all' repeated four times. Are we living by faith in the supreme authority of our Lord (verse 18), walking in the experience of His presence (verse 20), and working to fulfil the threefold task He has submitted to us (verse 19)?

Notes.—(1) xxvii. 62. 'The preparation'; i.e. the day before the sabbath, which, being in Passover week, was a special sabbath.

(2) xxviii. 5. 'Fear not *ye*'; i.e. in contrast to the panic-stricken soldiers (verse 4).

(3) xxviii. 19. 'All the nations.' The commission extended to all the world (cf. Mk. xvi. 15).

(4) xxviii. 20. 'Alway'; literally 'all the days'. 'World'; literally 'age'.

I and II CHRONICLES

INTRODUCTION

(See New Bible Handbook, pp. 175-179)

THESE two books, which are really one whole, were composed at a much later date than the other historical books, and frequent reference is made to former writings not now possessed by us. The date is after the carrying away to Babylon (1 Ch. vi. 15) and after the decree of Cyrus ordering the return (2 Ch. xxxvi. 22-23), which decree is found also in the first chapter of Ezra. The literary style is similar to the books of Ezra-Nehemiah, which suggests that all belong to the same period.

The books of Chronicles are placed last in the Hebrew Bible, being separated from the other historical books, forming part of the section of the Hebrew Canon known as *Hagiographa* or Writings. The Hebrew title for the books of Chronicles is *The Words of the Days*, and the Greek is *Omissions*. The name Chronicles comes from Jerome. The theme of the books is the need for God as central in the life of the nation, and the frequent sad departure from Him in the history of the monarchy, together with occasional times of reformation under such kings as Jehoshaphat, Hezekiah and Josiah. After the death of Solomon (2 Ch. ix) the story of the southern kingdom alone is told, with only occasional references to the northern kingdom. The work of the prophets as witnesses to the truth of God, when kings and even priests corrupted it, is shown again and again, as is the faithfulness of God to the people of His choice. The interest of the writer centres very largely in the temple, its priesthood and its worship. See *Analysis*.

ANALYSIS

1 Chronicles

i–ix.	Chiefly genealogies.
x–xxix.	Events leading up to the building of the temple. Reign of David.

      x–xii. Death of Saul and accession of David. The exploits of his mighty men.

      xiii–xvi. The ark brought to Jerusalem—services arranged.

      xvii. David's desire to build a temple and Jehovah's answer.

      xviii–xx. David conquers and subdues neighbouring peoples.

Week 8. I Chronicles I–XVII

Day 1. I Ch. i–ix.

These chapters, which at first sight appear to be a mere wilderness of names, are seen on closer inspection to contain an orderly arrangement, like a garden divided into separate beds. The writer begins with the line of descent from Adam to Noah, and then gives the descendants of each of Noah's three sons (i. 1-23). Arriving thus at Abraham, there follow the sons of Ishmael, and of Keturah, and Isaac's two sons Israel and Esau, with a list of the descendants of Esau (i. 24-54). With chapter ii begins the list of Israel's sons, with their descendants. Judah comes first and is given the largest space (ii. 3-iv. 23); then Simeon (iv. 24-43), Reuben, Gad, and the half tribe of Manasseh (chapter v), Levi (chapter vi), Issachar (vii. 1-5), Benjamin (vii. 6-12), Naphtali (vii. 13), Manasseh (vii. 14-19), Ephraim (vii. 20-29), Asher (vii. 30-40). It will be noticed that two tribes are omitted. In chapter viii the descendants

Benjamin are given more fully, leading up to the family of Saul and his descendants. Chapter ix gives a list of inhabitants of Jerusalem, and repeats the genealogy of Saul as an introduction to the story of his death in chapter x. Amidst these lists of names are a number of passages which may be spiritually applied with profit to ourselves.

(1) Consider the prayer of Jabez (iv. 9-10). What is said of his character (cf. 1 Sa. ii. 30, last clause)? What were the four petitions of his prayer? What was the result? See Ps. lxxxi. 10.

(2) iv. 23. The king's potters. Consider the application to ourselves of the description of these potters that they 'dwelt with the king for his work'. Can these things be said of us spiritually and of our service? Cf. Jn. xiv. 23; 2 Cor. vi. 15.

(3) v. 18-22. The victory of Reuben, Gad, and the half tribe of Manasseh. To what causes is their victory ascribed, and how may this be applied to the Christian life? With verse 18 compare Eph. vi. 17b; 2 Tim. ii. 15; and with verse 20 compare Col. iv. 2; 1 Jn. v. 4.

Day 2. 1 Ch. x and xi.

(1) Chapter x is a sad story of failure. To what is Saul's failure ascribed? Are our own lives free from the sins which brought about Saul's downfall? Cf. Ps. lxxxi. 13, 14; Is. viii. 19, 20 (R.V.).

(2) What instances are given in chapter xi of the valour, love and loyalty of the men who followed David? How does our devotion to our Lord compare with it? See Acts xx. 22-24; 1 Cor. ix. 24-27; Phil. i. 20, 21.

Notes.—(1) x. 12. The *body* of Saul had been exposed on the city wall of Bethshan; see 1 Sa. xxxi. 10.

(2) xi. 8. 'Millo'; see the note on 2 Sa. v. 9 (Vol. II, p. 158).

Day 3. 1 Ch. xii.

(1) Observe the unity prevailing at this time among the followers of David—though drawn from so many different tribes—and also the diversity of gifts which were found among them. Make a list of these gifts and compare them with the gifts of the Spirit, as set forth in 1 Cor. xii. 4-11.

(2) What was the secret of the unity that prevailed?

(3) What qualities are commended in the men of Zebulun? Are these, in their spiritual application, characteristic of the Christian Church today? Are they true of you?

Notes.—(1) Verse 15. The Gadites forded the Jordan when in flood and put to rout the people in the valleys on both sides of the river.

(2) Verse 18. 'The Spirit came upon Amasai'; literally 'clothed himself with Amasai'. This Amasai is probably the same as Amasa of ii. 17; 2 Sa. xvii. 25, xx. 10.

Day 4. 1 Ch. xiii and xiv.

(1) The story in chapter xiii will repay reflection. Was Uzza alone guilty, or was the spirit of deep reverence lacking also in king and people? Was it too much like a heathen idol procession? What lesson would the judgment upon Uzza impress upon the people? Cf. Heb. xii. 28, 29.

(2) The Philistines were not willing to submit to the ascendancy of David, and three times made an all-out effort to regain the upper hand. What may we learn from the way in which David met the challenge?

Notes.—(1) xiii. 6. The power and majesty of God are emphasized, as also His presence. Cf. the words 'before God' twice repeated in verses 8 and 10.
(2) xiv. 15. 'A sound of going'; better the 'sound of marching', as in R.V.

Day 5. 1 Ch. xv–xvi. 6.

(1) What reason does David assign for the failure of the first attempt to bring the ark to Jerusalem?

(2) Comparing chapter xv with chapter xiii, what was there common to both processions, and what peculiar to the second?

(3) 'With joy' (verse 16; see also verses 25, 28, 29). What made David so greatly to rejoice? What did the ark stand for in his eyes?

Notes.—(1) xv. 20. 'On Alamoth' may mean 'for the women's voices'; and 'on Sheminith' (verse 21), 'for the men's voices'. Cf. Ps. lxviii. 25.
(2) xv. 21. 'To excel'; better, 'to lead', as in R.V.

Day 6. 1 Ch. xvi. 7-43.

(1) Verses 8-22. What should be the response of God's people in return for all His goodness? Make a list of all the things the Psalmist calls upon them to do.

(2) Verses 23-33. Here the Psalmist looks beyond Israel, and summons all nations to worship Jehovah. What various aspects of Jehovah's greatness does he declare?

(3) Verses 34-36. A closing call to Israel to continue in prayer and praise. Are our hearts thus filled with thoughts of God's greatness and goodness, and our lips with His praise?

Notes.—(1) Verse 7. 'This psalm'; these words are not in the Hebrew, and are omitted in the R.V.

(2) Verses 37-42. Distinguish between those who were to lead the praise in connection with the ark in Jerusalem, as given in verses 37, 38, and those under Zadok who were to serve in the tabernacle at Gibeon, referred to in verses 39-42.

Day 7. 1 Ch. xvii.

(1) From this chapter and other passages where Nathan is mentioned (2 Sa. xii. 1-15, 25; 1 Ki. i *passim*, iv. 5) work out what an important place he had in the lives of David and of Solomon. The revelation here made to him and through him to David is one of the chief Messianic prophecies in the Old Testament, and had a profound influence upon the development of the Messianic hope (cf. e.g. Ps. lxxxix. 26, 27; Lk. i. 33; Heb. i. 5).

(2) In what sense did God deny David's desire, in what way modify it, and in what way answer it above all that David asked or thought? Note especially verses 4, 10b, 12a.

Week 9. 1 CHRONICLES XVIII–XXIX

Day 1. 1 Ch. xviii–xx.

(1) What indications do you find in chapter xviii of David's inward attitude towards God, and what in turn did God do for him?

(2) How do chapters xix and xx show what grave consequences may arise out of a misunderstanding, and what retribution may result from an act of folly?

(3) What good qualities are seen in Joab in today's portion? How, then, did he come to the sad end described in 1 Ki. ii. 31, 32, 34?

Notes.—(1) xx. 1. Kings went out to battle about the beginning of the Hebrew year, that is, about the end of March.

(2) xx. 3. Opinions differ as to what exactly is meant. Moffatt translates here and in 2 Sa. xii. 31 'Whom he set to work with saws and iron picks, and axes'. Others think that David punished the Ammonites with physical torture. Such things were done in ancient warfare (cf. Amos i. 3), but there is no other passage which attributes such cruelties to David.

Day 2. 1 Ch. xxi–xxii. 1.

The victories which David had won no doubt tended to engender pride, and Satan, observing this, sought to show that David, notwithstanding his proposed piety, was no different from others (cf. Jb. i. 9-12, ii. 3-7; Lk. xxii. 31). God, in His wisdom, permitted this (2 Sa. xxiv. 1), and turned it to good.

(1) Consider how the numbering of the people, in the circumstances of the time, might be displeasing to God. Cf. Je. xvii. 5.

(2) What evidences do you find in the chapter that David's repentance, when his eyes were opened to his sin, was deep and and genuine? See especially 8, 16b-17, 19, 24. Cf. 2 Cor. vii. 11.

(3) What two proofs are there in today's portion of God's forgiving mercy? See especially verse 15, verse 18 with xxii. 1, and 26b. Observe how God turned the incident into blessing by using it to show David the site of the temple. Cf. verse 18, xxii. 1; 2 Ch. iii. 1.

Note.—Verse 25. The price David paid is very much larger than that of 2 Sa. xxiv. 24, but the passage in Samuel speaks only of the threshing floor and the oxen, whereas the purchase now made includes 'the place of the threshing floor', that is, the whole area of the top of the hill.

Day 3. 1 Ch. xxii. 2-19.

The thought of building a house of the Lord had been in David's mind, but now the way for action was open. Today's portion tells (a) of the abundance of what he prepared; (b) of his charge to Solomon; and (c) of his charge to the leaders of the tribes.

(1) What may we learn from David's high conception of the kind of building that alone would be worthy (verse 5), and from the abundance of his preparations? Contrast the spirit of the people in Malachi's day (Mal. i. 6-8).

(2) David's charge to Solomon is rich in instruction. What lessons may be learned from verses 8-10, and from David's willing acceptance of God's decision that not he, but Solomon, should build the temple? Cf. 1 Cor. xii. 21; also Acts xxii. 17-21 with Gal. ii. 9. What did David lay down for Solomon as the all-important secrets of success?

(3) In his charge to the leaders of the tribes, what motive does David use to stir them to action (verse 18), and what does he first call upon them to do before undertaking the task of building (verse 19)? Cf. 2 Cor. viii. 5.

Notes.—(1) Verse 2. 'Strangers'; i.e. non-Israelites; cf. 2 Ch. ii. 17.

(2) Verse 14. 'Here have I prepared, with great pains, nine million six hundred thousand pounds' weight of gold, ninety-six million pounds' weight of silver, and bronze and iron past all weighing for their amount' (Moffatt).

INTRODUCTORY NOTE TO CHAPTERS XXIII–XXVII

THESE five chapters describe how David and the leaders of the tribes organized before David's death the administration of the kingdom. The first matter taken in hand was the ministry of the priests and Levites, who had charge of the temple and its worship and also administered judgment. This is set forth in chapters xxiii-xxvi. Chapter xxiii speaks of the Levites as a whole, chapter xxiv of the priests (verses 1-19) and their attendants (verses 20-31); chapter xxv of the choirs; chapter xxvi of the porters (verses 1-19), and of the officers and judges (verses 20-32). Then in chapter xxvii are given in lesser detail the civil and military leaders of the nation other than Levites.

Day 4. 1 Ch. xxiii and xxiv.

Chapter xxiii, after telling of the assembly at which these matters were decided (verse 2), first gives the division of the Levites according to their work (verses 3-5), and then their divisions according to families or houses, as descended respectively from the three sons of Levi—from Gershon (verses 7-11), from Kohath (verses 12-20), and from Merari (verses 21-23). The remainder of the chapter defines their duties. Chapter xxiv speaks of those who served within the temple, distinguishing between the sons of Aaron, who were priests (verses 1-19), and the rest who were attendants of the priests (verses 20-31). Together these made up the 24,000 of xxiii. 4a.

(1) What were the special duties of the priests? See xxiii. 13; also Ex. xxx. 7-8; Dt. xxi. 5; Nu. vi. 23. See also note below.

(2) What were the duties of other Levites who were not sons of Aaron? What part of their former duties were now no longer necessary, and why? See xxiii. 25-32.

(3) Why has all this elaborate organization passed away? Cf. Heb. vii. 11-25. What has taken its place? Cf. Heb. viii. 1, 2; 1 Pet. ii. 9; Rev. i. 6, v. 10.

Note.—Verse 13. 'That he should sanctify'; better, 'to sanctify him as most holy, him and his sons for ever', as in R.V.mg. The burning of incense implies also the offering up of the blood of the atonement. See Ex. xxx. 10; Lv. xvi. 12-14.

Day 5. 1 Ch. xxv–xxvii.

These chapters record the family divisions and the work of (a) the 4,000 choristers mentioned in xxiii. 4, 5 (see xxv), (b) the 4,000 doorkeepers (xxvi. 1-19), and (c) the 6,000 officers and judges (xxvi. 20-32). All these were Levites. Chapter xxvii records the leaders of the tribes, the commanders of the monthly courses, and the chief officers of state.

(1) Who were the three chief leaders of praise? See xxv. 1, also vi. 33, 39, 44, xv. 16, 17. Why is their ministry of praise called 'prophesying'? Does it imply that inspired praise may speak for God no less than preaching? Cf. Eph. v. 18-20.

(2) Amidst the many differences of function and service described in these chapters, do you find any suggestion that one

form of service was more necessary or more honourable than another? If not, is the same true also of Christian service? Cf. Eph. iv. 1-7, 11, 12; 1 Cor. xii. 18-21.

Notes.—(1) xxv. 1. 'The captains of the host'; the phrase seems to refer here to those in charge of the temple staff, 'the authorities of the temple' (Moffatt).

(2) xxv. 3. 'Jeduthun', elsewhere called 'Ethan'. See vi. 44, xv. 17, 19.

(3) xxvi. 1. 'Porters'; better, 'gatekeepers'. As guardians of the temple and the storehouse they rendered important service.

(4) xxvi. 29. 'Officers and judges'. The officers collected the tithes and other revenue and the judges gave judgment in matters of law.

(5) xxvii. 1. 'The courses'. It would appear that David had at his command a force of 24,000 for each month of the year, each course being under a trusted leader.

Day 6. 1 Ch. xxviii.

When David had done all he could in his private and personal capacity in preparation for the building of the temple, he summoned an assembly of the leaders in all departments of the nation's life to commend the scheme to them, and as the next chapter shows was greatly gratified by their response.

(1) 'As for me, I had in mine heart to . . . but God said unto me, "Thou shalt not" ' (verses 2 and 3). Have we known some such experience in our service of God? How does David bring out that God's plan was far better?

(2) There are two charges to Solomon in today's portion, in verses 9-10 and 20-21. Considering them together, what was to be Solomon's first duty, what the character of the God with whom he had to do, what the ground of his confidence, and what consequently the manner and spirit of his service?

(3) Have we also not been given a pattern for our life and service? Cf. Mt. xi. 29; Jn. xiii. 14, 15; 1 Pet. ii. 21b.

Notes.—(1) Verse 12. 'By the spirit'; it would seem better, in view of verse 19, to translate this 'by the Spirit'.

(2) Verse 19. Notice the distinct claim here made that the pattern of the temple and of its service was given to David by revelation.

Day 7. 1 Ch. xxix.

(1) What did David ask of the people, and what were the grounds of his appeal? See verses 1-5. What guidance may we find in his words for any appeal we may make, as, for example, for foreign missions?

(2) What three characteristics of the people's giving are specially emphasized? Cf. 2 Cor. viii. 3, ix. 7.

(3) Consider in David's prayer (verses 10-19) (a) what he says

of God, (b) what he says of man and of his own attitude of heart, (c) what he prayed for.

Week 10. 2 CHRONICLES I–XII

Day 1. 2 Ch. i and ii.

(1) How did Solomon inaugurate his reign? Cf. Mi. vi. 6-8; Ps. l. 9-15.

(2) How do Solomon's request (i. 10) and God's response illustrate Mt. vi. 33?

(3) 'Now Solomon purposed' (ii. 1, R.V.). What is your purpose in regard to your service of God? Observe in this second chapter with what zeal and practical wisdom Solomon prepared to execute his purpose.

Notes.—(1) i. 3. 'The tabernacle of the congregation'. This was the tabernacle used in the wilderness. After the Israelites entered Canaan, it was first pitched at Shiloh (Jos. xviii. 1), then moved to Nob (1 Sa. xxi. 1, 6), and thence to Gibeon. Later Solomon brought it to Jerusalem (v. 5), where it was probably stored and finally perished.

(2) ii. 13. 'Of Huram my father's'. Better, 'even Huram my father', as in R.V.; the term 'my father' being equivalent to 'my trusted adviser' (Moffatt). So also in iv. 16. Cf. Gn. xlv. 8.

Day 2. 2 Ch. iii–v. 1.

Today's portion describes the temple and its furnishings: first, the site and date of building (iii. 1-2); second, the holy place (called 'the greater house') and porch (iii. 3-7); third, the holy of holies (called 'the most holy house'), with its cherubim and veil (iii. 8-14) then the two pillars in front of the porch (iii. 15-17); and finally the brazen altar, the 'sea', the lavers, the candlesticks, the tables of shewbread, the golden altar of incense, and all the various vessels and instruments (iv).

(1) All that human skill and wealth could do (note how many times the word 'gold' occurs in these chapters) was done. Yet it was still inadequate. Why? See Heb. ix. 1-10, which, though spoken of the tabernacle, is equally applicable to the temple.

(2) Solomon's temple has long since passed away (see xxxvi. 19), and the temples that succeeded it also. Is there, then, today a place where men may draw nigh to God? And if so, where is it? See Heb. x. 19-22; Eph. ii. 13, 18. 'Let us then draw nigh'.

Notes.—(1) iii. 3. 'The first measure'; a reference to the cubit in use before the exile, which was a handbreadth longer than that used later.

(2) iii. 4. 'An hundred and twenty'. The original reading was probably

twenty cubits'. It is not known how the figure 'an hundred' crept in, but the porch could not have towered to such a height above the building (cf. 1 Ki. vi. 2; also verse 15 below).

(3) iii. 6. 'Parvaim'; a place not known, but supposed by some to be in Arabia.

(4) iii. 16. 'As in the oracle'; more probably, 'like a necklace'.

(5) iv. 20. 'Before the oracle'; literally, 'before the innermost part', that is, 'before the holy of holies' or 'the inmost shrine' (Moffatt). So also in v. 7, 9.

Day 3. 2 Ch. v. 2–vi. 11.

(1) This was one of the great days in Israel's history. How does Solomon interpret its significance in vi. 1-11?

(2) We, who belong to the new Covenant, are ourselves the temple of God (1 Cor. iii. 16, vi. 19). Is there any parallel between the place given here to the ark and the place we should give to Christ in our hearts? What is the ground of Christian praise and what corresponds to the glory which 'filled the house'?

(3) Is there not also a typical significance in this day of days, pointing forward to Christ's return? Cf. e.g. Eph. ii. 20-22; Col. iii. 1-4.

Notes.—(1) v. 5. See i. 3, note.

(2) v. 9. Read as in R.V. and cf. Ex. xxv. 15. Comparing what is said here with 1 Ki. viii. 8, it would appear that the ark was laid in the centre of the holy of holies, with the staves projecting outwards so that they could be seen 'from the holy place' in the darkness of the inner shrine.

(3) v. 11, 12. 'Did not then wait by course'; normally the priests were divided into twenty-four courses, which served in turn (1 Ch. xxiv. 7-18); but on this occasion all the priests were in attendance, and also all the choristers.

Day 4. 2 Ch. vi. 12-42.

(1) On what grounds does Solomon base his prayer? See verses 14-15 and 42. What three main petitions does he present in verses 16-21, and into what seven specific requests does he expand the third of these?

(2) What conditions does Solomon's prayer suggest as being essential to effective prayer?

Day 5. 2 Ch. vii and viii.

(1) God's immediate answer to Solomon's prayer is given in vii. 1-3. Cf. Lv. ix. 24; Jdg. vi. 21, xiii. 19-20; 1 Ki. xviii. 38; 1 Ch. xxi. 26. What effect had it upon the people? Does your heart echo their words of praise as you reflect upon God's mercies?

(2) But God gave also a further answer to Solomon privately in the form of a promise and a warning (vii. 12-22). Observe care-

fully the conditions upon which Solomon's petitions were granted. Reflect also how literally the warning was fulfilled in Israel's later history.

Day 6. 2 Ch. ix and x.

(1) What was the Queen of Sheba's testimony (verse 6)? Has this been your experience of Christ? Cf. Phil. iii. 8.

(2) Wherein did Solomon, notwithstanding all his wisdom, and wealth, and outward glory, fail? In your answer refer to Dt. vi. 4, 5 and Lv. xix. 18 quoted by our Lord in Mt. xxii. 34-40. For example, Dt. vi. 5 with 1 Ki. xi. 4, and Lv. xix. 18 with 2 Ch. x. 4. How does our life stand in the light of these tests?

(3) What led Rehoboam to make such a disastrous mistake? What did he lack that Solomon possessed? Cf. 1 Ki. iii. 28.

Day 7. 2 Ch. xi and xii.

(1) What, according to the Chronicler, was the fundamental fault in Rehoboam's life? Cf. Jas. i. 8.

(2) Observe how one man of God twice profoundly influenced king and nation. What was the secret of his power, and what parallel is there between his calling and that of a Christian today?

(3) What lesson did God design to teach by means of Shishak's invasion? In what ways is God's service better than bondage to the world? Write down as many points as you can.

Notes.—(1) xi. 14-15. See 1 Ki. xii. 25-33.

(2) xi. 23. 'He desired many wives'. Better, 'He sought for them (his sons) many wives', as in R.V. 'He made many marriages for them' (Moffatt). The number of his sons was an embarrassment to Rehoboam. Therefore he dispersed them, and sought to keep them contented.

(3) xii. 2. 'Shishak king of Egypt'. Shishak's invasion of Judah and the submission of Rehoboam are recorded not only here, but also in a temple at Karnak in Egypt.

Week 11. 2 CHRONICLES XIII–XXIV

Day 1. 2 Ch. xiii and xiv.

Today's portion contains two signal instances of victory through faith.

(1) xiii. Jeroboam had the advantages of numbers (verse 3) and of military skill (verse 13), and he, too, had received promises from God (cf. 1 Ki. xi. 29-39). What, then, gave Judah the victory? Cf. verse 18 with 1 Ki. xii. 28-33.

(2) **xiv.** Consider Asa's position over against the huge army of the Ethiopian king. Is God as near and real to you, and as strong and mighty as He was to Asa? What is the connection between xiv. 2-4 and xiv. 11, 12? Cf. 1 Jn. iii. 21, 22, v. 3, 4. If Asa had not set God and His commandments in the forefront of his endeavours, could he have prayed with the same confidence or won so great a victory? Observe that faith provided for Asa a place of rest, a source of courage, and a stimulus to action (xiv. 11).

Notes.—(1) xiii. 5. 'By a covenant of salt'. That is, a binding covenant, not to be broken; cf. Nu. xviii. 19.

(2) xiii. 15. 'Gave a shout'; a religious battle-cry; cf. Jos. vi. 10, 20; Jdg. vii. 20, 21.

(3) xiv. 11. 'It is nothing with Thee to help', etc.; the R.V. gives here another and probably more exact rendering.

Day 2. 2 Ch. xv and xvi.

Today's portion tells the story of the remainder of Asa's reign. The victory over Zerah led, under prophetic guidance, to a still more vigorous religious reformation. A wave of revival swept the country, culminating in a renewed covenant with Jehovah. Yet, after all this, Asa in his last years became a backslider.

(1) Note how deeply Azariah's message influenced king and nation. Cf. xi. 2, 4. Can you find in the prophet's words (a) a fundamental principle of divine government, (b) illustration of the working of this principle in the facts of Israel's national history (as, for example, in the book of Judges), (c) an exhortation, and (d) a promise?

(2) Note in chapter xv the zeal and thoroughness with which idolatry was stamped out. What lessons are taught us in verse 15? Cf. Ps. xxxii. 11; Je. xxix. 13; Mt. xi. 29.

(3) On behalf of whom does the Lord show Himself strong? What do His eyes see as they gaze into your heart? What did Asa lose by failing to trust in God? See xvi. 7b.

Notes.—(1) xv. 3. 'For a long season'; better, 'for long seasons', as in R.V. The reference is to Israel's history.

(2) xv. 8. The LXX here reads Azariah, as in verse 1.

(3) xv. 16. Maachah seems to have been Asa's grandmother (1 Ki. xv. 2), and to have continued as queen mother during Asa's reign. As such she would enjoy a position of great influence.

(4) 'An idol in a grove'; better, 'an abominable image for Asherah', as in R.V. mg. The 'Asherah' was properly a sacred tree or pole beside the altar of an idol shrine, but seems here to be used as the name of a goddess, perhaps 'Ashtoreth'.

Day 3. 2 Ch. xvii and xviii.

(1) The Chronicler gives four chapters to the reign of Jehoshaphat, who was one of the best of the kings of Judah. What, according to chapter xvii, were the reasons for his prosperity? Note the word 'therefore' in verse 5. What method did Jehoshaphat introduce to give religious instruction to the people?

(2) Contrast the character of Jehoshaphat and Ahab.

(3) What are the qualifications of a true prophet, and how does Micaiah illustrate them? Cf. Mal. ii. 5-7. See also xvi. 10.

Notes.—(1) xvii. 3. 'Baalim'; better, 'the Baalim', as in R.V. That is, the idols, by whom the people were so often attracted.

(2) xvii. 6. 'His heart was lifted up'; i.e. his heart was full of desire and longing; cf. La. iii. 41.

Day 4. 2 Ch. xix and xx.

(1) In the beginning of Jehoshaphat's reign he continued the policy of maintaining fortified cities for defence against Israel. But later he made peace with Israel through a marriage alliance (xviii. 1, xxi. 6). How was this alliance with Ahab rebuked, and on what grounds? Cf. 2 Cor. vi. 14; also xx. 35-37 below.

(2) After this rebuke, what further steps did Jehoshaphat take to establish true religion in the land?

(3) When peril came, what did Jehoshaphat do first? What impresses you most in this story?

Notes.—(1) xix. 11. The last words of the verse should be 'The Lord be with the good' (as in R.V.), or 'with each honest man' (Moffatt).

(2) xx. 1. 'Other beside the Ammonites'; see R.V. mg.

(3) xx. 2. 'En-gedi'; on the western shore of the Dead Sea, not far from Jerusalem.

(4) xx. 16. 'Ziz . . . Jeruel'; places not now known.

Day 5. 2 Ch. xxi–xxii. 9

(1) Enunciate the sins here recorded of Jehoram.

(2) Show how the low estate of Judah under Jehoram and Ahaziah is directly traceable to the mistaken step of Jehoshaphat as recorded in xviii. 1.

Day 6. 2 Ch. xxii. 10–xxiii.

Today's portion relates how a great danger to Judah was averted. The story may be summed up under three words: planning, action, success.

(1) The period of planning. Why had Jehoiada to wait seven years? What lesson may we learn here for ourselves? Cf. Hab. ii. 3.

(2) The time of action. Observe how thoroughly organized the whole affair was. Would you say that careful planning and organization are equally required in the service of Christ?

(3) Success. Jehoiada, in the hour of success, was not content with half measures. How did he follow up his victory? See verses 16-20.

Notes.—(1) xxiii. 2, 3. This was a preliminary gathering, secretly convened in the temple, in which all present pledged their loyalty to the boy king.

(2) xxiii. 11. 'The testimony'; that is, the book of the law; cf. Dt. xvii. 18-20.

(3) xxiii. 14. 'Have her forth of the ranges'; better, 'have her forth between he ranks', as in R.V.

Day 7. 2 Ch. xxiv.

(1) In what state was the temple when Joash came to the throne, and how had this come about? What steps were taken to collect funds, and with what negative result? What other method was then introduced which was abundantly successful? Cf. Ex. xxxv. 22-24, xxxvi. 3, 6. Ought we to learn from this not to be too stereotyped in our methods?

(2) How does the story of Joash illustrate the perils that beset weakness of character? Joash leaned upon others: first upon Jehoiada, who led him in right ways; then upon the princes, who led him in wrong ways. Are you learning to lean, not upon human support, but upon God Himself? Cf. 2 Tim. ii. 1.

(3) Why was the stoning of Zachariah a peculiarly flagrant crime?

Notes.—(1) Verse 16. This was a signal and unique honour.

(2) Verse 25. 'In great diseases'; possibly as a result of his wounds.

Week 12. 2 Chronicles xxv-xxxvi

Day 1. 2 Ch. xxv.

(1) What would you say was the chief fault in Amaziah's character? How does the chapter illustrate the Chronicler's description of him in verse 2? See, on the one hand, verses 4 and 7-10; also xxvi. 4; and, on the other, verses 14-16 and 27. Cf. Je. xvii. 9.

(2) How does Amaziah's career, with its gradual drift away from God, show the peril of a half-hearted loyalty to Christ? Compare the story of Demas in the New Testament (Phm. 24; Col. iv. 14; 2 Tim. iv. 10).

Notes.—(1) Verse 2. 'Not with a perfect heart'; i.e. not wholeheartedly. Cf. 1 Ki. xi. 4.

(2) Verse 8. The meaning is that if Amaziah is set upon his present course, let him pursue it; but it will end in defeat, for God will be against him.

(3) Verse 10. The hired soldiers had been hoping for loot and plunder, hence their anger. Cf. verse 13.

Day 2. 2 Ch. xxvi–xxviii.

Today's portion tells the story of three kings of Judah: Uzziah, Jotham and Ahaz. Uzziah proved himself a man of great gifts, as a military leader (xxvi. 6-8), as a builder (xxvi. 9), in agriculture (xxvi. 10), and in administration (xxvi. 11-15). During his reign the kingdom of Judah reached a high degree of prosperity, and this continued through the reign of his son Jotham (xxvii. 3-6). But all was frittered away by the weakness and folly of Jotham's son Ahaz (xxviii. 19).

(1) How was it revealed that in Uzziah's heart, notwithstanding his piety (xxvi. 5), there lurked the same evil tendency that had marred the life and reign of his father Amaziah before him? With xxvi. 16 cf. xxv. 19; Dt. xvii. 18-20. What forms might his sin take today?

(2) How did the sin of Ahaz affect (a) God, (b) His people, (c) himself?

(3) In the midst of a godless age the actions, first of Oded the prophet, and then of the men mentioned in xxviii. 12, are conspicuously noble. What may we learn from their example? Cf. 1 Tim. v. 20.

Notes.—(1) xxvi. 5. 'Zechariah'; not otherwise known. 'The visions of God'; see R.V. mg.

(2) xxvi. 18. See Nu. xvi. 40, xviii. 7.

Day 3. 2 Ch. xxix–xxxi. 1.

The story of Hezekiah's reign occupies four chapters, as did that of an earlier godly king, Jehoshaphat.

(1) On ascending the throne Hezekiah acted at once with great energy and on a definite plan. Note the sense of urgency running through today's portion. What period of time does it cover? Cf. 1 Sa. xxi. 8; Ec. ix. 10.

(2) Politically, the nation was in a bad way (cf. xxviii. 16-21). But with what did Hezekiah begin, and on what grounds? See xxix. 3-11; also xxx. 1-9. What followed the cleansing of the temple? What is the spiritual significance of the sacrifices and of the *order* in which they were offered (see specially xxix. 24, 27, 31)?

(3) What evidence do you find in chapter xxx that this celebration of the Passover was not merely an outward form, but be-

tokened a genuine turning back to God? What may we learn as to the signs of true revival? Cf. vii. 13, 14.

Notes.—(1) xxix. 25. See R.V. The meaning is that David's arrangements for the praise in the temple worship were by commandment of the Lord through His prophets.

(2) xxx. 2-3, 13, 15. The king availed himself of the provision in the law which allowed the Passover to be kept in the second month, instead of the first (see Nu. ix. 10, 11). Otherwise they would have had to wait a year. The great national Passover held by Josiah was in the first month. See xxxv. 1.

(3) xxx. 5. 'Of a long time'; better, 'in great numbers', as in R.V.

(4) xxx. 27. 'The priests the Levites'; the LXX has 'the priests and the Levites', as in verse 25.

Day 4. 2 Ch. xxxi. 2–xxxii.

(1) Observe the thoroughness with which Hezekiah acted in all matters connected with religion. How far was this the secret of his success? See especially xxxi. 20, 21; cf. Rom. xii. 11; Col. iii. 23.

(2) Enumerate the lessons that we can learn from the way in which Hezekiah met opposition.

Notes.—(1) xxxi. 20. 'Truth'; better, 'faithful', as in R.V.

(2) xxxii. 1. 'And the establishment thereof'; better, 'and this faithfulness', as in R.V. This reference to Hezekiah's faithfulness (xxxi. 20) is introduced to show that the coming of Sennacherib was not because Hezekiah had sinned.

(3) xxxii. 8. Cf. Is. xxxii. 2.

(4) xxxii. 31. 'The wonder that was done'; see verse 24 (R.V. mg.) and 2 Ki. xx. 1-11.

Day 5. 2 Ch. xxxiii.

Manasseh's story is like that of the prodigal son in our Lord's parable. Unfortunately his son followed his father in his wickedness but not in his repentance.

(1) Make a list of Manasseh's idolatrous deeds, as described in verses 3-9. It has been termed 'a very delirium of idolatry' and was done in the face of protest and rebuke (verses 10, 18).

(2) What means did God use to bring Manasseh to his senses, and what may we learn from this as to one of the purposes of human suffering?

(3) What marks of true repentance are seen in Manasseh after his restoration?

Notes.—(1) Verse 6. A reference to human sacrifice in honour of the god Molech; cf. 2 Ki. xxiii. 10; Je. vii. 31.

(2) Verse 14. 'Ophel'; a mound south of the temple; cf. xxvii. 3.

Day 6. 2 Ch. xxxiv and xxxv.

The outstanding events of Josiah's reign, as recorded in today's portion, are (i) his purging of the land from idols (xxxiv. 3-7); (ii) his repair of the temple and finding of the book of the law (xxxiv. 8-28); (iii) a renewed covenant with God (xxxiv. 29-33); (iv) the holding of a great national Passover (xxxv. 1-19); and (v) the king's untimely death (xxxv. 20-27).

(1) What was the effect of the finding of the book of the law (a) upon Josiah, and (b) through him upon the nation? Cf. Ps. cxix. 59, 60. What effect is the Word of God having upon your life?

(2) What does xxxiv. 23-28 teach as to the inevitable consequences of sin, whether immediate or delayed?

(3) At what age did Josiah begin to seek after God? What would you say were the outstanding features in his character?

Notes.—(1) xxxiv. 4 (R.V.). 'The sun images'; probably pillars to the sun god.

(2) xxxiv. 6. 'With their mattocks round about'. The text seems doubtful (see R.V. mg.). Some think the original text was 'he destroyed their houses round about'. That is, the houses of the idols, as in 2 Ki. xxiii. 19.

(3) xxxiv. 12. 'And other of the Levites', etc.; better, 'And the Levites, all skilled in instruments of song'. In this and the next verse emphasis is laid on the fact that only Levites were engaged to supervise the temple repairs.

(4) xxxiv. 14. 'A book of the law', etc.; better, 'the book', etc., as in R.V. Cf. Dt. xxxi. 26.

(5) xxxv. 3. It is usually assumed that the ark had been taken out of the holy of holies during the repairs and that the Levites were now bidden to restore it, with the assurance that they would not again be asked to undertake this work. Cf. 1 Ch. xxiii. 26.

Day 7. 2 Ch. xxxvi.

(1) Neither the actions of the great powers, Egypt (verse 4) and Babylon (verse 6), nor the doings of the remaining kings of Judah were of interest to the Chronicler. What is the one outstanding event in this chapter that overshadows all else? With verse 19 cf. vii. 11.

(2) In the indictment against Manasseh, stress was laid upon his idolatries (xxxiii. 3-10), but in the indictment of this chapter on what sin does the emphasis lie (verses 12-16)? How would you express in your own words the cause of Judah's downfall? Cf. vii. 19-22.

(3) What is the character of God as revealed in this chapter?

Notes.—(1) Verse 3. 'The king of Egypt'. The king of Egypt, taking advantage of Assyria's weakness, had advanced eastwards; but meantime Babylon had defeated Assyria, and met and overthrew the Egyptian armies at Carchemish. Cf. 2 Ki. xxiv. 7.

(2) Verse 6. Apparently Jehoiakim made submission, and the king of Babylon relented and allowed him to continue to reign, as verse 8 indicates. See also 2 Ki. xxiv. 2 and 6.

(3) Verse 14. Cf. Ezk. viii. 6-18.

(4) Verse 17. 'The king of the Chaldees'; i.e. the king of Babylon.

(5) Verse 21. Cf. Lv. xxv. 2, 4 and xxvi. 34, 35. The thought is that during the captivity the land enjoyed the rest from cultivation which it ought to have had every seventh year, according to the law.

JEREMIAH

INTRODUCTION

(See New Bible Handbook, pp. 219-225)

ANATHOTH, the home of Jeremiah, was a small town some three miles north-east of Jerusalem. Jeremiah's father was a priest, possibly a descendant of Abiathar (cf. 1 Ki. ii. 26), and the family owned some property in Anathoth (xxxii. 8). Jeremiah's fellow townsmen were among those who turned against him and sought to slay him (xi. 21).

Born probably towards the end of the reign of Manasseh, Jeremiah lived through the reigns of Josiah (thirty-one years), Jehoahaz (three months), Jehoiakim (eleven years), Jehoiachin (three months), and Zedekiah (eleven years). Of these kings Josiah alone was loyal to Jehovah. Jehoiakim was hostile to Jeremiah, and Zedekiah, though personally friendly, was weak and unstable. Under these two kings Jeremiah endured much physical suffering at the hands of his enemies. His life, however, was preserved, and after the fall of Jerusalem he was permitted to stay with the remnant left in the land, and was by them carried into Egypt (xliii. 4-7).

In the earlier years of his ministry, though his outward lot was easier, Jeremiah suffered great mental conflict. He saw more and more clearly that the nation was thoroughly corrupt, and that judgment was at hand. The false prophets who cried 'Peace, Peace', were misleading the people (xiv. 13, 14). The inevitability of disaster filled Jeremiah's heart with dismay and sorrow. It seemed as if God were annulling His covenant and casting off His people, and if that were to happen what hope was left? God, however, revealed to Jeremiah that He still had a purpose of good beyond the judgment, and that He could and would make a new covenant of a different kind, in which He would give His people a new heart and put His fear in their inmost being: and the hope of this glorious future sustained him as he watched the dying agonies of his nation, and suffered with them.

Jeremiah was appointed a prophet not only to Judah, but to the nations (i. 5, 10), and he kept an ever-watchful eye on the movements of neighbouring peoples. In Josiah's reign the power of Assyria was waning, and both Egypt and Babylon sought to take advantage of this for their own ends. Three events especially affected the kingdom of Judah, and had a profound influence upon Jeremiah's life and outlook. The first was the battle of Megiddo, when king Josiah was slain. The second was the capture of Nineveh and of the Assyrian Empire by Babylon. The third was the battle of Carchemish, when Pharaoh-Necho of Egypt and Nebuchadnezzar of Babylon met face to face in a trial of strength and the Egyptian armies were routed. From that time Jeremiah was assured that Babylon was to reign supreme for many years, and that Judah would be wise to yield submission. In fearlessly proclaiming this he seemed in the eyes of many a traitor to his own nation, and aroused great opposition and enmity against himself; but his devotion to Jehovah and to his fellow countrymen stands out clearly on every page, though from time to time he breaks out into passionate cries for vengeance upon his persecutors.

The prophecies are not all in chronological order. In some, mention is made of the king in whose reign they were uttered, but in others the date must be judged from the contents. The following may be taken as a rough guide:

The reign of Josiah i–vi.

The reign of Jehoiakim vii–xx, xxii, xxv, xxvi, xxx, xxxi, xxxv, xxxvi, xlv.

The reign of Zedekiah xxi, xxiii, xxiv, xxvii–xxix, xxxii–xxxiv, xxxvii–xxxix.

ANALYSIS

i.   Call of Jeremiah in the thirteenth year of Josiah (626 B.C.).

ii–vi.   The sin of Israel. Call to repentance.

vii–x.   In the temple gate. Prophecies of judgment. Jeremiah's sorrow.

xi, xii.   The broken covenant. Jeremiah's complaint and God's answer.

xiii.   The linen girdle and other prophecies.

xiv, xv.   The drought. Jeremiah's pleadings and God's reply.

Week 13. JEREMIAH I–X

Day 1. Je. i.

(1) What did God require from Jeremiah, and what did He promise to him? See verses 4-10 and 17-19. Have you had any such experience?

(2) What is the divine interpretation of the two visions which Jeremiah saw?

(3) What aspects of God's character are brought before us in this chapter?

Notes.—(1) Verse 5. 'Knew'; in the sense of 'regarded'; almost equivalent to 'chose'. 'I sanctified thee'; set thee apart for Myself. 'Prophet'; one who would speak for God. Cf.. verse 9.

(2) Verse 11. 'A rod'; probably meaning a straight shoot just beginning to blossom. The word for almond tree is from the same root as the word 'hasten'

(or 'watch over' R.V.) in verse 12. Moffatt translates 'Wake tree'. The almond was so called because it was the first to awake after the sleep of winter.

(3) Verse 13. See R.V. 'From the north'. The cauldron is ready to pour out its fiery contents southwards.

(4) Verse 15. 'Every one his throne'; that is, his throne of judgment.

Day 2. Je. ii–iii. 5.

Today's portion is a review of Israel's backsliding from the beginning.

(1) How are Israel's beginnings described? Under what figures is her backsliding depicted?

(2) 'Living' water means fresh water from an ever-flowing spring. With verse 13 cf. xvii. 13 and Jn. iv. 13, 14. What do the 'fountain of living waters' and the 'broken cisterns' stand for in spiritual experience?

(3) What evil results does Jeremiah say have already followed from the nation's forgetfulness of God?

Notes.—(1) See R.V. and R.V. mg. in ii. 8, 18, 20, iii. 1.

(2) ii. 10. 'Isles of Chittim' is a name for Cyprus. 'Kedar' was a tribe to the east of the Jordan. The whole phrase, therefore, means 'from west to east'.

(3) ii. 16. 'Noph' and 'Tahapanes'—cities of Egypt.

(4) ii. 25. 'Do not run thy foot bare, and thy throat dry in the eager pursuit of strange gods' (Driver).

(5) iii. 4. 'Wilt thou not?' etc.; better, 'Hast thou not been crying to me?' —an allusion probably to the feigned penitence of many at the time of Josiah's reform (2 Ch. xxxiv. 33). Then the last half of verse 5 gives God's verdict upon their words of penitence and trust: 'So you say, but what you do is vilest of the vile' (Moffatt).

Day 3. Je. iii. 6–iv.

(1) iii. 6-20. What sin is condemned in these verses, and what appeal does God make? Why is Judah's sin accounted greater than that of the northern kingdom of Israel? What form does this sin take today? Cf. Jas. iv. 4.

(2) Trace the process of restoration as outlined in iii. 21–iv. 4. What is meant by such phrases as 'Break up your fallow ground' and 'Circumcise yourselves to the Lord'? Cf. ix. 26; Dt. x. 16; Rom. ii. 28, 29.

(3) iv. 5-31. A vivid picture of the approach of an invader from the north. Note the reasons why he is permitted by God to come.

Notes.—(1) iii. 10. An allusion to the reformation under Josiah.

(2) iii. 16-17. The ark was a symbol of God's presence. But now God promises that His presence will be so real that they have no need of a symbol to represent it.

(3) iii. 19. Read as in R.V. mg. God's purpose had been to treat them as sons and heirs, but they would not (verse 20).

(4) iii. 23. See R.V. mg. A reference to the noisy, excited worship of the mountain sanctuaries.

(5) iii. 24. 'Shame'; better, 'the shameful thing', as in R.V.; that is, the idols. Cf. iv. 1.

(6) iv. 16. 'Watchers' here seems to mean 'blockaders'.

Day 4. Je. v and vi.

Chapter v shows (a) how all, high and low alike, are corrupt (verses 1-9), and (b) the nature and the cause of the impending judgment (verses 10-31). Chapter vi opens with a picture of the siege (verses 1-6), declares again Israel's wickedness (verses 7-8), and shows the greatness of the ruin that is near and its cause (verses 9-19). Rich offerings are no substitutes for obedience (verses 20, 21). A time of terror lies ahead, because of the nation's grievous condition (verses 22-30).

(1) Why was judgment inevitable? Was God not willing to pardon?

(2) Make a list of the sins charged against the people in chapter v. They can be divided into seven categories. How many of them find further confirmation in chapter vi?

(3) In what ways is the coming judgment described? Have all these things any message for us?

Notes.—(1) v. 4, 5. 'Judgment' here means 'ordinance'. See viii. 7, R.V. and R.V. mg.

(2) vi. 1. Tekoa and Beth-Haccerem were a few miles south of Jerusalem. 'A sign of fire'; better, as in R.V., 'a signal'; probably a beacon. Cf. Jdg. xx. 38.

(3) vi. 2-5. 'Shepherds with their flocks' here means kings and their armies. Verses 4 and 5 give their very words.

(4) vi. 16. 'In the ways'; i.e. 'at the cross roads'.

(5) vi. 27, 28. 'Tower'; better, 'trier', as in R.V. mg. Jeremiah's work is compared to that of a tester of silver. But no pure silver results from the process of refining. Cf. ix. 7.

Day 5. Je. vii–viii. 3.

It is thought by many that this is the address given by Jeremiah in the fourth year of Jehoiakim, as described in xxvi. 1-9.

(1) How does today's portion show the uselessness of ritual and outward worship when separated from the daily practice of godliness? What does God require in His worshippers which the people of Jerusalem failed to render?

(2) In what ways may we in our day act in a spirit exactly similar to that rebuked in vii. 10?

(3) What terrible retribution is here pronounced upon the temple and the people?

Notes.—(1) vii. 4. 'Lying words'; cf. verse 8. What is meant is words that declared the temple in itself to be a protection. Cf. 1 Sa. iv. 3, vi. 3.

(2) vii. 10b. 'Thinking you are now quite safe—safe to go on with all these abominable practices' (Moffatt).

(3) vii. 12. Shiloh was probably destroyed at the time of the disaster recorded in 1 Sa. iv.

(4) vii. 32. 'The valley of the son of Hinnom'; a valley on the south side of Jerusalem, where the city refuse was cast. The day will come, says the prophet, when the slain will be so many that they will have to be buried even in this unclean spot.

Day 6. Je. viii. 4–ix. 22.

Further exposure of the moral and spiritual condition of the nation, and descriptions of the coming judgment. Jeremiah's heart is almost broken.

(1) What specific charges does God level against His people in these chapters? Can you find traces of these faults in your own life?

(2) Note the questions in viii. 19, 22 and ix. 12b. What answers does God give?

(3) Do these things cause you sorrow, as they did to Jeremiah? Are you pleading with men, as he did, to consider their ways? Cf. xxv. 3.

Notes.—(1) viii. 19, 20. The people are pictured as already in exile. The words 'The harvest is past', etc. are probably a proverbial saying expressing the thought that it is too late.

(2) ix. 14. 'The imagination'; better, 'the stubbornness', as in R.V.; a phrase that occurs frequently in the book.

Day 7. Je. ix. 23–x.

(1) What is better than wisdom, power and wealth? See ix. 23, 24 and compare Phil. iii. 8-11.

(2) Set down on the one hand the characteristics here mentioned of the idols of the heathen, and on the other the character of the living God.

(3) Have we learned the truth of x. 23? If man is thus unable to direct his steps, what is he to do? Cf. Pr. iii. 5, 6.

Notes.—(1) ix. 24. 'Judgment' here means a right dealing with offenders.

(2) ix. 25. 'Circumcised with the uncircumcised'; better, 'circumcised in (their) uncircumcision', as in R.V.; that is, circumcised in body but not in heart. Judah's condition in God's sight is no better than that of an uncircumcised nation. Cf. Rom. ii. 28, 29. Observe Judah's place in the list, between Egypt and Edom.

(3) x. 17. 'Thy wares'; better, 'bundle', as in R.V. mg.; a few hastily gathered possessions for immediate flight.

(4) x. 21. 'Pastors'; see ii. 8, note.

(5) x. 24. 'With judgment'; i.e. 'in measure'; cf. xxx. 11.

Week 14. JEREMIAH XI–XXII

Day 1. Je. xi and xii.

These chapters fall into three sections: xi. 1-17, xi. 18-xii. 6, and xii. 7-17. The first deals with Judah's hardness of heart and abounding idolatries. The next is a complaint of the prophet because of plots against his life, and God's answer to his questionings. The third seems to refer to the attacks of surrounding peoples (see 2 Ki. xxiv. 1, 2), and closes with a remarkable promise to these nations on condition of their turning from idols to the worship of Jehovah.

(1) With xi. 21 and xii. 6 cf. Mk. iii. 21; Lk. iv. 24, xxi. 16.

(2) What did Jeremiah do with his perplexities, and what answer did he receive? See xii. 1-6. Does verse 5 suggest that the pathway of obedience grows easier or more difficult for God's servants as life goes on?

Notes.—(1) xi. 15. Read as in R.V. mg. Cf. vi. 20, vii. 9-11.

(2) xii. 5. See R.V. The 'pride' of Jordan is the thick growth by the river, the haunt of wild beasts.

(3) xii. 13. 'They'; i.e. the people of Judah.

Day 2. Je. xiii.

(1) What is the purpose of the story of the girdle? Does your life answer more nearly to the girdle as God meant it to be, or to the girdle as marred?

(2) Ponder the images of the bottle (earthenware jar), darkness, the flock, stubble driven by the wind. Cf. Is. li. 17; Ps. lx. 3 (R.V.); Is. v. 20, viii. 22; Mi. iii. 6, 7, and notes below. How far are these images applicable in gospel preaching today? See Ps. i. 4; Jn. xii. 35.

Notes.—(1) Verses 13, 14. 'Drunkenness' is used in a figurative sense to describe mental fear and bewilderment, when men in their panic turn against each other.

(2) Verse 16. 'God'. A Hebrew expression for confession of sin, recognizing and turning from sin to obedience. Cf. Jos. vii. 19; Mal.

(3) Verse translation is: 'What wilt thou say, when He whom thou hast thyself taught to be viii. 13, 44; La. i. 5 (R.V.).

buy between Jeremiah and God. ought (xiv. 1-6).

before God in xiv. 7-9, Cf. Is. lix. 1, 2.

ge in his second and

third prayers (verses 13 and 19-22)? What are God's answers in each case?

(3) The prophet, ceasing to pray for the people, breaks into a lament (xv. 10) and prays for himself (xv. 15-18). Observe carefully God's answer, especially in xv. 19-21. Test your quiet time in the light of xv. 16, and your whole life in the light of xv. 19. Cf. 2 Tim. ii. 19-21.

Notes.—(1) xiv. 7, 21. 'For Thy Name's sake'; because Thou art Jehovah, our covenant God.

(2) xv. 12. 'The northern iron'; a reference to the Chaldeans. There is no hope of breaking their power.

(3) xv. 13, 14. These verses seem to refer to the nation, and to be out of place in their present setting. Cf. xvii. 3, 4.

(4) xv. 19. The tone is severe. Jeremiah must return to a more undivided allegiance. Then he will stand before God (cf. 1 Ki. xvii. 1, xviii. 15), receive God's Word to speak, and abide under His protecting care.

Day 4. Je. xvi–xvii. 18.

(1) Consider how hard it must have been for a man of Jeremiah's affectionate and sympathetic nature to obey the commands of xvi. 2, 5 and 8. Why did God lay this burden upon him? What other trials that Jeremiah had to bear are referred to in xvii. 14-18? Cf. Phil. iii. 7.

(2) How does the passage illustrate Jeremiah's oft-repeated statement concerning God's dealings with His people, 'I will not make a full end with you'? See iv. 27, v. 10, 18, xxx. 11, xlvi. 28. Cf. Ps. xciv. 14; Rom. xi. 2a.

(3) Contrast, clause by clause, verses 5 and 6 of chapter xvii with verses 7 and 8. Why must it be so, from the very nature of God and man? See verses 9-13. Which way of life have you chosen? Cf. Ps. cxlvi.

Notes.—(1) xvi. 6, 7. Read as in R.V. The practices here described were used in time of mourning. Cf. Am. viii. 10; 2 Sa. xii. 17; Pr. xxxi. 6b.

(2) xvi. 16-18. God's punishment of His people. The phrase 'the carcases of their detestable things' refers to the idols, here called 'carcases' in contempt.

(3) xvii. 1, 2. 'The table of their heart'; i.e. their inmost being. 'The horns of your altars'; a reference to the defiling blood of idolatrous sacrifices (cf. Lv. iv. 7, 30) at the various shrines or high places (verse 2; cf. ii. 20).

(4) xvii. 16. 'From being a pastor'. The words may also be rendered 'because of evil'. The meaning is that Jeremiah's prophesying did not spring from delight in predicting calamity.

Day 5. Je. xvii. 19–xviii.

(1) The issue between God and His people turned on the question of obedience. How was it brought in xvii. 19-27 to a single

test? What is the test for men today? See Acts xvi. 31; Jn. iii. 18.

(2) To the prophet the condition of the people made the destruction of the kingdom inevitable; yet the destruction of the kingdom seemed to involve the failure of God's purposes. How did the illustration of the potter throw light upon this problem? See especially xviii. 4. What other lessons about God does it teach?

(3) What in Jeremiah's teaching specially aroused the people's anger and opposition? Cf. xviii. 18b with xviii. 16, 17.

Notes.—(1) xviii. 14, 15. Read as in R.V. The Hebrew text is uncertain, but the meaning is clear. The snows of Lebanon remain, and its streams do not run dry; but God's people have failed.

(2) xviii. 18. 'The law shall not perish', etc. The people refused to believe that the present order of things would be destroyed.

Day 6. Je. xix and xx.

(1) Reflect on Jeremiah's courage, and what it must have cost him to deliver the message of xix. 1-13. What was his immediate reward? See xix. 14–xx. 6.

(2) The strain and tension caused the prophet to break out into a more bitter lament than he had yet uttered (xx. 7-18). In the midst of it his faith triumphed in the assurance of God's protection, and he was able even to sing His praise (xx. 11-13). Then once more the waves of sorrow swept over him. In the light of this passage, try to enter into the loneliness, hardship and suffering of Jeremiah's life. Note especially verse 9. Do we know anything of the prophet's burning passion in proclaiming God's message?

Notes.—(1) xix. 1. 'Ancients'; better, 'elders', as in R.V. That Jeremiah could persuade these civil and religious leaders to go with him shows the measure of his influence.

(2) xix. 5-6, 11b. See vii. 31-33 and notes there.

(3) xix. 13. The houses, defiled by dead bodies, would like Tophet be accounted unclean.

Day 7. Je. xxi and xxii.

These two chapters refer in turn to the last five kings of the kingdom of Judah, namely Josiah (xxii. 15, 16), Jehoahaz or Shallum (xxii. 10-12), Jehoiakim (xxii. 13-19), Jehoiachin or Coniah (xxii. 24-30), and Zedekiah (xxi).

(1) Zedekiah's hope was that God might work a miracle, as He had done in the days of Hezekiah, a little over a century before (xxi. 2; 2 Ch. xxxii. 20-22). What was Jeremiah's answer, and why did not God hear Zedekiah's prayer? Cf. Is. lix. 1, 2.

(2) If Jeremiah were alive today, what would his attitude be to social injustice and wrongs? See xxii. 3-5, 13-19.

(3) Make a list of incidents in Judah's history which justify the statements in xxii. 21. Note that the northern kingdom of Israel had behaved in the same way. See iii. 25.

Notes.—(1) xxii. 6. Gilead and Lebanon typify prosperity.

(2) xxii. 15. 'Closest thyself'; better, 'strivest to excel', as in R.V.; an ironical comment.

(3) xxii. 20. 'From the passages'; better, as in R.V., 'Abarim', a mountain range to the south-east of Palestine.

(4) xxii. 22a. 'All thy shepherds the wind shall shepherd' (Driver); i.e. their rulers would be scattered.

(5) xxii. 23. 'Gracious'; better, 'greatly to be pitied' (R.V.).

Week 15. JEREMIAH XXIII–XXXII. 5

Day 1. Je. xxiii.

The first eight verses are a condemnation of the rulers ('pastors' or 'shepherds') of Judah, and a prophecy of the Messiah's coming. This passage belongs probably to the reign of Zedekiah. The rest of the chapter is a lament over the prophets of the time and a pronouncement of divine judgment against them.

(1) Observe how Jeremiah's hopes for the future now centre in a Person, a King who is to come. How much of the prophecy has already been fulfilled? What does the name given to the Lord in verse 6 mean for you and me? See 1 Cor. i. 30; Rom. x. 4.

(2) What does Jeremiah say concerning (a) the religious life, worship and ministry of the prophets of his day; (b) of their moral character and conduct; and (c) of their influence?

(3) How does God regard these prophets, and what does He say will happen to them?

Notes.—(1) Verse 4. 'Neither shall they be lacking'; i.e. none shall be lost or missing. Cf. Jn. xvii. 12.

(2) Verse 5. 'Branch'; the word 'shoot' is perhaps better. See R.V. mg. Cf. xxxiii. 15; Is. xi. 1.

(3) Verse 9 describes the effect of God's words upon Jeremiah himself.

(4) Verses 13, 14. 'Folly'; better, 'unseemliness'; literally, 'unsavoury'. The word 'horrible' in verse 14 is much stronger: in God's sight the prophets of Jerusalem are worse than those of Samaria.

(5) Verses 33-40. The Hebrew word translated 'burden' may mean either literally a burden or, figuratively, a solemn utterance. It would seem that Jeremiah's utterances were jestingly spoken of as 'burdens' and those who spoke thus are here rebuked. Verse 33 should probably read: 'When the people . . . shall ask thee saying, What is the burden of the Lord? thou shalt then say unto them, Ye are the burden. I will even cast you off, saith the Lord.'

Day 2. Je. xxiv and xxv.

Chapter xxiv dates from the reign of Zedekiah. Chapter xxv belongs to the fourth year of the reign of Jehoiakim, and declares to Judah and the surrounding nations that they shall all be brought under the power of Babylon with great slaughter, and made to drink the cup of God's wrath.

(1) Who are the good figs and who are the bad figs, and what will happen to them respectively? Cf. Ezk. xi. 14-16.

(2) xxv. 1-11. The fulfilment of the vision of the boiling cauldron (i. 13-15). Much of what is said in these verses is found in preceding chapters. See e.g. vii. 6, 7, 13, xvi. 9, xviii. 11, 16. What, however, do you find here that is new?

(3) 'The supreme factor in history for the Hebrew is the activity of the eternal God.' Illustrate this statement from today's portion. How does chapter xxv show God's loving warning coming before His judgment? Cf. Lk. xiii. 34, 35.

Notes.—(1) xxiv. 2. See R.V.

(2) xxv. 12-14. These verses break the sequence of thought, and may have been introduced into the prophecy at a later date; so also the last clause of verse 26 (see R.V. mg.).

(3) xxv. 18. 'As it is this day'. These words must have been added later. They are not in the LXX.

(4) xxv. 23. See R.V. Dedan, Tema and Buz were tribes of Northern Arabia. Unlike the Jews (Lv. xix. 27), they shaved the hair from the sides of their forehead. Cf. ix. 26, xlix. 32 (R.V.).

(5) xxv. 34, 35, 36. 'The principal (sheep) of the flock'; denoting men of wealth and position in the land.

Day 3. Je. xxvi.

Jehoiakim was a very different king from Josiah. In the beginning of his reign, therefore, God sent Jeremiah to warn the people against being led astray into further disobedience to Jehovah.

(1) The chapter gives a graphic account of what happened. What reason does God give for sending His servant on this dangerous mission? See verse 3 and cf. 2 Ch. xxxvi. 15; Mt. ix. 36; 2 Pet. iii. 9.

(2) Consider the three prophets mentioned in this chapter— Micah, Uriah and Jeremiah—all faithful to Jehovah. What treatment did each receive? What, as Christ's witnesses, may we expect in the world? See Mt. x. 16-22; Jn. xvi. 33; 1 Pet. iv. 12, 13.

Notes.—(1) Verses 4-6. It seems probable that this brief summary of Jeremiah's words is given more fully in chapter vii.

(2) Verse 18. 'Micah the Morasthite'. See Mi. i. 1, iii. 12.

(3) Verse 24. 'Ahikam the son of Shaphan'. One of those sent by King Josiah to consult the prophetess Huldah (2 Ki. xxii. 12, 13), and the father of Gedaliah, who was made governor after the fall of Jerusalem (xl. 5, 6).

Day 4. Je. xxvii and xxviii.

Five kings of the surrounding nations seek Zedekiah's co-operation in an attempt to throw off the yoke of Babylon. Jeremiah opposes the plan.

(1) What means did Jeremiah use to impress upon the five kings the futility of their resistance to Babylon? Notice the claim which God made for Himself in His message to these heathen rulers (xxvii. 4-7).

(2) What did Jeremiah condemn in the propaganda of the prophets?

(3) In chapter xxviii we have a leading prophet of the time attacking Jeremiah, and we can consider the two men at close range. In what respects did they resemble each other, and in what respects did they differ?

Notes.—(1) xxvii. 1. 'Jehoiakim', should be Zedekiah. See verse 3, xxviii. 1.

(2) xxvii. 16-22. Only a part of the vessels of the temple had at this time been carried off to Babylon.

Day 5. Je. xxix.

Those who had been carried into exile in the first captivity under Jehoiachin (2 Ki. xxiv. 14-16) were being made restless and unsettled by prophets who prophesied falsely that they would soon be set free. Jeremiah therefore wrote a letter to them declaring the exile would last seventy years.

(1) What, as revealed to Jeremiah, were the Lord's thoughts (a) towards the exiles in Babylon, and (b) towards Zedekiah and those who remained in Jerusalem? With verse 17 compare chapter xxiv.

(2) What three prophets are mentioned by name by Jeremiah, what accusations did he bring against them, and what judgment did he pronounce upon them? Do you gather that God regards it as a serious offence when men speak falsely in His Name?

Notes.—(1) Verse 24. 'Shemaiah'; that he, too, was a prophet is seen from verse 31.

(2) Verse 25. 'Zephaniah'; probably the same as the Zephaniah who in lii. 24 is called 'the second priest'; i.e. second to the high priest.

Day 6. Je. xxx–xxxi. 30.

Today's portion forms part of a group of prophecies. See *Analysis*. It was a time of darkness and despair, and Jeremiah himself apparently derived much comfort from the message. See xxxi. 26.

(1) Today's portion falls into sections which are all variants of the same theme that after judgment will come restoration. See xxx. 1-3, 4-11, 12-22, 23, 24, xxxi. 1-9, 10-14, 15-20, 21-22, 23-30. What are the blessings promised?

(2) To what extent have these prophecies been fulfilled? Observe that they are spoken of northern Israel as well as of Judah (xxx. 4, xxxi. 1).

(3) Are not the great blessings spoken of in xxx. 22, xxxi. 3, xxxi. 14 even now part of our inheritance in Christ? Let us then possess our possessions, and greatly rejoice. Cf. Jn. xv. 9-11, xvi. 27.

Notes.—(1) xxx. 14. 'All thy lovers'; i.e. nations with whom Israel had sought an alliance. Cf. verse 17b.

(2) xxxi. 2. 'The wilderness'; here denoting the place of their exile.

(3) xxxi. 15. 'Rachel weeping for her children'; a graphic picture of the sorrows of the exile. Rachel, the mother of Joseph and Benjamin, is depicted as weeping in her grave, which was near Ramah, as the exiles pass by; cf. xl. 1; also Mt. ii. 17, 18.

Day 7. Je. xxxi. 31–xxxii. 5.

(1) xxxi. 31-34. If Israel has broken the covenant between herself and Jehovah, how can there be any future blessing for her? What is God's answer to this question?

(2) What four features of the new covenant are set forth in xxxi. 33-34? The foundation is free and full forgiveness. Rom. iii. 21-26 and Heb. x. 14-18 show how this is possible in Christ. With verse 33 contrast Ex. xxxi. 18; and with verse 34 contrast Ex. xx. 19. Cf. also Eph. ii. 18; Jn. xiv. 7, xvii. 3; 1 Jn. iv. 7, v. 20.

Notes.—(1) xxxi. 32. The writer to the Hebrews, in quoting this passage, follows the LXX; see Heb. viii. 3-12.

(2) xxxi. 34. The word 'know' is used in the meaning not of intellectual knowledge, but of personal intimacy.

(3) xxxi. 39, 40. The localities Gareb and Goath are not now known. 'The valley of the dead bodies' is the valley of Hinnom. The meaning is that in the new city all shall be holy.

(4) xxxii. 2. 'The court of the prison'; better, 'the court of the guard', as in R.V. Jeremiah's friends would be able to visit him, but he could not go outside the court.

Week 16. JEREMIAH XXXII. 6–XLIII

Day 1. Je. xxxii. 6–xxxiii.

(1) Jeremiah is perplexed by the command to buy land and prays to God. Do we make a habit of unburdening our perplexities before God as we seek to walk by faith? Cf. Is. l. 10.

(2) Why was God giving the city into the hand of the Chaldeans? And what was the significance of His command to Jeremiah to buy property at such a time?

(3) Whence did Jeremiah derive his strong assurance that, notwithstanding the desolation around him (xxxii. 43, xxxiii. 10, 12), God's purpose of blessing was not exhausted? What blessings are promised in chapter xxxiii? May we take xxxiii. 3 as a promise to ourselves? Cf. Eph. i. 17-19a; 1 Cor. ii. 9, 10.

Notes.—(1) xxxiii. 3. 'Great and mighty things'; better, 'great things and difficult', as in R.V. That is, not easily attainable. The original reading may, however, have been 'hidden', as in Is. xlviii. 6b.

(2) xxxiii. 13. 'Telleth'; i.e. 'counts'. Cf. Lv. xxvii. 32.

Day 2. Je. xxxiv.

This chapter describes two incidents that occurred during the siege of Jerusalem at the end of Zedekiah's reign.

(1) Nebuchadnezzar doubtless thought that he, with his numerous and powerful forces (verse 1), was master of the situation. But who is revealed here as the controlling power, deciding the fate of cities and kings? Cf. Is. xl. 15, 17, 21-23.

(2) Verses 8-22. Have you ever gone back, because of altered circumstances, upon a solemn promise made before God? How does God regard such conduct? Cf. Lk. ix. 62.

Notes.—(1) Verses 2-5. Cf. xxxii. 3-5, lii. 11; Ezk. xii. 13.

(2) Verse 17. 'A liberty to you'; that is, freedom from God's protecting care.

(3) Verse 18. 'When they cut the calf in twain'; part of the ceremony of the covenant. See Gn. xv. 10.

Day 3. Je. xxxv.

The Rechabites were a small class or sect who regarded Jonadab (see 2 Ki. x. 15) as their father or founder, and had received a charge from him to abstain from wine, from settled dwellings and from agriculture. They normally lived a nomad life; but, in fear of the advance of the armies of the north, they had taken refuge in Jerusalem. The incident belongs to the reign of Jehoiakim.

(1) What test did Jeremiah at God's command apply to the Rechabites? And what message did God then give him to take to the people of Jerusalem?

(2) Verse 17b. May not these words be said of multitudes today? Cf. vii. 13; Pr. i. 24-33; Jb. xxi. 14, 15.

(3) What traits of the Rechabites should be the distinguishing features of Christians today? Cf. Mt. xxiv. 12, 13; Heb. x. 38, 39.

Day 4. Je. xxxvi.

(1) The events of this chapter cannot have been very long after those of chapter xxvi. (Compare the dating in verse 1 and xxvi. 1.) God in His compassion bids Jeremiah make one more appeal.

In what respects does it differ from that of chapter xxvi (a) in its content, (b) in the manner of its delivery, and (c) in its outcome?

(2) Why do you think the princes felt that they must tell the king (verse 16)? Was it to get Jeremiah silenced (cf. Am. vii. 12, 13), or was it in the hope that the king might hearken to God's Word, as Josiah had done (2 Ki. xxii. 10, 11)? Do you have the impression that this was a fateful moment for the nation, and that very much depended on the king's action?

(3) If so, how great the king's responsibility, and how great his guilt in what he did! It was all the more so because a fast was being held to seek Jehovah's aid (verse 9). Cf. Mt. xviii. 7 and verses 30, 31 below. With verses 27, 28 and 32 cf. 2 Tim. ii. 9; Acts xii. 23, 24.

Notes.—(1) Verse 5. 'I am shut up'; better, 'I am detained'. Jeremiah may have been prevented from going to the temple by some ceremonial defilement. Cf. 1 Sa. xxi. 7.

(2) Verse 8. This verse sums up in brief the story of the following verses.

(3) Verses 22, 23. 'On the hearth'; better, 'in the brasier', as in R.V. 'When Jehudi had read'; better, 'As often as Jehudi had read'.

Day 5. Je. xxxvii and xxxviii.

These chapters belong to Zedekiah's reign. Although Egypt had been decisively defeated by the armies of Babylon at Carchemish twenty years before (xlvi. 2), now a new king had arisen in Egypt who sought to oppose Nebuchadnezzar's southward advance. He sent an army, while Nebuchadnezzar was besieging Jerusalem, whose approach forced the Chaldeans to raise the siege. This excited great hopes, but Jeremiah was not deceived. The Chaldeans, he said, would come back and burn the city with fire.

(1) Today's portion tells of two occasions about this time when Jeremiah was arrested. What was the cause of the arrest, and what happened to the prophet? How do these incidents illustrate i. 18, 19?

(2) Do you think the physical sufferings or the reproaches hurled at him were harder to bear? Why did he not keep silent and so escape censure? See xx. 7-11.

(3) What can we learn from the character of Zedekiah as revealed in these chapters? How does he exemplify the truth of Pr. xxix. 25a; Jas. i. 8?

Notes.—(1) xxxvii. 12. See R.V. The meaning is not fully clear. There seems to have been an exodus from the city. Jeremiah went with the crowd apparently in connection with some property.

(2) xxxvii. 16. See R.V.

(3) xxxviii. 6. 'Dungeon'; better, 'cistern'; an underground pit to store water.

(4) xxxviii. 22. The king's womenfolk will tell him that the men he trusted had led him on, and now that he is sinking they have deserted him.

Day 6. Je. xxxix–xli.

These chapters relate the fall of Jerusalem and the events immediately following.

(1) What message did Jeremiah give to Ebed-melech, and why? Cf. Mt. x. 40-42.

(2) Note carefully xl. 2, 3. Could the matter be better summed up than was done in these words by this heathen officer? Cf. Pr. xxix. 1; Is. xxx. 9-15.

Notes.—(1) xxxix. 3. 'Rabsaris' and 'Rabmag' are titles of the men whose names precede them; Rabsaris meaning chief of the princes, and Rabmag, chief of the magi.

(2) xxxix. 4. 'Betwixt the two walls'; i.e. of the city, probably 'the wall along the west side of the east hill, and along the east side of the west hill' (Driver).

(3) xxxix. 5. 'Riblah'; in the far north, fifty miles south of Hamath.

(4) xxxix. 9. 'Remnant (or residue) of the people'. The phrase occurs twice here, but in lii. 15 the second time it is 'residue of the artificers' (R.V. mg.).

(5) xli. 1. Read as in R.V. Ishmael was probably jealous that Gedaliah had been appointed governor, and sought to get the remnant of the Jews under his control (xli. 10).

Day 7. Je. xlii and xliii.

(1) It is clear that the remnant of the people left in the land were obsessed by fear—fear of the Chaldeans (xlii. 11) and fear of famine (xlii. 16). From both these evils Egypt appeared to offer a secure place of refuge (xlii. 14). But what did God say they ought to do? And what did He say would happen to them if they went to Egypt?

(2) Why did the people, in spite of their promise to obey God, take a wrong course? What did they lack spiritually that they failed so badly? Read carefully xlii. 20, 21 and cf. Mt. xv. 7; Heb. iii. 18, 19. Are we, as a nation, seeking more what Egypt offers than to obey God? Cf. 2 Tim. iii. 1-5; 2 Pet. ii. 20-22.

(3) Contrast the character of Jeremiah. God had made the same promise to Jeremiah that He now made to these Jews (see i. 18, 19), but how different was the response in Jeremiah's case? What are the outstanding features that you observe in Jeremiah in these chapters?

Notes.—(1) xlii. 21. During the days of waiting (verse 7) preparation for going to Egypt had probably been going on apace, and Jeremiah recognizes that this was their fixed resolve.

(2) xliii. 2, 3. To the human judgment of these men it seemed incredible that any one should counsel staying in the land.

(3) xliii. 10-13. Nebuchadnezzar did invade Egypt and defeat its king a few years later.

Week 17. JEREMIAH XLIV–LII

Day 1. Je. xliv and xlv.

This is the last scene which is recorded of Jeremiah. The now aged prophet, exiled in Egypt, visits some place where his fellow countrymen are gathered and delivers a last message from their God—a message which they resolutely reject, thus drawing upon themselves their own destruction. Chapter xlv is a much earlier fragment, belonging to the fourth year of Jehoiakim.

(1) How would you sum up Jeremiah's message in xliv. 2-14?

(2) What was the spiritual condition of the people as revealed in their reply (cf. Is. xliv. 20)? And what was God's final word to them through His servant? Cf. 1 Jn. v. 21.

(3) Chapter xlv. Baruch was the son of a princely house. His brother Seraiah held an important office under the king (see li. 59), and he himself probably had ambitions (verse 5). His work for Jeremiah would reveal to him the doom of the city and the kingdom. What were his natural reactions (see verse 3)? What was God's message to him, and what may we learn from it for ourselves? Cf. Mk. x. 42-45; 1 Cor. vii. 29-31.

Notes.—(1) xliv. 17. 'The queen of heaven'; probably Ashtoreth, a goddess widely worshipped.

(2) xliv. 26. 'Shall no more be named'; i.e. because of their destruction; see verse 27.

(3) xliv. 27. 'I will watch'; better, 'I am wakeful'. Cf. i. 12, where the same word occurs.

Day 2. Je. xlvi and xlvii.

Chapter xlvi falls into four sections, namely verses 3-6, 7-12, 14-26, 27-28. Verses 1, 2 and 13 are introductory notes. The first two sections are descriptions of Egypt's bid for power, and defeat at Carchemish; the third is a prophecy of Nebuchadnezzar's invasion of Egypt; and the fourth section is a message of comfort to Israel. Chapter xlvii refers to the Philistines.

(1) Read each section aloud, in the Revised Version, or, if possible, in Moffatt's translation, that you may catch something of the rhythm and force of these utterances. What is the relation of Jehovah to the clash of these mighty powers?

(2) How is Egypt described (a) before the battle, (b) after it, and (c) during the invasion? Compare all this with her boast in verse 8, and read again ix. 23-26.

(3) What will happen to the Philistines? Cf. 2 Cor. v. 10; Heb. x. 31.

Notes.—(1) xlvi. 7, 8. Read as in R.V.

(2) xlvi. 16. 'And they said'. The reference must be to foreign traders in Egypt or to foreign mercenaries (verse 21).

(3) xlvi. 18. 'As Tabor . . . as Carmel'; towering above the nations.

(4) xlvi. 22. The two parts of the verse are in contrast, the first clause referring to the armies of Egypt, gliding away like a rustling serpent, and the second to the invaders, marching like woodcutters. Egypt's cities are compared to a dense forest (verse 23).

(5) xlvii. 1. 'Before that Pharaoh smote Gaza'. It is not known to what this refers. The LXX omits it.

(6) xlvii. 5. 'Baldness' and 'cut thyself' are tokens of mourning; cf. xlviii. 37.

(7) xlvii. 6. 'O thou sword of the Lord'; cf. xii. 12, xlvi. 10, 16, l. 35-37.

Day 3. Je. xlviii.

(1) This long chapter on Moab falls into five sections, each of which is complete in itself. These are (a) verses 1-10; (b) verses 11-19; (c) verses 20-28; (d) verses 29-39; (e) verses 40-47. What heading would you give to each of these sections to sum up its contents?

(2) What reason is given in verse 11 for the judgment upon Moab? What other reasons are also set forth in this chapter?

Notes.—(1) Verse 2. No such place as 'Madmen' is known. The LXX renders it thus: 'Yet thou (i.e. Moab) shall be brought to silence.'

(2) Verses 7, 13. 'Chemosh'; the god of Moab.

(3) Verses 11, 12. An illustration from the treatment of the juice of the grapes. It is left in a vessel until a sediment called lees has formed at the bottom; then the liquid is poured into another vessel, and so repeatedly, until the liquid is clear. Moab had experienced no such purifying process, and so retained its original unrefined character.

(4) Verse 26. 'Make ye him drunken'; i.e. stagger with grief and despair. Cf. xxv. 16.

(5) Verse 34. See R.V. 'Eglath-shelishiyah'; possibly 'Eglath the third' (Moffatt); i.e. the third city built on the same site.

Day 4. Je. xlix.

This chapter contains prophecies on five nations, namely Ammon (verses 1-6), Edom (verses 7-22), Damascus (verses 23-27), Kedar and the kingdom of Hazor (verses 28-33), and Elam (verses 34-39). Kedar was a pastoral people, on the east of Palestine, though the exact position where they lived, like that of the kingdom of Hazor, is not certainly known. Elam was a country north of the Persian Gulf.

(1) What was Ammon's sin against Israel? Cf. Am. i. 13; Ex. xx. 17; Lk. xii. 15. In what was her trust placed? Cf. Mk. x. 23, 24. What was to be her punishment?

(2) Notice the vivid metaphors describing the severity of Edom's fate, as e.g. in verses 9, 10, 19 and 20. Yet how does the divine compassion also find expression? Why is the judgment against Edom (Esau's descendants) so severe? Cf. verse 16; Mal. i. 2, 3; Heb. xii. 16, 17.

(3) The sins that brought judgment upon Damascus, Kedar and Elam are not specified. Observe, however, the phrase 'my fierce anger' in verse 37, and compare xxv. 31, 32, 37, 38; Rev. vi. 16, 17; also Jn. iii. 36; Rom. i. 18, ii. 5.

Notes.—(1) Verse 1. 'Their king'; the Hebrew is *Malcam* (see R.V.), but the LXX reads *Milcom*, which was the name of the god of the Ammonites. So also in verse 3.

(2) Verses 2 and 3. The word 'daughters' here refers to towns and villages which looked to Rabbah as their head. In verse 4 'daughter' refers to the whole people.

(3) Verse 8. 'Dwell deep'; i.e. hidden away from observation. Cf. verse 30.

(4) Verse 17. 'Hiss'; i.e. draw in the breath with astonishment.

(5) Verses 19, 20. The picture of a lion coming up out of the jungle on the fringe of the Jordan and doing what it pleases with the flock, no shepherd being able to challenge him.

(6) Verse 25. See R.V. A difficult verse. It appears to be an exclamation of distress, put into the mouth of a citizen of Damascus, that the city was not forsaken by its inhabitants before the slaughter described in the next verse.

Day 5. Je. l.

Jeremiah had persistently declared that Babylon was God's instrument of judgment upon the nations. But as he looked further ahead, he saw that Babylon in turn would herself be judged. Today's portion may be divided as follows: Babylon's fall (verses 1-3); a message of comfort to Israel (verses 4-7); renewed declaration of Babylon's doom (verses 8-13); summons to the attackers to begin their work (verses 14-16); Israel's return to her land and to her God (verses 17-20); the attackers bidden to press on (verses 21-28, 29-34, 35-40); description of the attackers (verses 41-46).

(1) Whence did the prophet derive hope for his people?

(2) Consider the solemn truth that while God may use a nation as His instrument, this does not in any way absolve that nation from responsibility before God. Because Babylon was ruthless in her exercise of power, she would receive no mercy. See especially verses 11, 12, 13, 15, 24, 27, 29.

Notes.—(1) Verse 2. 'Bel' and 'Merodach' are names of the supreme god of Babylon.

(2) Verse 7. Cf. xl. 3.

(3) Verse 12. Read as in R.V.

(4) Verse 16. A reference to foreigners in Babylon; cf. xlvi. 16.

(5) Verse 21. 'Merathaim'; a name for Babylonia. 'Pekod' is the name of a people in Babylonia.

(6) Verse 36a. Better, 'A sword is upon the empty talkers (i.e. the diviners), and they shall become foolish'; cf. Is. xliv. 25.

Day 6. Je. li. 1-58.

The divisions of this chapter are as follows: Babylon's doom and Israel's vindication (verses 1-10); summons to the attackers to press home their assault (verses 11-14); Jehovah in contrast with idols (verses 15-19); Jehovah's fierce anger against Babylon (verses 20-26); capture of the city (verses 27-33); Israel's wrongs avenged: let her hasten her escape (verses 34-57); summing up of God's judgment upon Babylon (verse 58).

(1) In the time of her prosperity the idols of Babylon seemed powerful and mighty; but now in the hour of her fall how do they appear? See verses 15-19, and cf. 1, 2; Ps. cxlvi. 5-10.

(2) What, according to chapters l and li, were the sins of Babylon which called down upon her such terrible vengeance? How far are these sins prevalent in the world today?

Notes.—(1) In verses 1 and 32 read as in R.V. mg.

(2) Verse 3. Read as in R.V. The meaning is that the defenders of Babylon need not trouble to fight, for it will be of no avail. Cf. verse 30; also xxi. 4, xxxii. 5b.

(3) Verse 5. It is probable that the words 'their land' refers to Chaldea. See next verse. In the whole of verses 5-10 the voice of Israel seems to be speaking, as in verses 34, 35 and 51.

(4) Verse 14. 'Caterpillers'; probably locusts in the pupal stage; so also in verse 27. The meaning is that the attackers will be without number.

(5) Verse 20. 'Thou art my battle axe'. A reference to Cyrus, the conqueror of Babylon.

(6) Verse 36. 'Her sea'; Nebuchadnezzar had had a great lake made to ensure the safety of the city.

(7) Verse 55a. 'The great voice'; i.e. the noise of the great city. Verse 55b speaks in contrast of the voice of the attackers, their shouts and cries as they pressed forward.

(8) Verse 58. 'So ends the toil of nations, ends in smoke, and pagans waste their pains' (Moffatt).

Day 7. Je. li. 59–lii.

(1) li. 59-64. Note the date of this incident. At the time Babylon was rising to the height of her power and glory, and Jeremiah was convinced that she would enjoy complete supremacy over the nations. See xxviii, which belongs to the same year. How, then, does this commission which Jeremiah gave to Seraiah illustrate the words of Heb. xi. 1, that 'faith is . . . the evidence of things not seen'?

(2) In chapter lii is told once more the story of the fall of Jerusalem, the destruction of the temple, and the captivity of the

people, perhaps to emphasize how complete was the fulfilment of Jeremiah's words. For example, compare verse 3 with vii. 15; verse 6 with xiv. 15-18; verses 8-11 with xxxiv. 3; verse 13 with vii. 14, ix. 11, xix. 13, xxxii. 28, 29; verse 15 with xvi. 9-13, xxi. 9; verses 18-19 with xxvii. 19-22.

Notes.—(1) li. 59. 'And this Seraiah was a quiet prince'; literally, 'a prince (or captain) of the camping place'. The meaning is that he prepared the king's camping place on a journey. See R.V. mg.

(2) The R.V. is clearer in li. 61, lii. 25.

(3) li. 64. 'And they shall be weary'; words repeated from verse 58, perhaps by mistake.

(4) lii. 24. 'The three keepers of the door' (or threshold, R.V. mg.); denoting three high officials of the temple who had charge of the three gates.

LAMENTATIONS

INTRODUCTION

(See The New Bible Handbook, pp. 225, 226)

THE book of Lamentations consists of five songs or elegies, the theme of which is the sorrows of Judah and Jerusalem in the siege and destruction of the city. The cause of these calamities is traced to the sin of the people bringing Jehovah's judgment upon them, and the songs contain confessions of sin, statements of faith and hope, and prayers for the restoration of God's favour.

Tradition (from the time of the Septuagint translation of the Old Testament) has assigned the authorship of the songs to the prophet Jeremiah. In the Hebrew Bible, however, the book is anonymous, and is placed not among the prophets, but in the section known as 'The Writings'. What is certain is that the book has close affinities with Jeremiah and his teaching, and if not written by him must have been written by one or more of his spiritual children, such as the scribe Baruch.

The songs are written in acrostic form. In chapters i, ii, and iv each verse begins with a fresh letter of the Hebrew alphabet. In the poem of chapter iii there are twenty-two groups of three verses each, and each verse of each group begins with the same letter of the alphabet. In chapter v the acrostic form is not followed. The metrical structure of the songs is more clearly seen in the R.V., which should be used in the study of this book.

ANALYSIS

i. The deep sorrows of Jerusalem, with contrite confession of sin.

ii. It is Jehovah who has done it according to His Word. Seek Him in prayer.

iii. Speaking on behalf of the nation, the writer pours out his grief before God, and, staying himself upon Jehovah, pleads earnestly for help.

iv. The miseries of the siege. The guilt of prophets and priests. The capture of the city.

v. A prayer describing the nation's suffering, confessing sin, and pleading for salvation.

Week 18. Lamentations and Nahum

Day 1. La. i.

(1) What ingredients made up Jerusalem's cup of sorrow? Do you find the following: (a) loneliness; (b) bereavement; (c) captivity; (d) defeat; (e) humiliation; (f) spoliation; (g) consciousness of sin? Or would you make a different list?

(2) How and why had Jerusalem come to such a pass? See especially verses 5, 8, 9, 12, 14, 17, 18, 20; and cf. Heb. x. 31, xii. 29; Lv. xxvi. 27-33.

(3) What lessons may we learn as to the consequences of persistent sinning? Cf. Jas. i. 12-15; Rom. ii. 5, 6.

Notes.—(1) Verse 2. 'Lovers' . . . 'friends'; i.e. neighbouring States with which she had sought alliance.

(2) Verse 3. 'Between the straits'; i.e. in time of distress.

(3) Verse 6. 'Her princes', etc.; cf. Je. xxxix. 4, 5.

(4) Verse 9. 'She remembered not', etc.; 'she never thought of what would follow' (Moffatt).

(5) Verse 15. 'A solemn assembly' (r.v.); 'a triumphant host' (Moffatt).

Day 2. La. ii.

Verses 1-9a describe what was done to the buildings in Judah and Jerusalem, including the temples, and in the remaining part of the chapter we are told what happened to the various classes of the inhabitants.

(1) Try to imagine the desolation here portrayed and the intensity of the people's sorrow. Cf. i. 12.

(2) What is said of God's 'right hand' in verses 3 and 4? Contrast with this such passages as Ex. xv. 6, 12; Ps. lxiii. 8, cxxxix. 10.

(3) Verses 18-22. Notice that this summons to pray follows the

acknowledgment and confession of sin in chapter i, and the recognition in this chapter that the judgment was from God. What does this suggest in the light of 2 Ch. vii. 14?

Notes.—(1) Verse 2. 'Habitations'; that is, country dwellings, as opposed to 'strongholds'.

(2) Verse 4. 'Tabernacle'; better, 'tent', as in R.V. The word here denotes the city, but in verse 6 'tabernacle' refers to the temple, as also does 'His place of assembly' (R.V.).

(3) Verse 11. The reference to 'bowels', 'liver', etc., is the Eastern way of expressing strong and painful emotion. We use 'heart' in a similar sense.

Day 3. La. iii.

(1) In verses 1-20 the poet, speaking in the name of the community, 'pours out his heart like water before the face of the Lord' (ii. 19b). Notice the change from the minor to the major key at verse 21. What causes it? Does David's experience in Ps. lxii. 8 provide a clue?

(2) What aspects of God's character are most emphasized in verses 21-42, and what in time of affliction or chastisement should be our attitude of soul? Cf. Joel ii. 12-14. Why is it both wrong and foolish for a man to complain and murmur in time of chastisement (verses 37-39)? Cf. Je. v. 19-24; Pr. xix. 3.

(3) In verses 45-54 the poet, in the name of the people, again pours out his heart before the Lord and, having done so, is strengthened to pray again, and receives comfort. What is his prayer (verses 55-66)? We may think it does not rise very high; but if we feel inclined to condemn, let us ask what is the level of our own praying. Cf. Mt. v. 24.

Notes.—(1) Verse 37. Cf. Ps. xxxiii. 9.

(2) Verse 38. Read as in R.V. The word 'evil' is used here in the sense of a misfortune or calamity. Cf. Am. iii. 6; Is. xlv. 7.

(3) Verse 63. 'I am their musick'; better, 'song', as in R.V. Cf. Jb. xxx. 9.

Day 4. La. iv.

(1) Make a list of the statements in this chapter which emphasize the extraordinary severity of the divine judgment. Notice how all classes of the community are affected.

(2) What is the particular cause here assigned for so great a calamity? Cf. Je. xxiii. 9-14.

(3) With verse 17 cf. Je. ii. 36, 37, xxxvii. 7, 8; and with verse 20 cf. Ps. cxlvi. 3, 4; Je. xvii. 5, 6.

Notes.—(1) Verse 3. 'Sea monsters'; better, 'jackals', as in R.V.

(2) Verse 6. 'No hands stayed on her'; 'ere any could wring his hands' (Moffatt).

(3) Verse 7. 'Her Nazarites'; better, 'her nobles', as in R.V.

(4) Verse 8. 'Blacker than a coal'; literally, 'darker than blackness' (see R.V. mg.).

(5) Verse 10. 'Pitiful'; in the sense of compassionate or tender-hearted.

(6) Verse 11. The very foundations are destroyed.

(7) Verses 13-16. Read as in R.V.

(8) Verse 20. A reference to the king.

Day 5. La. v.

(1) Would you infer from this chapter that it was written some time after Jerusalem had fallen? How would you sum up the conditions in the land?

(2) How does this chapter illustrate what is said in Heb. xii. 11? Contrast the present disposition of the people with what they formerly said (Je. v. 11, 12, xviii. 18). What did they still lack?

(3) With verse 16 cf. Je. xiii. 18, and with verse 21 Je. xxxi. 18. Consider how much God's word spoken before through Jeremiah meant to the people at such a time. Cf. Jn. xiii. 19, xiv. 29, xvi. 4.

Notes.—(1) Verse 1. 'Consider'; or 'Behold', as in R.V. The same word as that translated 'look' in Is. lxiii. 15 and lxvi. 2.

(2) Verse 9. A reference to the danger of attack from desert robbers when the people ventured out to reap the harvest.

(3) Verse 13. 'Fell under the wood'; i.e. stumbled under loads of wood.

(4) Verse 22. 'But', or rather 'unless', as in R.V. mg.; faith cannot accept that they are utterly rejected, yet is without assurance of salvation.

NAHUM

INTRODUCTION

(*See New Bible Handbook, p. 252*)

IN the prophet Nahum God found a man who, with flaming conviction, proclaimed the astonishing message that great Nineveh, still at the height of her power, must fall and disappear. Nhaum does not treat of other things. He concentrates on this seemingly incredible event. With high poetic skill and vivid realism he portrays the attack upon the city and her final end. We can almost see the battle, the capture, the looting, and hear the noise of her fall and the silence of her desolation.

Nahum's purpose in writing, however, is not to gloat over the downfall of the great enemy of his people. It is to magnify Jehovah, to declaim that Jehovah is, on the one hand, faithful to His promises and strong to save those who put their trust in Him, and, on the other, the Holy One, who is the Adversary and Judge of the wicked. It is because the Assyrian Empire was built with ruthless cruelty upon the principle that might is right that Jehovah, the moral governor of the world, rises up to smite it to the dust.

Nahum prophesied between the overthrow of No-amon (Thebes) in Egypt, about 663 B.C. (to which he makes reference in his prophecy), and the fall of Nineveh in 612. There is no certain clue as to a more exact date, but the most likely period for his ministry seems to be in the early years of king Josiah. If so, he preceded Jeremiah by only a few years.

ANALYSIS

i. 1.   Title.
i. 2-15.   Jehovah, good to those who trust in Him, is terrible to His enemies, and will utterly destroy Assyria.
ii.   The attack upon the city, its capture and overthrow.
iii.   Nineveh's guilt and punishment. Her end is final, and all that hear of it shall clap their hands.

Day 6. Na. i.

(1) What do we learn in this chapter about God (a) in relation to His own people, and (b) in relation to His enemies? Cf. Lk. xviii. 7, 8; 2 Thes. i. 8; Nu. xiv. 17, 18; Ps. xlvi. 1.

(2) Nineveh's boastful spirit is seeu in Is. xxxvi. 18-20, xxxvii. 23-25; Zp. ii. 15. But how does Nahnm regard her in relation to Jehovah's power? See verses 3b-6, 9-12a, 14, and cf. Is. xl. 15, 17; Ps. xxxvii. 35, 36.

(3) Consider how verse 7 is illustrated in the story of 2 Ki. xviii–xix, which happened less than a century before Nahum's time. Have you your own illustration to give out of your own experience?

Notes.—(1) Verse 1. 'The Elkoshite'; a reference probably to Nahum's birthplace; but where Elkosh was is not known with certainty.

(2) Verses 2, 8 and 12 should be read as in R.V.

(3) Verse 2. 'God is jealous'. Behind this word lies the figure of the marriage relation used in Scripture of Jehovah and Israel. 'Just as jealousy in husband or wife is the energetic assertion of an exclusive right, so God asserts and vindicates His claim on those who belong to Him alone.' Cf. Ex. xxxiv. 14; 1 Cor. x. 20-22.

(4) Verse 11. Possibly a reference to Sennacherib; cf. Is. x. 7-10.

(5) Verses 12, 13 and 15 are addressed to Judah, and verses 11 and 14 to Nineveh.

(6) Verse 14. 'Vile'. The word here and in iii. 6 does not mean depraved, but rather abject, reduced to the meanest condition.

(7) Verse 15. The good tidings is the news of Nineveh's downfall.

Day 7. Na. ii and iii.

These two chapters are two separate odes describing the fall of Nineveh. In chapter ii the prophet depicts the approach of the enemy (verse 1a) and ironically summons the people to defend their city (verse 1b). Then follows description of the attackers (verses 3, 4). The defenders haltingly man the wall (verse 5); but the river gates are forced. The palace is in panic, the queen is captured, the people flee (verses 6-8), and looting follows (verse 9). The chapter ends with a picture of Nineveh overthrown, lying desolate in her ruin. Chapter iii declares the city's guilt and her punishment (verses 1-7), and bids her take warning from the fate of No-amon (verses 8-10). Nineveh's strength fails (verses 11-15a). Though her people are without number, and her merchants are as numerous as locusts, yet, like locusts, they will fly away (verses 15b-17). Her rulers perish, her people are scattered. All who hear of her fall will rejoice, clapping their hands.

(1) Read each chapter aloud, either from the R.V. or in Moffatt's translation.

(2) What were Nineveh's sins that brought upon her so terrible a retribution? 'Blood . . . lies . . . rapine . . . harlotry . . . wickedness'. What is meant by each of these terms? See also i. 11.

(3) How does Nahum show the converse of Rom. viii. 31; i.e. if God be against us, who can be for us? Cf. Ps. xxxiv. 16; Je. xxxvii. 9, 10.

Notes.—(1) ii. 2. A reference, not wholly clear, to Judah's restoration.

(2) ii. 5. 'Worthies'; one of a trio of words, whose meaning is obscure, as, e.g., Huzzab, usually taken to be a name or title of the queen. Compare iii. 17. 'Worthies' may denote in verse 5 the commanders of the army.

(3) ii. 8. Nineveh is compared to a reservoir that has been breached and whose water is flowing away.

(4) ii. 13. 'Messengers' or 'Envoys'; cf. 2 Ki. xix. 9, 23.

(5) iii. 1. 'The prey departeth not'; 'no end to your ravaging' (Moffatt).

(6) iii. 16. 'The cankerworm spoileth', etc.; better, 'the young locust strippeth itself and flieth away' (Driver).

(7) iii. 19. 'For upon whom', etc.; 'for whom have you not wronged unceasingly?' (Moffatt).

ZEPHANIAH

INTRODUCTION

(See New Bible Handbook, pp. 254, 255)

ZEPHANIAH prophesied in the reign of Josiah and probably in the early years of that reign, before Josiah began his religious reforms. For when Zephaniah delivered his message, idolatrous customs, which Josiah abolished, were still openly practised (cf. e.g. i. 4, 5 with 2 Ki. xxiii. 4, 5). Zephaniah was therefore a contemporary of Jeremiah and possibly began his ministry somewhat earlier. If the Hezekiah from whom his descent is traced (i. 1) was, as many think probable, the king of that name, then Zephaniah was related to the royal house.

The theme of his prophecy is the day of the Lord, which was about to break. It is pictured as a day of terrible judgment, under the imagery of war and invasion, in which Judah and Jerusalem would be thoroughly purged of those who practised wickedness. But the judgment would embrace all nations; it was to be a day of universal judgment.

When the judgment was completed there would be a remnant of Israel, a lowly but upright people who, trusting in the Lord, would rejoice in His favour. Zephaniah foresaw also that other nations would 'call upon the name of the Lord, to serve Him with one consent' (iii. 9). His message is marked by breadth of view and profound insight, and charged with an ardent vehemence of moral passion.

Zephaniah's words received a striking fulfilment in the fall of Nineveh, and a quarter of a century later in the fall of Jerusalem. But the fulfilment is not yet complete. Where sin abounds, there God will manifest Himself in judgment. 'For wheresoever the carcase is, there will the eagles be gathered together' (Mt. xxiv. 28).

ANALYSIS

i. The approaching day of the Lord, with special reference to Judah and Jerusalem.

ii–iii. 7. A summons to repentance, with prophecies of judgment against other nations, and the failure of Jerusalem to amend her ways.

iii. 8-20. The remnant that will survive the judgment; their character and their felicity.

Week 19. ZEPHANIAH AND HABAKKUK

Day 1. Zp. i.

The chapter, after an introductory statement respecting Zephaniah, begins with a declaration of universal judgment (verse 2), then describes the impact of this judgment upon Judah and Jerusalem in particular (verses 4-13), and ends with a vivid picture of 'the day of the Lord' (verses 14-18).

(1) What forms of religious error are rebuked in verses 4-6, and what classes of the people are threatened with punishment in verses 7-13? Are the sins mentioned here found in modern life, and if so, in what form?

(2) Notice how often the word 'day' occurs in verses 14-18. What may we learn about God's view of sin from the picture here given of 'the day of (His) wrath'? Cf. Pr. xi. 4a; Ezk. vii. 19.

Notes.—(1) The chapter should be read in the R.V., especially verses 2, 7, 9 and 10.

(2) Verse 4. 'Chemarim'; a name for the priests of idol cults.

(3) Verses 8, 9 refer most probably to Jews who aped foreign fashions and foreign religious rites. Cf. 1 Sa. v. 5.

(4) Verses 10, 11. 'Fish gate', 'the second quarter', 'the hills', and 'Maktesh' are all names of localities in Jerusalem.

(5) Verse 12. 'Settled on their lees'; cf. Je. xlviii. 11, *note*. The phrase means here men who had grown careless, and ignored God.

(6) Verse 18. 'Land'; probably should be rendered 'earth', as in ii. 11, iii. 8, 20.

Day 2. Zp. ii–iii. 7.

(1) 'Hid in the day of the Lord's anger.' Is there such a hiding-place? Cf. Je. xxiii. 24; Am. ix. 3; Rev. vi. 15; Ps. xvii. 8, xxvii, 5, xxxi. 20; Col. iii. 3.

(2) 'Nineveh . . . the rejoicing (or "joyous", R.V.) city that dwelt carelessly.' What is lacking in the joy of non-Christians? Cf. Is. xlvii. 6-11; Ec. xi. 9, xii. 14.

(3) How much more grievous is the indictment against Jerusalem than against Nineveh, Moab and Ammon! Cf. Lk. xii. 47, 48. Make a list of the evils which God found in her.

Notes.—(1) ii. 1. See R.V. 'Gather yourselves together', etc.; that is, in solemn assembly to seek the Lord. Cf. Joel ii. 14-16.

(2) ii. 2. 'Before the decree bring forth'; that is, before the decree of God's judgment take effect. Many think, however, that in the original text this and the next clause may have run 'before ye have become as chaff that passeth away'. Cf. Ps. i. 4.

(3) iii. 3. Read as in R.V.

(4) iii. 5-7. They do these evils, not discerning that God is among them daily exercising judgment. They do not perceive the lessons He would have them learn, but eagerly pursue their corrupt ways.

Day 3. Zp. iii. 8-20.

(1) Beyond the judgment the prophet declares the dawn of a better day. What will God do for the nations (verses 9, 10); for the remnant in Jerusalem (a) in their character, and (b) in the

blessings they will enjoy (verses 11-17); and for Israel in exile (verses 18-20)? How much of this is true for us *now* in Christ Jesus?

(2) Note the marginal rendering of verse 17: 'He will be silent in His love'—a love too deep for words. Comparing verses 17 and 18 with Eph. i. 18, 19 and 23, what do they teach us as to God's indwelling presence, His power, and the preciousness to God of His people?

Notes.—(1) Verse 9. Read 'Will I turn to the peoples a pure lip' (see R.V. mg.). Cf. Ho. ii. 17.

(2) Verse 10. 'The daughter of my dispersed' seems to mean dispersed Jews; cf. Is. xi. 11, 12. Some, however, prefer the R.V. mg. rendering; cf. Is. lxvi. 20

(3) Verse 18. Read as in R.V. 'Solemn assembly' means the appointed easts.

HABAKKUK

INTRODUCTION

(*See New Bible Handbook, pp. 253, 254*)

THE book of Habakkuk is singularly free from historical and geographical detail. Of the prophet himself nothing is said, except that he was a prophet. Nor is it stated in whose reign he prophesied. The date must be inferred from his prophecies, and can be fixed with fair certainty as the reign of Jehoiakim, king of Judah. For, on the one hand, the land was full of violence and wickedness and, on the other, God was beginning to use the Chaldeans as a scourge wherewith to smite the nations. Habakkuk was therefore a contemporary of Jeremiah, but the two men were very different. Jeremiah's heart was broken by the impending fall of Judah. His problem was how God could destroy His people. Habakkuk demanded God's judgment upon Judah. His problem was how God could use so evil a nation as the Chaldeans as the minister of His judgment. The problem is set forth in chapter i and God's answer is given in chapters ii and iii in words of extraordinary depth and significance and majestic grandeur.

ANALYSIS

i. 1.   Introductory statement.
i. 2-4.   Habakkuk's problem. God's delay in judgment.
i. 5-11. God's answer: the Chaldeans are His instrument of judgment.

i. 12-17.   A second problem.   How can God employ an evil
            nation?

ii. 1-4.   The prophet waits and receives God's answer.

ii. 5-20.   A series of woes, directed against the Chaldeans.

iii. 1-19. A psalm: consisting of a prayer, a theophany, and a
            confession of faith.

Day 4. Hab. i–ii. 4.

(1) What is the prophet's first complaint, and what is God's
answer? See i. 2-4 and 5-11.

(2) What further problem does this raise in the prophet's mind,
and what answer is he given? See i. 12-17 and ii. 2-4.

(3) What course of action does ii. 1 suggest that the Christian
should adopt when perplexed at God's dealings? Cf. Ps. lxxiii.
16, 17, cxii. 4; Is. l. 10. Have you had experience of this?

Notes.—(1) i. 5. 'Behold ye'. The words are addressed to the people of
Judah.

(2) i. 7. 'Their judgment', etc. They exalt themselves to give judgment and
to have pre-eminence over the nations.

(3) i. 9. This verse, as also i. 11 and ii. 3, should be read in the R.V.

(4) i. 10. 'They shall heap dust'; i.e. mounds of earth. Cf. Ezk. iv. 2.

(5) ii. 1. The Syriac version instead of 'I will answer' has 'He will answer'.

(6) ii. 2. 'Tables'; better, 'tablets'. The answer God gives is to be written
plainly upon tablets, so that men may read it quickly and easily.

(7) ii. 4. God's answer is in two parts: (a) The soul of the Chaldean is lifted
up with pride and is not upright. Therefore, it is implied, he will perish. Cf.
Is. ii. 12-17. (b) The righteous man shall not perish, but live, by his faith.
There lies here a profound truth, which is seen in its full significance in the
ight of the gospel. Cf. Rom. i. 16, 17.

Day 5. Hab. ii. 5-20.

Today's portion consists of five songs directed against the Chaldeans, each
of them beginning with 'Woe'. Verses 5-6a are an introduction to them.

(1) Sum up in one or two words each of the evils against which
the five 'woes' of these verses are pronounced. Are these evils
found in the world today?

(2) Show how each of these songs bears out the teaching of
verse 4a.

(3) Contrast what is said of the Lord. Babylon at the height
of her strength might seem invincible, but what was she in comparison to God?

Notes.—(1) Verse 5. The word 'wine' is not found in the LXX, and seems out
of place here. There has probably been some corruption of the original text.
The pronoun 'he' refers throughout to the Chaldeans.

(2) Verse 6. Read as in R.V. The Chaldean is compared to a usurer who

enriches himself with articles taken in pledge; but one day he will have to pay them back.

(3) Verse 13. 'Labour in the very fire'; better, 'for the fire', as in r.v.; that is, the fires of war will destroy the results of their labour.

(4) Verses 15-17. See r.v. Verses 15 and 16 refer not to literal drunkenness, but to the stupefaction of a conquered people.

(5) Verse 17. Read as in r.v.

Day 6. Hab. iii. 1-15.

This majestic psalm begins with the prayer that God would manifest Himself once again as in days of old (verses 1, 2), and then describes the vision given to the prophet of the coming of God for the deliverance of His people. Past and present are intermingled. The manifestations of Jehovah in the past—at Sinai, at the Red Sea, at the entrance into Canaan—are pictured under the image of a thunderstorm rolling up from the south and breaking upon Palestine. But the same 'Holy One' is at work also in the present, and the tumults of the nations are the tokens that He is come forth in judgment to effect salvation for His people.

(1) The prophet's contemplation of Jehovah's manifestations in former days had a twofold effect upon him (verses 1, 2). The first, his longing to see Jehovah manifesting Himself again as of old, we can understand. But why was he *afraid*? Do we know such longings and such fears? Cf. Ps. lxxxv. 6; Is. lxiv. 1-3; Acts iv. 24-30.

(2) Note the poetic imagery used to describe the political upheavals which were the prophet's real concern (cf. Is. xxix. 5-8, especially 6). How does the vision of God granted to him here teach us to regard the world-happenings of our own day? What is God's relation to them, and what is His purpose through them? Cf. Ps. lxxiv. 12-15; Lk. xxi. 25-28.

Notes.—(1) The passage should be read in the r.v.

(2) Verse 3. 'Teman . . . mount Paran'; these lie south of Palestine, in the region of Sinai.

(3) Verse 4. 'He had rays', etc. (r.v.); an allusion to flashes of lightning.

(4) Verse 5. 'Before him Pestilence strides, behind him the burning Plague' (Moffatt).

(5) Verse 6. 'Measured'; better, 'shook', as in r.v. mg. The second clause of the verse should read 'He looked, and made the nations start (with fear)' (Driver). The storm was perhaps accompanied by an earthquake.

(6) Verse 8. The answer is given in verses 13-15.

(7) Verse 9b. The meaning is uncertain. With 9c, cf. Ps. lxxiv. 15.

(8) Verses 10, 11. Cf. Ex. xiv. 22, xix. 18; Jos. x. 12. 'The sun and moon stood still'; a poetical expression meaning that their light was obscured by the darkness of the storm.

(9) Verses 13-15. It is probable that the prophet in these verses is speaking of the present victory of God in his own day, which by faith he sees as already accomplished. The second half of verse 13 pictures the foe under the image of a house, whose upper part has been destroyed. See r.v. mg.

Day 7. Hab. iii. 16-19.

(1) What two effects did the vision have upon the prophet? See verses 16 and 17-18. With verse 16 cf. Je. iv. 19; Dn. x. 8; Rev. i. 17; and with verses 17-18 cf. Ps. lxxiii. 25, 26; Phil. iv. 11-13; 2 Cor. vi. 10; Heb. xiii. 5, 6. Have we an inner source of joy when earthly comforts fail?

(2) What three things did God, thus trusted and rejoiced in, do for the prophet? Cf. Ps. xviii. 32, 39; Zc. iv. 6; 2 Sa. ii. 18; Is. xl. 31, lii. 7; Ps. lix. 1; Eph. iii. 16.

Notes.—(1) Verse 16. 'Rottenness entered into my bones'. A Hebrew idiom expressing complete loss of strength. See Pr. xii. 4, xiv. 30. The remainder of the verse is of uncertain meaning. Moffatt translates 'Yet calmly we await the day of doom that dawns upon the folk who would assail us'. Cf. 2 Thes. i. 6-8.

(2) Verse 19. 'To walk upon mine high places'; i.e. to take possession of the heights and to walk there in freedom.

EPHESIANS

INTRODUCTION

(*See New Bible Handbook, pp. 368-371*)

THIS Epistle, together with Philippians, Colossians and Philemon, form a group known as the 'Prison' Epistles, because all four were, as is generally believed, written from Rome when Paul was a prisoner there, as described in Acts xxviii. 16, 30, 31. The words 'at Ephesus' (i. 1) are omitted in a number of important MSS. (see R.V. mg.), and this has led many to suppose that the Epistle was not intended for Ephesus alone, but for all the churches of the Lycus valley, of which the church at Ephesus was the chief.

It was God's purpose from before the foundation of the world to form a people for Himself. But mankind fell into sin and death, and only when Christ came was it revealed that God's purpose was to find accomplishment through the creation of a new humanity in Christ, made up of both Jew and Gentile, reconciled to God and to one another through the blood of the Cross, and indwelt by the Holy Spirit. This 'new man' consists of the whole redeemed community of which Christ is the Head, and stands in contrast to the 'old man' whose head is Adam, and which is under the dominion of the world, the devil and the flesh, and is subject to divine condemnation.

This new humanity in Christ is the theme of the Epistle. The doctrine of individual salvation by faith, as expounded in Romans and Galatians, is here less prominent, and the apostle dwells rather upon the corporate aspects of salvation under the image of the Church as the body of Christ.

ANALYSIS

Theme: 'The New Humanity in Christ'

i–iii. God's purpose concerning His people.

iv–vi. 9. Conduct befitting Christians.

    iv–v. 21. In relation to fellow believers and to the world.

    v. 22–vi. 9. In family life.

vi. 10-18. Conflict with the powers of evil.

vi. 19-24. Final personal request, and benediction.

Week 20. Ephesians

Day 1. Eph. i. 1-14.

These verses deal with God's purpose to form a people for Himself, and to sum up all things in Christ.

(1) In verses 3-6 we are shown this people as conceived in the mind of God. How are they described (a) in their relation to God; (b) in their character; (c) in their relation to one another; and (d) in their privileges?

(2) In verses 7-14 we are shown this same people in process of redemption from sin. What part is played by God the Father, by God the Son, and by God the Holy Spirit in the work of redemption? What three gifts of grace are spoken of in these verses? See verses 7, 8, 13-14.

(3) Is every believer a partaker of the Holy Spirit, and for what purposes is the Holy Spirit here said to be given?

Notes.—(1) Verse 10. Read as in R.V.

(2) Verse 13. 'Sealed'; a mark of God's ownership.

(3) Verse 14. 'Earnest'; a sample given as a first instalment in token that all will be paid.

(4) Verse 3. 'In heavenly places'; a phrase signifying that the believers' blessings are spiritual, in contrast to the earthly blessings offered to Israel under the first covenant (see Dt. xxviii. 8). The phrase is used five times in the Epistle in the sense of super-terrestrial regions—what we today might term 'the spirit realm'.

Day 2. Eph. i. 15–ii. 10.

(1) What are the three great spiritual facts which the apostle prays that his readers may know? For the first of these facts see

1 Cor. ii. 9, 10; 1 Pet. v. 10a; for the second see i. 11 (R.V.); Dt. iv. 20, xxxii. 9; Jn. xvii. 9, 10, 22, 23; and for the third see questions (2) and (3) below.

(2) Consider Christ's present position as set forth in i. 20-23 in relation (a) to God; (b) to other powers and authorities; (c) to the universe; and (d) to the Church. In the light of these verses, has our conception of Christ been large enough?

(3) Work out the contrast between man's condition by nature (ii. 1-3) and his position in Christ (ii. 4-10). How has this amazing change been effected, and are you taking advantage of what Christ has won for you? Cf. Rom. vi. 1-4.

Notes.—(1) ii. 3. 'Children of wrath'; a Hebrew idiom meaning 'subject to wrath'; that is, exposed to the displeasure of God.

(2) i. 20, ii. 6. 'In the heavenly places'; see i. 3, note. The expression here refers to the realm where Christ now is, at God's right hand. Believers have communion with Him *there*.

Day 3. Eph. ii. 11-22.

The apostle expounds the new position of Jew and Gentile in Christ Jesus.

(1) Before Christ came Jew and Gentile remained separate, divided by a wall of partition (ii. 14). How did God deal with this problem through Christ's coming? And what is now the position of believers, whether Jews or Gentiles, in relation (a) to God, and (b) to one another (ii. 13-18)?

(2) What three metaphors are used in verses 19-22 to show the complete equality of privilege which Gentile believers enjoy in Christ with those of Jewish birth?

Notes.—(1) Verse 15. 'Make in Himself'. These words point back to ii. 4-10, for the word 'make' in Greek is the same word as 'create' in ii. 10, and 'in Himself' signifies the union with Christ described in ii. 5, 6.

(2) Verses 19-22. 'Strangers and sojourners' (R.V.). Gentile believers shared in the full privileges accorded to citizens of the city of God. More than this they were of God's family and a part of His house.

Day 4. Eph. iii.

The apostle shows that the union of Jews and Gentiles in one body in Christ was in God's purpose from the beginning.

(1) Notice how strongly in verse 6 the apostle emphasizes the parity of Gentile believers with those of Jewish race. Apply his teaching to the problems of racial discrimination and the 'colour bar' which face us today even within the churches.

(2) What was Paul's twofold commission, as set forth in verses 8-11?

(3) Comparing the prayer of iii. 14-19 with that of i. 17-19, what resemblances and what differences do you find? What petitions does Paul offer in the prayer of this chapter?

Notes.—(1) Verse 1. 'The prisoner of Christ Jesus'; cf. iv. 1; 2 Tim. i. 8; Phm. i. 9; also Jn. xviii. 11. Paul states his conviction that even his imprisonment is part of the Lord's will for him.

(2) Verse 2. 'The dispensation'. The Greek word is *oikonomia*, meaning the office or work of the *oikonomos*, the manager or steward of a house or estate, or, more generally, of any charge or trust. The particular thought expressed, therefore, is that of management or administration. In Eph. i. 10 and iii. 9 (R.V.) the reference is to *God's* administration or working out of His purpose in Christ. Here it is used of Paul's part in it; that is, the special commission assigned to Paul.

(3) Verse 4. 'The mystery of Christ'. The word 'mystery' as used in the New Testament denotes God's secret counsel, now made known through the gospel. It is used both of the Christian revelation as a whole, as here and in verse 9, and also of some particular part of that revelation, as in v. 32.

Day 5. Eph. iv–v. 2.

The apostle now passes to the kind of conduct that befits the people of Christ.

(1) Express in your own words the difference between the unity described in iv. 3-7, as already existing among Christians, and that mentioned in iv. 13-16, which Christians are to seek. How is the first to be preserved and how is the second to be attained?

(2) Does Paul's fourfold description of the life of the Gentile world (iv. 17-19) apply to the life of non-Christians today? In contrast, what three principles are to govern the behaviour of Christians (iv. 20-24)?

(3) In iv. 25–v. 2 what must be put away, and what is to take its place? Notice also the reasons given by the apostle why we must live thus.

Notes.—(1) Verse 7. 'Grace'; used here, as also in iii. 2, 7, of God's gifts to His people in Christ in appointing them each to his special work. Cf. Mk. xiii. 34; Mt. xxv. 14, 15.

(2) Verse 12 should be read with the first comma omitted, 'for the perfecting of the saints unto the work of ministering'.

(3) Verse 22-24. The tenses in the Greek show that the putting off of the old man and putting on of the new are definite acts, whereas the being renewed is a process. The living of this new Christian life is made possible for us through the continual renewing of the Spirit, enabling our minds to lay hold of the truth in Christ.

(4) Verses 26, 27. While there may be anger which is not sin, anger is dangerous. It may lead to some action which gives the devil room to strike a blow at the body of Christ.

Day 6. Eph. v. 3–vi. 9.

The apostle continues to set forth the kind of conduct that alone befits Christ's people.

(1) v. 3-21. Make two lists, one of actions, words and thoughts which belong to the old life and must be put away, and the other of those which belong to the new life. Test your own life in the light of these things.

(2) In what ways, according to v. 18-21, will the Spirit-filled life express itself?

(3) What teaching is given in v. 22–vi. 9 concerning the duties and relations of Christians to each other in a Christian household —of husband and wife, of parents and children, of masters and servants?

Notes.—(1) v. 14. Some think that Paul is here quoting from a Christian hymn, addressed to those who have not yet believed in Christ.

(2) vi. 5-9. 'Masters' and 'servants' in this passage have reference primarily to the slave society of Paul's day, but the principles laid down are applicable still.

Day 7. Eph. vi. 10-24.

Christian warfare with the powers of evil.

(1) How are our enemies described—in their leadership and in their organization, in their character and in their sphere of action? What two methods which Satan uses are particularly mentioned? Do you gather that Paul conceives Satan's attack to be upon the *mind* of the believer? Cf. 2 Cor. xi. 3, 13, 14.

(2) Some interpreters take 'truth' to mean inward sincerity and 'righteousness' to mean integrity and fidelity. Others think 'truth' here means 'the truth of the gospel', as in iv. 21, and 'righteousness' to mean God's righteousness, as in Rom. iii. 22. Can you find a decisive answer? What defensive weapons are mentioned, and how many offensive?

(3) What lessons may we learn regarding prayer from this passage?

Notes.—(1) Verse 12. 'Wrestle'; a word implying hand-to-hand conflict.

(2) Verse 13. 'The whole armour of God'; completely equipped with God's armour.

(3) Verse 15. 'The preparation of the gospel of peace'; better, 'preparedness'; that is, readiness to fight, being sure-footed with the peace the gospel brings.

(4) Verse 16. 'Fiery darts'; sudden thoughts or desires, evil in their nature and tending to influence the passions.

PHILIPPIANS

INTRODUCTION

(See New Bible Handbook, pp. 371-374)

THE heart of Paul flowed out in special love towards the brethren in the church at Philippi. Three times he addresses them as 'beloved' (ii. 12, iv. 1; see also i. 8). From the beginning they had entered into his labours and sufferings with financial support and prayerful personal interest (i. 5, 19, iv. 15, 16). Shortly before this letter was written they had sent a gift to Rome, where he was a prisoner, and had gladdened his heart (iv. 10, 14, 18). His letter, therefore, is marked to an unusual degree by personal affection for his readers, and consists largely of a recital of his personal experience of Christ, with special reference to his circumstances as a prisoner.

The church in Philippi seems to have been singularly free from both serious error in doctrine and moral lapses. At the same time there were threatening dangers. A measure of friction had arisen between certain members, and in the earlier part of the letter Paul urges the importance of being of one mind in the Lord. He warns also against other perils, and bids them stand fast in the Lord. It is in connection with these dangers that the main doctrinal passages of the letter occur, namely in ii. 5-11 and iii.

The letter is diffused with an atmosphere of heavenly joy and peace, and is an outstanding witness to the power of Christ to lift the soul above the sorrow and suffering of earth into a holy gladness in the Lord.

ANALYSIS

i. 1, 2. Greeting.

i. 3-11. Thanksgiving and prayer.

i. 12-26. Paul's present circumstances and outlook.

i. 27–ii. 16. Call to unity and concord, with an appeal to Christ's example.

ii. 17-30. Paul explains that Epaphroditus is about to return to Philippi and that he and Timothy will follow soon, if the Lord will.

iii. Warning against threatening dangers. The faith and aim of a Christian illustrated by Paul's own life.

iv. 1-9. Further marks of a Christian.

iv. 10-20. A gracious 'thank you' for the gift sent from Philippi,
            and a testimony to the power of Christ to meet
            every need.

iv. 21-23. Greetings and Benediction.

Week 21. PHILIPPIANS

Day 1. Phil. i. 1-11.

(1) In verses 1 and 2 how does Paul describe (a) himself and
Timothy, and (b) his readers? What is the meaning of the terms
he uses? What blessings does he desire for his readers?

(2) Note Paul's confidence for the believers in Philippi. What
grounds has he for this confidence? See verses 5, 6, 7.

(3) What four petitions does the apostle include in his prayer?
Put them in your own words. What kind of Christians does Paul
wish his readers to become?

Notes.—(1) Verse 1. 'Servants'; literally, 'bondservants' or 'slaves'. Cf. ii. 7.
'Saints'; a name for the people of Christ as set apart for God's use and service

(2) Verse 5. See iv. 15, 16.

(3) Verse 6. 'The day of Jesus Christ'; i.e. the era introduced by His promised return.

(4) Verses 7, 8. Read as in R.V. Cf. i. 29, 30.

Day 2. Phil. i. 12-26.

(1) 'The things that happened' to Paul must have seemed a
calamity to those who loved him. But what did Paul think about
it? See verses 12-18; Rom. viii. 28.

(2) What does Paul say will be the outcome of his sufferings for
himself? What did he require from man, and what from God, to
help him realize this fully (verse 19)? Meantime, what was his
eager hope and expectation? How far are you one with him in
this?

(3) To Paul both life and death were sweet (verse 21). How
different the attitude of Hezekiah in Is. xxxviii! Which would
Paul himself have chosen, and why? But what other consideration
had a decisive influence on his outlook?

Notes.—(1) Verse 13. 'In all the palace'; more probably 'throughout the
whole prætorian guard', i.e. the whole body of troops, about 9,000 strong, who
formed the imperial guard.

(2) Verse 19. 'My salvation'; some take this to mean deliverance from
prison (cf. verses 25, 26), but the verse as a whole seems to suggest that Paul
was thinking of the word's spiritual significance.

(3) Verse 22a. 'If it is to be life in the flesh, that means fruitful labour for
me' (R.S.V.).

Day 3. Phil. i. 27-ii. 11.

(1) Paul turns from his own circumstances to the situation at Philippi. He sees the believers there, a small company in a hostile world. What qualities does he desire to see manifested in their lives (i. 27, 28)? In what light does he regard their sufferings? Cf. Acts iv. 24-31, xiv. 22; 1 Cor. xvi. 13, 14; 1 Pet. iii. 14; 2 Thes. i. 7; Mt. v. 12.

(2) 'Fulfil ye my joy.' What was the one defect in the Philippian church, and what arguments and appeals does the apostle use in ii. 1-4 to urge his readers to remedy it?

(3) ii. 5-9. The supreme appeal is the example of our Lord Himself. How did He act, and how did God manifest His complete approval?

Notes.—(1) i. 27-30. Read as in R.V.

(2) ii. 1. 'So if there is any encouragement in Christ, any incentive of love, any participation in the Spirit, any affection and sympathy' (R.S.V.). Paul shows that the Philippians' love for Christ, their participation in the Spirit, and their sympathy for him should all encourage them to seek the highest.

(3) ii. 7. 'Made Himself of no reputation'; better, 'emptied Himself', as in R.V. The self-emptying was the exchanging of 'the form of God' for 'the form of a bondslave'.

Day 4. Phil. ii. 12-30.

(1) How do God and man co-operate in the achievement of man's highest good or salvation? See especially verses 12, 13.

(2) What ideal of conduct is set before us in verses 14-16 in regard to (a) personal character; (b) conduct towards other believers; and (c) our relation with the outside world?

(3) Consider the three Christian men whom we meet in this chapter, Paul, Timothy and Epaphroditus. What may we learn from each of them?

Notes.—(1) Verses 12, 13. 'Obeyed'; cf. verse 8 above. 'With fear and trembling'; conscious of the indwelling presence of God (verse 13). Cf. Is. lxvi. 2.

'Of His good pleasure'; i.e. to carry out His purposes of grace. Cf. Eph. i. 5, 9.

(2) Verses 17, 18. Paul here regards his blood, if he should be martyred, as wine poured upon the sacrifice of the Philippian believers (cf. Rom. xii. 1). It would not be a matter for sorrow, as it might seem to human judgment, but for rejoicing.

(3) Verse 28. 'The more carefully'; better, 'I am the more eager to send him' (R.S.V.).

(4) Verse 30. 'Risking his life to complete your service to me' (R.S.V.).

Day 5. Phil. iii. 1-11.

Paul now turns to another subject—possibly, as some think, resuming his writing after a break. His subject now is the essential character of the Christian life from its beginning in justification by faith to its glorious consummation at the coming of the Lord, and he illustrates the theme from his own life. He warns the believers at Philippi against three incipient errors: (a) making circumcision and observance of the law necessary to salvation (verse 2); (b) thinking that they had already become perfect (verse 12a); and (c) thinking that they can indulge sin in the body, and yet soar Godwards in spirit (verses 18, 19). Paul has spoken of these things before, but to reiterate them, he says, is not irksome for him and is safe for them (verse 1).

(1) What three characteristics of the true people of God are given in verse 3?

(2) Examine carefully the reasons for 'confidence in the flesh' which Paul enumerates in verses 5-6. Are there not many church-goers today who are relying for salvation on just such grounds as these? What, in contrast to all this, is the position of the true Christian?

(3) Faith in Christ as the sole ground for acceptance with God led, in Paul's case, to intense desire to know Christ; nothing else seemed to him of any value (verses 8, 9). Along what two lines in particular did he want a deeper knowledge (verse 10), and to what end (verse 11)?

Notes.—(1) Verse 2. Note the emphatic 'beware' repeated three times. The persons mentioned are one and the same. The phrase 'the concision' is used because the circumcision on which they insisted was not the true circumcision of the heart, but an outward rite only. Cf. Je. iv. 4; Rom. ii. 28, 29.

(2) Verses 3, 4. 'Confidence in the flesh'; reliance upon outward privilege and personal merit. See verses 5, 6, and also Mt. iii. 9; 2 Cor. xi. 22; Gal. i. 13, 14.

'We are the circumcision'; i.e. we are the true people of God.

(3) Verse 11. 'The resurrection of the dead'; literally, 'the resurrection which is out from the dead'.

Day 6. Phil. iii. 12-21.

(1) There were some who thought they had reached the summit of spiritual experience. Not so Paul. How does he describe his attitude in verses 12-14? Are we 'thus minded' (verse 15)?

(2) Others who professed to be Christians were living in sinful self-indulgence. They thought that the body might sin while the spirit soared. How does Paul show that a true vision of Christ's return shatters any such conceptions?

Notes.—(1) Verses 12-14. These verses should be read in the R.V.

'Perfect'; the word means properly 'having reached its end', but it was used of persons who were full grown or mature (cf. 1 Cor. ii. 6; Heb. v. 14, R.V. mg.).

(2) Verses 20, 21. Read as in the R.V. Christians belong to a heavenly commonwealth (R.V. mg.). Cf. Col. iii. 1.

Day 7. Phil. iv.

(1) What seven qualities should characterize the Christian life? See verses 1-9.

(2) What three great promises does this chapter contain?

(3) What may we learn in verses 10-18 from the example (a) of Paul in prison, and (b) of the Philippian believers in sending him a gift?

Notes.—(1) With verse 1 cf. i. 27, and with verse 2 cf. ii. 2.

(2) Verse 3. 'True yokefellow'; it is not known who this may be. Some think that it should be read as a proper name, thus, 'I beseech thee who art a true Syzygus (yoke fellow), help these women.'

(3) Verse 5. 'The Lord is at hand.' This may mean that the Lord is near in the sense of being beside them (cf. Ps. cxix. 151) or that His coming is near.

(4) Verse 18. 'An odour of a sweet smell.' A phrase used frequently in the Old Testament of acceptable offerings. Cf. Lv. i. 9; Eph. v. 2.

(5) 'They that are of Cæsar's household'; i.e. people in the domestic service of the emperor, probably mainly slaves.

COLOSSIANS

INTRODUCTION

(*See New Bible Handbook, pp. 374-377*)

COLOSSE was one of a group of three cities (of which the other two were Laodicea and Hierapolis; see Col. iv. 13), situated on the river Lycus about a hundred miles inland from Ephesus. Paul had not visited these cities himself (ii. 1), but was given a full account of the situation at Colosse by Epaphras, who had founded these churches (i. 7, ii. 5, iv. 12, 13).

While there was cause for thanksgiving (i. 3-5, ii. 5), yet there was ground also for deep concern because of the dissemination of a plausible false teaching, which, dressed in the garb of an enlightened philosophy (ii. 8), claimed to be a higher form of Christianity. Would they have full emancipation from evil? Then they must observe circumcision and practise a strict discipline. Would they have access to the divine presence? Then they must worship angelic beings, by whose mediation they might draw nearer to the throne of God. No doubt these teachers gave Jesus a place, but it was not the supreme place.

Paul's answer is to set forth Christ Jesus as pre-eminent in every sphere, and as all-sufficient for the believer's need. This is the main theme of the letter, which stands out among all Paul's Epistles for the fulness of its revelation about the Person and work of Christ. It contains also in brief compass a wealth of practical instruction in regard to Christian living.

ANALYSIS

i. 1, 2.	Greeting.
i. 3-8.	Thanksgiving.
i. 9-14.	Prayer.
i. 15-18.	Christ in relation to Creation and to the Church.
i. 19-23.	Christ the great Reconciler.
i. 24-ii. 3.	Paul's personal ministry.
ii. 4-15.	The all-sufficiency of Christ as Saviour.
ii. 16-iii. 17.	The principles and practice of the Christian life.
	ii. 16-23. Warnings against false teaching.
	iii. 1-4. The Christian's true attitude and outlook.
	iii. 5-17. A revolutionary change, viewed negatively (iii. 5-11) and positively (iii. 12-17).
iii. 18-iv. 6.	Particular instructions in regard to family life, prayer, etc.
iv. 7-17.	Personal references, greetings, etc.
iv. 18.	Final salutation in Paul's own writing.

Week 22. COLOSSIANS AND PHILEMON

Day 1. Col. i. 1-18.

(1) In verses 3-8 what is said concerning (a) the Colossian believers; (b) the true gospel; and (c) Epaphras? Consider the appositeness of this paragraph to the special circumstances of the Colossian church (see *Introduction* above).

(2) Make a list of the six divisions into which Paul's prayer may be divided (verses 9-14). Is there any significance in the order? How far are these blessings for which he prays found in us? With verses 12, 13 compare Acts xxvi. 18, and with verse 14, Eph. i. 7.

(3) What is revealed in verses 15-18 as to our Lord's relation to God, to creation, and to the Church? What practical effect should the revelation have on the Christian's life?

Notes.—(1) Verse 5. 'For the hope'; better, 'because of the hope', as in R.V. The hope set before us in the gospel promotes mutual love.

(2) Verse 15. In Christ the unseen God is manifested, the unknown God known. Cf. Jn. xiv. 9.

(3) Verse 16. Read as in R.V. Notice especially the changes in the prepositions.

Day 2. Col. i. 19-ii. 3.

(1) As with His work in creation, so also Christ's work as Reconciler is related to God, to the universe, and to the Church. What does Paul say here about these things? With verse 19 cf. ii. 9; with verse 21 cf. Eph. ii. 12; with verse 22 cf. Eph. i. 4; and with verse 23 cf. Heb. ii. 1, iii. 12-14, x. 39.

(2) In verses 24-28 what does the apostle say (a) of his sufferings; (b) of his commission; (c) of his theme; and (d) of the method, aim and manner of his ministry? With verse 29 cf. Mt. xxviii. 20.

(3) In ii. 1-3 how does Paul describe his praying? For whom did he pray, and what three things did he ask for them? Cf. i. 9, and with ii. 2 ('knit together in love') cf. i. 4; 1 Thes. iii. 12.

Notes.—(1) i. 20. 'Reconcile'. The Greek word gives the thought of complete reconciliation. Nothing further is required.

(2) i. 23. Paul identifies himself with the gospel preached by Epaphras. There is no other. Cf. Gal. i. 6-9.

(3) i. 29. 'Striving'. A metaphor from the Greek games. The same word in noun form is used in ii. 1 (translated 'conflict') and in its verbal form in iv. 12 (translated 'labouring fervently').

(4) ii. 2. Read as in R.V.

Day 3. Col. ii. 4-15.

(1) Note the two features in the church life at Colosse which gave the apostle cause for rejoicing. Describe in your own words the conditions of spiritual growth as set forth in verses 6, 7. Note that there is one central principle which branches out along four lines.

(2) What four defects does Paul find in the false teaching? See verse 8. What guidance may we receive here to help us to detect error? Cf. Mk. vii. 6-12; Gal. iv. 3 (note); 1 Cor. i. 30, 31.

(3) In verses 9-15 Christ is set forth as the one absolutely sufficient Saviour, because of what He is (9, 10), because of what He gives (11, 12), and because of what He has done (13-15). Take up these points one by one, express them in your own words, and try to grasp their profound significance.

Notes.—(1) Verse 7. The tense of 'rooted' is final, but of 'built up' and 'stablished' continuous.

(2) Verse 8. 'Philosophy and vain deceit'; i.e. a system of teaching which appeared very wise, but which in reality was empty and deceitful.

(3) Verses 11, 12. 'In putting off the body of the flesh' (R.V.). The false teachers advocated the rite of circumcision as a means of purification. Paul's answer is that in the believer's identification with Christ in His death and resurrection the body which had been governed by fleshly desires is put off, and a new man emerges. This far more than fulfils all that the rite of circumcision signified. Cf. Rom. vi. 1-14.

(4) Verses 13-15. The false teachers advocated also as part of the way of salvation a strict observance of legal precepts and a worship of angelic powers. Paul answers that the cross destroyed the law's claim against us, and also carried with it complete victory over all spiritual powers that might have held us in bondage.

Day 4. Col. ii. 16-iii. 4.

(1) It is quite clear that the false teachers stressed (a) the observance of holy days; (b) the worship of angels; and (c) ascetic practices. See ii. 16, 18, 21. On what grounds does the apostle show all these to be mistaken, useless, and hurtful as a means of salvation?

(2) What, in contrast, should be the attitude of the Christian? See especially ii. 19, 20, iii. 1, 2.

(3) 'Died with Christ' (ii. 20, R.V.). '. . . risen with Christ' (iii. 1). What do these phrases imply? Compare your answer with your own experience. Cf. ii. 12, iii. 3; Gal. ii. 20; Rom. vi. 4-6.

Notes.—(1) ii. 17. Christ, the real Saviour, travelling towards the time of His incarnation cast before Him a shadow consisting of rites and ordinances which, now that He had appeared, were no longer of value. They belonged to 'the rudiments' (ii. 20). Cf. Heb. viii. 13.

(2) ii. 18. 'Beguile'; better, 'disqualify', as in R.S.V. 'A voluntary humility'; read as in R.V. mg.

(3) ii. 20. 'As though living in the world'; i.e. according to its teachings and ways. Cf. Gal. vi. 14.

(4) ii. 23. Read as in R.V. 'Will worship' means 'self-imposed worship'.

(5) iii. 1, 2. 'Seek . . . set your mind upon.' 'The one points to the outward life of effort and aim; the other to the inward life of thought and longing.'

Day 5. Col. iii. 5-17.

(1) What evils must be slain, what sins put off by every Christian, and for what reasons? (See the word 'therefore' in verse 5, also verses 6, 7, and the word 'now' in verse 8 and verses 9b-11.) Are you tolerating any of these things in your life?

(2) They must be slain and put off, but how? What has Christ done in the matter, and what must we do? It is all-important to grasp the apostle's teaching here and to practise it.

(3) Mark carefully the garments of 'the new man', which are

to be worn by every Christian. In verses 15-17 what does Paul add about the peace of Christ, the Word of Christ, the Name of Christ, and about thanksgiving?

Notes.—(1) Verse 5. 'Mortify (better, 'put to death', as in R.S.V.) your members that are upon the earth.' Paul is speaking of the use of the bodily members in the service of sin. That must end absolutely. Cf. Rom. vi. 12-14.

(2) Verse 14. 'Which is the bond of perfection'; better, 'which binds everything together in perfect harmony', as in R.S.V. The R.S.V. should, if possible, be consulted for the whole of today's portion.

Day 6. Col. iii. 18–iv.

(1) Observe how, in giving directions about the life of a Christian household, the apostle urges 'upon each party its own duties and the other's rights'.

(2) In iv. 2-6 Paul speaks (a) of the Christian's prayer life; (b) of his behaviour in the world; and (c) of the words he utters. Are not hurried formal devotions, thoughtless disregard of others, and idle words, too, often characteristic of our lives also? How different the ideal set before us here!

(3) The names in the closing verses of the Epistle fall into groups: (a) the bearers of the letter; (b) those who send greetings, of whom there were three Jews and three Gentiles; (c) those to whom greetings are sent. From the references here and in other Epistles concerning these men, what may we learn from them?

Notes.—(1) iii. 19. 'Bitter'; a reference to harsh, biting speech.

(2) iii. 21. 'Provoke'; by undue fault-finding and little or no praise.

(3) iv. 5. 'Redeeming the time'; literally, 'buying up the opportunity', i.e. using each day and hour to the best advantage in winning others to faith.

(4) iv. 10. 'Aristarchus my fellow prisoner.' Cf. Phm. 23, 24. It has been suggested that Paul's friends took turns in sharing his captivity.

(5) iv. 11b. There were, no doubt, many other believing Jews in Rome, but they did not work in co-operation with Paul. Cf. Phil. i. 15, 17.

PHILEMON

INTRODUCTION

(See *New Bible Handbook, pp. 387-389*)

THE Epistle to Philemon contains no doctrinal teaching. It has one purpose only—to ask Philemon to receive back a runaway slave who had been in his service and had absconded with his money. The man had come into contact with Paul in Rome and had been converted and transformed into a new man. It was not easy for Paul to let him go; it was harder still for Onesimus to face his former master. But it was hardest of all for Philemon to take him back. These men were Christians, however, and that made all the difference. The letter is one of great charm, tact, gracious- ness, and love, and provides an unforgettable picture of Chris- tianity in action. Though no place-names are mentioned, it is clear that the letter was written at the same time as that to the Colossians.

Day 7. Philemon.

(1) What light does the letter throw upon Paul himself? Is he putting into practice Col. iii. 12-14? Consider closely the appeal he makes and the arguments by which he reinforces it.

(2) What does Paul find worthy of praise in Philemon, and what is his prayer for him? Why was Paul's request a hard one with which to comply?

(3) How does the letter illustrate Lk. xix. 10? How does it teach us also what attitude we should adopt to the fallen, both before and after their conversion?

Notes.—(1) Verse 6. 'That this faith which you share with us may have its perfect work in your recognition of this, that all the good which is in us is for Messiah Jesus' service' (Way).

(2) Verse 7. 'Bowels'; should be rendered here, and in verses 12 and 20, as 'heart', which is the corresponding English idiom.

(3) Verse 11. There is a play here upon the name 'Onesimus', which means profitable'.

PSALMS LXXIII-CVI

INTRODUCTION

(See Year II, p. 164 and New Bible Handbook, pp. 191-198)

WE begin here the third division of the Book of Psalms. The first ten psalms in this division are entitled 'A Psalm of Asaph'. The only other psalm bearing this title is Ps. l. Asaph was one of three chief musicians in the time of David. His sons and descendants formed a Levitical family or guild, and are mentioned in 2 Ch. xx. 14, xxix. 13, xxxv. 15; Ezr. ii. 41, iii. 10. It is probable that the title 'A Psalm of Asaph' means that the psalm in question was one specially associated with the guild of Asaph, if not actually composed by one of its members. The psalms bearing this title are marked by certain characteristic features, among which may be mentioned the representation of God as Judge and also as the Shepherd of His people. They are, in the main, national psalms, and look back to the past history of Israel to draw from it encouragement and warning.

Week 23. Psalms LXXIII–LXXX

Day 1. Ps. lxxiii.

(1) Does it sometimes seem to you, as it did to the Psalmist, that those who live without God in the world have a better time than those who fear Him? Observe how painfully this problem pressed upon the Psalmist's mind. See verses 2, 3, 16.

(2) How did the Psalmist discover the grossness of his error? What did he come to see with regard to the wicked (verses 17-20), and what did he find that he possessed in God (verses 23-26)? Cf. Jas. i. 12-15; Rom. viii. 16-18.

(3) What may we learn from the Psalmist's example (a) in verses 15-17; (b) in verses 21, 22; and (c) in verse 28? Do the three steps in verse 28 find a parallel in your experience?

Notes.—(1) Verse 10. 'Return hither'; better, 'turn hither', i.e. to the wicked. 'Wrung out to them'; better, 'drained by them', as in R.V. mg. The meaning is that they drink deeply of the pleasures of sin.

(2) Verse 15. The Psalmist had not spoken his thoughts aloud.

(3) Verse 21. 'Thus my heart'; better, 'when my heart', etc.

(4) Verse 22. 'As a beast'; seeking happiness only in material good.

(5) Verse 28. 'Draw near'; in contrast to 'far from thee' (verse 27). Cf. Heb. x. 22.

Day 2. Ps. lxxiv.

(1) Israel had suffered a shattering defeat (see 2 Ki. xxv). How does the Psalmist describe what the enemy had done, and the sorrowful condition of his country? Yet what does he believe concerning Jehovah, and what pleas does he present in prayer? Have you learned thus to *plead* in prayer, giving reasons why God should answer?

(2) Note the Psalmist's distress at the lack of such visible things as a sanctuary (verse 7), synagogues (verse 8, but see note (1) below), signs and prophets (verse 9), etc. Contrast Paul's words in Phil. iii. 8; 2 Cor. vi. 10.

Notes—(1) Verse 4. 'Congregations'; the Hebrew word *moed* may mean either the people assembled together, or the actual place of meeting. It is used here in this latter sense and signifies probably the temple. The same word is used in verse 8 where it is wrongly translated 'Synagogues'. It may refer here to traditional places of worship such as Bethel.

(2) Verses 5, 6. Read as in R.V. The enemy are likened to woodcutters.

(3) Verse 9. 'Our signs'; i.e. the outward and visible symbols of religion. Contrast the 'signs' introduced by the enemy (verse 4b).

(4) Verses 13-15. The Psalmist in poetical language recalls the miracles of the exodus.

Day 3. Pss. lxxv and lxxvi.

These two psalms, like Pss. xlvi–xlviii, appear to celebrate the deliverance of Jerusalem from the Assyrians in the reign of Hezekiah. Ps. lxxv, in a spirit of thanksgiving, draws lessons from the victory; Ps. lxxvi extols Jehovah's majesty.

(1) If verses 2-5 of Ps. lxxv are taken as a divine utterance, how does it confirm (a) the certainty of God's judgment, and (b) its character? What two things, according to this psalm, will God not tolerate?

(2) How does the teaching of Christ illustrate Ps. lxxv. 6 and 7? See e.g. Lk. xiv. 7-11; Mt. xx. 20-23. Do we really believe the teaching of these verses? How do we react to the promotion of ourselves and of others?

(3) Ps. lxxvi falls into four sections of three verses each. How would you summarize the contents of each section? Observe that the first two vividly depict God's act of judgment, and the second two extol Jehovah's greatness and man's consequent duty towards Him.

Notes.—(1) lxxv. 2. Read as in R.V. Cf. Dn. viii. 19b.

(2) lxxv. 3. 'When men in any panic melt away, I still uphold the order of the world' (Moffatt).

(3) lxxvi. 4. Read as in R.V. God is represented as a lion returning from hunting his prey upon the mountains. Cf. Is. xiv. 25.

(4) lxxvi. 5, 6. A vivid picture of the enemy silent in death.

(5) lxxvi. 10. The enemy's wrath, through his defeat, will turn to God's praise. The second half of the verse should be read as in R.V.

Day 4. Ps. lxxvii.

Jerusalem is destroyed. Israel is in exile. Hence the Psalmist's sorrow and his problem.

(1) Observe the depth of the writer's depression in verses 2-4. He turns to the past history of his nation and his own happier days. Was all the past to end thus? See verses 5-9.

(2) Gradually he sees more clearly *God Himself* (note how in the first part of the psalm the pronoun 'I' predominates, but in the second it is all 'Thou'). What aspects of God's character are mentioned in verses 10-20, and how did this vision of God answer the questions of verses 7-9?

Notes.—(1) Verse 13 should be read as in R.V. mg., and verse 19 as in R.V.

(2) Verses 16-19 are a poetical description of God's deliverance of Israel at the Red Sea.

Day 5. Ps. lxxviii. 1-39.

(1) A nation's history may teach many different lessons. We have seen what it taught the writer of Ps. lxxvii. What does the Psalmist say is the main purpose of Ps. lxxviii? See verses 1-8. What light do these verses throw upon the necessity and importance of family religion? Cf. Dt. vi. 6-9, 20-25.

(2) From verses 9-39 make a list (a) of God's wondrous works for His people; (b) of the nation's sins; and (c) of God's judgments. Does this portion of Scripture help you to understand better God's dealings in your own life and also your own shortcoming?

Note.—Verses 15, 16. Verse 15 refers to the miracle of Ex. xvii. 6, and verse 16 to that of Nu. xx. 8-10.

Day 6. Ps. lxxviii. 40-72.

Verses 40-55 relate to the period from the exodus to the entrance into Canaan, and verses 56-72 to the period from the entrance into Canaan to the accession of David.

(1) Why do you think the Psalmist recites in such detail six of the plagues of Egypt (see verses 43-51)? Was it to set in bolder relief the people's ingratitude and rebellion? See verses 40-42. Or was it simply to stir up their forgetful memories? Cf. Ps. ciii. 2; 2 Pet. i. 12, 13.

(2) When Israel entered the promised land, what new sin did they commit and with what result? See verses 56-64.

(3) How do the closing verses of this psalm illustrate Paul's words in Rom. v. 20b? See verses 65-72 and compare 1 Tim. i. 14.

Notes.—(1) The whole passage should be read in the R.V.

(2) Verse 61. A reference to the capture of the ark; cf. 1 Sa. iv. 21.

(3) Verse 67. The tent or tabernacle at Shiloh, which was in the territory of Ephraim, was not rebuilt, but Zion was chosen in the territory of Judah, and David was made king (verses 68-71).

Day 7. Pss. lxxix and lxxx.

These two psalms are national prayers in times of national disaster. Ps. lxxix closely resembles Ps. lxxiv.

(1) In what four facts does Ps. lxxix lay bare the sorrowful condition of the nation? See verses 1-4. By what different image does Ps. lxxx describe the nation's ruin (see verses 12, 13)?

(2) How does the prayer of Ps. lxxix differ from that of Ps. lxxx? Do these prayers conform to the conditions of revival laid down in 2 Ch. vii. 14?

(3) Ps. lxxx may be regarded as 'a permanent picture of Israel's woeful condition when banished from God's presence and scattered among the nations'. Viewed in this light, the thrice-repeated refrain (verses 3, 7, 19) shows how Israel's final salvation shall yet come. Cf. Zc. xii. 10–xiii. 1; Rom. xi. 26.

Notes.—(1) lxxx. 1, 2. The three tribes here mentioned camped west of the tabernacle in the wilderness and immediately followed the ark when the people were on the march. See Nu. ii. 17-24.

(2) lxxx. 17. The reference is to the nation, but points forward to the Messiah.

Week 24. Psalms LXXXI–LXXXIX

Day 1. Pss. lxxxi–lxxxiii.

(1) Ps. lxxxi falls into three parts: (a) a call to celebrate the God-ordained Feast of Tabernacles (verses 1-4); (b) God's voice declares His deliverance of His people in past days and the fundamental basis of His covenant (verses 5-10); (c) the door of blessing remains open still, in spite of failure (verses 11-16, R.V.). Note carefully the basic condition on which the weal or woe of Israel depended. Is it otherwise with the believer today? Cf. 1 Sa. xv. 22, 23; Jn. xv. 10, 11.

(2) Ps. lxxxii is a dramatic picture of the judgment and condemnation of divinely appointed judges who have failed to fulfil their office. What does God demand of such men (verses 2-4), and what is the effect upon society of their failure (verse 5b)?

(3) A strong coalition of enemy nations are plotting Israel's destruction. What does Ps. lxxxiii ask of God, and to what end? Contrast it with the prayer of the apostles in Acts iv. 29, 30. In its national aspect is the Psalmist's prayer still legitimate?

Notes.—(1) lxxxi. 5. The last clause may be taken as Israel's hearing the voice of Jehovah, whom at that time Israel did not know, in which case verses 6 onwards give what God said. Moffatt begins a new sentence and translates 'I heard one whom I knew not, saying . . .'

(2) lxxxi. 7. 'The secret place of thunder', i.e. from the midst of the thundercloud. Cf. Ex. xiv. 10, 24.

'The waters of Meribah'; cf. Ex. xvii. 7; Nu. xx. 1-13.

(3) lxxxi. 13. Instead of 'had hearkened' read 'would hearken', as in R.V.

(4) lxxxii. 1. 'Among the gods'. Cf. verse 6. From Jn. x. 34, 35 it is clear that earthly judges are meant. They were called 'gods' and 'sons of the most High' in virtue of their high office as dispensing divine justice.

(5) lxxxii. 8. A prayer for God Himself to judge the nations.

(6) lxxxiii. 13. 'Like a wheel'; better, 'like whirling dust', as in R.V.

Day 2. Ps. lxxxiv.

The three great annual feasts were outstanding events in the religious life of Israel, and men and women went up to them from all parts of the country. This psalm is a song of pilgrimage written by one who was familiar with the temple, but who, for some reason, was cut off from it. He pictures his longing to be there, the journey of the pilgrims, and their arrival in the temple. It should be read in the R.V.

(1) Verses 1-4. The Psalmist's longing. He sees in imagination the temple precincts and longs to be there. But what was his deepest desire? What titles does he give to God?

(2) Verses 5-8. A description of the journey. What five characteristics of the true pilgrim are mentioned in these verses?

(3) Verses 9-12. In the temple. If what is said here was true of the earthly Zion, how much more will it be true of the heavenly! Cf. 1 Cor. ii. 9. Notice especially verse 11. What is the condition of enjoying the 'gracious and glorious life' here spoken of?

Notes.—(1) Verse 6. 'The valley of weeping'. (Hebrew *Baca*, possibly meaning balsam trees, see R.V. mg.) It denotes some dry and barren valley which the travellers approach with dread, only to find that the early rains have carpeted it with grass and flowers and that springs of water are to be found there. So is it also with the 'weary glens' (Moffatt) of life.

(2) Verse 7. One would expect the pilgrims to be exhausted in 'weary glen', but they 'go from strength to strength'.

Day 3. Ps. lxxxv.

This psalm belongs to the period of the return from exile.

(1) Is. xl. 1, 2 had been fulfilled, but all was not as it should be in the restored community (verse 6). Did this mean that God was still angry? Note how the prayer of verses 4-7 expresses exactly the need of a lifeless and joyless Christian.

(2) God's answer marvellously anticipates the gospel. Where, for example, do the statements of verse 10 have their most complete fulfilment? See Rom. iii. 24-26, v. 1. Make a list of other words in the psalm which have a special gospel implication. Cf. Jn. i. 14, 17, xiv. 27.

Notes.—(1) Verse 9. 'Glory'; the manifested presence of Jehovah. Cf. Ex. xl. 34; Zc. ii. 5.

(2) Verses 10, 11. While it is primarily divine attributes that are spoken of here, yet verse 11a shows that earth will reflect the likeness of heaven. Cf. 2 Cor. iii. 18.

Day 4. Pss. lxxxvi and lxxxvii.

(1) List the Psalmist's petitions in Ps. lxxxvi, noting especially those in verse 11. What is meant by the phrase 'unite my heart'? Cf. Dt. vi. 4; Is. xxvi. 13; Je. xxxii. 39; Jas. i. 8; Phil. iii. 13, 14.

(2) List also the reasons which the Psalmist lays before God (introduced by the conjunctions 'for' or 'because') why God should hear his petitions. What is the Psalmist's conception of God?

(3) Ps. lxxxvii is a kind of prophetic expansion of Ps. lxxxvi. 9. Zion is seen as the city of Jehovah's choice, the centre of His world-wide dominion. Nations that were Israel's enemies will be reborn as citizens of Zion. Cf. Jn. iii. 3, 5; Gal. iii. 26-29.

Notes.—(1) lxxxvi. 2. 'For I am holy'. The meaning is, 'I am the object of thy lovingkindness'.

(2) lxxxvi. 13. 'The lowest hell'; i.e. the lowest part of Sheol, the place of the dead.

(3) lxxxvii. 5. 'This one and that one' (R.V.), meaning each and every one. All nations would be included and enrolled in the register of citizens (verse 6).

(4) lxxxvii. 7. Read as in R.V. The city resounds with joy.

Day 5. Ps. lxxxviii.

Jewish interpreters have regarded the psalm as depicting the sufferings of the Jewish *nation* in exile. Many Christian expositors see in it a picture of the sufferings of Christ. Both interpretations find some support in the Psalmist's words, but neither can be consistently applied throughout. See e.g. verse 15.

(1) Summarize briefly the main features of the sufferer's distress.

(2) Observe the intensity and persistence of his prayer (verses 1, 2, 9, 13). What evidence do you find in the psalm that his faith, in spite of everything, remained undismayed? Cf. Is. l. 10.

(3) Outline the Psalmist's view of the after-life (verses 5b, 10-12) and contrast it with that of the Christian (see e.g. Jn. xiv. 1-3, xvii. 24; Rom. viii. 35-39; 2 Tim. i. 10). Cf. also Lk. x. 23, 24.

Notes.—(1) The R.V. is clearer in verses 2, 3, 4, 5, 9, 13.

(2) Verse 3. Sheol, the place of the dead, is also called 'the pit' (verses 4, 6), 'darkness' (verses 6, 12), 'the deeps' (verse 6), 'destruction' (verse 11), and 'the land of forgetfulness' (verse 12).

(3) Verse 18b. 'My one companion is darkness' (Moffatt; cf. R.V. mg.).

Day 6. Ps. lxxxix. 1-37.

This psalm depicts vividly the conflict of faith. In the first part the Psalmist joyfully recalls God's character and promises, and in the second (verses 38-52) he sets forth the facts of Israel's overthrow and exile. The latter seem to contradict the former.

(1) Verses 1-4 give the theme which is expanded in verses 5-37. State in your own words what the Psalmist says concerning (a) God's character, and (b) God's promise. Note especially in verses 1, 2 the double repetition of the words 'mercy' and 'faithfulness', each of which occurs seven times in the psalm.

(2) Verses 5-18 expand verses 1 and 2. What attributes of God are extolled, and how is the blessedness of God's people described?

(3) Verses 19-37 expand the promise of verses 3 and 4. What points are emphasized?

Notes.—(1) The R.V. is clearer in verses 5, 7, 8, 14, 16, 18, 19, 23.
(2) In verses 9-14 the pronouns 'Thou' and 'Thine' are emphatic.
(3) Verse 15. 'The joyful sound'; or 'the shout of joy' as heard in the sacred feasts.

Day 7. Ps. lxxxix. 38-52.

(1) Observe the reiteration of the pronoun 'Thou' in verses 38-46. It is the same God of mercy, faithfulness and power extolled in the earlier part of the psalm, who has brought about the overthrow of David's throne and the desolation of the land. This constitutes the Psalmist's dilemma.

(2) What two pleas for God's speedy action are urged in verses 48-51?

(3) What may we learn from the Psalmist's example when circumstances seem to deny the promises and character of God? What is the Christian solution of his problem?

Notes.—(1) Verse 45. Some think this refers to Jehoiachin, who as a youth was carried off to Babylon; see 2 Ki. xxiv. 8.
(2) Verse 50b. The sense is not clear. It is possible that the original text may have been simply 'How I bear in my bosom the shame (or reproaches) of the peoples'. Cf. Ezk. xxxiv. 29, xxxvi. 15.
(3) Verse 52 is not part of the original psalm, but a doxology at the close of Book III. See R.V.

Week 25. PSALMS XC–C

Day 1. Ps. xc.

Light falls upon this sublime psalm if it is viewed as written towards the end of the wilderness wanderings of the children of Israel.

(1) In verses 2-11 what is said about (a) man, and (b) God?

(2) In view of these facts, what should be man's attitude? See verses 11, 12 (R.V.). What is meant by 'an heart of wisdom'? Cf. Pr. ix. 10; Je. ix. 23, 24; Jas. iv. 12-16.

(3) Set down in your own words the seven petitions of verses 13-17. How is it possible for man in his frailty and sinfulness to live thus in God's favour and fellowship? Cf. verse 1; 2 Cor. iii. 18; 1 Cor. iii. 7; 2 Thes. ii. 16, 17.

Notes.—(1) Verse 11b. Read as in R.V. The meaning is that men do not understand the intensity of God's wrath against sin, and so fail to reverence Him as they should.

(2) Verse 14. 'In the morning' (R.V.); i.e. when the dark night of trouble is passed.

Day 2. Ps. xci.

The theme of this psalm is the security and blessedness of a life lived in God's presence (see verse 1). The change of pronouns from 'I' to 'thee' and to 'he' (see verses 2, 3, 14) has been variously explained. It is perhaps simplest to regard the psalm as designed to be sung antiphonally. Verse 1 is the prelude, sung by the choir. A single voice is then heard (verse 2). The choir answers with assurances of blessing (verses 3-5). The solo voice again sings its song of trust (verse 9a, R.V.), and the choir respond with renewed assurances (verses 9b-13). Finally, God Himself speaks in words of gracious promise (verses 14-16).

(1) Do the assurances of verses 3-5 and 9b-13 run counter to experience and to other Scriptures? See e.g. Ps. xxxiv. 16, cv. 17, 18; Jn. xvi. 1-4. Is the solution of this apparent contradiction the fact that the Psalmist here leaves on one side the complementary truth that God for wise reasons permits His people to suffer? Examine the more complete statement in Rom. viii. 16-18, 28, 31, 32.

(2) Gather out God's seven promises in verses 14-16. Can you bear witness to these truths from your own experience and the experience of other believers? Cf. 2 Pet. i. 2-4.

Notes.—(1) Verse 9 should be read as in R.V.

(2) The evils mentioned in verses 3, 5, 10 and 13 are stock expressions for all kinds of evil, whether insidious and hidden or open and visible in their attack. 'Plague' in verse 10 means any stroke of misfortune. 'The young lion' and 'the dragon' of verse 13b represent evil at its greatest strength.

Day 3. Pss. xcii and xciii.

(1) Ps. xcii. The Psalmist's eyes have been opened to discern the principles of God's working, which are hidden from those who lack spiritual understanding (verses 4-8). What are these principles?

(2) Have you thought of the life of the godly as it is described in xcii. 12-14? What is the secret of their vigour and beauty? Cf. Ps. i. 3; Je. xvii. 7, 8; Is. xl. 29-31, xlvi. 4.

(3) Ps. xciii. The majestic thoughts of this psalm (as also of Pss. xcv–c) seem to have been kindled by the return from Babylon. Of what three divine attributes does the Psalmist specially speak?

Notes.—(1) xcii. 6. Notice the colon in R.V. after 'this', showing that 'this' refers to verses 7, 8.

(2) xcii. 10. Read as in R.V. The verse speaks of restored power and freshness.

(3) xciii. 3, 4. An emblem of the surging might of hostile powers. Cf. lxxxix. 9.

Day 4. Ps. xciv.

If this psalm belongs to the same general period as the other psalms of this series it may represent the sufferings of the nation in the closing years of the exile. It is a prayer for God's coming in judgment to avenge the wrongs of His people (verses 1-7).

(1) What rebuke does the Psalmist give to those in Israel who thought God was indifferent to His people's need, and what purpose does he see in the nation's present sufferings? See verses 8-15 (R.V.) and cf. Pr. iii. 11, 12; Is. xlix. 14-16, li. 7, 8.

(2) In what does the Psalmist find comfort in the midst of distress? See verses 16-23. Make a list of the grounds on which his confidence rests.

Notes.—(1) The psalm should be read in the R.V. throughout.

(2) Verse 16. The meaning is that there is no help save in Jehovah.

(3) Verse 19. 'Thoughts', i.e. distracting thoughts; cf. R.V. mg., 'doubts'. Cf. 1 Sa. xxx. 3-6.

Day 5. Pss. xcv and xcvi.

Pss. xcv–c, with Ps. xciii, form a group of national psalms composed, it may be, to be sung at the dedication of the temple after the return from exile (Ezr. vi. 15-18). These psalms borrow much from earlier Scripture, but are marked by an unusual breadth of vision. Ps. xcv is a summons to His people to worship Jehovah and a warning against backsliding. Ps. xcvi bids all nations and the whole creation to join in His worship.

(1) What is said in these two psalms to show that worship from all creation is Jehovah's due? What should characterize the worship of such a God?

(2) Assuming the date of these psalms to be as mentioned above, what special significance would the word 'today' have for the original worshippers? What application has it for us? See Heb. iii. 7–iv. 13.

(3) What, according to Ps. xcvi, is the world's greatest need? When and how will the Psalmist's vision be fully realized, and

what is our duty meantime? See 1 Cor. xv. 22-26; Rom. viii. 15-20, x. 11-15.

Notes.—(1) xcv. 6. 'Our Maker'; i.e. the Maker of Israel as a nation.

(2) xcv. 8. Read as in r.v. and cf. Ex. xvii. 1-7; Nu. xx. 1-13; Ps. lxxxi. 7.

(3) xcvi. 11. 'In the establishment of God's righteous rule the Psalmist sees the prelude of the Messianic age, which is to bring harmony and peace to all creation' (Kirkpatrick).

Day 6. Pss. xcvii and xcviii.

The triumphant pæan of praise continues. In Ps. xcvii there are four sections of three verses each, and in Ps. xcviii three sections.

(1) Under what four aspects is Jehovah described in xcvii. 1-3, and what further illustrations of these attributes are found in verses 4-9?

(2) What in verses 10-12 is Jehovah's attitude towards His people, and what should be their response towards Him? Test your own life in the light of the Psalmist's teaching. Is your love to God, for example, begetting in you a hatred of evil?

(3) Consider in Ps. xcviii, and in this group of psalms generally, to what *exuberance* of praise men and even nature are summoned. Is our praise thus jubilant?

Notes.—(1) xcvii. 11. Many ancient versions read 'has arisen' for 'sown'.

(2) xcviii. 4-6. Shoutings and songs with harps, and cornets and trumpets.

Day 7. Pss. xcix and c.

In Ps. xcix the thrice-repeated refrain divides the psalm into three sections; see r.v. The first section exalts God as holy in Himself; the second as holy in His righteous government; and the third as holy in His dealings with individuals.

(1) Is there in your heart a passion, such as the Psalmist had, to see God exalted in holiness? Cf. Is. vi. 1-3.

(2) This holy God permits His people to approach Him in prayer and intercession (verse 6). What is the condition for the answering of their cry? See verse 7. What is the connection between forgiveness and retribution? Cf. Ex. xxxii. 35; Nu. xx. 12.

(3) Ps. c is a twice-repeated call to all lands to praise Jehovah (verses 1-2, 4). What in His Being and character makes Him worthy of man's praise?

Notes.—(1) xcix. 3. 'Terrible'; i.e. to be feared, the same word as in Ps. lxxvi. 7, 12, cxi. 9.

'Holy is He' (r.v.). The word means 'not only moral purity, but separation from, by elevation, above the finite and imperfect' (Maclaren).

(2) xcix. 4. The word 'king' here denotes Jehovah, as in xcv. 3, xcviii. 6.

(3) c. 3. Read as in r.v.

Week 26. PSALMS CI–CVI

Day 1. Ps. ci.

See verse 2b and cf. 2 Sa. vi. 9. The meaning is clearer if we assign the psalm to the beginning of David's reign, when he longed for the ark of God (and the God of the ark) to come to him in Jerusalem, and resolved to make his life, his court, and the whole city worthy of God's presence.

(1) Verses 1-4. David's worship. What attributes of Jehovah are to be the chief theme of his meditation and his song? What is he resolved to do in regard to his own conduct and what not to do?

(2) Verses 5-8. What kinds of people will he refuse to employ or have about him? Whom will he favour and how will he purify the city? Cf. 2 Tim. ii. 19-22.

Note.—The psalm should be read in the R.V. Note also the R.V. mg. reading in verses 2 and 3.

Day 2. Ps. cii.

This psalm was probably written towards the close of the exile (see verse 13 and cf. Je. xxix. 10; Dn. ix. 2). A description of the present distress (verses 1-11) is followed by a vision of a restored Zion (verses 12-22). The closing section records the Psalmist's rest and assurance in God's eternal and changeless Being (verses 23-28).

(1) What does the psalm teach us to do in time of trouble? See the title and cf. Ps. lxii. 8.

(2) Observe the metaphors and similes in which the nation's sad condition is described (verses 1-11). Contrast with this extreme misery the vision of faith in verses 12-22. What has happened? Where is your gaze fixed—upon earth's sorrows, or upon God? Cf. 2 Cor. iv. 8, 9, 18.

Notes.—(1) The psalm should be read in the R.V.
(2) Verses 19, 20. Cf. Ex. iii. 7, 8. As then, so now.

Day 3. Ps. ciii.

(1) Enumerate the spiritual blessings in this psalm, noting how praise for personal benefits opens out into thanksgiving which is universal.

(2) Have you known these blessings in your own experience? If so, what does the psalm call upon you to do now?

(3) What is the significance of the threefold recurrence of the phrase 'them that fear Him'? Cf. also verse 18.

Notes.—(1) Verse 4. 'Destruction'; or 'the pit' as in R.V. mg., i.e. Sheol.
(2) Verse 5. 'Mouth' is not a satisfactory translation, but other suggested renderings are equally uncertain.

'Like the eagle's'; better, 'like the eagle', as in R.V. The meaning is 'made strong as an eagle'.

(3) Verse 13. 'Pitieth'; better, 'hath compassion'. Cf. verse 8 (R.V.).

Day 4. Ps. civ.

(1) The psalm in its general outline is based upon the creation story in Gn. i. For example, verse 2a covers the first day (Gn. i. 3-5), verses 2b-4 the second day (Gn. i. 6-8), verses 5-18 the third day (Gn. i. 9-13), etc. Can you complete the outline?

(2) How is the dependence of the creature on the Creator brought out in verses 27-30? Cf. Gn. i. 29, 30. Ponder the beautiful picture in verses 27-28 of God as the great householder, dispensing to all creatures their necessary food.

(3) Do we share the desires and resolves of the Psalmist's heart, as expressed in verses 31-35 (R.V.)?

Notes.—(1) Verses 3, 4. These verses are additional to the Genesis story. The ancient Hebrews conceived that there was a reservoir of water above the firmament (Gn. i. 7) and that God had His dwelling there (cf. verse 13).

(2) Verse 26. 'Leviathan'; meaning here sea monster. Cf. Gn. i. 21, though the Hebrew word there used is different.

(3) Verse 31. Better, 'let the glory of the Lord', etc., as in R.V., and in the second half of the verse 'let the Lord rejoice'.

Day 5. Ps. cv.

This psalm and Ps. cvi belong, in all probability, to the time of the return from exile. The returned Jews, comparatively few in number and faced with many problems and difficulties, could derive encouragement and warning from their early history.

(1) How many things should we do because of what God has done? See verses 1-5. Think of appropriate times during the day when you might do one or more of these things. Cf. Ps. cxix. 164.

(2) What reason is given in verses 7-10 (cf. also verse 42) for God's intervention on behalf of the Children of Israel? Cf. Lk. i. 72-74. For what similar reason do we know He will not fail or forsake us? See Heb. xiii. 5b, 6, 20, 21.

(3) Make a list of all the ways in which God helped His people. What may we learn from these things about the way in which God protects, delivers, trains, and provides for His chosen?

Notes.—(1) Verse 2. 'Talk'; better, 'meditate', as in R.V. mg.

(2) Verse 5. 'The judgments of His mouth', i.e. His decrees as Judge.

(3) Verse 19. God's word to Joseph was a promise of blessing, but it also tested him until the time came for its fulfilment. Cf. verse 25.

(4) Verse 28b. A difficult clause. The LXX omits 'not', which may be the original reading. Cf. Ex. x. 28.

Day 6. Ps. cvi. 1-33.

In today's portion the Psalmist, after a summons to praise Jehovah and a prayer of singular beauty, recites seven instances of Israel's sin from the exodus to the entry into Canaan. See verses 7-12, 13-15, 16-18, 19-23, 24-27, 28-31, 32-33.

(1) What feature of Israel's failure is mentioned three times in these verses, and what were some of the consequences? See Dt. viii. 11-20.

(2) Note in verses 14 and 15 what inspired the Israelites' request, and the serious spiritual consequence which followed. What ought we to do first if we are to be saved from making wrong requests? See Pr. iii. 5, 6.

(3) Why did God, after delivering the Children of Israel, later overthrow them in the wilderness? Note the four things mentioned in verses 24 and 25 which caused Him to change His attitude. See Heb. iii. 12, 17-19, iv. 1.

Notes.—(1) The R.V. is clearer in verses 9b, 29 and 32.

(2) Verse 26. 'Against them'. More correctly, 'unto them', as in R.V. The meaning is that God swore an oath that He would overthrow them. See Nu. xiv. 28, 29, 32.

(3) Verse 33. 'Provoked his spirit'; better, 'were rebellious against His Spirit' (R.V.).

Day 7. Ps. cvi. 34-48.

(1) A new generation entered Canaan (see Nu. xiv. 29-32 xxvi. 64-65); but the sinning went on. What was their first failure, and to what sins of ever deeper degradation did it lead? See verses 34-39. How can Christians avoid similar entanglement? See 2 Cor. vi. 14-vii. 1; Jas. iv. 4; 1 Jn. ii. 15-17.

(2) Verses 34-46 present a summary of Israel's later history. In spite of punishment and deliverance, what remained their general attitude? See verse 43 note below. Yet how does the Psalmist show his firm assurance that God's compassion would win in the conflict? See verses 1-5, 45-47. Cf. also Is. i. 18; Lk. xv. 18-24; Jn. iii. 16; Rom. xi. 25-29.

Notes.—(1) The meaning is clearer in the R.V. in verses 34, 35 and 39.

(2) Verse 43. 'They provoked Him with their counsel'; better, 'they were rebellious in their counsel' (R.V.), i.e. they followed their own self-willed ways.

(3) Verse 48. It is uncertain whether this verse belonged to the original psalm or was appended later as a doxology to mark the end of Book IV. It corresponds to the opening verses and suitably follows the prayer of verse 47.

JAMES

INTRODUCTION

(See New Bible Handbook, pp. 394-397)

IT is generally believed that this letter was written by James, the brother of our Lord. During Christ's life on earth he was an unbeliever (Jn. vii. 5), but was converted when Jesus appeared to him after His resurrection (1 Cor. xv. 7). He was austere in disposition and practical in character. In the book of Acts (see xii. 17, xv. 13-21, xxi. 18, and also Gal. ii. 9) he appears as leader of the church at Jerusalem. He was killed by the Jews about A.D. 62.

The letter is addressed 'to the twelve tribes which are of the Dispersion' (i. 1, R.V.); that is, to fellow Jews living outside Palestine. It is terse and forceful, yet vivid and dramatic in style. It begins and ends abruptly, without any opening thanksgiving or final benediction. James seeks to encourage those who were passing through a period of trial and suffering; but at the same time rebukes such failings as profession of faith without the practice of it, sins of speech, strife and envying, eagerness to take the position of teachers, and a lack of steadfast endurance. He urges his readers to be 'doers of the Word, and not hearers only'; to express their Christian faith not in outward formality and barren profession, but by seeking to obey from the heart God's perfect law of liberty in the manifold relationships of life.

The central thought is that 'faith without works is dead' (ii. 20). Justification is by faith, but the faith that justifies is a living faith that brings forth the fruit of good works.

ANALYSIS

The teaching of the Epistle gathers round certain main subjects which seem on the surface to be without systematic arrangement, but are nevertheless closely connected.

i. 1-18.   The endurance of temptation.
i. 19-27.   Hearing and doing God's Word.
ii. 1-13.   Respect of persons.
ii. 14-26.   Relation between faith and works.
iii. 1-12.   Control of the tongue.
iii. 13-18.   Earthly and heavenly wisdom.
iv.   The wickedness of strife, worldliness, and evil speaking.

v. 1-11.   The sins of the rich; comfort and counsel for patient
            sufferers.
v. 12-20.   Oaths; the power of prayer; the blessedness of con-
            verting others.

Week 27. JAMES

Day 1. Jas. i. 1-18.

(1) What are the rewards of overcoming temptation? See verses
3, 4, and 12, and cf. Heb. v. 8, 9, xii. 3. What on the other hand,
is the result of yielding to it? See verses 13-15. How should the
Christian believer regard temptation and trial?

(2) Find in today's portion three characteristics of God as the
great Giver, and two conditions to be fulfilled by those who would
obtain His gifts.

Notes.—(1) Verse 2. 'Temptation' is regarded in this chapter in two senses.
Here and in verse 12 it refers to outward trials which test faith (cf. 1 Pet. i. 7),
but in verses 13, 14 it is rather the enticement to evil, arising out of our desires.

(2) Verses 3, 4. 'Patience'; better, 'endurance', as in verse 12a and v. 11.
Another Greek word is used in v. 7, 8, 10.

(3) Verse 6. 'Nothing wavering'; better, 'with no doubting', as in R.S.V.

(4) Verse 17. 'Father of lights'; a comprehensive expression. God is the
source of all light; cf. 1 Jn. i. 5.

'Neither shadow of turning'; or 'shadow due to change' (R.S.V.). The whole
clause means that God does not change within Himself, nor is affected by
change from without.

(5) Verse 18. 'Begat'; better, 'brought forth'. The Greek word is the same
as that in verse 15.

'A kind of firstfruits'; proclaiming a new order of things about to appear.
Cf. Rom. viii. 19-23.

Day 2. Jas. i. 19-27.

It is characteristic of James to pass from one paragraph to another by
repetition of a key word. Here, having spoken of God's Word in regeneration
(verse 18), he goes on to speak of the place God's Word should have in the
believer's life.

(1) First the Word, already planted in the heart, is to be received with meekness (verses 19-21). In what two ways may this
be hindered? Cf. Gal. v. 15; 1 Pet. ii. 1, 2.

(2) Second, it is not sufficient merely to hear. What else is all-
essential? What illustration does James use to enforce this? With
verse 25 cf. Lk. viii. 15.

(3) Finally, what are the distinguishing marks of true and false
religion? Looking at today's portion as a whole, make a list of

the faults against which warning is given, and of the qualities which should characterize the believer.

Notes.—(1) Verse 19. 'Wherefore'; better, 'Know this', as in R.V. mg. The R.V. should be read in verse 20.

(2) Verse 25. 'Looketh into'; literally, 'to bend over for close examination' (cf. Jn. xx. 5, 11), and hence to look carefully into.

'The perfect law of liberty', i.e. the divine law accepted by the free choice of the heart. In ii. 8 it is called 'the royal law', as the law of the kingdom of God.

Day 3. Jas. ii. 1-13.

(1) Can you find in verses 4-7 five grounds on which James condemns the conduct described in verses 2, 3?

(2) We, too, believe in Jesus Christ as 'the Lord of glory' (verse 1). Is the Church of today free from the fault which is here rebuked? Are we ourselves guiltless?

(3) How does James show in verses 8-13 that this is not a matter of minor importance?

Notes.—(1) Verse 3. 'Under my footstool', i.e. on the floor at my feet.

(2) Verse 4. 'Have you not made distinctions among yourselves, and become judges with evil thoughts?' (R.S.V.). Cf. iv. 11.

Day 4. Jas. ii. 14-26.

James is still seeking to warn against unreal religion (i. 23). Another form in which it may manifest itself is in a profession of faith without corresponding action.

(1) Notice the word 'say' in verse 14. What illustration does James use to show the emptiness of mere words? See verses 15-17.

(2) What two instances does James adduce in verses 20-26 to support his position? How in these two instances did faith lead to action and thus show itself a living faith? What similar actions have resulted from your faith?

Notes.—(1) Verse 14. 'Save him', i.e. from condemnation.

(2) Verse 17. 'Being alone'; better, 'in itself', as in R.V.

(3) Verse 18. Moffatt translates: 'Someone will object, "And you claim to have faith!" Yes, and I claim to have deeds as well; you show me your faith without any deeds, and I will show you by my deeds what faith is!'

(4) Verse 22. 'By works was faith made perfect', i.e. by active exercise faith reached its full development.

(5) Verse 25. 'Justified by works'; cf. Rom. iii. 20, 28; Gal. ii. 16. Paul and James seem to contradict each other. But the faith against which James is contending is not what Paul means by faith, and the works which James insists upon are not 'the works of the law' which Paul condemns. The reconciliation is found in Gal. v. 16.

Day 5. Jas. iii.

In this section James takes up two subjects, which have previously been mentioned. See i. 5 and i. 26 (cf. also i. 20). The meaning is clearer in the R.V.

(1) Observe the warning James gives regarding the desire to become religious teachers and the ground of his warning. How does he in verses 2-5a set forth and illustrate the power of the tongue?

(2) How in verses 5b-8 does James show the power of mischief that lies in the tongue, and in verses 9-12 that the result of its misuse would be regarded as monstrously unnatural if it occurred in nature?

(3) What are the marks and results of the two kinds of wisdom described in verses 14-18? Consider how the wisdom from above spoken of in verses 17 and 18 is seen in our Lord Himself.

Notes.—(1) Verse 6. Moffatt translates as follows: 'And the tongue is a fire, the tongue proves a very world of mischief among our members, staining the whole of the body and setting fire to the round circle of existence with a flame fed by hell.'

(2) Verse 14. 'Lie not against the truth.' To boast of an intellectual wisdom when the heart is full of bitter animosity is to be false to the truth. Cf. i. 26.

(3) Verse 18. Righteousness and peace go together, as do an evil heart and strife (verse 16).

Day 6. Jas. iv.

(1) Verses 1-3 give a vivid picture of the spiritual condition of the recipients of the letter. What faults are specially mentioned, and what reason is given for their prevalence? Cf. also verse 4.

(2) Verses 4-10 sketch the open road to the recovery of spiritual health. Can you find in these verses seven steps that must be taken? In this endeavour what mighty helper is there for us, and what must be resolutely put away? See verses 4-6.

(3) In verses 11-17 two other wrong lines of action are mentioned. What are these and why are they condemned? Cf. Mk. iv. 24, 25, and then check your own behaviour in the light of verse 17.

Notes.—(1) Verse 4. 'Ye adulteresses' (R.V.). As a woman may be unfaithful to her husband, so are they unfaithful to God.

'Will be a friend of the world', i.e. definitely makes this their wish and desire.

(2) Verse 5. 'The spirit that He made to dwell in us, yearns for us even with jealousy.' See R.V. mg.

Day 7. Jas. v.

In the opening verses James speaks like one of the Old Testament prophets. His mind is burdened with a sense of impending judgment and views with horror the wickedness and folly of those who set store by riches. At the same time he exhorts the oppressed to bear with patience their afflictions.

(1) What two sins in particular are charged against the rich, and what outstanding fact makes their actions all the more foolish?

(2) How many links with the teaching of our Lord in the Gospels can you find in today's portion?

(3) In what ways are we called to help others? In particular, what illustrations are here given of the power of prayer, and what conditions of effective prayer are laid down?

Notes.—(1) Verse 6. Some have seen here a reference to Christ, as in Acts vii. 52. Probably, however, the words are of more general application, and reveal the state of social life at the time.

(2) Verse 9. 'Grudge not'; better, 'murmur not', as in R.V. James is thinking of muttered grumbling against others. Cf. iv. 11, where open criticism is also condemned.

(3) Verse 11. 'The end of the Lord', i.e. what the Lord does in the end.

(4) Verse 16. 'Confess your faults.' There must be no hushing up of sin if prayer is to prevail.

I TIMOTHY

INTRODUCTION

(See New Bible Handbook, pp. 382-385)

TIMOTHY was Paul's dearly loved companion and helper whom he first found at Lystra (Acts xvi. 1-3) and ever afterwards regarded as a son (1 Tim. i. 2, 18; 2 Tim. i. 2, ii. 1). He was with Paul on his missionary journeys and during his imprisonment in Rome (Col. i. 1), and was sent by Paul from time to time on important missions (1 Thes. iii. 1-6; 1 Cor. iv. 17, xvi. 10, 11; Phil. ii. 19). At this time he had been left at Ephesus to check tendencies to false teaching (1 Tim. i. 3, 4) and to superintend the affairs of the church as the apostle's representative (1 Tim. iii. 14, 15, R.V.). The letter belongs to the last period of Paul's life, between his first and second imprisonments in Rome.

Paul's main purpose in writing was to guide and encourage Timothy in his work. The letter is full of practical advice concerning church affairs and the preservation of purity of life and doctrine. It exhorts the worker for God to be uncompromising in his loyalty and devotion to his duty.

ANALYSIS

Week 28. I Timothy

Day 1. I Tim. i.

Timothy is reminded of the purpose for which he was left at Ephesus. Verses 12-17 are a digression in which Paul breaks out into thanksgiving for God's mercy towards himself.

(1) What is Paul's complaint against the teachers and teaching which he charges Timothy to oppose? Note especially to what it leads. What, in contrast, are the things on which Timothy should lay stress? See verses 5 and 19.

(2) The teaching which Paul is here combating evidently made much of the law as a means of promoting righteousness. How does Paul indicate in verses 8-15 that it is the gospel, not the law, which has saving power?

(3) Compare your own experience of the gospel with that described by Paul in verses 12-17. What outstanding features does he emphasize?

Notes.—(1) Verse 4. 'Fables and endless genealogies'. Speculative allegories and attempts to find hidden meanings in names.

(2) Verse 5. 'Commandment' or 'charge'; the same word in the Greek as in verse 3.

(3) Verse 20. 'Hymenæus and Alexander'. Nothing is known of these men; but see 2 Tim. ii. 17, iv. 14.

'Delivered unto Satan'. A solemn judgment by the apostle, involving physical suffering or even death, with a view to the spiritual restoration of the offender. Cf. Acts v. 9; 1 Cor. v. 3-5.

Day 2. 1 Tim. ii.

(1) Verses 1-7. What truths mentioned here indicate the simplicity of the main tenets of the Christian faith? Cf. 1 Cor. viii. 5, 6. And what two truths about Christ constitute Him a sufficient Saviour for men? Cf. Heb. ii. 14, 15. Are you experiencing His sufficiency for your own needs today?

(2) In the light of these truths, why should we take part in public worship and why can we pray 'for all men' (verse 1)? In thus praying, from what should our own lives and thoughts be free (verse 8)?

(3) Verses 8-15. The method of conducting public prayer today differs widely from what was customary in Paul's day. See verse 8, note (1) below. May changes be permitted also in woman's part in public worship if the general principles which lie behind Paul's detached instructions are not infringed? What are these principles?

Notes.—(1) Verse 8. 'Everywhere'; better, 'in every place', as in R.V.; i.e. in every church. Cf. 1 Cor. xiv. 33, 34.

'Lifting up holy hands'. It was customary to stand when praying and to spread out the hands before God. Cf. 1 Ki. viii. 22. See also Ps. xxiv. 4.

'Without wrath and doubting'. The prayers must be offered in love and faith. Cf. Mk. xi. 24, 25.

(2) Verse 14. Read as in R.V.

(3) Verse 15. 'In childbearing' or 'in her child bearing', as in R.V. mg. In view of the context there may be a reference to Gn. iii. 15, 16. Paul is speaking of married women, and indicates that in the discharge of their vocation as mothers women will work out their own salvation if they continue in faith, etc. Cf. and contrast iv. 16.

Day 3. 1 Tim. iii. 1-13

(1) What are the qualities required in those who are chosen to exercise oversight in a congregation? Note what Paul says (a) about their personal character; (b) about their abilities; (c) about their Christian experience; and (d) about their general reputation. See verses 1-7.

(2) What qualities are necessary for deacons (verses 8-10, 12, 13) and deaconesses (verse 11)? Compare your answer with the answer to question (1). Are you a fit person to be put in charge of others in God's service?

Notes.—(1) The whole passage should be read in the R.V.

(2) Verse 1. 'Bishop'; the Greek word literally means 'one who has oversight'. There were a number of such men in each congregation (Phil. i. 1) and they were also called 'elders': see v. 17; cf. Tit. i. 5, 7. 'Bishop' in the modern sense is a later development.

(3) Verse 2. 'The husband of one wife'; cf. verse 12 and v. 9. Opinion is

divided as to whether this means married only once or having only one wife, i.e. not a polygamist. The second is the more probable meaning in view of such passages as Rom. vii. 1-3; 1 Cor. vii. 8, 9; 1 Tim. v. 14.

(4) Verse 6. 'The condemnation of the devil', i.e. the condemnation incurred by the devil for his pride.

(5) Verse 9. 'The mystery of the faith', i.e. the revelation of the gospel.

(6) Verse 11. 'Their wives'; literally, 'women', as in R.V., but meaning here women deacons, such as Phœbe (Rom. xvi. 1).

Day 4. 1 Tim. iii. 14–iv. 5.

(1) By what three expressions does Paul in iii. 15 bring out the dignity and importance of the Church? Consider each in turn in the light of such passages as Eph. ii. 19; Heb. iii. 6, x. 21; 2 Cor. vi. 16; Heb. xii. 22; Jn. xvi. 13; Col. i. 5, 6.

(2) Whence would spring the false teaching described in iv. 1-5, and by what kind of men would it be propagated? What, according to Paul's teaching here, is the true Christian position with regard to marriage and to foods? Cf. Heb. xiii. 4; Rom. xiv. 17.

Notes.—(1) iii. 15. 'Ground'; better, 'bulwark' or 'stay', as in R.V. mg. The Church is represented as a massive pillar, upholding and displaying the revelation of the gospel.

(2) iii. 16. Read as in R.V.

(3) iv. 1. 'Giving heed'; cf. i. 4, iv. 13 (R.V.).

(4) iv. 3. 'Know' means 'have a clear knowledge of'.

Day 5. 1 Tim. iv. 6-16.

(1) In iv. 6-11 Paul recommends to Timothy (a) a positive teaching of the truth of the gospel, and (b) a wholehearted pursuit of godliness. What reward would attend such singlehearted devotion?

(2) What counsel does Paul give in verses 12-16 regarding (a) Timothy's personal character, and (b) how he might keep fit to do work for God? Are you qualified to be a 'life saver', or are you liable to 'go under' yourself? See verse 16 and 1 Cor. ix. 27.

Notes.—(1) Verses 6 and 12 should be read as in R.V.

(2) Verse 7. 'Profane and old wives' fables'; better, 'godless and silly myths' (R.S.V.).

(3) Verse 10b. The gospel is for all, but salvation is through believing.

(4) Verse 13. The three forms of ministry mentioned here all refer to public worship.

Day 6. 1 Tim. v–vi. 2.

In today's portion counsel is given concerning four matters: (a) rebuking (v. 1-2); (b) the granting of church support to widows (v. 3-16); (c) elders (v. 17-25); and (d) the relation of slaves to their masters (vi. 1, 2).

(1) In the case of widows, what two classes are not to be enrolled as receiving church support, and why? Notice the qualifications of those widows who are to be accepted.

(2) In verses 19-22 what four dangers are to be avoided? Are there not useful lessons to be learned here for our own Christian service?

(3) How does today's portion show the need of wisdom in church matters, as well as of keenness? Cf. Acts vi. 3.

Notes.—(1) Verse 3. The word 'honour' probably implies financial aid. Cf. verse 17 below.

(2) Verse 7. 'These things'; a reference to verse 4, as verse 8 shows. Cf. also verse 16.

(3) Verse 8. 'Infidel'; better, 'unbeliever', as in R.V. Cf. Mt. v. 47.

(4) Verses 11-15. In verse 12 read 'and so they incur condemnation for having violated their first pledge' (R.S.V.). When a widow was enrolled as such it was implied that she would remain unmarried. Young widows, however, might become restive under this restriction and in other ways lack discretion. Paul therefore advised them to marry again.

(5) Verses 22-25. 'Lay hands suddenly upon', i.e. for ordination as an elder. The reason is given in verses 24, 25 that *time* is needed to know a man's real character. Verse 23 is an aside, and should be read as in the R.V.

Day 7. 1 Tim. vi. 3-21.

(1) In today's portion Paul deals again with the false teachers who were disturbing the Church. Where did their chief interest lie? What were their ruling motives, and what was the outcome of their teaching? See verses 3-5, 9-10. Cf. Jas. iii. 14-16.

(2) What, on the contrary, should be the chief interest of the Christian? What should be his ruling motives and the outcome of his faith? See verses 6-8, 11-16. Cf. Tit. ii. 11-14.

(3) What advice is given to rich people in verses 17-19? What should be the central aim of all their living?

Note.—Verses 3-5, 10 and 20 should be read as in the R.V.

TITUS

INTRODUCTION

(See New Bible Handbook, pp. 385, 386)

TITUS was a Gentile convert (Gal. ii. 3), led to faith by the apostle himself (i. 4), who accompanied Paul on some of his journeys and was sent by him on important missions to churches, as, for example, to Corinth (2 Cor. viii. 16-18, 23, xii. 17, 18) and to

Dalmatia (2 Tim. iv. 10). This letter reveals that Paul left him in Crete to establish the churches of that island (i. 5).

The Epistle is very similar to 1 Timothy and was probably written about the same time, in the interval between Paul's two imprisonments. It is therefore earlier than 2 Timothy. It emphasizes the importance of order and discipline in the Church. The gospel had evidently made rapid headway in Crete, but church government was as yet undeveloped (i. 5). False teaching also had to be countered, and the apostle has some strong words to say on this subject. But, above all else, the Epistle stresses the Christian's calling and obligation to live a holy life. It contains also two great doctrinal passages (ii. 11-14, iii. 4-7), which stand out like mountain ranges in the landscape.

ANALYSIS

i. 1-4. Opening greeting.

i. 5-16. The need to appoint elders in the churches as a safeguard against the spread of doctrinal error.

ii. 1-10. Instructions concerning the conduct of various classes in the Christian community: the aged, the young, Titus himself, slaves.

ii. 11-15. The doctrinal basis for the appeal to holy living.

iii. 1-7. Exhortation to submission and gentleness, leading up to a further doctrinal statement.

iii. 8-11. The Christian's obligation to maintain good works, and to avoid profitless discussion.

iii. 12-15. Personal closing messages.

Week 29. TITUS AND 2 TIMOTHY

Day 1. Tit. i.

(1) To what extent does our salvation depend upon the fidelity (a) of God; (b) of the preachers of the gospel; (c) of ourselves in the response we make? See verses 1-11 and cf. Rom. x. 13-16.

(2) What three sources of weakness in the church life at Crete does Paul refer to? What action does he counsel Titus to take in regard to each of these?

(3) Compare in detail the qualifications for Christian ministry given in verses 6-9 with those in 1 Tim. iii.

Notes.—(1) Verse 1. 'According to the faith'; better, 'to further the faith', as in R.S.V.

(2) Verses 6-9 should be read as in the R.V.

Day 2. Tit. ii.

(1) Observe the emphasis (a) upon sound doctrine, (b) upon holy character. If these are secured, what three results will follow? Cf. 1 Pet. ii. 11, 15; Phil. i. 27 (R.V.).

(2) What are the two sides of the change that comes into a man's life when he is saved? What should he leave behind and what should be his aim? See verses 11-15. Are we living thus? The verses should be read as in R.V.

Day 3. Tit. iii.

(1) What personal reason is given in verses 1-3 for showing meekness in our treatment of others? Cf. Jn. viii. 7; Gal. vi. 1; 1 Cor. xv. 9, 10. What might be your spiritual condition but for the grace of God?

(2) In the doctrinal statement of verses 4-7 what is said concerning (a) the source and method of salvation, (b) our present state and future hope? Can your Christian life be described as 'abundant'? With verse 6 cf. Jn. x. 10.

(3) What should mark the life of believers, and what should they avoid? See verses 8-11, 14.

Notes.—(1) Verse 10. 'Heretick'; better, 'factious', as in R.V. mg.
(2) Verse 11. 'Subverted'; better, 'perverted', as in R.V.

II TIMOTHY

INTRODUCTION

(See New Bible Handbook, pp. 386, 387)

THIS letter is of peculiar interest because it is Paul's last, written during his final imprisonment in Rome when he was aware that his death could not be for long delayed. It reveals that his last days were spent without material comfort. There was no immediate earthly reward to crown his long years of labour. For one reason or another his friends had left him (i. 15, iv. 10, 12, 16). Amid the dreary limitations of his imprisonment he asks for his old cloak to be brought to keep him warm and his books for him to read (iv. 13). He urges Timothy to come quickly that he may see him before his death (i. 4, iv. 9, 21).

In such difficult circumstances he exhorts his son in the faith to be faithful to the truth. He is more concerned for Timothy and for the future of the gospel than for himself. Steadfast and confident to the end, he has still the same message to give to all who are called to the service of Christ. What the Lord requires in His workers is faithfulness, even unto death; to watch, to endure, to work and fully to discharge the obligation of their office; to finish their course; and to live in anticipation of the crowning day that is coming. For all such is laid up in store 'eternal glory'.

ANALYSIS

Day 4. 2 Tim. i.

(1) Apart from Paul and Timothy, five persons are mentioned by name in this chapter. What may we learn from them?

(2) Picture Paul's circumstances. What evidence do you find that he felt his loneliness keenly? Note the threefold use of the word 'ashamed', and compare verses 4a and 8; iv. 10, 11, 16; Jn. xvi. 32. Yet he was filled with quiet confidence. What was his secret?

(3) Consider Timothy's position: he was about to lose his beloved leader and to be left in a hostile world. Express in your own words the chief points of Paul's counsel and exhortation to him in this chapter, and observe how exactly fitted they were to meet Timothy's need. Cf. 2 Cor. iv. 17, 18.

Notes.—(1) Verse 1. 'An apostle . . . according to', etc. or 'in the service of' (Moffatt).

(2) Verse 3. 'I thank God'; to be connected with 'When I call to remembrance' in verse 5.

(3) Verse 7. Cf. Acts iv. 31; 1 Thes. ii. 2. The whole verse should be read as in the R.V.

(4) Verse 14. 'Guard the truth that has been entrusted to you' (R.S.V.).

(5) Verse 16. Many infer from the fact that Paul sends greetings to 'the

houshold of Onesiphorus' that Onesiphorus himself had died (cf. iv. 19). This, however, is not certain, and even if it be the case, Paul's wish that Onesiphorus might be rewarded for his kindness to him gives no support to the practice of praying for the dead.

Day 5. 2 Tim. ii.

(1) What do verses 1-13 teach about the Christian life (a) in what it demands from those who embrace it, (b) in the source of its strength (with verse 1 cf. i. 8 'according to the power of God', i. 14; Eph. i. 19), (c) in its final end? Consider the illustrations used.

(2) In verses 14-26 find five evil consequences of wrong talking. See Ps. cxli. 3.

(3) What should be the Christian's central aim and purpose? And what should be his attitude (a) to things evil, and (b) to those who oppose the truth?

Notes.—(1) Verse 5. 'Lawfully', i.e. according to the rules of the contest. Cf. 1 Cor. ix. 25.

(2) Verse 6. 'Laboureth'; implying hard toil.

(3) Verses 11-13. Some think that this may be a fragment of a Christian hymn. Verse 13 means that if we fail, God does not fail—an encouragement to hold fast.

(4) Verse 15. 'That needeth not to be ashamed', i.e. when his work is inspected.

(5) Verse 21. 'If a man purge himself from these', i.e. from the false teachers and their ways.

(6) Verse 26. ,Who are taken captive', etc. The literal translation is 'having been taken captive by him unto the will of him'. The two pronouns 'him' are different in the Greek, and it is difficult to decide to whom they refer. Besides the A.V. and R.V. translations, another possible rendering is: 'That they who had been taken captive by the devil may recover themselves out of his snare, so as to serve the will of God.'

Day 6. 2 Tim. iii.

(1) What may we learn by contrast from verses 1-9 of what true Christians ought to be? What is the Christian worker to do when the conditions described here arise within the church?

(2) What two great things can the right use of the Bible do for us (verses 15 and 17)? What two things must we do to gain these benefits (verses 14 and 15)? Cf. Jn. v. 39, 40, viii. 31, 32.

Notes.—(1) Today's portion is clearer in the R.V., except that in verse 16 the R.V. mg. is better. See also R.S.V.

(2) Verses 8, 9. Jannes and Jambres are not mentioned by name elsewhere in the Scriptures.

Day 7. 2 Tim. iv.

(1) What are the nine points of Paul's final charge to Timothy, as given in verses 1-6?

(2) How does this chapter illustrate the possibility of failure to be a good soldier of Jesus Christ, and one common cause of such failure?

(3) Consider Paul as he appears in the closing verses of the Epistle: (a) in the greatness of his sufferings; (b) in his human frailty; (c) in the strength of his faith; (d) in the victory of his life; and (e) in the reward that awaited him. Are we following in his steps? Cf. 1 Cor. xi. 1.

PSALMS CVII-CL

(See Year II, p. 164 and New Bible Handbook, pp. 191-198)

Week 30. PSALMS CVII–CXIV

Day 1. Ps. cvii. 1-32.

This psalm is addressed to the Jews who had returned from exile in Babylon. It falls into two parts, and today's study is of the first.

(1) Note the various causes of the trouble and distress here described. What was the remedy? What is frequently the good consequence of being brought to the end of human resources? See Ps. l. 15; 2 Cor. i. 9.

(2) How many different blessings are here said to have been given in answer to prayer? Is there among them one which you need to ask God to give to you just now? Are you giving praise for His abounding mercies? Cf. Ps. ciii. 1, 2.

Notes.—(1) Verse 10. 'Such as sit in darkness'; better, 'sat', as in R.V. The deep darkness ('shadow of death') is the darkness of an unlighted dungeon.

(2) Verses 8, 15, 21 and 31. 'Oh that men', etc.; better, 'Let them', etc. It is a call to the particular people mentioned rather than to men in general.

(3) Verse 26. 'They mount up', i.e. the sailors.

Day 2. Ps. cvii. 33-43.

The second part of this psalm sets forth God's dealings with nations and peoples in judgment and blessing.

(1) Observe the evidences given here of God's all-sovereign control over the varied circumstances of life. With verse 34 cf. Joel i. 19, 20, ii. 3; Dt. xxix. 22-26, and with verse 35 cf. Ps. cxiv. 8; Is. xliii. 19, 20.

(2) Can the words of today's portion be applied spiritually to the dealings of God with His people? See e.g. the revival that sprang up in the region of Lydda and Saron in Acts ix. 32-35, and the warning given to the church in Ephesus in Rev. ii. 4, 5.

Day 3. Ps. cviii.

The first five verses of this psalm are taken from Ps. lvii. 7-11, and the remainder from Ps. lx. 5-12.

(1) Verses 1-5. In what three ways has the Psalmist made up his mind to give praise to God? And what is his chief desire? Cf. verse 5 with Rev. v. 13. Is your heart 'fixed' like the Psalmist's upon these things, or does his eager intensity rebuke you?

(2) Upon what strong grounds of confidence does the Psalmist base his prayer? With verse 7a cf. Heb. vi. 17; with verses 7b-9 cf. Is. xliii. 4; and with verses 11-13 cf. 1 Sa. xii. 22. In praying for victory over our spiritual foes, have we not the same grounds of confidence? See e.g. Jn. xiv. 13, 14, xvi. 26, 27; Heb. xiii. 5b, 6.

Notes.—(1) Verse 1. 'My glory', i.e. my soul, the noblest part of me.

(2) Verse 2. 'Awake early'; literally, 'awake the dawn'; see R.V. mg.

(3) Verses 7-9. Shechem and Succoth are both connected with the story of Jacob (see Gn. xxxiii. 17, 18). Shechem is on the west side of Jordan and Succoth on the east. The two places may thus represent the whole land. For verse 9 see lx. 8, note.

Day 4. Ps. cix.

This psalm falls into three parts. Verses 1-5 are a prayer to God for speedy deliverance from deceitful and cruel enemies. The Psalmist then invokes a terrible retribution upon the leader of his foes and upon all that belongs to him (verses 6-20). The third section (verses 21-31) is a further prayer, rising at the close to the thanksgiving of faith.

(1) Leaving out for the moment verses 6-20 (see note below) and considering only David's prayer in verses 1-5 and 21-31, in what ways is he an example to us? On what grounds does he base his appeal for God's help?

(2) Note how desperate is his condition; yet his faith rises into a confident assurance of deliverance and into triumphant praise. Is this assurance of faith characteristic also of our praying? See Mk. xi. 24 (R.V.); 2 Cor. i. 8-11.

Notes.—(1) Verse 4. 'I give myself unto prayer'. The Heb. is simply 'prayer'. It may refer equally to the past—'I gave myself unto prayer', which seems to fit better with verse 5.

(2) Verse 6. 'Satan'; better, 'an adversary', as in R.V. Contrast verse 31, where God stands at the right hand of 'the needy' (R.V.).

(3) Verses 6-20. Note how the retribution invoked includes the man him-

self, his person and office, his wife and children, his property, and his posterity. The place and significance of the imprecatory psalms (of which this is one), as part of the fulness of revealed truth, belong to the general subject of the progress of revelation. It is to be remembered that in pre-Christian days New Testament standards were not yet revealed. Old Testament believers lived in a dispensation in which retribution was a fundamental principle. Their very faith in a God of righteousness who would reward the righteous, and condemn the wicked, encouraged them to pray for His blessing upon themselves and for His vengeance upon their persecutors, and in this they had Scriptural support (see e.g. Lv. xxiv. 19; Pr. xvii. 13). Retribution was therefore prayed for as part of the practical vindication of God's actual and righteous sovereignty, and these prayers and imprecations are often prophetic (e.g. see verse 8 above and Acts i. 20. Cf. also Rev. vi. 9, 10; 2 Thes. i. 6-9). But the New Testament teaches men to leave vengeance to God, and to love and pray for them that despitefully use them (Mt. v. 43-45; Rom. xii. 19-21).

Day 5. Ps. cx.

(1) To whom does this psalm refer (see Mk. xii. 35-37), and what sure prospect does it reveal? Cf. verses 1 and 2 with Heb. x. 12, 13 and 1 Cor. xv. 25. Has this expectation made you offer yourself willingly (verse 3, R.V.)?

(2) The promised King is also to be a *priest*, but not after the Aaronic line. How does the writer to the Hebrews expound verse 4? See Heb. v. 6-10, vi. 20-vii. 28.

(3) Verses 5, 6 look forward to the final triumph. Cf. Rev. xix. 11-18. What picture of the great Leader is presented in verse 7? Cf. Jn. iv. 7, xix. 28; Heb. xii. 2.

Notes.—(1) Verse 1. Two Hebrew words are here rendered as 'Lord'. One is Jehovah or the 'LORD', verses 1, 2 and 4. The other is 'Adonai' or 'my Lord' used in verse 5 of Jehovah, but in verse 1 of the Messianic King.

(2) Verse 3. Read as in R.V.

(3) Verse 7. The subject is suddenly changed from Jehovah (verses 5, 6) to the King.

Day 6. Pss. cxi and cxii.

These are acrostic psalms, each line in the Hebrew text beginning with a fresh letter of the alphabet in regular order. They are closely connected, both in structure and content.

(1) Does your delight in the works of the Lord make you inquire into them (cxi. 2)? From what Ps. cxi says about His works, how many reasons can you find for praising the Lord with your whole heart (verse 1)?

(2) What are the marks of the upright man (Ps. cxii)? How does he act (a) towards God, (b) towards men? What consequent blessings does he enjoy (a) in his heart, (b) in his home?

(3) Where in the character of an upright man, as portrayed in Ps. cxii, do you find a reflection of the character of God Himself, as depicted in cxi?

Notes.—(1) cxi. 5. 'Meat'; the Heb. word literally means 'prey' (see R.V. mg), but is used here in the general sense of food, and is chosen because of the acrostic.

(2) cxi. 9, 10. 'Reverend', i.e. to be feared. The word is translated 'terrible' in Ps. xcix. 3. It is in Heb. from the same root as 'fear' in verse 10. Thus verses 9 and 10 are closely connected. With verse 10b cf. Jn. vii. 17.

(3) cxii. 5. The R.V. is better in 5a. Verse 5b may be rendered 'who manages his affairs with rectitude' (Kirkpatrick).

(4) cxii. 7a. Contrast Jb. xv. 23b-25; Pr. x. 24a.

Day 7. Pss. cxiii and cxiv.

With Ps. cxiii begins the Hallel, or Hymn of Praise, extending to Ps. cxviii, which was sung at Jewish festivals, and may have been sung by our Lord and His disciples in the upper room when they observed the Passover. Ps. cxiii celebrates God's grace towards the weak and lowly, and Ps. cxiv the notable example of this given in the exodus.

(1) What two truths about God call for unceasing and universal praise (cxiii. 1-6)? Consider how the second found expression in the incarnation. See Phil. ii. 6-11.

(2) In what sense is cxiii. 7 true of all Christians? See Eph. ii. 1-10; Rom. v. 17. Are you 'reigning in life' through Jesus Christ?

(3) What point of great significance about the journey of the Israelites from Egypt to Canaan is emphasized in Ps. cxiv? Cf. Ex. xxxiii. 14-16; Mk. xvi. 20. What two things must God's people become in order to enjoy the full benefits of this blessed privilege (verse 2)? Cf. 2 Cor. vi. 16, 17; Is. xxvi. 13; 2 Ki. xviii. 6, 7.

Notes.—(1) cxiii. 6. The phrase 'in heaven' is probably to be taken with verse 5b, 'who hath His seat on high' (R.V.) and the words 'in earth' with 'Who humbleth Himself to behold'.

(2) cxiii. 7-9. These verses are reminiscent of the story of Hannah, see 1 Sa. i–ii; but the Jews were wont to see in verse 9 an allusion to Zion, as in Is. liv. 1.

(3) cxiv. 2. The meaning is that Israel became Jehovah's dwelling-place and kingdom.

(4) cxiv. 3, 4. A poetical description of the crossing of the Red Sea and the Jordan, and of the earthquake at Mount Sinai. Cf. Ex. xix. 18. Verse 8 refers to the miracles at Rephidim (Ex. xvii. 6) and Kadesh (Nu. xx. 11).

Week 31. PSALMS CXV–CXIX. 96

Day 1. Ps. cxv.

This psalm was probably written after the return from exile, at such a time as that described in Ezr. iii. 3 or iv. 23, 24. The nation was in weakness; its enemies were mocking (verse 2).

(1) What was the Psalmist's chief distress? See verses 1, 2.

(2) Yet what does he see to be the true situation, as beheld by the eye of faith? What contrast does he draw between God and the idols, and between what each can do?

(3) Through the power of faith the Psalmist is able to exhort his fellow countrymen. What does he say to them in this hour of outward humiliation? See verses 9-18. Note how his confidence swells to a note of triumphant praise. Can we speak with the same confidence about our God? Cf. 2 Tim. i. 12.

Day 2. Ps. cxvi.

While this psalm is written in the first person, there are indications that, like the other psalms of this group, it has a national character, and sets forth the reaction of the nation to the deliverance from exile. At the same time it is applicable to the case of individual believers of all generations.

(1) What does the Psalmist say concerning the peril and the deliverance on the one hand, and concerning his own resolves on the other?

(2) What is the connection as seen in this psalm between affliction, prayer, praise, and a life of loving devotion?

(3) If we apply the psalm in a spiritual sense to our salvation from our sin and death, are verses 7-8 and 12-14 true to our experience?

Notes.—(1) Verse 4. 'Then called I'; or 'Then continued I to call'.

(2) Verses 10, 11. The meaning is not wholly clear. If the R.V. mg. is followed the Psalmist confesses that though his faith was sorely tried and he lost confidence in man, he did not lose faith in God.

(3) Verse 15. God sets a high value on the life of His people, and does not regard their death lightly.

Day 3. Pss. cxvii and cxviii.

(1) In Ps. cxvii on what grounds are the nations summoned to praise Jehovah? The thought lies near that if Jehovah is a God of this character He will bless not only Israel, but all peoples. Cf. Rom. iii. 29, xv. 8-11.

(2) Ps. cxviii may have been composed to be sung by the worshippers on their way to the temple at the Feast of Tabernacles, described in Ne. viii. With verse 14, cf. Ex. xv. 2, and note the quotations from it in the New Testament (see Heb. xiii. 6; Mk. xii. 10, 11; Mt. xxi. 9). Which verses of the psalm speak most powerfully to your heart?

(3) Are you prepared for God to work wondrously on behalf

of those that trust in and call upon Him? Do you believe He can still fulfil His purpose when men seem completely to have frustrated it?

Notes.—(1) cxvii. 1. Read as in R.V. Two different words for 'praise' are used in the Heb.

(2) cxviii. 13. 'Thou' refers to Israel's enemies and 'me' to Israel. Israel is the speaker throughout, except in verse 26, when the priests speak, blessing the worshippers.

(3) cxviii. 27. The sentence 'Bind the sacrifice with cords', etc. is in the Heb. of obscure meaning. Some think it refers to a sacred dance round the altar, waving branches.

Day 4. Ps. cxix. 1-24.

The psalm consists of twenty-two stanzas of eight verses each and goes through the Hebrew alphabet letter by letter. Each stanza begins with a new letter and each verse in the stanza begins with that letter. See R.V. It is remarkable how, within these limitations, the Psalmist expresses the depth of his devotion for the law and for God who gave the law, coupled with delicate variety of phrase.

(1) Find four statements in these verses that indicate how we may both make and keep our life pure and free from sins. Is your study of the Bible having this full practical result? See Jas. i. 21-25.

(2) What were the joy and delight of the Psalmist's life? And what condition of heart and eye is necessary if we wish to enter into the same experience?

Notes.—(1) The R.V. is clearer in verses 1, 7, 11, 17, 19. In verse 21 read as in R.V. mg.

(2) Verse 13. 'Declared'; better, 'recounted'.

Day 5. Ps. cxix. 25-48.

(1) In verses 29 and 30 (note changes in R.V.), what two ways are set in contrast, between which men must choose? Find four other descriptions of the way which the Psalmist confesses he has chosen to follow. What does the Psalmist say he needs from God, and what attitude in himself is necessary to keep to the way of truth? Cf. Jn. viii. 31, 32.

(2) Have you come to the point of making up your mind to 'stick to' (verse 31) the Word of God against the opinions of men, and even against your own judgment? Can you adopt for yourself the Psalmist's prayers, and affirm his resolves in verses 41-48?

Notes.—(1) Read as in R.V. in verses 27b, 38 and 42.

(2) Verse 38. 'Which belongeth to the fear of Thee'; i.e. which belongs to those that fear Thee, or possibly 'which tendeth to promote the fear of Thee'. The confirming of God's promises leads others to fear Him. Cf. Ps. cxvii, cxxx. 4.

(3) Verse 48. 'I will lift up my hands', i.e. in the attitude of prayer. Cf. Ps. xxviii. 2; 1 Tim. ii. 8.

Day 6. Ps. cxix. 49-72.

(1) What verb occurs seven times in today's portion (A.V.) with reference to what we should do with God's Word? Cf. Jn. xiv. 15, 21, 23, 24; 1 Jn. ii. 3-5.

(2) The Psalmist three times speaks of suffering affliction (verses 50, 67, 71). What comforted him in affliction, and what gain did it bring him? Can you find any indication of the form the affliction took? Are you equally responsive to the Lord's correction? See Je. ii. 30; Heb. xii. 6, 9-11.

(3) How does today's portion show the preciousness to the Psalmist of God's Word?

Notes.—(1) The R.V. is better in verses 52, 56, 61.

(2) Verse 61. 'The cords of the wicked have wrapped me round' (R.V.), i.e. entangled me.

(3) Verse 69. 'Forged a lie against me'; more literally, 'bespatter me with lies' (Moffatt).

Day 7. Ps. cxix. 73-96.

(1) What does the Psalmist pray for in verses 73-80, and to what end? What pleas does he put forward why his prayer should be answered? Can you make these prayers and pleas your own?

(2) State in your own words the various ingredients in the Psalmist's cup of sorrow, as described in verses 81-88. Yet what, even in such circumstances, was his attitude to God's Word? See also verse 92.

(3) What do verses 89-91 declare to be a common characteristic of both God's words and His works? Cf. 1 Pet. i. 25; Ps. civ. 5. Are you sure, because of His unchanging Word, that the Lord has done abiding work in your heart? See Jn. v. 24.

Notes.—(1) In verses 78, 80, 82 and 90 read as in R.V.

(2) Verse 73. The meaning is 'Thou hast made my bodily frame, perfect my spirit' (Kirkpatrick).

(3) Verse 83. 'Bottle'; better, 'wineskin' (R.V. mg.), hung up out of use, and blackened by smoke.

(4) Verse 96. Earthly perfection is limited, but not so Jehovah's commandment.

Week 32. Psalms cxix. 97–cxxviii

Day 1. Ps. cxix. 97-120.

(1) How do verses 97-104 illustrate from the Psalmist's experience the truth already emphasized (see e.g. Week 31, Day 6 (1)), that uncompromising obedience is the practical condition of true progress in understanding of and appreciation of the truth? Cf. Je. xv. 16; Jn. vii. 17.

(2) Do you gather from verses 105-112 that the Psalmist's devotion to the law was the reason why he was persecuted? Have you had any experience of this, and are you equally resolved to tread the way of the cross? Cf. Jn. xv. 19-21.

(3) What in verses 113-120 does the Psalmist say God is to him, and does for him? Can you say from the heart each statement in this section?

Notes.—(1) The r.v. is clearer in verses 98, 100, 101, 113, 115 and 118.

(2) Verse 108. 'The freewill offerings of my mouth', such as prayer, praise, vows.

Day 2. Ps. cxix. 121-144.

(1) What evidence is there in today's portion that the Psalmist had many in opposition to him (cf. also verse 157), and what was his own reaction to their neglect and transgression of God's Word?

(2) Note one by one the various phrases that are explicit prayers. Compare them with your own praying. Are your requests as personal, definite, and comprehensive?

(3) How in today's portion does the Psalmist describe God's Word, and what His words give to the seeking heart? With verse 130 cf. 105, and with verse 133 verse 9.

Notes.—(1) The r.v. is to be preferred in verses 126, 130, 131 and 138.

(2) Verse 130. 'The entrance of Thy Words'; better, as in r.v., 'the opening of Thy Words' or 'the interpretation of Thy Words' (Moffatt).

Day 3. Ps. cxix. 145-160.

(1) What prayer occurs four times in today's portion? How many times does it occur in the psalm as a whole? Do you need to pray thus, and are you doing it?

(2) When and how did the Psalmist find time for prayer and the study of God's Word? See note (2) below, and cf. verse 62; Ps. v. 3, lxiii. 6. What may we learn from his example?

(3) How does the Psalmist in verses 153-160 speak of his perse-

cutors? How does his attitude fall short of that taught in the New Testament?

Notes.—(1) The R.V. is clearer in verses 145, 146, 152, 158 and 160. In verse 150 read as in R.V. mg.

(2) Verses 147, 148. Moffatt translates verse 147 thus: 'I am up before the dawn to pray.' Verse 148 may refer to the author's duties in the temple if, as some suppose, he was a Levite. 'Before the hour when he must rise for his watch, he is awake and meditating on God's words.'

(3) Verse 158. 'The treacherous dealers' (R.V.) refers to apostate Israelites. The Psalmist felt loathing against them (see R.V. mg.).

Day 4. Ps. cxix. 161-176.

(1) In verses 161-168 find at least three characteristics of the Psalmist's heart attitude to the Word of God, and three blessings which devotion to it brings into a man's life. Cf. Mt. xiii. 52; Pr. iii. 1, 2 and 21-24.

(2) 'Give me understanding' (verse 169b) is an oft-repeated prayer on the Psalmist's lips (see verses 34, 73, 125, 144, and also verses 18 and 27), though he was already a deeply taught man (see verses 98-100). Indeed, right through this section (169-176) he takes the position of one in great need. What may we learn from this? See Phil. iii. 11, 12; 1 Tim. i. 15.

(3) In the Psalmist's case knowledge of the Word led to a lif of praise (verses 164, 171, 172, 175; cf. also Col. iii. 16). Are you beginning to find this true of your own experience? Why should there be this connection between the Word in the heart and praise on the lips?

Note.—The R.V. is clearer in verses 165b, 171, 172 and 173.

Day 5. Pss. cxx-cxxii.

Pss. cxx-cxxxiv form a group, each of which bears the title 'A Song of Degrees' (or better, 'Ascents'; see R.V.). They may originally have formed a separate collection and have been used by pilgrims on their ascent or going up to Jerusalem at the time of the feasts. See e.g. Ps. cxxii in today's portion.

(1) What passage in the Epistle of James does Ps. cxx recall?

(2) Why does the writer of Ps. cxxi contemplate the mountains and meditate upon the creation of heaven and earth? Cf. Ps. cxxiv. 8; Je. x. 10-12; Acts xiv. 15. When, where, and for how long does he declare that this God will keep His people?

(3) What was the rallying centre of the true Israelite, and what his first interest? See Ps. cxxii and cf. Dt. xii. 5-7; Ps. lxxxvii. 2, 3. Where do you go to find your most coveted fellowship? And what is your ruling ambition? See Heb. x. 25; Mt. vi. 33.

Notes.—(1) The R.V. is to be preferred in cxx. 5b, cxxi. 1 and 7.

(2) cxx. 3, 4. Verse 4 is the answer to verse 3. 'Coals of juniper' means charcoal made from broom, which gives out a strong heat.

(3) cxx. 5. 'Meshech . . . Kedar'. 'Meshech' was the name of a people living near the Black Sea. 'Kedar' was a nomad tribe of the Arabian Desert. The Psalmist's meaning is that he had to live among people as barbarous as those of Meshech and Kedar.

(4) cxxii. 2. 'Our feet shall stand'; better, 'are standing', as in R.V. The pilgrims have just reached the city gates and verse 3 gives their excited exclamation.

Day 6. Pss. cxxiii–cxxv.

These three psalms probably all belong to the time of Nehemiah. With Ps. cxxiii. 3-4 cf. Ne. ii. 19, iv. 1-4. With Ps. cxxiv cf. Ne. iv. 7, vi. 16, and with Ps. cxxv cf. Ne. vi. 9.

(1) What kept the Psalmist and his fellow Israelites from despair? See Ps. cxxiii and cf. Heb. iv. 16.

(2) By what four metaphors is the danger from which Israel was delivered described in Ps. cxxiv? Can you make Ps. cxxiv into a personal confession?

(3) Of what two things did the mountain beneath and the mountains around Jerusalem speak to God's people? See Ps. cxxv. 1, 2 and cf. Pr. x. 25 and 30; Dt. xxxiii. 27; 2 Ki. vi. 16, 17. Note the last two words in verse 1 and verse 2 of the psalm. Cf. Jn. xiv. 19b; Heb. vii. 25.

Day 7. Pss. cxxvi–cxxviii.

(1) According to Ps. cxxvi what are, or should be, the desire, the task, and the sure hope of those who have already experienced the wonder of divine deliverance? Do you get inspiration to endure the trials of Christian service, both from your remembrance (verse 3) and from your anticipation (verses 5, 6) of spiritual joy? Cf. Hab. iii. 17, 18; Heb. xii. 2.

(2) What is the one simple secret of true prosperity, as revealed in Pss. cxxvii and cxxviii? Cf. Ps. xxxvii. 5-9; Pr. iii. 5-7.

Notes.—(1) cxxvi. 4. The word 'south' (or better, 'South', as in R.V.) refers to the Negeb, the district south of Judah which has little water—save when the autumn rains come, filling the dry beds of the streams and making the people rejoice. The Psalmist longed to see some such rich outpouring of God's power and blessing.

(2) cxxvi. 6. 'Bearing precious seed'; better, 'bearing forth the seed', as in R.V. The thought of the seed's preciousness is not in the Hebrew.

(3) cxxvii. 2. 'Sleep' or 'in sleep', as in R.V. mg.

Week 33. PSALMS CXXIX–CXXXIX

Day 1. Pss. cxxix and cxxx.

Both these psalms may belong to the time of Nehemiah. In the first the writer looks back over Israel's history, and argues from God's deliverances in the past to the certainty of His judgment upon those who would seek Zion's downfall. In Ps. cxxx the Psalmist assures Israel that not even sin can thwart God's purpose of good for His people.

(1) May not the Christian Church, equally with Israel, use the language of Ps. cxxix. 1-4? What two abiding truths concerning the life of the servants of God in the world are here set forth? Cf. Jn. xvi. 33; Rom. viii. 35-37; 2 Cor. iv. 8-10. Are you ready for the one and rejoicing in the other?

(2) With us there is iniquity; with God forgiveness (Ps. cxxx. 3, 4). How is this confirmed in the New Testament? See Rom. iii. 19-23, iv. 7. Have you acknowledged your iniquity, and have you received God's forgiveness?

(3) On what sure foundation does the Psalmist's hope rest? Thus encouraged he is able to exhort others and to rise in faith to strong assurance (cxxx. 7). For an apt illustration of this, see Acts xxvii. 25, 33-36. Are you causing others to hope in the Lord?

Notes.—(1) cxxix. 5. It is possible to regard verses 5 and 6 as a word of faith; thus 'Ashamed and turned backward shall all they be that hate Zion. They shall be as the grass', etc.

(2) cxxx. 3. In the first clause the word translated 'LORD' is Jah; in the second clause the word 'Lord' is Adonai. Cf. Ps. cx. 1, note.

Day 2. Pss. cxxxi and cxxxii.

These two psalms also belong to the period after the return from exile. The exiles returned with high hopes, which were not fulfilled in the way they had expected. In Ps. cxxxi the Psalmist tells how he had learned contentment, and bids Israel hope in the Lord. Ps. cxxxii is a word of encouragement based upon 2 Sa. vii that God will yet fulfil His promises to David.

(1) What four things does the Psalmist say about himself in Ps. cxxxi? Cf. Mt. xi. 29; Phil. iv. 11-13, 17, 18.

(2) In Ps. cxxxii the opening verses describe in poetical form David's eagerness to build the temple (verses 1-5); then follow the response and prayer of the people (verses 6-10); and finally Jehovah's promise is given and His sure fulfilment of it (verses 11-18). Consider the faith that had such confidence in God. Cf. Heb. xi. 1.

(3) Promises have been made also concerning our Lord Jesus Christ. What place are we giving in our lives to the Lord and His Kingdom? Does not this Psalmist, with his faith and his zeal, put our apathy to shame?

Notes.—(1) Ps. cxxxi. 2. The weaned child is content to do without the food that has been its life.

(2) Ps. cxxxii. 6. 'The fields of the wood' refers to Kirjath-jearim, where the ark had rested before David removed it to Zion (1 Ch. xiii. 5). The meaning of Ephratah is uncertain, but it may have been a name given to the district of Kirjath-jearim.

(3) Ps. cxxxii. 17. See R.V. mg. and cf. Je. xxiii. 5; Zc. vi. 12, 13.

Day 3. Pss. cxxxiii and cxxxiv.

Some refer Ps. cxxxiii to the time of Nehemiah's efforts to re-people Jerusalem (see Ne. xi. 1, 2). Ps. cxxxiv is a temple song, consisting of the greeting of the worshippers as they left the temple at evening to the priests who were to serve during the night (verses 1, 2), and the answering blessing from the priests or from their leader (verse 3). It forms an appropriate ending to the 'Songs of Ascents'. See introductory note to Ps. cxx.

(1) By what two similes does the Psalmist in Ps. cxxxiii bring out the copiousness of the blessing that flows from brotherly concord? See note below. How far is this mutual love and unity apparent in your church? See Jn. xiii. 34, 35; Eph. iv. 1, 3, 16.

(2) What were the unique favours bestowed upon Zion? And what did all this typify and foreshadow? Cf. Ps. lxxxvii. 3, 5, 6; Heb. xii. 22-24; Rev. xxi. 2, 10, 27.

(3) What should the servants of God be continually doing? See Ps. cxxxiv. How suggestive, too, the reciprocal action here recorded. See note above and cf. Heb. x. 23-25.

Note.—cxxxiii. 2, 3. Read as in R.V. and for 'skirt' read 'collar', as in R.V. mg. Notice the repetition of the word 'like', introducing the two similes which the Psalmist uses. Both these indicate copiousness. The oil was poured upon Aaron's head so plentifully that it reached even the collar of his robe. The dew of Hermon was also noted for its abundance.

Day 4. Ps. cxxxv.

This psalm is in many ways like Ps. cxv. Its beginning and ending are a call to praise.

(1) Who are summoned thus to praise the Lord, and why? What three reasons for praise are given in verses 3-5?

(2) In what ways is Jehovah's greatness manifested? See verses 6-14. What still greater manifestation has He given through Christ? Should not our praises therefore swell louder even than those of Israel? Cf. Rom. xvi. 25-27.

Notes.—(1) Verse 13. 'Name' and 'memorial' are here synonymous. 'Jehovah's Name is called His memorial as bringing to mind all that He is and does. Such as He has once revealed Himself to be He will continue for ever. Cf. Heb. xiii. 8' (Kirkpatrick).

(2) Verse 14. 'Judge' is here used in the sense of 'vindicate' or 'right His people's wrongs', as Moffatt renders it. Cf. Dt. xxxii. 36; Ps. cvi. 45.

Day 5. Ps. cxxxvi.

The psalm may be divided as follows: verses 1-3, a call to give thanks; verses 4-9, God in His creative acts; verses 10-15, God in His acts of deliverance; verses 16-22, God in His gift of the land; verses 23-26, God in His redemption of His people from exile, and His provision of food for all flesh.

(1) By what *titles* is God described? See verses 1-3, 26, and cf. Dt. x. 17; Ne. i. 4, 5.

(2) What *acts* of the Lord does the Psalmist adduce to demonstrate that these titles are true? Also, how do these acts show His *mercy*?

(3) Going back upon your own life, can you recall and testify to similar experiences of God's mercy, particularly in the spiritual sphere?

Day 6. Pss. cxxxvii and cxxxviii.

(1) What is the one heart interest of the writer of Ps. cxxxvii? Are you as concerned about the condition of the Church, which today has the honour of bearing God's Name before men? With verse 1 cf. 2 Sa. i. 19, 20, and with verse 6, 1 Thes. ii. 19, iii. 8, 9.

(2) Whence does the writer of Ps. cxxxviii gain the conviction that God is at work in his life? And what does that fact guarantee? Cf. Rom. viii. 14, 16, 26; Phil. i. 6.

(3) 'Before the gods' (Ps. cxxxviii. 1). The Psalmist is not ashamed to magnify Jehovah against all the idolatrous pomp of Babylon and Egypt. Are we also ready to exalt the Lord Jesus against all that the world trusts in? Whence did the Psalmist gain his courage? See verse 3 (R.V.), and cf. Acts iv. 13; 2 Tim. iv. 17.

Notes.—(1) cxxxvii. 8, 9. Such words do not reach the height of Christ's command to love our enemies, but they do express the necessary truth that goodness can only be preserved when there is also a justice that punishes evil-doers.

(2) cxxxviii. 2. 'Thou hast magnified', etc. The recent fulfilment of God's promises in the deliverance from Babylon excels all that the past revelation of Himself has shown.

(3) Verse 4. 'All the kings'. The Psalmist is writing in the name of Israel, and it is God's dealings with Israel that impresses the nations and their rulers.

Day 7. Ps. cxxxix.

(1) What three truths about God are emphasized in verses 1-6, 7-12, and 13-18 respectively?

(2) Note the Psalmist's personal reflections as he meditates on these tremendous realities. See verses 6, 10, 14, etc. Note further how often the personal pronouns 'me', 'my', and 'Thou', 'Thy' occur. Is God thus near and real to you?

(3) What four petitions are there in the prayer of verses 23, 24? Can you and do you pray each one of them with your whole desire?

Notes.—(1) The R.V. should be read in verses 3, 8, 11, 12, 15, 16 and 19b; and R.V. mg. in verses 13, 16b and 19a.

(2) Verse 13. 'My reins', i.e. my inmost nature.

(3) Verses 23, 24. 'Search'. A strong word, implying a deep and thorough disclosure of what is within. 'Try' or 'test' by any discipline, however severe. 'Wicked way'; literally, way of pain or sorrow; here implying wrongdoing that leads to ruin.

Week 34. PSALMS CXL–CL

Day 1. Pss. cxl and cxli.

Pss. cxl–cxliii form a group of four psalms, all of them in their titles ascribed to David and all of them reflecting similar circumstances. They show the conflict of faith in one who is subjected to the attacks and plottings of wicked men.

(1) In Ps. cxl note carefully the Psalmist's description of his enemies—their character, their methods, their purpose. In these circumstances of dire peril, what does the Psalmist do, what does he pray for, and how is his faith sustained?

(2) The Psalmist had to do with human enemies. This may not be true at the moment in our case, but what help may we learn from the Psalmist's example in regard to our conflict with temptation and with spiritual foes? Cf. Eph. vi. 10-13.

(3) In Ps. cxli the pressure is such that the Psalmist is tempted to give up the struggle (verse 4). What does he pray for, and what correction was he ready to receive if only he might be kept from sin? Are you as prepared to pay heed to divine restraint and friendly reproof? Cf. Eph. iv. 30; Pr. ix. 8, xxvii. 6.

Notes.—(1) cxli. 5. The R.V. is clearer in the last two lines of the verse.

(2) cxli. 6, 7. These verses are obscure and do not appear to belong to the context; they remain an unsolved problem.

Day 2. Pss. cxlii and cxliii.

(1) In Ps. cxlii the Psalmist is at his wit's end. Note the terms in which he describes his extremity (verses 3, 4, 6, 7a). In such circumstances what did he believe, do, and expect? The Christian application of this may be found in 2 Cor. i. 8-11.

(2) In Ps. cxliii the Psalmist's danger and distress are no less great, but his spirit is more composed. What is now the burden of his prayer?

(3) Observe how to almost every petition is attached a reason why it should be granted. Find all of these, and the prayers based upon them, and consider how appropriate many of them are to your own morning quiet time.

Notes.—(1) cxlii. 7. 'Bring my soul out of prison'. Not probably a literal prison, but equivalent to 'out of trouble' in Ps. cxliii. 11.

(2) cxliii. 7. 'Into the pit', i.e. 'to death'.

(3) cxliii. 8. 'Cause me to know the way', etc.; cf. cxlii. 3b.

Day 3. Ps. cxliv.

(1) Do you begin your prayers as the Psalmist does, with an outpouring of praise to God for all that He has been and is to you? See verses 1, 2. 'See how he multiplies words to express the satisfaction he had in God, and in His interest in him' (Matthew Henry).

(2) Such praise makes us conscious of our own nothingness (verses 3, 4). Yet what boldness it gives in asking great things of such a God, even complete victory (verses 5-8 and 9-11). Cf. the outburst of praise in Eph. i. 3-14 and the prayer which follows (verses 15-19).

(3) What was the Psalmist's vision of a prosperous community (verses 12-15)? What is your conception of the spiritual blessings you desire in Christ?

Notes.—(1) Verse 8. The meaning is that when they raised their right hand in solemn oath, they lied.

(2) Verse 12. A prayer for sons strong like well-grown saplings, and daughters graceful as stones carved for a palace.

(3) Verse 14. No war, no cry of mourning.

Day 4. Ps. cxlv.

From this point to the end of the Psalter all the psalms are songs of *praise*.

(1) Why should God be praised? Can you find in this psalm at least fifteen main reasons connected with His being, His character, and His works?

(2) Who should praise God? See verses 4, 6, 7, 10, 11, 21. What should be the manner of their praise? Are you resolved, as the Psalmist was, to extol, bless and praise God 'every day', and 'for ever'?

(3) In what ways is the Lord 'good to all' (verse 9), and what

additional things does He do only for those that fulfil certain conditions? How do these additional and conditional blessings far exceed those which all alike receive? Contrast Mt. v. 45 with Rom. iii. 22 and viii. 28.

Note.—Verse 13. The psalm is an alphabetical poem, each verse of two lines beginning with a fresh letter in alphabetic order. The verse beginning with the letter Nun is wanting in the Heb. text, and is supplied in the LXX between verses 13 and 14 as follows:

> 'Faithful is the Lord in all His Words
> And holy in all His works.'

But the second line of the couplet occurs again in verse 17, and whether the couplet is original must remain uncertain.

Day 5. Ps. cxlvi.

(1) In verses 3, 4 the Psalmist is warning Israel against trust in human alliances, which had been so disastrous in the past. Cf. Is. xxx. 1, 2. Why is trusting in man a mistake? See verse 4 and cf. Is. ii. 22; Je. xvii. 5.

(2) Can you find in the history of Israel actual instances of what is here said of Jehovah, taking verses 7-9 clause by clause? For example, to illustrate verse 6c see Jos. xxiii. 14-16; to illustrate verse 7a see Ex. iii. 7, 8; verse 7b, Ex. xvi. 12-14; verse 7c, Ps. cxxvi. 1, etc.

(3) How many of these statements find a fulfilment also in the miracles and works of mercy recorded in the Gospels? What does this correspondence prove? Cf. Mt. xi. 2-5. If, then, the Psalmist praised God as he did (verses 1, 2), how much more should we?

Day 6. Ps. cxlvii.

(1) The psalm falls into three sections, verses 1-6, 7-11, and 12-20, each of which is a summons to praise Jehovah. How would you summarize the main theme for praise in each section?

(2) Observe how the Psalmist delights to meditate upon God's character and upon what He has done. As you read thoughtfully phrase by phrase all the things said about the Lord, ask yourself after each: 'If this God is on my side, what is there to fear?'

(3) What do we learn from this psalm as to what is needed to please God and to secure His continual help? Cf. Is. lvii. 15; Ps. xxxiii. 18, 19.

Notes.—(1) Verses 2, 3. The reference is to the return of the exiles and to the rebuilding and repeopling of Jerusalem.

(2) Verse 10. The community restored from exile did not possess the war-

horses and swift-footed warriors of earlier days. But it was not in these that the Lord took delight.

(3) Verse 16. 'Showering snow white as wool, scattering hoar-frost thick as ashes, casting hail-stones down like crumbs' (Moffatt).

(4) Verses 19, 20. 'Judgments', i.e. ordinances. Israel's peculiar privilege was God's Word; cf. Rom. ix. 4.

Day 7. Pss. cxlviii–cl.

(1) The Psalmist in Ps. cxlviii first summons the heavens and all that are therein to praise Jehovah (verses 1-6); then the earth and all that are in it (verses 7-13); and finally records Israel's special ground of praise (verse 14). Have you also something that God has done for you, for which you have cause specially to praise Him?

(2) What four activities of God mentioned in Ps. cxlviii demonstrate that He is all-sovereign in the universe? Cf. Ps. xxxiii. 6, 9, cxix. 90, 91; Jb. xxxvii. 9-13; 1 Sa. ii. 6-8. See also Ps. cl. 1, 2.

(3) To what one end should everything be used, and all creation be united (see all three psalms)? There are discordant elements preventing the full realization of this end; but what people are expected to be always pursuing it, with all the powers of their being? Cf. 1 Cor. x. 31.

Notes.—(1) cxlviii. 6. Another rendering of the last line is: 'He hath given them a statute which none (of them) shall transgress' (Kirkpatrick; cf. R.V. mg.).

(2) cxlviii. 14. Read as in R.V. The meaning is that God has restored Israel to a place of power.

(3) cxlix. 9. 'The judgment written'; possibly a reference to Dt. xxxii. 40-43. This commission has not been given to Christ's followers in this dispensation; but the Word remains, for the Scripture cannot be broken. (Jn. x. 35; cf. 2 Thes. i. 7-9; Jude 14, 15; Rev. xix. 11-15, 19-21.)

(4) cl. 1. 'His sanctuary', i.e. heaven.

(5) cl. 3-5. 'Trumpet, psaltery', etc. All used in Old Testament worship.

(6) cl. 6. Cf. Rev. v. 13.

EZRA AND NEHEMIAH

INTRODUCTION

(See New Bible Handbook, pp. 179-183)

THE books of Ezra and Nehemiah continue the history of the Israelites from the point reached at the end of 2 Chronicles. The two books are closely linked together and cover between them a space of about one hundred years, from the first year of the reign of Cyrus, King of Persia (538 B.C.) to soon after the thirty-second year of Artaxerxes (432 B.C.). Other books of Scripture belonging to this period are Haggai, Zechariah, Malachi, and Esther.

The events recorded in the books of Ezra and Nehemiah gather round three periods, as follows:

First Period (Ezr. i–vi), from the first return of exiles under Zerubbabel (or Sheshbazzar) and Jeshua the High Priest (536 B.C.) to the completion of the temple (515 B.C.). It is to be noted that, though these events are recorded in the book of Ezra, they occurred more than sixty years before Ezra himself appeared on the scene.

Second Period (Ezr. vii–x), describing the return of a second large company of exiles under Ezra, with some account of Ezra's ministry in Jerusalem (458 B.C.).

Third Period (Ne. i–xiii), describing the arrival of Nehemiah as governor (444 B.C.), and his building of the city walls, together with his joint activity with Ezra.

Ezra and Nehemiah were men raised up of God to render invaluable service at a critical time in Israel's history. Ezra was a priest of the house of Aaron, a man of outstanding piety, a diligent student and capable teacher of the Law of God, and a zealous reformer. Nehemiah was a public servant and a true patriot, who devoted himself to the improvement of the moral and material condition of his country. He combined watchfulness with prayerfulness, and energetic activity with conscious dependence upon God. While both men rendered notable service, the work of Ezra was the more enduring, for he gave to the Law of God a place of supreme authority in the life of the people.

ANALYSES

Ezra

i, ii.	The return of exiles to Jerusalem to rebuild the temple.
iii.	The altar erected, and the temple foundations laid.
iv.	The work opposed, and made to cease.
v.	The resumption of the work, promoted by the prophets Haggai and Zechariah.
vi.	The completion of the temple.
vii, viii.	After an interval of nearly sixty years, Ezra's journey to Jerusalem in 457 B.C.
ix, x.	Reformation, including expulsion of foreign wives, promoted by Ezra.

Nehemiah

Week 35. EZRA

Day 1. Ezr. i and ii.

(1) With i. 1 cf. Je. xxix. 10; Nu. xxiii. 19. Of what then can we be sure in a changing world? See Mt. xxiv. 35; 2 Cor. i. 18-20.

(2) Make a list of the definite acts of God, which made possible a return to Jerusalem and which furthered its successful accomplishment. With ii. 69 cf. 1 Ch. xxix. 9; 2 Cor. viii. 1-5.

(3) Imagine the excitement caused among the exiles by the transfer of the sacred vessels of the house of the Lord from the idol temple to the returning Jews. See i. 7-11. Yet only a small proportion of the exiles set out to return to Jerusalem (ii. 64). Have you known in your life opportunities let slip? Are you tempted now to choose the place of ease rather than go forth with God at His call?

Notes.—(1) i. 4. 'Whosoever remaineth in any place', etc., may be rendered 'Wherever any such survivor resides' (Moffatt). Verse 6 shows that the reference is to those who were intending to go back to Jerusalem.

(2) ii. 63. 'Tirshatha.' A Persian title for a high official appointed by the king. Here it denotes the governor. See R.V. mg.

Day 2. Ezr. iii.

(1) The arrival of the date of the Feast of Tabernacles stirred the returned exiles tremendously, and brought them all to Jerusalem. What were the motives and purposes in their hearts, as recorded in verses 1-5, and in what respects are they an example to us today? Cf. Acts ii. 46, v. 42; Jos. i. 8; Phil. i. 27.

(2) Note the references to the house of the Lord in ii. 68 and iii. 8. How could they come to something which was not yet built? Do you realize that you already belong to, and yet are called to work for the completion of the Church of Christ? Cf. Eph. i. 4, 5, ii. 19-22, iv. 11-13.

(3) What attributes of Jehovah specially called forth the praises of His people when the foundations of the house of the Lord were laid? Why did the old men who were present weep? Had they real cause for their grief?

Day 3. Ezr. iv.

(1) Is not co-operation with others in work for God most desirable? Why, then, did the Jews refuse to co-operate with those who claimed to share their faith, and who offered to help them to achieve their great spiritual objective? Note the word 'adversaries' in verse 1, and with the claim in verse 2, 'We seek your God, as you do', cf. 2 Ki. xvii. 24, 32, 33. See also Mt. vii. 15, and contrast 3 Jn. 8 with 2 Jn. 11.

(2) Can you recall other instances in Scripture where adversaries have sought (as here) to represent the people of God as disloyal and dangerous to the government? See e.g. Am. vii. 10; Lk. xxiii. 2; Acts xvii. 7. Have we as much concern for the honour of our queen as those adversaries professed to have for their king? See verse 14.

(3) What was the price Zerubbabel and his fellow Jews had to pay for their faithfulness? See verses 4, 5, and 24.

Notes.—(1) Verses 1-3. 'The proposal to unite in building the temple was a political move; for in old-world ideas, co-operation in temple-building was incorporation in national unity. The calculation, no doubt, was that if the returning exiles could be united with the much more numerous Samaritans, they would soon be absorbed in them' (Maclaren).

(2) **Verse 5.** 'Until the reign of Darius'; cf. verse 24. It was a period of about sixteen years.

(3) Verses 6-23. Ahasuerus and Artaxerxes are kings who succeeded Darius

(cf. vii. 1). This indicates that these verses refer to a later period than do verses 1-5, and this is confirmed by the fact that the letters of verses 11-16 and 17-22 concern the re-building of the *city* of Jerusalem, not of the temple. Some think the passage belongs chronologically to the time between Ezr. x and Ne. i.

Day 4. Ezr. v and vi.

(1) When the work of rebuilding the temple had ceased for many years (iv. 24), by what various means did God cause it to begin again and bring about the fulfilment of His purpose? How does today's portion strengthen faith and give guidance for prayer? Cf. Gn. l. 20; Pr. xxi. 1; Hg. i. 14; 1 Tim. ii. 2.

(2) Find in vi. 21 three characteristics of the people whom the Lord made joyful, when they kept the feast. How may this be applied spiritually to ourselves? See 1 Cor. v. 7, 8; 1 Jn. i. 4-7.

(3) 'They builded and finished it' (vi. 14, 15). Consider how great their rejoicing as they looked upon the completed temple. Is it the purpose of your heart to finish the task God has given you? Cf. Jn. xvii. 4; Acts xx. 24; Col. iv. 17; 2 Tim. iv. 7; Rev. iii. 2.

Notes.—(1) v. 4. 'Then said we'. The LXX reads 'they' as R.V. mg.

(2) v. 5. 'The eye of their God'; i.e. God's favourable regard. Cf. Pss. xxxiii. 18, xxxiv. 15.

Day 5 Ezr. vii.

This chapter begins the second period of the book (see *Introduction*). Some sixty years have elapsed since the end of chapter v.

(1) What in Ezra's character and conduct had impressed Artaxerxes, and how did he expect and desire Ezra to act? Are people prepared to trust us for the same reason? Cf. Gn. xli. 41-43; Dn. vi. 3; 1 Pet. ii. 15, 16.

(2) What are the two things we must set our hearts to do (see verse 10 R.V.), before, like Ezra, we can become able and effective teachers of the Word of God? See Acts xvii. 11; Jas. i. 25. Considering how long you have been a Christian, are you what you ought to be? See Heb. v. 12-14.

(3) What called forth the doxology of verses 27, 28? Observe how Ezra ascribes all praise and glory to God. Cf. 2 Cor. iii. 5.

Notes.—(1) Verse 6. 'A ready scribe'; i.e. one who was expert in expounding and teaching the law. Cf. verse 10.

(2) Verse 7. 'Porters' or 'doorkeepers' (1 Ch. xxvi. 1 R.V.). The meaning of the word 'Nethinim' is obscure. They were 'temple-attendants' (Moffatt).

(3) Verse 12. 'Perfect'. Not a reference to Ezra's character, but a word of greeting. 'And at such a time'. 'And so forth' (R.V.), having the force of our 'etc.' cf. iv., 10, 11, 17.

Day 6. Ezr. viii.

(1) How many males, all told, were with Ezra? These, with women and children (verse 21), would make a large company. They had also their goods and provision for the way, and a number of precious vessels and a large quantity of silver and gold. The journey was long (vii. 9) and dangerous (viii. 31). Would it have been wrong for Ezra to ask the king for an escort? Cf. Ne. ii. 9. Why did he not do so? Are we as careful as he to live out what we profess?

(2) From Ezra's actions before setting out, what may we learn regarding our undertaking work for God? See especially verses 15-19, 21-23, 24-30, 33-35, 36, and cf. in contrast Jos. ix. 14; Is. xxxi. 1; Je. xlviii. 10a (R.V.); Mt. xxv. 3.

(3) What treasure has been placed in our hands who in Christ are 'a royal priesthood' (1 Pet. ii. 9)? Do not Ezra's injunctions to the priests to whom he entrusted the treasure apply also to us? See verses 24-29.

Day 7. Ezr. ix and x.

(1) What state of affairs was brought to Ezra's notice soon after his arrival in Jerusalem? Cf. Dt. vii. 1-4. Note carefully how he acted. See especially ix. 6 and cf. Dn. ix. 3-6. How do you act when you discover something wrong being done in the Christian fellowship to which you belong?

(2) Are prayer and confession sufficient? Notice how Ezra seemed paralysed (ix. 15, x. 1) until one of the congregation bade him take the matter in hand and deal with it boldly. Is there any step we can take to persuade others that resolute action is needed if revival is to come? Cf. 2 Ch. xv. 7, 8; Heb. iii. 13.

(3) How was conviction of sin produced, and what part did the Word of God play in the matter? What proved that the people's repentance was genuine? Cf. 2 Cor. vii. 9-11.

Notes.—(1) ix. 1. 'Princes'; better, perhaps, 'Leaders' (Moffatt).

(2) ix. 3. All the actions described were signs of Ezra's grief and sorrow.

(3) ix. 8. 'A nail'; i.e., a fixed and secure hold. The expression 'a wall' is also figurative, signifying God's protective care, like a 'fence' (R.V. mg.) round a vineyard.

Week 36. Nehemiah i–vii

Day 1. Ne. i.

(1) How long did Nehemiah brood over the news about Jerusalem before he took action (see Note (1) below)? Observe that he

was first moved with a deep concern, which then drove him to prayer, resulting finally in sacrificial action. Is not this the usual sequence in those who hear God's call to the mission field or elsewhere? Do you know anything of this?

(2) What evidence do you find in Nehemiah's prayer that he knew the Scriptures? What four things does he mention before God as the ground of his hope of an answer to his prayer? Cf. 1 Ki. viii. 51-53; Ps. cxix. 49; Lk. xviii. 13; 1 Thes. v. 24. What may we learn from this as to how we should pray?

(3) Consider what it meant for Nehemiah to give up his position. Cf. Heb. xi. 24-26.

Notes.—(1) Verse 1. The month 'Chisleu' corresponded to our November-December, and Nisan (ii. 1) to our March-April.

(2) Verse 2. 'Concerning the Jews that had escaped', etc.; i.e. 'the Judaean remnant that had survived the exile' (Moffatt).

(3) Verse 11. 'Cupbearer'. A high official, who had the duty of tasting wine before it was handed to the king, lest it should have been poisoned.

Day 2. Ne. ii.

The chapter describes (a) Nehemiah's request of the king; (b) the journey to Jerusalem; (c) the night exploration of the city wall, and (d) the conference with the leading Jews, and the mockery of the enemy.

(1) Observe how at every stage difficulties had to be overcome. Are you prepared to face difficulties in Christ's service?

(2) What light does the chapter throw upon Nehemiah's secret communion with God? In the midst of daily activity, when suddenly confronted by some demand or danger, do you lift brief heart prayers to the present Lord? Cf. Ps. cxxxviii. 3; Pr. xviii. 10; Mt. xiv. 30.

(3) On what grounds was Nehemiah confident that God would prosper him in the work he was taking in hand? May we have a similar confidence? See verses 18 and 20, and cf. Phil. i. 6, ii. 13; 1 Thes. v. 24.

Notes.—(1) Verse 2. Nehemiah had probably transgressed court etiquette in letting his grief be seen in the king's presence.

(2) Verse 10. 'Sanballat'. An important official, probably governor of Samaria. Tobiah may have been his secretary. They were opposed to any restoration of Jerusalem. In verse 19 an Arabian chief, Geshem, is mentioned as being with them.

Day 3. Ne. iii.

(1) Contrast the busy scenes of this chapter with the picture of the walls and gates lying desolate, broken, and burned, in ii. 13, 14. What brought about the change?

(2) Note how all classes in the city took part in the work, each being assigned his special place and task. What may we learn from this chapter of the value (a) of thorough organization; (b) of willing co-operation? Cf. 1 Cor. xiv. 40; Phil. i. 27; 1 Pet. iv. 10, 11.

(3) How does the chapter show also the necessity of individual effort on the part of all? Nehemiah alone could have achieved nothing. Are you doing your part in backing up your leaders in the work?

Notes.—(1) Verse 5. The word 'Lord' should probably be 'lord' as in R.V., the reference being to Nehemiah. These men from Tekoa took part in the rebuilding (cf. also verse 27), but they were not submissive to Nehemiah. For the metaphor see Je. xxvii. 12.

(2) The *Century Bible* divides the chapter as follows: Verses 1-5, the north and north-west wall; verses 6-12, the west wall; verses 13, 14, the south wall and gates; verses 15-27, the south-east wall and gates; verses 28-32, the north-east wall.

(3) Verse 20. The LXX omits the word 'earnestly'. Its presence in the Hebrew text may be due to a copyist's error known as 'dittography'.

Day 4. Ne. iv.

(1) The successful progress of the work brought increasing opposition. What various kinds of discouragement did Nehemiah meet with at this time? See verses 1-12.

(2) What was his reply and how did he act in each case? Notice especially his refuge against ridicule (verses 1-6) and his defence against threatened attack (verses 9 and 13-18).

(3) In verses 19-23 notice how Nehemiah shared in the hard work. Where did he plan to be if fighting broke out? What does this teach us as to the nature of true leadership?

Notes.—(1) Verse 12. The Hebrew is uncertain in meaning. Moffatt renders it 'And when the Jews who lived beside our enemies came in, they kept telling us "They are gathering against us from all quarters" '.

(2) Verse 16. It is better to take the last words 'all the house of Judah' as belonging to verse 17, and read as in R.V. mg. Verse 16 will then refer to Nehemiah's own men, and verse 17 to the general body of the people.

Day 5. Ne. v.

(1) What features of his conduct made Nehemiah an excellent governor? At least four are mentioned in this chapter.

(2) What social evil did Nehemiah put right (see verses 1-13), and how did he do it? Do you find evidence here that Nehemiah had acquired very great moral influence in the community of which he was the head?

(3) What consideration ought to keep God's people from doing some things, which others do as a matter of course? Cf. Ps. xxxiv. 11-13; 1 Cor. viii. 13. Have you had to apply this principle yourself recently?

Notes.—(1) Verses 1-5. The well-to-do Jews were evidently demanding repayment at high interest of money lent by them to their poorer brethren, and were seizing the lands and property and even the persons of the debtors whenever their demands were not met.

(2) Verse 10. 'On usury' (R.V.). There is clearly some textual error here, for Nehemiah did not exact interest, as the context shows. In verse 11 the phrase 'the hundredth part' should probably be 'the interest'.

(3) Verse 15. 'Were chargeable unto'; better, 'laid burdens upon', as in R.V. mg.; i.e. burdens of taxation.

Day 6. Ne. vi.

(1) Nehemiah's enemies now tried intrigue. The proposal to confer together is attractive to many minds. What made Nehemiah persistently refuse it? Contrast Eve's folly in discussing the question raised by the serpent (Gn. iii. 1-5). Do you ever parley with questions that ought never to be allowed?

(2) What was the special subtlety of the attempts to ensnare Nehemiah which are described in verses 5-9 and 10-14? Notice how Nehemiah's singleness of purpose and loyalty to God were as a shield about him. Note also how the narrow path of faith and duty lies between folly on the one hand and fear on the other. With verses 6 and 7 cf. Lk. xxiii. 2; Acts xvii. 7; and with verse 10 cf. Pr. xxix. 25.

(3) There were those among the Jewish nobles who had collaborated with the enemy. Are the thoughts of your heart free from sinful entanglements? Cf. 1 Ki. xi. 4, xv. 3; 2 Ch. xxv. 2; Jn. xiv. 30.

Notes.—(1) Verse 5. 'An open letter'. So that others besides Nehemiah might see its contents.

(2) Verse 10. 'Who was shut up'. Probably by some ceremonial uncleanness; see 1 Sa. xxi. 7, where the same Heb. word is rendered 'detained'. If this be so, then Shemaiah tempted Nehemiah to permit a double trespass, in meeting Shemaiah in the inner temple (cf. Je. xxxvi. 5) and in going there himself as a layman (cf. verse 11 R.V. mg.).

Day 7. Ne. vii.

(1) What were the two qualities which marked out Hananiah as fit to be put in charge of Jerusalem? See Lk. xix. 17 and 1 Tim. i. 12; Ex. xviii. 21, and Col. iv. 1. Remembering that you may

be called to undertake responsibility in work for God, what are
you doing to develop these two qualities?

(2) What makes a register of names so important? See verses
64, 65, and cf. Rev. xx. 15, xxi. 27. See also Dn. xii. 1; Lk. x. 20.

Notes.—(1) Verse 2. The 'he' refers to Hananiah. Possibly the appointment
of two men in charge of the city means, as in iii. 9, 12, that each was ruler of
half the district of Jerusalem.

(2) Verse 3. 'Appoint watches'; i.e. men were appointed to be on guard
during the night watches.

Week 37. NEHEMIAH VIII–XIII

Day 1. Ne. viii.

Chapters viii, ix, and x describe a remarkable revival. It was characterized
by a hunger to know God's commandments, confession of sin, prayer, and the
making of a covenant to keep God's law.

(1) 'The ears of all the people were attentive unto the book of
the law' (verse 3). Consider how great a change of heart had taken
place since the days before the exile. See Je. xi. 6-8, xxxii. 36-40.
How are these verses an illustration of Ps. cxix. 71 and Heb.
xii. 11?

(2) Have you the desire and determination to acquire the
things which will equip you to fulfil the important ministry of
helping others to understand the Scriptures? See 1 Cor. xiv. 1, 3,
12, 19; 1 Tim. iv. 12-16; 2 Tim. ii. 15, iii. 14-17.

(3) Verses 9-12 show that drawing near to God in His appointed
way brings joy and gladness (cf. Acts viii. 30-39). Are you strong
in that joyful confidence in God, which is given to those who
from their hearing (or reading) of the Word of God daily see the
light and walk in it? Cf. Phil. iv. 4; 1 Jn. i. 4-7.

Notes.—(1) Verse 10. 'Send portions', etc. See Dt. xvi. 11, 14; Est. ix. 19,
22.

(2) Verse 17. The Feast of Tabernacles had been observed (see e.g. 2 Ch.
vii. 9, viii. 13), but not, it would appear, the making of booths.

Day 2. Ne. ix. 1-21.

(1) What marks do you find in today's portion of a genuine
repentance? See 2 Cor. vii. 10, 11.

(2) Do you ever recall in God's presence, for God's glory and
your own encouragement, the great things God has done, whether
in your own personal experience, or in the past history of our
country and of His Church? Cf. Ps. ciii. 1-5.

(3) Meditate upon God's 'great kindness', and 'manifold

mercies' in spite of 'great provocation', as seen in today's portion. Cf. Ps. lxvi. 16-20; 2 Tim. ii. 19.

Day 3. Ne. ix. 22-38.

(1) What may we learn here about the heart of God, and the heart of man? Have you considered (a) how much you need to look to yourself; and (b) to what extent you can look to the Lord? See (a) Heb. iii. 12, 13; 2 Jn. 8; (b) Phil. i. 6; Heb. xii. 2.

(2) The Jews had learned by bitter experience the hard lesson that disobedience brings penalty. Yet had God acted only in punishment? Cf. Ps. cxxx. 3, 4. What may we learn here about the principles of God's action towards His people when they sin?

Note.—The prayer follows the course of Israel's history from the covenant with Abraham (7, 8), through the deliverance from Egypt (9-11), and the wilderness period (12-21), to the conquest of Canaan (22-25) and the period of the Judges (26-29); and then, in brief summary, the period of the prophets (30) and the deliverance from exile (31)—all leading up to the fervent plea of verses 32-38 based upon their present condition.

Day 4. Ne. x.

(1) Make a list of the seven specific ordinances embraced within the general resolve and covenant to walk in God's law (verse 29) and not to 'forsake the house of our God'.

(2) What did the people agree to give up that they might 'Observe and do all the commandments?' Cf. 1 Jn. ii. 15; 2 Cor. vi. 14–vii. 1. What price are you paying for whole-hearted consecration?

(3) Note the different kinds of offering made by the people for the maintenance of the work and worship of God. What can we learn from this about how to give? Cf. Pr. iii. 9, 10; Mal. iii. 10; 1 Cor. xvi. 1, 2.

Notes.—(1) Verse 29. 'Entered into a curse and into an oath'; i.e. pledged themselves by an oath, invoking divine vengeance upon themselves, if they failed to observe it.

(2) Verse 31b. Cf. Ex. xxiii. 10; Dt. xv. 1-3.

(3) Verses 35-39 give a general summary of such laws as Ex. xxiii. 19 and Nu. xviii. 8-32. The translation 'heave offering' (r.v.) is misleading. The root meaning of the Hebrew word is something lifted off or separated, that is, an offering or contribution. It is better to omit the word 'heave' as in a.v.

Day 5. Ne. xi.

(1) Though the temple had been rebuilt and the city walls repaired, Jerusalem remained unattractive to dwell in (cf. ii. 3,

17), and the bulk of the people preferred to live in the country. By what two methods according to verses 1 and 2 were more inhabitants for the city secured? Are you willing to volunteer to serve in the place of greatest need? Cf. Is. vi. 8.

(2) In verses 3-24 is given a list of those who dwelt in Jerusalem, in the following categories: (a) Heads of families of the tribe of Judah (4-6); (b) of the tribe of Benjamin (7-9); (c) officials of the temple—priests (10-14), Levites (15-19), other attendants, including singers (21-24). Try to picture the life of the city. Observe the prominence given to the house of God and its worship. Others helped in other ways, and some of them are described as 'valiant' or 'mighty men of valour' (lit. 'men of strength and force'). Are you playing your part in the community to which you belong, helping it to become strong? Cf. Ec. ix. 10a; Rom. xii. 11a; 1 Cor. xv. 58.

Day 6. Ne. xii.

(1) How did the people celebrate the completion of the wall? Does the joy of success make us remember God or forget Him? See Lk. xvii. 15-18; Dt. viii. 10-18.

(2) As you read this passage and follow in imagination the two companies as they marched in procession, each round half of the wall, remember Nehemiah's solitary journey as described in ii. 12-15. Cf. 1 Cor. xv. 10. Who knows what God can do through you if your life is yielded to Him for the fulfilling of His purpose?

(3) 'Nehemiah the governor, and Ezra the scribe' (verse 26). Consider and contrast the office and character of these two great men, and how both alike were needed in this critical period of Israel's history.

Notes.—(1) Verse 9. 'In wards' (R.V.). The word literally means keeping guard or watch. Here it denotes the bands or courses of Levites who in turn served in the temple. In verse 24 the phrase 'ward against ward' seems to mean that one band sang responsively to another.

(2) Verse 25. 'Who were warders in charge of the storehouses at the gates' (Moffatt).

(3) Verse 30. 'Purified'; by sprinkling the blood of sacrifices. Cf. Ezk. xliii. 19, 20.

(4) Verse 45. 'They kept the ward of their God', etc.; i.e. they discharged the duties of their office, in regard to worship and purification.

Day 7. Ne. xiii.

Nehemiah at some point in his governorship returned to king Artaxerxes and later came again to Jerusalem (see verses 6 and 7), only to find that during his absence various abuses and backslidings had taken place.

(1) Note in this chapter five references to definite actions taken to deal with and to bring to an end unsatisfactory features in the conduct and condition of the people. Are you zealous, as Nehemiah was, against the encroachments of evil?

(2) Sanballat and Tobias, having been defeated in their frontal attack, now succeed, during Nehemiah's absence, in gaining a footing in the Jewish community in Jerusalem. How does this illustrate the need of watchfulness against our besetting sins, lest, having kept them out for a time, they should at length find entrance in another way?

Notes.—(1) Verse 5. With Nehemiah's departure, the practice described in xii. 44 had quickly fallen into desuetude. Hence the store room was left empty, and Tobiah got in.

(2) Verse 30. 'Appointed wards'; i.e. watches or courses; cf. xii. 9 and 45 notes.

HAGGAI

INTRODUCTION

(See New Bible Handbook, pp. 255-257)

THE prophets Haggai and Zechariah are mentioned together in Ezra v. 1 as prophesying at that time in Jerusalem. Ezra v and vi should be read in order to fit the ministry and God-given messages of these prophets into their historical setting.

The exact date of Haggai's prophesying is given in Hg. i. 1 as being the second year of Darius, king of Persia, i.e. 520 B.C. (cf. Zc. i. 1). Sixteen years before, in 536 B.C., the first company of exiles, under Zerubbabel, had returned from Babylon to Jerusalem, and had set about the work of rebuilding the temple. But Samaritan opposition and intrigue proved too strong, and the work ceased (see Ezr. iv. 1-5, 24). The people became occupied with their own concerns, and said with regard to the temple, 'The time is not come, the time that the Lord's house should be built' (Hg. i. 2).

The prophecies of Haggai consist of four utterances (see *Analysis*), which contain repeated promises of God's presence and blessing, if only the people will give themselves to the work of building the Lord's house. Haggai's words express for our hearing the abiding truth that God gives Himself and His best to those who fully honour Him, and seek first His kingdom. There is no other hope of survival in the day of trouble and judgment when

God Himself will shake all things and reveal the worthlessness of every other boasted confidence (see Hg. ii. 21-23, and cf. Heb. xii. 25-27). Thus did Haggai, by the light of the Spirit of God, discern the truth about life's immediate circumstances, and foresee the similar, if greater, certainties of the final consummation in the day of the Lord.

ANALYSIS

i.		First utterance. A call to the people to recommence the building of the temple. The work resumed.
ii.	1-9.	Second utterance. The builders encouraged. God is with them to prosper the work.
ii.	10-19.	Third utterance. The people and their offerings have been unclean in God's eyes. But now He will bless them.
ii.	20-23.	Fourth utterance. The kingdoms of this world shall be overthrown, and the Lord's elect servant be exalted.

Week 38. HAGGAI–ZECHARIAH VIII

Day 1. Hg. i

(1) How does this chapter show the unprofitableness of a life that forgets God, and why it must be so? What was God's interpretation of the situation through His servant Haggai? With verse 3, 4 cf. Mt. vi. 33; with 5 and 6 cf. 1 Cor. xv. 58; and with verse 13 cf. Ps. cxxx. 3, 4.

(2) For what purpose had the people been brought back from Babylon? See Ezr. i. 3-5. Contrast their first beginnings with the condition of things described by Haggai, and think back over your own experience. See Ezr. ii. 68, iii. 8. How does today's portion show (a) that the Lord sees our backsliding (cf. Rev. ii. 4), and (b) that He desires to restore us?

Notes.—(1) Verse 1. 'The sixth month'; corresponding to our August-September.

(2) Verse 4. 'Cieled'. More probably 'panelled' (Moffatt); i.e. the walls covered with wood panelling.

Day 2. Hg. ii.

(1) Picture the desolate scene and the despondency of the people (verse 3). But how did the prospect appear to Haggai's

eye of faith (verses 4-9)? On what grounds did he reassure them, and to what vision did he direct their eyes? Cf. Heb. xii. 26, 27.

(2) Verses 10-19. How does Haggai show that in the sanctified life contact with unholy things must be avoided and that mere contact with holy things is not sufficient? Are you deceiving yourself in either direction, as the people in Haggai's day had been deceiving themselves? See Is. i. 11-18; 2 Tim. ii. 19-22.

(3) What will be the fate of all human activity and organization carried on without God, and what is the work that will stand, whose doers are blessed from the day they set their hand to it? See 1 Cor. iii. 11-15; 1 Jn. ii. 17.

Notes.—(1) Verse 3. 'In its former glory' (R.V.); see 2 Ch. iii-v.

(2) Verse 5. 'Abode' (R.V.); better 'abideth' as in R.V. mg. Cf. 'I am with you' (verse 4).

(3) Verse 6. 'It is a little while'. 'The prophecy is not completely fulfilled even now, and it covers the entire development of "the kingdom that cannot be moved" until the end of time. . . . So the chronology of prophecy is not altogether that of history; and while the events stand clear, the perspective is foreshortened' (Maclaren).

(4) Verse 7. 'The desire of all nations'. Better 'the desirable things of all nations' as in R.V.

(5) Verse 23. 'As a signet'—a symbol of honour and authority. Cf. Je. xxii. 24. The prophecy was not finally fulfilled in Zerubbabel, and points forward to Christ.

ZECHARIAH

INTRODUCTION

(See New Bible Handbook, pp. 257-259)

ZECHARIAH began his prophetic ministry two months after Haggai (see Zc. i. 1; Hg. i. 1). His book falls into two parts (chapters i–viii and ix–xiv), and these are so different in character that many have thought that the second part must have been written by someone other than Zechariah. Such a supposition, however, is by no means necessary. The differences may be explained by the change of theme, and by the fact that the second part was written many years later than the first. A close study also reveals remarkable resemblances between the two parts.

The first part of the book has to do mainly with the rebuilding of the temple, and contains Zechariah's words of encouragement and warning to the people and their rulers. After an opening call to repentance (i. 1-6) there follows a series of eight visions, which supply an answer to doubts and questionings in the people's

minds. The first part closes with the prophet's reply to an enquiry
from the people of Bethel (vii. 1-3 R.V.) about the continuance of
the Fasts which the Jews had been observing in mourning for the
calamities that had overtaken them.

The second part of the book consists of two oracles (ix–xi and
xii–xiv). Both sections, as David Baron says in his valuable
commentary, treat of war between the heathen world and Israel,
but 'in the first the judgment through which *Gentile world power
over Israel is finally destroyed*, and Israel is endowed with strength
to *overcome all these enemies*', is the main theme: and in the second
the judgment through which '*Israel itself is sifted and purged* in
the final great conflict between the nations, and transformed into
the holy nation of Jehovah, forms the leading topic'.

Zechariah's writings foreshadow the appearance of Zion's king
both in meekness and in majesty, and declare both His rejection
and His dominion over the whole earth. They are therefore
frequently quoted in the New Testament with reference either
to Christ's first or to His second coming to the earth.

ANALYSIS

xiv. Messiah's appearing, and the establishment of His kingdom on earth.

Day 3. Zc. i and ii.

(1) What do we learn from Zc. i. 1-6 about the Word of the Lord and the different consequences of obeying and rejecting it? What is and always will be true of it, whatever men do? With verse 6 (R.V.) cf. Dt. xxviii. 1, 2, 15. See also Mt. v. 18, xxiv. 15.

(2) In today's portion are three visions (i. 7-17, i. 18-21, ii. 1-13). How do these answer the following questions? (a) What is God's real attitude towards Jerusalem? (b) How can the nations which oppress them be subdued? (c) Can the city, now desolate, have any future?

(3) Consider how much that is said here of Jerusalem is true spiritually for us in Christ. See, for example, ii. 5, 8b, 10, 11, 12. Is there not the same call to us to believe, as there was to the people of Zechariah's day? Cf. 2 Cor. i. 20.

Notes.—(1) i. 6. 'take hold of'; better, 'overtake' as in A.V. mg. Cf. Dt. xxviii. 15, 45.

(2) i. 11. There was no sign of any stirring among the nations to fulfil God's purposes towards Israel.

(3) i. 15b. The nations had exceeded their commission. 'For while I was slightly angry with Israel, they have pushed my anger for their own evil ends' (Moffatt).

(4) i. 20, 21. 'Four carpenters'; i.e. agents appointed by God to destroy the 'horns' (strength) of the nations.

'Fray'; i.e. affright.

(5) ii. 4, 5. The proposed measurement of Jerusalem is cancelled, for the reasons here given.

(6) ii. 6. 'The land of the north'; i.e. Babylon (or Persia), see verse 7.

Day 4. Zc. iii and iv.

In chapter iii Joshua the high priest, and in chapter iv the golden candlestick, are emblems of the nation. Both visions speak of Christ.

(1) Consider how these two visions answer the two questions: Can our guilt and defilement be removed and by what power can the building of the temple and the restoration of Israel be achieved?

(2) By whose intervention was Satan rebuked and Joshua cleansed? Note that these things were a sign of what God was going to do (verses 8 and 9 R.V.). Cf. Heb. ix. 26; Jude 9. Note carefully Rom. viii. 31-34; Heb. vii. 25.

(3) Try to picture how discouraging the outward circumstances were in regard to the building of the temple. See iv. 7, 10; Hg.

ii. 3. What promises are here given to Zerubbabel, and what was the guarantee of their fulfilment? Cf. Ho. i. 7; 2 Cor. x. 4, 5.

Notes.—(1) iii. 4, 5. 'Change of raiment': signifying probably the special dress of the high priest. When finally the mitre was put on his head, his equipment was complete for the fulfilment of his office. See Ex. xxviii. 36-38.

(2) iii. 8, 9. 'My servant' . . . 'the Branch' . . . 'the Stone'. All titles of the Messiah. See e.g. Is. xxviii. 16, xlii. 1; Je. xxiii. 5. The 'seven eyes' may represent the omniscience of the Messiah. Cf. Rev. v. 6.

Day 5. Zc. v and vi.

(1) God has declared that His purpose is to re-establish Jerusalem (i and ii), to cleanse the nation (iii), and to prosper the building of the temple (iv). But what is the necessary complement of such divine blessing? What of those who still practise wickedness, and what of wickedness itself? See chapter v and also 2 Tim. ii. 19; 2 Thes. i. 7-10; Rev. xxi. 1-4, 8, 27. Contrast Rom. i. 17 and 18.

(2) What is foreshadowed in vi. 9-15 by the crowning of the high priest, and by the prophetic declaration that 'the man' (verse 12) thus signified shall be a priest *upon his throne*, and shall build the temple of the Lord? See Eph. ii. 13, 19-22; Heb. viii. 1, x. 11-13; 1 Pet. ii. 5.

Notes.—(1) v. 1-4. A vision of God's judgment pursuing the transgressor.

(2) v. 6. 'An ephah'; barrel-shaped measure, having here a circular lid of lead.

(3) v. 11. 'The land of Shinar'; i.e. Babylonia.

(4) vi. 1-8. The vision is in its details difficult to interpret, but in general reveals Jehovah ruling over the earth (verse 5), and exercising His judgments by unseen agents. Cf. 2 Ki. vi. 15-17.

(5) vi. 10, 11. A deputation from the Jews in Babylon had come to Jerusalem. Zechariah is commanded to make 'a crown' (R.V. mg.) from some of the silver and gold which they had brought and to set it on the head of the high priest.

(6) vi. 14. The names are slightly different from those given in verse 10. The form Helem is due probably to a scribal error, and the word 'Hen' is not a proper name at all, but means 'kindness' (see R.V. mg.).

Day 6. Zc. vii.

See *Introduction*. Zechariah's answer to the delegation from Bethel consists of four parts, each beginning 'And Jehovah's word came unto me'. The first two parts of his reply are contained in today's portion, and the last two in chapter viii.

(1) With what did God find fault in these fasts? See verses 5 and 6 and contrast 1 Cor. x. 31. In the light of this part of the

prophet's reply, is there not much in men's worship today that is not acceptable to God?

(2) With verses 9 and 10 cf. Is. lviii. 6, 7. Where does a man's enmity towards his brother take its rise? Cf. Mk. vii. 21-23.

(3) What attitude of heart towards God had the Jews shown? Do you realize that this is a peril against whose beginnings God warns us to be daily on our guard? See Heb. iii. 7-13.

Notes.—(1) Verse 3. 'Separating myself'; i.e. from food and drink.

(2) Verse 7. 'Should ye not hear?' The LXX reads 'Are not these the words?' etc.

(3) Verse 13. Cf. Pr. i. 25, 26.

Day 7. Zc. viii.

(1) Enumerate the blessings which God here promises concerning Jerusalem, noticing also the emphasis placed upon them by the number of times the phrase 'saith the Lord' occurs. Is God less willing to fulfil to us the 'great and precious promises' (2 Pet. i. 4), which He has given us in Christ? Cf. Heb. vi. 11-18.

(2) What, however, are the conditions for obtaining the promises of God? In the light of the evidence we have of God's willingness to give, where does the hindrance lie if we are not enjoying in personal experience the things promised?

(3) Observe how the prophet repeats here earlier utterances. With verse 2a cf. i. 14b; with verse 2b, i. 15; and with verse 3, i. 16 and ii. 10. What does he say in verses 19-23 will ultimately happen to the fasts about which the deputation from Bethel had enquired (vii. 2, 3)?

Note.—Verse 10. Three evils are here spoken of from which the people suffered when God's house was neglected, namely, scarcity, absence of security, and disunion.

Week 39. ZECHARIAH IX–MALACHI IV

Day 1. Zc. ix and x.

(1) The opening verses (ix. 1-8) are a prophecy of an invasion of Syria, Phoenicia, and the country of the Philistines. The prophecy was historically fulfilled in the conquests of Alexander the Great. But to whom is the prophet's eye directed? How does this account for the fall of Tyre, notwithstanding its wisdom, strong defences, and wealth and, on the other hand, for the preservation of Jerusalem? Cf. verse 15a and ii. 5.

(2) In verses 9 and 10 of chapter ix a picture is presented of Zion's King, in which, as often in the Old Testament, His first

and second advents are merged into one. What is said (a) of His character; (b) of the manner of His coming; (c) of the final extent of His rule, and (d) of the benefits He brings?

(3) The remaining portion of today's study (ix. 11–x) has for its theme what God will yet do for His people Israel. It is profitable if time permits to make a list of the things here promised, and to reflect how they are types and symbols of spiritual blessings which are ours in Christ.

Notes.—(1) ix. 7. A prophecy of the abolition of idolatrous sacrifices, and the incorporation of the remnant of the Philistines among God's people. 'Jebusite' here means inhabitant of Jerusalem.

(2) ix. 11, 12. A promise that Jews still captive will be delivered. Cf. Ps. xl. 2, 3. 'The strong hold' may mean God Himself. Cf. Joel iii. 16b. For the meaning of 'double' see Is. lxi. 7.

(3) ix. 13-17. Prophecy of victory for Israel, when the enemy shall be trodden down like sling stones (verse 15 r.v.) and Israel lifted up like the stones of a crown (verse 16). The latter half of verse 15 is another figure, representing the Israelites as drinking the blood of their enemies as full as the bowls used in sacrifice, or the corners of the altar that were drenched in blood.

(4) x. 2. 'Teraphim' (r.v.). Household idols, used, as here, in divination. Cf. Ezk. xxi. 21 r.v.

(5) x. 3. 'He-goats' (r.v.). Means the leading people of the community. God promises that He will transform Israel from the defencelessness of sheep to the strength of the war horse.

(6) x. 4. Best taken as a fourfold picture of the Messiah—Corner stone (Is. xxviii. 16; Eph. ii. 20); Nail (Is. xxii. 22-24 r.v.); Battle bow (Ps. xlv. 5); and Ruler (r.v. mg.). The last clause of the verse is obscure. David Baron renders 'He that will exercise all rule'. 'From him' means 'from Judah'.

Day 2. Zc. xi.

While plain in its main teaching, this chapter is obscure in many of its details. Its theme is grace and judgment. It opens with a vision of judgment, sweeping over the land, and making it desolate (verses 1-3). God shows to the prophet that the promises of the preceding chapter will not be realized without further uprisings of evil (cf. x. 2, 3a). In verses 4-17 the prophet is bidden impersonate first a good shepherd, and when he was rejected and despised, a worthless shepherd, under whom the flock will suffer many sorrows. The section is a vivid foreshadowing of the coming of Christ (verses 12, 13; cf. Mt. xxvi. 14, 15, xxvii. 9, 10).

(1) The good Shepherd's two staves (cf. 'rod and staff' in Ps. xxiii. 4) were named 'Graciousness' (r.v. mg.) and 'Union' (r.v. mg.), that is, He came in grace to bind the flock into one. Do you see here a picture of Christ? Cf. Jn. i. 14, xvii. 20-22.

(2) When the good shepherd was loathed (verse 8 r.v.), and His services not valued (verse 12), what did He do? Note the significant change from 'I fed the flock' (verse 7) to 'Then said I,

I will not feed you' (verse 9). See also verses 6 and 10. Compare with this the contrast between 'My house' (Mt. xxi. 13) and 'your house' (Mt. xxiii. 38).

(3) How is the lot of those who deliberately refuse the good further described in verses 15 and 16? Cf Lk. xv. 14-16. With verse 17 cf. 2 Thes. ii. 8.

Notes.—(1) Verse 4. 'The flock of the slaughter', i.e. exposed to slaughter.

(2) Verses 5, 6. Cf. Mt. ix. 36; Zc. xiii. 7.

(3) Verse 7b. 'Even you, O poor of the flock'; see R.V. mg. The meaning of this clause is uncertain, as also of verse 8a.

(4) Verse 12. Thirty pieces of silver, 'The price of an injured slave'. Ex. xxi. 32.

Day 3. Zc. xii and xiii.

Today's portion contains a prophecy of a combined attack of many peoples upon Jerusalem, and of the deliverance God will give (xii. 1-9) together with the repentance and cleansing which will be wrought within the nation by their vision and recognition of Him whom they pierced (xii. 10-xiii). The ultimate fulfilment of this prophecy will take place at the time of Christ's second coming (cf. Rom. xi. 25-27), but it has a present application spiritually to all who belong to Him.

(1) What is to be the secret of Jerusalem's survival, when threatened by so many enemies gathered together against it (xii. 1-9; cf. xiv. 3)? Has the Christian similar hope of overcoming the world, the flesh, and the devil? See Ps. xxvii. 1-5; 1 Jn. iv. 4, v. 4.

(2) What four experiences of God's people are set forth in xii. 10–xiii? Do you know them in your experience? With xii. 10-14 cf. Jn. xvi. 8, 9 and Acts ii. 37-40; with xiii. 1, Heb. ix. 13, 14; with xiii. 2-5, 2 Cor. vii. 1; and with xiii. 7-9, 1 Pet. i. 5-7.

Notes.—(1) xii. 12-14. Both the intensity and the universality of Israel's repentance are here emphasized.

(2) xiii. 2-6. The prophets, having been proved false, shall be ashamed, and seek to disguise the fact that they prophesied. The wounds spoken of in verse 6 are either wounds self-inflicted in their prophetic frenzy (cf. 1 Ki. xviii. 28), or more probably wounds received by them through the attacks of people upon them (cf. verse 3, last clause).

Day 4. Zc. xiv.

(1) Verses 1-7 describe the breaking in of 'the day of the Lord'. Who will at that time be gathered against Jerusalem, what will happen to the city and its inhabitants, when and in what manner will the Lord appear, and what will be the first result?

(2) In the day of the Lord what further results will come to

pass (a) as regards Jerusalem (verses 8-11); (b) as regards those who attacked Jerusalem (verses 12-15), and (c) as regards the remnant of the nations that has escaped (verses 16-19)?

(3) Picture the city as described in verses 20, 21 (see Note (3) below). Are we seeking that our lives may become thus holy? Cf. 2 Cor. vii. 1; 1 Thes. iii. 13; 1 Pet. i. 15, 16.

Notes.—(1) Verse 5. The people remaining in Jerusalem (verse 2b) will flee by the valley cleft in the Mount of Olives.

(2) Verse 10. The land generally will sink and become as a plain, while Jerusalem remains exalted.

(3) Verses 20, 21. Every aspect of the city's life shall bear the impress of holiness, the business life, the religious life, and the domestic life. The meaning of verse 20b is that the pots which were employed for mean uses shall be as holy as the bowls that held the blood of sacrifice.

MALACHI

INTRODUCTION

(See New Bible Handbook, pp. 259-261)

MALACHI (the name means 'My messenger'—see iii. 1) was doubtless a contemporary of Ezra and Nehemiah. He attacked the evils which arose at Jerusalem after the temple was rebuilt and its services re-established, evils of which we have historical record in the book of Nehemiah. 'The religious spirit of Malachi is that of the prayers of Ezra and Nehemiah.' There is an ancient tradition which regarded 'Malachi' as a pen name, and assigned the authorship to Ezra himself.

This book is the more significant because it closes the Old Testament revelation. As a link between the law and the gospel, it combines severe insistence on the necessity of purity and sincerity of heart with the sure promise of the coming of a Deliverer to them who fear the Lord. Finally (iv. 4-6), it appeals back to the Law and the Prophets (of whom Elijah is the chosen representative). The fuller revelation will not contradict its preparatory stages. The people are to find in the spiritual authorities they already know (i.e. in the Old Testament) their assurance for accepting Him who should come. So, on the mount of Transfiguration, when the Father called men to hear the Son, Moses and Elijah stood by to give their assent and to provide evidence that He was the fulfilment of all their anticipations. See Mt. xvii. 3-5; Jn. v. 46.

ANALYSIS

i. 1-5.   God's love for Israel.

i. 6–ii. 9.   The sins of the priests.

ii. 10-17.   The sins of the people.

iii. 1-6.   Warning that the Lord will come to judge and to purify.

iii. 7-12.   How to give practical expression to their repentance.

iii. 13–iv.   The future day of judgment.

Day 5. Mal. i–ii. 9.

(1) Verses 1-5. The people of Judah, looking upon their condition and circumstances, were depressed and murmuring against God. What proof did the prophet adduce to show that God did love them as a nation? Cf. Ps. xxxiv. 15, 16, lxxiii. 26-28.

(2) What light is thrown by today's portion on what it means to 'hallow God's Name' (Mt. vi. 9)? How did these priests behave, and what does God say He would do to those who did not 'give glory to His Name'?

(3) What, by contrast, do we learn should be the quality and objectives of our service as 'messengers of the Lord of Hosts'? See ii. 5-7 and cf. 2 Cor. vi. 3 (R.V.); 2 Tim. ii. 15; 1 Pet. iv. 10, 11.

Notes.—(1) i. 5b. Render 'The Lord is great beyond the border of Israel', as in R.V. mg. The people had too small a conception of their God, and this the prophet seeks to correct. Cf. verses 11 and 14b.

(2) i. 7. The sacrificial meat (here called 'bread') was polluted by their contempt of God's altar.

(3) i. 9. It was the duty of the priests to intreat God's favour, but how could they find acceptance when they were acting as they were?

Day 6. Mal. ii. 10–iii. 6.

(1) In ii. 10-16 the sin of divorce is rebuked, as something that God hates (ii. 16). The people were putting away their wives, and causing many tears (verse 13), in order to marry foreign women (verse 11) which would lead to idolatry (Dt. vii. 2). What was the root cause of their wrongdoing? Cf. Heb. iii. 12, 13, and the occurrence five times in these verses of the phrase 'deal treacherously'.

(2) Note how iii. 1-6 is an answer to the people's complaint in ii. 17. What similes are used to describe the 'day of the Lord's coming'? What must be put away, and on what must my heart

be set if I am to be ready to welcome Him at His appearing? See 1 Thes. iii. 12, 13; 1 Jn. iii. 2, 3.

Notes.—(1) ii. 10, 11. 'Profaning the covenant of our fathers'; i.e. by marrying wives of other nations. Cf. Ex. xix. 5, xxxiv. 16. 'The daughter of a strange god' means a foreign woman of another religion.

(2) ii. 15. A difficult verse, the meaning of which is obscure. Cf. R.V. mg.

(3) iii. 6. Cf. Je. xxx. 11.

Day 7. Mal. iii. 7–iv.

(1) Of what are the people accused in verses 7-15? What must we make our chief concern if we wish to obtain God's promised blessings? Cf. Pr. iii. 9, 10; Mt. vi. 30-33, xvi. 25; Lk. vi. 38.

(2) Two different classes of people are described in iii. 13-16. To which do you belong? The wicked may seem to have the best of it, but God says here that, in contrast to present circumstances, He is going to make a day (iii. 17 and iv. 3, both R.V.) in which the righteous and the wicked shall be openly distinguished and justly recompensed; how will this be effected? Cf. iv. 1, 2 with 2 Thes. i. 7-10; 1 Jn. ii. 28, iii. 2; Rev. vi. 15-17.

Notes.—(1) iii. 10. 'The whole tithe' (R.V.). Not a part only.

(2) iii. 11. 'The devourer'; i.e. the locust.

ESTHER

INTRODUCTION

(*See New Bible Handbook, pp. 183-185*)

THE book of Esther is apt to be regarded at first sight with suspicion and even dislike. But it is part of the inspired Scriptures which, as the apostle Paul says, are profitable for doctrine, for reproof, for correction, for instruction in righteousness (2 Tim. iii. 16). It is a thrilling drama which ought to be read at a sitting. The story moves swiftly through its various phases until right overcomes evil, and the wicked fall into the pit which they have dug for themselves.

The name of God is not mentioned in the book, but the unseen presence of God pervades it. It has been said that the story was written to glorify the Jews. Rather was it written to show how God provides for His people in the time of need. Many fundamental principles of God's government of this world are more clearly set forth in this book than in almost any other book of Scripture.

The author of the book is unknown and the date of its composition. The opening verses note only that it was written after the reign of Ahasuerus, but the details given in it suggest that it was written not long after that date. It is quite unnecessary to push its composition back to the second century B.C. as some wish to do.

The story of Zerubbabel, Ezra, and Nehemiah tells how God helped the Jews who returned to Jerusalem. The book of Esther shows how God also watched over His people in exile, saving them from destruction, and giving them favour with the Persian king Xerxes. This in turn may have facilitated the work of Ezra and Nehemiah some year later. Chronologically the events recorded in the book of Esther and the books of Ezra and Nehemiah supplement one another.

The Jewish feast known as Purim had its origin in the events recorded in this book.

ANALYSIS

Week 40. ESTHER

Day 1. Est. i.

(1) Read this chapter as an illustration of 1 Jn. ii. 16, 17. Cf. also Ps. xxxix. 5, 7; 2 Cor. iv. 18; Jas. iv. 13, 14.

(2) What lessons may we learn from the character and actions of Ahasuerus, Vashti, and Memucan respectively, as revealed in today's portion? With verse 12 (last clause) cf. ii. 1, vii. 7, 10; Pr. xvi. 14, xx. 2.

Notes.—(1) Verse 2. 'Shushan the palace' (or castle as in R.V. mg.). The meaning would appear to be that there was a fortress called Shushan, in the city of Shushan.

(2) Verse 3. 'Princes'; i.e. officials. 'Servants'; i.e. those who served at court. 'Nobles'; i.e. those belonging to the nobility.

(3) Verse 14. 'Which saw the king's face'; i.e. belonging to the inner circle of the king's counsellors.

Day 2. Est. ii. 1-18.

(1) By what steps did Esther reach the position of queen? None of those concerned, unless it were Mordecai and Esther, saw in what was happening the unseen hand of God; yet He was over-ruling in it all. What comfort may we derive from this? Cf. Ps. cxiii. 5-8; Rom. viii. 28.

(2) See verses 18-20; Are you an individualist, or can you fit in, like Esther, with the plans of others? Mark her humility towards Mordecai, and cf. Phil. ii. 3, 4; Heb. xiii. 17; 1 Pet. v. 5.

Note.—Verse 6. 'Who had been carried away'; these words must refer to Kish.

Day 3. Est. ii. 19–iii.

(1) Why did Mordecai, so loyal in the matter of the plot (ii. 21-23), break the king's commandment in this instance (verse 2)? Cf. Ex. xx. 5; Dn. i. 8; Rom. i. 25. Can you discover a principle here to guide your own actions? See Mt. xxii. 21; Acts xxiv. 16.

(2) What were the outstanding features in Haman's character?

(3) Observe how suddenly the outlook for the Jews was changed from one of hope through Esther's promotion to one of threatening disaster. Why are such things permitted?

Notes.—(1) ii. 19. Moffatt translates 'It was during a second levy of girls'. The girls were brought to the palace in two or more groups.

'Sat in the king's gate'. The phrase may imply that he was in the king's service in some way.

(2) ii. 21. 'Which kept the door'; i.e. of the king's sleeping apartments.

Day 4. Est. iv.

(1) Try to put yourself in Esther's place. Consider (a) her loving concern for Mordecai in his sorrow; (b) her sudden and most difficult summons to personal action; (c) her first reaction to this; (d) Mordecai's compelling argument, and (e) how Esther prepared herself. Cf. Dn. ix. 3, 4.

(2) Consider verse 14 in its application to yourself. Are you concerned about the present situation? Is your faith in God leading you to *action*? What would have been the consequences (a) for God's people, and (b) for Esther, if she had failed to respond to God's call?

Day 5. Est. v and vi.

(1) What may we learn about the need, the possibilities, and the conditions of prayer from Esther's approach to the king? Note also in v. 1-8 how she remains timid and hesitant in spite of the king's repeated promise. Is not this often characteristic of our praying?

(2) When Mordecai saved the king's life (ii. 21-23), he was not allowed, in the providence of God, to receive any reward at the time. What light does this throw upon delays and disappointments in our own lives, which at the time seem strange and unaccountable? See Ps. xxxvii. 7; Heb. x. 35, 36.

(3) Read the story of Haman in the light of such verses as Ps. xxxiv. 15, 16, xxxvii. 32-36.

Day 6. Est. vii and viii.

(1) How does chapter vii illustrate Ps. lxxiii. 17b-20?

(2) After the enemy was defeated, what did Esther and the Jews still have to do to make their deliverance complete? What parallel is there in Christian experience? Cf. Eph. vi. 11-18; 2 Tim. ii. 24-26 (R.V.); Heb. ii. 14, 15.

(3) Picture the change in the lives and outlook of the Jews, when the second decree went forth. What was the effect also on their adversaries? What similar results has your experience of salvation produced? Cf. Acts ii. 46, 47, xix. 17.

Day 7. Est. ix and x.

(1) Gather out from these and earlier chapters outstanding features in Mordecai's character. What lay behind his moral strength?

(2) Notice the severity of the judgment on the wicked. Are we in danger of underestimating or failing to declare to others this part of 'the whole counsel of God' (Acts xx. 27 R.V.)? See 2 Thes. i. 8, 9; Rev. xx. 10-15.

(3) What was the purpose of the institution of the Feast of Purim? See ix. 22 and cf. Ex. xii. 14-17. See also Ps. ciii. 1, 2; 2 Pet. i. 12, 13, iii. 1. Do you ever 'stir yourself up' by the remembrance of God's mercies? Cf. 1 Cor. xi. 24-26.

II PETER

INTRODUCTION

(See New Bible Handbook, pp. 401-403)

THE second Epistle of Peter was written just before his death (i. 14, 15). We may regard it as his last word, and this fact lends added significance to the final message, 'Grow in grace, and in the knowledge of our Lord and Saviour Jesus Christ' (iii. 18).

Peter is obviously concerned about the heresies and moral evil which have crept into the Church, and is writing to warn, to exhort, and to comfort. In contrast with the gloomy picture which he draws is the prominence he gives to the hope of our Lord's return. He explains that this is delayed, not through any slackness on God's part, but through His long-suffering (iii. 9). He is afraid that the Christians, under the stress of persecution and temptation, will forget the commandments which have been delivered to them through the prophets and the apostles. He writes to remind them of their calling and to stir them up (i. 9, 12, 13, 15, iii. 1 and 2).

Chapter ii is strikingly similar in content to the Epistle of Jude. As Peter dwells on the evil which is rampant, he stresses more than ever the call to holiness which he had given in his first letter. 'Ye therefore, beloved, knowing these things beforehand, beware lest, being carried away with the error of the wicked, ye fall from your own steadfastness' (iii. 17, R.V.). And so Peter, who knew the bitterness of falling, closes his earthly ministry with a call to holiness, stability, and expectant faith.

ANALYSIS

i. 1-2.   Introduction.

i. 3-15.   The call to progress in Christian character and fruitfulness.

i. 16-21.   The veracity of the Christian message.
      ii.   Description and condemnation of evildoers and false
            prophets.
iii. 1-7.   Warnings for the last days.
iii. 8-18. The long-suffering of the Lord, and the certainty of
            His coming.

Week 41. 2 Peter and Jude

Day 1. 2 Pet. i. 1-11.

(1) How are those to whom this letter is written described?
See especially verses 4, 9, 10. From what have they been delivered,
and to what height does God design to raise them? How is this
being brought about?

(2) Observe the twice repeated emphasis on *diligence* (verses 5,
10). In what is the Christian to be thus diligent, and what reward
will he gain thereby?

(3) Analyse the picture of the fully developed Christian, given
in verses 5-7, in relation to (a) his personal character; (b) his
attitude to God; (c) his dealings with others. Observe that all
rests upon a basis of faith, but faith without these added qualities
is not enough.

Note.—The passage is clearer in the R.V. and still more so in the R.S.V.

Day 2. 2 Pet. i. 12-21.

(1) What does Peter say three times? Cf. iii. 1, 2, also i. 9. Why
is he thus urgent? What are the implied dangers, and what steps
are you taking to avoid them? Cf. Dt. xxxii. 18, 19; Heb. ii. 1.

(2) By what twofold witness is 'the power and coming of our
Lord Jesus Christ' attested? And what gives this witness its
authority? What does the apostle say 'the word of prophecy' will
do for us?

Note.—Verse 19 should probably be read as in R.V. 'The written word of
prophecy has been confirmed by the vision of the Lord's glory . . . on the mount
of Transfiguration, and Christians may well trust themselves to its guidance
in this dark world, till a light has dawned, which will render the lamp of an
external revelation unnecessary' (Swete). This lamp is referred to again in
iii. 2.

Day 3. 2 Pet. ii.

(1) Although we have the lamp of prophecy, it is necessary to
beware of *false* teachers. Note from today's portion the forms of

evil in which the false teachers, of whom the apostle speaks, indulged. By which are you most liable to be ensnared? What class of people did the teaching and example of the false teachers specially endanger (see verses 16, 18-22)?

(2) What three historical examples of God's judgment upon sinners are given in verses 4-8, and what conclusion is drawn in verse 9 for the comfort of true believers? Does your experience lead you to say Amen to Peter's statement?

Notes.—(1) The chapter is more clearly translated in the R.S.V.

(2) Verses 4-10a are parenthetical, interrupting the description of the false teachers, which is resumed in verse 10b.

Day 4. 2 Pet. iii. 1-10.

(1) How will Christians be tested 'in the last days'? Have you felt the power of this temptation? What sure defence against it is mentioned in verse 2? Cf. Ps. cxix. 49-52; Je. xv. 16.

(2) What made Peter certain that the Day of the Lord 'would come'? See verses 5-7, noticing especially the phrases 'by the word of God', 'by the same Word', and 'His promise'. Cf. 1 Pet. i. 25.

(3) Why is 'the Day' slow in coming? Cf. Ezk. xviii. 23, 32; but also Ezk. xii. 28.

Notes.—(1) Verse 5 is clearer in R.V. and R.S.V.

(2) Verse 10. 'Elements'; the material elements of the universe, but, as many think, with specific reference to the heavenly bodies.

Day 5. 2 Pet. iii. 11-18.

(1) What practical conclusions does Peter base on the certainty that the Day of the Lord will come? Make a list of these, that we may know what effect this great fact should have on our own lives. How can we 'hasten' that Day? (See verse 12, Note (2) below.)

(2) Verses 17, 18. These are probably the last words of the apostle (see *Introduction*). On what two things does he lay stress, the one negative, the other positive? Are you holding fast, and growing, and with Peter, giving all glory to our Lord and Saviour Jesus Christ?

Notes.—(1) Verse 11. 'In all holy conversation'. Better 'holy living', as in R.V.

(2) Verse 12. 'Hasting unto'. Better 'hastening', as in R.V. mg.

JUDE

INTRODUCTION

(*See New Bible Handbook, pp. 405-407*)

THE writer of this Epistle has been generally identified with Judas, one of the brethren of the Lord (Mt. xiii. 55). The letter was probably written shortly before the Fall of Jerusalem, between the years A.D. 60 and 70.

The message of the Epistle is very similar to that of 2 Peter. Both authors write out of a sense of deep urgency (cf. Jude 3, 'I was constrained', R.V.). Evil men and evil ways had crept into the Church, and were endangering its life. This evil must be fought; and the object of both Epistles is to stir up the Christians. Jude, like Peter, looks to the past for illustrations of divine judgment upon sin, and declares that judgment will fall as certainly as in the past upon those who are now turning their backs upon truth and righteousness. Finally, he exhorts his readers to keep themselves in the love of God, who will hold them fast, through Jesus Christ our Lord.

ANALYSIS

1-4. Introduction, and purpose of the letter.
5-7. God's judgments in the past.
8-16. Description and condemnation of the evil which has crept in.
17-25. Exhortation and benediction.

Day 6. Jude 1-16.

(1) Contrast clause by clause the threefold description in verse 1 of the faithful believers to whom Jude is writing, with the description in verse 4 of the false intruders into the Church, whom he condemns.

(2) Comparing Jude's characterization of these false brethren (verses 4, 8-13, and 16, 19) with the description of them in 2 Pet. ii, what resemblances and what differences do you find?

(3) On what grounds does Jude declare their certain condemnation?

Note.—The Epistle is more clearly translated in the R.V. and R.S.V.

Day 7. Jude 17-25.

(1) What five injunctions are given in verses 17, 20, 21? Con-

sider their meaning and ask yourself concerning each of them, Am I doing this?

(2) Note the complementary truths suggested by the two occurrences of the word 'keep' (verses 21 and 24). Cf. Phil. ii. 12, 13. If there is failure, what must be the cause?

(3) What should be our attitude as Christians to those around us who may be going astray, and what to the sin that has defiled them?

EZEKIEL

INTRODUCTION

(See New Bible Handbook, pp. 226-232)

EZEKIEL was one of the many taken captive by Nebuchadnezzar in the first captivity, commonly referred to as the captivity of King Jehoiachin (e.g. i. 2), because this king himself was among those carried away. This occurred in 597 B.C., eleven years before the actual destruction of Jerusalem.

Ezekiel was a priest as well as a prophet. He commenced prophesying in 592 B.C. and continued till at least 570 B.C. See i. 2 and xxix. 17. His ministry was divided into two distinct periods by the destruction of Jerusalem (586 B.C.). Before this event it was his painful task to disillusion his fellow-exiles, to proclaim that all hopes of the early deliverance of the city and a speedy return of the exiles were vain. Jerusalem must fall. After this event the character of his ministry completely changed. He sought to rebuke despair and to afford comfort and hope by promises of future deliverance and restoration.

To witness with the object first of overthrowing men's natural hopes, and then of overcoming men's inevitable despair, is a work that can be undertaken and carried through only under the constraint and by the inspiration of a divine commission. Such a commission was Ezekiel's compelling urge. He was a man whose whole life was dominated by his sense of vocation and responsibility as a prophet—as God's messenger to his fellows. Similar necessity is laid upon us to be God's witnesses, and the essential truth of Ezekiel's message should be the unchanging truth of our own. Because God is righteous, sin must be punished; old things must pass away. But because God is gracious, and has provided a salvation for sinners, there is a gospel of hope for the hopeless: in Christ all things can become new.

ANALYSIS

Week 42. EZEKIEL I–XI

Day 1. Ezk. i.

The vision of this chapter was of supreme importance in Ezekiel's life. It called him to be a prophet, and through it was revealed a conception of God which moulded his prophetic ministry.

(1) It is a vision of God in His heavenly chariot. We must imagine it to be great in size, as it was also awe-inspiring in appearance. Follow the prophet's description of it, part by part, first the living creatures (verses 5-14), then the wheels (verses 15-21), then the firmament above them, with the throne upon it, and finally

Him who sat there. Meditate upon the vision until you experience something of the awe that cast Ezekiel upon his face (verse 28).

(2) What does the vision suggest to your mind concerning God? Write down what you find symbolized by the living creatures, the wheels, the throne, etc.

Notes.—(1) Verse 3. 'The hand of the Lord was there upon him'. A phrase used also elsewhere in the book to signify a prophetic trance or ecstasy. See iii. 22, viii. 1, xxxiii. 22, xxxvii. 1.

(2) Verse 5. 'Four living creatures'; heavenly beings, yet representing also the highest forms of life on earth, and indicating, perhaps, that all created things are under God's control for the execution of His purposes.

(3) Verse 18. 'Full of eyes'; signifying that nothing is unseen by God.

(4) Verses 19-21. Observe that there was no mechanical framework to the chariot. All was spiritual, and responsive to the Spirit.

Day 2. Ezk. ii–iii. 21.

(1) To whom was Ezekiel sent, and how are they described? See ii. 3-5, iii. 4-9, 10-11. Consider in the light of these verses how difficult his task was. Cf. Je. xv. 20, 21.

(2) What two meanings are symbolized by the eating of the scroll, one having reference to the prophet himself (ii. 8), and the other to his ministry (iii. 4)? Consider the application of these things to all who would be God's messengers.

(3) What consolations and warnings are there in today's portion for one called to witness for the Lord among those who are obstinately opposed to the gospel? Why is such opposition no excuse for ceasing to witness (ii. 5b)?

Notes.—(1) ii. 1, 3. 'Son of man', or 'child of man'; a phrase indicating human weakness and insignificance and occurring over ninety times in the book. Only as he was strengthened by the Spirit could Ezekiel hear God's words.

(2) ii. 6. 'Briers and thorns . . . scorpions'; symbols of the trials he would suffer.

(3) iii. 15. 'Astonished. . . seven days'; so great was the effect of the vision.

Day 3. Ezk. iii. 22–v.

Jerusalem, under king Zedekiah, had recovered a measure of strength after its capture by Nebuchadnezzar in 597 B.C., and false prophets were prophesying a period of divine favour (see Je. xxviii. 1-4). These reports reached the exiles in Babylon, and the burden of Ezekiel's message at this time was that, on the contrary, Jerusalem was about to experience God's judgments.

The closing verses of chapter iii are best regarded as an introduction to the prophecies of chapters iv-xxiv, which all relate to the approaching judgment on Jerusalem. During this time the prophet was commanded to live in seclusion, as if bound and dumb, except when God gave him some message to deliver (iii. 25-27).

(1) **In chapters iv. 1–v. 4** the prophet is directed to show by four symbolic actions the impending siege of Jerusalem, with its privations and sufferings, and also the plight of those who would be carried into exile after the city's fall. What were these actions? Which of them refer to the siege, and which to the sufferings of those who would be carried into captivity? With iv. 13 cf. Ho. ix. 3, 4, and note the explanation of v. 1-4 in v. 12.

(2) What is said in v. 5-17 of (a) the reasons; (b) the nature, and (c) the purposes of the terrible judgment that was about to fall upon Jerusalem? Some Christians are less Christian in their lives than many who reject or ignore Christ. In the light of these verses what may we infer to be God's attitude to this sad fact?

Notes.—(1) iv. 4, 5. 'Lay the iniquity', etc.; i.e. as the prophet's side bore the weight of his body, so Israel must bear the weight of the divine punishment of her sin. Instead of '390 days' the LXX has '190 days', which is probably the original reading.

(2) iv. 10, 11. Food restricted to eight ounces, and water to two pints or less. Cf. iv. 16.

Day 4. Ezk. vi and vii.

The coming judgment (a) upon the whole land (vi. 1-vii. 9), and (b) upon the city (vii. 10-27).

(1) Chapter vi. Against what sin is the Lord's anger specially directed? What was that sin in its essence and in what forms is it manifested today? Cf. vii. 19; Col. iii. 5 (last clause).

(2) Contrast the phrase 'I will judge thee according to thy ways' (vii. 3, 4, 8, 9, 27, and xxiv. 14) with Ps. ciii. 10; and see Pr. i. 24, 29-31; 2 Cor. vi. 1, 2. What warning for the careless and indifferent does this contrast suggest?

(3) What refrain frequently recurs in these two chapters? What very common attitude towards God is here rebuked, and its folly exposed? Cf. Ps. x. 4-6, 13.

Notes.—(1) vi. 3. 'Your high places'; the word originally meant a height or eminence, but as these were used as the sites of temples, and shrines, the word came to mean 'sanctuaries', as here. Cf. Dt. xii. 2, 3.

(2) vii. 7. 'The morning'; better 'thy doom', as in R.V.; so also in verse 10.

(3) vii. 20. 'They prided themselves upon the beauty of their silver and their gold, and made out of them . . . idols' (Moffatt). Cf. Ho. ii. 8.

(4) vii. 23. 'Make a chain'; the LXX renders 'They shall work disorder'.

Day 5. Ezk. viii.

Chapters viii-xi describe what Ezekiel was shown in a prophetic trance fourteen months after his first vision (see viii. 1 and i. 1, 2).

(1) The prophet is carried 'in the visions of God' to Jerusalem, and is there shown four forms of idolatry, practised in or at the gate of the temple. If you were asked what these practices were, how would you describe them? Observe also what classes of the community are seen engaging in them.

(2) The idol-worshipping elders said 'The Lord hath forsaken the land' (verse 12, R.V. mg.). In what sense were their words true (cf. verse 6), and in what sense false? How does this chapter show that all that was happening was under the eyes and under the judgment of Jehovah?

(3) If the temple be regarded as a type of the human heart, what wrong attitudes towards God are represented by the 'abominations' here described? Cf. Dt. v. 8, 9; Mt. xxiii. 27, 28; Rom. i. 21, 25.

Notes.—(1) Verse 3. 'Image of jealousy'; i.e. which provoked God's jealous anger. Cf. Dt. xxxii. 21; 2 Ch. xxxiii. 7.

(2) Verse 14. 'Women weeping for Tammuz'; i.e. taking part in the heathen festival of mourning the death of the god Tammuz, later known in Greek mythology as Adonis.

(3) Verse 16. 'Between the porch and the altar'. These men must therefore have been priests. Cf. Joel ii. 17.

Day 6. Ezk. ix and x.

These chapters give a picture of God acting in judgment in the destruction of the people (ix) and of the city (x) according to His Word in viii. 18.

(1) Chapter ix. What was God's answer to the prophet's cry of distress? Cf. Je. xiv. 19, xv. 1.

(2) Who alone were spared, and how are they distinguished from others? Cf. Rev. vii. 1-3, xiv. 1; 2 Tim. ii. 19. What effect should open sin in church or nation have upon us? Cf. Ps. cxix. 53, 136, 158; Mt. v. 4.

(3) What caused the blindness of the people of Jerusalem to the true facts? See verse 9. How may we avoid like errors? Cf. Jn. viii. 12; 2 Cor. iv. 6; i Jn. ii. 10.

Day 7. Ezk. xi.

The prophet, still in the trance which began at viii. 1, is given two further messages from the Lord, one concerning the political leaders in Jerusalem (verses 1-13), and the other concerning those with him in exile (verses 14-21).

(1) The political leaders in Jerusalem thought they were safe within the fortification of Jerusalem, as flesh in a pot is safe from the fire (verse 3). What does God say concerning them? For the fulfilment of the prophecy, see 2 Ki. xxv. 18-21.

(2) The people of Jerusalem thought that they were the favoured of the Lord, and would be given possession of the land, while those in exile would be cut off (verse 15). But what was God's purpose concerning those in exile (verses 16-20)? Cf. Pr. xvi. 9, xix. 21; also Je. xxiv.

(3) Trace the steps by which the glory of Jehovah withdrew from His temple. See viii. 3, 4, ix. 3, x. 4, 19, xi. 1, xi. 23. What hint is given in chapter xi as to the possibility of the return of the glory and under what conditions? Cf. xliii. 1-4, 9.

Notes.—(1) Verse 1. 'Jaazaniah, the son of Azur'; a different man from the Jaazaniah of viii. 11. 'Princes' here means men of high position.

(2) Verse 16. Read as in R.V.

(3) Verse 23b. 'The mountain', etc.; i.e. the Mount of Olives.

Week 43. EZEKIEL XII–XXI

Day 1. Ezk. xii and xiii.

(1) xii. 1-20 declares by two vivid symbolic actions on the part of the prophet the doom that was in store both for the people of Jerusalem (verses 3, 4, 18, 19) and for the king (verses 5, 6, 10-16). Having grasped the significance of the prophecy, turn to 2 Ki. xxv. 4-7 to see how exactly it was fulfilled.

(2) Note the two scoffing remarks in xii. 22 and 27. Does the answer which God gave through Ezekiel apply to similar taunts today? Cf. 2 Pet. iii. 8-10.

(3) Chapter xiii. Condemnation of false prophets. By what two vivid images are they described (see verses 4 and 10-11), and what is the effect of their prophesying (verses 6, 10a, 22)? What phrase differentiating them from true prophets occurs twice in the chapter?

Notes.—(1) xii. 4-6. During the day the prophet is to carry to a certain place the things which would be needed by a person who was escaping: then at night he is to dig a hole through the (city) wall and flee, bearing his 'stuff' with him.

(2) xiii. 4, 5. 'The foxes in the desert'; better, 'jackals in the waste places'; 'burrowing among the ruins' (Moffatt). Instead of being a defence to the nation's battlements by their counsel, the false prophets spoke lies and only made things worse.

(3) xiii. 18-20. Read as in R.V. In verse 20 'to make them fly' should be 'as birds', as in R.V. mg. It is not certain what the 'pillows' and 'kerchiefs' were—possibly arm bands and veils which the prophetesses used to delude their victims.

Day 2. Ezk. xiv and xv.

(1) xiv. 1-11. (a) If men whose hearts are inwardly alienated

from God come professing to seek guidance from Him, will God answer them? What must they first do, and if they do not so do, what will be their end? (b) If a prophet should fail to follow this rule, and attempt to give guidance, how will God deal with him?

(2) People might ask 'Will not the presence of righteous men among a sinful nation save it from destruction?' Cf. e.g. Gn. xviii. 23-26. How does God in reply show that in the present instance the righteous will be saved out of the destruction, but will not be able to save others. Cf. ix. 4-6; Je. xv. 1. If any should escape, what purpose will this accomplish (see xiv. 22, 23)?

(3) But is not Israel God's vine? Will He suffer it to be destroyed? See Is. v. 1-7. What is God's answer in chapter xv to this unspoken question? Observe how God through His servant seeks to take away every false hope concerning the impending judgment.

Day 3. Ezk. xvi.

In this vivid allegory the prophet seeks to break down the pride of Jerusalem. She appears as the bride of Jehovah, who loved her from infancy, and did everything for her, but whose love she has requited with persistent and shameful idolatry. The chapter falls into four sections: (1) Jerusalem as a child and as a bride (verses 1-14); (2) her sin (verses 15-34); (3) her judgment (verses 35-58); (4) her restoration (verses 59-63).

(1) What was Jehovah's complaint against Jerusalem? With verses 22 and 32 cf. Dt. xxxii. 15-18. Notice also that God regards her sin as greater than that of Samaria and of Sodom. See verses 46-52 and cf. Mt. xi. 23, 24.

(2) How may the teaching of this chapter be applied to one who has been truly converted, but has backslidden? What can we learn here for our warning of the peril and folly of the sin of unfaithfulness? Cf. Je. ii. 13, 19; Ho. viii. 3; Jas. iv. 4-10 (R.V.).

Notes.—(1) Verses 4, 5. A helpless, uncared for, castaway babe.

(2) The R.V. is better in verses 12, 13, 38, 53, 63.

(3) Verse 29. 'Land of Canaan'. Better, 'land of merchants or traffick' (cf. xvii. 4). A description of Chaldea. The Canaanites, especially the Phoenicians, were traders, and so the word came to mean 'merchants'. Cf. Ho. xii. 7 and Zp. i. 11 where it is so translated.

(4) Verse 52. 'Thou hast justified thy sisters'; i.e. by her wickedness making them appear less guilty.

(5) Verse 61. 'Not by thy covenant'. The wonderful events that are promised here will not happen as a result of God's former covenant, but in a new covenant of grace.

Day 4. Ezk. xvii.

(1) The parable in verses 1-10, as its interpretation in verses

11-21 shows, is based upon the story of Jehoiachin and Zedekiah, as recorded in 2 Ki. xxiv. 8–xxv. 7. Whom does 'the top of the cedar' represent (verse 3) and whom 'the seed of the land' (verse 5)? Who was the first eagle, and who the second?

(2) What sin is the prophet specifically rebuking here? With verses 13-16 cf. 2 Ch. xxxvi. 13 and with verses 7 and 15 cf. Je. xxxvii. 5-8. See also Ps. xv. 4c.

(3) How do verses 22-24 show that neither the ambitious designs nor the perfidies of men can frustrate God's purposes? Notice the emphatic and repeated 'I'. Cf. Pr. xix. 21; Is. xlvi. 8-13.

Notes.—(1) Verse 3. 'Unto Lebanon'. Lebanon is here spoken of figuratively as representing the glory of Israel, and its cedar as representing the Davidic house.

(2) Verse 6. 'Whose branches turned'. Better, 'might turn' (Moffatt). Cf. verse 14.

(3) Verses 22, 23. God's cedar will be planted high up, that all nations may see it. Cf. Is. ii. 2, xi. 10.

Day 5. Ezk. xviii and xix.

The teaching of national retribution in chapter xvi and other passages seems to have raised doubts as to the justice of God's dealings with individuals (xviii. 2, 29). This is the subject of chapter xviii. Chapter xix is a lament.

(1) What two principles are stated in xviii. 4 in answer to the people's complaint in xviii. 2? Try to express these in your own words.

(2) In the remainder of chapter xviii two questions are answered. (a) Is each man responsible to God for his own acts, and for these alone (see verses 5-20)? (b) If a man turn from his past way of life, will that past affect God's judgment upon him (see verses 21-29)? How does this teaching reveal not only God's justice, but His mercy, and constitute a call to immediate repentance? (See xviii. 30-32.)

(3) Over what three kings of Judah is chapter xix a lament? With verses 3 and 4 cf. 2 Ki. xxiii. 31-34; with verses 5-9, 2 Ki. xxiv. 8-15; and with verses 10-14, 2 Ki. xxv. 4-11.

Notes.—(1) xviii. 6, 11, 15. 'Eat upon the mountains'; i.e. to join in idolatrous forms of worship. Cf. vi. 1-4.

(2) xix. 10. 'In thy blood'; the meaning is uncertain.

(3) xix. 11. 'Among the thick branches'; better, 'to the clouds' (R.V. mg.). The meaning of the first part of the verse is that the nation had had strong rulers.

(4) xix. 14. The fire that brought destruction sprang from the ruler himself, i.e. Zedekiah; see xvii. 19-21.

Day 6. Ezk. xx. 1-44.

Today's portion is a review of Israel's history (verses 5-29), with a prophecy of what God will yet do (verses 30-44). The review of history covers (a) the time in Egypt (verses 5-9); (b) in the wilderness (verses 10-17 and 18-26) and (c) in the land of Canaan (verses 27-29). With verses 1-3, cf. xiv. 1, 2.

(1) What restrained God from 'pouring out His fury upon Israel to consume them'? See verses 9, 14, 22, 44. What does this reveal of God's character? Also how does it show what is the one and only guarantee of our salvation? See Ps. cvi. 6-8; 1 Sa. xii. 22.

(2) To what two conclusions does God say He will ultimately bring His people Israel (verses 42-44) and by what means? Has a like conviction been wrought in us? Cf. 1 Tim. i. 12-17.

Notes.—(1) Verse 9. 'Polluted'; better, 'profaned', as in R.V., the opposite of 'sanctify' or 'hallow'.

(2) Verse 25. Such evil statutes were allowed by God to be established as a punishment for previous sins. It was 'a judicially inflicted blindness'.

(3) Verse 37. 'Pass under the rod'. As the eastern shepherd makes his sheep pass one by one under his staff, held horizontally, to count and examine them. Cf. Lv. xxvii. 32; Je. xxxiii. 13.

Day 7. Ezk. xx. 45–xxi.

The prophet is bidden to prophesy (a) against the south (of Palestine) (xx. 45-49), and (b) against Jerusalem and the land of Israel (xxi. 1-17). The sword of the Lord is drawn from its sheath (xxi. 1-7), sharpened and polished (xxi. 8-13), and smites repeatedly in its deadly work (xxi. 14-17). In xxi. 18-27, the explanation is given. The king of Babylon is seen, standing at the parting of the ways, seeking guidance by divination—Ammon? or Jerusalem? The decision falls for Jerusalem, the city is taken, and the king (Zedekiah) slain. The closing verses of the chapter are a short prophecy of utter doom upon Ammon.

(1) Who kindles the fire? Whose sword is drawn? Yet it was by a heathen king that the judgment was effected. What does this teach us concerning God's methods of accomplishing His purposes of judgment in the world? Cf. Je. xxv. 9 (My servant); Is. xxv. 1-4. Whose hand then should the child of God be always looking for in the happenings of life in whatever form they may come?

(2) When human leaders and confidences all fail and are overthrown, where can we still look for the establishment of a reign of peace? See verses 25-27; Ps. ii. 6-9; Lk. xxi. 25-28.

Notes.—(1) The passage as a whole is very vivid, but the exact text in some places is uncertain. The R.V. is clearer in verses 12, 15, 21, 25.

(2) xxi. 21. A description of guidance by divination. Arrows inscribed with names (here Rabbah and Jerusalem) were placed in a bag and shaken before the teraphim (R.V.), or image of the god, and one was then drawn, this being

taken as the god's answer. The mention of 'looking in the liver' implies that there has also been a sacrifice followed by an examination for some reason not now known of the animal's liver.

Week 44. EZEKIEL XXII–XXXII

Day 1. Ezk. xxii.

This chapter falls into three divisions: (a) a description of the sins committed within the city (verses 3-16); (b) the certainty of judgment (verses 17-22), and (c) an indictment of all classes of the community (verses 23-31).

(1) Group the sins enumerated in verses 1-12 under the following two heads: (a) religious; (b) social. Notice how with the loss of a true conception of Jehovah, there follows the loss of filial piety, moral purity, and civic justice. How far are the sins mentioned here prevalent in our land today?

(2) What four classes are mentioned in verses 24-29, and what charges are made against them? What is the saddest feature of the situation, as stated in verse 30? Cf. verse 19 ('all become dross') and Je. v. 1-5.

Notes.—(1) Verse 4. 'Thy days . . . thy years'; i.e. thy times of judgment; cf. xxi. 25-29.

(2) Verse 6 should be read as in R.V., so also verses 10, 16.

(3) Verse 13. 'Smitten mine hand'; a gesture of horror; cf. xxi. 14, 17.

(4) Verse 24. 'The land that is not cleansed'; the LXX renders 'not rained upon', which gives a better meaning. 'You are a land bereft of rain and shower' (Moffatt).

(5) Verse 25. 'A conspiracy of her prophets'. Better, as in LXX, 'whose princes in the midst of her are like', etc.

(6) Verse 30. There was no protest against these abominations, no one to turn back the approaching judgment.

Day 2. Ezk. xxiii.

This chapter resembles chapter xvi. Samaria and Jerusalem are condemned for their unfaithfulness in seeking alliances with foreign nations and their gods. Their conduct is represented in unusually realistic figures to make it appear how loathsome and repulsive it has been.

(1) What is the main content of each of the four divisions of this chapter, namely verses 1-10, 11-21, 22-35, and 36-49?

(2) Trace how Jerusalem walked in the way of Samaria and even exceeded her in wickedness, and therefore must drain to the dregs the same cup of judgment. In spiritual things whose are the greatest responsibilities and dangers? See Heb. x. 26, 27.

(3) What is meant by the words in verse 49 'Ye shall bear the sins of your idols'? Cf. verse 35, xiv. 10, xvi. 58. How alone can we

escape from 'bearing our sins' in this sense? See Lv. xvi. 21; Is.
liii. 4; Heb. ix. 28; 1 Pet. ii. 24.

Notes.—(1) Verses 8, 19, 27. The idolatrous tendencies in Israel as a nation
are here traced back to her sojourn in Egypt.

(2) Verses 17, 22, 28. 'Her soul was alienated from them' (R.V.); see 2 Ki.
xxiv. 20b; Ps. cxxxvii. 8, 9.

Day 3. Ezk. xxiv.

A last picture of Jerusalem before its destruction—a rusted pot set on a fire,
with flesh being boiled in it. The flesh is taken out and scattered, symbolizing
the dispersion of the people of the city, and the pot is then left on the fire,
symbol of the city lying waste and burned.

(1) The prophecy was spoken on the day Jerusalem was
invested (verse 2). Where was the prophet when he spoke it?
Yet how clearly he saw what was happening! What was this
prophetic revelation designed to prove? See verses 24, 27, and
cf. Jn. xiii. 19, xiv. 29.

(2) Compare what the chief men of Jerusalem said in xi. 3
(see note (3)), and what God says here concerning the city and its
people. What may we learn from this? Cf. 1 Thes. v. 3; 2 Pet.
iii. 4.

(3) The same evening Ezekiel's wife died. How is she described
in verse 16? Yet God made this so painful experience also a means
of ministry. Can you think of other instances where the sufferings
of a servant of God have been made to subserve God's ends, no
matter at what cost to the sufferer? Cf. Col. i. 24.

Notes.—(1) Verse 6. 'Scum'; better 'rust', as in R.V. So also in verses 11, 12
(2) Verse 10. 'Consume'; better, 'boil well', as in R.V.
(3) Verse 13. Read as in R.V.
(4) Verse 23. The people would be too stunned by the evil tidings to take
any action.
(5) Verse 27. Cf. iii. 26, 27.

INTRODUCTORY NOTE TO CHAPTERS XXV–XXXII

THESE chapters are a series of prophetic utterances against seven
foreign nations. They are intended to show that the calamities
which were falling on Judah were not arbitrary, nor an evidence
of Jehovah's weakness, but that, on the contrary, He is supreme
over all peoples and all His acts are governed by fixed moral
principles which reveal His holy nature. By their position in the
book they separate the prophecies that belong to the period of
Ezekiel's ministry prior to the Fall of Jerusalem, from those that
followed later. (See *Introduction*.)

Day 4. Ezk. xxv and xxvi.

Chapter xxv contains four prophecies directed against Ammon, Moab, Edom, and the Philistines respectively. Chapter xxvi is a prophecy of the approaching destruction of Tyre through the armies of Nebuchadnezzar, together with a vivid description of the far-reaching effects of her overthrow.

(1) In chapter xxv find four ways in which unbelievers and enemies of the truth act towards the people of God when the latter are brought low by calamity. How will such adversaries be dealt with, and why? Cf. Ps. xciv. 1-5, 21-23, xlvi. 8-10; Is. xxvi. 9b.

(2) What, according to xxvi. 2, 3 was the ground of God's judgment upon Tyre? As we try to imagine the scenes described in xxvi. 7-14, and measure the fame and worldly greatness of Tyre by the dismay caused by her fall (xxvi. 15-18), what lessons may we learn? Cf. Je. ix. 23, 24; Lk. xii. 15-21.

Notes.—(1) The R.V. is clearer in xxv. 13, 15, xxvi. 2, 4, 14, 17.

(2) xxv. 10. Read as in R.V. mg., 'The children of the east' are the tribes of the desert.

(3) xxvi. 2. Jerusalem had been as an open gate, by which commerce had been diverted from Tyre.

(4) xxvi. 6. 'Her daughters which are in the field'; i.e. inland towns dependent upon Tyre.

(5) xxvi. 20. 'In the low parts of the earth'; better, 'nether parts', as in R.V.; i.e. the underworld of the dead. Instead of 'and I shall set glory', the LXX reads 'nor arise (i.e. resume thy place) in the land of the living'. Cf. R.V. mg.

Day 5. Ezk. xxvii and xxviii.

Further prophecies concerning Tyre. In chapter xxvii the city is pictured as a stately ship. Verses 5-11 give a description of the ship; verses 12-25 of her cargo; and verses 26-36 of her shipwreck and total loss, with the widespread mourning that ensued. In chapter xxviii the prince of Tyre is regarded as personifying the genius or spirit of the city, and as incarnating in his person the principle of evil which animated it. The terms used concerning him (especially in verses 11-19) are such that the figure of the human ruler seems to merge into Satan himself, the originator of the sins of which Tyre was guilty.

(1) Contrast men's judgment of Tyre (xxvii. 4, 33) and Tyre's view of herself (xxvii. 3) with God's judgment of her (xxviii. 2-8). What was the pre-eminent sin of Tyre? Cf. Dn. iv. 29-32; 2 Thes. ii. 3, 4, 8, 9.

(2) In what sense did Tyre become 'a terror' (xxvii. 35, 36)? See also xxvi. 21, xxviii. 19. To what kind of fear should such a catastrophe give rise in our own hearts? Cf. Dt. xvii. 12, 13; Rom. xi. 20; 1 Tim. v. 20.

(3) xxviii. 20-26 is a short prophecy against Sidon, which was closely linked with Tyre. What is said in verses 20-26 to be the

twofold purpose of God's judgments (a) in relation to Himself, and (b) in relation to His people?

Notes.—(1) xxvii. 4. The meaning probably is 'Thy moorings are in deep waters'.

(2) xxvii. 12. 'In thy fairs'; better, 'for thy wares', as in R.V. So also in verses 14, 16, 19, etc.

(3) xxvii. 20. 'Precious clothes for chariots'; better, 'precious cloths for riding', as in R.V.; i.e. saddle-cloths.

(4) xxviii. 10. 'The deaths of the uncircumcised'; i.e. a death without the rites of honourable burial.

(5) xxviii. 22, 25. 'Sanctified'; i.e. shown forth as the Holy One (or God alone) through Israel's restoration.

Day 6. Ezk. xxix and xxx.

The prophet's gaze is now directed towards Egypt, pictured in xxix. 1-16 as a great dragon or crocodile, whose destruction is at hand. The remainder of today's portion consists of three further prophecies of similar import, namely xxix. 17-20, xxx. 1-19, and xxx. 20-26.

(1) Compare the explanation of the allegory in xxix. 8-12 with the allegory itself in xxix. 3-7. What are the two sins in particular which caused God's judgment to fall upon Egypt? With xxix. 7 cf. verse 16 R.V. and Is. xxx. 5.

(2) 'The pride of her power shall come down' (xxx. 6; ct. xxx. 18). Why cannot anyone ultimately prosper who trusts, as Pharaoh did, in his own resources and achievements? See Is. ii. 11-17, and with Ezk. xxx. 13, cf. Is. ii. 18. Cf. also Lk. i. 51; Jb. ix. 4.

Notes.—(1) xxix. 10. 'From the tower', etc.; better, from Migdol to Syene, as in R.V. mg.; i.e. 'the extreme limits of the country'. So also in xxx. 6.

(2) xxix. 14, 15. Egypt is not to be finally destroyed, like Tyre (xxvi. 21, xxvii. 36, xxviii. 19), but reduced in status.

(3) xxix. 17-21. A prophecy dated sixteen years after that of verses 1-16. It appears to indicate that Nebuchadnezzar had not gained the spoils of war at Tyre as he expected, and is now promised a recompense from the conquest of Egypt.

Day 7. Ezk. xxxi and xxxii.

These chapters contain three more prophecies concerning Egypt. In chapter xxxi Egypt is likened to a mighty cedar, whose fall causes the other trees to mourn. In xxxii. 1-6 the figure of the dragon or crocodile is resumed (cf. xxix. 3-5), and in xxxii. 7-8 Egypt is likened to a bright star. The imagery is very vivid, depicting the utter destruction of Pharaoh and his hosts. In xxxii. 17-32 the prophet in vision follows Pharaoh and his armies into Sheol, and sees them there among others also slain by the sword who bear the shame of their lack of proper burial.

(1) How does chapter xxxi further enforce the lesson of chapter xxx? See Day 6 (2) above.

(2) Observe how often in these chapters the personal pronoun 'I' occurs. Do we realize enough that God is the chief actor in the developments of history? Over what realms, in addition to that of Israel, is His dominion here asserted? Cf. Ps. xxxiii. 8.

Notes.—(1) xxxi. 3. The introduction of the word 'Assyrian' is almost certainly a textual error. The original reading probably was 'a stately cedar'. The reference is to Egypt: see verse 18.

(2) xxxi. 4. 'The trees of the field'; i.e. the smaller nations. The 'cedars in the garden of God' (verse 8) were the great powers, and 'the trees of Eden' were likewise trees (nations) of special stature.

(3) xxxi. 10. 'The thick boughs'. Better, 'clouds', as in R.V. mg. So also in verse 14.

(4) xxxii. 17-32. This is not to be regarded as a literal description of the state of men after death, but as an imaginative picture intended to show that all who use violence and lawless might, causing terror on the earth (cf. verses 23, 24, 25, 26, 27, etc.), shall alike meet with retribution.

Week 45. EZEKIEL XXXIII–XXXIX

THE chapters in this week's study all belong to the second period of the prophet's ministry after the fall of Jerusalem (see *Introduction* and *Analysis*). The only mention of a date is in xxxiii. 21, but the prophecies all presuppose that God's judgment upon the guilty city and nation, long predicted, has come to pass.

Day 1. Ezk. xxxiii.

The prophet had known from the first that part of his commission was to be as a watchman (cf. iii. 16-21), but now the time had come to put it into practice; for in the new era that was dawning, only those who individually repent and return to God will live.

(1) What is God's attitude and desire, and what is the alternative presented to each and all alike? See verses 11-20, noticing the emphasis on individual action.

(2) Compare the two current sayings quoted in verses 10 and 24. Observe *where* they were current, and how the one is despairing, the other confident. What is God's answer in each case?

(3) Why did the prophet suddenly become more bold to speak, and the people more curious to hear his words? See verses 30-33. What, however, was lacking in their new interest? Cf. Mt. vii. 26, 27.

Note.—The R.V. is clearer in verses 2, 16, and 30.

Day 2. Ezk. xxxiv.

The new era will be different from what has gone before, because of a change of shepherd, i.e. ruler.

(1) What, according to verses 1-10, was the inherent vice of the rulers of the past, which brought disaster upon the nation? Contrast their methods (verses 4-6) with those of Jehovah (verses 11-16). Cf. 1 Pet. v. 1-4.

(2) What blessings are declared in verses 23-31 as following the coming of the Messiah? Interpreting them spiritually, what may we learn from these verses concerning God's gifts to us in Christ? Cf. Ps. xxiii; Heb. xiii. 20, 21.

Notes.—(1) Verse 17. 'Cattle'; the word is misleading here, as the reference is to a flock. The Heb. word means 'sheep'. The 'rams' and 'he-goats' represent the strong and wealthy among the nation, who tended to oppress the weak.

(2) Verse 29. 'A plant of renown'; better 'a plantation for renown' as in R.V., referring to the fertility of the land in the times of the Messiah. Cf. Joel ii. 23-27.

Day 3. Ezk. xxxv–xxxvi. 15.

In today's portion the prophet declares that the new era will be better than the past, because of the greater fertility of the land. When he uttered this prophecy, the land of Israel seemed ruined. Edom was seeking to obtain possession (xxxv. 10, xxxvi. 5), and the mountains of Israel lay desolate (xxxvi. 4). The prophet declares, first a judgment upon Edom (xxxv), and, second, a return of Israel to enjoy times of unprecedented prosperity (xxxvi. 1-15).

(1) What are the three sins of Edom, mentioned in verses 5 and 10, for which they will be judged? With whom did their boasted intention to possess the countries of Israel and Judah bring them into conflict, and why? Cf. Acts ix. 4, 5. What reassurance may this give also to us? See Is. xliii. 1-3; Ps. v. 11.

(2) What evidence does today's portion afford that God hears and knows what men say against Him and His, and will not allow His enemies finally to triumph? Do you find any blessings, which we may enjoy in Christ, typified in xxxvi. 8-15?

Notes.—(1) xxxv. 10. 'Whereas the Lord was there'; better, 'Though the Lord', etc., as in R.V. mg. The gravamen of the charge is that Edom was deliberately ignoring and defying Jehovah.

(2) xxxvi. 13. The land had gained an ill repute because of droughts, etc. Cf. verse 30.

Day 4. Ezk. xxxvi. 16-38.

(1) Consider carefully in this remarkable passage the following points: (a) Why the Lord cast the people into exile (verses 16-19);

(b) why He brought them back (verses 20-24); (c) the change wrought in their moral and spiritual condition (verses 25-31).

(2) Reflect how closely the prophet's teaching here anticipates the New Testament revelation of the steps by which God transforms a sinner into a saint. See particularly Rom. iii, v, vi, and viii.

(3) How will the change in the people and their restored prosperity affect the surrounding nations? See verses 35, 36, and cf. Jn. xvii. 21, 23. With verse 37 cf. Eph. iii. 14-19; Col. iv. 12.

Notes.—(1) Verse 20. 'They profaned my holy Name'; because the nations, seeing them cast out, concluded their God could not protect them. Cf. Ps. xlii. 10.

(2) Verse 26. 'Stony heart'; cf. ii. 4, iii. 7; Zc. vii. 12. 'A heart of flesh'; i.e. sensitive to the divine Word.

Day 5. Ezk. xxxvii.

(1) Why were the people unable to believe Ezekiel's prophecies of restoration and blessing? See verse 11. Did the vision of verses 1-10 show that things were not so bad as or worse than they seemed? Yet what happened, and why?

(2) Apply this to the raising of the spiritually dead. Are souls receiving life through your ministry? What may this vision teach us, and how may it give new faith and courage? Note that God uses His Word and His Breath or Spirit, working together, to produce life, and that Ezekiel had a part to play in the change that was wrought. What qualities in Ezekiel were necessary?

(3) Verses 15-28. A glorious picture of a purified, restored, and reunited Israel. What light does the passage throw upon the conditions and upon the blessings of Christian unity? Cf. Gal. v. 15; 2 Cor. vi. 16-18; Jn. x. 16 (R.V.); Acts iv. 32, 33.

Notes.—(1) Verse 11. 'Cut off for our parts'; better 'clean cut off', as in R.V.

(2) Verse 23. 'Out of all their dwelling places'; or 'backslidings'. See R.V. mg. and cf. xxxvi. 29.

Day 6. Ezk. xxxviii.

In this chapter and the next the prophet foresees in the far distant future an invasion of Israel by nations lying beyond the circle of those with which Israel hitherto has had to do. They, too, must learn that Jehovah alone is God, and they will learn it through meeting the power of Jehovah as they seek to plunder His land, and through being brought by Him to total defeat.

(1) In what two different ways are the causes of Gog's invasion described? Contrast verses 4 and 16 with verses 10-12. And yet

may not all these verses describe one and the same cause? Cf. Rom. ix. 17, 18.

(2) Cf. verses 18-23 with xxxvii. 25-28. In what two ways will God bring the nations to know that He is God alone? See Rom. i. 16-18, ix. 22, 23, xi. 17-22.

Notes.—(1) Verse 2. 'The chief prince'; better, 'the prince of Rosh, Meshech', etc., as in R.V. So also in verse 3. Little is known about these nations. In their onward march they gathered in other nations also (verses 4-6).

(2) Verse 13. These are merchant nations, stirred to excitement by Gog's invasion.

(3) Verses 19, 20. Description of a shattering earthquake.

Day 7. Ezk. xxxix.

(1) A further prophecy against Gog emphasizes the completeness of his overthrow. In what three ways is this brought out in verses 9-20, and what attributes of God's character are thereby revealed (verses 21-29)?

(2) What is meant by the expression 'I hid my face from them' (verse 23)? Cf. Dt. xxxi. 17; Ps. xxx. 7, civ. 29; Is. viii. 17, lxiv. 7. Consider what great blessedness is contained in the promise of verse 29. Cf. Nu. vi. 25; Ps. iv. 6, lxxx. 3, lxxxix. 15.

Notes.—(1) Verse 11 should be read as in R.V. The meaning is that the way will be closed to travellers by reason of the multitude of graves.

(2) Verse 14. The LXX omits the words 'with the passengers', which makes the meaning much clearer. Read verse 15 as in R.V., and also verse 26

INTRODUCTORY NOTE TO CHAPTERS XL–XLVIII

THESE chapters describe a vision given to Ezekiel some twelve years after the prophecies of chapters xxxiii–xxxvii (cf. xl. 1 with xxxiii. 21). In these earlier prophecies he had declared to the exiles in Babylon God's purpose to restore Israel to the holy land as a nation purified, redeemed, and re-united. The question must have been much in the prophet's mind how this restored community would be fashioned in its religious and political life; and in these chapters God gives to the prophet the answer to his questionings. There is first a description of the sanctuary, to which Jehovah will come in glory, and in which He will take up His dwelling (xl–xliii); second, regulations with regard to the ministers of the sanctuary, and to the 'prince' who shall rule over the people (xliv–xlvi); and third, the boundaries of the land are defined, and the territories of the tribes (xlvii–xlviii).

The question is sometimes asked, whether the vision will be

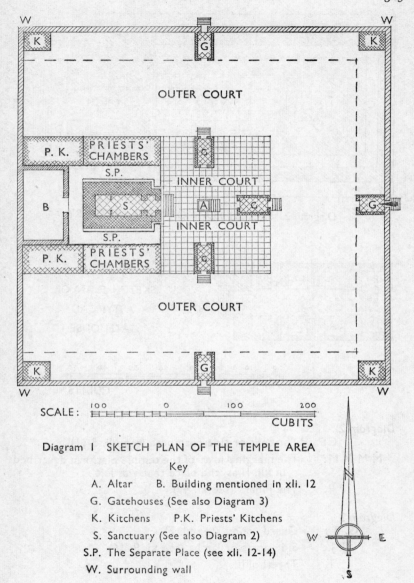

SCALE: 100 ___ 0 ___ 100 ___ 200
CUBITS

Diagram 1   SKETCH PLAN OF THE TEMPLE AREA
Key

A. Altar   B. Building mentioned in xli. 12

G. Gatehouses (See also Diagram 3)

K. Kitchens   P.K. Priests' Kitchens

S. Sanctuary (See also Diagram 2)

S.P. The Separate Place (see xli. 12-14)

W. Surrounding wall

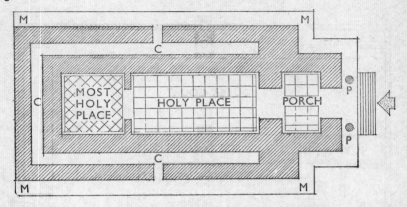

Diagram 2. SKETCH PLAN OF THE SANCTUARY

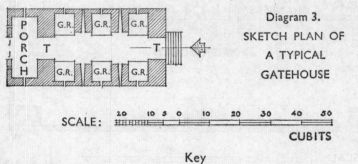

Diagram 3.

SKETCH PLAN OF

A TYPICAL

GATEHOUSE

SCALE: 20 10 5 0   10   20   30   40   50

CUBITS

Key

Diagram 2

C:	The cells or side-chambers (see xli. 5-11).
M M M M:	The marginal area of the temple platform described in xli. 11 as 'the place that was left'.
P P:	The Pillars (see xl. 49).

Diagram 3

G. R.:	Guard rooms (see xl. 7).
J. J.:	Side posts or jambs (see xl. 9, 16).
T:	Thresholds.

literally fulfilled. Why, however, should we suppose this, any more than that the vision of chapter i is a literal portrait of the divine Being? It is true that the prophets generally associate great changes in nature with the advent of 'the Day of the Lord', and this is affirmed also in the New Testament (see e.g. Rom. viii. 21), but this is not to say that the vision which Ezekiel saw will find literal fulfilment. It is rather a setting forth, within the limits of Old Testament symbolism, of fundamental principles concerning God's relation to His redeemed and sanctified people when He dwells in their midst in His glory.

Week 46. EZEKIEL XL–XLVIII

Day 1. Ezk. xl. 1-47.

Having been cast into a trance, and brought in spirit to the holy land, he saw on the top of a high mountain what at first he thought to be a city, but was in fact the temple, with its courts and buildings. It was, however, a new temple. While the sanctuary itself was similar to that of Solomon's temple, the surroundings were very different. The prophet was met by a heavenly messenger, who had a measuring-tape of flax and a measuring-rod, and who acted as his guide.

(1) What two responsibilities did the heavenly messenger place upon the prophet? See verse 4. Cf. 1 Cor. ii. 9-12; Je. xxix. 13; 1 Jn. i. 1-3. When judged by these standards, how far is your own Bible study a success?

(2) With the aid of Diagram 1, p. 509, follow the prophet's route as he was shown the outer gateway on the east (verses 6-17), the outer court (verses 17-19), and the gateways on the north and south (verses 20-26); then the inner court on a higher level, also with three gateways (verses 28-37). In the inner court, alongside the north gate, were a chamber and tables (verses 38-43), and there were two chambers for the priests, one near the north gate and another near the south gate (verses 44-47).

(3) Note the symmetry of the ground plan of the temple. Has this anything to teach us about God? Reflect upon the balance and symmetry of Christ's character, and cf. Dt. xxxii. 4; Ps. xviii. 30; Mt. v. 38; Jas. i. 4; Rev. xxi. 16.

Notes.—(1) The R.V. is clearer throughout, and Moffatt's translation may be consulted with advantage.

(2) Verse 5. Two cubits were in use, one longer by an extra handbreadth. It is the longer that is employed here. The measuring-rod was probably between 9 ft. and 10 ft. Some make it 10 ft. 6 in.

(3) Verse 7. 'Little chambers'. Or rather 'guardrooms', see R.V. mg.

(4) Verse 12. 'The space', etc. A reference to the projecting front wall of the guardrooms into the passage-way.

(5) Verse 14. The LXX reads 'and he measured the porch, 20 cubits'.

(6) Verses 15, 16. The word translated 'arches' is most probably another name for the 'porch'. The 'posts' are the walls at either side of an entrance, i.e. 'jambs'. For the position of the porch see Diagram 3.

(7) Verse 44. The word 'singers' is a textual error. The LXX renders 'two chambers in the inner court, one at the side of the north gate, and its prospect', etc.

Day 2. Ezk. xl. 48–xli.

(1) Follow with the aid of Diagrams 1 and 2 the prophet's further examination of the temple, as he comes first to the sanctuary itself (here called 'house'), with its porch and two pillars (xl. 48, 49), holy place (called 'temple' and 'tabernacle', xli. 1, 2), most holy place (xli. 3, 4), and side chambers or cells built in three storeys (xli. 5-11). The *interior* of the sanctuary is described in xli. 15b-26. For xli. 12-15a see Notes below.

(2) Note that Ezekiel as a priest (i. 3, cf. xliv. 16), entered into the porch and holy place, but not into the most holy place (xli. 3, 4). Why did he not enter the most holy place? Contrast our privileges in Christ. See Heb. ix. 6-9, 24, x. 19-22.

(3) There were palm trees both in the inner sanctuary (xli. 18-20), and also on the gate posts of the outer and inner courts (xl. 16, 22, 31). So also in Solomon's temple. See 1 Ki. vi. 29, vii. 36. Applying this to the temple of our lives, what does it suggest both as to the hidden life of communion with God, and the outer life seen by all? Cf. Ps. xcii. 12-14; Je. xvii. 7, 8; Mt. vi. 5, 6.

Notes.—(1) Verse 7. See R.V. The meaning is that at each storey the walls facing the cells were made less thick, to leave a ledge for the beams to rest on, and thus the rooms on each floor were a little broader than the rooms below.

(2) Verse 11b. The sanctuary stood upon a raised platform six cubits higher than the level of the inner court (verse 8), and occupied the whole platform except for a marginal strip, running round three sides on the outer edge (see Diagram 2 MMMM). This narrow strip is what is here called 'the place that was left'.

(3) Verses 12-14. Another strip of ground, at the level of the inner court, encompassed the sanctuary platform, and is here called 'the separate place', because it marked off or 'separated' the sanctuary from other buildings near by (see Diagram 1 SP). One of these buildings, on the west side, is mentioned in verses 12 and 13 (see Diagram 1 B), but its use is not specified. Other buildings are mentioned in xliii. 1-14, xlvi. 19, 20.

(4) Verse 15. 'Galleries'; a word of uncertain meaning, used only here and in verse 16 and xlii. 3-5.

'On their **three** stories'; or rather 'to the three of them'. Render 'and the temple (holy place) and the inner house (holiest) and the porch of the court (sanctuary porch) were covered with a roof work, and they three had their closed windows, and their galleries round about'.

(5) Verse 22. The table here spoken of, which looked like an altar of wood, was probably the table of shewbread.

Day 3. Ezk. xlii–xliii. 12.

Today's portion opens with a description of other buildings in the inner court (xlii. 1-12), together with the purposes they are intended to serve (xlii. 13, 14). See Diagram 1. The measurements of the outer wall, and of the whole temple area are then stated (xlii. 15-20). In xliii. 1-9 the prophet sees in vision the glory of the Lord returning by the east gate; the gate by which, years before, he had seen Him depart (xi. 1, 22, 23).

(1) Observe the emphasis on the *holiness* of Jehovah. See especially xlii. 13, 14, xliii. 7-9, 11, 12. As you look back upon the design of the temple as a whole, in what other ways is the same thought stressed? Consider, for example, (a) the separation of Jehovah's dwelling-place from all that is common, and (b) the gradation from the outer court to the inner court and to the sanctuary, and from the people to the Levites, and to the priests.

(2) How, for us, have the barriers that separate us from the Holy One been removed? And on what conditions may we draw nigh to God and render Him acceptable service? See 2 Cor. vii. 1; Heb. vii. 24, x. 14; 1 Pet. ii. 5.

(3) What is God's great objective in His relations with men? Cf. Jn. i. 14; Rev. xxi. 3. Why then does He sometimes do the very opposite? See xi. 20-23; Is. liv. 7, 8; 2 Cor. vi. 16-18.

Notes.—(1) xlii. 1. 'Into the chamber'; better, 'into the chambers'. The position of these chambers is marked in Diagram 1, but not their structure. They were placed to the north and south of the sanctuary platform and had three storeys. A 'walk' or passage ran down the centre of each block (xlii. 4). Many details are obscure.

(2) xlii. 10. 'Toward the east' is a textual error. It should be 'toward the south'.

(3) xliii. 7-9. In Solomon's temple there was no walled-off outer court separating between the temple and the unconsecrated ground without (cf. xlii. 20). The temple, royal palace, and other buildings all stood together in one great enclosure, and the burial ground of the kings was not far distant.

Day 4. Ezk. xliii. 13–xliv.

The section opens with a description of the great altar in the centre of the inner court, together with the sacrifices by which it is to be 'cleansed and purged' (xliii. 13-27). The altar rested upon a square base and was built of three square blocks of stone, each smaller than the one below, so as to leave at each level a projecting ledge. The uppermost block had four horns and was twelve cubits square. It was reached by steps on the east side. Chapter xliv lays down three ordinances, the first concerning the use of the east gate (verses 1-3), the second concerning the Levites (verses 4-14), and the third concerning the priests (verses 15-31).

(1) Why had the altar to be cleansed before the offerings made upon it were acceptable to God? See xliii. 27 and cf. Lv. xvi. 18, 19; Col. i. 19-22; Heb. ix. 23.

(2) What lessons are taught in xliv. 10-16 regarding God's judgments upon faithful and unfaithful service? Cf. Lk. xix. 17; 2 Cor. v. 9, 10 (R.V.); 1 Tim. i. 12.

(3) What is the main principle running through all the regulations given here concerning the priesthood? Cf. Lv. x. 3, xi. 44, 45; 1 Pet. i. 15, 16. Note the special privileges of the priests, and the conditions on which they were allowed to exercise them. How can we enjoy the corresponding Christian privileges? See 1 Pet. ii. 5, and cf. Heb. vii. 26; 2 Tim. ii. 20, 21.

Notes.—(1) xliii. 26. 'They shall consecrate themselves'; better, 'so shall they consecrate it', as in R.V.

(2) xliv. 7, 8. It had evidently been the custom before the exile to allow foreigners to officiate in the sanctuary and in its ministry, even though it may have been only in menial duties. 'Ye have set keepers'; i.e. allowed foreigners to act as keepers.

(3) xliv. 19. They shall not bring their holy garments into contact with the people. Cf. Ex. xxx. 29.

Day 5. Ezk. xlv–xlvi.

Not only was the temple different in many respects from that of Solomon, but the whole land was to be divided up in a new way. A broad strip of land, extending right across the country from the Mediterranean to the Jordan and including the temple was to be set apart for the Lord (xlv. 1-8). How it was to be used is shown in the accompanying diagram. Verses 9-17 lay down

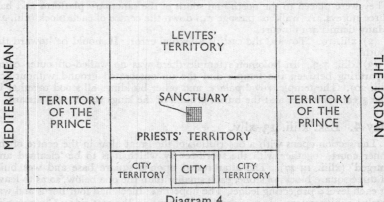

Diagram 4.

regulations as regards weights and measures, and the dues to be paid by the people to the prince. The remainder of today's portion is chiefly concerned with the feasts and offerings (xlv. 18-xlvi. 15), but at the end are two notes, one about the right of the prince to bestow part of his territory upon his sons or servants (xlvi. 16-18), and the other about rooms in the temple courts to be used as kitchens for boiling the flesh of the sacrifices (xlvi. 19-24).

(1) Note the large portions assigned in the vision to priests and to the prince. Cf. Rev. i. 6. Do you see any connection between the completeness of their sanctification and the greatness of their reward?

(2) How does xlv. 8-12 show that the holiness which Jehovah requires is not only religious but moral? What light do these verses throw upon God's attitude to injustice and oppression, and to commercial dishonesty? Cf. xlvi. 18; Lv. xix. 35, 36; Pr. xi. 1; 1 Pet. i. 14-16.

(3) What is said three times in xlv. 15-20 (R.V.) to be the purpose of the sacrifices? If they had not been offered, could the people have had any assurance in drawing nigh to God? What in the New Testament is revealed as the true ground of atonement? See Heb. x. 4-10; 1 Jn. ii. 1, 2.

Notes.—(1) The R.V. is clearer throughout this section.

(2) xlv. 2. 'Suburbs'; i.e. a strip of land surrounding the temple area. Cf. Nu. xxxv. 4. The city also had 'suburbs' of this kind. See xlviii. 15, 17.

(3) xlv. 5. 'For twenty chambers'; read with LXX 'for cities to dwell in'. See R.V. mg.

(4) xlv. 9. 'Exactions'; more probably 'evictions'. Cf. R.V. mg. and xlvi. 18.

(5) xlv. 11, 12. 'The ephah was a tenth of the homer—dry measure; and the bath a tenth of the homer—liquid measure' (Camb. Bible). Read verse 12 following LXX 'the shekel is to be twenty gerahs; five shekels are to count five, ten shekels ten, and the "maneh" is to be fifty shekels' (Moffatt).

(6) xlv. 20. The LXX reads 'In the seventh month, on the first day of the month'. Thus atonement was made half-yearly, cf. verse 18. 'For him that is simple' means a person who transgresses through lack of knowledge or of understanding.

(7) xlvi. 19 defines the position of the priests' kitchens, as verses 21-24 do the position of the people's kitchens. See Diagram 1 'PK' and 'K'.

Day 6. Ezk. xlvii. 1-12.

The prophet is shown another aspect of what it means when Jehovah dwells in the midst of His redeemed and reconciled people. 'Blessings abound where'er He reigns'.

(1) Notice particularly where the river comes from. What may those who seek reform, whether it be social, political, or moral, learn from the revelation here given to Ezekiel? Cf. Ps. xlvi. 4; Is. xxxiii. 21; Rev. xxii. 1, 2.

(2) What is symbolized by the increasing depth and extent of the waters? How long is it since you first came to Christ, and became a temple for His indwelling? Are the living waters flowing from your life in increasing measure? If not, what is wrong? Cf. Jn. vii. 37-39.

(3) The river of life sought out the most desolate and seemingly irrecoverable region in all the land, and brought life and healing. Recall how this was also Christ's method. Cf. Mk. ii. 16, 17; Lk. xv. 1, 2, xix. 10, xxiii. 42, 43. What have these things to say to us?

Notes.—(1) Verse 1. The waters flowed from the sanctuary across the inner court, south of the altar, and appeared on the right-hand side of the outer east gate.

(2) Verse 8. 'The sea'; i.e. the Dead Sea, in which nothing can live.

(3) Verse 12. 'According to his months'; better, 'every month', as in R.V. With this verse cf. Ps. i. 3; Je. xvii. 8; Rev. xxii. 2.

Day 7. Ezk. xlvii. 13-xlviii.

Finally the prophet is shown in vision the boundaries of the land (xlvii. 13-21) and the portions of the tribes (xlviii. 1-29). The land was to be divided into parallel zones, running from the west coast to the Jordan.

(1) What gospel principle is foreshadowed in xlvii. 22, 23? Cf. Eph. ii. 11-13, 19; Col. iii. 11.

(2) How many tribes had their portion north of the broad zone assigned to the Lord (xlv. 1, Diagram 4, p. 514), and how many south of it? What attributes of God's character and rule are symbolized by these arrangements? Cf. xviii. 25, 29, xxxvii. 26, 27.

(3) What does the new name of the city reveal as to God's purpose in relation to His people? Looking back upon the vision as a whole, write down the main lessons which it teaches, and consider how these stand out still more clearly in the light of the revelation given us in Christ.

DANIEL

INTRODUCTION

(*See New Bible Handbook, pp. 232-238*)

THE book of Daniel is rich in spiritual instruction, and will reward prayerful study. It shows, first of all, how those who believe in God can take their place in the society where they find themselves, play their part in current affairs, and yet remain true to God, thereby bringing glory to Him and blessing to men. Such men and women are needed among the nations today.

The book of Daniel is also a tonic to faith. The overthrow and exile of the Jews raised the question 'Where is now their God?' (Ps. cxv. 2). The book of Daniel reveals God as sovereign over the nations, watchful over those who trust in Him, and working all things 'according to the counsel of His own will'. The earlier chapters helped to bring home to the Jews the great truth of the sole Deity of Jehovah, which weaned them from idol-worship (cf. Ps. cxv. 3-11). The later chapters of the book, with their exact prediction of the course of events, were the means by which the faith of the remnant was sustained amid the troubles and persecutions that they endured. This book should help also to sustain our own faith in days of darkness.

The book of Daniel is also an integral part of Scripture in its revelation of things to come. This assumes that the book is a true record and prophecy belonging to the time of the exile. There has been a strong trend in recent times to dispute this, and to assign the composition of the book to a period 400 years later, when many of its predictions had already become facts of history. The older view is not without its difficulties, but the progress of archæology has already removed some of these (see *The New Bible Handbook*, p. 235), and in holding to the authenticity of the book we are in line with the New Testament, which bears witness to its miracles and predictions (see e.g. Heb. xi. 33, 34; Mt. xxiv. 15), and quotes from or alludes to it frequently, especially in the synoptic Gospels and the book of Revelation.

ANALYSIS

History (Chapters i–vi).

<ol type="i">
<li>Daniel, and three other youths selected, proved, educated.</li>
<li>Nebuchadnezzar's dream and its interpretation.</li>
<li>Nebuchadnezzar's golden image, and the fiery furnace.</li>
<li>Nebuchadnezzar's second dream, with its fulfilment, and his testimony.</li>
<li>Belshazzar's feast, the writing on the wall, the fall of Babylon.</li>
<li>Darius' edict. Daniel in the den of lions.</li>
</ol>

Prophecy (Chapters vii–xii).

    vii. Vision of the four great beasts, in the first year of Belshazzar.

    viii. Vision of the ram and he-goat, and of four kingdoms, and of the little horn, in the third year of Belshazzar.

    ix. The prayer of Daniel; the revelation concerning Messiah.

    x–xii. Vision of the future, and of 'the time of the end' in the third year of Cyrus.

Week 47. Daniel i–vi

Day 1. Dn. i.

(1) Consider the *purpose* of Daniel and his friends, their *reason* for acting as they did (cf. Lv. iii. 17, xx. 24-26; 1 Cor. viii. 7-12, x. 31), their *demeanour*—firmness mingled with tact (verse 12, cf. 1 Pet. ii. 11-15; Jas. i. 5), and their *reward* (verse 17, cf. Mt. xiii. 12; 1 Sa. ii. 30).

(2) What light does the story throw upon what it means to be 'in the world' (Jn. xvii. 11), but 'not of the world' (Jn. xvii. 16)? Reflect also how firmness of conviction in youth laid a foundation for later steadfastness. Cf. Pr. iv. 18.

Notes.—(1) Verse 2. 'Shinar'; an ancient name for Babylon.

(2) Verse 21. Cf. vi. 28, x. 1. It has been suggested that some words may have fallen out, and that what is meant is that Daniel remained at the king's court until the first year of Cyrus.

Day 2. Dn. ii. 1-30.

(1) Daniel and his friends were brought suddenly into great peril through no fault of their own. Note carefully what steps Daniel took. What may we learn from his example as to how to act in any such time of sudden danger? Cf. Acts iv. 23, 24, xii. 5.

(2) Watch the four at prayer. They might have asked God to change the king's mind, for he was acting very unreasonably, but what did they ask? Consider the faith behind their petition, and how God answered them above what they had asked. See ii. 47-49; Eph. iii. 20, 21.

Note.—Verse 4. 'In Syriack'; better 'in the Syrian language', as in R.V.; i.e. Aramaic. It is an interesting feature of the book of Daniel that the section from the words 'O King' in ii. 4 to the end of chapter vii is written in Aramaic, and the rest of the book in Hebrew. It has been suggested that the words 'in Aramaic' were originally a marginal note, to mark the point in the book where the Aramaic text begins.

Day 3. Dn. ii. 31-49.

The great image, though strange to our eyes, as we try to picture it, was not incongruous with the sculpture of ancient Babylon, nor out of keeping with the thoughts of a king, who had recently succeeded to the fallen empire of Assyria, and might well wonder what the future of his own kingdom was to be.

(1) Observe that the four kingdoms, though historically appearing one after the other, are yet all parts of the one image. Also it is not only the last kingdom of the four, but the whole image that is broken to pieces by the stone that smites it. What does the dream reveal as to God's final purpose, and what differences do you find between 'the kingdoms of the world' that compose the image and the kingdom prefigured by the stone? Cf. Gn. xlix. 24; Ps. cxviii. 22; Is. xxviii. 16; Acts iv. 11; Rev. xi. 15.

(2) What divine purposes did the dream serve in relation to (a) Nebuchadnezzar, (b) Daniel and his friends, and (c) all who knew, or know of it?

Notes.—(1) Verses 39, 40. Those who assign the book of Daniel to the Maccabean period take the four kingdoms to be those of Babylon, the Medes, the Persians, and the Greeks. This, however, apart from other objections, seems to go contrary to the book itself, which regards Medo-Persia as one kingdom (see v. 28, vi. 8, viii. 20, 21). The older interpretation, therefore, which takes the four kingdoms to be Babylon, Medo-Persia, Greece, and Rome is to be preferred.

(2) Verses 48, 49. 'Daniel sat in the gate of the king'. The meaning is that Daniel, who had been given by Nebuchadnezzar a dual office (verse 48), asked that the rule of the province of Babylon might be transferred to his friends, while he remained at court as chief of the king's sages.

Day 4. Dn. iii.

In the opening part of this chapter the king manifests a very different attitude towards Jehovah from that of ii. 47. The reason is that between chapters ii and iii there is an interval of several years, during which Nebuchadnezzar had destroyed Jerusalem and burnt the temple there with fire. This to him would be evidence that his own god was greater than Jehovah (cf. verse 15b). It accounts also for the enmity of the Chaldean officials against Shadrach, Meshach, and Abed-nego. They would resent Jews continuing to hold rule over the province of Babylon.

(1) What threefold accusation was brought against the three Hebrews? Consider how subtly it was worded to stir the king's anger.

(2) How does this trial of faith differ from anything these men had had to meet hitherto? For similar instances of courage see Acts iv. 8-12, v. 29-32; 2 Tim. iv. 16, 17. What purposes were served by the miracle of deliverance which God wrought?

Note.—Verse 25. 'Like the Son of God'; better, 'like a son of the gods', as in R.V.; i.e. a heavenly being or angel (cf. verse 28).

Day 5. Dn. iv.

Nebuchadnezzar was a great builder (cf. verse 30) and took pleasure also in forestry and woodcutting. The dream, therefore, was shaped by one of his chief interests. With what delight he would look upon the mighty tree of his dream, and with what dismay would he hear the sentence from heaven to cut it down, especially when the speaker went on to indicate that the tree represented a living person! This explains the king's fear. (Verse 5.)

(1) Reflect on the nature, and the purpose, of the king's humbling. See especially verses 22, 25, 32.

(2) Was it effective? Contrast his attitude to God, and confession of Him in this chapter, with his previous utterances in ii. 47, iii. 29. How would you define the change?

(3) Write out the main truths which the chapter teaches. With verse 27 cf. Mi. vi. 8.

Notes.—(1) Verse 11. 'The sight thereof', etc.; i.e. the tree was visible to the ends of the earth. The phrase 'all the earth' here and in verse 1 denotes the then known world.

(2) Verse 12. 'Meat'; better, 'food'. The peoples looked to Nebuchadnezzar for supplies.

(3) Verse 13. 'A watcher and an holy one'; i.e. an angel in God's service.

(4) Verse 17. 'The basest of men'; better, 'lowest' or 'lowliest', with reference to social position. Nebuchadnezzar's father, king Nabopolassar, records in an inscription that he sprang from very humble beginnings.

Day 6. Dn. v.

Babylon fell twenty-three years after Nebuchadnezzar's death. A quarter of a century, therefore, has elapsed since the events of chapter iv.

(1) Picture the scene as described in verses 1-12. How does it illustrate such passages of Scripture as Ps. xxxix. 4-6, xc. 8; Lk. xii. 20; Jas. iv. 14?

(2) What four accusations did Daniel bring against Belshazzar? In what two ways was Belshazzar's sin aggravated, and made more heinous?

(3) Consider the judgment pronounced upon Belshazzar as symbolizing the divine judgment upon all ungodliness, whether in national or individual life. See verses 26-28 and cf. Pr. xv. 3, 9; Ec. viii. 11-13.

Notes.—(1) The identity of Belshazzar was for long unknown, but it has been discovered that he was the eldest son of Nabonidus, the last ruler of the empire of Babylon, and shared with his father the duties of the throne.

(2) Verse 10. 'The queen'; probably the queen mother, widow of Nebuchadnezzar.

(3) Verses 25-28. 'Numbered thy kingdom'; i.e. numbered (the days of) thy kingdom.

'Pharsin' and 'peres' both mean 'divided'. The 'U' in U-pharsin simply means 'and'.

Day 7. Dn. vi.

Who Darius the Mede was is not fully clear. No doubt further light will come, as in the case of Belshazzar. See Day 6, Note 1.

(1) Neither pressure of business nor the threat of death kept Daniel from prayer. How is it with you? Do you think that other qualities in Daniel's character revealed in this chapter were the outcome of his prayer life? Cf. Is. xl. 29-31; Phil. iv. 5, 6.

(2) Is your faith of such a kind that you can stand alone in obedience to God without external support? Are we so living that even our keenest critics take it for granted that we would sooner perish than do what we know to be wrong before God?

Notes.—(1) The r.v. is clearer in verses 2, 3, 7, and 23.

(2) Verse 6. 'Assembled together'; better, 'came tumultuously', as in r.v. mg. So also in verses 11 and 15. There was a vehemence of animosity against Daniel that caused excited movement.

Week 48. DANIEL VII–XII

WE now come to that portion of the book which contains visions communicated to Daniel himself, and recorded by him (vii. 1, viii. 1, x. 1). A full enquiry into their meaning would require close and prolonged study. Many varied interpretations have been given, and different views are still held by Christian people. Three guiding principles which we shall do well to bear in mind are, first, to keep a watchful eye upon the text, lest imagination lead us astray; second, that the burden of Daniel's heart was for his own people, the Jews, and it is upon their future that the visions principally throw light (cf. ix. 20 and 23, 24, x. 14, xii. 7); and third, that we should therefore consider in the first instance, how the visions and the interpretations given to him would be understood by Daniel himself.

Day 1. Dn. vii.

The chapter records, first, the vision (verses 2-14); then, the general interpretation (verses 15-18); then, Daniel's enquiry concerning three features of the vision (verse 19, 20); and lastly, the answer given to these enquiries.

(1) Assuming the four kingdoms to be the same as those which

Nebuchadnezzar saw in his dream (chapter ii), what is there new in this vision which caused Daniel such distress and agitation of spirit (verses 15, 28)?

(2) To Nebuchadnezzar 'the kingdoms of this world' appeared in the glittering splendour of material wealth and power, whereas by Daniel they are seen as beasts of prey. What is the difference between these points of view, and which is the deeper and truer view? Cf. 1 Sa. xvi. 7; Mt. iv. 8; 1 Jn. ii. 16, 17.

(3) What is to be the final goal of history? Observe that the figure of Christ, dimly symbolized in Nebuchadnezzar's dream by the image of a stone, here stands out more distinctly in a form which our Lord Himself took up and used. Cf. Mt. xxvi. 64; Acts xvii. 31.

Notes.—(1) Verse 2. The sea is used figuratively for mankind (see Rev. xvii. 15 and cf. verse 17, where 'the great sea' becomes 'the earth'). The verse describes times of great agitation in world affairs.

(2) Verse 3. Taken alone, this verse might suggest that the beasts came up from the sea simultaneously. But the words 'after this' in verses 6 and 7 show that it was not so.

(3) Verse 4. Explained by chapter iv.

(4) Verse 5. 'Raised up itself on one side'; possibly a reference to the dominance of Persia in the Medo-Persian kingdom. Cf. viii. 3, last clause.

'Three ribs'. The Medo-Persians were voracious in absorbing new territory.

(5) Verse 6. 'Wings of a fowl'; or 'bird', indicating swiftness. Cf. viii. 5.

(6) Verse 9. 'The thrones were cast down'; better, 'placed', as in R.V., or 'set'. They are the thrones of angels assisting in the judgment. Cf. Rev. iv. 4.

(7) Verse 12. 'For a season and time'; i.e. for a certain period.

(8) Verse 18. 'The saints of the most High'. See also verses 21, 22, 25. The word 'saints' is used in the New Testament of the people of Christ (2 Cor. i. 1, xiii. 13, etc.). To Daniel, however, it would mean the people of Israel. He seems to have had no inkling of what Paul calls 'the mystery' of the Church (Eph. iii. 4-6).

(9) Verse 25. 'And the dividing of time'; better, 'and half a time', as in R.V. The whole phrase means three and a half years, the word 'time' being used for a year as in iv. 16, xii. 7.

Day 2. Dn. viii.

The vision of this chapter received historical fulfilment in the overthrow of Persia by Alexander the Great (330 B.C.), the division of his kingdom into four ('with less power', verse 22, Moffatt), and the rise of Antiochus Epiphanes, who did what is here foretold of him in verses 9-12 and 23-25 (170-164 B.C.). Gabriel's emphasis, however, upon the vision having to do with '*the time of the end*' (see verses 17 and 19) suggests that its meaning is not exhausted in Antiochus, but that he is only a type of one greater than he, and yet to come, who will act in a similar way. Cf. vii. 24-26 and Mt. xxiv. 15; 2 Thes. ii. 8-10. God's purposes have many unfoldings.

(1) What expression is used both of the ram and of the he-goat in the time of their prosperity, and also of the king of verse 23? See verses 4, 8, 25. Yet what was the end of these kingdoms? Notice the repetition of 'brake' and 'broken' (verses 7, 8, 22, 25), and cf. 1 Sa. ii. 9c; Is. ii. 12-17; Ezk. xxi. 27; Lk. xiv. 11.

(2) Why was Daniel so deeply affected by this vision? Consider how the prophecies of Jeremiah and Ezekiel seemed to indicate that the return from exile would coincide with the advent of the kingdom of God (see e.g. Je. xxxii. 38-44; Ezk. xxxvii. 21-28); but this vision shows long vistas of history stretching into the future, and *further suffering for the Jews*. Cf. Ps. lxxiv. 10, 11; Zc. i. 12.

Notes.—(1) Verse 9. 'The glorious land' (R.V.); i.e. Palestine.

(2) Verse 10. 'The host of heaven . . . stars'. Used figuratively of Israel and her leaders.

(3) Verse 11. 'The prince of the host'; i.e. God Himself. Cf. verse 25.

(4) Verse 12. Read as in R.V. Israel was to be given over into the power of the 'horn' because of transgressions.

'Cast down truth', etc. The suppression of the true religion.

(5) Verses 13, 14. 'Saint'; better, 'a holy one', as in R.V., i.e. an angel.

'Days' (verse 14) is literally 'evenings-mornings', as in R.V. (cf. verse 26). If the burnt-offering ceased for 2,300 times that would be 1,150 days, which is a little more than three years. It is known that Antiochus did suspend the burnt-offering for three years and possibly a little longer.

Day 3. Dn. ix. 1-19.

(1) Consider the effect of the fall of Babylon upon one who, like Daniel, saw in it a fulfilment of prophecy (verse 2, cf. Je. xxv. 11, xxix. 10-14, l. 1-5). What did it lead him to do (cf. Ezk. xxxvi. 37), and what light do verses 2 and 3 throw upon the use of Scripture in our praying?

(2) As you read through Daniel's prayer, how would you describe his praying? See especially verses 3 and 19, and cf. Lk. xi. 8; Col. ii. 1, iv. 12, 13; Eph. vi. 18; Heb. v. 7. In his *confession*, how does he speak of God, how of himself and his people? In his *petition*, on what does he base his plea for mercy, and for what does he ask?

Day 4. Dn. ix. 20-27.

Daniel had assumed that a period of seventy years would finish 'the desolations of Jerusalem' (verse 2), and in his prayer pleaded with God for this (verse 18). God sends Gabriel to give him fuller understanding (verses 20-23), by conveying to him a 'commandment' (literally a 'word'), which speaks not of seventy years, but of seventy weeks of years. The message is very condensed, and every clause is significant.

(1) Verse 24. What are the six things here mentioned? Notice that they all concern the Jews and the holy city, and are to come to pass at the end of the full seventy weeks of years.

(2) The seventy weeks of years are divided into three periods of seven weeks, sixty-two weeks, and one week respectively. What the first period signifies is not certainly known, unless it be the time taken to build the city (verse 25, A.V.). What event, however, is stated as happening at the end of the second period? Cf. Is. liii. 8; Mk. ix. 12.

(3) The remainder of the passage has been variously interpreted, even by those who regard it as inspired prophecy. If verse 26a be a reference to the cross of Christ, then verse 26b seems to point to the destruction of Jerusalem and the temple by the Romans in A.D. 70. But such questions as these arise (i) Does the fall of Jerusalem in A.D. 70 exhaust the prophecy? (ii) Who is 'the prince that shall come', and is he to be identified with 'the little horn' of vii. 8, 24, 25? See note below.

Notes.—(1) Verses 26, 27 should be read as in R.V.

(2) Verse 24. 'To finish transgression' and 'to make an end of sins' are parallel expressions meaning to bring Israel's sinning to an end. Cf. Rom. xi. 26, 27.

'To make reconciliation' or 'purge away', as in R.V. mg. Cf. Zc. xiii. 1.

'To bring in everlasting righteousness'. Cf. Je. xxiii. 5, 6.

'To seal up the vision and prophecy'; i.e. to ratify it as fulfilled.

'To anoint the most Holy'; i.e. sign of Jehovah's return to dwell in the midst of His people.

(3) From the time of Ne. ii. 5, 8 (445 B.C.), sixty-nine weeks of years (the sacred year of 360 days) brings us to the period of Christ's ministry. This prophecy of Daniel may account for the widespread expectation of a Messiah at the time Jesus appeared (cf. Mt. ii. 1, 2; Lk. ii. 25, 26, iii. 15), and may lie behind our Lord's own words in Mk. i. 15a.

(4) Verses 26, 27. Many hold that in this prophecy, as in other Old Testament passages, the beginning and end of the Christian era are telescoped together, and that the prophecy here leaps forward to the end of the age. If so, the last 'week' is separated from the first sixty-nine by the whole interval between Christ's first and second comings. With verse 27 cf. 2 Thes. ii. 8.

Day 5. Dn. x–xi. 1.

(1) This chapter is introductory to Daniel's last vision. Consider the date (verse 1) and trace out from Ezr. i and iii and iv. 4, 5 what was happening at that time to the first contingent of those who returned from exile. What light does this throw upon the mourning of Daniel (verse 2) and upon the purpose of the vision? Cf. Mt. v. 4.

(2) What does today's portion teach of the *costliness* of communion with God, and of true prayer?

(3) Read Eph. vi. 10-13 in the light of this chapter; also 2 Ki. vi. 16-18; Ps. xxxiv. 7. In the presence of the mysterious spirit-world, what comfort may we draw from the New Testament revelation that our Lord is supreme there also? See Eph. i. 20-23; Col. i. 16, ii. 15.

Notes.—(1) Verse 1. 'The time appointed was long'; better, 'even a great warfare' (R.V.). Moffatt renders the whole clause 'the true revelation of a great conflict'.

(2) Verse 4. 'Hiddekel'; i.e. the Tigris, see R.V. mg.

(3) Verses 5, 6. It is not said who this august being was. Some features of his appearance and person remind us of the visions of Ezekiel and John (Ezk. i. 13-16; Rev. i. 13-15).

(4) Verse 8. 'No strength'; 'before God gives strength and power unto His people He makes them sensible of their own weakness'.

(5) Verse 13. 'Prince'; used here of guardian angels of the kingdoms.
'I remained there with the kings of Persia'. The LXX renders 'beside the prince of the kings of Persia'.

(6) Verse 19. 'And said'; better, 'and he said', as in R.V. The speaker is the august being whom Daniel saw, to be distinguished from the strengthening angel of verses 16a and 18.

Day 6. Dn. xi. 2-20.

Today's passage is a forecast of history, not continuous, but selective. The period is one of nearly 400 years, from the time of Daniel's vision to the reign of Antiochus Epiphanes. Verses 2-4 are introductory, having reference (a) to the rulers of Persia, up to Xerxes (verse 2), and (b) to the rise of Alexander the Great nearly 150 years later, and to the division of his kingdom into four (verses 3, 4). From this point the prophecy confines itself to two of these four kingdoms: Egypt, whose ruler is called 'king of the south', and Syria, whose ruler is called 'king of the north'. The successive rulers of these kingdoms in historical succession were (a) Egypt: Ptolemy I (305-285 B.C.); Ptolemy II (285-247 B.C.); Ptolemy III (247-222 B.C.); Ptolemy IV (222-205 B.C.); Ptolemy V (205-182 B.C.); Ptolemy VI (182-146 B.C.); (b) Syria: Seleucus I (312-280 B.C.); Antiochus I (280-261 B.C.); Antiochus II (261-246 B.C.); Seleucus II (246-226 B.C.); Seleucus III (226-223 B.C.); Antiochus III, called the Great (223-187 B.C.); Seleucus IV (187-175 B.C.); Antiochus IV, called Epiphanes (175-164 B.C.).

Verse 5a of our chapter refers to Ptolemy I, and verse 5b (to be read as in R.V. mg.) to Seleucus I, who for a time was one of Ptolemy's generals, but became ruler of a wider empire than Ptolemy's. Verse 6 refers to Ptolemy II, who gave his daughter Berenice to Antiochus II in marriage upon certain conditions. The conditions were, however, broken, and Berenice lost her life. Verses 7 and 8 refer to Ptolemy III, brother of Berenice, who successfully attacked the kingdom of Syria under Seleucus II and returned with great spoil, Seleucus II later invaded Egypt; but without success (verse 9). Verses 10-19 predict continued wars between the kings of Syria and Egypt in the reigns of Antiochus III, Ptolemy IV, and Ptolemy V. The victory turned now to the north (verse 10), and now to the south (verses 11, 12). Then Antiochus brought Egypt low (verses 13-17), but, wishing to press westwards (verse 18), made an alliance with Egypt by giving to Ptolemy V his daughter Cleopatra in marriage (verse 17). The plans for a conquest westward were, however, defeated by a Roman commander (verse 18), and Antiochus had to retire to his own kingdom, where he died (verse 19). Verse 20 refers to Seleucus IV, who imposed heavy taxes upon Palestine to build up his kingdom's finances. In all this time Palestine, named 'the glorious land' (verse 16) and 'the glory of the kingdom' (verse 20), was the pathway of marching armies, and a bone of contention between the warring nations. But it had not yet suffered what it was soon to suffer under Antiochus IV.

(1) What was the purpose of this detailed prediction? In what way would it help the remnant during the persecution which was to come? Cf. Is. xli. 21-24, xlvi. 10; Jn. xiii. 19, xiv. 29, xvi. 4.

(2) Ponder the words in verses 3 and 16 'shall do according to his own will'. See also verse 36, and contrast Jn. iv. 34; Rom. xii. 1, 2; 1 Jn. ii. 17. Are you learning to say with Christ Mt. xxvi. 42 and Heb. x. 7?

Notes.—(1) The chapter should be read as in the R.V.

(2) Verse 14. A party among the Jews will rise up, thinking by violence to bring to pass the fulfilment of prophecy.

(3) Verse 17, last sentence. Read as in R.V.

Day 7. Dn. xi. 21–xii.

At chapter xi. 21 the predicted course of events as told in the vision reaches the reign of Antiochus Epiphanes, and the historical fulfilment can be traced with accuracy up to verse 35. The career of Antiochus is revealed in four main features: (a) the craft by which he obtained the throne and won his way to power (verses 21-23;) (b) his love of munificent and lavish giving (verse 24a); (c) his plans for war (verse 24b), and especially his wars against Egypt (verses 25-30), and (d) his acts of sacrilege against the temple in Jerusalem, and persecution of the Jews (verses 31-35).

The remainder of today's passage (xi. 36–xii. 13) seems at first sight to be a continuation of the career of Antiochus, but on closer examination is seen to go beyond it, alike in its description of the king (verse 36; cf. 2 Thes. ii. 4), in the events which it records (e.g. xii. 1, 2), and in the emphasis laid upon its being 'the time of the end' (xi. 35, 36, 40, xii. 4). The figure of Antiochus seems here to merge into the more sinister figure of the Antichrist. With xii. 2, 7, cf. vii. 25, ix. 27.

(1) Gather out the evidence given here, on the one hand of man's sinfulness and lust for power, and on the other of God's overruling control and purpose. Cf. Je. xvii. 5-14.

(2) What are the characteristics of those who will be glorified and of those who will be put to shame at the last?

Notes.—(1) Today's passage should be read in the R.V.

(2) Verse 21. 'Not given the honour', etc.; i.e. he was not the recognized heir to the throne.

(3) Verses 22-24. It is not wholly clear who is meant by 'the prince of the covenant'. 'The strong holds' are those of Egypt.

(4) Verse 27. Antiochus actually captured the king of Egypt, but they pretended to be friendly.

(5) Verse 30. 'Ships of Chittim'; i.e. Roman ships, which refused Antiochus liberty to proceed. He vented his anger, therefore, upon Palestine.

(6) Verse 31. 'The abomination that maketh desolate'. A small altar was placed upon the altar of burnt offering and sacrifices were offered to idols.

(7) Verse 37. 'The desire of women'. Possibly refers to the god Tammuz. See Ezk. viii. 14.

REVELATION

INTRODUCTION

(See New Bible Handbook, pp. 408-413)

MANY have been repelled from the study of the book of Revelation by fears of its difficulty, or the intricate nature of some interpretations. But the fears are imaginary, and no book of the Bible will more surely reward the student who approaches it as a spiritual guide to his present life and not as an eschatological enigma. It is important to remember that the visions which occupy so large a part of it are not to be regarded as literal pictures, but as setting forth symbolically heavenly and spiritual realities.

It is generally agreed that it was written by John the apostle, and in days of persecution, as his exile proves (i. 9). Some think that his exile was suffered under Nero, who died in A.D. 68; some under Domitian (81-96). The later date seems more probable. The struggle between the people of Christ and the power of Rome had now reached a state more advanced than that which is reflected in the Acts of the Apostles. Emperor worship became common from Nero's reign onward, and the outlook was dark and threatening.

The reference to Rome in chapter xvii is but thinly veiled. Some interpreters ('Praeterist') regard all the references as being to contemporary events, so that for us the book speaks of things already past; some ('Historicist') see in chapters ii–xix references to Christian history before and after the fall of Rome, and to the conflict of evangelical religion with the Roman Church, so leading on to the times of the end; others ('Futurist') regard chapters ii and iii as an epitome of Christian history, and the rest of the

book as a prophecy looking forward to events at the time of the
Lord's return.

A true interpretation will probably find something of value in
all these points of view. It is best to study the book with the assurance (1) that it had a real message for its own time; (2) that its
lessons have been illustrated by the history of the Church, and
(3) that it contains prophetical references to the future. Let the
student not be unduly troubled by obscurities that puzzle him,
but contemplate with joy and wonder what is clear. We may learn
lessons of the utmost value regarding the place of Christ's people
in the purposes of God and the glorious future awaiting them, of
the heavenly nature of our earthly conflict, which can be carried
on only with divine aid, of the need to overcome in the struggle,
of the eternal judgment of God upon Satan and sin, and of the
certainty of the coming and the complete victory of Jesus Christ
our Lord.

ANALYSIS

i. 1-8.	Prologue.
i. 9–iii.	Vision of Christ, alive for evermore, in the midst of the churches.
iv–v.	Vision of the throne of God, and of the Lamb in the midst of the throne, to whom is committed the sealed book of the judgments of God.
vi–viii. 5.	Vision of the 'seal' judgments, with two visions interposed for the comfort of Christ's people (vii. 1-8, 9-17).
viii. 6–xi.	Vision of the 'trumpet' judgments, with three visions for the comfort of Christ's people (x, xi. 1-2, 3-12).
xii–xiv.	Vision of the man-child, and of the dragon and the two beasts, with three visions for the comfort of Christ's people (xiv. 1-5, 6-13, 14-20).
xv–xvi.	Vision of the 'bowl' judgments.
xvii–xix. 10.	Visions of Babylon, the harlot city, and her destruction.
xix. 11–xx.	Vision of Christ's return in judgment, of His reign for 1,000 years, of His triumph over all His enemies, and of the last judgment.
xxi–xxii. 5.	Vision of a new heaven and earth, and of the new Jerusalem.
xxii. 6-21.	Epilogue.

Week 49. REVELATION I–III

Day 1. Rev. i. 1-8.

(1) Trace in verses 1 and 2 the course of the 'revelation' from its source in the mind of God by four successive steps to us who read and receive it. How is it described in its content, character and value, and what is required in those who read?

(2) Observe the place given to Jesus Christ in relation to God, and consider each title given to Him in verse 5a. See Jn. iii. 11, 32, 33, xviii. 37; Col. i. 18; Rev. xix. 11-16. How does John describe His attitude to us, and what He has done for us? Cf. Jn. xiii. 1; Eph. i. 7; 1 Pet. ii. 9.

(3) With i. 7 cf. Dn. vii. 13 and Acts i. 9-11. Is the thought of His coming a joy to you? Cf. vi. 15-17; 1 Thes. iv. 15-18, v. 1-4; 2 Thes. i. 7-10.

Notes.—(1) Verse 1. 'The Revelation of Jesus Christ'; i.e. communicated by Him.

(2) Verse 3. 'He that readeth'; i.e. the one who reads this book aloud to his fellow believers.

(3) Verse 4. 'The seven Spirits'; i.e. the Spirit in His sevenfold fulness.

(4) Verses 5, 6 should be read as in R.V.

Day 2. Rev. i. 9-20.

(1) What, according to verse 9, is the twofold experience in which all believers share, and what should characterize their lives? Cf. verse 6a; Jn. xvi. 33; 2 Tim. ii. 12.

(2) We are not for a moment to suppose that Christ is literally like this. What John sees is a vision, each feature of which is symbolic of some aspect of our glorified Lord. Write down against each feature here portrayed what trait in our Lord's character it suggests. What is the total impression left upon your mind?

(3) What does Christ say of Himself and of His relation to the churches in verses 17-20? With verse 17 cf. Dn. x. 8-11, 15-19, and with the figure of the 'lampstands' (R.V. mg.) cf. Mt. v. 14-16.

Notes.—(1) Verse 11. 'I am Alpha and Omega'. Christ applies to Himself the words which in verse 8 were spoken by God. See also verse 17 and xxii. 13.

(2) Verse 18. 'The keys of death and of Hades' (R.V.). According to the teaching of the Rabbis these keys are in the hands of God alone.

(3) Verse 20. 'Mystery'; i.e. something with a hidden meaning. Cf. xvii. 7; Mt. xiii. 11.

'The angels of the churches'. Sometimes taken to mean the pastors or bishops of each church, but more probably denoting a guardian angel (cf. Dn. x. 21; Mt. xviii. 10).

Day 3. Rev. ii. 1-7.

The seven letters of chapters ii and iii are all similar in structure, beginning with a self-description of the speaker, taken from the vision in i. 9-20; then giving His message to the church, and closing with a summons to hear 'what the Spirit saith to the churches', and a promise to 'him that overcometh'. In the last four letters, however, the promise precedes the summons to hear.

(1) State in your own words what Christ found to commend in the church at Ephesus (verses 2, 3, 6).

(2) Observe how a decline of love may have taken place in the heart while outward activities continue. If the loss of love be not remedied, to what end will it lead? What is the remedy? See verse 5.

(3) With verse 7a cf. Mk. iv. 9, 23, vii. 16, viii. 18. How may the hearing ear be obtained?

Notes.—(1) Verse 6. 'The deeds of the Nicolaitans'. See also verses 14, 15. A tendency towards moral slackness was creeping in to some of the Asian churches.

(2) Verse 7. 'The tree of life'. In contrast to the corrupt fruits of sensual self-indulgence, Christ gives to the one who overcomes fruit which yields perfect and abiding satisfaction. Cf. xxii. 2, 19.

Day 4. Rev. ii. 8-17.

(1) Reconstruct from verses 8-11 the situation with which the believers in Smyrna were confronted. What does Christ declare concerning (a) their immediate, and (b) their final future? Ponder the words in brackets 'but thou art rich', and set down some of their riches.

(2) Satan could not break the rocklike steadfastness of the church in Pergamos by frontal attack (verse 13), so he employed another method, tempting believers to ask, 'Is it necessary to be so uncompromising in our attitude towards idolatrous practices and pagan morals?' What is Christ's answer to this sort of question?

Notes.—(1) Verse 10. 'Ten days'; i.e. for a short period.

(2) Verse 11. 'The second death'; cf. xx. 14, xxi. 8.

(3) Verse 13. 'Where Satan's seat is'. Pergamos was the official residence the Roman proconsul of the province, and the chief centre of the worship of the emperor.

(4) Verse 17. 'The hidden manna'. The Rabbis taught that the Messiah when He came would give the people to eat of manna, now hidden in heaven. What is said here is that Christ is the true manna, the bread of life; cf. Jn. vi. 48-51.

'A white stone'. Stones engraved with names supposed to possess magical qualities were highly valued in heathen circles. Christ gives privileges, personal to each recipient, which exceed all that can be found outside of Him.

Day 5. Rev. ii. 18-29.

(1) Note the close correspondence in each letter between Christ's self-description at the beginning, and the message that follows. This is specially clear in the letter to Thyatira. What may we learn from this as to the universality of Christ and His complete suitability to every need of the churches and of individual believers? Cf. Heb. i. 10, ii. 9.

(2) The moral laxity that was creeping into the churches seems to have proceeded further in the case of Thyatira, and to have become a doctrine and almost a sect. What responsibility had the church as a whole in regard to the presence of evil in their midst, and what may we learn from this regarding the necessity of church discipline? Cf. 1 Sa. iii. 11-14.

(3) What qualities did the searching eyes of the Lord see in the church in Thyatira that He could approve?

Notes.—(1) Verse 20. 'Sufferest'. The church as a whole took no effective action.

'That woman Jezebel'. So called because of her moral likeness to Jezebel of old, cf. 1 Ki. xxi. 25. She appears to have advocated compromise with idolatrous and immoral practices on the principle that the way to overcome evil is to know it by experience.

(2) Verse 22. 'Into a bed'; i.e. of sickness.

(3) Verse 24. 'The depths of Satan'. Better, 'the deep things of Satan'. Jezebel's followers may have claimed to be more deeply instructed than others, and the Lord calls it 'the deep things of Satan'.

(4) Verse 28. 'The morning star'; the same image is used in xxii. 16 of Christ Himself. 'The glory of the Lord is to be the glory of His saints' (cf. 2 Cor. iii. 18).

Day 6. Rev. iii. 1-13.

(1) Christ bestows the Spirit in fulness (verse 1). If, then, in any Christian circle, as in the church in Sardis, there is but the outward form of Christian profession, and no abounding life, or if service for Christ is ineffective and incomplete in His sight, what must be the cause? Cf. Gal. v. 16, 24, 25.

(2) What promise did Christ make to the church in Philadelphia, and why? Compare the church of Christ there and the synagogue of the Jews. In what were they alike, and in what different?

(3) Write down in your own words the place to be given to the overcomers in the eternal glories of the perfected kingdom. Cf. xxii. 2-5

Note.—Verse 8. 'An open door'; or 'a door opened' (R.V.); i.e. a missionary opportunity. Cf. 1 Cor. xvi. 9; 2 Cor. ii. 12.

Day 7. Rev. iii. 14-22.

(1) How do you think the church in Laodicea had become so blind to its true spiritual condition? Cf. Mt. xxiii. 25, 26; 2 Cor. iv. 18. See also note below.

(2) What three qualities of Christian character are symbolized by 'white raiment', 'gold tried in the fire', and 'eye salve' respectively? See for the first verses 4 and xix. 8; Ps. li. 7; for the second 1 Pet. i. 7; and for the third Ps. cxix. 18; 2 Pet. i. 9; Eph. i. 18, 19. How may these things be obtained? See Lk. xiv. 33, xviii. 22.

(3) If a church as a whole be 'lukewarm', may individuals within it enjoy a close relationship with the Lord? What does the Lord promise to such? Are you resolved by God's grace so to fulfil the conditions that you may obtain what is promised?

Note.—Verse 18. Laodicea was famous for its banking and exchange, for its sheep from whose wool warm white garments were made, and for its medical school and eye powder.

Week 50. REVELATION IV–XI

WE are now entering upon the main revelation of the book (see i. 1 and iv. 1). We have seen the condition of the churches. Persecution had begun, and times of greater trial loomed ahead (see ii. 10, 13, iii. 10). The question 'What of the future?' must have troubled every thoughtful Christian, and is now about to be answered. But first in chapters iv and v God shows John a vision of the heavenly realities which abide unshaken behind and above the changes and uncertainties of earth.

Day 1. Rev. iv.

(1) Try to visualize what John saw in this vision. Where in relation to the throne were (a) the lamps of fire; (b) the four living creatures; (c) the thrones of the elders, and (d) the sea of glass?

(2) What attributes of the divine nature stand out in this chapter? Consider the symbolism of verses 3-8. What meaning is suggested by each part of it?

(3) What impression is left upon you of the character of heaven's worship? How does the vision illustrate the words of the Lord's prayer—'as it is in heaven'?

Notes.—(1) Verse 3. 'Jasper'; lustrous. Cf. xxi. 11.
'Sardine stone'; 'sardius' (R.V.) or 'cornelian'; red like fire or blood.
'A rainbow . . . like an emerald'. The rainbow suggests God's faithfulness,

and the emerald with its green colour the blessings of His bounty (cf. Ps. xxiii. 2; Acts iii. 19).

(2) Verse 4. 'Seats'; better, 'thrones', as in R.V. These elders are normally taken to represent the church of Old and New Testaments, an idea suggested by the reading 'us' in v. 9, 10 (A.V.). Another view is that they are angelic beings. Cf. Is. xxiv. 23 (R.V. mg.); Col. i. 16 ('thrones').

(3) Verse 6. 'As it were a glassy sea like unto crystal' (R.V.); transparent, nothing hidden, nor place to hide; cf. xv. 2, xxi. 18, 21.

'Four living creatures' (R.V.); similar to the 'cherubim' of Ezekiel's vision, 'the personification of the forces set in motion by the will of God, whereby His throne is supported, His authority maintained'.

'Full of eyes' (verses 6 and 8), symbolizing God's perfect knowledge of all that happens.

Day 2. Rev. v.

(1) What two great truths are symbolized by the vision of the book of the future being in the hand of God, and then committed for its fulfilment into the hand of Christ? Cf. Mt. xxviii. 18; Acts iv. 28.

(2) What place is given to Christ in this vision (a) in relation to God; (b) in the worship of heaven, and (c) in the worship of all creation? Cf. Jn. x. 30; Col. i. 16, 17; Heb. i. 6.

(3) How is the transcendent worth and efficacy of Christ's atoning sacrifice indicated? What reassurance does the contemplation of this twofold vision of heavenly realities in chapters iv and v bring to us who are fighting on earth 'the good figh of faith'?

Notes.—(1) Verse 1. 'A book'; i.e. the book of God's judgments. Cf. Ezk. ii. 9, 10; Dn. xii. 4, 9.

(2) Verse 6. 'Seven horns and seven eyes'; fulness of power and fulness of vision.

(3) Verses 9, 10 should be read as in R.V.

Day 3. Rev. vi.

(1) As the book of future events is opened seal by seal, what points of correspondence do you find with Mt. xxiv. 4-14? Compare, for example, verses 4, 6, and 9 with Mt. xxiv. 6, 7, and 9. For the meaning of the white horse, see note below.

(2) To what climax of judgment do all these things mount up? See verses 12-17 and note (4) below. Men, in their terror, think that the day of God's wrath has come; but see chapter viii. Cf. Is. ii. 19-21.

(3) What answer is given in this chapter to those who see their friends slain because of their faithfulness to the gospel, and God seems to take no action?

Notes.—(1) Verses 1, 3, 5, 7. 'Come and see'; better, 'Come', as in R.V., a summons to the four riders.

(2) Verse 2. Two principal interpretations have been given of the white horse and his rider. Many take it to be a picture of Christ, going forth in the conquests of the gospel. Cf. Mt. xxiv. 14; Ps. xlv. 3-5. Others regard it as a picture of invasion and lust of conquest, leading to the miseries of war. The latter seems more likely. It is difficult to conceive of the Lamb as opening the seals, and at the same time going forth (verses 2, 3).

(3) Verse 6. Such was the scarcity that a day's wage (Mt. xx. 2) would suffice only to buy a small measure of wheat (R.V. mg.). But luxuries such as wine and oil were still plentiful.

(4) Verses 12-14. The imagery of these verses is such as is frequently used in the Old Testament to symbolize great upheavals among the nations. See e.g. Is. xiii. 9-11, 13; Ezk. xxxii. 7-9; Na. i. 5.

Day 4. Rev. vii.

Before the revelation of further judgments, two visions are interposed for the comfort of believers. In all that has been shown, nothing has been said of the Church, except with regard to those who have been martyred. Today's portion shows the Church first in this life, on earth (verses 1-8), and then in heaven, having life for evermore.

(1) What assurance is given in verses 1-8 that God is watchful over His people and will secure their safety in the midst of His judgments, so that not one is missing? Cf. Jn. x. 27-29; Ezk. ix. 3-6.

(2) In verses 9-17 who compose the great multitude, and where are they standing? How came they to be there, and what is now their occupation? Make a list of the blessings that they enjoy, translating the symbols into the realities which they represent.

(3) What are the marks of those who truly belong to Christ's Church?

Notes.—(1) Verses 4-8. Some have thought that those who are 'sealed' represent believers from among the Jews, but in the light of xiv. 1-4 it is better to regard the vision as including the whole 'Israel of God' (Gal. vi. 16).

(2) Verse 14. 'Great tribulation'. Better 'the great tribulation'. Cf. iii. 10. The vision shows that all who are the Lord's will be brought through safely.

Day 5. Rev. viii and ix.

We are brought back, after the interlude of chapter vii, to the opening of the seventh seal. Will it usher in the final end? All heaven is silent, as if in suspense, and expectancy (cf. Mk. xiii. 32), but there follows a new series of judgments (cf. Mk. xiii. 7, 8).

(1) In viii. 3-5 we see, in the heavenly sanctuary (Heb. viii. 1, 5), what happens to the prayers of Christ's people. What are we taught as to the efficacy of prayer when mingled with the incense

of Christ's intercession, and fire from the altar of His sacrifice? Cf. Jn. xiv. 13, 14; Rom. viii. 26; Eph. vi. 18, 19.

(2) Contrast the first four trumpet judgments with the fifth and sixth, (a) in the objects affected, (b) in the severity of their character and result. What was the purpose of these trumpet judgments? See viii. 13, ix. 20, and note (2) below.

(3) What do we learn from today's portion concerning God's control over all that happens? See especially ix. 1, 4, 13, 14, 15.

Notes.—(1) viii. 3, 5. Two altars are to be distinguished, the altar of sacrifice, and the 'golden altar' of incense. See Ex. xxxvii. 25–xxxviii. 7.

(2) viii. 6. 'Trumpets'; indicating that these judgments were sent in warning. Cf. Am. iii. 6; Ezk. xxxiii. 1-4.

(3) viii. 7-11. 'The third part'; cf. vi. 8, 'the fourth part'.

(4) ix. 1. 'The bottomless pit'. Better, 'the abyss' (R.V.), the abode of the powers of evil. Cf. xi. 7, xvii. 8.

(5) ix. 11. 'Abaddon' and 'Apollyon'; both mean 'destruction'.

(6) ix. 13. 'The golden altar'; indicating that the prayers of the saints were being answered.

Day 6. Rev. x–xi. 13.

Today's passage is an interlude between the sixth and seventh trumpets, corresponding to chapter vii (see *Analysis*). The seer first tells of his new commission (x. 1-11), and then describes the Church as God's sanctuary (xi. 1, 2), and as bearing witness in the world (xi. 3-12).

(1) In what two ways does chapter x show that the revelation thus far given to John, though it extends to the end of the age (verses 6, 7), is by no means a complete disclosure of the hidden counsel of God? Cf. Dt. xxix. 29; Jb. xxvi. 14; 1 Cor. xiii. 9, 12.

(2) What made God's Word sweet to taste, but bitter to digest? Before John could declare it, it must pass through his own mind and heart. Are you prepared for the cost of the personal application in your own life of truth you have delighted to meditate upon, or have preached to others? Cf. Jb. iv. 3-5; Acts xx. 26, 27.

(3) The question, who are the two witnesses in xi. 3-12 has received many answers. Assuming that they represent the witness of the Church throughout the present age, what lessons may we learn from the passage concerning true witness for Christ, the authority of His witnesses (verses 5, 6), their suffering unto death (verses 7-10), and their final triumph? Cf. Lk. x. 19; Jn. xvi. 2; Acts vii. 54-56.

Notes.—(1) x. 6. 'That there should be time no longer'. Better, 'that there should be no more delay' (R.S.V.).

(2) xi. 1, 2. The purpose of the measuring was to mark out what was to be preserved. If the temple represents Christ's people (1 Cor. iii. 16) the outer court may represent the Jews in their unbelief (Lk. xxi. 24).

'Forty and two months'. The same length of time as the 1260 days of xi. 3, and the 'time, times, and half a time' of xii. 14 (cf. xii. 6). It appears to be in John's use of it a conventional term for the duration of the present age between the first and second comings of Christ.

Day 7. Rev. xi. 14-19.

These verses bring us to the time of the end, which is described more fully in chapters xix and xx. The book might have ended here but for the further revelation which John was given (x. 11).

(1) Who is seen to be triumphant at the last, in spite of the wrath of the nations? Cf. Ps. ii.

(2) What two attributes of God are mentioned which make certain His triumph over all opposition?

(3) What is symbolized by the ark of the covenant (verse 19)? And what reassurance does this vision of the ark in the heavenly sanctuary give us that we may draw right into the very presence of the divine holiness? Cf. Ex. xxv. 21, 22; Heb. x. 19-22.

Week 51. REVELATION XII–XIX. 10

AT this point a new division of the book begins, and a new series of prophecies (cf. x. 11). The earlier part of the book has been occupied mainly with outward events and acts of divine judgment, together with visions of the Church and her sufferings; and it has been shown that behind all is God's throne, and that all that is happening is under His control, and in the hand of Christ. The present section of the book reveals another and graver aspect in the situation, namely, the enmity of powerful spiritual foes, of Satan and the world. This has so far only been hinted at (ii. 9, 13, 24, iii. 9, ix. 11, xi. 7), but is now brought into full view, and it is shown that the sufferings of the Church have their origin in the conflict between Satan and Christ.

Day 1. Rev. xii.

The chapter gives a symbolic picture of the birth of Christ, and of His return to the throne of God, but its main purpose is to show the power and malignity of Satan as the enemy of Christ and His people.

(1) Gather out what is said about Christ. With verse 5 cf. Ps. ii. 6-9; Eph. i. 19-21.

(2) How is the fearful power of Satan depicted? And how the intensity of his hatred of Christ? Verse 4b covers the whole attack of Satan upon Jesus on earth, see e.g. Mt. ii. 16-18, iv. 1-11; Lk. xxii. 43, 44, 53b. With verses 7-10a cf. Lk. x. 18; Jn. xii. 31.

(3) Why, according to this chapter, is the lot of the Church on earth one of constant conflict? Cf. Eph. vi. 10-13; 1 Pet. v. 8.

Notes.—(1) Verses 1, 2. The woman represents the true Israel, who, after Christ's ascension, formed the Christian Church of the first days. Cf. Rom. xi. 4, 5. For the imagery, see Gn. xxxvii. 9; Ct. vi. 4, 10; Is. lxvi. 7-10.

(2) Verses 3, 4a, 'Red'; the colour of blood. Cf. Jn. viii. 44. The seven heads and diadems (R.V.) indicate far-reaching dominion, the ten horns, great power, and the tail (verse 4a) his vast size and strength.

(3) Verses 6, 14-16. The exact meaning of the symbolism is obscure, but the general sense is clear, that the Church is under God's protection, and although Satan will seek to destroy her, his plans will be thwarted. The number 1260 days in John's use of it seems to cover the whole of this present age, cf. xi. 2, note.

Day 2. Rev. xiii.

Satan in his war against the saints uses two chief instruments: (a) totalitarian world power, hostile to the true God, subservient to Satan, and claiming worship for itself (verses 1-10); and (b) established religion, supporting the claims of the world power, by false miracles and signs (verses 11-18). Such 'beasts' were found in John's day in the Roman Empire, and the cult of Emperor worship. They have appeared also in later history, and may appear again.

(1) What do the various characteristics of the beast from the sea symbolize (verses 1-3)? Note that it combined the characteristics of the first three beasts of Daniel's vision. See Dn. vii. 4-6. Whatever particular meaning verse 3 may have, it certainly signifies extraordinary vitality.

(2) In what respects did the second beast differ in outward appearance from the first? Cf. 1 Pet. v. 8 with 2 Cor. xi. 14. How did its aims and methods bring Christians into direct conflict with it? Cf. Dn. iii. 4-6; Jn. xv. 18-21.

(3) What qualities were specially called for in Christians? Cf. Mk. xiii. 13.

Notes.—(1) Verse 10. Read as in R.V. The meaning seems to be that whatever be their fate, Christ's people must not retaliate by violence.

(2) Verse 12. This second beast is called the false prophet in xvi. 13, xix. 20, xx. 10. Cf. Mt. vii. 15.

(3) Verse 18. Many take the number 666 to mean 'Nero Caesar', others, because every digit falls short of the perfect number, regard 666 as a symbol of Antichrist. The name Nero would be more appropriate to the first beast.

Day 3. Rev. xiv.

This chapter, like chapters vii and x–xi. 13, is an interlude introduced for the comfort of believers.

(1) Verses 1-5 present a picture of the true followers of Christ. Although outwardly scattered, suffering, and in danger of death,

spiritually they are with the Lamb on the impregnable rock of Mt. Zion, owned of God, not one missing (verse 1), and sharing in the worship of heaven (verses 2, 3). To what do they owe their position and what four characteristics mark their life? See verses 4 and 5, and cf. Mt. v. 3; Lk. xiv. 27; Eph. iv. 25; Phil. ii. 15. How does your own life appear in the light of these standards?

(2) In verses 6-12 are shown three angels, each with a message for all who dwell upon the earth. Examine the contents of their threefold message. Verse 13 is addressed to believers. What encouragement does it give to those who may have to die for Christ's sake?

(3) In the twofold vision of verses 14-20 what are the differences between the two parts of it (verses 14-16 and 17-20)? Cf. Ps. i; Mal. iii. 16–iv. 3; Mt. xiii. 40-43.

Notes.—(1) Verse 3b. The song is 'from heaven' (verse 2); the saints on Mt. Zion are learning to sing it.

(2) Verse 4. A symbol of purity of heart. Cf. 2 Cor. xi. 2.

(3) Verse 6. 'An eternal gospel' (R.V.). Cf. Ec. xii. 13, 14; Pr. ix. 10; Acts xiv. 14-18.

(4) Verse 13b. The weariness of labour will be over, the reward of their deeds awaits them. Cf. Mt. xxv. 35-40.

Day 4. Rev. xv and xvi.

The series of judgments here described, though similar to those of the seals and trumpets, is not connected with them, but is seen as a separate sign ('portent', R.S.V.) in heaven. They fall upon the kingdom of the beast, and immediately precede the Lord's coming in judgment (xv. 1).

(1) John is looking at the seven angels, when his eye is caught by another vision, which he describes in xv. 2-4, no doubt for the comfort of believers, in face of the terrible judgments which are about to fall. What points of resemblance, and what of contrast are there between the vision and the story of Ex. xiv. 30–xv. 19?

(2) In what respects are the 'bowl' judgments more severe than those of the seals and the trumpets? What was the reaction to them (a) of men, (b) of the dragon and his allies?

(3) What attributes of God are conspicuous in these chapters? By whom is testimony borne to Him, and who refuse to give Him glory? With xvi. 15 cf. Mt. xxiv. 42-44.

Notes.—(1) xv. 3. 'Thou King of saints'; better, 'thou King of the ages', as in R.V.

(2) xvi. 6. 'They are worthy'. Or 'It is their due' (R.S.V.).

(3) xvi. 16. 'Armageddon'. Meaning 'the hill of Megiddo'; i.e. the plain of Megiddo where more than one famous battle was fought (Jdg. v. 19; 2 Ch. xxxv. 22) and the hills around.

(4) xvi. 21. 'Every stone about the weight of a talent'. Better, 'heavy as a hundred weight', as in R.S.V.

Day 5. Rev. xvii.

The people of Christ have another enemy—Babylon. Babylon is the name of a city, and John uses it to denote the Rome of his day, seated upon her seven hills (verse 9), and also upon many waters, i.e. upon nations and kingdoms making up the empire (verses 1, 15). But Babylon, like the two beasts of chapter xiii, is a symbol also of the world, not, like the first beast, a symbol of material power, nor, like the second beast, of false religion, but rather a symbol of the world's lust, love of gain, pride and corruption. Wherever these aspects of the worldly spirit find embodiment in a great city, there is Babylon, and there God's judgment will fall, unless men repent.

(1) John's wonder at the woman (verse 6) should lead us to examine her closely. What does each feature of the picture symbolize? Contrast the woman and her brood with the woman of chapter xii and her seed (verse 14; cf. xii. 17).

(2) Verses 7-13, as the interpreting angel himself admits, require for their understanding a mind that has wisdom (verse 9). Observe that two different meanings are assigned to the heads of the beast. Note carefully also the difference between the heads and the horns. Do you gather that the horns arise later than the seven kings, and belong to the time of the end? Cf. Dn. vii. 24.

(3) The main lesson of the chapter is the certain 'doom' of Babylon. What is the end of the woman, and by whom is it inflicted? What light is thrown also upon the future of those who are her destroyers?

Notes.—(1) Verse 2. 'Committed fornication'; a reference to the immoral practices which kings and rulers committed in response to the seductions of Rome, and which drew them away from God.

(2) Verse 4. 'Purple and scarlet'; colours associated with wealth, pomp, and royalty.

(3) Verse 6. Probably an allusion to the persecutions under Nero.

(4) Verses 10, 11. The emperor Nero committed suicide, and the historian Tacitus says that a rumour spread abroad that he was not dead and would return. It is commonly thought that there is an allusion to this belief in verses 8a and 11. Assuming that the seven kings of verse 10 were Roman emperors, the most probable theory sees in the five who 'have fallen', Augustus, Tiberius, Caligula, Claudius, and Nero; in the one who 'is', Vespasian (A.D. 69-79), and in the one who 'is not yet come', Titus. (*Century Bible*). After Titus came Domitian, who would be the 'eighth' (verse 11), and who resembled Nero so closely, especially in his persecution of the Christians, that he might well seem to be Nero come to life again.

Day 6. Rev. xviii. 1-20.

(1) Consider first the messages of the two angels. What two aspects of Babylon's destruction do these emphasize? With verse 4 cf. 2 Cor. vi. 14-18.

(2) In contrast listen to the voices of earth on Babylon's fall. Who are the speakers? To what fact about Babylon's fall do they refer, and what was the cause why they thus mourned for Babylon? Observe the difference between the points of view of heaven and of the world.

(3) If time permit, read Is. xiii and xlvii; Je. l and li; and Ezk. xxvii to see how deeply steeped is the mind of John in the visions and prophecies of the Old Testament.

Day 7. Rev. xviii. 21–xix. 10.

(1) What thoughts does the action of the angel in xviii. 21 suggest as to the purpose of God towards 'Babylon'? Notice especially how many times the phrase 'no more at all' occurs in these verses. What indications do you find that the 'Babylon' here spoken of is not merely Rome, but the whole system of godless luxury and lust which the name 'Babylon' represents? Cf. 1 Cor. vii. 31b; 1 Pet. i. 24, 25; 1 Jn. ii. 17.

(2) What calls forth the praises of verses 1-3, 4, 5-8, and by whom respectively were they spoken? With verses 1-3 cf. v. 11, 12; with verse 4 cf. iv. 8-11; and with verses 5-8 cf. xiv. 1-5.

(3) Consider the measure of the blessedness described in verse 9. What effect has the vision upon John himself, and what important truths were revealed to him (verse 10)?

Notes.—(1) Verse 3b. Symbolic of final destruction. Cf. Is. xxxiv. 10.

(2) Verse 7. 'The marriage of the Lamb'. The fulfilment of God's purpose as described in Eph. i. 3, 4; Tit. ii. 14.

(3) Verse 8. 'The righteousness of saints'; i.e. their holy character ('righteous acts', R.V.), resulting from their cleansing in Christ's blood, and their sanctification by the Spirit. Cf. Eph. ii. 10.

(4) Verse 10. 'The testimony of (borne by) Jesus is (constitutes) the spirit of prophecy'; i.e. the revelation given in and through Jesus is the Truth, to which all prophecy inspired by the Spirit conforms. Cf. Jn. xiv. 6, 17a, xvi. 13, 14.

Week 52. REVELATION XIX. 11–XXII

Day 1. Rev. xix. 11-21.

Following upon the destruction of 'Babylon', the beast, and the kings in alliance with him (cf. xvii. 12-14), make war upon Christ, who comes forth from heaven in judgment to overthrow them. The end of the present age, prophesied throughout the book, has now come, and we have in today's portion Christ's second coming described, in its aspect of judgment upon His enemies, as in 2 Thes. i. 6-8 and Ps. ii.

(1) Comparing the symbolic picture of Christ in verses 11-16 with that of i. 12-20, what parallels and what additional features do you find? As you translate each symbol into its corresponding reality, what attributes and glories of our Lord are revealed?

(2) Verses 17-21. This is the battle of Armageddon, spoken of in xvi. 16. Note carefully the results of it, as here described, first as regards the beast and the false prophet, and second as regards 'the rest' (verse 21).

Notes.—(1) Verse 11. 'Faithful and True'; cf. i. 5, iii. 7, 14; 1 Jn. v. 20.
(2) Verse 12. 'Many diadems' (R.V.); cf. verse 16; Ps. lxxii. 11.
(3) Verse 13a. Cf. verse 15b; Is. lxiii. 2, 3.
(4) Verse 14. These are armies of angels; cf. Mt. xvi. 27, xxvi. 53.
(5) Verse 20. 'The lake of fire'; so also in xx. 10, 14, 15, xxi. 8, elsewhere called 'the eternal fire' or 'the Gehenna of fire' (Mt. xviii. 8, 9, xxv. 41, R.V. and R.V. mg.), also 'the furnace of fire' (Mt. xiii. 42, 50). It is the place of final destruction.

Day 2. Rev. xx. 1-6.

It is assumed here that these verses describe events which follow upon those described in the previous chapter. John, having been shown the end of three of the enemies of Christ's people, namely, Babylon, the beast, and the false prophet, is now shown what happens to the arch-enemy Satan, and is given a vision also of the blessedness of those who have gained the victory over the beast.

(1) Contrast the treatment meted out to Satan with that given to the beast and false prophet (verses 1-3, xix. 20). What difference does the arrest of Satan make to the nations?

(2) What other events are associated in verses 4-6 with the thousand years here spoken of? Can you find other indications in Scripture that there will be more than one resurrection of the dead, and, if so, who will be partakers of the first of them? See e.g. Lk. xiv. 14; Jn. v. 29; 1 Thes. iv. 16; Phil. iii. 11 ('the resurrection which is out from the dead').

(3) With verse 4 cf. Mk. xiii. 12, 13 and Lk. xxii. 28-30; and with verse 6 cf. i. 6, v. 10. Are we gaining the victory even now (cf. xii. 11) so as to be numbered among the 'blessed' of verse 6 at Christ's appearing?

Notes.—(1) Verses 1-3. The 'abyss' as the abode of evil spirits (cf. ix. 11) is to be carefully distinguished from 'the lake of fire'.
(2) Verse 3. 'Must'. For reasons hidden in the divine will.

(3) Verse 4. 'Reigned with Christ a thousand years'. A reign of Christ on (or rather over) the earth at His second coming finds, as many think, strong support in Scripture and is closely linked with the fulfilment of prophecies concerning the Jewish people. It seems to form part, e.g. of Paul's statement in 1 Cor. xv. 20-28, see especially verses 24 and 25. Opinion, however, is divided. Many (as e.g. Hendriksen in *More Than Conquerors*) regard the whole idea of a 'millennium' as mistaken, and interpret John's words here as referring to the present age.

Day 3. Rev. xx. 7-15.

(1) What will Satan do when he is released, and what success will he have? What is his final end?

(2) The first beast, representing totalitarian world power, and the second beast representing the false religion of the world, and Satan, the arch deceiver of the nations, all having been cast into the lake of fire, there remains but one final act of judgment before the new heaven and the new earth are established. Who are the subjects of it, what are the matters enquired into, and what sentence is pronounced?

Notes.—(1) Verse 8. 'Shall go out to deceive'. Cf. verses 3 and 10; also xii. 9; Gn. iii. 4, 5.

(2) Verse 9. 'The camp of the saints' . . . 'the beloved city'; i.e. Jerusalem. Notice that in this final conflict the beast and false prophet are absent; see verse 10 and xix. 20.

(3) Verses 13, 14. 'Death and hell'. Better, 'death and Hades', as in R.V. With verse 14, cf. 1 Cor. xv. 26.

Day 4. Rev. xxi. 1-8.

(1) The description of the city in verse 2 is continued in verse 9, but what five things are said of it in verse 2, which differentiate it from the cities of this world?

(2) The new heaven and new earth, as depicted in verses 1, 3, is the full development of the new life which all who are in Christ have already begun to live. Cf. 2 Cor. v. 17; 1 Cor. i. 9, 10. How many of the blessings here spoken of are you experiencing? Cf. 2 Cor. vi. 16b, i. 3, 4; 2 Tim. i. 10.

(3) In verses 5, 6 the voice of God breaks through. Let your mind dwell on His gracious offer and solemn warning.

Notes.—(1) Verse 1. 'A new heaven'; the word translated 'new' means new as to its form and quality, not that it did not exist before. So also in verses 2 and 5.

'There was no more sea'; or 'the sea is no more'. As John in vision surveyed the new heaven and earth, he saw no sea there. The sea in Scripture speaks of separation (i. 9), and of the restless striving of the nations (xiii. 1). All this was now done away.

(2) Verse 3. 'The tabernacle of God'; literally 'tent of God'. But here used in the sense of 'dwelling' (R.S.V.).

'His people'; better, 'peoples', as in R.V., denoting not only Israel but all peoples.

(3) Verse 8. 'Fearful'; i.e. cowardly or craven. Cf. 2 Tim. i. 7.

Day 5. Rev. xxi. 9-21.

This vision of the city of God is no more to be taken literally than was the vision of Christ in i. 12-20. It is a symbolic picture, and we have to see in and through the symbols the spiritual realities which they represent.

(1) For example, the size of the city (verse 16; cf. note 2 below) expresses the same thought as the phrase 'which no man could number' in vii. 9, the shape of the city as a cube (verse 16b) suggests its perfection of design and permanence, the gold and precious stones its brilliance and perfection of quality (cf. note 3 below), and so forth. What other spiritual realities does today's portion suggest to you?

(2) How is the contrast between this city and the harlot city Babylon brought to the mind of the reader? Cf. verse 9 with xvii. 1. Work out this contrast in some of its features. What are the outstanding differences between Babylon and the New Jerusalem? Cf. Zc. xiv. 20, 21; Lk. xvi. 15; 1 Jn. ii. 16, 17.

Notes.—(1) Verses 12-14. The city, while open to all, lies within the revelation given through patriarchs and apostles.

(2) Verse 16. 'Twelve thousand furlongs'; about 1,500 miles.

(3) Verse 18. 'Pure gold, like unto clear glass'; see also verse 21. There is nothing not genuine, nothing not transparent.

Day 6. Rev. xxi. 22–xxii. 5.

(1) Make a list of all that is said not to be found in the perfected kingdom of God, i.e. of all in xxi–xxii. 5 of which the words 'no' or 'no more' or 'in no wise . . . anything' are used. Over against these set the positive blessings here spoken of. Comparing these blessings with those of the Garden of Eden (Gn. i. 28, 29, ii. 8-25), how do they transcend them, and what is their chief glory? Cf. 1 Cor. xv. 46; Eph. i. 3.

(2) Would a non-Christian be able to enter the city (see xxi, 27), and if he did enter would he find satisfaction in its blessings (cf. Eph. ii. 3; 1 Cor. ii. 14)? In the light of this, consider the absolute necessity of 'the blood of the Lamb' and of regeneration for every man.

Note.—xxii. 1, 2. Some interpret this to mean that there is one broad street which intersects the city, beside which the river flows, with trees on either bank. Others take 'street', 'river', and 'tree of life' as being collective nouns and picture many streets and streams of the river flowing by them and many trees bearing fruit every month, all being symbolic of 'the superabundant character of God's provision'.

Day 7. Rev. xxii. 6-21.

(1) Compare the seven beatitudes in this book, i. 3, xiv. 13, xvi. 15, xix. 9, xx. 6, and verses 7 and 14 in today's portion. Are we observing the conditions, and in so far as is yet possible to us, beginning to know the wealth of the blessedness?

(2) What word of Christ is repeated three times in these verses? See also iii. 11, and cf. i. 7, xvi. 15. How are we to reconcile this word with the fact that even now, after the lapse of 1,850 years He has not come? What should be our attitude and response to this word of our Master? See 2 Pet. iii; Mt. xxiv. 43-51; Heb. x. 36-39. Can you join in the prayer of verses 17 and 20 as the spontaneous yearning of your heart?

(3) How are the truth and the importance of the contents of this book confirmed to us in today's portion? By what name is it four times described? What is its origin, and whence does it derive its authority?

Notes.—(1) Verse 6. This book springs from the same divine source from which all the prophets have derived their inspiration.

(2) Verses 8, 9. Cf. xix. 10. John emphasizes both the attraction and the error of angel worship. The same might be said of the worship of the saints.

(3) Verse 11. An emphatic warning that the time of the end is near, and the opportunity of a change of character is passing. Cf. Dn. xii. 10; 2 Tim. iii. 13. Yet see verse 17b below, and xxi. 6.

(4) Verse 14. Read as in R.V. With verse 15, cf. xxi. 8.

(5) Verse 16. 'The root and offspring'. All sprang from Christ, and finds its fruition in Him. Cf. Mk. xii. 35-37.